C#™ Network Programming

Richard Blum

SYBEX

San Francisco · London

Associate Publisher: Joel Fugazzotto
Acquisitions Editor: Denise S. Lincoln
Developmental Editor: Carol Henry
Editor: Sally Engelfried
Production Editor: Erica Yee
Technical Editor: Dan Frumin
Graphic Illustrator: Jeff Wilson, Happenstance Type-O-Rama
Electronic Publishing Specialists: Scott Benoit, Judy Fung
Proofreaders: Emily Hsuan, Dave Nash, Laurie O'Connell, Yariv Rabinovitch, Nancy Riddiough
Indexer: Ted Laux
Cover Designer:Carol Gorska, Gorska Design
Cover Photographer: Carlos Navajas, The Image Bank

Library of Congress Card Number: 2002111958

ISBN: 0-7821-4176-5

Manufactured in the United States of America

10 9 8 7 6 5 4 3

This book is dedicated to Sister Marie Imelda, C.S.C, who in the late 1970s fought and struggled to teach a bunch of goofy high school kids how to program. Thanks, Sister. "Trust in the Lord with all your heart and lean not on your own understanding; in all your ways acknowledge him, and he will make your paths straight." Prov. 3:5-6 (NIV)

Acknowledgments

First, all honor, glory, and praise goes to God, who through His Son, all things are possible, and who gives us the gift of eternal life.

I would like to thank all the great people at Sybex for their help, guidance, and professionalism. Thanks to Denise Santoro Lincoln, the Acquisitions Editor, for offering me the opportunity to write this book. Also, thanks to Carol Henry, the Developmental Editor, for all her work guiding this book along and helping make my paragraphs make sense.

Many thanks to Sally Engelfried, the Copy Editor, for turning my poor grammar into perfect sentences, and to Dan Frumin, the Technical Editor, for going above and beyond the call of duty fixing my programs and pointing out my technical blunders. Also, thanks to Carole McClendon at Waterside Productions for her help in arranging this book for me.

Finally, I would like to thank my parents, Mike and Joyce Blum, for their dedication and support, and my wife Barbara and daughters Katie Jane and Jessica for their faith, love, and understanding, especially while I was writing this book.

Contents at a Glance

Introduction   *xix*

Part I   **Network Programming Basics**

Chapter 1:   The C# Language   3

Chapter 2:   IP Programming Basics   41

Chapter 3:   C# Network Programming Classes   87

Chapter 4:   DNS and C#   125

Part II   **Network Layer Programing**

Chapter 5:   Connection-Oriented Sockets   167

Chapter 6:   Connectionless Sockets   209

Chapter 7:   Using The C# Sockets Helper Classes   249

Chapter 8:   Asynchronous Sockets   291

Chapter 9:   Using Threads   333

Chapter 10:   IP Multicasting   375

Part III   **Application Layer Programming Examples**

Chapter 11:   ICMP   411

Chapter 12:   SNMP   441

Chapter 13:   SMTP   477

Chapter 14:   HTTP   511

Chapter 15: Active Directory   **535**

Chapter 16: Remoting   **563**

Chapter 17: Security   **593**

Index   *623*

Contents

Introduction   *xix*

Part I   Network Programming Basics   1

Chapter 1   The C# Language   3

Basics of .NET   4
    Common Language Runtime (CLR)   4
    MSIL Code   5
Installing a C# Development Environment   6
    C# Development Options   7
    Downloading the .NET Framework SDK   8
    Installing the .NET Framework SDK   9
The C# Runtime Environment   10
    Downloading and Installing the C# Runtime Package   11
    Developing with the C# Runtime   11
C# Programming Basics   12
    Creating C# Programs   12
    Compiling and Running C# Programs   15
    Using Multiple Source Files   16
    Debugging C# Programs   17
    Debugging MSIL Code   22
C# Features   23
    C# Namespaces   24
    Using Strings in C# Programs   28
    C# Streams   33
    C# Exception Programming   36
Summary   39

Chapter 2	**IP Programming Basics**	**41**
	Watching Network Traffic	42
	Installing the WinPcap Programs	43
	The WinDump Program	44
	The Analyzer Program	48
	Analyzing Network Packets	51
	The Ethernet Layer	51
	The IP Layer	56
	The TCP Layer	61
	The UDP Layer	68
	Programming with TCP and UDP	69
	TCP Programming Features	70
	UDP Programming Features	71
	Finding IP Address Information	72
	Using ipconfig	72
	Using the Registry	74
	Using WMI	80
	Using DNS	83
	Summary	84
Chapter 3	**C# Network Programming Classes**	**87**
	A Primer on Socket Programming	88
	Socket Programming in Windows	98
	C# Socket Programming	103
	IP Addresses in C#	103
	Using C# Sockets	108
	C# Socket Exceptions	119
	C# Socket Helper Classes	120
	TcpClient	120
	TcpListener	122
	UdpClient	123
	Summary	124
Chapter 4	**DNS and C#**	**125**
	The Domain Name System (DNS)	127
	DNS Structure	127
	Finding a Hostname in DNS	130

The DNS Database   131
A Sample DNS Database   136
Windows DNS Client Information   138
DNS Configuration   138
Using C# to Investigate the DNS Configuration   141
Resolving Hostnames with nslookup   144
DNS Classes in C#   153
Synchronous Methods   153
Asynchronous Methods   159
Summary   164

Part II   Network Layer Programing   165

Chapter 5   Connection-Oriented Sockets   167

A Simple TCP Server   168
Creating the Server   168
Testing the Server   172
Watching the Server   172
A Simple TCP Client   173
Creating the Client   174
Testing the Client   176
When TCP Goes Bad   177
Problems with Data Buffers   177
Problems with TCP Messages   180
Solving the TCP Message Problem   184
Using C# Streams with TCP   198
The NetworkStream Class   198
The StreamReader and StreamWriter Classes   202
Summary   207

Chapter 6   Connectionless Sockets   209

A Simple UDP Application   210
The UDP Server   211
A UDP Client   215
Testing the Client and Server Programs   217
Using Connect() in a UDP Client Example   219

	Distinguishing UDP Messages	220
	When UDP Goes Bad	223
	Preventing Lost Data	223
	Preventing Lost Packets	228
	A Complete UDP Application	242
	Catching Multiple Exceptions by Monitoring Error Codes	242
	The Complete Client Program	245
	Summary	247
Chapter 7	**Using The C# Sockets Helper Classes**	**249**
	The TcpClient Class	250
	The TcpClient Class Constructors	250
	The TcpClient Class Methods	251
	Creating a Simple Client Program	252
	Testing the Program	254
	The TcpListener Class	255
	The TcpListener Class Constructors	255
	The TcpListener Class Methods	256
	A Simple Server Program	257
	Incorporating the StreamReader and StreamWriter Classes	258
	The UdpClient Class	259
	The UdpClient Class Constructors	259
	The UdpClient Class Methods	260
	Using the UdpClient Class in Programs	260
	A Simple UdpClient Server Program	262
	A Simple UdpClient Client Program	263
	Testing the Sample Programs	264
	Moving Data across the Network	265
	Moving Binary Data	265
	Communicating with Other Host Types	272
	Moving Complex Objects	280
	Summary	288
Chapter 8	**Asynchronous Sockets**	**291**
	Windows Event Programming	292
	Using Events and Delegates	293

The AsyncCallback Class   297
Using Asynchronous Sockets   298
    Establishing the Connection   298
    Sending and Receiving Data   301
Sample Programs Using Asynchronous Sockets   304
    The Client Program   305
    The Server Program   312
Using Non-blocking Socket Methods   319
    The Poll() Method   319
    The Select() Method   324
Summary   331

Chapter 9   Using Threads   333
How Applications Run in Windows   334
    Finding Process Information Using C#   335
    Threads   343
Creating Threads in a Program   350
    The Thread Class   350
    Using the Thread Class   351
Using Threads in a Server   354
    Creating a Threaded Server   354
    Testing the Server   357
    Watching the Threads   357
Using Threads for Sending and Receiving Data   358
    The TcpChat Program   359
    Testing the Chat Program and Watching the Threads   363
Thread Pools   364
    The ThreadPool Class   365
    A Sample ThreadPool Program   366
    Testing the Program and Watching the Threads   367
Using Thread Pools in a Server   369
    A ThreadPool Server   369
    Testing the Program and Watching the Threads   371
Summary   373

Chapter 10	**IP Multicasting**	**375**
	What Is Broadcasting?	376
	Local versus Global Broadcasts	376
	Implementing Broadcasting with C#	377
	Using Broadcast Packets to Advertise a Server	382
	The Advertising Loop	382
	What Is Multicasting?	390
	Multicast Techniques	391
	Sending Multicast Packets through Routers	392
	C# IP Multicast Support	393
	C# Socket Multicasting	394
	C# UdpClient Multicasting	399
	Sample Multicast Application	402
	Testing the Multicast Chat Program	405
	Summary	406
Part III	**Application Layer Programming Examples**	**409**
Chapter 11	**ICMP**	**411**
	The ICMP Protocol	412
	ICMP Packet Format	412
	ICMP Packet Types	413
	Using Raw Sockets	415
	Raw Sockets Format	415
	Sending Raw Packets	416
	Receiving Raw Packets	417
	Creating an ICMP Class	417
	The ICMP Class Constructors	417
	The ICMP Packet Creator	420
	The ICMP Checksum Method	420
	Putting It All Together	422
	A Simple Ping Program	423
	Testing SimplePing	425
	An Advanced Ping Program	426
	Testing AdvPing	431

The TraceRoute.cs Program   432
   Testing TraceRoute.cs   434
The FindMask Program   435
   The Subnet Request Packet   435
   Testing FindMask.cs   437
Summary   438

Chapter 12   **SNMP**   **441**

Understanding SNMP   442
   SNMP Commands   443
   Community Names   444
   Common Management Information Base   445
Working with SNMP Packets   448
   SNMP Packet Format   448
   SNMP Packet Layout   450
   SNMP Communication   452
Creating a Simple SNMP Class   452
   The SNMP Class Program   453
   Walking through the Class   455
The SimpleSNMP Program   457
   Testing the Program   461
   Watching the Packets   462
Using Vendor MIBs   463
   The Cisco CPU MIB   463
   The CiscoRouter Program   466
Using GetNextRequest Queries   469
   Extracting the Next MIB   469
   The getnextMIB() Method   470
   The MAC Address Program   471
   Testing the Program   473
Summary   474

Chapter 13   **SMTP**   **477**

E-mail Basics   478
   The MTA Process   478

The MDA Process   480
The MUA Process   481
SMTP and Windows   483
Collaboration Data Objects (CDO)   483
SMTP Mail Service   484
The SmtpMail Class   485
Class Methods and Properties   486
Using the SmtpMail Class   487
Using Expanded Mail Message Formats   488
The RFC2822 Mail Format   488
The MailMessage Class Properties   491
Using the MailMessage Class   493
Mail Attachments   494
uuencode   495
MIME   495
The MailAttachment Class   499
A POP3 Client   501
The POP3 Protocol   501
Writing a POP3 Client   504
Summary   510

Chapter 14   **HTTP**   **511**

The WebClient Class   512
Downloading Web Data   512
Viewing HTTP Headers   515
Uploading Web Data   516
Using Credentials   519
Advanced Web Classes   521
The HttpWebRequest Class   522
The HttpWebResponse Class   523
Advanced Web Client Example   525
Web Services   528
Creating the Web Service Server   529
Testing the Web Service   531
Creating the Web Service Proxy   532
Creating a C# Web Service Client   533
Summary   534

Chapter 15	**Active Directory**	**535**
	Network Directory Basics	536
	The LDAP System	536
	LDAP Objects and Attributes	537
	Working with Active Directory	539
	Parts of an Active Directory	539
	Connecting to an Active Directory Server	543
	Using C# to Access a Network Directory	543
	Modifying Directory Data	546
	Working with Object Properties	546
	Working with Objects	550
	Searching the Network Directory	556
	Step 1: Defining the Search Properties	556
	Step 2: Retrieving the Search Results	557
	Step 3: Extracting the Search Results	558
	Performing a Search	558
	Advanced Search Features	560
	Summary	561
Chapter 16	**Remoting**	**563**
	Moving Data, Revisited	564
	Using a Serialization Class	564
	Problems with Serialization	571
	An Overview of Remoting	574
	The Remote Class	575
	The Remoting Server	576
	The Communication Channel	577
	The Proxy Class	577
	The Client Program	577
	Using Remoting	578
	Creating the Remote Class Proxy	578
	Creating the Server Program	579
	Creating the Client Program	583
	Creating a Proxy Class Using soapsuds	585
	Viewing the Remote Class Interfaces	585
	The soapsuds Program	586
	Summary	590

Chapter 17   Security   **593**

   Application Security: What's Involved?   594
      Security Policies   594
      Security Groups   595
      Security Permissions   596
      Security Tools   597
   Socket Permissions   603
      Implementing Declarative Security   604
      Using Declarative Security   606
   Protecting Network Data   610
      Data Encryption   610
      Using Data Encryption   612
      Network Data Encryption   615
   Summary   621

   Index   *623*

Introduction

Networks (and network programming) have come a long way over the past 20 years. In the early days of network computing (the '80s), network programming was left to the advanced programmer, who typically built applications using the C programming language in (mostly) Unix environments. Now, networks are everywhere, from large corporations to small home users. With so many computers connected together via networks, network-aware applications are an accepted necessity. Existing applications must incorporate network features to stay competitive in the marketplace, and adding network communication to applications is essential. Network programs are used for everything from children's games to advanced corporate database systems.

Network programming has always been a key feature of the Microsoft Windows operating system. Unfortunately, you've had to know advanced C or C++ programming concepts to utilize the network programming features in Windows programs. Now, though, the .NET Framework languages simplify the task of adding network features to your applications. The .NET libraries provide many network classes that can integrate network programming.

As a network administrator, I've written many network programs using the C and Java languages for both Windows and Unix platforms. Today's network management and security requirements make it essential to communicate with network devices and track workstations on the network. Trying to quickly write clean network code can be difficult when you are working within the structure of the C socket APIs (especially in WinSock), and running Java applications is often a painful experience due to slow processing speeds and poor Windows support.

The C# language has solved many of my network programming problems by allowing me to quickly prototype and deploy network applications using C# classes. Combining the C# Forms library to write the graphical code with the C# Socket library to write the networking code makes creating professional network applications simple. With C# network classes, what used to take a day to write often only takes an hour or less.

Who Should Read This Book

Obviously, if you are a C# programmer who is interested in creating network programs, this book is specifically intended to help you out. I've described each network C# class in detail, and you'll find lots of examples to help you implement the classes in your own work. If you have never before written a network program, I've included useful explanations of the concepts and ideas behind network programming in general, including common techniques for passing data between network devices.

You may already be familiar with writing network programs using other languages, such as C, C++, or Java. In that case, you'll be interested in seeing how easy it is to do this with the C# language.

If you are new to the C# language, the first chapter describes the basics of creating and compiling C# programs. You may want to skip other chapters in the first part of the book, which discuss network programming basics, and dive right into the C#-specific network programming classes.

How This Book Is Organized

This book is organized into four separate sections that cover a particular aspect of network programming.

Part I: Network Programming Basics

The first four chapters are intended for programmers just starting out in network programming and looking for some background information about how network programming works and the pieces that are required for network programming.

Chapter 1, "The C# Language," provides some basic information for the reader new to C#, such as which C# package to use for development work and how to compile C# programs.

Chapter 2, "IP Programming Basics," demonstrates how network programming has evolved from the Unix world to the world of Windows, via the WinSock interface, and how .NET uses the WinSock interface to access network resources.

Chapter 3, "C# Network Programming Classes," offers a quick introduction to the entire C# network libraries and shows the basic formats of the classes.

Chapter 4, "DNS and C#," rounds out the introductory section by showing network novices how DNS can resolve host addresses and how to use the C# DNS classes.

Part II: Network Layer Programming

The next group of chapters presents the core of network programming topics in the book. Each of these chapters discusses a major topic using in creating C# network programs.

Chapter 5, "Connection-Oriented Sockets," starts the discussion of network programming by introducing stream programming using TCP. In addition to the standard C# Socket class used for stream programming, common pitfalls are discussed to help you create stream programs that will work on real networks.

Chapter 6, "Connectionless Sockets," discusses how to use the Socket class to create UDP applications. In addition to showing you how to create UDP applications, this chapter also discusses pitfalls related to UDP programming and shows examples of creating applications that will withstand the problems inherent in real networks.

Chapter 7, "Using the C# Socket Helper Classes," discusses the C# `TcpClient`, `TcpListener`, and `UdpClient` classes. These are special classes in .NET to help programmers create network programs with minimal effort. This chapter also discusses the basics of sending different data types across the network.

Chapter 8, "Asynchronous Socket Programming," discusses the technique of using asynchronous programming (prevalent in Windows programs) within the network programming world.

Chapter 9, "Using Threads," presents information for using multi-threaded application techniques in network programs. This technology is often used in server applications that must service multiple clients at the same time.

Chapter 10, "IP Multicasting," describes how to use broadcasting and multicasting to send packets to multiple clients, cutting down on network bandwidth.

Part III: Application Layer Programming Examples

The last part of the book describes specific network applications and how to implement them using the C# network classes.

Chapter 11, "ICMP," shows how to use C# raw sockets to implement a protocol-specific application. The common ping and traceroute programs are shown within the C# network programming context.

Chapter 12, "SNMP," describes how to write network management applications using C#. SNMP allows you to communicate with many devices on the network to retrieve network statistics. This chapter shows specific examples of reading a vendor MIB sheet and creating a C# application to extract the MIB data from the network device.

Chapter 13, "SMTP," describes the C# e-mail classes and shows examples of using them to send mail using SMTP to remote mail servers. Also, an example of using other mail protocols (such as POP3) is shown.

Chapter 14, "HTTP," presents the C# web classes and how you can use them to create web-enabled C# applications. Also, .NET web services , and how you can use them to host your application methods on an IIS server, are discussed.

Chapter 15, "Active Directory," shows the C# classes for contacting Microsoft Active Directory servers. Examples are presented that show how to query, change, add, and delete entries in the Active Directory.

Chapter 16, "Remoting," discusses the .NET concept of remoting, allowing an application to share methods with clients across the network. Examples are shown that demonstrate how to create both a remoting server and client.

Chapter 17, "Security," closes out the book by describing how the .NET Framework handles program security, and how you can implement security in your network applications using encryption techniques.

Keeping Up to Date

All of the examples in this book have been created and compiled using the .NET Framework 1.0 package. Each of the examples willeasily compile using any of the Microsoft Visual Studio packages (including Visual C#).

At the time of this writing (2002) the current version of the .NET Framework was version 1.0, with Service Pack 1. Microsoft maintains the .NET Framework website at `http://www.microsoft.com/netframework`, where all .NET announcements are posted.

PART I

Network Programming Basics

Chapter 1: The C# Language

Chapter 2: IP Programming Basics

Chapter 3: C# Network Programming Classes

Chapter 4: DNS and C#

CHAPTER 1

The C# Language

- Basics of .NET

- Installing a C# development environment

- The C# runtime environment

- C# programming basics

- C# features

In its short history, the Microsoft .NET technology has quickly become a popular programming platform for developing applications for Microsoft Windows workstations and servers. Although most of the media attention has focused around the web application capabilities of .NET, there are many other features that are useful to Windows programmers.

One of those features is the new C# programming language, developed specifically for .NET. C# is becoming a widely used programming platform for programmers wanting to create both network-aware and stand-alone applications for Windows systems. The language provides many resources to help create robust Windows-based applications. Many programmers are migrating to the C# language to take advantage of these resources.

Before learning the basics of network programming in C#, it is important that you understand the C# programming environment, the fundamentals of .NET, and how to create and distribute C# applications. This chapter shows how to create a C# development environment on your system and how to ensure that C# applications you create will run on other Windows workstations and servers. Finally, I'll present a brief introduction to the C# language, along with some C# programming topics relevant to network programming. All together, the concepts presented in this chapter will help you get ready for C# network programming.

Basics of .NET

The .NET group of programming languages differs from previous versions of Windows programming languages in the way programs are created and run on the Windows systems. If you are not familiar with how C# programs operate, this section briefly describes the basics you should know to be able to deploy applications based on the .NET technologies.

Common Language Runtime (CLR)

The core of the Microsoft .NET technology is the *Common Language Runtime (CLR) environment*. This environment enables programmers to create programs using a multitude of programming languages and run them on any platform that supports the CLR. The idea of the CLR is to provide a middle layer of Application Program Interfaces (APIs) that operate between the low-level Windows Win32 API functions and the application program code. By providing a common middle layer, Microsoft has given a larger number of application languages access to core Windows technologies (such as network support).

The layout of how application programs run in the CLR environment is shown in Figure 1.1. High-level applications written in various .NET languages, such as Visual Basic .NET, Visual C++ .NET, Visual J# .NET, and of course Visual C# .NET, are compiled into a special intermediate language called *Microsoft Intermediate Language (MSIL)*. The MSIL code is interpreted by the CLR as the program runs; MSIL runs on the host operating system as a normal executable program. Of course, legacy programs that do not use the CLR can still directly access the low-level Windows Win32 APIs as before.

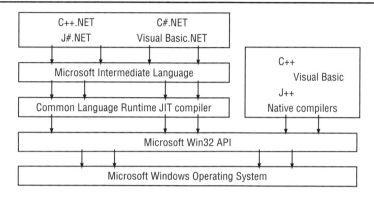

This CLR model also pertains to other operating systems. Because the CLR is ported to other operating systems, .NET programs will be able to run without recompiling them on the new host systems. Currently, Microsoft supports the Shared Source Common Language Interface (CLI) project (nicknamed Rotor), which ports the CLR environment to the FreeBSD operating system. It is expected that the Rotor project will branch out to other operating systems as well. At the time of this writing you can get more information about Rotor at the following website:

```
http://msdn.microsoft.com/downloads/default.asp?URL=/downloads/sample.asp?url=
/msdn-files/027/001/901/msdncompositedoc.xml
```

For programs to run in the CLR, they must be compiled into the special MSIL format. The .NET C# compiler is used to convert C# language programs to MSIL code that runs in the CLR environment. The next section describes the MSIL code.

MSIL Code

When you compile a C# program, it produces an executable file. However, this executable file is different from the ones you may be used to seeing produced from other Windows compilers. Instead of a low-level assembly program that can run directly in Windows, this executable file contains two parts:

- A *stub* assembly language program to start the CLR compiler
- The MSIL code of the compiled application

The stub program starts the CLR just-in-time (JIT) compiler, which compiles the MSIL program code to native Win32 code that can be run on the system. Unlike native Windows applications, which interact directly with the low-level Win32 API system, .NET applications rely on the .NET Framework CLR to run. Running a .NET application on a system that does not have the .NET Framework installed will produce an error message like the one in Figure 1.2. The .NET Framework is crucial to any .NET application, whether it is running on a Windows workstation or server. Without it the MSIL code cannot run. Any Windows workstation or server expected to run .NET programs must have the .NET Framework installed.

FIGURE 1.2:
Trying to run a .NET
application without
the .NET Framework

Microsoft is committed to ensuring the .NET Framework will be installed on all future versions of the Windows OS. However, older versions of Windows must have the .NET Framework manually installed. The following section includes instructions for installing the .NET Framework for a developer environment to allow you to create, compile, and run .NET applications.

Installing a C# Development Environment

Before you can begin programming in C#, you must have a C# development environment—a system for creating, compiling, and debugging C# programs. Unfortunately, one of the most stringent requirements for .NET application development is the designation of OS platform to use for development. Currently, .NET requires one of the following systems for full C# program development:

- Windows NT 4 Workstation or Server (with Service Pack 6a)
- Windows 2000 Professional or Server (with Service Pack 2)
- Windows XP Home Edition or Professional

Programmers without access to any of these systems will not be able to develop C# programs—but there is a solution to this, as will be explained later in the C# Runtime Environment section.

C# Development Options

Microsoft offers three development environments for C# developers. Each environment has its own set of pros and cons. This section describes these C# development environments and how they differ.

- Visual Studio .NET

- Visual C# .NET

- .NET Framework software development kit (SDK)

NOTE   All of the example programs in this book can be compiled in any of the .NET development environments. To simplify things, this book's examples are shown using the .NET Framework command-line compiler. This ensures that anyone can use the examples, no matter which development environment you are using.

Visual Studio .NET

The Visual Studio .NET package is the flagship development product for Microsoft .NET. This Integrated Development Environment (IDE) offers many features to assist your Windows application programming tasks. Microsoft describes the Visual Studio package as "a rapid application development (RAD) tool, enabling programmers to quickly code and debug .NET applications." It includes a complete graphical environment for creating Windows forms, typing code, and debugging programs. In addition to containing a fancy development environment, Visual Studio also supports all the .NET programming languages—Visual Basic .NET, Visual C++ .NET, Visual J# .NET, and Visual C# .NET. If you are looking at developing with all of the .NET languages, the Visual Studio package is well worth the extra expense.

In Visual Studio .NET, applications can be created in a graphical environment using any of the four programming languages. The IDE provides separate windows for developing code and for visually laying out Window controls for the application, including text boxes, list boxes, buttons, and scrollbars. Visual Studio .NET offers an easy way to create, test, and debug .NET applications, whether they are stand-alone Windows applications or ASP.NET web pages.

There are several package levels for Visual Studio .NET, depending on your development requirements (and budget). Each package level includes progressively more development functionality, and also comes with a progressively higher price tag.

Visual C# .NET

If you are interested only in programming using the C# language, you do not have to buy the full Visual Studio .NET package. Instead, Microsoft offers the Visual C# .NET package, which has the same functionality of Visual Studio .NET but supports only the C# language. This is a much less expensive method of development for C# programmers. Similar to Visual Studio, the Visual C# package also comes in various package levels, from a bare-bones student version to a full-featured professional developer version. Before you choose this version, however, be aware that it does not include some of the advanced features, such as automatic database support, that are in Visual Studio .NET.

Both the Visual Studio and C# development options require that you purchase a commercial software development package from Microsoft. Both are excellent software development packages that can save you hours of time in creating Windows and debugging applications. However, many first-time and hobbyist programmers might find the cost of these IDE packages too great.

.NET Framework SDK

If you are looking for an inexpensive way to get started with C# programming, the .NET Framework SDK is the way to go. The SDK is available free from Microsoft and contains command-line tools for compiling and debugging .NET programs, including C#. This package allows you to get the feel for developing C# applications without investing in an expensive IDE development environment. You can obtain the .NET Framework SDK package by downloading the complete package via Microsoft's .NET Framework website, or by ordering a minimal-cost CD directly from Microsoft. (See the upcoming section for website information.)

If you are completely new to C#, you may want to start by downloading the .NET Framework SDK and giving it a try. It is often said that the best way to learn a programming language is to hand-code all your programs and suffer the consequences—I think this is especially true of network programming. As you progress in your C# programming skills, you can migrate to the Visual C# .NET package for creating Windows forms and debugging complex applications. To get you started, the following section describes how to download and install the .NET Framework SDK.

Downloading the .NET Framework SDK

At the time of this writing, the current version of the .NET Framework SDK is release 1. As mentioned, it can be downloaded free or you can purchase a CD from Microsoft. If you choose to download the package from Microsoft, there are two methods that can be used. Because the SDK is so large (131MB), you can either download it in one piece, or as ten smaller (13.1MB) packages that can be assembled after the download. Both methods require the same amount of data to be downloaded, but people with slower connections may want the convenience of downloading the individual pieces one at a time.

The .NET Framework website URL is currently www.microsoft.com/netframework/. As is common on the Web, this location may change by the time you read this. If so, just go to the Microsoft home page (www.microsoft.com) and look for the .NET stuff.

The .NET Framework site contains lots of information about the SDK, including a link to the separate software download page. The download page shows the various options for downloading the software. The single-file download is a file named setup.exe, which can be downloaded to your workstation or server for installation. If you select the multipart download option, you must download all of the split SDK files, along with the separate setup.bat file, to a temporary directory. After all of the files are downloaded, you must run the setup.bat file. This file creates the master setup.exe file from all of the SDK split files.

In either download scenario, the resulting file will be a setup.exe file. You must run this file to install the .NET Framework SDK package. The following section describes this process.

Installing the .NET Framework SDK

Once the setup.exe file is obtained, either by single download, multipart download, or CD, you can install the .NET Framework SDK. You start the installation by running the setup.exe file from a DOS command prompt, or by double-clicking it in Windows Explorer.

When the installation starts, a dialog box asks if you want to install the .NET Framework SDK. Click the Yes button to start the installation.

The .NET installation process first extracts the working installation files into a temporary directory, pointed to by the TEMP environment variable. This allows you to place the temporary working files on a drive other than the system drive (usually C:\) if you are tight on disk space. After the working files are extracted, the installation updates the Windows installer package on the workstation and then launches Windows installer with the .NET Framework installation.

After the opening screen and a license agreement screen, you are asked which components of the SDK package you want installed. This is shown in Figure 1.3.

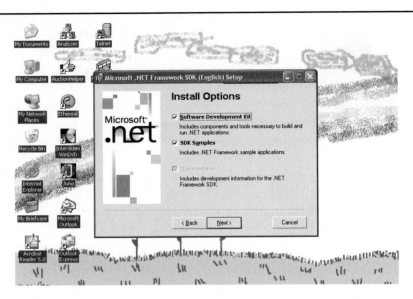

FIGURE 1.3:
.NET Framework
Install Options screen

If you are tight on disk space, you can prevent the SDK samples from being loaded on the workstation by deselecting the SDK Samples checkbox. After the Install Options screen, the program asks where to install the SDK components. This only applies to some of the components, as the DLLs and executable files used by the .NET Framework must be installed on the system drive (usually C:\). After you select the installation destination, the installation begins. When it's completed, you should be ready to compile and run C# programs.

TIP   It"s a good idea to check out the Microsoft .NET Framework home page occasionally to see if new service packs are released, and then to install them as directed.

The C# Runtime Environment

The .NET Framework provides not only a development environment, but also a CLR environment for Windows workstations and servers that only run .NET programs. The .NET Framework contains lots of DLL files used to supply libraries to support .NET application programs. These libraries must be loaded on any workstation or server you want your .NET program to run on. However, you do not need to load the .NET Framework SDK on every machine that runs your program. As alluded to previously, Microsoft has a solution to this aggravation.

Microsoft has indicated that all future Windows operating systems will include the .NET Framework runtime (CLR) environment, starting with the Windows .NET Server release. This will ensure that .NET applications will run on the new OSes without your having to manually install any .NET Framework libraries. Unfortunately, this is not the case with older versions of Windows (98, Me, NT, 2000, and XP). The solution for these systems is manually installing a runtime version of the .NET Framework libraries.

The .NET Framework runtime version is a much smaller distribution than the SDK package. It includes only the files necessary to run .NET applications on the Windows workstation or server. The following section describes how to download and install the .NET Framework runtime files on older Windows platforms.

Downloading and Installing the C# Runtime Package

The C# runtime package is part of the .NET Framework Redistributable package. The Redistributable package contains runtime environments for all .NET languages. Similar to the SDK package, the Redistributable package can be obtained from the .NET Framework home page at www.microsoft.com/netframework/. Because this is a much smaller distribution, there is no multipart download option. The entire package must be downloaded as a single piece (about 20MB).

The download file, dotnetredist.exe, is actually a compressed file that must be uncompressed into a working directory. When you run the program, it will ask for a working directory to use. You can choose any location that has enough space (about 22MB). The extracted file is named dotnetfx.exe.

There is not much to installing the .NET Framework Redistributable package. After starting the dotnetfx.exe file, you're asked to confirm the installation, and then the files are installed. You don't have any choice as to locations for the Redistributable package files; they all go into default locations on the system drive.

Developing with the C# Runtime

Currently, the .NET Framework Redistributable package includes the C# compiler program, csc.exe. This allows developers who do not have workstations or servers running Windows NT 4, 2000, or XP to compile C# programs without installing the .NET Framework SDK. Any machine that supports the .NET Framework runtime can be used to compile C# applications using the csc.exe program. This includes Windows 98 and Me workstations. Though the compiler is included, none of the documentation or debugging programs are, so this is pretty much a bare-bones development environment.

If you want to compile C# programs from the Redistributable package, you must add the location of the csc.exe program to the PATH environment variable of your system. This differs depending on the system you are using.

- For Windows 98 and Me systems, you can add the PATH statement in the autoexec.bat file located in the C:\ directory. There may already be an autoexec.bat file present, and it may already have a PATH statement in it. If so, you can append the csc.exe path to the existing PATH statement.

- For release 1 of the .NET Framework Redistributable package, csc.exe is located in the C:\Windows\Microsoft.Net\Framework\v1.0.3705 directory. (Remember that on Windows 98 and Me, the Windows system directory is called Windows; on Windows NT and 2000 systems, it is Winnt.)

After rebooting the system you should be able to access the csc.exe compiler program from the command-line prompt, as in the following example:

```
C:\>csc
Microsoft (R) Visual C# .NET Compiler version 7.00.9466
for Microsoft (R) .NET Framework version 1.0.3705
Copyright (C) Microsoft Corporation 2001. All rights reserved.

fatal error CS2008: No inputs specified

C:\>
```

You are now ready to start programming using the C# language.

C# Programming Basics

Though it's considered a bare-bones development environment, the .NET Framework SDK contains quite a few tools that allow you to create, compile, and debug C# programs. This section describes some of the tools that are at your disposal.

Creating C# Programs

If you are using one of the Microsoft Visual products to develop your programs (Visual Studio .NET or Visual C# .NET), you have a complete program editing environment, including help files, graphical wizards, and command completion wizards. If you are using the .NET Framework SDK package, you are on your own for producing and compiling your C# code. Although this SDK's features pale in comparison to the fancy Visual packages, it is nonetheless just as valid a way to produce C# applications.

The first step to working with C# programs in the .NET Framework development environment is to associate the C# source code filename extension with a text editor. This will make editing programs much easier; you can just double-click a program from within the Windows Explorer program to begin editing. The type of editor you select is important. Choose one that allows you to save your source code files in text mode rather than a Microsoft Word .doc file or other word processing document, because the C# compiler must be able to interpret each line of code. If you do select a word processing package to edit your C# programs, make sure that you save all of the files in text format.

After you select an editor, associate the .CS file type to the editor application within the Windows Explorer: right-click a C# program, select the Open With option, and select the appropriate application from the list.

If you are new to C#, you may want to practice compiling and debugging C# programs. To do that, you must first have a sample program to work with. Listing 1.1 shows a simple program that demonstrates some basic C# programming principles.

Listing 1.1   **SampleClass.cs program**

```
class DataClass
{
    private int a;
    private int b;

    public DataClass(int x, int y)
    {
        a = x;
        b = y;
    }

    public int addem()
    {
        return a + b;
    }
}

class SampleClass
{
    static int sampleX;
    static int sampleY;

    public SampleClass()
    {
        DataClass sample = new DataClass(sampleX, sampleY);
        System.Console.WriteLine("The result is: {0}", sample.addem());
    }

    public static void Main(string[] argv)
    {
    if (argv.Length != 2)
```

```
        {
            System.Console.WriteLine(" Usage: SampleClass x y");
            return;
        }
        sampleX = System.Convert.ToInt16(argv[0]);
        sampleY = System.Convert.ToInt16(argv[1]);
        SampleClass starthere = new SampleClass();
    }
}
```

The sample program contains two separate C# classes, DataClass and SampleClass. DataClass declares two private integers (that is, they are only accessible from the DataClass class), a constructor for the class, and a method that manipulates the data. The DataClass constructor defines what happens when DataClass is instantiated from a program:

```
public DataClass(int x, int y)
    {
        a = x;
        b = y;
    }
```

The default constructor requires two integers. The two integers are assigned to the internal private variables *a* and *b* defined in the class. The one method that is defined, addem, returns an integer value that is the addition of the two private variables:

```
public int addem()
    {
        return a + b;
    }
```

NOTE   Once DataClass is defined in the program, other classes in the program can use it. In C#, unlike C^{++}, you can use classes before they are defined without first declaring them. The SampleClass code could just as easily have been defined first, before the DataClass definition. The C# compiler will realize that the required class is located later in the program. You can even declare classes in separate files, as long as you include them on the command line when compiling. The compiler will only complain if declared classes are never found in any of the program files listed on the command line.

SampleClass contains two static integer variables, a constructor, and a Main() method, which instructs the C# compiler where to start execution of the program. The Main() method first checks to ensure that two command-line parameters have been entered, converts them to integer values, and assigns them to the two integer variables defined. It then creates an instance of SampleClass using the statement

```
SampleClass starthere = new SampleClass();
```

This forces the CLR to execute the SampleClass constructor to create a new instance of the class.

The SampleClass constructor code creates an instance of DataClass, passing the two integers to the DataClass class constructor. The addem() method is called from the instantiated SampleClass variable and returns the result of the addition method. The following line is used to display the result of the addem() method to the console screen:

```
System.Console.WriteLine("The result is: {0}", sample.addem());
```

The symbol {0} is used as a placement value to represent a variable listed after the text string, in this case replaced with the return value of the sample.addem() method. You can add additional variables by continuing the placement numbers ({1}, {2}, and so on). Each additional variable is added to the variable list separated by commas.

After typing the program code, you must save the file using a .CS extension, which identifies the file as a C# code file. Once you save the file, you are ready to compile it.

Compiling and Running C# Programs

The .NET Framework SDK and Redistributable packages both contain the C# compiler, csc.exe. Any C# program, no matter how complex, can be compiled using just this compiler. Many different switches can be used on the command line to control the behavior of the compiler function. Some of the most common are listed in Table 1.1.

TABLE 1.1: csc Command Line Switches

Switch	Function
/out:*filename*	Defines the executable filename of the program
/main:*classname*	Defines the class that contains the Main() method
/target:*target*	Defines the type of program. The *target* can be exe for console-based apps, winexe for Windows graphical apps, library for Windows DLL files, or module for assembly modules
/debug:*type*	Creates debugging information for the executable file. The *type* can be full (the default), which enables attaching the debugger to a running process, or it can be pdbonly, which only creates a .pdb database file for debugging within a debugging tool
/resource:<*res*>	Embeds the resource specified in the executable file

After you determine what command-line options (if any) you need, compiling the C# program using the csc command-line compiler is simple:

```
C:\>csc SampleClass.cs
Microsoft (R) Visual C# .NET Compiler version 7.00.9466
for Microsoft (R) .NET Framework version 1.0.3705
Copyright (C) Microsoft Corporation 2001. All rights reserved.

C:\>
```

The compile was successful if the command prompt returns with no text messages. If any errors or warnings are indicated by the C# compiler, you must edit the source code file to correct them. Each error or warning produced by the compiler indicates the line where the error occurred. Here is an example of the error produced by `csc` when a typo occurs within the source code:

```
C:\>csc SampleClass.cs
Microsoft (R) Visual C# .NET Compiler version 7.00.9466
for Microsoft (R) .NET Framework version 1.0.3705
Copyright (C) Microsoft Corporation 2001. All rights reserved.

SampleClass.cs(36,12): error CS0117: 'System.Convert' does not contain a
        definition for 'oInt16'

C:\>
```

Note the line number, along with position in the line, shown in parentheses within the error message. Also, you get a fairly descriptive error message, helping you to determine the cause of the error. If you are using a text editor that supports line numbers, it is easy to go back into the source code and correct the mistake. If not, happy counting!

Once you successfully compile the program, you can run it from the command line:

```
C:\>SampleClass 5 10
The result is: 15

C:\>
```

You can see that the program has successfully run and displayed the result of the addition of the command-line arguments. Of course, this simple example does not do much error checking on the command-line arguments, so be careful to only enter numbers or the program will blow up and produce an error message—but more on that later in the C# Exception Programming section.

Using Multiple Source Files

The `SampleClass.cs` example program defined two separate classes in one source code file. This was easy to do for a small example, but larger programs can get confusing when you're combining classes into one source code file. Often it is best to create a separate source code file for each class used in the application. This allows better code management, especially when several people are working on an application that contains hundreds of classes. For example, two separate files could be created:

- `DataClass.cs` for the `DataClass` class code
- `SampleClass2.cs` for just the `SampleClass` class code

There are a few things to be careful of when you separate classes out into discrete source code files. First, you must ensure that the C# compiler can find them at compile time. The easiest way to do this is to include all related source code files on the command line, as follows:

```
C:\>csc SampleClass2.cs DataClass.cs
```

Be careful when you do this, however, because the source code file listed first will be the default .exe filename. If you want to change the .exe filename, you can use the /out: command line switch:

```
C:\>csc /out:SampleClass2.exe DataClass.cs SampleClass2.cs
```

Another issue is the importance of telling the compiler where the program execution starts. If only one class has a Main() section defined, this will work fine. However, sometimes different classes can use methods from other classes, but both classes may contain a Main() method. This would confuse the compiler, as it would not know from which Main() method to start to run the program.

A command-line switch for the csc.exe program solves this problem. The /main:*switch* defines the class that contains the Main() method you want to use:

```
C:\>csc /main:SampleClass SampleClass2.cs DataClass.cs
```

Notice that you must specify the class that the Main() method is in, not the source code filename.

Debugging C# Programs

The .NET Framework SDK offers two excellent ways to debug C# programs:

- dbgclr is a GUI debugging program
- cordbg is a command-line text debugging program

The graphical dbgclr program and the text mode cordbg program have similar features but present different interfaces. Both allow you to step through the C# program and watch variables and outputs as execution proceeds. To do this, though, you must compile the executable program using the /debug option on the csc compiler:

```
C:\>csc /debug SampleClass.cs
```

This command performs two actions: an attribute is set in the executable file that informs the CLR JIT compiler that code tracking must be done, and a programmer database (PDB) file is created that contains code tracking information for the debugger. The added attribute is called the JIT Tracking flag. It informs the CLR JIT compiler that the code must be disassembled from the generated native code back to MSIL instructions and ultimately mapped back to the original source code. All of this information is contained in the PDB file for the executable file.

Using the dbgclr Program

The dbgclr program provides a Windows environment that can be used to watch and trace a running C# program to look for coding errors. The dbgclr program is located under the Microsoft.Net directory you specified when installing the SDK. The default location is as follows:

```
C:\Progam Files\Microsoft.Net\FrameworkSDK\GuiDebug\dbgclr.exe
```

When dbgclr is run, you must specify the source code and executable file location for the application. To do this, follow these steps:

1. From the Menu Bar, click Debug ➤ Program to Debug.

2. Next to the Program text box, click the ellipsis (...) button and select the SampleClass.exe program you want to debug. (Remember that the executable program must have been compiled with the /debug switch.) The Working Directory text box will automatically display the directory location of the executable file. Also, in the Arguments text box, type in any required arguments for the program; for the SampleClass program, type in any two numbers. Click OK when you are finished.

3. Click File ➤ Open ➤ File. Select the SampleClass.cs source code file for the application, and click Open.

At this point, the dbgclr program will display four separate windows:

- The source code file
- The Solution Explorer
- The application output
- The command window

You should see the SampleClass.cs file in the source code window, and the Solution Explorer should list this file in the Miscellaneous Files section. To start debugging, from the menu bar, click Debug ➤ Step Into. This starts the program and allows you to single step though the code (see Figure 1.4).

FIGURE 1.4:

Using dbgclr to
single-step through
an application

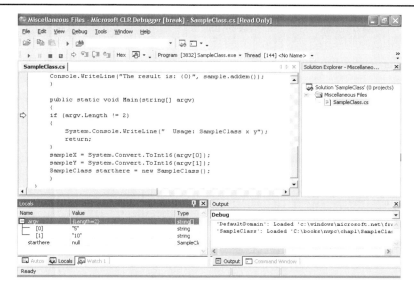

When the debugging process starts, a new window appears showing various variables used within the application code. Note in Figure 1.4 that the command-line argument values you entered are displayed under the Locals tab, along with the Length value (which should be 2). This allows you to easily watch variable values throughout the execution of the program. This is handy if you are getting a corrupt variable value within the program and want to investigate.

The Step Into function starts executing the program line by line, starting at the Main() section. The current code line is highlighted in yellow. By pressing F11, you can single step through the entire program. You can also click buttons on the toolbar to step over code, as well as step out of (or back up from) a code segment. This gives you great control in watching the program execute.

Using the cordbg Program

The cordbg command-line tool has similar functionality to that of dbgclr, without the graphical windows. It, too, allows you to single step through a program and monitor variable values as you go along, but with allowing text input and providing a text output. Listing 1.2 shows a sample debug session using cordbg.

Listing 1.2   Sample output from cordbg

```
C:\>cordbg
Microsoft (R) Common Language Runtime Test Debugger Shell Version 1.0.3705.0
Copyright (C) Microsoft Corporation 1998-2001. All rights reserved.

(cordbg) run SampleClass.exe 5 10
Process 356/0x164 created.
Warning      couldn't load symbols for
c:\winnt\microsoft.net\framework\v1.0.3705\ms
corlib.dll
[thread 0xff] Thread created.

031:     if (argv.Length != 2)
(cordbg) sh
026:     System.Console.WriteLine("The result is: {0}", sample.addem());
027:       }
028:
029:      public static void Main(string[] argv)
030:       {
031:*    if (argv.Length != 2)
032:       {
033:          System.Console.WriteLine("  Usage: SampleClass x y");
034:          return;
035:       }
036:     sampleX = System.Convert.ToInt16(argv[0]);
(cordbg) pro

PID=0x164 (356)  Name=C:\SampleClass.exe
          ID=1  AppDomainName=SampleClass.exe
(cordbg) p argv
argv=(0x00e718b8) array with dims=[2]
  argv[0] = (0x00e718d0) "5"
  argv[1] = (0x00e718e4) "10"
(cordbg) s

036:     sampleX = System.Convert.ToInt16(argv[0]);
(cordbg) so

037:     sampleY = System.Convert.ToInt16(argv[1]);
(cordbg) so

038:    SampleClass starthere = new SampleClass();
(cordbg) s

023:     public SampleClass()
(cordbg) s

[0007] nop
```

```
(cordbg) s

[001c] mov            ecx,0B65210h
(cordbg) s

006:     public DataClass(int x, int y)
(cordbg) s

[0007] nop
(cordbg) s

[0014] mov            dword ptr [esi+4],edi
(cordbg) s

009:     b = y;
(cordbg) s

010:     }
(cordbg) s

025:     DataClass sample = new DataClass(sampleX, sampleY);
(cordbg)
```

Note that when the cordbg program is started, you can use the run command with the file-name of the executable program, along with any pertinent command-line parameters for the executable program. Alternatively, you can run the cordbg command with the executable program and arguments on the command line.

The cordbg program uses text commands to step through the program and display pertinent information. Table 1.2 describes some of the text commands that can be used.

TABLE 1.2: cordbg text commands

Command	Function
s	Step into one line of source code
si	Step into one line of source code
so	Step over the next line of code
ss	Step into the next native or IL instruction
p *arg*	Print the current value of the variable *arg*
pro	Show the system process information for the running program
reg	Display the CPU registers for the current thread
run *prog*	Run the progam *prog* in the debugger
break	Set or display a breakpoint in the code
sh	Show the current line of code, along with five lines before and after

As demonstrated, you can do everything in `cordbg` that you can in `dbgclr`. In fact, many advanced developers prefer to use `cordbg` because it can be faster than waiting for the graphical `dbgclr` program to do its thing.

Watching the C# program execute is one way to debug your application. The next section describes a tool for observing the actual MSIL code generated by the `csc` compiler and run by the CLR.

Debugging MSIL Code

If you really want to get under the hood of your program, you must look at the MSIL code—the actual code that is compiled by the CLR JIT compiler to create the native system code for the host. The .NET Framework SDK gives you a tool that helps you do this: the Microsoft Intermediate Language Disassembler (IL DASM). You must run the `ildasm.exe` program from the command line, along with the name of the CLR executable program to monitor to see the code:

```
C:\>ildasm SampleClass.exe
```

Figure 1.5 shows the IL DASM window with the classes and variables that are contained in the program. IL DASM gives you a hierarchical view of the code, separating the classes and the variables and methods within classes. To see the actual MSIL code, double-click an individual section. Figure 1.6 shows the result from clicking the `addem()` method. Even without knowing much about MSIL, you can see that this section of code retrieves two values from memory and adds them.

FIGURE 1.5:

The IL DASM window

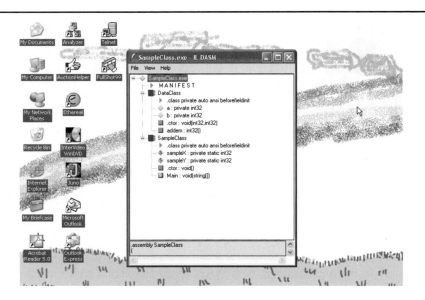

FIGURE 1.6:

MSIL code generated for the `addem()` method

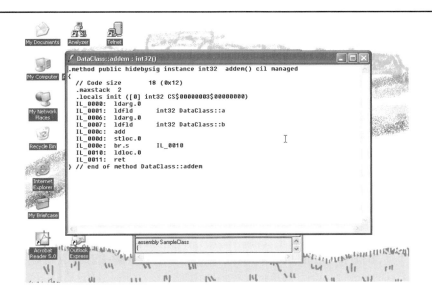

NOTE   If you want to debug your applications at the CLR level, you must learn the MSIL assembly code, which is way beyond the scope of this book.

Now that you are familiar with the C# development environment, it is time to start working on C# code. Let's begin by looking at some features of C# that are different from other programming languages and that are often used in network programs. If you are already familiar with the C# language, feel free to skip to the next chapter.

C# Features

C# is an object-oriented language created by Microsoft that incorporates many features that may be new to experienced C, C++, and Visual Basic programmers. If you are not familiar with the C# programming language at all, I suggest you purchase a book on C# programming, such as Sybex's *Mastering Visual C# .NET* by Jason Price and Michael Gunderloy, or *Visual C# .NET Programming* by Harold Davis, also from Sybex. Texts like these fully explore the features of this exciting language. The following sections provide a brief synopsis of some unique C# features that are crucial to understand before you begin network programming.

C# Namespaces

With all of the classes provided in the .NET Framework, it's easy to get confused about which classes perform which functions and the methods that should be used from particular classes. To help simplify things, Microsoft uses *namespaces* in classifying .NET Framework classes.

What Are Namespaces?

As shown in the SampleClass program, each C# application consists of one or more classes. Each class defines an object that can contain data and methods to manipulate the data. At least one class in each application must contain a program interface method called `Main()`. The `Main()` method lets the C# compiler know where to begin execution of the program. Other classes can be defined within the program (such as the `DataClass`), or can even be shared with other programs.

Sharing classes among programs is the goal of object-oriented programming. One of the issues involved in class sharing is the importance of unique and meaningful class names. If you are working alone and on simple projects, it is unlikely that you will run into the problem of calling two (or more) classes by the same name. However, on a large development team that needs to create hundreds of classes, having a class naming structure in place is critical to success.

C# namespaces are used to identify a higher-level hierarchy of class names, allowing you to group similar classes together within a single namespace. The namespace is defined in the source code file before the class definition, using the `namespace` directive:

```
namespace Test1;

class testProgram
{

}

namespace Test2;
class testProgram
{

}
```

For programs that do not declare a namespace (such as the `SampleClass` program) the defined classes become part of a *global namespace*. These classes are globally available to any application in the CLR.

Each namespace uniquely identifies the programs within it. Notice that both of the sample namespaces just shown contain a class called `testProgram`; most likely they perform separate functions. If your program needs to use one or both of the `testProgram` classes, you must specify which class you mean to use by referencing the namespace.

The .NET Framework contains many classes separated into namespaces, which help classify the various classes into groups of common functions. You must know how to properly declare the classes you use so that there is no confusion by the compiler when your program is compiled. Let's examine the specific namespaces used in the .NET Framework.

.NET Framework Namespaces

The .NET Framework uses namespaces to help categorize library classes used in the CLR. This helps programmers determine the location of various classes and how to define them in their programs.

Many .NET Framework namespaces make up the core CLR classes. Table 1.3 lists some of the common namespaces you will encounter in your C# network applications.

TABLE 1.3: .NET Framework Class Namespaces

Namespace	Description of Classes
Microsoft.Win32	Handles events raised by the OS and Registry handling classes
System	Base .NET classes that define commonly used data types and data conversions
System.Collections	Defines lists, queues, bit arrays, and string collections
System.Data	Defines the ADO.NET database structure
System.Data.OleDb	Encapsulates the OLE DB .NET database structure
System.Drawing	Provides access to basic graphics functionality
System.IO	Allows reading and writing on data streams and files
System.Management	Provides access to the Windows Management Instrumentation (WMI) infrastructure
System.Net	Provides access to the Windows network functions
System.Net.Sockets	Provides access to the Windows sockets (Winsock) interface
System.Runtime.Remoting	Provides access to the Windows distributed computing platform
System.Security	Provides access to the CLR security permissions system
System.Text	Represents ACSII, Unicode, UTF-7, and UTF-8 character encodings
System.Threading	Enables multi-threading programming
System.Timers	Allows you to raise an event on a specified interval
System.Web	Enables browser and web server functionality
System.Web.Mail	Enables sending mail messages
System.Windows.Forms	Creates Windows-based application using the standard Windows graphical interface
System.XML	Provides support for processing XML documents

Using Namespaces in Programs

As explained, each namespace provides support for a specific group of classes. Once you have located the namespaces that contain the classes you need for your program, you must define them in your program to access the classes. There are two methods of identifying .NET Framework classes in your programs.

The first method was demonstrated in the SampleClass program:

```
System.Console.WriteLine("The result is {0}", sample.addem());
```

This command uses the `WriteLine()` method of the `Console` class, found in the `System` namespace. Notice the hierarchy used in referencing the method. First the namespace is declared, followed by the class name, and finally the method name. You can reference all of the .NET Framework classes in your program using this method, but you might quickly get tired of typing.

An easier way is to declare the namespace with the C# `using` directive at the beginning of the program. Any classes contained within a namespace declared with `using` do not have to be referenced by their namespace name:

```
using System;

Console.WriteLine("The result is {0}", sample.addem());
```

The C# compiler searches all declared namespaces for the `Console` class and automatically references the proper namespace.

WARNING Be careful using this method of declaring namespaces, because you can run into situations where two declared namespaces have classes with the same name (such as the Timer class). In that case, you must supply the full namespace name when referencing the class. If you don't, the C# compiler will complain that it cannot determine which class you are trying to reference.

After the namespaces have been declared and you use the namespace classes in your program, you must ensure that the C# compiler can find the proper class libraries when you compile your program. The next section explains how this is done.

Compiling Programs with Namespaces

The .NET Framework implements the CLR class library as a set of DLL files. Each DLL file contains a specific subset of classes from one or more namespaces. Not only must the DLLs be available when you run your .NET program, they must also be referenced on the command line when you compile the program.

You must reference each DLL that is necessary to support all of the namespaces declared in your program. To reference a DLL, you use the /resource command-line switch for the csc compiler:

```
C:\> csc /r:System.dll SampleClass.cs
```

(The /resource switch can be abbreviated /r.) Here, the classes for the System namespace are contained in the System.dll file, so you need to reference the System.dll file on the command line for the SampleClass.cs program to compile properly. You may be wondering why you didn't have to do this when you compiled the program earlier. There is a trick involved.

The csc.exe compiler program uses a configuration file that sets a few standard command-line parameters, including default DLL files to reference. The configuration file is called csc.rsp and is located in the same directory as the csc.exe program file.

You can examine the csc.rsp file with any text editor, such as Microsoft Notepad. Listing 1.3 shows the default csc.rsp file that was installed with my version of the .NET Framework.

Listing 1.3   **Default csc.rsp file**

```
# This file contains command-line options that the C#
# command line compiler (CSC) will process as part
# of every compilation, unless the "/noconfig" option
# is specified.

# Reference the common Framework libraries
/r:Accessibility.dll
/r:Microsoft.Vsa.dll
/r:System.Configuration.Install.dll
/r:System.Data.dll
/r:System.Design.dll
/r:System.DirectoryServices.dll
/r:System.dll
/r:System.Drawing.Design.dll
/r:System.Drawing.dll
/r:System.EnterpriseServices.dll
/r:System.Management.dll
/r:System.Messaging.dll
/r:System.Runtime.Remoting.dll
/r:System.Runtime.Serialization.Formatters.Soap.dll
/r:System.Security.dll
/r:System.ServiceProcess.dll
/r:System.Web.dll
/r:System.Web.RegularExpressions.dll
/r:System.Web.Services.dll
/r:System.Windows.Forms.Dll
/r:System.XML.dll
```

Notice that the majority of the prevalent namespace DLLs are referenced in the `csc.rsp` file. This is a handy feature that keeps you from having to reference lots of files on the command line if you are using classes from several namespaces. As shown in the comment text from the `csc.rsp` file, you can also override the `csc.rsp` values by using the `/noconfig` command-line switch:

```
C:\>csc /noconfig /r:System.dll SampleClass.cs
```

This command will compile the SampleClass program with just the reference to the `System.dll` file.

NOTE   Adding references to additional DLL files does not increase the size of the resulting executable file. The references are only for the purpose of telling the compiler where to find the namespace definitions, not for compiling in the DLL code. The library class code is still run from the DLL. That is why the .NET Framework must be installed on the target workstation or server.

Using Strings in C# Programs

One of the most difficult parts of C programming is dealing with strings. Many program security holes develop from string *buffer overflows*, in which programmers have used character arrays for strings, and hackers place more characters than memory bytes allocated for the string. To alleviate some of the problems of dealing with strings in C# programs, Microsoft has incorporated two string handling classes into the C# language. Because many network protocols are concerned with sending and receiving text strings, it's a good idea to get a handle on using strings properly in C# network programs. This section will help you do that by discussing the use of .NET string classes in the C# language.

The String Class

The basic part of string support in C# is the `String` class. The `String` class allows you to assign a series of characters to a variable and handle the variable in your program as a single unit. The `String` class also contains several methods that can be used to perform operations on string objects, such as determining the length of the string and comparing two strings.

The `String` constructor is overloaded, providing several ways to create a string variable. Table 1.4 describes the string constructors.

TABLE 1.4: String Constructors

Constructor	Description
string(*char[]*)	Creates a string from a specified character array
string(*char*, *int*)	Creates a string from a specified character repeated *int* number of times
string(*char[]*, *int1*, *int2*)	Creates a string from a specified character array, starting at position *int1* with a length of *int2* bytes

In one of the few quirks of C#, you can define strings using either a capital S or a lowercase s in the String declaration. The following are a few examples of declaring string variables:

```
string test = "This is a test string";
string test2 = test;
string anotherTest = new string('a', 10);
```

The first technique just listed is the most common way to create new strings. After the string is created, several other methods are available for manipulating and operating on the string. Table 1.5 shows some of the more popular methods.

TABLE 1.5: String Methods

Method	Description
Clone	Returns a reference to the string
Compare	Compares two specified strings
CompareTo	Compares a string with another object
Concat	Concatenates two strings
Copy	Creates a new string with the value of an existing string
CopyTo	Copies a specified number of characters from one string, starting at a specified location, to another string
EndsWith	Determines if a string ends with a specified string
Equals	Determines if two strings have the same value
IndexOf	Returns the first occurrence of a specified string within the string
Insert	Inserts a specified string at a specified location of the string
Intern	Retrieves the system reference for the string
Join	Concatenates a specified string between each element of the string array

Continued on next page

TABLE 1.5 CONTINUED: String Methods

Method	Description
LastIndexOf	Returns the index location of the last occurrence of the specified string in the string
PadLeft	Right-aligns the characters of the string and sets the left-most characters to spaces
PadRight	Left-aligns the characters of the string and sets the right-most characters to spaces
Remove	Deletes a specified number of characters from the string
Replace	Replaces all occurrences of a specified character or string with another specified character or string
Split	Identifies substrings in the string based on a specified separation character
StartsWith	Determines if a string starts with a specified string
ToCharArray	Copies the characters in the string to a character array
ToLower	Returns a copy of the string, setting all characters to lowercase
ToString	Converts the value of the object to a string
ToUpper	Returns a copy of the string, setting all characters to uppercase
Trim	Removes all occurrences of a set of specified characters from the beginning and end of a string
TrimEnd	Removes all occurrences of a set of specified characters from the end of a string
TrimStart	Removes all occurrences of a set of specified characters from the beginning of a string

With all of these string methods at your disposal, it is easy to work with strings in C# programs. Much of the hard work of manipulating and comparing strings has been done for you. Listing 1.4 shows a sample string program to illustrate some of these features.

Listing 1.4   **Sample string program StringTest.cs**

```
using System;

class StringTest
{
    public static void Main ()
    {
        string test1 = "This is a test string";
        string test2, test3;

        test2 = test1.Insert(15, "application ");
        test3 = test1.ToUpper();

        Console.WriteLine("test1: '{0}'", test1);
        Console.WriteLine("test2: '{0}'", test2);
        Console.WriteLine("test3: '{0}'", test3);

        if (test1 == test3)
            Console.WriteLine("test1 is equal to test3");
```

```
        else
            Console.WriteLine("test1 is not equal to test3");

        test2 = test1.Replace("test", "sample");
        Console.WriteLine("the new test2: '{0}'", test2);

    }
}
```

The output from this program should look like this:

```
C:\>StringTest
test1: 'This is a test string'
test2: 'This is a test application string'
test3: 'THIS IS A TEST STRING'
test1 is not equal to test3
the new test2: 'This is a sample string'

C:\>
```

C# creates a set amount of memory for each new string created. Because of this, strings are *immutable*, that is, they cannot be changed. That said, you may see C# code like the following:

```
string newString = new string("test");
string newString += "ing";
```

The resulting value for the variable *newString* is testing.

If strings are immutable, how can you modify an existing string? The answer is, you don't; C# just does some trickery. Instead of modifying the existing string, C# creates a brand new string with the new value. The memory area reserved for the old string is now unused and will be cleaned up on the next garbage collection cycle (CLR's automatic recovery of lost memory). If you do a lot of string manipulation in your programs, these operations can create additional memory overhead. To compensate for this, Microsoft has created another type of string class just for modifying string objects.

The StringBuilder Class

As its name suggests, the StringBuilder class allows you to create and modify strings without the overhead of recreating new strings each time. It generates a mutable sequence of characters that can change size dynamically as the string is modified, allocating more memory as required.

The amount of memory used by the string is called the *capacity*. The default capacity of a StringBuilder string is currently set to 16 bytes (StringBuilder documentation indicates that this value may change in the future). If you create a string larger than 16 bytes, StringBuilder will automatically attempt to allocate more memory. When you want to control exactly how much memory StringBuilder can use, you can manually increase or decrease the string capacity using StringBuilder methods, as well as various StringBuilder constructors when the instance is initially created.

Six constructors can be used to create a `StringBuilder` instance, as shown in Table 1.6.

TABLE 1.6: The StringBuilder Class Constructors

Constructor	Description
StringBuilder()	Initializes a new default instance with a size of 16
StringBuilder(*int*)	Initializes a new instance with a capacity of *int*
StringBuilder(*string*)	Initializes a new instance with a default value of *string*
StringBuilder(*int1*, *int2*)	Initializes a new instance with a default capacity of *int1* and a maximum capacity of *int2*
StringBuilder(*string*, *int*)	Initializes a new instance with a default value of *string* and a capacity of *int*
StringBuilder(*string*, *int1*, *int2*, *int3*)	Initializes a new instance with a default value starting at position *int1* of *string*, *int2* characters long, with a capacity of *int3*

Once the `StringBuilder` instance is created, you have access to several properties, methods, and operations for modifying and checking properties of the string. One of the most useful properties is `Length`, which allows you to dynamically change the capacity of the string. Listing 1.5 shows an example of changing the capacity of the `StringBuilder` string using the `Length` property.

Listing 1.5   **The SampleBuilder.cs program**

```
using System;
using System.Text;

class SampleBuilder
{

    public static void Main ()
    {

        StringBuilder sb = new StringBuilder("test string");
        int length = 0;

        length = sb.Length;
        Console.WriteLine("The result is: '{0}'", sb);
        Console.WriteLine("The length is: {0}", length);

        sb.Length = 4;
        length = sb.Length;
        Console.WriteLine("The result is: '{0}'", sb);
        Console.WriteLine("The length is: {0}", length);
```

```
        sb.Length = 20;
        length = sb.Length;
        Console.WriteLine("The result is: '{0}'", sb);
        Console.WriteLine("The length is: {0}", length);

    }
}
```

The output from the StringSample program should look like this:

```
C:\>SampleBuilder
The result is: 'test string'
The length is: 11
The result is: 'test'
The length is: 4
The result is: 'test
The length is: 20

C:\>
```

The original string is 11 bytes long, but after setting the string length to 4, the resulting string is only the first 4 bytes of the original string. After setting the string length to 20, the string becomes 20 bytes long, but the data originally located after the fourth byte has been lost, with spaces used to pad the extra bytes.

After the final string is built using a `StringBuilder` object, you may need to convert it to a string object to send it to a network stream. This is a simple process using the `ToString()` method:

```
string outbound = sb.ToString();
```

Now the `string outbound` can be used as a normal string object. Just remember that it is now an immutable string, and as such should not be modified (or be aware that you may suffer additional overhead if it is).

Streams, mentioned in the preceding paragraph, are another feature of C# that you should know intimately for network programming. The next section describes C# streams and their uses.

C# Streams

Data handling is one of the most important jobs of programs. There are many methods for storing and retrieving data in the C# world—files, memory, input/output devices, interprocess communication pipes, and networks. There are also many ways of reading data to and writing it from objects. Most objects allow data to be read or written on a byte-by-byte basis. This method transfers one byte of data into or out of the data object at a time. Certainly this works, but it is not the most efficient manner of handling data.

The C# language supplies an interface to assist programmers in moving large chunks of data to and from data objects. The data *stream* allows multiple bytes of data to be transferred simultaneously to a data object so that programs can work on blocks of data instead of having to build data elements one byte at a time.

Streams can support three fundamental operations:

- Transferring data from a stream to a memory buffer (reading)
- Transferring data from a memory buffer to a stream (writing)
- Searching the stream for a specific byte pattern (seeking)

Not all streams support all of these functions. Obviously, a CD-ROM device cannot support streams that write data, and network connections do not support streams that seek data patterns.

The .NET System.IO namespace contains various stream classes that can be used to combine the bytes from a data source into manageable blocks that are easier to manipulate.

The FileStream class is a good example of using a stream to simplify reading and writing data. This class provides a stream interface to easily read and write data to a disk file. Let's look at an example.

If you were writing a program that logged messages to a log file, you most likely would be logging (writing out) one text line of information at a time. You would write the code to place each string in the file byte-by-byte, and ensure that the proper carriage return was added to each text line as it was written. Then, when you wanted to read the log file with a program, you would have to create the code to read the file byte-by-byte. As the file was read, you would have to know that each log file entry ended with the carriage return and that a new entry would start. Each byte read would have to be examined to determine if it was a carriage return.

Instead of this tedious process, you can take advantage of the FileStream class, along with the StreamWriter class, to easily write and read lines of text in a log file. Listing 1.6 shows a sample program that uses streams to simplify file access.

Listing 1.6   **Sample log writing program TestLog.cs**

```
using System;
using System.IO;

class TestLog
{
    public static void Main ()
    {
        string logFile = "LOGFILE.TXT";

        FileStream fs = new FileStream(logFile,
```

```
                     FileMode.OpenOrCreate, FileAccess.ReadWrite);

           StreamWriter sw = new StreamWriter(fs);
           StreamReader sr = new StreamReader(fs);

           sw.WriteLine("First log entry");
           sw.WriteLine("Second log entry");

           while(sr.Peek() > -1)
           {
               Console.WriteLine(sr.ReadLine());
           }

           sw.Close();
           sr.Close();
           fs.Close();
       }
   }
```

Take note of the following things in this example:

- The `FileStream` object can be used for both reading data from and writing data to the stream.

- Both the `StreamReader` and `StreamWriter` objects reference the same `FileStream`, but they perform different functions.

- Each stream object has its own pointer in the stream. After the `StreamWriter` object inserts two new lines in its stream, the `StreamReader` object reads the first object in its stream, which is the first line in the file.

- Each stream opened must be explicitly closed, including the base `FileStream` object. Many novice programmers forget to close the base stream and inadvertently leave it hanging.

The most common stream technique is to create two separate streams for reading and writing:

```
StreamWriter sw = new StreamWriter(fs);
StreamReader sr = new StreamReader(fs);
```

This enables you to have complete control over data access to and from the stream using separate streams.

One thing this program doesn't do is error checking on the file open attempt. If the program is not able to open the log file, it will produce an ugly error message to the user. The next section shows how you can gracefully handle error conditions within C# programs.

C# Exception Programming

One of the biggest problems for programmers is dealing with abnormal conditions in a program. Inexperienced programmers often forget to compensate for error conditions such as dividing by zero. This results in ugly and annoying error messages and programs blowing up in customers' faces. To ensure that your code is user-friendly, try to compensate for most types of error conditions. Such error conditions, or other unexpected behavior occurring when a program executes, are called *exceptions*. Listing 1.7 shows an example.

Listing 1.7   **The BadError.cs program**

```csharp
using System;

class BadError
{
    public static void Main ()
    {
        int var1 = 1000, var2 = 0, var3;

        var3 = var1 / var2;
        Console.WriteLine("The result is: {0}", var3);
    }
}
```

As you can see, this program is doomed from the start. The arithmetic function in line 9 is destined for disaster because of a divide-by-zero error. Compile and run this example and watch what happens:

```
C:\>csc BadError.cs
Microsoft (R) Visual C# .NET Compiler version 7.00.9466
for Microsoft (R) .NET Framework version 1.0.3705
Copyright (C) Microsoft Corporation 2001. All rights reserved.


C:\>BadError

Unhandled Exception: System.DivideByZeroException: Attempted to divide by zero.
   at BadError.Main()

C:\>
```

The csc compiler had no problem compiling this code. It was oblivious to the impending error. When the program runs, a pop-up window indicates that an error occurred and asks you if you want to debug the application. This is exactly the kind of thing you do not want your customers to see. After clicking the OK button, the text error message is produced on the console, indicating the error that was encountered. The program halts at the line of code that produced the error, and no other lines are executed.

C# helps programmers code for exceptions by providing a way to watch and capture exceptions as they occur. By catching exceptions, programmers can efficiently provide for readable error messages and the continuation of the program, or they can stop the program gracefully if necessary. In C#, the `try-catch` block accomplishes this.

The `try-catch` block tries to execute one or more statements. If any of the statements generates an exception, the `catch` block of code is executed instead of the program stopping. Depending on what you include in the `catch` block, the program can either be terminated gracefully, or allowed to continue as if nothing were wrong. Here is the format of a `try-catch` block:

```
try
{
    // one or more lines of code
}
catch ()
{
    // one or more lines of code to execute if an error
}
finally
{
    // one or more lines of code to execute at all times
}
```

The statements in the `try` block are executed as normal within the course of the program. If an error condition occurs within the `try` block, program execution moves to the `catch` block. After the code in the `catch` block is executed, control passes back to the main program statements that follow the `try-catch` block, as if no error had occurred (unless of course the code in the `catch` block stops or redirects the program execution).

Optionally, you can add a `finally` block, which will be executed after the `try` or the `catch` blocks are finished. Sometimes the `finally` block is used for clean-up functions that *must* run whether the functions succeed or fail; most often, however, `finally` is not used.

NOTE Notice the parentheses in the `catch` statement. This is a filter, allowing you to define what types of exceptions you want to attempt to catch. You can define a specific exception to watch for, depending on the type of actions being done in the `try` block; or you can define the generic `Exception` class, which will catch any exception that occurs. You can even define more than one `catch` block. Catch blocks are evaluated in order, so specific exceptions must be listed before general ones.

Listing 1.8 shows an example of a simple `try-catch` block.

Listing 1.8   **The CatchError.cs program**

```
using System;

class CatchError
{
    public static void Main ()
    {
        int var1 = 1000, var2 = 0, var3;

        try
        {
            var3 = var1 / var2;
        }
        catch (ArithmeticException e)
        {
            Console.WriteLine("Exception: {0}",
                    e.ToString());
            var3 = -1;
        }
        catch (Exception e)
        {
            Console.WriteLine("Exception: {0}",
                    e.ToString());
            var3 = -2;
        }
        Console.WriteLine("The result is: {0}", var3);
    }
}
```

In CatchError, the original program is modified by adding a try-catch block. There are two catch statements: one to watch specifically for ArithmeticExceptions, and one to watch for any general Exception. Notice that the specific ArithmeticException was listed first, otherwise the general Exception block would handle all of the exceptions before the more detailed exception appeared. Also note that the catch blocks set a value for the result variable that can then be checked later on in the program. The result of this program is as follows:

```
C:\>csc CatchError.cs
Microsoft (R) Visual C# .NET Compiler version 7.00.9466
for Microsoft (R) .NET Framework version 1.0.3705
Copyright (C) Microsoft Corporation 2001. All rights reserved.


C:\>CatchError
Exception: System.DivideByZeroException: Attempted to divide by zero.
   at CatchError.Main()
The result is: -1

C:\>
```

The `try-catch` block gracefully catches the arithmetic exception, displays the error as instructed in the `catch` block, and sets the variable to a special value that can later be checked in the program logic.

NOTE   Network functions are frequently used within `try-catch` blocks. In network programming, it is often impossible to determine whether an action will succeed. For example, packets sent out on the network may not get to their intended destination because of a down router or destination host. Instead of the program blowing up because of an unexpected network issue, the problem can be reported to the user.

Summary

The Microsoft .NET technology supplies an excellent programming environment for network programmers. The C# programming language allows programmers to easily prototype applications in a short amount of time and lets them design robust network applications that take advantage of the Windows networking features.

Creating a C# development environment is easy with the two comprehensive Microsoft Visual .NET products or the new .NET Framework SDK package. All three environments include compilers and debuggers for creating C# application programs.

The C# language also offers many features that smooth the way for programmers writing network applications. For instance, using the `StringBuilder` class instead of creating and modifying string objects may save your application some performance time. Also, putting streams to work in network programming can simplify handling of data into and out of the network transport. Using exceptions in your programs can make your applications look more professional and save your customers lots of grief.

This chapter discussed the basics of the C# language, and you'll find more basics in Chapter 3. There we'll get into the specific C# classes used for network programming. With the addition of network programming helper classes, C# makes network programming a snap. First, though, Chapter 2 presents a helpful review of IP programming fundamentals.

CHAPTER 2

IP Programming Basics

- Watching network traffic

- Analyzing network packets

- Programming with TCP and UDP

- Finding IP address information

The Internet Protocol (IP) is at the core of network programming. IP is the vehicle that transports data between systems, whether within a local area network (LAN) environment or a wide area network (WAN) environment. Though there are other network protocols available to the Windows network programmer, IP provides the most robust technique for sending data between network devices, especially if they are located across the Internet.

Programming using IP is often a complicated process. There are many factors to consider concerning how data is sent on the network: the number of client and server devices, the type of network, network congestion, and error conditions on the network. Because all these elements affect the transportation of your data from one device to another, understanding their impact is crucial to your success in network programming. Often what you think is happening in your programs is not happening on the network. This chapter describes a method of watching IP traffic on the network to help you debug your network programs.

This chapter also examines the parts of IP communications necessary to your understanding of network communications, along with the inner workings of the two most popular protocols that use IP: the Transmission Control Protocol (TCP) and the User Datagram Protocol (UDP). Finally, one of the most confusing network issues is IP network addressing. This chapter finishes up with a helpful look at Microsoft Windows systems' handling of IP addresses, and how you can programmatically determine the IP address configuration of the system on which your program is running.

Watching Network Traffic

One of the biggest difficulties for network programmers is not being able to see exactly what is happening on the network. Often you think you have created the perfect client/server application, spending hours working out the mechanics of sending and receiving application data among machines, only to find out that somewhere along the network your data is not getting through. A *network analyzer* can be the network programmer's best friend in finding out what is happening "on the wire." Programming errors can often be detected by watching application data pass from one device to another.

This section shows how to install a simple public-domain network analyzer on your Windows workstation or server to help you debug network programming problems.

NOTE   If you are developing C# programs on a Windows NT 4 or 2000 server, you already have a network analyzer program built into your system: netmon. This program offers a way to capture and view network packets that enter and leave the server. Unfortunately, this program is not available on other Windows platforms. Therefore, to be consistent for all C# development platforms, this chapter discusses implementation of a public-domain network analyzer that operates on all Windows platforms on which the .NET Framework runs. This analyzer is the WinPcap driver and its associated tools, WinDump and Analyzer.

Installing the WinPcap Programs

The NetGroup at the Politecnico di Torino developed the WinPcap driver to allow Windows systems to capture network packets. The NetGroup has released a complete set of network monitoring tools to the public domain that use the WinPcap driver and operate on all Windows systems. These tools allow the network programmer to "look under the hood" of the network and see what is happening. The network tools available are WinDump, a command-line packet capture tool; and Analyzer, a Windows-based packet capture tool.

The WinPcap driver is the core of the package. It allows most types of network cards on a Windows workstation or server to be placed in *promiscuous* mode. In promiscuous mode, the network card can receive all traffic on the network, no matter where the packet is destined. (Ordinarily, the network card driver only accepts packets destined for the individual device address, or for a broadcast address.) The WinDump and Analyzer programs can display the network data as readable Ethernet and IP packets, allowing you to watch your application data as it passes between devices on the network.

The WinPcap driver and network tools can be downloaded from the NetGroup home page at `http://netgroup-serv.polito.it/netgroup/tools.html`. Each package tool has its own separate home page that is referenced from the main tool's web page. Each package must be downloaded and installed separately.

At the time of this writing, the current WinPcap driver is version 2.3. After downloading the install file (currently `winpcap_2_3.exe`), double-click the file from within Windows Explorer. An installation window appears, guiding you through the simple installation steps. The WinPcap driver files are stored in preset locations, so you do not have any choices to make during the installation. If you ever need to uninstall the WinPcap drivers (recommended before you upgrade to a newer version), select the WinPcap software from the Add/Remove Programs icon in the Control Panel, and select the Remove option.

WARNING If you happen to find an older version of the WinPcap drivers, be careful. The 2.3 version is the first one certified to work properly with Windows XP systems.

After the WinPcap driver is loaded, install the WinDump and/or Analyzer programs from their individual home pages. At the time of this writing, the latest versions are WinDump 3.6.2 and Analyzer 2.2. The WinDump program downloads as a single executable file that is ready to run. It can be stored anywhere on your system. The Analyzer program downloads as a self-extracting installation program that must be run to extract the Analyzer program and supporting files into a separate directory.

Once you have downloaded and installed the WinPcap driver and network monitoring tools, you can begin watching IP traffic on your network. The next section describes how to use the WinDump command-line network monitor to watch your data.

The WinDump Program

If you have worked on a Unix system, you may be familiar with the tcpdump program, a popular text-based network monitoring tool for the Unix environment. It can either display a summary of each packet that it sees on the network, or a detailed hexadecimal dump of each packet's contents. tcpdump uses simple command-line options to determine what type of packets to capture. The goal of the WinDump program is to re-create the look and feel of the tcpdump program for the Windows command-line environment.

Command-Line Options

The first part of using the WinDump tool is to determine which network interface you want to monitor. Many computers have several network interfaces, including network cards and modems used to dial into Internet Service Providers (ISPs) using the Point-to-Point Protocol (PPP). To see a list of current network interfaces on your system, use the -D option on the WinDump command line:

```
C:\monitor>windump -D
1.\Device\Packet_{E0D13BFC-D26F-45D6-BC12-534854E3AD71} (Novell 2000 Adapter.)
2.\Device\Packet_NdisWanIp (NdisWan Adapter)
3.\Device\Packet_NdisWanBh (NdisWan Adapter)


C:\monitor>
```

The configuration on the workstation illustrated here contains one network card (emulating a Novell 2000 network adapter), and a modem that has two separate PPP connections configured. By default, WinDump will monitor traffic on the number 1 interface. If you want to monitor traffic on a different interface, you must specify it on the command line using the -i option:

```
C:\monitor>windump -i 2
windump: listening on\Device\Packet_NdisWanIp
```

The WinDump program is very versatile. As you might guess, it has lots of available command-line options for modifying its behavior. Table 2.1 shows some of the more common options you might need to use.

TABLE 2.1: WinDump Command-Line Options

Option	Description
-a	Attempts to convert network and broadcast addresses to names
-B *size*	Sets the receive buffer size to *size* bytes
-c *count*	Captures only *count* number of packets
-D	Displays all of the available network interfaces on the system

Continued on next page

TABLE 2.1 CONTINUED: WinDump Command-Line Options

Option	Description
-e	Prints the link-level information on each line of the output
-F *file*	Reads the filter expression from the filename *file*
-i *interface*	Monitors the network *interface*, which can be either the interface name, or a number shown from the –D command
-n	Specifies not to convert addresses to names
-N	Specifies not to print fully qualified domain names
-q	Prints quick (less) packet information
-r *file*	Reads the packets from dump file *file*
-S	Prints absolute TCP sequence numbers
-s *snaplen*	Captures *snaplen* bytes from the packets; the default value is 68
-t	Specifies not to print a timestamp on each line
-w *file*	Writes the output to *file*
-X	Prints each packet in hex and ASCII
-x	Prints each packet in hex

Multiple options can be combined on the command line to create the network monitoring environment you need. For example, the following command will capture the first 200 bytes of each packet, print them in hex, and write the output to a file:

```
C:\monitor>windump -s 200 -x -w testcap
```

Filter Expressions

By default, WinDump attempts to capture all packets it sees on the network interface. Depending on your network (and the placement of your Analyzer workstation on the network), "all packets" may represent a substantial amount of traffic. Often it is difficult to track a single IP session within a bunch of irrelevant network packets. With WinDump, you can specify a filter to decrease the amount of traffic captured to just the information you are interested in monitoring.

WinDump uses a shorthand method of defining filters. A *filter expression* defines the network traffic you want WinDump to capture. By using different filter expressions, you can be as general or as specific as you need to be in instructing WinDump to watch for various packet features.

The filter expression comprises one or more *primitives*. A primitive describes a specific item to filter and consists of a network name or number, along with one or more *qualifiers*. There are three types of qualifiers:

- The type of object referred to by the ID name or number

- The direction the packet flows in relation to the filtered object
- A specific protocol for the filter to address

In practice, using these qualifiers is very simple. If you are interested in seeing only the IP packets on the network, use the following command:

```
windump ip
```

This command captures all IP packets, no matter what the source or destination addresses are. If you want to see traffic from a specific IP address, use a command like this one:

```
windump ip host 192.168.1.6
```

This causes WinDump to capture only IP packets associated with the host, 192.168.1.6. By default, WinDump will capture packets that are either coming from or going to the specified device. Should you only want to see the packets coming from that address, you could add a direction qualifier:

```
windump ip src 192.168.1.6
```

This command causes WinDump to capture only IP packets coming from the 192.168.1.6 device (the source). No reply packets to that address are captured.

You can also specify network addresses to capture packets from all hosts on a specific subnet:

```
windump ip host 192.168.1
```

This command captures IP packets from any host on the 192.168.1.0 subnetwork.

WARNING   Always be aware of the type of network on which you are developing network applications. If your development workstation is plugged into a network switch, you will not see any traffic from other devices on the network, because the switch will block that traffic. Often it is best to use network hubs rather than switches when trying to debug network applications so you can see all of the network traffic.

Running WinDump

The output of the `windump` command shows the necessary information from each packet captured. By default, WinDump will attempt to determine the network name of the device and display each network packet using the device's network name rather than the IP address. You can track a network session based on the device names of the two communicating devices. Listing 2.1 shows a sample Telnet session WinDump capture.

Listing 2.1   **Sample WinDump session**

```
C:\monitor>windump
windump    listening on\Device\Packet_{E0D13BFC-D26F-45D6-BC12-534854E3AD71}
18:46:49.583176 arp who-has SHADRACH tell ABEDNEGO
```

```
18:46:49.583677 arp reply SHADRACH is-at 0:e0:7d:74:df:c7
18:46:49.583717 ABEDNEGO.1037 > SHADRACH.23: S 334792806:334792806(0) win 16384
<mss 1460,nop,nop,sackOK> (DF)
18:46:49.584169 SHADRACH.23 > ABEDNEGO.1037: S 1564900369:1564900369(0) ack 334
92807 win 32120 <mss 1460,nop,nop,sackOK> (DF)
18:46:49.584271 ABEDNEGO.1037 > SHADRACH.23: . ack 1 win 17520 (DF)
18:46:49.996842 SHADRACH.23 > ABEDNEGO.1037: P 1:13(12) ack 1 win 32120 (DF)
18:46:49.997496 ABEDNEGO.1037 > SHADRACH.23: P 1:7(6) ack 13 win 17508 (DF)
18:46:49.997955 SHADRACH.23 > ABEDNEGO.1037: . ack 7 win 32120 (DF)
18:46:49.998081 SHADRACH.23 > ABEDNEGO.1037: P 13:16(3) ack 7 win 32120 (DF)
18:46:49.998174 ABEDNEGO.1037 > SHADRACH.23: P 7:16(9) ack 16 win 17505 (DF)
18:46:49.998657 SHADRACH.23 > ABEDNEGO.1037: P 16:28(12) ack 16 win 32120 (DF)
18:46:49.998986 ABEDNEGO.1037 > SHADRACH.23: P 16:25(9) ack 28 win 17493 (DF)
18:46:50.002249 SHADRACH.23 > ABEDNEGO.1037: . ack 25 win 32120 (DF)
18:46:50.002334 ABEDNEGO.1037 > SHADRACH.23: P 25:41(16) ack 28 win 17493 (DF)
18:46:50.012285 SHADRACH.23 > ABEDNEGO.1037: . ack 41 win 32120 (DF)
18:46:50.177333 SHADRACH.23 > ABEDNEGO.1037: P 28:40(12) ack 41 win 32120 (DF)
18:46:50.177966 ABEDNEGO.1037 > SHADRACH.23: P 41:44(3) ack 40 win 17481 (DF)
18:46:50.192238 SHADRACH.23 > ABEDNEGO.1037: . ack 44 win 32120 (DF)
18:46:50.192334 ABEDNEGO.1037 > SHADRACH.23: P 44:53(9) ack 40 win 17481 (DF)
18:46:50.193672 SHADRACH.23 > ABEDNEGO.1037: P 40:114(74) ack 53 win 32120 (DF)
18:46:50.194002 ABEDNEGO.1037 > SHADRACH.23: P 53:56(3) ack 114 win 17407 (DF)
18:46:50.212238 SHADRACH.23 > ABEDNEGO.1037: . ack 56 win 32120 (DF)
18:46:50.212437 ABEDNEGO.1037 > SHADRACH.23: P 56:59(3) ack 114 win 17407 (DF)
18:46:50.232199 SHADRACH.23 > ABEDNEGO.1037: . ack 59 win 32120 (DF)
18:46:50.753865 SHADRACH.23 > ABEDNEGO.1037: P 114:121(7) ack 59 win 32120 (DF)
18:46:50.859647 ABEDNEGO.1037 > SHADRACH.23: . ack 121 win 17400 (DF)
```

Each line of the WinDump output shows a separate network packet captured. The first two packets show the client workstation (abednego) using the ARP protocol to find the network address of the server (shadrach). After the device determines the proper address, it begins the IP session.

Each IP line in the WinDump output contains the following information:

- Timestamp
- Source IP address (or hostname) and TCP or UDP port
- Destination IP address (or hostname) and TCP or UDP port
- TCP or UDP packet information

The WinDump capture shows the pertinent information for each network packet captured in the text mode listing. If you want to see more detailed information, you can increase the length of the packet captured using the -s command, and you can also print out the data in hex and ASCII using the -X command. The next section shows how WinDump's companion program, Analyzer, gives you the same packet information but in a much easier to read graphical format.

The Analyzer Program

The Analyzer program provides a graphical environment for capturing and analyzing network packets. It has the same functionality as the WinDump program, but with a more convenient user interface.

To start the Analyzer program, double-click the `analyzer.exe` file, or click the Analyzer desktop icon if you selected to create it during the installation. A blank Analyzer window, as shown in Figure 2.1, should appear.

FIGURE 2.1:

The Analyzer window

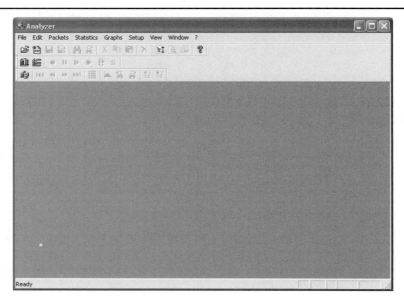

There are four basic functions the Analyzer program can perform:

- Capture and display network packets
- Display packets stored in a file
- Capture network statistics
- Perform real-time network monitoring

Since the point of this section is to discuss capturing network packets, I will not describe the network statistics and real-time monitoring functions of the Analyzer program. These are, however, useful for doing network troubleshooting, and you should investigate them on your own.

To capture network packets, you must click the packet capture icon, which is the first icon on the third row of toolbars. When you click the icon, the Filter Selection window appears, as shown in Figure 2.2.

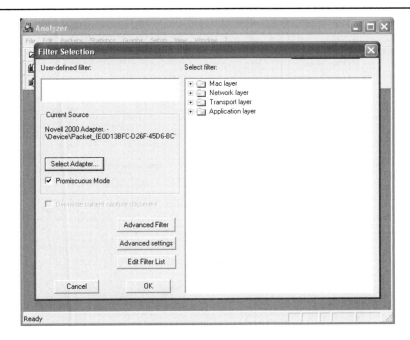

The Filter Selection window allows you to select the network interface to capture packets from, and to define a filter for the packet capturing. By clicking the Select Adapter button, you can select which network adapter to use. The list that appears should be the same as from the windump -D command-line option. Again, any PPP connections that you have defined will show up here as well.

WARNING   Be careful with monitoring PPP connections. At the time of this writing, version 2.3 of the WinPcap driver had some difficulty monitoring PPP connections on WinDows 2000 and XP PCs. Let's hope this will be resolved in future releases

If you want to capture all network packets, you must check the Promiscuous Mode check box; otherwise, all you will see are packets destined to your local device. After you select the network adapter to use, you may define a specific filter to use. In the right side window, the Analyzer program shows a tree of several common filters. By expanding a particular network layer, you can select a specific packet type to capture. Figure 2.3 shows some of the possible filter options available.

FIGURE 2.3:

Analyzer Filter
Selection options

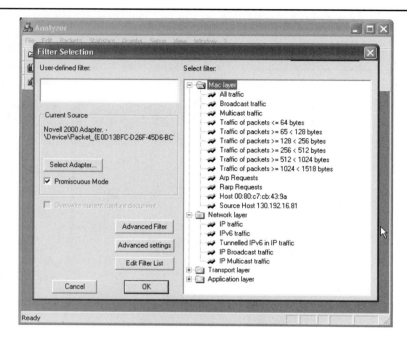

After you select the desired filter options and click the OK button, the Analyzer program begins capturing packets. The Capture in Progress window appears, showing the elapsed time the capture has been running, how many packets have been accepted by the filter, how many packets have been analyzed by the Analyzer, and how many packets have been lost (dropped). To end the capture session, press the Stop button.

When you stop the capture, a Capture document window appears. (You'll see examples of this window in Figures 2.5, 2.6, and 2.7.) It has three sections:

Packet index   This is the top frame of the window, showing all of the packets, captured in order.

Packet details   This is a tree view of the packet-type information, shown in the bottom-left frame of the window. It gives you detailed information about the packet, divided into sections on the various protocols present in the packet data. For example, for a typical TELNET session packet, the following protocols would be represented:

- Ethernet layer transport information
- IP network layer information
- TCP transport layer information
- TELNET application data

Hex and ASCII printout of the current packet   This information is in the bottom-right frame of the window. It shows the raw information for the entire packet (you may have to scroll up/down or left/right to see all of the information). There are two parts to this information: the raw hexadecimal representation of each byte in the packet, and the ASCII code for each byte. This helps you to easily decode the data portion of packets.

To successfully trace and debug a network application, you should know how to decode and understand each of these layers of information contained in the network packet. The next section explores the layers and describes how to decode their information.

Analyzing Network Packets

The ability to watch an IP session and decode its meaning is a crucial skill for a network programmer. To fully understand the concepts behind network programming, you must first understand the IP protocol and how it moves data among network devices. Getting familiar with this information could save you countless hours of troubleshooting network programs that aren't behaving the way you think they should.

The network packets that you capture contain several layers of information to help the data get transported between the two network devices. Each layer of information contains bytes arranged in a predetermined order, specifying parameters specific for the protocol layer. Most packets that you will use in IP network programming will contain three separate protocol layers of information, along with the actual data being transmitted between network devices. Figure 2.4 illustrates the protocol hierarchy used for IP packets, as discussed in the sections that follow.

FIGURE 2.4:

Network protocol
layers in packets

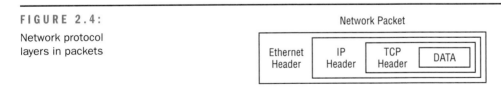

The Ethernet Layer

The first layer of the network packet shown in the Analyzer capture is called the *Ethernet header*. You may see three types of Ethernet protocol packets on your network: Ethernet 802.2, Ethernet 802.3, and Ethernet version 2.

The Ethernet 802.2 and 802.3 protocols are IEEE standard protocols defined for Ethernet layer traffic. Ethernet version 2 is a legacy protocol that is not a standard protocol per se, but it is the most common protocol used on Ethernet networks. Almost all devices (including

Windows systems) use the Ethernet version 2 protocol to transmit IP packets by default. Take a look at the packet details frame in Figure 2.5.

FIGURE 2.5:

Ethernet header data in the Packet Details section of the Analyzer

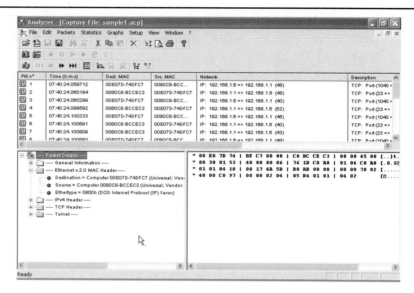

The Ethernet version 2 header shows the Media Access Card (MAC) addresses that are used to identify individual devices on the Ethernet network, along with an Ethernet protocol number that identifies the next layer protocol contained in the Ethernet packet. Each Ethernet packet conforms to a predetermined layout:

- A 6-byte destination Ethernet (or MAC) address
- A 6-byte source Ethernet (or MAC) address
- A 2-byte next-layer protocol identifier
- A data payload of 46 to 1500 bytes
- A 4-byte checksum

The data payload must contain a minimum of 46 bytes to ensure that the Ethernet packet is at least 64 bytes long. (This helps prevent collisions, because sending shorter packets could cause a collision on the network after the packet has been sent, and the sending device would never know.) If the data is not 46 bytes long, padding characters are added. The checksum value supplies a rudimentary error checking mechanism for the data on the network. If the packet becomes corrupt in transit, the checksum will not compute properly, and the packet is marked as bad.

Let's take a closer look at the most important values in the Ethernet header that you will need to check: the Ethernet addresses and protocol identifier.

Ethernet Address

The Ethernet addresses of devices are assigned by the network card vendor and should not be changed (even though in some instances software allows you to override that address). Each device on an Ethernet network must have a unique MAC address. The MAC address consists of two parts:

- A 3-byte vendor identifier, or Organizationally Unique Identifier (OUI)

- A 3-byte device serial number unique to the vendor

The resulting 6-byte network address uniquely identifies the network card on the network, no matter how large the network is. The Internet Assigned Numbers Authority (IANA) assigns vendors MAC addresses to ensure there is no duplication. The assigned numbers are published in Internet Request For Comments (RFC) documents (the most recent Assigned Numbers RFC is RFC 1700). The IANA also maintains a web page (www.iana.org) that contains the most current Ethernet vendor information. Table 2.2 lists a few vendor identifiers for MAC addresses.

TABLE 2.2: Vendor MAC identifiers

Identifier	Vendor
00000C	Cisco
00001D	Cabletron
00002A	TRW
00005E	IANA
000065	Network General
0000A2	Wellfleet
0000A6	Network General (internal assignment, not for products)
0000A9	Network Systems
0000AA	Xerox machines
0000C0	Western Digital
0000E2	Acer Counterpoint
0020AF	3COM
008064	Wyse Technology / Link Technologies
0080C2	IEEE 802.1 Committee
0080D3	Shiva
00AA00	Intel
00DD00	Ungermann-Bass

Continued on next page

TABLE 2.2 CONTINUED: Vendor MAC identifiers

Identifier	Vendor
00DD01	Ungermann-Bass
020701	Racal InterLan
02608C	3Com IBM PC; Imagen; Valid; Cisco
080002	3Com (formerly Bridge)
080009	Hewlett-Packard
08000B	Unisys
080011	Tektronix, Inc.
08001A	Data General
08001B	Data General
08001E	Apollo
080020	Sun machines
08002B	DEC
08002F	Prime Computer Prime 50-Series LHC300
080046	Sony
080047	Sequent
08004C	Encore
08005A	IBM
080069	Silicon Graphics
800010	AT&T

After the 3-byte vendor portion, a 3-byte unique serial number is added to produce the unique 6-byte address. You may see Ethernet addresses referenced in several ways; here are some of the traditional formats:

- As a single value: 0020AFCCEC3

- Using colons: 00:20:AF:BC:CE:C3

- Using hyphens: 00-20-AF-BC-CE-C3

- Using a single hyphen: 0020AF-BCCEC3 (as used by the Analyzer program)

In addition to individual device addresses, the Ethernet addressing scheme allows for broadcast and multicast addresses. In the *broadcast address*, all of the destination address bits are set to 1 (FFFFFFFFFFFF in hexadecimal). Every device on the Ethernet should accept packets addressed to the Ethernet broadcast address. This address is useful for protocols that must send a query packet to all devices on the network; ARP, for example, when a workstation is looking for a device that has a particular IP address.

Ethernet *multicast addresses* are a special form of Ethernet address; only a subset of the network devices will accept the packet. The Ethernet software on the network device must be configured to accept the particular type of multicast address. Table 2.3 is a list of some Ethernet multicast addresses.

TABLE 2.3: Ethernet Multicast Addresses

Address	Description
01-80-C2-00-00-00	Spanning tree (for bridges)
09-00-09-00-00-01	HP Probe
09-00-09-00-00-01	HP Probe
09-00-09-00-00-04	HP DTC
09-00-2B-00-00-00	DEC MUMPS
09-00-2B-00-00-01	DEC DSM/DTP
09-00-2B-00-00-02	DEC VAXELN
09-00-2B-00-00-03	DEC Lanbridge Traffic Monitor (LTM)
09-00-2B-00-00-04	DEC MAP End System Hello
09-00-2B-00-00-05	DEC MAP Intermediate System Hello
09-00-2B-00-00-06	DEC CSMA/CD Encryption
09-00-2B-00-00-07	DEC NetBios Emulator
09-00-2B-00-00-0F	DEC Local Area Transport (LAT)
09-00-2B-00-00-1x	DEC Experimental
09-00-2B-01-00-00	DEC LanBridge Copy packets (all bridges)
09-00-2B-02-00-00	DEC DNA Lev. 2 Routing Layer Routers
09-00-2B-02-01-00	DEC DNA Naming Service Advertisement
09-00-2B-02-01-01	DEC DNA Naming Service Solicitation
09-00-2B-02-01-02	DEC DNA Time Service
09-00-2B-03-xx-xx	DEC default filtering by bridges
09-00-2B-04-00-00	DEC Local Area System Transport (LAST)
09-00-2B-23-00-00	DEC Argonaut Console
09-00-4E-00-00-02	Novell IPX
09-00-77-00-00-01	Retix spanning tree bridges
09-00-7C-02-00-05	Vitalink diagnostics
09-00-7C-05-00-01	Vitalink gateway
0D-1E-15-BA-DD-06	HP
CF-00-00-00-00-00	Ethernet Configuration Test protocol (Loopback)

Ethernet Protocol Type

The other important part of the Ethernet header is the Protocol Type field. The difference between the Ethernet version 2 packet and the Ethernet 802.2 and 802.3 packets occurs in the Protocol Type field. The 802.2 and 802.3 packets both contain a 2-byte value in the same location of the packet, and they both use the value to indicate the total size of the Ethernet packet. The Ethernet version 2 protocol uses those same 2 bytes to define the protocol type used in the next level packet that is contained within the Ethernet packet (see Figure 2.5). This allows network applications to quickly identify the next layer protocol in the packet data.

Similar to the Ethernet vendor addresses are the IANA-assigned values for various protocols that can be identified within the Ethernet protocol type field. Table 2.4 lists some of the assigned protocol values.

TABLE 2.4: Ethernet Protocol Values

Value	Protocol
0800	IP
0806	ARP
0BAD	Banyan VINES
8005	HP Probe
8035	Reverse ARP
809B	AppleTalk
80D5	IBM SNA
8137	Novell
8138	Novell
814C	Raw SNMP
86DD	IPv6
876B	TCP/IP compression

NOTE   Because this book deals with the subject of using IP to transport data across a network, you will see the 0800 value in the protocol type field of all captured packets in the book's examples. This value identifies the protocol of the next layer as being IP.

The IP Layer

The next protocol layer in the Analyzer capture packet is the IP packet. In Figure 2.6, the packet details frame shows the IP layer section of the Analyzer capture for a specific packet. As you can see, the IP protocol defines several additional fields of to the Ethernet protocol information. Table 2.5 describes the IP fields found in the Analyzer capture.

FIGURE 2.6:

IP layer network information shown in Analyzer

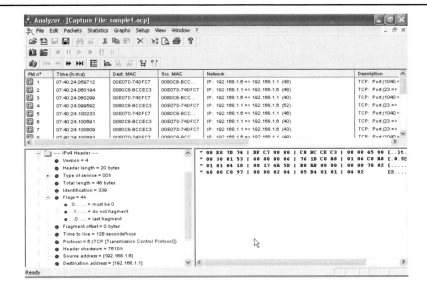

TABLE 2.5: IP Fields

Field	Bits	Description
Version	4	IP header version format (current version is 4)
Header Length	4	The length of the header part of the IP packet, in octets
Type of Service	8	The Quality of Service (QoS) type desired for the packet
Total Length	16	The length of the total IP packet, in octets
Identification	16	An ID value that uniquely identifies the individual IP packet
Flags	3	Indicate whether the IP packet can be fragmented, or if there are more fragments
Fragment offset	13	Location of the fragment in the IP packet
Time to Live (TTL)	8	The maximum time the packet is allowed to remain in the network (in seconds)
Protocol	8	The protocol type of the next level data
Header Checksum	16	A checksum of the IP header data
Source Address	32	The IP address of the sending device
Destination Address	32	The IP address of the receiving device
Options	variable	Optional fields that further define the IP packet characteristics

The value of each field can be seen in the Analyzer packet details frame. Fields that contain more than one type of information, such as the Type of Service and Flags fields, can be expanded to show all of the values in the field.

The following sections describe some of the more important fields of the IP packet that you might have to watch for in your traces.

Address Fields

While Ethernet addresses are good for uniquely identifying devices on a LAN, they do not help at all for identifying remote devices. It is impossible to look at an Ethernet address and determine what network it is on. To help uniquely identify the devices on separate networks, the IP addressing scheme uses particular bits of the 32-bit address to identify address features. The IP address is divided into three parts:

- A preset number of high bits used to identify the packet address scheme used

- A predetermined network address

- A device address on the network

From 1 to 4 *high bits* identify how the network and device addresses are determined within the total 32 bits of the IP address. The network address identifies the unique network where the device is located. Every network should have a unique IP network address assigned to it. IP routers can use the network address information to decide the routing of individual IP packets to the proper remote network, even when they are located across the Internet. The device address uniquely identifies the device within the network address. No two devices with the same network address can have the same device address.

By default the IP address specification uses the 4 high bits to define four classes of network addresses, as shown in Table 2.6

TABLE 2.6: IP Network Address Classes

High Bits	Network Address	Host Address	Type
0	7 bits	24 bits	Class A
10	14 bits	16 bits	Class B
110	21 bits	8 bits	Class C
1110	0 bits	28 bits	Class D

This may seem confusing, but in practice it is fairly straightforward. The 32-bit IP address is almost always broken down into four 8-bit (1 byte) segments, which can then be represented by decimal numbers with periods between them, called *dotted decimal notation*. This is the IP address format you are likely most used to seeing. The decimal numbers are ordered with the network address part on the left side and the host part on the right side.

Using the dotted decimal notation of the IP address, the network class ranges become as follows:

Class A	0.x.x.x–127.x.x.x
Class B	128.x.x.x–191.x.x.x
Class C	192.x.x.x–223.x.x.x
Class D	224.x.x.x–254.x.x.x, which has been further divided into two sections:

IP multicast addresses: 224.x.x.x–239.x.x.x

Experimental networks: 240.x.x.x–255.x.x.x

To complicate things even more, individual class networks can be further divided into other networks, or *subnets*. Each subnet must use a common network address scheme to identify it among the other subnets in the class network. To identify the network part of the IP address, a *subnet mask* is defined for a particular subnet. The subnet mask identifies the bits of the IP address that are used to define the network address part, and the bits used to define the host address.

Let's clarify all this with an example. By default, a class B network address would have a subnet mask of 255.255.0.0, indicating that the upper 16 bits (or first two decimal numbers) are devoted to the network address. The lower 16 bits (or second two decimal numbers) are used to define individual host addresses on the network. Thus, in a default class B network, hosts 130.100.1.6 and 130.100.10.5 are on the same network. Using subnets, however, you can add extra bits to the network address to create subnets of the class B network. For example, if the class B network address 130.100. uses a subnet mask of 255.255.255.0, the third octet also becomes part of the network portion of the address. Thus the individual subnets become 130.100.*x*.0, where *x* can be anything from 0 to 255. This causes address 130.100.1.6 to be a separate network from address 130.100.10.5 because the third octets are different.

The hosts on the subnet network can have addresses ranging from 130.100.*x*.1 to 130 .100.*x*.254 (the host address of all 1s, 192.168.*x*.255, is reserved as a subnet broadcast address). This allows for a single class B address to contain up to 256 subnets, all supporting different networks. This technique is used most often for large building LANs as well as campus LANs to help divide the total number of devices on a network to a manageable number.

Fragmentation Flags

One of the many complexities of IP packets is their size. The maximum size of an IP packet can be 65,536 bytes. This is a huge amount of data for an individual packet. In fact, most lower-level transports (such as Ethernet) cannot support carrying a large IP packet in one piece (remember, the Ethernet data section can only be 1,500 bytes long). To compensate for this, IP packets employ *fragmentation* to divide the IP packet into smaller parts for transport to the destination. When the pieces arrive at the destination, the receiving software must have a way to recognize the fragmented packet and reassemble the pieces back into a single IP packet.

Fragmentation is accomplished using three fields of the IP packet, the fragmentation flags, the fragment offset, and the identification fields. The fragmentation flags consist of three 1-bit flags:

- A reserved flag, which must be zero
- A Don't Fragment flag, which indicates that the IP packet may not be fragmented
- A More Fragment flag, which indicates that this packet is an IP fragment and more fragments are on the way

The IP Identification field uniquely identifies each IP packet. All the fragments of any packet will have the same identification number. This tells the receiving software which packets need to be joined together to create the original IP packet. The fragment offset field indicates the location for the fragment in the original packet.

Type of Service Field

The Type of Service field identifies a Quality of Service (QoS) type for the IP packet, to mark an individual IP packet (or a stream of IP packets) as having a particular priority. In the past this field was not used much. However, recently there has been a push for using this field to prioritize real-time data such as video and audio streams. This will help routers and other network devices to give real-time data packets a higher priority of service to reduce the delay in their transmission. In most network traffic, the Type of Service field will be set to all zeros, indicating normal, routine data. However, with the increased use of IP for transporting real-time data, you may encounter applications that use the Type of Service field to prioritize packets.

The Type of Service (ToS) field contains 8 bits of information, divided into the following subfields:

- 3 bits used as a precedence field
- 1 bit used to denote normal or low delay
- 1 bit used for normal or high throughput
- 1 bit used for normal or high reliability
- 2 bits reserved for future use

The 3-bit precedence field allows for eight levels of packet priority, defined in Table 2.7.

TABLE 2.7: IP Packet Priorities Defined in the ToS Field

Bits	Priority
000	Routine
001	Priority
010	Immediate
011	Flash
100	Flash Override
101	CRITIC/ECP
110	Internetwork Control
111	Network Control

Protocol Field

The Protocol field is used to identify the next layer protocol contained in the IP packet. The IANA has defined 135 values for this field that can be used in IP packets, but in practice on a typical network you will see just a few. Table 2.8 defines some of the more popular values.

TABLE 2.8: IP Protocol Field Values

Value (Decimal)	Description
1	Internet Control Message (ICMP)
2	Internet Group Message (IGP)
6	Transmission Control (TCP)
8	Exterior Gateway (EGP)
9	Interior Gateway (Cisco IGP)
17	User Datagram (UDP)
88	Cisco EIGRP

The two protocols in this table discussed in this book are TCP (protocol 6) and UDP (protocol 17). Most of the applications that you will code using C# will use one of these two higher-level protocols. They are described in the following two sections.

The TCP Layer

The Transmission Control Protocol (TCP) adds connection information to the data packet. This allows programs to create an end-to-end connection between two network devices, providing a consistent path for data to travel. TCP guarantees the data will reliably be delivered to the destination device or that the sender will receive indication that a network error occurred.

Because of this feature, TCP is called a *connection-oriented* protocol. Each TCP connection, or session, includes a certain amount of packet overhead related to establishing the connection between the two devices. Once the connection is established, data can be sent between the devices without the application having to check for lost or out-of-place data.

For a network programmer, it is a good idea to have a basic understanding of how TCP works, and especially how it moves data between devices on the network. Figure 2.7 shows the Analyzer capture window with the TCP Header fields expanded in the packet details tree. These fields contain the information necessary for TCP to implement its advanced connection and data reliability features.

FIGURE 2.7:

The TCP Header fields displayed in Analyzer

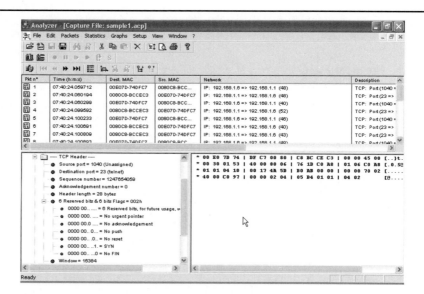

Each of the many fields in the TCP Header is associated with a particular function in the TCP session. The functions worth looking at are as follows:

- The tracking of multiple connections between devices (source and destination ports)
- The tracking of packet order and requests for retransmission of lost packets (sequence and acknowledgement numbers)
- The opening and closing of connection streams between devices for data transmission (TCP flags)

The following sections describe these functions and their roles in network programming.

TCP Application Ports

The first two entries in the expanded TCP Header in the Analyzer capture window are the source and destination *ports*. TCP uses ports to identify individual TCP connections on a network device. The port value identifies a TCP endpoint on the device to be used for a particular application. To communicate with an application on a remote device, you must know two pieces of information:

- The remote device's IP address

- The TCP port assigned to the remote application

For a TCP connection to be established, the remote device must accept incoming packets on the assigned port. Because there could be many applications running on a device that uses TCP, the device must allocate specific port numbers to specific applications. This tells the client which port to use for a particular application and tells the host which application an incoming packet should be forwarded to. Figure 2.8 illustrates an example of how clients and servers use TCP ports to channel data between applications.

FIGURE 2.8:

Sample TCP connection

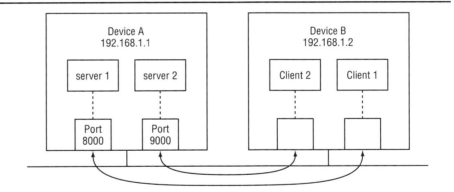

In Figure 2.8, network device A is running two server applications, waiting for incoming packets from remote devices. One application is assigned TCP port 8000 on the device, and the other is assigned port 9000. Network device B is a client that wants to connect to the applications on the server. For a device to send a packet to a remote device, it too must obtain a free TCP port from the operating system, which remains open for the duration of the session. The client TCP port number is usually not important and can be assigned to any available port on the device. The client forwards the packet from an available port on Device B to the application TCP ports on Device A.

The combination of an IP address and a port number defines an *IP endpoint*. A TCP session is defined as the combination of a local IP endpoint and a remote IP endpoint. Only one session can have both these properties the same. A single network application can use the same local IP endpoint, but each remote connection must have either a separate IP address or remote port number.

The IANA has defined a list of standard TCP ports assigned to specific applications. This ensures that any host running the specific application will accept connections on that TCP port for that application. Table 2.9 shows a partial listing of the many different assigned application port numbers.

TABLE 2.9: TCP Application Ports

Port	Description
7	Echo
13	Daytime
17	Quote of the day
20	FTP (data channel)
21	FTP (control channel)
22	SSH
23	Telnet
25	SMTP
37	Time
80	HTTP
110	POP3
119	NNTP
123	Network Time Protocol (NTP)
137	NETBIOS name service
138	NETBIOS datagram service
143	Internet Message Access Protocol (IMAP)
389	Lightweight Directory Access Protocol (LDAP)
443	Secure HTTP (HTTPS)
993	Secure IMAP
995	Secure POP3

Ports that are numbered from 0 to 1023 are called *well-known* ports because they are assigned to specific, common applications. If you are creating a new application, avoid assigning it to one of these ports to avoid confusion. In fact, if an application is already using a port, the system will not allow you to use that port. Ports numbered from 1024 to 65,535 are open for use by any application; even in this wide range, it is still possible to run into two applications that chose to use the same port. For this reason, many custom-made applications give users the choice of defining their own port number to use.

For the network programmer, TCP ports are crucial elements. All server applications must use a valid (and available) port on the network device. It is up to you to decide how to use the TCP port assignment for your application. As mentioned, it is always a good idea to give your customer the option of changing the TCP port number of your application. Just remember that if the server port number changes, the client application must know about this change, or it will never find the server application.

Ensuring Packet Reliability

After the ports, the next fields in the TCP header are the sequence and acknowledgement numbers. These values allow TCP to track packets and ensure they are received in the proper order from the network. If any packets are missing, the TCP system can request a retransmission of the missing packets and reassemble the data stream before passing it off to the application.

Each packet sent has a unique *sequence* number for the TCP session. A random number is chosen for the first packet sent in the session. Each subsequent packet sent by the device increases the sequence number by the number of TCP data bytes in the preceding packet. This ensures that each packet is uniquely identified within the TCP data stream.

The receiving device uses the *acknowledgement* field to acknowledge the last sequence number received from the remote device. The receiving device can receive multiple packets before sending an acknowledgement. The returned acknowledgement number should be the highest consecutive sequence number of data received. This technique is called a *sliding window*. Packets received out of order can be held in a buffer and placed in the right order when the other packets are successfully received, rather than being retransmitted. If a packet it dropped, the receiver will see the missing sequence number and send a lower acknowledgement number to request the missing packet. Without the sliding window each packet would have to be individually acknowledged, resulting in an increase of network traffic and delay.

When troubleshooting TCP problems, the sequence and acknowledgement numbers are often the most difficult part to debug. Often it is best to create a list of packet sequence numbers for each packet from each individual device. By comparing the TCP sequence numbers of each packet, you can determine if packets are being frequently retransmitted (repeated or overlapping sequence numbers in a TCP session). This could mean a network problem somewhere along the line.

Establishing a TCP Session

After the header length field, the TCP Header shows a Flags field that can be expanded to view the fields defined in Table 2.10. The flags are used to control the TCP connection between the two devices.

TABLE 2.10: TCP Flags

Flag	Description
6 bits that are reserved	Reserved for future use—always zero
1-bit URG flag	Marks the packet as containing urgent data
1-bit ACK flag	Acknowledges receiving a packet
1-bit PUSH flag	Indicates data is to be pushed to the application immediately
1-bit RESET flag	Resets the TCP connection to the initial state
1-bit SYN flag	Indicates a TCP synchronization packet (start-of-session)
1-bit FIN flag	Indicates a TCP end-of-session

TCP uses *connection states* to determine the status of a connection between devices. A specific handshaking protocol is used to establish these connections and to monitor the status of the connection during the session. The TCP session has three phases:

- Opening handshake
- Session communication
- Closing handshake

Each phase requires the flag bits to be set in a certain order. The opening handshake is often called the *three-way handshake* and requires three steps to establish the connection:

1. The originating host sends a SYN flag to indicate the start of a session.

2. The receiving host sends a both a SYN flag and an ACK flag in the same packet to indicate it accepts the start of the session.

3. The originating host sends an ACK flag to indicate the session is open and ready for packets.

After the session is established, you will see the ACK flag set on packets, indicating that the device is acknowledging the receipt of a packet with a particular sequence number. To close the session, another handshake is done using the FIN packets:

1. The host initiating the close sends a FIN flag.

2. The remote host sends both an ACK flag and a FIN flag in the same packet to indicate it accepts the end of the session.

3. The initiating host sends an ACK flag to officially close the session.

Sometimes it helps to visualize these steps. Figure 2.9 shows the TCP handshake protocol in action.

FIGURE 2.9:

The steps of the TCP handshake protocol

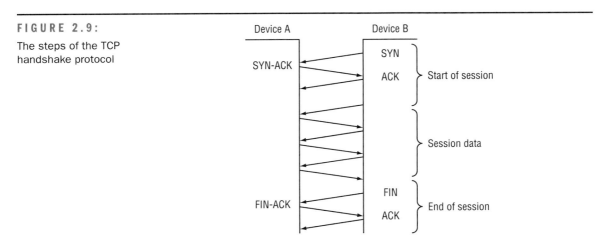

The phases of the TCP session are associated with connection state names. Each connection state indicates the session's current position in the handshaking sequence. The connection states apply equally to clients as well as servers. Both devices in the TCP session follow the same TCP states. Table 2.11 lists the TCP connection states and describes their associated flags.

TABLE 2.11: TCP Connection States

State	Description
CLOSED	The session is not active.
LISTEN	The device is waiting for incoming data on a specific port.
SYN-SENT	The device sent a SYN flag to start a session and is waiting for the remote device to acknowledge and return a SYN flag.
SYN-RECEIVED	The device received a SYN flag, returned both a SYN flag and an ACK flag to complete the start of session, and is waiting for an ACK flag.
ESTABLISHED	Both devices completed the opening handshake and can pass data packets between each other.
FIN-WAIT-1	The device sent a FIN flag to end the session.

Continued on next page

TABLE 2.11 CONTINUED: TCP Connection States

State	Description
FIN-WAIT-2	The device received a FIN flag and returns FIN and ACK flags.
LAST-ACK	The device has sent a FIN flag in response to receiving a FIN flag and is waiting for the final ACK flag from the remote device.
TIME-WAIT	After the LAST-ACK state a device will wait a preset amount of time before officially closing the session port to ensure the remote device does not send additional data.

NOTE   On a Windows system, you can watch these TCP connection states in action using the netstat command-prompt program. The netstat program allows you to list the current status of all the TCP and UDP ports on your Windows workstation or server.

The UDP Layer

The User Datagram Protocol (UDP) is another popular high-level protocol used in IP communications. After studying TCP, UDP will seem like a snap. Unlike TCP, UDP provides a *connectionless* path between network devices to transmit data, and thus does not need all of the overhead of session establishment flags and connection states. Each UDP "session" is nothing more than a single packet transmitted in one direction. Figure 2.10 shows a sample UDP packet in the packet details frame of the Analyzer capture window.

FIGURE 2.10:

The UDP header shown in Analyzer

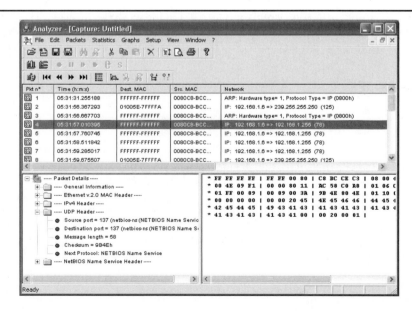

The UDP header fields are pretty straightforward:

- Source Port
- Destination Port
- Message Length
- Checksum
- Next Level Protocol

Like TCP, UDP tracks individual connections using port numbers and assigns port numbers from 0 to 1023 to reserved application ports. Ports 1024 to 65536 are available for you to use in your applications. Table 2.12 shows a list of some of the well-known UDP port numbers.

TABLE 2.12: Well-known UDP Port Numbers

Port	Description
53	Domain Name System
69	Trivial File Transfer Protocol
111	Remote Procedure Call
137	NetBIOS name service
138	NetBIOS datagram
161	Simple Network Management Protocol

Many applications have both a TCP and a UDP port reserved for their use, even though in practice the application only uses one or the other. Either way, it is always safest to use port numbers that are above the reserved port number area to avoid possible conflicts in future protocol changes.

The next section of this chapter describes what you should know about how to use the TCP and UDP protocols for your programs.

Programming with TCP and UDP

Now that you have looked under the hood of TCP and UDP, let's go over what each protocol means to you as a network programmer. These two protocols move data between network devices in very different ways. The following sections describe the features and pitfalls that each protocol presents to network programmers to help you decide which protocol is best to use for your application.

TCP Programming Features

The most important thing to remember about using TCP is that it is a connection-oriented protocol. Once a connection exists between two devices, a reliable data stream is established to ensure that data is accurately moved from one device to the other. Although with TCP your applications do not need to worry about lost or out-of-order data, there is one huge consideration when you are programming with TCP: the buffers.

Because TCP must ensure the integrity of the data, it keeps all sent data in a local buffer until a positive acknowledgement of reception is received from the remote device. Similarly, when receiving data from the network, TCP must keep a local buffer of received data to ensure that all of the pieces are received in order before passing the data to the application program. Because of the separate TCP buffer, data moving between your program and the destination program on the remote host is handled somewhat differently than what you might expect. Figure 2.11 shows how this works.

FIGURE 2.11:

TCP data transfer

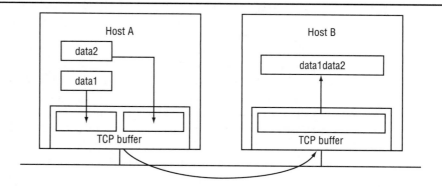

The TCP subsystem on the Windows OS is responsible for accepting data from your application and the incoming data from the remote device. Instead of being immediately sent out on the network, the data will sit in the buffer for a set amount of time. In the meantime, your application may send more data to the remote host, which in turn will also be added to the buffer (as shown by the data1 and data2 data packets). When the TCP subsystem is ready to send the data to the remote device, it will attempt to send all of the contents of the buffer, not just individual pieces, so both the data1 and data2 buffers are sent as a single packet. The receiving host then receives a single packet of data, comprising both the data1 and data2 buffers. It is up to the application program to determine if this is really two separate chunks of data or one large chunk of data.

What does this mean to you as a network programmer? When you send data in messages to a remote device, the remote device won't necessarily receive the data in the same number of message units. The TCP subsystem will place all of the individual messages of data into the

TCP buffer. Depending on the rate at which you are sending data and the rate at which the receiving device is receiving data, those messages (or at least some of them) may get pushed together in the data stream. This "feature" of TCP communications surprises many a novice network programmer.

Because TCP does not preserve data message boundaries, you must compensate for that in your network programs. There are two ways to handle this:

- Create a protocol that requires a one-for-one response to each data message sent from the host

- Design a data message marker system to distinguish data message boundaries within the data stream

Both techniques require a fair amount of forethought before coding begins. Most Internet protocols that use TCP implement the first way of separating data. FTP and similar protocols implement a command/response system where the client sends one message command at a time and waits for the response for each command from the remote host.

UDP Programming Features

UDP was created to solve the message boundary problem of TCP. UDP preserves data boundaries of all messages sent from an application to the network. Because UDP was specifically designed not to worry about reliable data transport, it does not need to use local buffers to keep sent or received data. Instead, each message is forwarded as a single packet as it is received from the application program. Also, each message received from the network is forwarded to the application program as a single message. UDP preserves the message boundary in the network packet, as illustrated in Figure 2.12.

FIGURE 2.12:

UDP data transfer

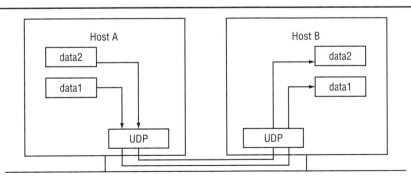

Apart from UDP's capability to preserve message boundaries, it has another problem. Because UDP does not guarantee data delivery, your application must perform that function if it is concerned about the data getting to its destination. Just because a device sends a UDP data packet doesn't necessarily mean that the receiving device received it. You must ensure that your program can deal with missing data packets.

One way around this is to always expect some type of answer from the remote host after you send out a data packet (the *command/response* method). When no answer is received, you should assume that your data packet did not make it through the network to the remote device. This makes sending data via UDP a four-step process:

1. Send data to the remote device.
2. Start a timer, set for a predetermined period of time.
3. Wait for a response from the remote device. When it arrives, stop the timer and go on with your program.
4. If the timer expires before you receive a response, go back and repeat step 1. After you have repeated step 1 a set number of times (the *retry count*) without an answer, assume that you cannot communicate with the remote host.

Although sending data using UDP is somewhat easier as far as message boundaries go, it is a lot more complicated than TCP because you need to do your own checking for lost data packets.

Finding IP Address Information

One of the biggest challenges of network programming is dealing with network configurations of individual workstations and servers. When sending data across the network, you often need to determine the IP network information for the system running your program. The Windows OS family offers many ways to determine IP configuration information, both manually and from within a program. This section demonstrates a few of the ways that you can use to determine IP configuration information both manually and within your C# programs.

Using ipconfig

The ipconfig program displays IP network information for each active network interface on the system. The default form of ipconfig displays basic information for each network device:

```
C:\>ipconfig

Windows NT IP Configuration

Ethernet adapter E190x1:

        IP Address. . . . . . . . . : 192.168.1.6
        Subnet Mask . . . . . . . . : 255.255.255.0
```

```
            Default Gateway . . . . . . : 192.168.1.1

    PPP adapter NdisWan5:

            IP Address. . . . . . . . . : 0.0.0.0
            Subnet Mask . . . . . . . : 0.0.0.0
            Default Gateway . . . . . . :

    C:\>
```

Here, the ipconfig program found two network interfaces configured on the workstation. The first interface is an Ethernet card configured for a LAN with a static IP address assigned to the workstation. The second device is a PPP connection configured to use a modem in the workstation. Because the PPP connection obtains its IP information dynamically when the PPP session starts, the values set by default in the workstation are zeroed. When the PPP connection is enabled, the assigned IP information is displayed.

To obtain more detailed information about a device, use the /all switch for the ipconfig command, as shown here:

```
    C:\>ipconfig /all

    Windows NT IP Configuration

            Host Name . . . . . . . . . : shadrach.blum.lan
            DNS Servers . . . . . . . . : 192.168.1.1
                                          192.168.1.2
                                          192.168.1.3
            Node Type . . . . . . . . . : Broadcast
            NetBIOS Scope ID. . . . . . :
            IP Routing Enabled. . . . . : No
            WINS Proxy Enabled. . . . . : No
            NetBIOS Resolution Uses DNS : No

    Ethernet adapter E190x1:

            Description . . . . . . . . : 3Com EtherLink PCI
            Physical Address. . . . . . : 00-50-DA-10-78-67
            DHCP Enabled. . . . . . . . : No
            IP Address. . . . . . . . . : 192.168.1.6
            Subnet Mask . . . . . . . : 255.255.255.0
            Default Gateway . . . . . . : 192.168.1.1

    PPP adapter NdisWan5:

    Description . . . . . . . . : NdisWan Adapter
            Physical Address. . . . . . : 00-00-00-00-00-00
```

```
DHCP Enabled. . . . . . . . : No
IP Address. . . . . . . . . : 0.0.0.0
Subnet Mask . . . . . . . . : 0.0.0.0
Default Gateway . . . . . . :
```

```
C:\>
```

Using the Registry

The Registry is a treasure chest of information for Windows workstations and servers. It contains lots of information regarding installed software and hardware, including specific configuration information. You can use the C# Registry classes to walk through the Registry on the system to determine many features, including the current IP network configuration. This section describes where to find IP information in the Registry, and how to extract it with a C# program.

IP Info in the Registry

The Registry consists of individual *keys* that store one or more *data items*. Each key stores information for an entity on the system, such as a network card. Each data item has a *value* that defines the data information. The Registry key organization is similar to a directory/ subdirectory structure. A key may contain data as well as several subkeys. Each subkey itself may contain data and additional subkeys; the structure can go several levels deep.

The Windows Registry comprises six base keys from which all other keys are built:

CLASSES_ROOT

CURRENT_CONFIG

CURRENT_USER

DYN_DATA

LOCAL_MACHINE

USERS

The Registry base keys are prefixed with the term HKEY, thus the LOCAL_MACHINE base key is accessed using the key HKEY_LOCAL_MACHINE. For shorthand purposes, this is often called HKLM.

Subkeys are referenced using a directory-like convention, using a backslash (\) to separate levels of subkeys:

```
HKLM\SOFTWARE\Microsoft\Windows NT\CurrentVersion
```

WARNING   Note that the Registry contains key names that can be all uppercase, a mixture of upper- and lowercase, and words with spaces in them. This inconsistency often leads to problems when programming for the Registry.

The Registry contains network information for each installed network device on the system. Unfortunately, the various Windows platforms have their own storage locations for this information. Some platforms relate network information to the individual network interface cards (NICs), while others keep all network information in a common location. The following sections shows you how to find it for each platform.

Windows 98 and Me

Windows 98 and Me devices store network information in a single location, no matter how many network cards are configured on the system. You can always look in the same subkey to find all the IP configurations for the system:

    HKLM\SYSTEM\CurrentControlSet\Services\Class\NetTrans

Within this subkey, the information for each network interface is stored as a separate subkey, named sequentially starting with 0000. Each subkey contains data values that define the IP information for an individual network device. Table 2.13 lists the IP data values contained in the subkey for a network interface.

TABLE 2.13: Network Information Registry Data Names

Data Name	Description
IPAddress	The IP address assigned to this interface
DefaultGateway	The IP router assigned to this interface
IPMask	The subnet mask used to define the network address used on this interface

Windows NT, 2000, and XP

If you are looking for network information on a Windows NT, 2000, or XP system, you must first know what network cards are configured on the system. Network information on these platforms is stored within the individual network card Registry keys and not in a single location as it is for Windows 98 and Me. To obtain the IP address information, you must search for each network card and extract the network information from each location.

The first step is to find the Registry keys of all the network devices configured on the system. Windows NT, 2000, and XP systems have a single Registry key that lists all network interfaces configured on the system. This key is listed under the HKEY_LOCAL_MACHINE (HKLM) root key. The actual subkey is as follows:

    HKLM\Software\Micrososft\Windows NT\CurrentVersion\NetworkCards

It has subkeys for each network interface on the system. Each subkey is numbered sequentially and will contain information about a single network interface installed on the system, stored as a data value to the subkey. The pertinent data value that you need to extract is the *ServiceName* data value. This value points to the network device entry in the `Services` Registry key where the IP information is stored.

Once the *ServiceName* value is obtained for each network device, the next step is to look at the `Services` information area for each network interface *ServiceName*. The appropriate *ServiceName* key will appear as a subkey under the base system services key:

```
HKLM\SYSTEM\CurrentControlSet\Services
```

Each system service has a subkey under this key that contains information for the particular service. The network interface *ServiceName* retrieved from the first step is used as the subkey name, so finding the proper information once you have a listing of all the *ServiceName*s is easy.

The IP information is stored as data values under the `parameters\tcpip` subkey of the `Service` key. The data names used for IP information in the subkey are similar to those shown for the Windows 98 and Me systems:

```
IPAddress
```

```
SubnetMask
```

```
DefaultGateway
```

It is a simple matter to get the IP information stored in the data values. The only tricky part is that on Windows NT, 2000, and XP, each individual network device may have more than one set of IP information. This means that the Registry IP data values for each device can contain more than one value. You must ensure that you retrieve all possible values for the IP data values

---

NOTE   This method only works for network cards with static IP addresses. If your network is using DHCP to assign IP addresses, you will have to check the `DhcpIPAddress` Registry key values for your Windows platform instead.

Using C# to Search the Registry

Once you have determined where to find the network information in the Registry of your target system, you can create C# code to search for it and display the information to the user (or use it in your program). In this section, we'll examine a C# program to query the system Registry for IP information.

The .NET Framework provides a set of classes that help you query and manipulate Registry entries. The .NET Registry classes are contained in two separate namespaces:

Microsoft.Win32.Registry The `Microsoft.Win32.Registry` namespace contains all the base classes needed to access the base Registry key names: `Current_User`, `Local_Machine`, `Classes_Root`, `Current_Config`, `Dyn_Data`, and `Users`. You must use one of the base Registry key names to build your specific Registry subkey.

Microsoft.Win32.RegistryKey The `Microsoft.Win32.RegistryKey` namespace contains the classes and methods necessary to query and modify Registry keys and data. The `OpenSubKey()` method allows you to open a subkey of a known key and access any data values contained in the subkey. Once you have the appropriate subkey, you can use the `GetValue()` method to get the data values assigned to the subkey.

Listing 2.2 presents the `CardGrab.cs` program, which will find the network devices installed on a Windows NT, 2000, or XP system using the system Registry, and display the IP information for each device.

Listing 2.2   **CardGrab.cs program**

```
using System;
using Microsoft.Win32;

class CardGrab
{
   public static void Main ()
   {
   RegistryKey start = Registry.LocalMachine;
   RegistryKey cardServiceName, networkKey;
   string networkcardKey = "SOFTWARE\\Microsoft\\ ➡
           Windows NT\\CurrentVersion\\NetworkCards";
   string serviceKey =
           "SYSTEM\\CurrentControlSet\\Services\\";
   string networkcardKeyName, deviceName;
   string deviceServiceName, serviceName;

   RegistryKey serviceNames =
                     start.OpenSubKey(networkcardKey);
   if (serviceNames == null)
   {
       Console.WriteLine("Bad registry key");
       return;
   }

   string[] networkCards = serviceNames.GetSubKeyNames();
   serviceNames.Close();
```

```
foreach(string keyName in networkCards)
{
    networkcardKeyName = networkcardKey + "\\" + keyName;
    cardServiceName = start.OpenSubKey(networkcardKeyName);
    if (cardServiceName == null)
    {
        Console.WriteLine("Bad registry key: {0}",
                networkcardKeyName);
        return;
    }
    deviceServiceName =
            (string)cardServiceName.GetValue("ServiceName");
                deviceName =
                    (string)cardServiceName.GetValue("Description");
    Console.WriteLine("\nNetwork card: {0}", deviceName);

    serviceName = serviceKey + deviceServiceName +
        "\\Parameters\\Tcpip";
    networkKey = start.OpenSubKey(serviceName);
    if (networkKey == null)
    {
        Console.WriteLine("    No IP configuration set");
    } else
    {
        string[] ipaddresses =
            (string[])networkKey.GetValue("IPAddress");
        string[] defaultGateways =
            (string[])networkKey.GetValue("DefaultGateway");
        string[] subnetmasks =
            (string[])networkKey.GetValue("SubnetMask");

        foreach(string ipaddress in ipaddresses)
        {
            Console.WriteLine("    IP Address: {0}",ipaddress);
        }
        foreach(string subnetmask in subnetmasks)
        {
            Console.WriteLine("    Subnet Mask: {0}",
                subnetmask);
        }
        foreach(string defaultGateway in defaultGateways)
        {
            Console.WriteLine("    Gateway: {0}",
                    defaultGateway);
        }
        networkKey.Close();
    }
}
start.Close();
    }
}
```

You must define a root key to begin the key search. This is done using the Registry class:

```
RegistryKey start = Registry.LocalMachine;
```

This creates a Registry key object `start` and sets it to the root class `HKLM_LOCAL_MACHINE`.

Next, you drill down and set a key object to the pertinent subkey where the network device information is located:

```
string networkcardKey = "SOFTWARE\\Microsoft\\ ➡
            Windows NT\\CurrentVersion\\NetworkCards";
RegistryKey serviceNames =
                    start.OpenSubKey(networkcardKey);
```

Now the key object `serviceNames` points to the location of the installed network device subkeys.

Next you use the `GetSubKeyNames()` method to iterate through each of the network device subkey names. Because the same key name is used for the service keys, you can add that value to the known service key location and open the subkey using the `OpenSubKey()` method, again referenced from the root key:

```
serviceName = serviceKey + deviceServiceName + "\\Parameters\\Tcpip";
networkKey = start.OpenSubKey(serviceName);
```

Once each subkey is opened, the IP information is retrieved from the service key using the `GetValue()` method of the key object. Because each IP information data entry can have multiple values, you must assign the result to a string array and display the complete array using the `foreach` function:

```
string[] ipaddresses =
                (string[])networkKey.GetValue("IPAddress");
foreach(string ipaddress in ipaddresses)
{
    Console.WriteLine("    IP Address: {0}",ipaddress);
}
```

A sample output of the CardGrab program should look like this:

```
C:\>CardGrab

Network card: D-Link DE660 PCMCIA LAN adapter
    IP Address: 192.168.1.6
    Subnet Mask: 255.255.255.0
    Gateway: 192.168.1.1


C:\>
```

You can use a similar technique to find the IP information for Windows 98 or Me devices. In fact, that technique is much simpler because you only have to search in one location for the IP information.

Using WMI

In addition to the Registry, there's another source available to you for obtaining IP network information from Windows systems. The *Windows Management Instrumentation (WMI)* is the Microsoft implementation of *Web-Based Enterprise Management (WBEM)*, which is a standard for accessing system information in a network environment, developed by the Distributed Management Task Force, Inc. (DMTF). Since Windows 2000, Microsoft has included in the OS a database that contains information regarding system hardware and software, as well as current hardware status. The C# language can query the database to determine the status of managed hardware and software components, including network devices.

TIP   Older Windows systems can have the WMI system installed as a separate download from the WMI Sofware Developers Kit. This download is freely available on the Microsoft software download website (`http://www.microsoft.com/downloads/search.asp?`).The WMI consists of multiple database tables that store system information, and they are updated as the status of each monitored device changes. These tables each track information for particular system functions. The C# WMI classes allow you to query the database and extract up-to-date information related to the running system.

IP Info in WMI

The WMI Win32_NetworkAdapterConfiguration table within WMI contains information related to the network devices installed on the system. The result of the table query is a collection of information for each network interface. Each network interface represents one record in the returned collection. The IP information for the network interface appears as separate fields within the record.

A wide variety of network data values are contained in the WMI database. Table 2.14 describes some useful IP data fields contained in the Win32_NetworkAdapterConfiguration table.

TABLE 2.14: The Win32_NetworkAdapterConfiguration Data Fields

Field	Description
DefaultIPGateway	An array of IP router addresses assigned to the device
Description	The description of the network device
DHCPEnabled	Whether the device dynamically assigns its IP address

Continued on next page

TABLE 2.14 CONTINUED: The Win32_NetworkAdapterConfiguration Data Fields

Field	Description
DHCPServer	The DHCP server used to assign an IP address
DNSHostName	The DNS host that is used for resolving hostnames
IPAddress	An array of IP addresses assigned to the device
IPEnabled	Whether the device uses IP on the network
IPSubnet	An array of IP subnet addresses used on the device
MACAddress	The Ethernet MAC address assigned to the network device

Applications can access the WMI database using standard SQL syntax queries. The queries must specify a table to query, along with the fields to return (or the * wildcard character to return all the fields). A sample SQL query would look like this:

```
SELECT IPAddress, IPSubnet from Win32_NetworkAdapterConfiguration
```

This SQL statement returns the IP address and subnet mask for each network interface configured on the system. Again, remember that any one interface can have multiple IP addresses, so this information is returned in the form of a multivalue array.

Now that you know where the WMI network information is stored, let's look at an example of using C# to extract the information.

Using C# to Query WMI

The .NET System.Management namespace contains classes used for querying the WMI databases. You can create a C# program to query WMI for each network interface installed on the system and then display the IP information returned. The steps to use to query the WMI database from a C# program are as follows:

1. Create a ManagementObjectSearcher object that contains a SQL Select statement for the database table.

2. Create a ManagementObjectCollection object to obtain the result set from executing the SQL query.

3. In a foreach loop, assign a new ManagementObject for each object in the ManagementObjectCollection.

4. Assign the desired data fields to regular type variables.

Listing 2.3 shows the WMICardGrab.cs program, which uses the C# WMI classes to obtain the network interface IP information.

Listing 2.3   **WMICardGrab.cs program**

```
using System;
using System.Management;

class WMICardGrab
{
    public static void Main ()
    {
        ManagementObjectSearcher query = new
        ManagementObjectSearcher("SELECT * FROM ➡
          Win32_NetworkAdapterConfiguration WHERE IPEnabled = 'TRUE'");
        ManagementObjectCollection queryCollection = query.Get();
        foreach( ManagementObject mo in queryCollection )
        {
            string[] addresses = (string[])mo["IPAddress"];
            string[] subnets = (string[])mo["IPSubnet"];
            string[] defaultgateways =
                    (string[])mo["DefaultIPGateway"];

            Console.WriteLine("Network Card: {0}",
                    mo["Description"]);
            Console.WriteLine("    MAC Address: {0}",
                    mo["MACAddress"]);

            foreach(string ipaddress in addresses)
            {
                Console.WriteLine("    IP Address: {0}",
                    ipaddress);
            }
            foreach(string subnet in subnets)
            {
                Console.WriteLine("    Subnet Mask: {0}", subnet);
            }
            foreach(string defaultgateway in defaultgateways)
            {
                Console.WriteLine("    Gateway: {0}",
                    defaultgateway);
            }
        }
    }
}
```

The C# WMI class ManagementObjectSearcher defines the SQL query that will be performed against the WMI database. You can use the IPEnabled field to your advantage, filtering out any network devices that do not have IP configured:

```
ManagementObjectSearcher query = new
        ManagementObjectSearcher("SELECT * FROM ➡
        Win32_NetworkAdapterConfiguration WHERE IPEnabled = 'TRUE'");
ManagementObjectCollection queryCollection = query.Get();
```

The result of the query is stored in a `ManagementObjectCollection`. Each collection item represents one record in the result set, and each record represents one network interface. The handy `foreach` C# function can be used to iterate through the retrieved recordset collection, examining each record individually and assigning it to a `ManagementObject` object. Fields within the record are referenced using their proper field name:

```
string[] addresses = (string[])mo["IPAddress"];
string[] subnets = (string[])mo["IPSubnet"];
string[] defaultgateways = (string[])mo["DefaultIPGateway"];
```

Similar to the Registry version, the `IPAddress`, `IPSubnet`, and `DefaultIPGateway` values are arrays that can contain more than one value. To accommodate this, you must assign the result to a string array, and step through the string array, again with a `foreach` statement.

The IP information retrieved from the WMICardGrab program should be the same as from the Registry version:

```
C:\>WMICardGrab
Network Card: D-Link DE660 PCMCIA LAN adapter
    MAC Address: 00:80:C8:BC:CE:C3
    IP Address: 192.168.1.6
    Subnet Mask: 255.255.255.0
    Gateway: 192.168.1.1

C:\>
```

Using DNS

The last way to determine system IP information is to utilize the C# DNS (Domain Name System) classes. Chapter 4, "DNS and C#" contains a substantial discussion of how to use the DNS to obtain Internet hostnames and IP addresses. You can exploit this system to obtain the local IP address(es) of the system your program is running on.

The C# `System.Net` namespace contains the `Dns` class, which comprises several methods that allow you to obtain DNS information about hosts. The `GetHostName()` method retrieves the hostname of the local system. The `GetHostByName()` method attempts to find the IP address of a hostname. You can combine these two functions to find the IP address of the local system. Listing 2.4 shows the `DNSName.cs` program, which demonstrates using these functions to find the local IP address(es) of the system.

Listing 2.4   **DNSName.cs program**

```
using System;
using System.Net;

class DNSName
{
    public static void Main ()
    {
```

```
        string hostName = Dns.GetHostName();
        Console.WriteLine("Local hostname: {0}", hostName);
        IPHostEntry myself = Dns.GetHostByName(hostName);
        foreach (IPAddress address in myself.AddressList)
        {
        Console.WriteLine("IP Address: {0}", address.ToString());
        }
    }
}
```

Again, similar to the Registry and WMI programs, you must take into account the possibility of the local system having more than one IP address assigned to it. The `AddressList` property of the `IPHostEntry` class is an array of type `IPAddress`. You can use the `foreach` function to extract each of the IP addresses in the array. The output of this program is very simple:

```
C:\>DNSName
Local hostname: abednego
IP Address: 192.168.1.6

C:\>
```

This is a very common method to use to get the local system IP address for determining the local IP address to use for creating server network connections. You will see this code used many times in later chapters.

Summary

This chapter tells you how IP is used to transfer data across a network, and how you can watch that data. The WinPcap driver can be used to make any Windows system capable of capturing network packets for monitoring. The WinDump and Analyzer programs display the network data captured from the WinPcap driver.

Once you have captured network packets, you must know how to decode them and thus understand how data is traversing the network. You need a good understanding of the Ethernet and IP layer protocols, along with the higher-level TCP and UDP protocols. Each protocol builds on the previous one, adding more information related to how the data traverses the network. Part of your skill as a C# network programmer will involve understanding the effects of these protocols on your network programs. In transporting data across your network, TCP does not preserve data message boundaries, and UDP does not guarantee message delivery. Both protocols have their pros and cons for network programming.

Finally, the chapter described a few methods that you can use to determine the IP address of Windows systems, using the C# Registry, the Microsoft WMI implementation of WBEM, and DNS classes. The Windows Registry contains network information that can be accessed using the .NET Registry and RegistryKey classes. By querying the Registry for network card information, you can obtain static and dynamic IP addresses of systems your program is running on.

The `System.Management` namespace contains classes to access the WMI database found in Windows 2000 and later systems (earlier Windows platforms can have the WMI database manually installed). By using standard SQL queries and the `ManagementObjectSearcher` and `ManagementObjectCollection` classes, you can determine all the necessary IP address information.

The .NET library also contains standard DNS classes that allow you to query to local hostname and IP addresses. This method will be shown in greater detail in Chapter 4, which explores all of the DNS functions available in the .NET library and shows how to use them in C# network programs.

CHAPTER 3

C# Network Programming Classes

- A Primer on Socket Programming

- Socket Programming in Windows

- C# Socket Programming

- C# Socket Helper Classes

This chapter begins your journey into C# network programming by introducing the C# network programming classes. You learned in Chapter 2 about TCP and UDP and their roles in transporting data across networks to remote devices. Now you'll see how that is accomplished within C# network programs.

It is no secret that many of the features and functions found in Windows were borrowed from the Unix world. Network programming is one of those functions, and socket programming is the core of the C# network programming process.

Before you dive into the C# network socket classes, it is a good idea to get a little history of where they came from, and why they work the way they do. If you are already familiar with Unix socket programming, and/or the Windows Winsock interface, you can probably skip right to the "Using C# Sockets" section. If not, sit back, and enjoy a brief history lesson in network programming. It will be time well spent.

A Primer on Socket Programming

The Unix operating system revolutionized many features in the programming world. Among these is the *file descriptor*. A file descriptor provides a programming interface to a file object. Because nearly every object contained in a Unix system is defined as a file, the file descriptor can be used to send and receive data that has many objects across the Unix system. This makes life much simpler for Unix programmers. The same type of programming model works no matter what type of device (or file) you are trying to access.

Starting in the 4.2BSD Unix release, network access was also defined using file descriptors. A network file descriptor is called a *socket*. Unix (and Windows) network programs both utilize sockets for all network communication. This section describes the features of socket network programming in general so that you will be better prepared to understand the concepts behind C# network programming. Following this is the "Socket Programming in Windows" section, which describes the Windows Winsock implementation of sockets. Winsock is the base on which the C# Socket class implementation is built.

Sockets

In socket-based network programming, you do not directly access the network interface device to send and receive packets. Instead, an intermediary file descriptor is created to handle the programming interface to the network. The Unix operating system handles the details of determining which network interface device will be used to send out the data and how.

The special file descriptors used to reference network connections are called *sockets*. The socket defines the following:

- A specific communication domain, such as a network connection or a Unix Interprocess Communication (IPC) pipe
- A specific communication type, such as stream or datagram
- A specific protocol, such as TCP or UDP

After the socket is created, it must be bound to either a specific network address and port on the system, or to a remote network address and port. Once the socket is bound, it can be used to send and receive data from the network. Figure 3.1 shows what this process looks like.

FIGURE 3.1:

The socket interface

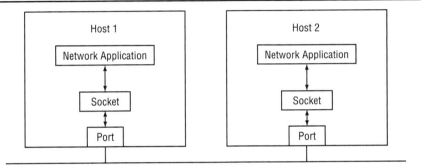

Unix provides the socket() C function to create new sockets:

```
int socket(int domain, int type, int protocol)
```

The socket() function returns a socket descriptor which can then be used to send and receive data from the network (more on that later). The three parameters used to create the socket define the communication's *domain*, *type*, and *protocol* used. Let's look first at the possible *domain* values that can be used; see Table 3.1.

TABLE 3.1: Values for the Socket's Domain Parameter

Domain Value	Description
PF_UNIX	Unix IPC communication
PF_INET	IPv4 Internet protocol, which is the type covered in this book
PF_INET6	IPv6 Internet protocol
PF_IPX	Novell protocol
PF_NETLINK	Kernel user interface driver

Continued on next page

TABLE 3.1 CONTINUED: Values for the Socket's Domain Parameter

Domain Value	Description
PF_X25	ITU-T X.25 /ISO-8208 protocol
PF_AX25	Amateur radio AX.25 protocol
PF_ATMPVC	Access to raw ATM PVC's
PF_APPLETALK	AppleTalk protocol
PF_PACKET	Low-level packet interface

The *type* value defines the type of network communication used for transmitting the data packets on the domain. Table 3.2 shows the *type* values that can be used.

TABLE 3.2: Values for Socket Type

Type Value	Description
SOCK_STREAM	Uses connection-oriented communication packets
SOCK_DGRAM	Uses connectionless communication packets
SOCK_SEQPACKET	Uses connection-oriented packets with a fixed maximum length
SOCK_RAW	Uses raw IP packets
SOCK_RDM	Uses a reliable datagram layer that does not guarantee packet ordering

The two most popular *type* values used for IP communications are SOCK_STREAM, for connection-oriented communication, and SOCK_DGRAM, for connectionless communication.

The specific *protocol* value used to create the socket depends on which *type* value you choose. Most socket types (such as SOCK_STREAM and SOCK_DGRAM) can be safely used only with their default protocols (TCP for SOCK_STREAM, and UDP for SOCK_DGRAM). To specify the default protocol, you can specify a zero value in the *protocol* parameter instead of the normal *protocol* value.

Using these guidelines, creating a socket in Unix for network communication is fairly straightforward. For instance:

```
int newsocket;
newsocket = socket(PF_INET, SOCK_STREAM, 0);
```

This example creates a standard TCP socket for transferring data to a remote host. Creating the socket itself does not define where the socket will connect. That will come later.

Once the socket is created, you can reference it using the returned value; in the example just shown, it is the *newsocket* variable. Unix also allows the programmer to modify some of the characteristics of the socket to control the communication parameters. The next section describes how to set socket options in Unix.

Socket Options

The Unix socket interface offers a method to change the Protocol parameters that are used for communications with the socket: the `setsockopt()` function, which alters the default behavior of the created socket. Here is the format of the `setsockopt()` function:

```
int setsockopt(int s, int level, int optname,
        const void *optval, socklen_t optlen);
```

The *s* parameter references the socket created with the `socket()` function.

The *level* parameter references the level of the changes. For IP sockets, there are two levels of options that can be used:

- `SOL_SOCKET`
- `IPPROTO_IP`

If you are working with TCP sockets, you can also use the `IPPROTO_TCP` level.

Each change level contains *optname* parameters, which describe the socket option to change. The *optval* and *optlen* parameters define the value and length of the option change.

Some of the socket options you'll see most often are `SO_BROADCAST`, which allows the socket to send broadcast messages, and `IP_ADD_MEMBERSHIP`, which allows the socket to accept multicast packets.

Network Addresses

After the socket is created, it must be bound to a network address/port pair. The way that the Unix socket system uses IP addresses and TCP or UDP ports is one of the more confusing parts of socket network programming. A special C structure, `sockaddr`, is used to designate the address information. The `sockaddr` structure contains two elements:

sa_family   An address family, defined as a short type

sa_data   An address for a device, defined as 14 bytes

The address family (`sa_family`) is designed to allow the `sockaddr` structure to reference many types of addresses. Because of this, the 14-byte address element (`sa_data`) is difficult to use directly. Instead, Unix offers an IP-specific address structure, `sockaddr_in`, which uses the following elements. Using the `sockaddr_in` structure requires placing the appropriate IP address and port values in the proper data element.

sin_family   An address family, defined as a short type

sin_port   A port number, defined as a short type

sin_addr   An address, defined as a long type (4-byte) IP address

sin_data   8 bytes of padding

To summarize use of these functions, here is some sample code to obtain an IP address/port pair for a host:

```
sruct sockaddr_in myconnection;
myconnection.sin_family = AF_INET;
myconnection.sin_addr.s_addr = inet_addr("192.168.1.1");
myconnection.sin_port = htons(8000);
```

Note that the sin_addr element is also a structure that uses elements to define the network address. The s_addr element is used to represent the IP address.

Now that you know how to define IP address/port pairs, you can match the sockets to an IP address and start moving data. You must choose between two function calls depending on whether the socket is connection-oriented or connectionless. The following sections describe the difference between the types of communication and the methods they use.

Using Connection-Oriented Sockets

The world of IP connectivity revolves around two types of communication: connection-oriented and connectionless. In a connection-oriented socket (one that uses the SOCK_STREAM type) the TCP protocol is used to establish a session (connection) between two IP address endpoints. There is a fair amount of overhead involved with establishing the connection, but once it is established, data can be reliably transferred between the devices. To create a connection-oriented socket, separate sequences of functions must be used for server programs and for client programs (see Figure 3.2).

FIGURE 3.2:

Connection-oriented socket programming functions

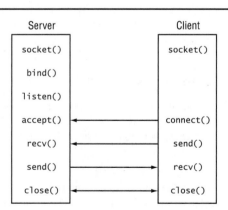

The Server Functions

For the server program, the created socket must be bound to a local IP address and port number that will be used for the TCP communication. The Unix bind() function is used to accomplish this:

```
int bind(int socket, sockaddr *addr, int length);
```

In bind(), the *socket* parameter references the return value from the socket() function. The *addr* parameter references a sockaddr address/port pair to define the local network connection. Because the server usually accepts connections on its own IP address, this is the IP address of the local device, along with the assigned TCP port for the application. If the IP address of the local system is unknown, the INADDR_ANY value can be used to allow the socket to bind to any local address on the system.

After the socket is bound to an address and port, the server program must be ready to accept connections from remote clients. This is a two-step process: first, the program looks for an incoming connection, next it sends and receives data.

The program must first use the listen() function to "listen" to the network for an incoming connection. Next it must use the accept() function to accept connection attempts from clients. The format of the listen() function is as follows:

```
int listen(int socket, int backlog);
```

As you'd expect, the *socket* parameter refers to the socket descriptor created with the socket() function. The *backlog* parameter refers to the number of pending connections waiting to be processed that the system can accept. For example, suppose this value is set to 2. If two separate clients attempt to connect to the port, the system will accept one of the connections for processing and hold the other connection until the first one is done. If a third connection attempt arrives, the system refuses it because the backlog value has already been met.

After the listen() function, the accept() function must be called to wait for incoming connections. The format of the accept() function is as follows:

```
int accept(int socket, sockaddr *from, int *fromlen);
```

By now, you're familiar with the *socket* parameter. The *from* and *fromlen* parameters point to a sockaddr address structure and its length. The remote address information from the client is stored in this structure in case it's needed.

Once the connection has been accepted, the server can send and receive data from the client using the send() and recv() function calls:

```
int send(int socket, const void *message, int length,
              int flags)
int recv(int socket, void *message, int length, int flags)
```

Here, the *socket* parameter again references the open socket for the connection. The *message* parameter references either the buffer of data to send, or an empty buffer to receive data into. The *length* parameter indicates the size of the buffer, and the *flags* parameter indicates if any special flags are necessary (such as for tagging the data as urgent in the TCP packet).

The Client Functions

In a connection-oriented socket, the client must bind to the specific host address and port for the application. For client programs, the connect() function is used instead of the listen() function:

```
int connect(int socket, sockaddr *addr, int addrlen);
```

As in server functions, the *socket* parameter references the created socket() function value. The *addr* parameter points to a created sockaddr structure containing the remote IP address and TCP port number.

Once the connect() function succeeds, the client is connected to the server and can use the standard send() and recv() functions to transmit data back and forth with the server.

Closing the Connection

When the client and server are finished sending data, two commands should be used to properly terminate the connection:

- shutdown(int *socket*, int *how*)

- close(int *socket*)

It is possible to use the close() function alone (and often you will see programs that use only this function to close the connection). However, the kinder, more gentler way is to use shutdown()first, and then close(). The shutdown() function uses the *how* parameter to allow the programmer to determine how gracefully the connection will close. The options available are as follows:

0   No more packets can be received.

1   No more packets can be sent.

2   No more packets can be sent or received.

By selecting values 0 or 1, you can disable the socket from receiving or sending more data, yet allow the socket to either finish sending pending data, or finish receiving pending data. After the connection has a chance to flush out any pending data, the close() function is called to terminate the connection without any data loss.

Using Connectionless Sockets

Because SOCK_DGRAM-type sockets use the UDP protocol, no connection information is required to be sent between network devices. Because of this, it is often difficult to determine which device is acting as a "server", and which is acting as a "client". If a device is initially waiting for data from a remote device, the socket must be bound to a local address/port pair using the bind() function. Once this is done the device can send data out from the socket, or receive incoming data from the socket. Because the client device does not create a connection to a specific server address, the `connect()` function need not be used for the UDP client program. Figure 3.3 illustrates the function sequence used for programming a connectionless socket.

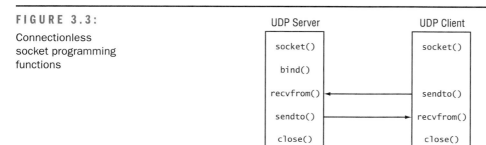

An established connection does not exist, so the normal `send()` and `recv()` functions cannot be used because they do not allow specification of the data's destination address. Instead, sockets provide the `sendto()` and `recvfrom()` functions:

```
int sendto(int socket, char *message, int length,
        int flags, sockaddr *dest, int destlength);
int recvfrom(int socket, char *message, int length,
        int flags, sockaddr *from, int *fromlength);
```

These two functions use the UDP address/port pair to specify the destination address for the *dest* parameter and to specify the sending host for received packets with the *from* parameter. After communication is finished between the two devices, you can use the `shutdown()` and `close()` functions for the sockets, as described for the TCP method.

Non-blocking I/O Methods

One drawback to the standard Unix network programming model is that the I/O functions (the functions used for sending and receiving data) *block* if they cannot be processed immediately. *Blocking* refers to stopping execution of the program and waiting for a specific statement to complete. For example, when a program gets to a `recv()` function, it will stop and wait until data is available on the socket to read. In effect, the `recv()` function blocks further execution of the program until data is present on the socket. If the remote device does not send any data, the program does not continue.

Although this principle may work fine for a single-connection client/server program where you can control the sending and receiving data patterns, it causes a problem for any type of program that must continue to process other events despite errors in sending or receiving data. There are two techniques that can be used to solve this problem: using non-blocking sockets or using socket multiplexing.

Non-blocking Sockets

A simple rudimentary solution for preventing undesirable blocking is to set a socket to not block when an I/O function is called. The non-blocking feature can be set as a special socket option on the socket using the `fcntl()` function. The `fcntl()` function is used to perform miscellaneous low-level operations on file descriptors. Setting blocking on a socket is one of those operations.

Here is the format of the `fcntl()` function:

```
int fcntl(int fd, int cmd, int arg)
```

The *fd* parameter should be an open file descriptor (or socket, in this case). The *cmd* parameter specifies what operation will be done on the file descriptor. For example, the command F_SETFL is used to read or set a file descriptor's flag options. The *arg* parameter is used to specify the flag to set (or query).

So, to set a socket to non-blocking mode, you would use the following:

```
int newsocket;
newsocket = sock(PF_INET, SOCK_STREAM, 0);
fcntl(newsocket, F_SETFL, O_NONBLOCK);
```

Here the O_NONBLOCK flag indicates that the socket should be set to non-blocking mode. Whenever a `recv()` function is performed on the *newsocket* socket, the program will not wait for data. If no data is immediately present, the `recv()` function will return a value of –1, and the Unix `errno` value would be set to EWOULDBLOCK.

Using non-blocking sockets, you can poll any open socket to look for incoming data or to determine if it is ready for outgoing data.

Multiplexed Socket

Another solution to the socket blocking problem uses the `select()` function to multiplex all the active sockets. The `select()` function lets you watch multiple sockets for events (such as data to be read from or written to the socket), and process only the sockets that need to be processed. Sockets without any pending events are skipped so they won't block the program execution.

The format of the `select()` function is as follows:

```
int select(int numfd, fd_set *readfds, fd_set *writefds,
    fd_set *exceptfds, struct timeval *timeout)
```

The *numfd* parameter specifies the highest value of the file descriptors (sockets) that the select function is monitoring, plus one. The `select()` function can thus know how high to iterate when testing the socket sets.

The *readfds*, *writefds*, and *exceptfds* parameters specify the following lists (or sets) of sockets to be monitored by select() for the specific data function:

readfds   Sockets that are checked if data is available to read

writefds   Sockets that are checked if ready to write

exceptfds   Sockets that are checked for exceptions

The *timeout* parameter defines a timeval structure to set how long the select() function should wait for any of the sockets to have an event.

The tricky part of socket multiplexing is assigning sockets to the *readfds*, *writefds*, and *exceptfds* parameters. Indeed, there is another whole set of functions that do that, as listed in Table 3.3.

TABLE 3.3: select() Helper Functions

Function	Description
FD_ZERO(*set*)	Zeros out a multiplex set *set*
FD_SET(*socket*, *set*)	Adds *socket* to the multiplex set *set*
FD_CLR(*socket*, *set*)	Removes *socket* from the multiplex set *set*
FD_ISSET(*socket*, *set*)	Tests to see if *socket* is contained in the multiplex set *set*

The helper functions must be used to set the individual socket sets for each select() call. A select() call cancels out any previous select() calls. Thus you must add or remove any new sockets to or from the existing set before the next call to the select() function.

Here is an example of using the select() method:

```
sock1 = socket(PF_INET, SOCK_STREAM, 0);
sock2 = socket(PF_INET, SOCK_STREAM, 0);
connect(sock1, addr, addrlen);
connect(sock2, addr2, addr2len);
FD_ZERO(&sockset);
FD_SET(sock1, &sockset);
FD_SET(sock2, &sockset);
if (sock1 > sock2)
   maxfd = sock1 + 1;
else
   maxfd = sock2  + 1;
timeout.tv_sec = 30;
timeout.tv_usec = 0;
```

```
select(maxfd, &sockset, NULL, NULL, &timeout);
if (FD_ISSET(sock1, &sockset))
    recv(sock1, buffer1, sizeof(buffer1), 0)
if (FD_ISSET(sock2, &sockset))
    recv(sock2, buffer2, sizeof(buffer2), 0)
```

This example shows how the select() function can be used to monitor two separate socket connections. Once select() is called with the appropriate socket sets, you can use the FD_ISSET helper function at any time in the program to test if data is available for an individual socket. After select()finishes (either by receiving an event or from the timeout) the *socketset* value contains only those sockets that have had an event trigger. By using FD_ISSET, you can determine whether either socket is receiving data. If either socket does not have any data, it is not part of the set and does not block the rest of the program.

Socket Programming in Windows

When you are familiar with network programming in the Unix environment, understanding Windows network programming is easy. This section describes the relationship between the Windows network programming interface and the Unix network programming model, and how Windows socket programming has formed the foundation of the .NET Framework network classes.

Windows Socket Functions

It makes sense that the Windows network programming model is derived from the comparable Unix model. Many features of the Windows operating systems have their roots in Unix systems. Much of Windows network programming was modeled after the Unix Berkeley socket method. It was called, not surprisingly, Windows Sockets, or Winsock for short. The Winsock interface was designed to allow network programmers from the Unix environment to easily port existing network programs, or to create new network programs in the Windows environment without a large learning curve.

The Winsock APIs were implemented as a set of header and library files for developers and DLL files to be used by applications. There are two basic Winsock library versions: the 1.1 version was originally released with Windows 95 workstations and provided basic socket functionality. Later, version 2 was released as an add-on for Windows 95 machines. It added significantly more socket functions and protocols that could be deployed by network programmers. By the time Windows 98 was released, the Winsock library had matured to version 2.2, which is still a part of the current Windows operating system releases.

NOTE   The lone exception to this arrangement is the Windows CE platform. At this writing, Windows CE still only supports the Winsock 1.1 libraries.

The core of the Winsock environment is, of course, the socket. Just as in Unix, all Windows network programs create a socket to establish a link with the underlying network interface on the Windows system. All of the standard socket function calls employed in the Unix world were ported to the Windows system. However, there are a few differences between Unix sockets and Winsock. The following sections describe these differences.

WSAStartup()

To begin a Winsock program, you make a call to the WSAStartup() function. This function informs the operating system which Winsock version the program needs to use. The OS attempts to load the appropriate Winsock library from which the socket functions will operate.

The format of the WSAStartup() function is as follows:

```
int WSAStartup(WORD wVersion, LPWSDATA lpWSAData)
```

The first parameter defines the required version for the program. If the program requests version 2.2 of Winsock and only version 1.1 is available, the WSAStartup() function will return an error. However, if the application requests version 1.1 and version 2.2 is loaded, the function will succeed.

When the function succeeds, the lpWSAData parameter points to a structure that will contain information regarding the Winsock library after it's loaded, such as the actual Winsock version used on the system. This information can then be used to determine the network capabilities of the system the program is running on.

WSACleanup()

A Winsock program must release the Winsock library when it is finished. The WSACleanup() function is used at the end of each Winsock program to indicate that no other Winsock functions will be used, and the Winsock library can be released. The WSACleanup() function does not use any parameters, it just signals the end of the Winsock functions in the program. If any Winsock functions are used after the WSACleanup() function, an error condition will be raised.

Winsock Functions

In between the WSAStartup() and WSACleanup() functions, the Winsock program can behave just like the Unix socket program, using socket(), bind(), connect(), listen(), and accept() calls. In fact, the Winsock interface uses the same structures for addresses (sockaddr_in) and the same values to define protocol families and types (such as the SOCK_STREAM protocol family) as Unix does. The goal of this was to make porting Unix network programs to the Windows environment as easy as possible.

In addition to the standard Unix network functions, the Winsock version 2 interface includes its own set of network functions, all preceded by WSA. These functions extend the functionality of the standard Unix network functions. For example, the WSARecv()

function can be used in place of the standard Unix recv() function call. WSARecv() adds two additional parameters to the original function call, allowing for the Windows-specific functionality of creating overlapped I/O and partial datagram notifications. Figure 3.4 shows how the Winsock WSA functions can be used to replace standard Unix functions.

FIGURE 3.4:

The Winsock WSA programming functions for servers and clients

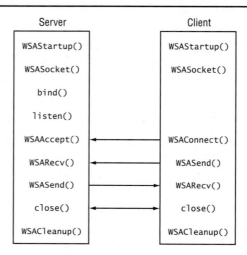

Server	Client
WSAStartup()	WSAStartup()
WSASocket()	WSASocket()
bind()	
listen()	
WSAAccept()	WSAConnect()
WSARecv()	WSASend()
WSASend()	WSARecv()
close()	close()
WSACleanup()	WSACleanup()

Winsock Non-blocking Socket Functions

Another similarity to the Unix network environment is that Winsock supplies ways to prevent network I/O functions from blocking the program execution. Winsock supports the standard Unix methods of setting a socket to non-blocking mode using the ioctlsocket() function (similar to the Unix fcntl() function) and the select() function to multiplex multiple sockets.

The ioctlsocket() format is as follows:

```
ioctlsocket(SOCKET s, long cmd, u_long FAR* argp)
```

The socket to be modified is *s*, the *cmd* parameter specifies the operation to make on the socket, and the *argp* parameter specifies the command parameter.

In addition to these standard socket functions, the Winsock interface offers additional methods of allowing non-blocking network I/O.

WSAAsyncSelect()

One of the features that differentiates Windows from standard Unix programs is the concept of *events*. Unlike common structured programs that have a set way of executing, Windows programs are usually event driven. Methods are executed in the program in response to events occurring while the program is running—buttons are clicked, menu items are selected, and so on. The standard technique of waiting around for data to occur on network sockets does not fit well in the Windows event model. Event-driven access to network sockets is the answer.

The WSAAsyncSelect() function expands on the standard Unix select() function by allowing Windows to do the work of querying the sockets. A WSAAsyncSelect() method is created that includes the socket to monitor, along with a Windows message value that will be passed to the window when one of the socket events occurs (such as data being available to be read, or the socket being ready to accept written data). The format of the WSAAsyncSelect() function is as follows:

```
int WSAAsyncSelect(SOCKET s, HWND hWnd,
              unsigned int wMsg, long lEvent)
```

The socket to monitor is defined by the *s* parameter, and the parent window to receive the event message is defined by *hWnd*. The actual event to send is defined by the *wMsg* parameter. The last parameter, *lEvent*, defines the events to monitor for the socket. You can monitor more than one event for a socket by performing a bitwise OR of the events shown in Table 3.4.

TABLE 3.4: WSAAsyncSelect() Event Types

Event	Description
FD_ACCEPT	A new connection is established with the socket.
FD_ADDRESS_LIST_CHANGE	The local address list changed for the socket's protocol family.
FD_CLOSE	An existing connection has closed.
FD_CONNECT	The socket has completed a connection with a remote host.
FD_GROUP_QOS	The socket group's Quality of Service value has changed.
FD_OOB	The socket has received out-of-band data.
FD_QOS	The socket's Quality Of Service value has changed.
FD_READ	The socket has data that is ready to be read.
FD_ROUTING_INTERFACE_CHANGE	The socket's routing interface has changed for a specific destination.
FD_WRITE	The socket is ready for writing data.

An example of the WSAAsyncSelect() function would look like this:

```
WSAAsyncSelect(sock, hwnd, WM_SOCKET, FD_READ | FD_CLOSE);
```

In this example, if the socket has data available to be read, or if it detects that the remote host closed the connection, the WM_SOCKET message would be sent to the *hwnd* window in the wParam of the Window message. It would then be the responsibility of the *hwnd* window to detect and handle the WM_SOCKET message and perform the appropriate functions depending on which event was triggered. This is almost always handled in a Windows procedure (WindowProc) method for the window using case statements.

WSAEventSelect()

Instead of handling socket notifications using Windows messages, the `WSAEventSelect()` uses an *event object handle*. The event object handle is a self-contained method defined in the program that is called when a unique event is triggered. This technique allows you to create separate Windows methods to handle the various socket events.

For this technique to work, a unique event must first be defined using the `WSACreateEvent()` function. After the event is created, it must be matched to a socket using the `WSAEventSelect()` function:

```
WSASelect(SOCKET s, WSAEVENT hEvent, long lNetworkEvents)
```

As usual, the *s* parameter defines the socket to monitor, and *hEvent* defines the created event that will be called when the socket event occurs. Similar to the `WSAAsyncSelect()` function, the *lNetworkEvent* parameter is a bitwise combination of all the socket events to monitor. The same event definitions are used for the `WSAEventSelect()` function as for the `WSAAsyncSelect()` function. When a socket event occurs, the event method registered by the `WSACreateEvent()` function is executed.

Overlapped I/O

Possibly one of the greatest features of the Winsock interface is the concept of overlapped I/O. This technique allows a program to post one or more asynchronous I/O requests at a time using a special data structure. The data structure (`WSAOVERLAPPED`) defines multiple sockets and event objects that are matched together. The events are considered to be *overlapping*, in that multiple events can be called simultaneously as the sockets receive events.

To use the overlapped technique, a socket must be created with the `WSASocket()` function call using the overlapped enabled flag (the `socket()` function does not include this flag). Likewise, all data communication must be done using the `WSARecv()` and `WSASend()` functions. These Winsock functions use an overlapped I/O flag to indicate that the data will use the `WSAOVERLAPPED` data structure.

Although using overlapped I/O can greatly improve performance of the network program, it doesn't solve all of the possible difficulties. One shortcoming of the overlapped I/O technique is that it can define only 64 events. For large-scale network applications that require hundreds of connections, this technique will not work.

Completion Ports

Another downside to the overlapped I/O technique is that all of the events are processed within a single thread in the program. To allow events to be split among threads, Windows introduced the *completion port*. A completion port allows the programmer to specify a number of threads for use within a program, and assign events to the individual threads. By combining the overlapped I/O technique with the completion port method, a programmer can handle overlapped socket events using separate program threads. This technique produces really interesting results on systems that contain more than one processor. By creating a separate thread for each processor, multiple sockets can be monitored simultaneously on each processor.

C# Socket Programming

The .NET Framework network classes were created to provide easy interfaces to the native Winsock network API for programmers using the .NET programming languages. Now that you have seen how the Winsock API handles network programming, you're ready to examine C#'s way of handling sockets. The following sections describe the C# network programming classes and how to use them in network programs.

IP Addresses in C#

One of the biggest advantages you will notice in the .NET network library is the way IP address/port pairs are handled. It is a fairly straightforward process that represents a welcome improvement over the old, confusing Unix way. .NET defines two classes in the System.Net namespace to handle various types of IP address information:

- IPAddress
- IPEndPoint

IPAddress

An IPAddress object is used to represent a single IP address. This value can then be used in the various socket methods to represent the IP address. The default constructor for IPAddress is as follows:

```
public IPAddress(long address)
```

The default constructor takes a long value and converts it to an IPAddress value. In practice, this default is almost never used. (How many times do you happen to have the long value of an IP address handy?) Instead, several methods in the IPAddress class can be used to create and manipulate IP addresses. Table 3.5 defines these methods.

TABLE 3.5: IPAddress Methods

Method	Description
Equals	Compares two IP addresses
GetHashCode	Returns a hash value for an IPAddress object
GetType	Returns the type of the IP address instance
HostToNetworkOrder	Converts an IP address from host byte order to network byte order

Continued on next page

TABLE 3.5 CONTINUED: IPAddress Methods

Method	Description
IsLoopBack	Indicates whether the IP address is considered the loopback address
NetworkToHostOrder	Converts an IP address from network byte order to host byte order
Parse	Converts a string to an IPAddress instance
ToString	Converts an IPAddress to a string representation of the dotted decimal format of the IP address

The Parse() method is most often used to create IPAddress instances:

```
IPAddress newaddress = IPAddress.Parse("192.168.1.1");
```

This format allows you to use a standard dotted quad IP address in string format and convert it to an IPAddress object.

The IPAddress class also provides four read-only fields that represent special IP addresses for use in programs:

Any   Used to represent any IP address available on the local system

Broadcast   Used to represent the IP broadcast address for the local network

Loopback   Used to represent the loopback address of the system

None   Used to represent no network interface on the system

Listing 3.1 shows an example program that demonstrates using the IPAddress class methods and fields.

Listing 3.1   **The AddressSample.cs program**

```
using System;
using System.Net;

class AddressSample
{
   public static void Main ()
   {
      IPAddress test1 = IPAddress.Parse("192.168.1.1");
      IPAddress test2 = IPAddress.Loopback;
      IPAddress test3 = IPAddress.Broadcast;
      IPAddress test4 = IPAddress.Any;
      IPAddress test5 = IPAddress.None;
      IPHostEntry ihe =
                  Dns.GetHostByName(Dns.GetHostName());
      IPAddress myself = ihe.AddressList[0];
      if (IPAddress.IsLoopback(test2))
         Console.WriteLine("The Loopback address is: {0}",
```

```
                                    test2.ToString());
      else
         Console.WriteLine("Error obtaining the loopback address");
         Console.WriteLine("The Local IP address is: {0}\n",
                           myself.ToString());
      if (myself == test2)
         Console.WriteLine("The loopback address is the ➥
                 same as local address.\n");
      else
         Console.WriteLine("The loopback address is not the local address.\n");
      Console.WriteLine("The test address is: {0}",
                        test1.ToString());
      Console.WriteLine("Broadcast address: {0}",
                        test3.ToString());
      Console.WriteLine("The ANY address is: {0}",
                        test4.ToString());
      Console.WriteLine("The NONE address is: {0}",
                        test5.ToString());
   }
}
```

The AddressSample.cs program shows a few of the things that can be done with IPAddress objects. One of the more interesting ones is the method used to obtain the local IP address:

```
IPHostEntry ihe =
            Dns.GetHostByName(Dns.GetHostName());
IPAddress myself = ihe.AddressList[0];
```

This code was introduced in Chapter 2, "IP Programming Basics." It uses the GetHostBy-Name() and GetHostName() methods of the System.Net.Dns class to determine the local IP address(es) and create an IPHostEntry object. Chapter 4, "DNS and C#" will describe the IPHostEntry object in much more detail, but for now it is sufficient to say that it contains the AddressList property, which is an array of IPAddress objects. The AddressSample.cs program takes the first address in the list and assigns it to the *myself* IP address object.

The output from this program should look similar to this:

```
C:\>AddressSample
The Loopback address is: 127.0.0.1
The Local IP address is: 192.168.1.6

The loopback address is not the local address.

The test address is: 192.168.1.1
Broadcast address: 255.255.255.255
The ANY address is: 0.0.0.0
The NONE address is: 255.255.255.255

C:\>
```

What's interesting about this output is the resulting values of the Any and None addresses. These values might look backward to what you would expect: the Any IPAddress object points to the 0.0.0.0 address, which you might think represents nothing. However, this address is most often used when a system has multiple network interfaces and you do not want to bind a socket to any particular interface. The None IPAddress object points to the 255.255.255.255 address, which is often used when a system wants to create a dummy socket and not bind it to any interfaces.

IPEndPoint

Similar to the Unix sockaddr_in structure, the .NET Framework uses the IPEndPoint object to represent a specific IP address/port combination. An IPEndPoint object is used when binding sockets to local addresses, or when connecting sockets to remote addresses. We'll first examine all the pieces of IPEndPoint and then look at a program that puts it to work.

Two constructors are used to create IPEndPoint instances:

- IPEndPoint(long *address*, int *port*)

- IPEndPoint(IPAddress *address*, int *port*)

Both constructors use two parameters: an IP address value, represented as either a long value or an IPAddress object; and the integer port number. As you can probably guess, the most common constructor used is the IPAddress form.

Table 3.6 describes the methods that can be used with IPEndPoint objects.

TABLE 3.6: IPEndPoint Methods

Method	Description
Create	Creates an EndPoint object from a SocketAddress object
Equals	Compares two IPEndPoint objects
GetHashCode	Returns a hash value for an IPEndPoint object
GetType	Returns the type of the IPEndPoint instance
Serialize	Creates a SocketAddress instance of the IPEndPoint instance
ToString	Creates a string representation of the IPEndPoint instance

The SocketAddress class is a special class within the System.Net namespace. It represents a serialized version of an IPEndPoint object. This class can be used to store an IPEndPoint instance, which can then be re-created using the IPEndPoint.Create() method. The format of the SocketAddress class is as follows:

- 1 byte represents the AddressFamily of the object.

- 1 byte represents the size of the object.
- 2 bytes represent the port number of the object.
- The remaining bytes represent the IP address of the object.

In addition to the methods, the `IPEndPoint` class also contains three properties that can be set or obtained from an instance:

Address   Gets or sets the IP address property

AddressFamily   Gets the IP address family

Port   Gets or sets the TCP or UDP port number

Each of these properties can be used with an `IPEndPoint` instance to obtain information about individual parts of the `IPEndPoint` object. The `Address` and `Port` properties can also be used to set the individual values within an existing `IPEndPoint` object.

There are also two fields that can be used with the `IPEndPoint` object to obtain the available port ranges from a system:

MaxPort   The maximum value that can be assigned to a port number

MinPort   The minimum value that can be assigned to a port number

Example of IPEndPoint at Work

Listing 3.2 shows a sample program that demonstrates the `IPEndPoint` class and its methods, properties, and fields.

Listing 3.2   **The IPEndPointSample.cs program**

```
using System;
using System.Net;

class IPEndPointSample
{
    public static void Main ()
    {
        IPAddress test1 = IPAddress.Parse("192.168.1.1");
        IPEndPoint ie = new IPEndPoint(test1, 8000);

        Console.WriteLine("The IPEndPoint is: {0}",
                    ie.ToString());
        Console.WriteLine("The AddressFamily is: {0}",
                    ie.AddressFamily);
        Console.WriteLine("The address is: {0}, and the ➥
                port is: {1}\n", ie.Address, ie.Port);
        Console.WriteLine("The min port number is: {0}",
                IPEndPoint.MinPort);
        Console.WriteLine("The max port number is: {0}\n",
```

```
                    IPEndPoint.MaxPort);

        ie.Port = 80;
        Console.WriteLine("The changed IPEndPoint value ➥
                is: {0}", ie.ToString());
        SocketAddress sa = ie.Serialize();
        Console.WriteLine("The SocketAddress is: {0}",
                    sa.ToString());
    }
}
```

The `IPEndPointSample.cs` program demonstrates several important `IPEndPoint` features. Note that you can display the complete `IPEndPoint` object as one string, or you can extract individual parts of the object:

```
Console.WriteLine("The IPEndPoint is: {0}",
                ie.ToString());
Console.WriteLine("The AddressFamily is: {0}",
                ie.AddressFamily);
Console.WriteLine("The address is: {0}, and the ➥
                port is: {1}\n", ie.Address, ie.Port);
```

The program also demonstrates how to change the port value of the `IPEndPoint` object individually, using the `Port` property:

```
ie.Port = 80;
```

This allows you to change individual address and port values within the object without having to create a new object.

The output from this program should look like this:

```
C:\>IPEndPointSample
The IPEndPoint is: 192.168.1.1:8000
The AddressFamily is: InterNetwork
The address is: 192.168.1.1, and the port is: 8000

The min port number is: 0
The max port number is: 65535

The changed IPEndPoint value is: 192.168.1.1:80
The SocketAddress is: ➥
InterNetwork:16:{0,80,192,168,1,1,0,0,0,0,0,0,0,0,0,0}

C:\>
```

Using C# Sockets

The `System.Net.Sockets` namespace contains the classes that provide the actual .NET interface to the low-level Winsock APIs. This section gives a brief overview of the C# `Socket` class.

Subsequent chapters will build on this overview, presenting detailed descriptions and examples of several types of socket programs.

Socket Construction

The core of the `System.Net.Sockets` namespace is the `Socket` class. It provides the C# managed code implementation of the Winsock API. The `Socket` class constructor is as follows:

```
Socket(AddressFamily af, SocketType st,
        ProtocolType pt)
```

As you can see, the basic format of the `Socket` constructor mimics the original Unix `socket()` function. It uses three parameters to define the type of socket to create:

- An *AddressFamily* to define the network type
- A *SocketType* to define the type of data connection
- A *ProtocolType* to define a specific network protocol

Each of these parameters is represented by a separate enumeration within the `System.Net.Sockets` namespace. Each enumeration contains the values that can be used. For normal IP communications on networks, the `AddressFamily.InterNetwork` value should always be used for the `AddressFamily`. With the *InterNetwork AddressFamily*, the *SocketType* parameter must match a particular *ProtocolType* parameter. You are not allowed to mix and match *SocketTypes* and *ProtocolTypes*. Table 3.7 shows the combinations that can be used for IP communications.

TABLE 3.7: IP Socket Definition Combinations

SocketType	Protocoltype	Description
Dgram	Udp	Connectionless communication
Stream	Tcp	Connection-oriented communication
Raw	Icmp	Internet Control Message Protocol
Raw	Raw	Plain IP packet communication

Using the enumeration values makes it easy to remember all the options (though it does make for some fairly long `Socket()` statements!). For example:

```
Socket newsock = Socket(AddressFamily.InterNetwork,
        SocketType.Stream, ProtocolType.Tcp);
```

Several properties of the `Socket` class can be used to retrieve information from a created `Socket` object, as described in Table 3.8.

TABLE 3.8: Socket Properties

Property	Description
AddressFamily	Gets the address family of the Socket
Available	Gets the amount of data that is ready to be read
Blocking	Gets or sets whether the Socket is in blocking mode
Connected	Gets a value that indicates if the Socket is connected to a remote device
Handle	Gets the operating system handle for the Socket
LocalEndPoint	Gets the local EndPoint object for the Socket
ProtocolType	Gets the protocol type of the Socket
RemoteEndPoint	Gets the remote EndPoint information for the Socket
SocketType	Gets the type of the Socket

NOTE All of the Socket class properties except the LocalEndPoint and RemoteEndPoint are available for a socket immediately after it is created. The LocalEndPoint and RemoteEndPoint properties can only be used on bound sockets.

Listing 3.3 is a simple program that demonstrates the Socket properties. Because the LocalEndPoint property needs a bound Socket object, I used the Bind() method to bind the socket to the loopback address of the system (127.0.0.1).

Listing 3.3 **The SockProp.cs sample socket properties program**

```
using System;
using System.Net;
using System.Net.Sockets;

class SockProp
{
    public static void Main ()
    {
        IPAddress ia = IPAddress.Parse("127.0.0.1");
        IPEndPoint ie = new IPEndPoint(ia, 8000);

        Socket test = new Socket(AddressFamily.InterNetwork,
                    SocketType.Stream, ProtocolType.Tcp);

        Console.WriteLine("AddressFamily: {0}",
                    test.AddressFamily);
        Console.WriteLine("SocketType: {0}",
                    test.SocketType);
        Console.WriteLine("ProtocolType: {0}",
```

```
                              test.ProtocolType);
           Console.WriteLine("Blocking: {0}", test.Blocking);

           test.Blocking = false;
           Console.WriteLine("new Blocking: {0}",test.Blocking);
           Console.WriteLine("Connected: {0}", test.Connected);

           test.Bind(ie);
           IPEndPoint iep = (IPEndPoint)test.LocalEndPoint;
           Console.WriteLine("Local EndPoint: {0}",
                             iep.ToString());

           test.Close();
     }
 }
```

The output of the program should look like this:

```
C:\>SockProp
AddressFamily: InterNetwork
SocketType: Stream
ProtocolType: Tcp
Blocking: True
New Blocking: False
Connected: False
Local EndPoint: 127.0.0.1:8000

C:\>
```

By setting the Blocking property to false, you can use non-blocking sockets, similar to the Unix fcntl() function—but more on that later.

Socket Options

Like Unix sockets, .NET sockets allow you to set protocol options for the created Socket object. However, because C# is an object-oriented language, there is a twist.

Instead of being a stand-alone function, the call is a method. Like its Unix counterpart, SetSocketOption() configures the socket parameters that you want to tweak to customize the communication parameters. The SetSocketOption() method is overloaded, using three different formats:

```
SetSocketOption(SocketOptionLevel sl,
     SocketOptionName sn, byte[] value)
SetSocketOption(SocketOptionLevel sl,
     SocketOptionName sn,int value)
SetSocketOption(SocketOptionLevel sl,
     SocketOptionName sn, object value)
```

The parameters used are similar to the Unix `setsockopt()` function. The *sl* defines the type of socket option to set. Table 3.9 lists the available `SocketOptionLevels`.

TABLE 3.9: SocketOptionLevel Values

Value	Description
IP	Options for IP sockets
Socket	Options for the socket
Tcp	Options for TCP sockets
Udp	Options for UDP sockets

The *sn* defines the specific socket option that will be set within the `SocketOptionLevel`. Table 3.10 lists the available `SocketOptionNames`.

TABLE 3.10: SocketOptionName Values

Value	SocketOptionLevel	Description
AcceptConnection	Socket	If true, socket is in listening mode
AddMembership	IP	Adds an IP group membership
AddSourceMembership	IP	Joins a source group
BlockSource	IP	Blocks data from a source
Broadcast	Socket	If true, permits sending broadcast messages
BsdUrgent	IP	Uses urgent data (can only be set once and cannot be turned off)
ChecksumCoverage	Udp	Sets or gets UDP checksum coverage
Debug	Socket	Records debugging information if true
DontFragment	IP	Doesn't fragment the IP packet
DontLinger	Socket	Closes socket gracefully without waiting for data
DontRoute	Socket	Sends packet directly to interface addresses
DropMembership	IP	Drops an IP group membership
DropSourceMembership	IP	Drops a source group
Error	Socket	Gets and clears the error status
ExclusiveAddressUse	Socket	Enables a socket to be bound for exclusive access
Expedited	IP	Uses expedited data (can only be set once, and cannot turned off)
HeaderIncluded	IP	Indicates that the data sent to the socket will include the IP header
IPOptions	IP	Specifies IP options to be used in outbound packets
IpTimeToLive	IP	Sets the IP packet time-to-live value

Continued on next page

TABLE 3.10 CONTINUED: SocketOptionName Values

Value	SocketOptionLevel	Description
KeepAlive	Socket	Sends TCP keep-alive packets
Linger	Socket	Waits after closing the socket for any extra data
MaxConnections	Socket	Sets the maximum queue length used
MulticastInterface	IP	Sets the interface used for multicast packets
MulticastLoopback	IP	IP multicast loopback
MulticastTimeToLive	IP	Sets the IP multicast time to live
NoChecksum	Udp	Sends UDP packets with checksum set to zero
NoDelay	Tcp	Disables the Nagle algorithm for TCP packets
OutOfBandInline	Socket	Allows receiving out-of-band data
PacketInformation	IP	Returns information about received packets
ReceiveBuffer	Socket	Sets the total per-socket buffer reserved for receiving packets
ReceiveLowWater	Socket	Receives low water mark
ReceiveTimeout	Socket	Receives time-out
ReuseAddress	Socket	Allows the socket to be bound to a port address that is already in use
SendBuffer	Socket	Sets the total per-socket buffer reserved for sending packets
SendLowWater	Socket	Sends low water mark
SendTimeout	Socket	Sends timeout value
Type	Socket	Gets socket type
TypeOfService	IP	Sets the IP type-of-service field
UnblockSource	IP	Sets the socket to non-blocking mode
UseLoopback	Socket	Bypasses the network interface when possible

The *value* parameter defines the value of the socket option name to use. The format of the value is different depending on the SocketOptionName used.

Once the socket is created and modified, you are ready to either wait for incoming connections, or connect to remote devices. The following sections describe how to communicate using the C# Socket class, using connection-oriented and connectionless communication sockets in C#.

Using Connection-Oriented Sockets

Once again, the .NET Framework concepts are similar to Unix network programming. In the .NET Framework, you can create connection-oriented communications with remote hosts across a network. Because C# is an object-oriented language, all the Unix socket functions are implemented as methods of the Socket class. By referring to the method from the Socket instance, you can perform network operations using the indicated socket.

NOTE   This section describes the C# methods in the Sockets class that are used for connection-oriented communication. Chapter 5, "Connection-Oriented Sockets" will expand on this explanation, showing much more detailed information along with lots of examples.

The Server Functions

Similar to the Unix server, once a server socket is created, it must be bound to a local network address on the system. The Bind() method is used to perform this function:

```
Bind(EndPoint address)
```

The *address* parameter must point to a valid IPEndPoint instance, which includes a local IP address and a port number. After the socket is bound to a local address, you use the Listen() method to wait for incoming connection attempts from clients:

```
Listen(int backlog)
```

The *backlog* parameter defines the number of connections that the system will queue, waiting for your program to service. Any attempts by clients beyond that number of waiting connections will be refused. You should remember that specifying a large number here might have performance consequences for your server. Each pending connection attempt uses buffer space in the TCP buffer area. This means less buffer space available for sent and received packets.

After the Listen() method is performed, the server is ready to accept any incoming connections. This is done with the Accept() method. The Accept() method returns a new socket descriptor, which is then used for all communication calls for the connection.

Here's a sample of C# server code that sets up the necessary socket pieces:

```
IPHostEntry local = Dns.GetHostByName(Dns.GetHostName());
IPEndPoint iep = new IPEndPoint(local.AddressList[0],
                8000);
Socket newserver = new Socket(AddressFamily.InterNetwork,
        SocketType.Stream, ProtocolType.Tcp);
newserver.Bind(iep);
newserver.Listen(5);
Socket newclient = newserver.Accept();
```

This program will block at the Accept() statement, waiting for a client connection. Once a client connects to the server, the *newclient* Socket object will contain the new connection information and should be used for all communication with the remote client. The *newserver* Socket object will still be bound to the original IPEndPoint object and can be used to accept more connections with another Accept() method. If no more Accept() methods are called, the server will not respond to any more client connection attempts.

After the client connection has been accepted, the client and server can begin transferring data. The `Receive()` and `Send()` methods are used to perform this function. Both of these methods are overloaded with four forms of the method. Table 3.11 shows the available methods to use for each.

TABLE 3.11: The Receive() and Send() Methods

Method	Description
Receive(byte[] *data*)	Receives data and places it in the specified byte array
Receive(byte[] *data*, SocketFlags *sf*)	Sets socket attributes, receives data, and places it in the specified byte array
Receive(byte[] *data*, int *size*, SocketFlags *sf*)	Sets socket attributes, receives the specified size of data, and places it in the specified byte array
Receive(byte[] *data*, int *offset*, int *size*, SocketFlags *sf*)	Sets socket attributes, receives the *size* bytes of data, and stores it at offset *offset* in the *data* byte array
Send(byte[] *data*)	Sends the data specified in the byte array
Send(byte[] *data*, SocketFlags *sf*)	Sets socket attributes and sends the data specified in the bytes array
Send(byte[] *data*, int *size*, SocketFlags *sf*)	Sets socket attributes and sends the specified size of data in the specified byte array
Send(byte[] *data*, int *offset*, int *size*, SocketFlags *sf*)	Sets socket attributes and sends *size* bytes of data starting at offset *offset* in the *data* byte array

The simple form of the `Send()` and `Receive()` methods sends a single byte array of data, or receives data and places it into the specified byte array. If you want to specify any special `SocketFlags`, you can add them into the method call as well. Table 3.12 shows the available `SocketFlag` values.

TABLE 3.12: SocketFlag Values

Value	Description
DontRoute	Sends data without using the internal routing tables
MaxIOVectorLength	Provides a standard value for the number of WSABUF structures used to send and receive data
None	Uses no flags for this call
OutOfBand	Processes out-of-band data
Partial	Partially sends or receives message
Peek	Only peeks at the incoming message

The other parameters available on the Receive() and Send() methods allow you to specify how many bytes of data to send or receive and where in the buffer you want the data. This will be demonstrated in much greater detail in Chapter 5.

The Client Functions

The client device must also bind an address to the created Socket object, but it uses the Connect() method rather than Bind(). As with Bind(), Connect() requires an IPEndPoint object for the remote device to which the client needs to connect:

```
IPAddress host = IPAddress.Parse("192.168.1.1");
IPEndPoint hostep = new IPEndPoint(host, 8000);
Socket sock = new Socket(AddressFamily.InterNetwork,
            SocketType.Stream, ProtocolType.Tcp);
sock.Connect(hostep);
```

The Connect() method will block until the connection has been established. If the connection cannot be established, it will produce an exception (see the section "Socket Exceptions" later in this chapter).

Once the connection has been established, the client can use the Send() and Receive() methods of the Socket class similar to the way the server uses them. When communication is done, the Socket instance must be closed. Like the Unix socket, the Socket class uses both a shutdown() method to gracefully stop a session, and a close() method to actually close the session. The shutdown() method uses one parameter to determine how the socket will shutdown. Available values for Socket.Shutdown() are described in Table 3.13.

TABLE 3.13: Socket.Shutdown() Values

Value	Description
SocketShutdown.Both	Prevents both sending and receiving data on the socket
SocketShutdown.Receive	Prevents receiving data on the socket. An RST will be sent if additional data is received.
SocketShutdown.Send	Prevents sending data on the socket. A FIN will be sent after all remaining buffer data is sent.

Here is the typical way to gracefully close a connection:

```
sock.Shutdown(SocketShutdown.Both);
sock.Close();
```

This allows the Socket object to gracefully wait until all data has been sent from its internal buffers.

Using Connectionless Sockets

.NET uses the same functionality for connectionless sockets as that employed by the Unix model. When you create a socket with the `SocketType.Dgram` socket type, the UDP protocol is used to transmit packets across the network. Similar to the Unix model, you must set up the `Bind()` method for the server to bind the socket to a particular port. Also similar to the Unix model, the server and client do not need to use the `Listen()` or `Connect()` methods.

Because there is no connection for communication, the standard `Receive()` and `Send()` methods will not work. Instead, you must use the special `ReceiveFrom()` and `SendTo()` methods. The formats for these methods comprise the same base parameters as the `Receive()` and `Send()` methods (as seen in Table 3.11). In addition, there is an extra parameter that is a reference to an `EndPoint` object. This parameter defines where the data is going (for `SendTo`) or where it is coming from (for `ReceiveFrom`). For example, the simplest format of the methods would be as follows:

```
ReceiveFrom(byte[], ref EndPoint)
SendTo(byte[], ref EndPoint)
```

For UDP communications, the `EndPoint` object will point to an `IPEndPoint` object. If you are new to C#, you may not have seen the `ref` keyword before. The `ref` keyword indicates that the method will access the `EndPoint` object by reference in memory, and not by its value. This is a popular technique in C and C++ programming, but it is not seen very often in C# programs.

Non-blocking Programming

The .NET `Socket` class I/O methods use blocking by default, just like the Unix network programming model. When a program reaches a network function that blocks, such as `Receive()`, the program waits there until the function completes, such as when data is received from the socket. Three C# techniques are available to avoid using blocking network calls: non-blocking sockets, multiplexed sockets, and asynchronous sockets.

Non-blocking Sockets

As mentioned earlier in the "Using C# Sockets" sections, C# `Socket` objects contain properties that can be queried for their values. However, one of the properties, `Blocking`, can also be set. You can set the `Blocking` property of a socket to false, putting the socket into non-blocking mode.

When the socket is in non-blocking mode, it will not wait for an I/O method to complete. Rather, it will check the method; if it can't be completed, the method will fail and the program will go on. For example, with `Blocking` set to false, the `Receive()` method will not wait for data to appear on the socket. Instead, the method will return a value of 0, indicating that no data was available on the socket.

Mutiplexed Sockets

Just as in Unix, the Socket class provides the Select() method. This method is used to multiplex multiple Socket instances to watch for the ones that are ready to be read or written to. In C#, however, the Select() method is used somewhat differently. Here is the format of the Select() method:

```
Select(IList read, IList write, IList error,
           int microseconds)
```

The *read*, *write*, and *error* parameters are IList objects, which are arrays that contain created sockets to monitor. The *microseconds* parameter defines the amount of time (in microseconds) the Select() method will wait for the events to happen.

The following is a small code fragment showing how the Select() method can be used:

```
ArrayList socketList = new ArrayList(5);

SocketList.Add(sock1);
SocketList.Add(sock2);

Socket.Select(socketList, null, null, 1000);

byte[] buffer = new byte[1024];
for (i = 0; i < socketList.Length - 1; i++)
{
    socketList[i].Receive(buffer);
    ConsoleWriteLine(Encoding.ASCII.GetString(buffer));
}
```

Notice that the Select() method will monitor both *sock1* and *sock2* for incoming data. If no data is present on either socket, the Receive() method will not block the program.

Asynchronous Socket Programming

It is no surprise that the .NET Framework uses the asynchronous socket model introduced by the Windows Winsock API. This method allows you to use a separate method when a socket is ready to receive or send data. Instead of using a Receive() method to wait for data from a client, you can use the BeginReceive() method, which will register a delegate to be called when data is available on the socket. Within the delegate method, you must use the EndReceive() method to stop the asynchronous read and retrieve the data from the socket. This concept is explained in more detail in Chapter 8, "Asynchronous Socket Programming."

C# Socket Exceptions

One feature of socket programming included in .NET Framework that is used neither by Unix nor the Winsock API is *socket exceptions*. So far, all of the examples and code fragments shown in this chapter assumed one important thing: that all socket calls will succeed. This is a dangerous assumption to make in today's networking world.

As shown in Chapter 1, "The C# Language," C# uses the `try-catch` mechanism to catch errors and exceptions as the program is running. You should always plan thoroughly for these exceptions and carefully determine what actions should be taken when an exception occurs.

All of the `Socket` class methods use the `SocketException` exception. Any socket programming you do should always check for `SocketException` exceptions and then attempt to recover from the error, or at least warn the user of the problem.

Listing 3.4 shows a simple socket client program that uses exception programming to determine if any errors occur during the normal network session. By using `try-catch` blocks around individual network calls, you can single out where problems occur in your program and give your customers better information so they can take the appropriate actions to fix the problem.

Listing 3.4   **The SocketExcept.cs program**

```
using System;
using System.Net;
using System.Net.Sockets;
using System.Text;

class SocketExcept
{
   public static void Main ()
   {
      IPAddress host = IPAddress.Parse("192.168.1.1");
      IPEndPoint hostep = new IPEndPoint(host, 8000);
      Socket sock = new Socket(AddressFamily.InterNetwork,
                   SocketType.Stream, ProtocolType.Tcp);

      try
      {
         sock.Connect(hostep);
      } catch (SocketException e)
      {
         Console.WriteLine("Problem connecting to host");
         Console.WriteLine(e.ToString());
         sock.Close();
         return;
```

```
        }
        try
        {
            sock.Send(Encoding.ASCII.GetBytes("testing"));
        } catch (SocketException e)
        {
            Console.WriteLine("Problem sending data");
            Console.WriteLine( e.ToString());
            sock.Close();
            return;
        }
        sock.Close();
    }
}
```

C# Socket Helper Classes

The .NET Framework supports the normal socket interface for advanced network programmers, but it also provides a simplified interface for easier network programming. The *simplified socket helper classes* help network programmers create socket programs with simpler statements and less coding—two important benefits for any programmer. This section introduces the C# socket helper classes. In Chapter 7, "Using the C# Sockets Helper Classes," you'll study detailed examples of how to use these classes in actual programs.

Here are the three helper classes used for socket programming:

- `TcpClient`
- `TcpListener`
- `UdpClient`

Each one is designed to support a specific socket programming function and to simplify the interfaces required to program for that function. Obviously, the `TcpClient` and `TcpListener` classes are used for creating TCP client and server programs; the `UdpClient` class is used for creating UDP programs.

TcpClient

The methods of the `TcpClient` class are used to create client network programs that follow the connection-oriented network model. The `TcpClient` methods mirror those in normal socket programming, but many of the steps are compacted to simplify the programming task.

For starters, there are three ways to create a `TcpClient` object and connect it to a remote host, and each technique makes creating a socket easier than using the manual `Socket` class methods.

The default constructor   The default constructor format creates a socket on any available local port. You can then use the Connect() method to connect to a specified remote host:

```
TcpClient newclient = new TcpClient();
newclient.Connect("www.isp.net", 8000);
```

The first statement creates a new TcpClient object and binds it to a local address and port. The second statement connects the socket to a remote host address and port number. Notice that the remote host address can be specified as a hostname. The TcpClient class will automatically attempt to resolve the hostname to the proper IP address. That's a lot of work already done for you!

A specific EndPoint object   The second constructor format goes one step further and allows you to specify a specific local EndPoint object to use when creating the socket:

```
IPAddress ia = Dns.GetHostByName(
                 Dns.GetHostName()).AddressList[0];
IPEndPoint iep = new IPEndPoint(ia, 10232);
TcpClient newclient2 = new TcpClient(iep);
newclient2.Connect("www.isp.net", 8000);
```

A specific remote host   The third constructor format is the most common. It allows you to specify the remote host address and port to connect to within the constructor, removing the need to use the Connect() method:

```
TcpClient newclient3 = new TcpClient("www.isp.net", 8000);
```

In one easy step, you create a new TcpClient object to a random local port number and connect it to the specified remote host. Again, if you use a hostname for the host address, the TcpClient object will attempt to resolve it automatically. Creating a socket and connecting to a remote host with one statement—what a system!'

Once a TcpClient instance is created, you will probably want to send and receive data with it. The GetStream() method is used to create a NetworkStream object that allows you to send and receive bytes on the socket. Once you have a NetworkStream instance for the socket, it is a snap to use the standard stream Read() and Write() methods to move data into and out of the socket. This code fragment demonstrates assigning a NetworkStream object to the TcpClient instance and writing data to and reading it from the socket:

```
TcpClient newclient = new TcpClient("www.isp.net", 8000);
NetworkStream ns = newclient.GetStream();
byte[] outbytes = Encoding.ASCII.GetBytes("Testing");
ns.Write(outbytes, 0, outbytes.Length);
byte[] inbytes = new byte[1024];
ns.Read(inbytes, 0, inbytes.Length);
```

```
string instring = Encoding.ASCII.GetString(inbytes);
Console.WriteLine(instring);
ns.Close();
newclient.Close();'
```

NOTE As in the Unix socket world, you must remember to properly close the TcpClient object with the Close()method when you are done with it. Note that closing the NetworkStream object still leaves the TcpClient object open. This is a small detail that many novice network programmers miss.

TcpListener

Just as the TcpClient class simplifies client socket programs, the TcpListener class simplifies server programs; their class constructors are similar as well. Here are the three constructor formats:

- TcpListener(int port)binds to a specific local port number
- TcpListener(IPEndPoint ie)binds to a specific local EndPoint
- TcpListener(IPAddress addr, int port) binds to a specific local IPAddress and port number

These three formats allow you to control how the underlying socket is created for the TcpListener object. Once the object is created, you can begin listening for new connection attempts using the Start() method.

After the Start() method, you must use either the AcceptSocket() or AcceptTcpClient() method to accept incoming connection attempts. As their names suggest, the two methods accept an incoming connection and return either a Socket or TcpClient object. You are already taking advantage of the TcpListener class, so you will probably want to use the AcceptTcpClient() method to create a new TcpClient object for the new connection.

Once the new TcpClient object is created for the connection, you can employ the standard TcpClient methods to begin communicating with the client. A sample code fragment would look like this:

```
TcpListener newserver = new TcpListener(9050);
newserver.Start();
TcpClient newclient = newserver.AcceptTcpClient();
NetworkStream ns = newclient.GetStream();
byte[] outbytes = Encoding.ASCII.GetBytes("Testing");
ns.Write(outbytes, 0, outbytes.Length);
byte[] inbytes = new byte[1024];
ns.Read(inbytes, 0, inbytes.Length);
string instring = Encoding.ASCII.GetString(inbytes);
```

```
Console.WriteLine(instring);
ns.Close();
newclient.Close();
newserver.Stop();
```

This program will block at the `AcceptTcpClient()` method, waiting for a new client connection. Once connected, the `GetStream()` method is used to create a `NetworkStream` object for reading and writing data to the connected socket.

Remember to close the `NetworkStream` as well as the `TcpClient` object when they are finished. You must use the `Stop()` method to close the `TcpListener`.

UdpClient

For applications that require a connectionless socket, the `UdpClient` class provides a simple interface to UDP sockets. You may be wondering why there is not a listener version of the UDP helper class. The answer is simple: you don't need one. Remember, UDP is a connectionless protocol, so there is no such thing as a client or server; there are only UDP sockets either waiting for or sending data. You do not need to bind the UDP socket to a specific address and wait for incoming data.

The `UdpClient` constructors follow the same format as `TcpClient`—they allow you to specify the amount of information necessary to create the UDP socket or reference a remote address and UDP port.

The `Receive()` method allows you to receive data on the UDP port. There is no connection session established, so when a UDP port receives data, you do not necessarily know where it came from (unless you specified it in the `UdpClient` constructor). To compensate for this, the `Receive()` method includes an `IPEndPoint` parameter that is filled with the IP information from the remote host. This is done as follows:

```
UdpClient newconn = new UdpClient(8000);
IPEndPoint remoteclient = new IPEndPoint(IPAddress.Any, 0);
byte[] recv = newconn.Receive(ref remoteclient);
string data = Encoding.ASCII.GetString(recv);
ConsoleWriteLine("From: {0}", remoteclient.ToString());
ConsoleWriteLine("  Data: "{0}", data);
newconn.Close();
```

The `UdpClient` object is instantiated using a port number on which you want the application to accept UDP packets. Note that the *remoteclient* object is instantiated using the `IPAddress.Any` value. This is used as a dummy value that will be replaced with the information from the remote client in the `Receive()` method.

The `Send()` method has three formats. If the `UdpClient` object references a remote host address and port, the `Send()` method does not need to specify the destination of the data.

However, if the UdpClient object does not reference a remote host, the Send() method must do that. This can be accomplished with either an IPEndPoint object, or a string hostname or address value and an integer port number. Sending data would look like this:

```
UdpClient newclient = new UdpClient(8001);
IPEndPoint remotehost = new
        IPEndPoint(IPAddress.Parse("192.168.1.6"), 8001);
byte[] bytes = Encoding.ASCII.GetBytes("test string");
newclient.Send(bytes, bytes.Length, remotehost);
newclient.Close();
```

The port number used on the UdpClient constructor does not have to be the same as for the remote host, but it often helps to keep them the same in order to track the ports that are being used by particular applications. The remote host address information is stored in an IPEndPoint object and used as a parameter in the Send() method.

Summary

This chapter covers a lot of ground in discussing the history of network programming and its relationships to C# network programming. Network programming got its real push in the early days of Unix systems with the Berkeley socket library. Version 4.2 of the BSD Unix operating system included a common socket interface to assist programmers in communicating with other systems across a network.

The Windows socket interface, Winsock, builds on the existing Unix network socket programming model, adding many Winsock-specific functions to enhance the standard socket programming model. Many of the enhancements center around adding the capability for asynchronous socket I/O. The WSAAsyncSelect() and WSAEventSelect() functions enable Winsock programs to use standard Windows messages and events to signal socket events.

The .NET Framework offers a socket interface to access the Winsock APIs. The System.Net .Sockets namespace provides the Socket class that uses managed code to provide Winsock functionality to C# programs. In addition to the normal Socket class, C# also offers the TcpClient, TcpListener, and UdpClient classes. These classes take care of much of the programming overhead associated with creating sockets, and they provide an easy interface for novice network programmers to work from.

As you can see, network addresses are crucial to socket programming. Unfortunately, these days there are lots of options for how to reference an address on the Internet (or even a local network). The next chapter describes how to use the Domain Name Service (DNS) classes in C# to resolve hostnames into IP addresses for your network programs.

CHAPTER 4

DNS and C#

- The Domain Name System (DNS)

- Windows DNS client information

- DNS configuration

- Using C# to investigate the DNS configuration

- Resolving hostnames with `nslookup`

- DNS classes in C#

- Synchronous methods

- Asynchronous methods

IP addresses and network programs go hand in hand. When writing socket programs, you must indicate the IP address of either the local host for server applications, or a remote host for client applications. Sometimes this is not an easy thing to do—equating IP addresses and hostnames can be complicated. If all we ever needed were IP addresses, life would be a lot simpler for the network programmer.

In the real world, however, everywhere you look—books, magazines, websites, television advertisements, and all the rest—you see hostnames thrown at you. The Internet has made the hostname a common household item. Because of this, almost all network programs must allow customers to enter hostnames as well as IP addresses, and it is up to the network programmer to ensure that the program can find the IP address that is properly associated with the hostname. The primary control mechanism for accomplishing this is the Domain Name System (DNS), which is used to control hostnames and provide information to hosts wanting to find the IP address of another hostname.

This chapter discusses the basics of DNS and how you can use DNS to resolve hostnames in your C# network programs. First, you'll look at an overview of DNS processes, and then you'll see how DNS is used on standard Windows workstations and servers. Finally, you'll get an in-depth look at how to use DNS in your C# network programs, along with sample programs showing the C# DNS classes in action.

The History of Computer Names

Back in the old days (the '80s) when the Internet was small, it wasn't too hard to locate other computers on the network. Each system on the Internet contained a database that matched hostnames with assigned IP addresses. Internet hostnames could be anything the system administrator wanted to use—Fred, Barney, acctg1, anything. A central clearinghouse kept track of all the hostnames and IP addresses used on the Internet and published a master database containing all the address information. Usually once a week or so, individual system administrators downloaded the master database of hostnames and addresses to their local systems.

This system worked fine for a while, but it wasn't long before it didn't scale very well. As more and more hosts were added to the Internet, the database grew. And of course, as it grew, the longer it took to download, and the more space it took up on the individual systems. Clearly a dramatic improvement was needed, and that improvement was the Domain Name System (DNS).

The Domain Name System (DNS)

To simplify the unwieldy state of computer naming, the Domain Name System (DNS) was created. It allows the master host database to be split up and distributed among multiple systems on the Internet. DNS uses a hierarchical database approach, creating levels of information that can be split and stored on various systems throughout the Internet.

In addition to splitting up the database, DNS also provides a means for clients to query the database in real time. All a client needs to know is the location of one DNS server (and maybe a backup or two) in the database hierarchy. If the client queries a DNS server with a hostname not stored on the DNS server's local database, the server can query another DNS server that does have the information and forward it to the client.

To implement the DNS concept, a new database and protocol were created to pass DNS information among clients and servers and to enable DNS servers to update one another. This section describes the workings of the DNS system and how clients can query DNS servers for hostname information.

DNS Structure

The structure of a hierarchical database is similar to an organization chart with nodes connected in a treelike manner (that's the hierarchical part). The top node is called the *root*. The root node does not explicitly show up in Internet host addresses, so it is often referred to as the "nameless" node. Multiple categories were created under the root level to divide the database into pieces called *domains*. Each domain contains DNS servers that are responsible for maintaining the database of computer names for that area of the database (that's the distributed part). The diagram in Figure 4.1 shows how the DNS domains are distributed.

FIGURE 4.1:
The Internet
DNS system

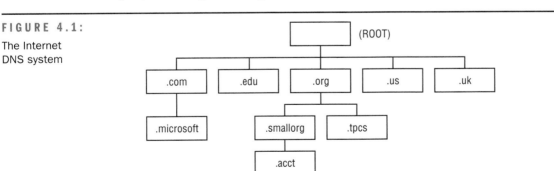

The first (or top) level of distribution is divided into domains based on country codes. Additional top-level domains for specific organizations were created to prevent the country domains from getting overcrowded. Table 4.1 describes the layout of the original top-level DNS domains.

TABLE 4.1: DNS Original Top-Level Domain Names

Domain	Description
.com	Commercial organizations
.edu	Educational institutions
.mil	U.S. military sites
.gov	U.S. government organizations
.net	Internet Service Providers (ISPs)
.org	Nonprofit organizations
.us	Other U.S. organizations (such as local governments)
.ca	Canadian organizations
.de	German organizations
(other countries)	Organizations from other countries

Recently, new top-level domains have been added to the DNS system. These new top-level domains allow identification of particular industries worldwide, and not just within a particular country. Corporations within those industries can register hostnames within their particular industry. Table 4.2 shows the seven new top-level domains.

TABLE 4.2: DNS Top-Level Domains Added in 2001

Domain	Description
.aero	Corporations in the air transport industry
.biz	Generic businesses
.coop	Cooperatives
.info	Unrestricted use
.museum	Museums
.name	Individuals
.pro	Professionals (doctors, lawyers, and so on)

As the Internet grows, the top-level domains are each divided into subdomains, or *zones*. Each zone is an independent domain in itself but relies on its parent domain for connectivity to the database. A parent zone must grant permission for a child zone to exist and is responsible for the child zone's behavior (just as in real life). Each zone must have at least two DNS servers that maintain the DNS database for the zone.

The original DNS specifications stipulated that the DNS servers for a single zone must have separate connections to the Internet and be housed in separate locations for fault-tolerance purposes. Because of this stipulation, many organizations rely on other organizations to host their secondary and tertiary DNS servers.

Hosts within a zone add the domain name to their hostname to form a unique Internet name. Thus, computer `fred` in the `smallorg.org` domain would be called `fred.smallorg.org`. This convention can become a little confusing because a domain can contain hosts as well as zones.

For example, the `smallorg.org` domain can contain host `fred.smallorg.org`, as well as grant authority for zone `acctg.smallorg.org` to a subdomain, which in turn can contain another host `barney.acctg.smallorg.org`. Although this simplifies the database system, it makes finding hosts on the Internet more complicated. Figure 4.2 shows an example of a domain and an associated subdomain.

FIGURE 4.2:

A sample domain and subdomain on the Internet

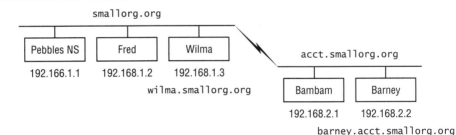

Control of Domain Names

Internet domain names have become a hot topic. In the past, one single entity, the Internic Corporation, controlled all U.S. domain names in the .com, .net, and .org domains. Today a nonprofit organization, the Internet Corporation for Assigned Names and Numbers (ICANN), controls this process. ICANN is responsible for the management of all U.S. domain names. The purchase of a domain name can be made from multiple vendors, not just one company. All domain names must be cleared by the ICANN for use in the U.S. domains.

Finding a Hostname in DNS

As mentioned, DNS enables clients to query a local DNS server to obtain hostname information. This process results in three possible scenarios for finding a hostname:

- Finding a host within the local domain
- Finding a remote host whose name is not on the local DNS server
- Finding a remote host whose name is on the local DNS server cache

Local Domain Hostnames

The simplest model for finding a hostname is a client attempting to find the hostname of another system within its local domain. In this scenario, the client uses the local DNS server as its default DNS server and sends the DNS query for the local hostname. The DNS server finds the hostname in its database section and returns the result to the client. This process is demonstrated in Figure 4.3.

FIGURE 4.3:

Client A is resolving a local hostname from the DNS server

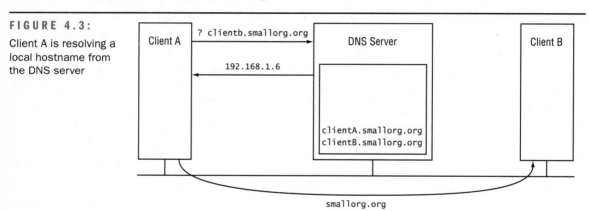

Remote Domain Hostnames

When a client wants to resolve the hostname for a system in a remote domain, there can be two possible scenarios:

- The remote hostname is not found on the local DNS server
- The remote hostname is found on the local DNS server cache

Remote Host Not Found on the Local DNS Server

When the client sends a query to the local DNS server to resolve a hostname for a system not contained within the local DNS server's database, the following actions occur:

1. The local DNS server queries a root DNS server for the hostname.

2. The root DNS server determines what domain the hostname should be found in and passes the request to a DNS server responsible for the host's domain.

3. The responsible local DNS server resolves the hostname to an IP address and returns the result to the root DNS server.

4. The root DNS server passes the result back to the client's local DNS server.

5. The client's local DNS server returns the resulting IP address to the client.

There's a lot of work going on behind the scenes in this process, but the end result is that the client receives the proper IP address for the remote system—all the client had to do was send one query to the local DNS server.

Remote Host Found in the Local DNS Server Cache

One advantage offered by DNS is that when the local DNS server has to query a root DNS server for a remote hostname, it can store the result in a local cache. When a local client queries the local DNS server for a remote hostname about which the server already has information, the local DNS server can return the cached information without having to go out and query a root DNS server. This greatly improves the response time of the query for the client.

There is one caveat to this process. When the root DNS server returns the IP address information for a hostname, it includes a time to live (TTL) value (the period for which the hostname information should be kept in a local DNS server's cache before expiring). The responsible local DNS server for the remote host sets this value. Depending on the volatility of local network hostnames, TTL values can be set anywhere from a few minutes to a few weeks. Once the TTL value has expired, the local DNS server must query the root DNS server when a new client query is received.

The DNS Database

Each DNS server is responsible for keeping track of the hostnames in its zone. To accomplish this, the DNS server must have a way to store host information in a database that can be queried by remote machines. The DNS database is a text file that consists of *resource records* (RRs) for hosts and network functions in the zone. The DNS server must run a DNS server software package to communicate the DNS information from the local domain database to remote DNS servers.

The DNS server's database must define various types of network resources, such as:

- The local domain definition
- Each registered host in the domain
- Common nicknames for hosts in the domain
- Special services, such as DNS servers and mail servers

RR formats were created to track all the information required for the DNS server. Table 4.3 describes some of the basic RRs that a DNS database might contain.

> **NOTE**   DNS database design has become a critical matter for researchers who constantly want to add more information to the database and to control the security of the information that is there. New record types are continually being added to the DNS database, but those in Table 4.3 are the core records for establishing a zone in the DNS database.

TABLE 4.3: Core DNS Database Records

Record Type	Description
SOA	Start of Authority
A	Internet address
NS	Name server
CNAME	Canonical name (nickname)
HINFO	Host information
MX	Mail server
PTR	Pointer (IP address)

There is one SOA record for the domain listed at the top of the database. Any other resource records for the domain can be added in any order after that. Each domain DNS server contains resource records for each registered host in the domain. The following sections describe the individual DNS record types in more detail.

Start of Authority Record (SOA)

Each database starts with an SOA record that defines the zone in which the database resides. The format for the SOA record is as follows:

```
domain name     [TTL] [class] SOA origin person (
                    serial number
```

```
refresh
retry
expire
minimum)
```

domain name   The name of the zone that is being defined. (The @ sign is often used as a placeholder to signify the computer's default domain.)

TTL   The length of time (in seconds) for which a requesting computer will keep any DNS information from this zone in its local name cache. Specifying this value is optional.

class   The protocol being used (for hosts on the Internet, it will always be class IN, for Internet).

origin   The name of the computer where the master zone database is located. A trailing period should be used after the hostname; otherwise, the local domain name will be appended to the hostname (of course, if you want to use that feature, omit the trailing period).

person   An e-mail address of a person responsible for the zone. The format of this value is a little different from what you might be used to seeing. The @ sign has already been used to signify the default domain name, so it can't be used in the mail address. Instead, a period is used. For example, instead of sysadm@smallorg.org, you would use sysadm.smallorg.org. If there are any periods in the name part, they must be escaped out by using a backslash \. An example of this would be the address john.jones@smallorg.org, which would translate to john\.jones.smallorg.org.

serial number   A unique number that identifies the version of the zone database file. Often what is used here is the date created plus a version count (such as 200210151).

refresh   The length of time (in seconds) a secondary DNS server should query a primary DNS server to check the SOA serial number. If the secondary server's SOA serial number is different from the primary server's, the secondary server will request an update to its database. One hour (3,600 seconds) is the common specification for this value.

retry   The time (in seconds) after which a secondary DNS server should retry in the event of a failed database refresh attempt.

expire   The period (in seconds) for which a secondary DNS server can use the data retrieved from the primary DNS server without getting refreshed. This value will usually be substantial, such as 3600000 (about 42 days).

minimum   The length time (in seconds) that should be used as the TTL in all RRs in this zone. Usually 86,400 (1 day) is a good value.

Internet Address Record (A)

Each host in the zone defined by the database should have a valid A record to define its hostname to the Internet. The format for the A record is as follows:

```
host    [TTL]    [class]    A    address
```

host   The fully qualified hostname for the computer (including the domain name).

address   The IP address of the computer.

TTL and class   These parameters are optional and have the same meaning as for the SOA record.

Canonical Name Record (CNAME)

In addition to a normal hostname, many computers also have nicknames. This is useful for identifying particular services without having to rename computers in the domain. For instance, you might assign the nickname www.smallorg.org to the host fred.acctg1.smallorg.org. The CNAME record links nicknames with the real hostname. The format of the CNAME record is as follows:

```
nickname    [TTL]    [class]    CNAME    hostname
```

The roles of the *nickname* and *hostname* parameters are fairly obvious. They represent the nickname assigned and the original hostname of the computer, respectively.

Here again, the *TTL* and *class* parameters are optional and have the same meaning as for the SOA record.

Name Server Record (NS)

Each zone should have at least two DNS servers. NS records are used to identify these servers to other DNS servers trying to resolve hostnames within the zone. The format of an NS record is as follows:

```
domain    [TTL]    [class]    NS    server
```

domain   The domain name of the zone for which the DNS server is responsible. If it is blank, the NS record refers to the zone defined in the SOA record.

server   The hostname of the DNS server. There should also be an associated A record in the database to identify the IP address of the hostname.

TTL and class   Again, these parameters are optional and have the same meaning as for the SOA record.

Host Information Record (HINFO)

Additional information about a computer can be made available to DNS servers by using the HINFO record. The format of the HINFO record is as follows:

```
host    [TTL]    [class]    HINFO    hardware    software
```

host   The hostname of the computer the information applies to.

hardware   The type of hardware the computer is using.

software   The OS type and version of the computer.

The TTL and class   Again, these parameters are optional and have the same meaning as for the SOA record.

Pointer Record (PTR)

In addition to an A record, each computer in the zone should have a PTR record. This allows the DNS server to perform reverse queries from the IP address of the computer. Without the PTR information, remote servers could not determine the domain name where an IP address is located. The format of a PTR record is as follows:

```
IN-ADDR name    [TTL]    [class]    PTR    name
```

IN-ADDR name   The reverse DNS name of the IP address. If that sounds confusing, it is. This name allows the DNS server to work its way backward from the IP address of the computer. The *IN-ADDR.ARPA* address is a special domain to support gateway location and Internet address to host mapping. Inverse queries are not necessary because the IP address is mapped to a fictitious hostname. Thus, the *IN-ADDR name* of a computer with IP address 192.168.0.1 would be 1.0.168.192.IN-ADDR.ARPA.

name   The hostname of the computer as found in the A record.

TTL and class   Again, these parameters are optional and have the same meaning as for the SOA record.

Mail Exchange Record (MX)

The MX record is used to signify a particular type of host in the domain. It instructs remote mail servers where to forward mail for the domain. The format of the MX record is as follows:

```
name    [TTL]    [class]    MX    preference    host
```

name   The domain name (or the SOA domain if *name* is blank). This can also be a hostname if you want to redirect mail for a particular host in the network.

preference   An integer signifying the order in which remote servers should try connecting if multiple mail servers are specified. The highest preference is 0, with decreasing preference represented by increasing numbers.

preference   This feature is used to create primary and secondary mail servers for a domain. When a remote mail server queries the DNS server for a mail server responsible for the domain, the entire list of servers and preferences is sent. The remote mail server should attempt to connect to the highest priority mail server listed, and if that fails, continue down the list in order of preference.

host   The hostname or IP address of the mail server. There should also be an associated A record to identify the IP address of the mail server.

TTL and class   Again, these parameters are optional and have the same meaning as for the SOA record.

WARNING   Be careful about using CNAME entries as MX hosts. Some e-mail server packages cannot work properly with CNAME (nickname) hosts.

A Sample DNS Database

When an ISP hosts a company's domain name, it will have records in its DNS database identifying the domain to the Internet. The SOA record will identify the domain name, but it will point to the ISP's host as the authoritative host. The NS records for the domain will point to the ISP's DNS servers. If the company has its own mail server, the MX record will point to it. If the ISP handles the e-mail server for the company, the MX records point to the ISP's mail servers.

As far as the rest of the Internet is concerned, these computers are part of the company domain—even if they do not really exist on the company network but rather are located at the ISP. Listing 4.1 presents a sample ISP record of the domain definitions in its DNS database.

Listing 4.1   **Sample DNS database entries**

```
smallorg.org  IN  SOA    master.isp.net. postmaster.master.isp.net
      postmaster.master.isp.net (
                               1999080501    ;unique serial number
                          8H        ; refresh rate
```

```
                               2H          ;retry period
                               1W          ; expiration period
                               1D)         ; minimum

                NS     ns1.isp.net.    ;defines primary namserver
                NS     ns2.isp.net.    ;defines secondary nameserver

                MX     10 mail1.isp.net.    ; defines primary mail server
                MX     20 mail2.isp.net.    ; defines secondary mail server

        www     CNAME     host1.isp.net     ;defines a www server at the ISP
        ftp     CNAME     host1.isp.net     ; defines an FTP server at the ISP

        host1.isp.net   A     10.0.0.1

        1.0.0.10.IN-ADDR.ARPA     PTR     host1.isp.net    ; pointer for reverse DNS
```

The first section of Listing 4.1 is the SOA record for the new domain. The ISP points the domain name smallorg.org to its server master.isp.net. Next, the primary and secondary DNS servers are defined using the NS record type. Following the NS records, the primary (mail1.isp.net) and secondary (mail2.isp.net) mail servers are defined with MX records. Because the preference number for the mail1.isp.net server is lower, it is considered the primary mail server. Any mail for the smallorg.org domain should be delivered to that server if it is available.

After the MX records, the CNAME record defines the hostname www.smallorg.org as a nickname that points to the ISP server, which hosts the company web pages. The address ftp.smallorg.org is also defined as a nickname pointing to the same ISP server, which also hosts the FTP site. Using alias addresses for web and FTP servers is a service that most ISPs provide to customers who cannot afford to have a dedicated connection to the Internet but want to provide web and FTP services to their customers.

The A and PTR recordsets provide the Internet hostname and IP address information for the ISP host so that remote clients can connect to this server.

NOTE   PTR records are often placed in a separate database file on the server to help simplify the databases. This isn't a problem in the Listing 4.1 example, which has just one PTR record, but it can be when there are dozens or hundreds of them.

Windows DNS Client Information

All Microsoft Windows platforms support the DNS protocol in one way or another. Each of the workstation platforms allows you to configure remote DNS servers for resolving hostnames in applications. In addition, on the Windows 2000 server platform you can also create a DNS server database to support the DNS for a domain.

For your C# DNS programs to work, the DNS settings must be set properly on the Windows platform. This section describes how to configure the DNS client components on Windows systems and how to obtain the system DNS client information from a C# program.

DNS Configuration

All Windows systems have the capability to resolve hostnames. There are two techniques for resolving hostnames to IP addresses:

- Accessing a local file of hostnames
- Querying a remote DNS server

Each technique resolves the hostname differently, as described in the following sections.

Using the hosts File

The simplest way to resolve a limited number of hostnames is to maintain a local hostnames file on the system. For remote hostnames that you frequently access, this is the most efficient arrangement for Windows because it allows more immediate access than going out to a remote DNS server. However, this is obviously not the preferred method to use for resolving lots of hostnames, as is the case during Internet surfing.

The hostnames file is named hosts, and its location depends on which version of Windows you are using:

- For Windows 95, 98, Me, and XP, hosts is located in the C:\WINDOWS\SYSTEM32\DRIVERS\ETC directory.
- For Windows NT, and 2000, hosts is located in the C:\WINNT\SYSTEM32\DRIVERS\ETC directory.

The hosts file is in text format, with each line representing a record for each host. The host IP address is listed first, followed by one or more spaces and then the hostname; for example:

```
127.0.0.1      localhost
192.168.1.1    shadrach.blum.lan
```

```
192.168.1.2    meshach.blum.lan
192.168.1.6    abednego.blum.lan
```

Notice the first entry in the hosts file. The 127.0.0.1 address represents the special loopback address and always points to the localhost hostname. The localhost hostname is itself special because it represents the internal network address of the system. Applications often use this address to direct IP packets to the same system—that's one way to communicate between programs running on the same system.

After the localhost definition, each remote host that you access frequently should be listed on its own line. Let's say you run a local in-house network using a fictitious domain name (as shown in the previous example); you can still use the hostnames in the network programs if you enter them in the hosts file on each system.

It's easy to see that this method will work fine for a limited number of hosts, but if you're trying to access lots of hosts, the hosts file will become pretty unwieldy. The obvious solution is to use the DNS system to resolve hostnames. The next section describes how to do this on a Windows platform.

Using a Remote DNS Server

When you need to resolve standard Internet hostnames, the easiest way is to find a DNS server to query. Most (if not all) ISPs provide one or more DNS server addresses for customers to use for DNS queries. Often you won't need to do anything at all to configure the DNS servers into your system. If your ISP dynamically assigns an IP address to your system, it most likely also assigns the DNS servers dynamically as well.

On the other hand, if your DNS servers are not assigned dynamically, it may be up to you to make sure they are configured. The DNS server entries are stored in the Internet Protocol Properties section of the system's network properties. You'll take a slightly different route to get to these properties based on the Windows platform you're working on. On a Windows 2000 or XP workstation, click Control Panel, and double-click the Network Connections entry. A list of all available network interfaces will be shown. Right-click the network interface for which you want to configure the DNS server, and select the Properties option.

Figure 4.4 shows the Properties window of a network interface. It indicates what protocols and services are loaded for the interface. The DNS configuration settings are stored in the Internet Protocol (TCP/IP) item.

The network interface properties, reached through Control Panel ➢ Network Connections

When you double-click to display the TCP/IP settings for the network interface, you see the Properties window shown in Figure 4.5 (for a Windows XP Professional workstation). Here you can set the appropriate IP address, subnet mask, and default gateway settings, as well as define two DNS servers. The first server listed will be the primary server. If Windows does not receive a response from that one, it will try the alternate server.

DNS Server Configurations and Windows

The various Windows platforms have their own ways of presenting the Internet Protocol Properties information. In all cases, the DNS server addresses are located in the IP Properties window, although the path you take to get there may vary.

Also, if you are using DHCP with your ISP, you may not have any DNS servers configured at all—they are configured dynamically when you connect to the ISP. The easiest way to tell if you have DNS configured correctly is to do a simple ping test. From a command prompt window, type **ping www.microsoft.com**, and see what happens. If the hostname resolves to an IP address, your DNS configuration is working fine.

The Internet Protocol
Properties window
in which the DNS
server addresses
are configured

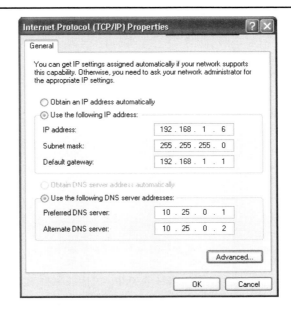

Using C# to Investigate the DNS Configuration

When your C# application is running on a customer's system, you have no guarantee that there are any DNS servers configured. You can find out what (if any) DNS servers are configured by using the .NET Registry class methods to examine the DNS Registry values.

Fortunately, all Windows platforms store the DNS server information in the same place:

```
HKLM\SYSTEM\CurrentControlSet\Services\Tcpip\Parameters
```

This key stores all the DNS parameters from the Internet Protocol Properties window as separate data values. Table 4.4 describes some of the values that are stored under this key.

TABLE 4.4: Registry Data Values for DNS Servers

Data Value	Description
DatabasePath	The location of the host's file
Domain	The name of the system's domain

Continued on next page

TABLE 4.4 CONTINUED: Registry Data Values for DNS Servers

Data Value	Description
Hostname	The name of the system's DNS host
NameServer	The list of DNS servers
SearchList	A list of DNS domains to append to the end of hostnames in DNS name searches

The value of most interest here is `NameServer`. This should contain a single string value representing all the configured DNS servers, separated by spaces. The primary DNS server will be listed first, followed by the alternate servers.

NOTE   If the workstation uses DHCP to dynamically assign an IP address, it may also dynamically assign DNS server addresses. These values are stored with the DHCP information of the connection, in place of the normal IP parameters section shown for this discussion.

You can create a C# program to query this Registry value using the .NET Registry class. Listing 4.2, the `FindDNSServers.cs` program, demonstrates how to do this.

Listing 4.2   **The FindDNSServer.cs program**

```csharp
using System;
using Microsoft.Win32;

class FindDNSServers
{
    public static void Main()
    {
        RegistryKey start = Registry.LocalMachine;
        string DNSservers = @"SYSTEM\CurrentControlSet\Services\Tcpip\Parameters";

        RegistryKey DNSserverKey = start.OpenSubKey(DNSservers);
        if (DNSserverKey == null)
        {
            Console.WriteLine("Unable to open DNS servers key");
            return;
        }

        string serverlist = (string)DNSserverKey.GetValue("NameServer");

        Console.WriteLine("DNS Servers: {0}", serverlist);
        DNSserverKey.Close();
        start.Close();

        char[] token = new char[1];
```

```
            token[0] = ' ';
            string[] servers = serverlist.Split(token);

            foreach(string server in servers)
            {
                Console.WriteLine("DNS server: {0}", server);
            }
        }
    }
```

In `FindDNSServer.cs`, the first step in the process is to create a base `RegistryKey` object with the HKLM value:

```
RegistryKey start = Registry.LocalMachine;
```

After the base key is set, you can use the `OpenSubKey()` method to create a `RegistryKey` object pointing to where the DNS information is located:

```
string DNSservers =
@"SYSTEM\CurrentControlSet\Services\Tcpip\Parameters";
RegistryKey DNSserverKey = start.OpenSubKey(DNSservers);
```

The `DNSservers` string points to the text version of the proper Registry key location for the DNS information.

TIP   Notice that this definition uses the @ symbol to tell the C# compiler that the backslash characters are not used as escape sequences, but as literal backslashes. This prevents your having to type two backslashes every time.

The `OpenSubKey()` method is used to assign the new key to the *DNSServerKey* `RegistryKey` object. Once you have a reference to the proper key, you can begin retrieving data values from it using the `GetValue()` method:

```
string serverlist =
        (string)DNSserverKey.GetValue("NameServer");
```

The *serverlist* variable should now contain the string value that includes all the configured DNS servers (if any), separated by spaces. To split them up into individual IP addresses, you use the `Split()` method of the string class.

The `Split()` method requires a character array specifying the characters on which to split the string. Because you know that each DNS server value is separated by a single space, you specify a character array that contains only a single entry, a space, and use the `Split()` method to divide the string into the string array:

```
char[] token = new char[1];
token[0] = ' ';
string[] servers = serverlist.Split(token);
```

Once you have an array of the DNS servers, you can use our old C# friend `foreach` to break them out into individual string values:

```
foreach(string server in servers)
    {
        Console.WriteLine("DNS server: {0}", server);
    }
```

If you need to use these addresses within the program, you could just as easily reference them using the server's array (`servers[0]` is the primary DNS server, `servers[1]` is the first alternate server, and so on).

The output from the program is simple—first the entire server string is shown, then the individual servers are split out to a separate line:

```
C:\>FindDNSServers
DNS Servers: 10.25.0.1 10.25.0.2
DNS server: 10.25.0.1
DNS server: 10.25.0.2

C:\>
```

This output should match what you see when you manually inspect the DNS server entries in the Internet Protocol Properties window. Both DNS server entries appear in the original string as extracted from the Registry. The individual servers are then separated using the `Split()` string method.

Resolving Hostnames with nslookup

Once the DNS server configuration is set, you can test the DNS functionality by manually using the command-line `nslookup` program to query the servers for DNS information. The `nslookup` program comes standard on all Windows platforms. This section shows how to use `nslookup` to obtain DNS information for domains and hosts.

Default nslookup Query

There are many ways to use the `nslookup` program. The easiest is to perform a single query for a hostname:

```
C:\>nslookup www.microsoft.com
Server: dns.ispnet.net
Address: 10.25.0.1

Non-authoritative answer:
Name:    www.microsoft.akadns.net
Addresses:  207.46.197.100, 207.46.230.218, 207.46.197.113, 207.46.197.102
          207.46.230.220, 207.46.230.219
```

```
Aliases:  www.microsoft.com
```

```
C:\>
```

The output from the `nslookup` command shows several pieces of information:

- The name and address of the DNS server queried:

  ```
  Server:  dns.ispnet.net
  Address:  10.25.0.1
  ```

- The status of the results:

  ```
  Non-authoritative answer:
  ```

- The results of the query:

  ```
  Name:     www.microsoft.akadns.net
  Addresses:  207.46.197.100, 207.46.230.218, 207.46.197.113, 207.46.197.102
          207.46.230.220, 207.46.230.219
  Aliases:  www.microsoft.com
  ```

Note that in this case, the www.microsoft.com DNS hostname is actually an alias for the host www.microsoft.akadns.net. This particular host also has six IP addresses assigned to it.

The status of the results tells you where the information came from. This example is a nonauthoritative answer, which means that the information came from a cache entry on the local DNS server and not from the DNS server assigned to that domain.

To verify if your local DNS server is caching queries, try to do a query on a new hostname that has not been previously queried, and then try the query a second time:

```
C:\>nslookup msdn.microsoft.com
Server:  dns.ispnet.net
Address: 10.25.0.1

Name:     msdn.microsoft.com
Addresses:  207.46.239.122, 207.46.196.115


C:\>nslookup msdn.microsoft.com
Server:  dns.ispnet.net
Address: 10.25.0.1

Non-authoritative answer:
Name:     msdn.microsoft.com
Addresses:  207.46.196.115, 207.46.239.122


C:\>
```

The first query does not display a status line with the results, which indicates that the results came directly from the DNS server for the domain of the remote host. However, the second query indicates that the results are nonauthoritative, which means that they came from the cache of the local DNS server. Indeed, this particular local DNS server is caching DNS results, which will help speed up your DNS queries.

You can also do reverse IP address queries to determine what hostname (if any) an IP address is assigned to:

```
C:\>nslookup 207.46.196.115
Server:  dns.ispnet.net
Address: 10.25.0.1

Name:    msdn.microsoft.com
Address:  207.46.196.115

C:\>
```

Unlike hostname queries, IP address queries are not cached on the local DNS server. If you perform this query a second time, it will still go to the DNS server for the domain and return an authoritative answer.

Watching the Query

You can use the WinDump or Analyzer programs to watch the DNS query from the local system. (These tools were described in Chapter 2, "IP Programming Basics.") Listing 4.3 shows a sample windump output during the sample nslookup command.

Listing 4.3   **nslookup windump output**

```
D:\winpcap>windump -s 200 udp port 53
windump    listening on\Device\Packet_E190x1
07:16:45.208103 192.168.1.6.1219 > dns.ispnet.net.53:  2+ A? www.microsoft.com
. (35)
07:16:45.208888 dns.ispnet.net.53 > 192.168.1.6.1219:  2 7/7/7 CNAME www.micro
soft.akadns.net., A microsoft.com, A microsoft.com, A microsoft.com, A www.inter
national.microsoft.com, A microsoft.com, (400)
07:16:50.260472 192.168.1.6.1222 > dns.ispnet.net.53:  3+ PTR? 100.197.46.207.
in-addr.arpa. (45)
07:16:50.261416 dns.ispnet.net.53 > 192.168.1.6.1222:  3 4/13/9 PTR microsoft.
com., PTR microsoft.net., PTR www.domestic.microsoft.com., PTR www.us.microsoft.
com. (499)
07:16:50.263891 192.168.1.6.1223 > dns.ispnet.net.53:  4+ PTR? 219.230.46.207.
in-addr.arpa. (45)
07:16:50.265999 dns.ispnet.net.53 > 192.168.1.6.1223:  4 4/13/8 PTR microsoft.
com., PTR microsoft.net., PTR www.international.microsoft.com., PTR www.us.micro
soft.com. (488)
07:16:50.268427 192.168.1.6.1224 > dns.ispnet.net.53:  5+ PTR? 218.230.46.207.
```

```
in-addr.arpa. (45)
07:16:50.270266 dns.ispnet.net.53 > 192.168.1.6.1224:  5 4/13/9 PTR microsoft.
com., PTR microsoft.net., PTR www.domestic.microsoft.com., PTR www.us.microsoft.
com. (499)
07:16:50.272684 192.168.1.6.1225 > dns.ispnet.net.53:  6+ PTR? 113.197.46.207.
in-addr.arpa. (45)
07:16:50.273576 dns.ispnet.net.53 > 192.168.1.6.1225:  6 2/13/11 PTR www.inter
national.microsoft.com., PTR www.us.microsoft.com. (498)
07:16:50.278458 192.168.1.6.1226 > dns.ispnet.net.53:  7+ PTR? 220.230.46.207.
in-addr.arpa. (45)
07:16:50.399074 dns.ispnet.net.53 > 192.168.1.6.1226:  7* 4/0/0 PTR microsoft.
com., PTR microsoft.net., PTR www.domestic.microsoft.com., PTR www.us.microsoft.
com. (147)

239 packets received by filter
0 packets dropped by kernel

D:\winpcap>
```

As you can see, there is a lot of action happening behind the scenes of a simple nslookup query. Here is the WinDump command that was used for this capture:

```
windump -s 200 udp port 53
```

This command uses the -s option to set the amount of displayed data to 200 bytes. Because DNS packets often contain lots of return data, this setting helps WinDump display more information from the packet than the default 64 bytes. It is still possible that more data will be present in the return packet, but for now this should be enough information to get your research started. Note also that the parameters are set to capture only DNS packets. The DNS protocol uses UDP and is assigned well-known port number 53. Fortunately, Win-Dump decodes the DNS queries to present the text information for you, so no protocol debugging is required here.

The first packet is as expected, a DNS query for the A record for the www.microsoft.com hostname:

```
07:16:45.208103 192.168.1.6.1219 > dns.ispnet.net.53:  2+ A? www.microsoft.com
. (35)
```

The return packet contains the information from the DNS query:

```
07:16:45.208888 dns.ispnet.net.53 > 192.168.1.6.1219:  2 7/7/7 CNAME www.micro
soft.akadns.net., A microsoft.com, A microsoft.com, A microsoft.com, A www.inter
national.microsoft.com, A microsoft.com, (400)
```

This indicates that the www.microsoft.com hostname was really an alias for another hostname. The A record information revealed that the real hostname of that system is www.microsoft.akadns.net.

The `nslookup` program then proceeds to query for the IP address information of the real hostname. The PTR record information shows the IP addresses assigned to the host, along with the assigned hostname for each IP address.

```
07:16:50.260472 192.168.1.6.1222 > dns.ispnet.net.53:  3+ PTR? 100.197.46.207.
in-addr.arpa. (45)
07:16:50.261416 dns.ispnet.net.53 > 192.168.1.6.1222:  3 4/13/9 PTR microsoft.
com., PTR microsoft.net., PTR www.domestic.microsoft.com., PTR www.us.microsoft.
com. (499)
```

The first IP address, 207.46.197.100, is used to query for the PTR record information. The returned information indicates that the address is assigned to the `microsoft.com` domain.

Advanced Queries

The default `nslookup` format described in the preceding sections provides good, simple information regarding the hostname requested. If you would like to see other DNS record types, you must use options for `nslookup`. The `nslookup` options can be specified on the command line, but it is often easier to use `nslookup` in interactive mode.

To enter interactive mode, simply type **nslookup** at the command prompt without any parameters. The default DNS server used will be displayed, along with an `nslookup` prompt:

```
C:\>nslookup
Default Server:  dns.ispnet.net
Address: 10.25.0.1

>
```

At the `nslookup` prompt, you can enter in a variety of special commands to modify the behavior of the `nslookup` query, as described in Table 4.5.

TABLE 4.5: nslookup Commands

Command	Description
NAME	Resolves the hostname NAME
NAME1 NAME2	Resolves the hostname NAME using DNS server NAME2
Help	Lists all the available `nslookup` commands and options
Set	Sets an `nslookup` option
Server NAME	Sets the default DNS server to NAME, using the current default server
Lserver NAME	Sets the default DNS server to NAME, using the initial server
Finger [USER]	Uses the Finger utility to find USER at the current default host
Root	Sets the current default DNS server to the root server
ls DOMAIN	Lists all registered addresses in DOMAIN
View	Views a file created with the `ls` command
Exit	Exits the `nslookup` command mode

As you can see in Table 4.5, you use the `set` command to establish various options for the DNS query. These options are defined in Table 4.6, and a few of the most commonly used are discussed in the sections that follow.

TABLE 4.6: nslookup Set Options

Option	Description
All	Prints the options, current server, and host
[no]debug	Prints (or doesn't print) debugging information
[no]d2	Prints (or doesn't print) exhaustive debugging information
[no]defname	Appends (or doesn't append) domain name to each query
[no]recurse	Asks for recursive answer to each query
[no]search	Uses domain search list
[no]vc	Always uses a virtual circuit
Domain=NAME	Sets default domain name to NAME
Srchlist=N1[N2/.../N6]	Sets domain to N1 and search list to N1, N2, etc.
root=NAME	Sets DNS root server to NAME
Retry=X	Sets number of retries to X
Timeout=X	Sets initial timeout interval to X seconds
type=X	Sets query type
Querytype=X	Sets query type
Class=X	Sets query class
[no]msxfr	Uses Microsoft fast zone transfer
Ixfrver=X	Sets the current version to use in IXFR transfer request

The debug Option

The debug option allows you to watch the DNS communication with the DNS server. Listing 4.4 shows a sample DNS query with the debug option turned on. This information shows exactly what you saw in the WinDump results: the original query for the www.microsoft.com hostname and the answer indicating that it was an alias for the www.microsoft.akadns.net host, along with all the IP addresses associated with it.

Listing 4.4   **nslookup query with debug on**

```
C:\>nslookup
Default Server     dns.ispnet.net
Address: 10.25.0.1

> set debug
> www.microsoft.com
Server:  dns.ispnet.net
```

```
Address:  10.25.0.1

_____
Got answer:
    HEADER:
        opcode = QUERY, id = 2, rcode = NOERROR
        header flags:  response, want recursion, recursion avail.
        questions = 1,  answers = 7,  authority records = 7,  additional = 7

    QUESTIONS:
        www.microsoft.com, type = A, class = IN
    ANSWERS:
    ->  www.microsoft.com
        canonical name = www.microsoft.akadns.net
        ttl = 7116 (1 hour 58 mins 36 secs)
    ->  www.microsoft.akadns.net
        internet address = 207.46.230.219
        ttl = 216 (3 mins 36 secs)
    ->  www.microsoft.akadns.net
        internet address = 207.46.230.220
        ttl = 216 (3 mins 36 secs)
    ->  www.microsoft.akadns.net
        internet address = 207.46.197.100
        ttl = 216 (3 mins 36 secs)
    ->  www.microsoft.akadns.net
        internet address = 207.46.230.218
        ttl = 216 (3 mins 36 secs)
    ->  www.microsoft.akadns.net
        internet address = 207.46.197.102
        ttl = 216 (3 mins 36 secs)
    ->  www.microsoft.akadns.net
        internet address = 207.46.197.113
        ttl = 216 (3 mins 36 secs)
    AUTHORITY RECORDS:
    ->  akadns.net
        nameserver = ZA.akadns.net
        ttl = 127117 (1 day 11 hours 18 mins 37 secs)
    ->  akadns.net
        nameserver = ZC.akadns.net
        ttl = 127117 (1 day 11 hours 18 mins 37 secs)
    ->  akadns.net
        nameserver = ZD.akadns.net
        ttl = 127117 (1 day 11 hours 18 mins 37 secs)
    ->  akadns.net
        nameserver = ZE.akadns.net
        ttl = 127117 (1 day 11 hours 18 mins 37 secs)
    ->  akadns.net
        nameserver = ZF.akadns.net
        ttl = 127117 (1 day 11 hours 18 mins 37 secs)
    ->  akadns.net
        nameserver = ZG.akadns.net
```

```
            ttl = 127117 (1 day 11 hours 18 mins 37 secs)
        ->  akadns.net
            nameserver = ZH.akadns.net
            ttl = 127117 (1 day 11 hours 18 mins 37 secs)
    ADDITIONAL RECORDS:
    ->  ZA.akadns.net
        internet address = 216.32.65.105
        ttl = 127117 (1 day 11 hours 18 mins 37 secs)
    ->  ZC.akadns.net
        internet address = 63.241.199.50
        ttl = 127117 (1 day 11 hours 18 mins 37 secs)
    ->  ZD.akadns.net
        internet address = 206.132.160.36
        ttl = 127117 (1 day 11 hours 18 mins 37 secs)
    ->  ZE.akadns.net
        internet address = 12.47.217.11
        ttl = 127117 (1 day 11 hours 18 mins 37 secs)
    ->  ZF.akadns.net
        internet address = 63.215.198.79
        ttl = 127117 (1 day 11 hours 18 mins 37 secs)
    ->  ZG.akadns.net
        internet address = 204.248.36.131
        ttl = 127117 (1 day 11 hours 18 mins 37 secs)
    ->  ZH.akadns.net
        internet address = 63.208.48.42
        ttl = 127117 (1 day 11 hours 18 mins 37 secs)


    ------
    Non-authoritative answer:
    Name:    www.microsoft.akadns.net
    Addresses:  207.46.230.219, 207.46.230.220, 207.46.197.100, 207.46.230.218
                207.46.197.102, 207.46.197.113
    Aliases:  www.microsoft.com

    >exit

    C:\>
    hostname
```

The querytype option

Another useful capability is setting the `querytype`. You can use this option to narrow down specific information regarding a host, or even regarding a complete domain. For example, you can set the query type to SOA to retrieve the SOA record for the domain:

```
C:\>nslookup
Default Server:  dns.ispnet.net
Address: 10.25.0.1

> set querytype=soa
> microsoft.com
```

```
Server:  dns.ispnet.net
Address: 10.25.0.1

microsoft.com
        primary name server = dns.cp.msft.net
        responsible mail addr = msnhst.microsoft.com
        serial  = 2002061201
        refresh = 900 (15 mins)
        retry   = 600 (10 mins)
        expire  = 7200000 (83 days 8 hours)
        default TTL = 7200 (2 hours)
dns.cp.msft.net internet address = 207.46.138.10
>
```

You can see the entire SOA record for the requested domain, as it is defined in the local DNS server. This will also work when you are trying to determine the mail servers for a particular domain, as shown in the following example:

```
C:\>nslookup
Default Server:  dns.ispnet.net
Address: 10.25.0.1

> set querytype=mx
> microsoft.com
Server:  dns.ispnet.net
Address: 10.25.0.1

microsoft.com   MX preference = 10, mail exchanger = maila.microsoft.com
microsoft.com   MX preference = 10, mail exchanger = mailb.microsoft.com
microsoft.com   MX preference = 10, mail exchanger = mailc.microsoft.com
maila.microsoft.com      internet address = 131.107.3.125
maila.microsoft.com      internet address = 131.107.3.124
mailb.microsoft.com      internet address = 131.107.3.123
mailb.microsoft.com      internet address = 131.107.3.122
mailc.microsoft.com      internet address = 131.107.3.126
mailc.microsoft.com      internet address = 131.107.3.121
>
```

The results show that there are three separate mail servers defined for the microsoft.com domain. The information shows the mail server hostnames, along with their individual IP addresses.

The Domain Dump Option (ls)

The ls option of the nslookup command allows system administrators to obtain a complete dump of the defined DNS database for a domain. With this option, you can investigate all the DNS records for an entire domain. Be forewarned, though—I say "can" because it is not guaranteed to work. Many DNS servers disable this command to prevent unauthorized users from seeing the entire DNS database.

If you do have access to the `ls` command on a DNS server, you can dump the complete DNS database to a file by using the redirection command (>):

```
C:\>nslookup
Default Server: dns.ispnet.net
Address: 10.25.0.1

> ls testdomain.com > td.txt
> view td.txt
```

The `view` command can then be used to view the downloaded text file, which contains the DNS database for the domain.

DNS Classes in C#

The `System.Net` namespace contains the `Dns` class, which provides all the necessary DNS functions for C# programs. This section describes the `Dns` class methods and shows how they can be used in C# programs to utilize the DNS capabilities of the system.

Synchronous Methods

There are four synchronous methods defined in the `Dns` class:

- `GetHostName()`
- `GetHostByName()`
- `GetHostByAddress()`
- `Resolve()`

GetHostName()

You have already seen this method in action back in Chapter 2. The `GetHostName()` method is used to determine the hostname of the local system the program is running on. This information is frequently needed for network programs, so you'll see this method used a lot. The format is simple: there are no parameters to enter, and the result is a string object:

```
string hostname = Dns.GetHostName();
```

The information retrieved by `GetHostName()`hostname should be the same name that appears in the Registry `Hostname` data value, along with the `Domain` data value, to create the complete fully-qualified domain name (FQDN) of the system. The FQDN includes the local hostname, along with the full domain name information.

GetHostByName()

The GetHostByName() method performs a DNS query for a specified hostname using the default DNS server configured on the system. The format of the method is as follows:

```
IPHostEntry GetHostByName(string hostname)
```

The IPHostEntry that is returned by GetHostByName() is itself an interesting object. It associates a DNS hostname with an array of alias names and IP addresses. It contains three properties:

- AddressList: An array of IPAddress objects, one for each assigned IP address

- Aliases: An array of string objects, one for each alias

- HostName: A string object for the hostname

The AddressList and Aliases objects must be separated into their individual array elements in order to retrieve the information stored. This is often done using the foreach function in C#.

Listing 4.5 is a sample program that demonstrates the GetHostByName() method.

Listing 4.5   **The GetDNSHostInfo.cs program**

```
using System;
using System.Net;

class GetDNSHostInfo
{
    public static void Main(string[] argv)
    {
        if (argv.Length != 1)
        {
         Console.WriteLine("Usage: GetDNSHostInfo hostname");
         return;
        }

        IPHostEntry results = Dns.GetHostByName(argv[0]);

        Console.WriteLine("Host name: {0}",
                        results.HostName);

        foreach(string alias in results.Aliases)
        {
            Console.WriteLine("Alias: {0}", alias);
        }
        foreach(IPAddress address in results.AddressList)
        {
            Console.WriteLine("Address: {0}",
                        address.ToString());
        }
    }
}
```

The `GetDNSHostInfo.cs` program is fairly straightforward. It takes the parameter entered on the command line, attempts to use it to perform a `GetHostByName()`, and dumps the `IPHostEntry` object returned from the method. If there is more than one IP address assigned to the hostname, each address will appear in the `AddressList` property. The `foreach` function is used to extract each individual IP address and display it. The output from a sample session looks like this:

```
C:\>GetDNSHostInfo www.microsoft.com
Host name: www.microsoft.akadns.net
Alias: www.microsoft.com
Alias: www.microsoft.com
Address: 207.46.197.102
Address: 207.46.230.220
Address: 207.46.230.218
Address: 207.46.230.219
Address: 207.46.197.100
Address: 207.46.197.113

C:\>
```

The `GetHostByName()` method returned the same information that was received by the default `nslookup` command. In fact, you can run `windump` or `analyzer` and watch the DNS query generated by the `GetHostByName()` method. It should look similar to the one generated by the default `nslookup` example in Listing 4.4.

As shown in Chapter 2, Listing 2.4, the `GetHostByName()` method is often used with the `GetHostName()` method to determine the IP address of the local system, like this:

```
IPHostEntry localaddrs = Dns.GetHostByName(Dns.GetHostName());
```

The resulting `IPHostEntry` object will contain all the IP addresses configured for the local host in the `AddressList` property.

GetHostByAddress()

When you use the `GetDNSHostInfo.cs` program in Listing 4.5 and enter an IP address, it unfortunately does not produce the hostname:

```
C:\>GetDNSHostInfo 207.46.197.100
Host name: 207.46.197.100
Address: 207.46.197.100

C:\>
```

Not too exciting. Obviously, the `GetHostByName()` method only works for resolving hostnames.

When you do need to find the hostname for a known IP address, use the `GetHostByAddress()` method. There are two formats for this method:

```
IPHostEntry GetHostByAddress(IPAddress address)
IPHostEntry GetHostByAddress(string address)
```

The first format is used when you have the IP address as an `IPAddress` object. The second format is used if you want to use the string representation of the dotted quad format of the IP address (such as 207.46.197.100).

The `GetDNSAddressInfo.cs` program shown in Listing 4.6 demonstrates the `GetHostByAddress()` method.

Listing 4.6   The GetDNSAddressInfo.cs program

```csharp
using System;
using System.Net;

class GetDNSAddressInfo
{
    public static void Main(string)[] argv)
    {
        if (argv.Length != 1)
        {
            Console.WriteLine("Usage: GetDNSAddressInfo address");
            return;
        }

        IPAddress test = IPAddress.Parse(argv[0]);

        IPHostEntry iphe = Dns.GetHostByAddress(test);

        Console.WriteLine("Information for {0}",
                    test.ToString());

        Console.WriteLine("Host name: {0}", iphe.HostName);
        foreach(string alias in iphe.Aliases)
        {
            Console.WriteLine("Alias: {0}", alias);
        }
        foreach(IPAddress address in iphe.AddressList)
        {
            Console.WriteLine("Address: {0}", address.ToString());
        }
    }
}
```

Just for fun (and experience), this program converts the string argument into an `IPAddress` object, which is used as the parameter to the `GetHostByAddress()` method. The output should look something like this:

```
C:\>GetDNSAddressInfo 207.46.197.113
Information for 207.46.197.113
Host name: www.international.microsoft.com
Address: 207.46.197.113

C:\>
```

Here again, you can use `windump` or `analyzer` to watch the DNS network traffic generated by this query.

WARNING The `GetHostByAddress()` method does not always work. You may run into many situations where an IP address does not resolve to a hostname. There are two common reasons for this. One is when there is no DNS hostname assigned to the address. Another is that, although a DNS A record might exist, the DNS administrator didn't use a PTR record pointing the address back to the hostname.

Resolve()

As you saw in the preceding sections, the main disadvantage with the `GetHostByName()` and `GetHostByAddress()` methods is that they are specific to one or the other types of address information. If you feed an IP address into the `GetHostByName()` method, it returns only the address. Even worse, if you try to feed a string hostname to the `GetHostByAddress()` method, it will produce an Exception (because it uses the `IPAddress.Parse()` method on the supplied string IP address).

Suppose you are creating a program where customers are entering the address of a remote host—you might not know which form the customers will use. Instead of worrying about trying to figure out whether the input is numeric or text so that you can use the proper `GetHostBy` method, the `Dns` class offers a simple solution: the `Resolve()` method. `Resolve()` accepts an address in either hostname or IP address format and returns the DNS information in an `IPHostEntry` object. Listing 4.7 demonstrates this method.

Listing 4.7   **The GetResolveInfo.cs program**

```
using System;
using System.Net;

class GetResolveInfo
{
    public static void Main(string[] argv)
```

```
    {
        if (argv.Length != 1)
        {
            Console.WriteLine("Usage: GetResolveInfo address");
            return;
        }

        IPHostEntry iphe = Dns.Resolve(argv[0]);

        Console.WriteLine("Information for {0}", argv[0]);

        Console.WriteLine("Host name: {0}", iphe.HostName);
        foreach(string alias in iphe.Aliases)
        {
            Console.WriteLine("Alias: {0}", alias);
        }
        foreach(IPAddress address in iphe.AddressList)
        {
            Console.WriteLine("Address: {0}",
                      address.ToString());
        }
    }
}
```

The Resolve() method attempts to fill the IPHostEntry object with information regarding the address entered as the parameter. You can use either hostnames or IP addresses, and Resolve() will return the proper information. It's a much friendlier way of handling any possible host information that a customer might throw at your program.

```
C:\>GetResolveInfo www.microsoft.com
Information for www.microsoft.com
Host name: www.microsoft.akadns.net
Alias: www.microsoft.com
Alias: www.microsoft.com
Address: 207.46.230.219
Address: 207.46.230.218
Address: 207.46.197.100
Address: 207.46.197.102
Address: 207.46.230.220
Address: 207.46.197.113

C:\>GetResolveInfo 207.46.197.100
Information for 207.46.197.100
Host name: microsoft.com
Address: 207.46.197.100

C:\>
```

Asynchronous Methods

The regular `Dns` methods might cause a problem for your C# program because they use blocking mode to communicate with the remote DNS server. If you ran the example programs offered earlier in this section on the DNS classes, you may have noticed that it often takes a few seconds for the DNS information to be returned from the remote DNS server. This may not seem like much of a problem, but it can cause serious difficulties in Windows programs that allow the user to do other things at the same time. While the program is waiting for the DNS server response, the user is prevented from clicking any buttons or entering any information in `TextBox` fields. For some applications, this can mean unacceptable performance.

Chapter 3, "C# Network Programming Classes," describes techniques that can be used to prevent network blocking calls. One of the techniques is to use the asynchronous socket methods (described in more detail in Chapter 8, "Asynchronous Socket Programming). These methods allow you to start a network function and specify a delegate to call when the network function completes. Meanwhile, the rest of the program can go happily on its way doing other things. When the network function is completed, it signals the program to run the delegate method.

The `Dns` class provides the following asynchronous methods to allow your programs to perform asynchronous DNS function calls:

- `BeginGetHostByName()`

- `BeginResolve()`

- `EndGetHostByName()`

- `EndResolve()`

Each of the asynchronous methods parallels the equivalent synchronous method. At this time there is no asynchronous `GetHostByAddress()` call.

The methods are called in pairs. The `Beginxxx` method is called from the program and points to a delegate method, which contains the `Endxxx` method. For example, `BeginResolve()` uses the following format:

```
public static IAsyncResult BeginResolve(string hostname,
        AsyncCallback requestCallback, object stateObject)
```

The method uses three parameters:

- A string representation, *hostname*, of a hostname or IP address

- An `AsyncCallback` object, *requestCallback*, which defines the delegate

- A generic object, *stateObject*, which defines the method state

The `AsyncCallback` object is created to point to the delegate method used when the DNS results are returned. To do this, you must first create the `AsyncCallback` object, then assign the delegate method to it:

```
private AsyncCallback OnResolved;
OnResolved = new AsyncCallback(Resolved);
Object state = new Object();
.
.
.
Dns.BeginResolve(addr, OnResolved, state);
.
.
}

private void Resolved(IasyncResult ar)
{
IPHostEntry iphe = Dns.EndResolve(ar);
}
```

The `OnResolved AsyncCallback` object points to the delegate method `Resolved`, which will contain the `EndResolve()` method to complete the DNS call. The *state* object allows you to pass information to the delegate method. The `EndResolve()` method has this format:

```
public static IPHostEntry EndResolve(IasyncResult ar)
```

The `IAsyncResult` object *ar* is what refers the `EndResolve()` method to the original `BeginResolve()` method. The result of the `EndResolve()` method is the standard `IPHostEntry` object, which can then be broken down to extract the returned information, similar to the standard `Resolve()` method discussed earlier.

Listing 4.8 shows a sample program that uses the `BeginResolve()` and `EndResolve()` methods in a Windows Forms environment.

Listing 4.8   The AsyncResolve.cs program

```
using System;
using System.Drawing;
using System.Net;
using System.Text;
using System.Windows.Forms;


class AsyncResolve  : Form
{

    TextBox address;
    ListBox results;
```

```
private AsyncCallback OnResolved;

public AsyncResolve()
{

    Text = "DNS Address Resolver";
    Size = new Size(400,380);
    OnResolved = new AsyncCallback(Resolved);


    Label label1 = new Label();
    label1.Parent = this;
    label1.Text = "Enter address to resolve:";
    label1.AutoSize = true;
    label1.Location = new Point(10, 10);

    address = new TextBox();
    address.Parent = this;
    address.Size = new Size(200, 2 * Font.Height);
    address.Location = new Point(10, 35);

    results = new ListBox();
    results.Parent = this;
    results.Location = new Point(10, 65);
    results.Size = new Size(350, 20 * Font.Height);

    Button checkit = new Button();
    checkit.Parent = this;
    checkit.Text = "Resolve";
    checkit.Location = new Point(235,32);
    checkit.Size = new Size(7 * Font.Height, 2 * Font.Height);
    checkit.Click += new EventHandler(ButtonResolveOnClick);
}

void ButtonResolveOnClick(object obj, EventArgs ea)
{
    results.Items.Clear();
    string addr = address.Text;
    Object state = new Object();

    Dns.BeginResolve(addr, OnResolved, state);
}

private void Resolved(IAsyncResult ar)
{
    string buffer;

    IPHostEntry iphe = Dns.EndResolve(ar);

    buffer = "Host name: " + iphe.HostName;
```

```
        results.Items.Add(buffer);

        foreach(string alias in iphe.Aliases)
        {
            buffer = "Alias: " + alias;
            results.Items.Add(buffer);
        }
        foreach(IPAddress addrs in iphe.AddressList)
        {
            buffer = "Address: " + addrs.ToString();
            results.Items.Add(buffer);
        }
    }

    public static void Main()
    {
        Application.Run(new AsyncResolve());
    }
}
```

Because Windows Forms programs operate in a graphical environment, they work more efficiently using asynchronous Dns methods rather than the synchronous methods. The first part of the AsyncResolve.cs program defines the constructor for the class. The constructor defines a standard Windows Form and adds four controls:

- A Label object to display some instructional text
- A TextBox object to allow the customer to enter the address to resolve
- A ListBox object to easily return the output of the DNS query to the customer
- A Button object to allow the customer to start the DNS query

After the constructor, two methods are defined. The ButtonResolveOnClick() method is registered as a delegate for the button using the Click property:

```
checkit.Click += new EventHandler(ButtonResolveOnClick);
```

Notice that the EventHandler object is added to the existing list of event handlers for the control. The EventHandler object references the delegate to call when the button Click event is detected.

When the Button object is clicked, the ButtonResolveOnClick() delegate is performed. It reads the value entered into the TextBox object and calls the BeginResolve() method using the value of the object, the AsyncCallback object created earlier, and an empty state object:

```
Dns.BeginResolve(addr, OnResolved, state);
```

The OnResolved parameter is defined as an AsyncCallback object, and defines the Resolved() method in the program class:

```
private AsyncCallback OnResolved = null;
OnResolved = new AsyncCallback(Resolved);
```

The `Resolved()` method calls the `EndResolve()` Dns class method, which completes the `BeginResolve/EndResolve` pair. It must use the `IasyncResult` object parameter as the parameter value:

```
private void Resolved(IAsyncResult ar)
    {
        string buffer;

        IPHostEntry iphe = Dns.EndResolve(ar);
```

The `IPHostEntry` object is then dissected using the standard methods used in the other DNS programs in this chapter, to find the hostname, any aliases, and any IP addresses returned from the DNS query. To make life a little simpler, the results are easily written to a `ListBox` object. Figure 4.6 shows a sample output from the program.

FIGURE 4.6:

AsyncResult
program results,
written to a `ListBox`
object

The `AsyncResult` program can show results from both hostname and IP address queries. Each time another address is queried, the `ListBox` is cleared to make it easier for the new information to be read. If you prefer to keep a log of all the queries processed, you can remove the following line from the `ButtonResolveOnClick()` method:

```
results.Items.Clear();
```

If you do this, you might also want to add some type of separator line after the DNS query information is written to the `ListBox`, to help distinguish between queries. Here's an example:

```
results.Items.Add("-----");
```

When the query log is too long for the `ListBox`, a vertical scrollbar will appear, allowing you to scroll through the entire query log. Pretty neat payoff for a short amount of code!

Summary

The Domain Name System (DNS) can be used by C# programs to determine the IP addresses of hostnames. DNS is a distributed hierarchical database system that assigns hostnames hierarchically, separating each level with a period. DNS servers are created to store the DNS database for individual domains. Clients can query the DNS servers to find the IP address associated with a hostname, or other domain information. If a local DNS server cannot answer the query, it goes to a higher-level DNS server until the query can be answered and returned to the client.

Windows systems can resolve hostnames in two ways. The first way is to use the hosts file to manually enter hostnames and provide quick hostname resolution. The second way is to configure DNS servers in the system to contact remote DNS servers and resolve DNS information. The C# language provides the RegistryKey class to query the local Registry for the addresses of DNS servers configured on the system.

Windows systems also include the nslookup program, which lets customers do manual DNS queries. The nslookup program has several options for altering the way it finds and displays DNS information. The debug option allows you to see the actual DNS query sent to the remote DNS server. The querytype option allows you to query for specific DNS record information for a domain.

C# contains the Dns class in the System.Net namespace to provide basic DNS query capability. The GetHostByName() and GetHostByAddress() methods allow C# programs to determine DNS information given particular host data. The Resolve() method can find DNS information for either a hostname or an IP address.

Also covered in this chapter are asynchronous Dns methods, for doing DNS queries in applications that don't allow you to tie up system resources while waiting for an answer from the DNS server. The asynchronous methods use the standard C# delegate system to call a method when the DNS query has returned. This can greatly improve the performance of Windows-based network programs.

PART II

Network Layer Programing

Chapter 5: Connection-Oriented Sockets

Chapter 6: Connectionless Sockets

Chapter 7: Using the C#Sockets Helper Classes

Chapter 8: Asynchronous Socket Programming

Chapter 9: Using Threads

Chapter 10: IP Multicasting

CHAPTER 5

Connection-Oriented Sockets

- Using connection-oriented sockets in a simple TCP server application

- A simple TCP client application using connection-oriented Sockets

- Solving problems with TCP buffer sizes

- Working around TCP's inability to protect message boundaries

- Using C# streams with TCP: three important classes to know

C hapter 5 begins Part II of this book, where the focus turns from dry socket definitions to actual socket programming. Each chapter in Part II presents real-world examples of how to use the C# socket classes in network programs. This chapter presents programs that use the connection-oriented socket model, utilizing TCP for all communication.

First, you'll examine a simplistic TCP server and client that use the basic Windows sockets interface and learn about their limitations. Next, you'll look at some advanced versions of the TCP server and client, which incorporate techniques to compensate for the inherent problems of TCP communication. Finally, I'll show you a way to use C# I/O stream classes demonstrated in Chapter 1, "The C# Language," to simplify reading and writing data. This technique will help make TCP communications easier for the novice network programmer.

A Simple TCP Server

As discussed in Chapter 3, you have four tasks to perform before a server can transfer data with a client connection:

- Create a socket
- Bind the socket to a local IPEndPoint
- Place the socket in listen mode
- Accept an incoming connection on the socket

This section shows how these procedures are accomplished for creating a simple TCP server. No bells or whistles here—just the bare necessities required to start the server and listen for a client connection. You will build on these basic principles as you work through other tasks later in the chapter.

Creating the Server

The first step to constructing a TCP server is to create an instance of a Socket object. The other three functions necessary for successful server operations are then accomplished by using methods of the Socket object. The following C# code snippet includes these steps:

```
IPEndPoint ipep = new IPEndPoint(IPAddress.Any, 9050);
Socket newsock = Socket(AddressFamily.InterNetwork,
          SocketType.Stream, ProtocolType.Tcp);
newsock.Bind(ipep);
newsock.Listen(10);
Socket client = newsock.Accept();
```

The Socket object created by the Accept() method can now be used to transmit data in either direction between the server and the remote client.

All these basic steps are demonstrated in the SimpleTcpSrvr.cs program, Listing 5.1.

Listing 5.1   **The SimpleTcpSrvr.cs program**

```
using System;
using System.Net;
using System.Net.Sockets;
using System.Text;

class SimpleTcpSrvr
{
    public static void Main()
    {
        int recv;
        byte[] data = new byte[1024];
        IPEndPoint ipep = new IPEndPoint(IPAddress.Any,
                                9050);

        Socket newsock = new
            Socket(AddressFamily.InterNetwork,
                        SocketType.Stream, ProtocolType.Tcp);

        newsock.Bind(ipep);
        newsock.Listen(10);
        Console.WriteLine("Waiting for a client...");
        Socket client = newsock.Accept();
        IPEndPoint clientep =
                    (IPEndPoint)client.RemoteEndPoint;

        Console.WriteLine("Connected with {0} at port {1}",
                        clientep.Address, clientep.Port);

        string welcome = "Welcome to my test server";
        data = Encoding.ASCII.GetBytes(welcome);
        client.Send(data, data.Length,
                        SocketFlags.None);
        while(true)
        {
            data = new byte[1024];
            recv = client.Receive(data);
            if (recv == 0)
                break;

            Console.WriteLine(
                    Encoding.ASCII.GetString(data, 0, recv));
            client.Send(data, recv, SocketFlags.None);

        }
        Console.WriteLine("Disconnected from {0}",
                        clientep.Address);
        client.Close();
        newsock.Close();
    }
}
```

As mentioned, there is nothing fancy about this program. First, an empty byte array is defined as a data buffer for incoming and outgoing messages. It is important to remember that the Socket Receive() and Send() methods work only with byte arrays, no matter what type of data is being transmitted. All data transmitted through the Socket must somehow be converted into a byte array. Since this example only uses text strings, the Encoding.ASCII methods found in the System.Text namespace are used to convert between strings and byte arrays and vice versa.

Next, an IPEndPoint object is defined for the local server machine:

```
IPEndPoint ipep = new IPEndPoint(IPAddress.Any, 9050);
```

By using the IPAddress.Any field, the server will accept incoming connection requests on any network interface that may be configured on the system. If you are interested in accepting packets from only one particular interface, you can specify its IP address individually using the following technique:

```
IPEndPoint ipep = new
    IPEndPoint(IPAddress.Parse("192.168.1.6"), 9050);
```

After determining the proper IPEndPoint object to use, the Socket() constructor can be called to create the TCP socket. Then the Bind() and Listen() methods are used to bind the socket to the new IPEndPoint object and listen for incoming connections.

Finally, the Accept() method is used to accept an incoming connection attempt from a client. The Accept() method returns a new Socket object, which must be used in all communications with the client.

After the Accept() method accepts a connection attempt, the IP address information of the requesting client is available from the returned socket using the RemoteEndPoint property:

```
IPEndPoint clientep =
            (IPEndPoint)client.RemoteEndPoint;
```

Because the RemoteEndPoint property specifies any type of EndPoint object, you must specifically typecast it to an IPEndPoint object. Once the IPEndPoint object is created using the remote client's information, you can access it using the Address and Port properties, as demonstrated in the program. This is a handy technique to use for identifying individual clients that connect to the server.

After the socket is established with the client, the client/server combination must agree upon a system to transfer data. If both the server and client use blocking sockets (the default) and try to receive data at the same time, they will be waiting forever in a deadlock mode. Likewise, they will deadlock if they both send data at the same time. Instead, there must be a "ping pong" effect, where one side sends data while the other side waits to receive it.

In this example, the server immediately sends a welcome message to the client, and then waits for messages from the client:

```
string welcome = "Welcome to my test server";
    data = Encoding.ASCII.GetBytes(welcome);
    client.Send(data, data.Length,
                      SocketFlags.None);
    while(true)
    {
       data = new byte[1024];
       recv = client.Receive(data);
       if (recv == 0)
          break;

       Console.WriteLine(
               Encoding.ASCII.GetString(data, 0, recv));
       client.Send(data, recv, SocketFlags.None);
    }
```

Clients wanting to communicate with this server must be prepared to accept the welcome banner as soon as the connection is established. After receiving the welcome banner, the client must alternate between sending and receiving data.

Because the socket sends and receives messages in byte format, you will have to convert any outbound string messages to a byte array type, and any incoming byte arrays to string objects. The easiest way to do this is to use the Encoding class in the System.Text namespace. If you are using ASCII characters for your server, the ASCII property can be used with the GetBytes() or GetString() methods to easily convert strings to byte arrays, and byte arrays to strings like this:

```
Byte[] data = Encoding.ASCII.GetBytes("test string");
string word = Encoding.ASCII.GetString(data);
```

As each message is received from a client, it is immediately sent back to the client. This functionality is called an *echo server* and is often used for testing communication channels. The interesting point to note about this code is how the server knows to stop waiting for more data. This code in the SimpleTcpSrvr program checks the value of the *recv* variable for a zero value.

A Word about the Receive() Method

You may have noticed in Listing 5.1 that the first line in the while loop resets the *data* variable to a new byte array. This is a crucial detail that is forgotten by many less-experienced network programmers. As the Receive() method places data in the data buffer, the size of the data buffer is set. If the data buffer is not reset to its original value, the next Receive() call using the buffer will only be able to place as much data as the previous call.

The `Receive()` method normally returns the amount of data received from the remote client. If no data is received, the `Receive()` method blocks, waiting for data to appear. You may be wondering how `Receive()` can possibly return a value of zero. It's simple: when the TCP structure has detected that the remote client has initiated a close session (by sending a TCP FIN packet), the `Receive()` method is allowed to return a zero value.

This allows you to check the `Receive()` return value for a zero value. If it is zero, the program must attempt to gracefully close the newly created client socket by using the `Close()` method along with the optional `Shutdown()` method. After the client `Socket` object is closed, no further communication can take place. Remember however, that the *original* main `Socket` object is still active and can still be used to accept more incoming connections until it is closed as well. If you do not want any additional connections at all, the original `Socket` object must also be closed.

Testing the Server

You can easily test the server code using the Microsoft Telnet program that comes standard on all Windows platforms. The Telnet version in Windows 98, Me, and NT is a graphical Windows-based system; the Windows 2000 and XP versions are text-based systems that operate in a command prompt window. The Telnet program allows you to connect via TCP to any address and any port.

To start the sample TCP server, open a command prompt window and type **SimpleTcpSrvr**. The server will display the opening greeting and wait for an incoming client:

```
C:\>SimpleTcpSrvr
Waiting for a client...
```

Once the server is running, open another command prompt window (either on the same system or another system on the network) and start the Telnet program. Connect to the address of the server and the 9050 port used:

```
C:\>telnet 127.0.0.1 9050
```

The connection should start, and the server welcome screen should appear.

At this point, the server is waiting for a message from the client. Using the Telnet program, a strange thing happens. If you try to type a message, each individual character is sent to the server and immediately echoed back. If you try to type in a phrase, each character is sent individually and returned by the server individually. This behavior is caused by the way the Telnet application transmits data to the remote server: it automatically sends each typed character to the remote server. It does not wait for a carriage return or line feed character to transmit data.

Watching the Server

If you are running the server and client on different machines, you can use the WinDump or Analyzer programs to watch the network traffic generated by the programs. Unfortunately, if you are testing using the same system for the server and Telnet, you will not be able to see the traffic with WinDump or Analyzer. Even if you bind the socket to the external IP address, Windows handles the network traffic internally instead of using the network card, so the WinPcap driver cannot capture the traffic. Figure 5.1 shows sample Analyzer output from using the simple server from Listing 5.1 and the Telnet program on separate network systems.

FIGURE 5.1:

Sample Analyzer output from server and remote client test

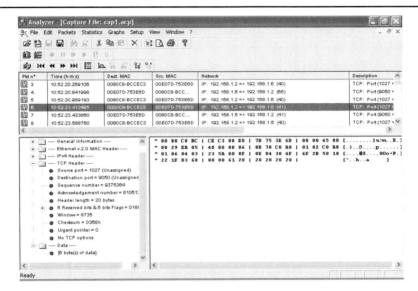

Sure enough, in the Analyzer output you can see in the data trace that the Telnet program sends each character entered as an individual packet to the server program (that is, there is only one data character in each packet). Because each character is separate, the server's `Receive()` method treats each one as a separate message and echoes back the individual characters.

The next section shows how to create a simple TCP client program that can solve this dilemma.

A Simple TCP Client

Now that you have a working TCP server, you can create a simple TCP client program to interact with it. As described in Chapter 3, there are only two steps required to connect a client program to a TCP server:

- Create a socket
- Connect the socket to the remote server address

This section describes in detail these steps for creating a basic TCP client program using C#.

Creating the Client

As it was for the server program, the first step of creating the client program is to create a Socket object. The Socket object is used by the Socket Connect() method to connect the socket to a remote host:

```
IPEndPoint ipep = new IPEndPoint(Ipaddress.Parse("192.168.1.6"), 9050);

Socket server = new Socket(AddressFamily.InterNetwork,
            SocketType.Stream, ProtocolType.Tcp);
server.Connect(ipep);
```

This example attempts to connect the socket to the server located at address 192.168.1.6. Of course, you can also use hostnames along with the Dns.Resolve() method. You may have noticed that I didn't use any fancy Exception programming for the server program. We will not have the same walk in the park for the client program. One huge challenge with the client's Connect() method is that if the remote server is unavailable, it will create an Exception. This can result in an ugly error message for customers. It is always a good idea to use a try-catch block to catch SocketExceptions when using the Connect() method so you can provide your own user-friendly message for your customers.

Once the remote server TCP program accepts the connection request, the client program is ready to transmit data with the server using the standard Send() and Receive() methods. Listing 5.2 is the SimpleTcpClient.cs program, which demonstrates these principles.

Listing 5.2   The SimpleTcpClient.cs program

```
using System;
using System.Net;
using System.Net.Sockets;
using System.Text;

class SimpleTcpClient
{
    public static void Main()
    {
        byte[] data = new byte[1024];
        string input, stringData;
        IPEndPoint ipep = new IPEndPoint(
                    IPAddress.Parse("127.0.0.1"), 9050);

        Socket server = new Socket(AddressFamily.InterNetwork,
                    SocketType.Stream, ProtocolType.Tcp);

        try
        {
            server.Connect(ipep);
```

```
    } catch (SocketException e)
    {
       Console.WriteLine("Unable to connect to server.");
       Console.WriteLine(e.ToString());
       return;
    }


    int recv = server.Receive(data);
    stringData = Encoding.ASCII.GetString(data, 0, recv);
    Console.WriteLine(stringData);

    while(true)
    {
       input = Console.ReadLine();
       if (input == "exit")
          break;
       server.Send(Encoding.ASCII.GetBytes(input));
       data = new byte[1024];
       recv = server.Receive(data);
       stringData = Encoding.ASCII.GetString(data, 0, recv);
       Console.WriteLine(stringData);
    }
    Console.WriteLine("Disconnecting from server...");
    server.Shutdown(SocketShutdown.Both);
    server.Close();
  }
}
```

Just like the simple server program, this client program has few frills. It simply creates an IPEndPoint for the server (if you want to connect to a remote server, you will have to plug your server's IP address in the *ipep* IPEndPoint value) and attempts to connect to that server:

```
IPEndPoint ipep = new IPEndPoint(
                    IPAddress.Parse("127.0.0.1"), 9050);

Socket server = new Socket(AddressFamily.InterNetwork,
                 SocketType.Stream, ProtocolType.Tcp);

try
{
   server.Connect(ipep);
} catch (SocketException e)
{
   Console.WriteLine("Unable to connect to server.");
   Console.WriteLine(e.ToString());
   return;
}
```

The Connect() method is placed in a try-catch block in hopes that it will ease the pain of the customer if the remote server is not available. Once a connection is established, the program waits for the welcome message sent by the server and displays the message on the console.

After that, the client program enters a loop, taking text entered at the console and sending it as a single message to the server. The resulting message received by the server is echoed to the console. When the input text is equal to the phrase exit, the while loop exits and the client closes the connection. When the server sees the connection closed—that is, when the Receive() method returns 0—the server, too, exits its while loop and closes the connection.

Testing the Client

The first thing to test is the Exception code used for the situation where the server is unavailable. This is an easy thing to do: just don't start the server program and do run the SimpleTcpClient program. This should produce the warning message you created in the Exception code:

```
C:\>SimpleTcpClient
Unable to connect to server.
System.Net.Sockets.SocketException: Unknown error (0x274d)
    at System.Net.Sockets.Socket.Connect(EndPoint remoteEP)
    at SimpleTcpClient.Main()

C:\>
```

Obviously, if this were a real production-quality client program, you would want to handle this error with more dignity, possibly allowing the customer to try the connection again. But even this terse bit of code is a much nicer solution than presenting the standard exception message generated by .NET when the SocketException occurs.

Now that the error test is out of the way, it is time to try connecting to the server. First, start the SimpleTcpSrvr program on the designated server machine. Once it has indicated it is waiting for clients, start the SimpleTcpClient program either in a separate command prompt window on the same machine, or on another machine on the network. When the client establishes the TCP connection, it should display the greeting banner from the server. At this point, it is ready to accept data from the console, so you can start entering data.

Notice that the entire phrase you enter at the console is sent to the server and displayed as a single message, and it's then returned back to the client as a single message, where it is also displayed. Because the client Send() method sends the data out as a block of bytes, it is received as a block of bytes at the server's Receive() method. Again, if you are running this test from two separate machines, you can watch this with the WinDump or Analyzer programs to verify that the data is being sent out as blocks instead of as characters.

Although the simple TCP programs are now behaving as expected, there is still a serious flaw lurking within. These test programs, as they are, use small blocks of data in a strictly controlled test environment, so they most likely worked just fine for you. I say "most likely," because the behavior is not guaranteed. There are many things that can go wrong with TCP communication processes. The next section demonstrates a few of the more common hitches that can occur with connection-oriented programs and tells you about some actions you can take to prevent them from happening in your own TCP client/server programs.

When TCP Goes Bad

The simple example programs studied so far in this chapter assumed a lot when sending and receiving data across the TCP channel. There are, however, plenty of possible glitches that weren't taken into consideration. In terms of connection-oriented client and server programs, the two problems that hit novice network programmers most often are as follows:

- Improper data buffer handling in programs
- Improper message handling across the network

Thankfully, each of these situations can be overcome with proper programming techniques.

Problems with Data Buffers

In the simple client and server samples shown, a byte array was used as a data buffer for sending and receiving data in the socket. Because the programs were operating in a controlled environment, and all of the messages were known to be a controlled size (small) as well as a controlled format (text), this kind of buffer was not a problem.

In the real world, however, you may not know the size or type of the incoming data when you're communicating with unknown remote servers or clients. What happens in the data buffer as messages of various sizes are received? How about when more data arrives than what you have defined in the data buffer? The following sections offer answers to these important questions.

Properly Using the Data Buffer

As data is received via TCP, it is stored in an internal buffer on the system. Each call to the Receive() method attempts to remove data from that TCP buffer. The amount of data read by the Receive() method is controlled by either of these factors:

- The size of the data buffer supplied to the Receive() method
- The buffer size parameter supplied to the Receive() method

In the `SimpleTcpSrvr.cs` program (Listing 5.1), the *data* variable was defined as a byte array with 1024 elements:

```
byte[] data = new byte[1024];
```

The simple form of the `Receive()` method was used to specify the buffer to store the incoming data. Because no data size was specified in the `Receive()` call, the buffer size was automatically set to the default size of the defined data buffer, 1024 bytes.

The `Receive()` method attempts to read 1024 bytes of data at a time and place it in the *data* variable:

```
recv = client.Receive(data);
```

At the time the `Receive()` method is called, if the TCP buffer contains less than 1024 bytes of data, the method will return with whatever data is available and set the *recv* variable to the amount of data actually read. This value is important because it represents the amount of valid data in the data buffer. You must always use it when referencing the data in the data buffer, or you may get surprised.

For example, the following command creates a `string` object using the first *recv* bytes of the *data* array:

```
stringData = Encoding.ASCII.GetString(data, 0, recv);
```

This is the proper way to reference the data in the buffer. The `GetString()` method only uses the number of bytes most recently placed in the buffer. If a larger data buffer were received before this `Receive()` method call, and you did not use the *recv* value to create the string, the extra bytes would be appended to the string, producing an incorrect data value.

You can see this problem occur if you remove the last two parameters of the `GetString()` method in the `SimpleTcpClient.cs` program and send varying sizes of strings to the server. The output from the SimpleTcpClient program will look like this (I removed the extra blank lines to shorten the output):

```
C:\>SimpleTcpClient
Welcome to my test server

test
testome to my test server

a bad test
a bad test my test server

exit
Disconnecting from server...

C:\>
```

Because the data buffer size was not defined in the `GetString()` method, the entire data buffer (all 1024 bytes) is displayed for each message, even though the majority of it was not part of the received data. Obviously, this is not a good thing. Without specifying the *recv* variable to show the amount of valid data, the data buffer will produce erroneous results.

Dealing with Small Buffers

The opposite of having too large a buffer is having one that's too small. A whole new set of challenges arises if the data buffer used in the `Receive()` call is too small for the incoming data.

As shown in Figure 5.2, the TCP subsystem on Windows contains its own data buffer, used to buffer both incoming and outgoing data. This is required because TCP must be able to retransmit data at any time. Once the data has been acknowledged, it can safely be removed from the buffer.

FIGURE 5.2:
The TCP buffers

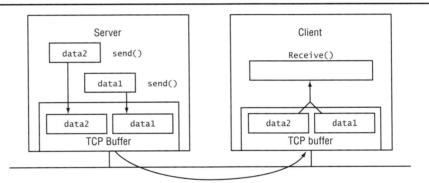

The incoming data works the same way. It will stay in the buffer until a `Receive()` method is used to read it. If the `Receive()` method does not read all the data in the buffer, the remainder stays there, waiting for another `Receive()` call. No data will be lost as long as more `Receive()` methods are used to read the data from the buffer, but you will not get the data chunks you want.

Let's set up a situation so you can see what happens. Set the data buffer size to a small number, such as 20 bytes, in the `SimpleTcpClient.cs` program:

```
byte data = new byte[20];
```

After recompiling the program, you can run the test. Here's what you get:

```
C:\>SimpleTcpClient
Welcome to my test s
test
erver
another test
test
oops
```

```
another test
exit
Disconnecting from server...
```

```
C:\>
```

Because the data buffer is not large enough to scoop up all the TCP buffer data in the `Receive()` method, it takes only what can fit in the buffer and leaves the rest for the next `Receive()` call. Thus, getting the entire server welcome banner required two calls to `Receive()`. On the next transmission, the next chunk of data from the buffer was read from the TCP buffer, and from then on the client was behind in the data transmission.

Because of this behavior, you must take care to ensure that all of the data is read from the TCP buffer properly. Too small a buffer can result in mismatched messages; on the other hand, too large a buffer can result in mixed messages. The hard part is trying to distinguish between messages as data is being read from the socket. The next section describes how to deal with message problems and ensure that the data is properly handled.

Problems with TCP Messages

One of the biggest pitfalls for novice network programmers is using message-oriented communications with TCP connections. The most important point to remember about using TCP for network communications is that TCP does not respect message boundaries. This section demonstrates this behavior using a badly written TCP program and some ways to fix it.

A Typical TCP Unprotected Message Boundary

The typical novice network programmer, having just read about the wonderful benefits of TCP programming, proceeds to create a client/server application that passes messages back and forth between two devices on the network using TCP sockets. However, not realizing the inherent disregard of message boundaries suffered by stream protocols such as TCP, the programmer writes a series of `Send()` methods on the client, along with a corresponding series of `Receive()` methods on the server. The processing setup is as illustrated in Figure 5.3:

FIGURE 5.3:

An improper TCP communication technique

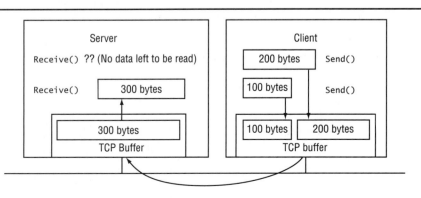

The critical drawback to using this way to communicate is that you are not guaranteed that the data from each individual `Send()` method will be read by each individual `Receive()` method. As shown in the preceding section on buffer issues, all of the data read by the `Receive()` method is not actually read directly from the network. Rather, the `Receive()` method reads data from the TCP buffer internal to the system. As new TCP packets are received from the network, they are placed sequentially into the TCP buffer. When the `Receive()` method is called, it reads all the data available in the TCP buffer, not just the first packet's worth. This exact behavior is what is occurring in Figure 5.4.

Let's demonstrate this problem using a couple of defective programs. First, Listing 5.3 is the bad server program.

Listing 5.3   **The BadTcpSrvr.cs program**

```
using System;
using System.Net;
using System.Net.Sockets;
using System.Text;

class BadTcpSrvr
{
    public static void Main()
    {
        int recv;
        byte[] data = new byte[1024];
        IPEndPoint ipep = new IPEndPoint(IPAddress.Any, 9050);

        Socket newsock = new Socket(AddressFamily.InterNetwork,
                        SocketType.Stream, ProtocolType.Tcp);

        newsock.Bind(ipep);
        newsock.Listen(10);
        Console.WriteLine("Waiting for a client...");

        Socket client = newsock.Accept();
        string welcome = "Welcome to my test server";
        data = Encoding.ASCII.GetBytes(welcome);
        client.Send(data, data.Length,
                    SocketFlags.None);
        IPEndPoint newclient = (IPEndPoint)client.RemoteEndPoint;
        Console.WriteLine("Connected with {0} at port {1}",
                        newclient.Address, newclient.Port);


        for (int i = 0; i < 5; i++)
        {
            recv = client.Receive(data);
            Console.WriteLine(Encoding.ASCII.GetString(data, 0, recv));
        }
        Console.WriteLine("Disconnecting from {0}", newclient.Address);
```

```
        client.Close();
        newsock.Close();
    }
}
```

This server program establishes a normal TCP socket to listen for incoming connections. When a connection is received, the server sends out a standard greeting banner message and then attempts to receive five separate messages from the client:

```
for (int i = 0; i < 5; i++)
{
    recv = client.Receive(data);
    Console.WriteLine(Encoding.ASCII.GetString(data, 0, recv));
}
```

Each call to the Receive() method attempts to read all the data available in the TCP buffer. After receiving the fifth message, the connection is closed, along with the original server socket.

Now we'll examine a bad client program to go along with the bad server program. Listing 5.4, the BadTcpClient.cs program, creates a socket and attempts to connect to the remote server (remember to replace the IP address or hostname shown with that of your server device). After connecting to the remote server, the client uses five separate Send() calls to transmit a text message to the server program.

Listing 5.4   The BadTcpClient.cs program

```
using System;
using System.Net;
using System.Net.Sockets;
using System.Text;

class BadTcpClient
{
    public static void Main()
    {
        byte[] data = new byte[1024];
        string stringData;
        IPEndPoint ipep = new IPEndPoint(
                    IPAddress.Parse("127.0.0.1"), 9050);

        Socket server = new Socket(AddressFamily.InterNetwork,
                    SocketType.Stream, ProtocolType.Tcp);

        try
        {
            server.Connect(ipep);
        } catch (SocketException e)
        {
            Console.WriteLine("Unable to connect to server.");
            Console.WriteLine(e.ToString());
```

```
            return;
        }


        int recv = server.Receive(data);
        stringData = Encoding.ASCII.GetString(data, 0, recv);
        Console.WriteLine(stringData);

        server.Send(Encoding.ASCII.GetBytes("message 1"));
        server.Send(Encoding.ASCII.GetBytes("message 2"));
        server.Send(Encoding.ASCII.GetBytes("message 3"));
        server.Send(Encoding.ASCII.GetBytes("message 4"));
        server.Send(Encoding.ASCII.GetBytes("message 5"));
        Console.WriteLine("Disconnecting from server...");
        server.Shutdown(SocketShutdown.Both);
        server.Close();
    }
}
```

Try running these programs multiple times from various clients and servers on the network. The results you will see are unpredictable. It is possible that each `Receive()` call on the server will read a single message sent by the `Send()` call on the client, which is what might be expected. But this behavior is not guaranteed. I tried it a few times, with different results. It appears that when the client and server are on the same system, the expected result usually occurs. However, when using the client on a system other than the server's (as you would assume in a normal network program environment), some very interesting things happen.

Here are two representative results from the server output:

```
C:\>BadTcpSrvr
Waiting for a client...
Connected with 192.168.1.6 at port 2345
message 1message 2
message 3message 4
message 5


Disconnecting from 192.168.1.6

C:\>BadTcpSrvr
Waiting for a client...
Connected with 192.168.1.6 at port 1065
message 1
message 2message 3message
 4message 5


Disconnecting from 192.168.1.6

C:\>
```

In the first try, the first server `Receive()` call picks up the complete messages from the first two client `Send()` calls. Then, the second server `Receive()` call gets the next two client `Send()` calls. Finally, the third server `Receive()` call grabs the data from the last client `Send()` call. Once the client disconnects, the remaining server `Receive()` calls return with no data, and the server properly closes the connection.

The second try is even more interesting. The first server `Receive()` call picks up a complete message from the first client `Send()` call—so far, so good. Then, the second server `Receive()` picks up the next two client `Send()` calls, plus part of the fourth client `Send()` call. This is a classic example of a message being split between `Receive()` calls. Finally, the third server `Receive()` call gets the rest of the data from the fourth client `Send()` call, plus the data from the last `Send()` call. What a mess!

There are two lessons that can be learned from this example:

- Never test your network programs only on a local client and server and expect those programs to work the same way on a network.
- Never assume that TCP will send message data in the same way you are employing in your program.

The next section offers some programming tips for getting your data to a remote system via TCP and being able to make sense out of it.

Solving the TCP Message Problem

To solve the unprotected boundary problems of our bad server and bad client programs, you must devise some technique to distinguish between separate messages on the remote system. There are three common ways to distinguish messages sent via TCP:

- Always send fixed-sized messages
- Send the message size with each message
- Use a marker system to separate messages

Each of these techniques offers a way for the remote system to separate out individual messages as they are received across the network. These techniques also have their own set of pros and cons. This section takes you through these techniques and their idiosyncrasies when they're employed in C# network programs.

Using Fixed-Sized Messages

The easiest but most costly way to solve the TCP message problem is to create a protocol that always transmits messages of a fixed size. By setting all messages to the same size, the receiving TCP program can know without doubt when an entire message has been received from the remote device.

Another advantage to using fixed-size messages is that when multiple messages are received, they can be clearly separated based on the number of bytes in the message. This way, messages received together can be separated with some accuracy. The following sections describe how to implement fixed-size messages for the Send() and Receive() methods.

Sending Fixed-Size Messages

When sending fixed-size messages, you must ensure that the entire message is sent from the Send() method. Don't assume that the complete message was sent by the TCP system. On a simple Send() method, you might see the following code:

```
byte[] data = new byte[1024];
.
.
.
int sent = socket.Send(data);
```

On the basis of this code, you might be tempted to presume that the entire 1024-byte data buffer was sent to the remote device and go on with your program. But this might be a bad assumption.

Depending on the size of the internal TCP buffer and how much data is being transferred, it is possible that not all of the data supplied to the Send() method was actually sent. The Send() return value sent indicates how many bytes of the data were actually sent to the TCP buffer. It is your job to determine whether *all* of the data was sent, however. If it wasn't, it is also your job to try and resend the rest of it. This is often done using a simple while() statement loop, checking the value returned from the Send() method against the original size of the data buffer. Of course, if the size does not match, you must provide a way to send the rest of the data.

The code using this method looks something like this:

```
int SendData(Socket s, byte[] data)
{
    int total = 0;
    int size = data.Length;
    int dataleft = size;
    int sent;

    while (total < size)
    {
        sent = s.Send(data, total, dataleft, SocketFlags.None);
        total += sent;
        dataleft -= sent;
    }
    return total;
}
```

Because you know the size of the data buffer before sending it, you can loop through the Send() method until you know that all of the expected bytes have been sent. This code snippet demonstrates how to loop through the Send() method, sending chunks of the data buffer until all of it has been properly sent. Each new call to the Send() method must obviously pick up where the previous call left off. Of course, it is entirely possible that all of the data will be sent on the first attempt, which is also fine.

Here is the more complicated format of the Send() method that does all this:

```
sent = s.Send(data, total, dataleft);
```

The first parameter points to the entire data buffer to be sent. The second parameter indicates at what position in the buffer to start sending, and the last parameter indicates how many bytes to attempt to send. Like the plain-vanilla Send() method, this more-capable version returns the total number of bytes sent to the remote device.

Receiving Fixed-Size Messages

As is so with sending data, you are not always guaranteed to receive all of the data message in a single Receive() method call. Looping through the Receive() method can also be done to ensure that you have received the entire amount of data expected. Of course, this works only when you know exactly how much data to expect to receive from the server. The following code snippet demonstrates the ReceiveData() method:

```
byte[] ReceiveData(Socket s, int size)
{
    int total = 0;
    int dataleft = size;
    byte[] data = new byte[size];
    int recv;

    while(total < size)
    {
        recv = s.Receive(data, total, dataleft, 0);
        if (recv == 0)
        {
            data = Encoding.ASCII.GetBytes("exit ");
            break;
        }
        total += recv;
        dataleft -= recv;
    }
    return data;
}
```

The ReceiveData() method requires the socket to receive data on and the set size of the data messages. In turn, it loops through the Receive() method, reading data until the set number of bytes have been received. Once finished, ReceiveData()can ensure that the proper number of bytes has been received before the message is returned to the calling application.

Testing the Fancy Send() and Receive() Methods

Using the SendData() and ReceiveData() methods is simple. Listing 5.5 presents the FixedTcpSrvr.cs program, in which the earlier bad TCP server example is re-created using the new methods.

Listing 5.5   **The FixedTcpSrvr.cs program**

```csharp
using System;
using System.Net;
using System.Net.Sockets;
using System.Text;

class FixedTcpSrvr
{
   private static int SendData(Socket s, byte[] data)
   {
      int total = 0;
      int size = data.Length;
      int dataleft = size;
      int sent;

      while (total < size)
      {
         sent = s.Send(data, total, dataleft, SocketFlags.None);
         total += sent;
         dataleft -= sent;
      }
      return total;
   }

   private static byte[] ReceiveData(Socket s, int size)
   {
      int total = 0;
      int dataleft = size;
      byte[] data = new byte[size];
      int recv;

      while(total < size)
      {
         recv = s.Receive(data, total, dataleft, 0);
         if (recv == 0)
         {
            data = Encoding.ASCII.GetBytes("exit");
            break;
         }
         total += recv;
         dataleft -= recv;
```

```
        }
        return data;
    }

    public static void Main()
    {
        byte[] data = new byte[1024];
        IPEndPoint ipep = new IPEndPoint(IPAddress.Any, 9050);

        Socket newsock = new Socket(AddressFamily.InterNetwork,
                        SocketType.Stream, ProtocolType.Tcp);

        newsock.Bind(ipep);
        newsock.Listen(10);
        Console.WriteLine("Waiting for a client...");

        Socket client = newsock.Accept();
        IPEndPoint newclient = (IPEndPoint)client.RemoteEndPoint;
        Console.WriteLine("Connected with {0} at port {1}",
                        newclient.Address, newclient.Port);

        string welcome = "Welcome to my test server";
        data = Encoding.ASCII.GetBytes(welcome);
        int sent = SendData(client, data);

        for (int i = 0; i < 5; i++)
        {
            data = ReceiveData(client, 9);
            Console.WriteLine(Encoding.ASCII.GetString(data));
        }
        Console.WriteLine("Disconnected from {0}", newclient.Address);
        client.Close();
        newsock.Close();
    }
}
```

The "fixed" version of the server now incorporates the SendData() and ReceiveData() methods in order to guarantee that the proper number of bytes are sent and received. The section of the program that receives the five data packets from the client now ensures that only 9 bytes of data are received for each message:

```
for (int i = 0; i < 5; i++)
{
    data = ReceiveData(client, 9);
    Console.WriteLine(Encoding.ASCII.GetString(data));
}
```

Now that the server is expecting each TCP message to be exactly 9 bytes, you need to create a client that sends only 9-byte messages. Listing 5.6, the FixedTcpClient.cs program, does this.

Listing 5.6   **The FixedTcpClient.cs program**

```
using System;
using System.Net;
using System.Net.Sockets;
using System.Text;

class FixedTcpClient
{
   private static int SendData(Socket s, byte[] data)
   {
      int total = 0;
      int size = data.Length;
      int dataleft = size;
      int sent;

      while (total < size)
      {
         sent = s.Send(data, total, dataleft, SocketFlags.None);
         total += sent;
         dataleft -= sent;
      }
      return total;
   }

   private static byte[] ReceiveData(Socket s, int size)
   {
      int total = 0;
      int dataleft = size;
      byte[] data = new byte[size];
      int recv;

      while(total < size)
      {
         recv = s.Receive(data, total, dataleft, 0);
         if (recv == 0)
         {
            data = Encoding.ASCII.GetBytes("exit ");
            break;
         }
         total += recv;
         dataleft -= recv;
      }
      return data;
   }

   public static void Main()
   {
      byte[] data = new byte[1024];
      int sent;
```

```
IPEndPoint ipep = new IPEndPoint(IPAddress.Parse("127.0.0.1"), 9050);

Socket server = new Socket(AddressFamily.InterNetwork,
                    SocketType.Stream, ProtocolType.Tcp);

try
{
   server.Connect(ipep);
} catch (SocketException e)
{
   Console.WriteLine("Unable to connect to server.");
   Console.WriteLine(e.ToString());
   return;
}

int recv = server.Receive(data);
string stringData = Encoding.ASCII.GetString(data, 0, recv);
Console.WriteLine(stringData);

sent = SendData(server, Encoding.ASCII.GetBytes("message 1"));
sent = SendData(server, Encoding.ASCII.GetBytes("message 2"));
sent = SendData(server, Encoding.ASCII.GetBytes("message 3"));
sent = SendData(server, Encoding.ASCII.GetBytes("message 4"));
sent = SendData(server, Encoding.ASCII.GetBytes("message 5"));
Console.WriteLine("Disconnecting from server...");
server.Shutdown(SocketShutdown.Both);
server.Close();
   }
}
```

With the new version of the client, each message sent to the server is always 9 bytes:

```
sent = SendData(server, Encoding.ASCII.GetBytes("message 1"), 9);
sent = SendData(server, Encoding.ASCII.GetBytes("message 2"), 9);
sent = SendData(server, Encoding.ASCII.GetBytes("message 3"), 9);
sent = SendData(server, Encoding.ASCII.GetBytes("message 4"), 9);
sent = SendData(server, Encoding.ASCII.GetBytes("message 5"), 9);
```

NOTE   You can test the new `FixedTcpSrvr` and `FixedTcpClient` programs with various clients on your network and with various fixed-message sizes (although each program can only use one set message size). Using the new versions of the programs, I experienced no message difficulties, even when running them on separate machines on a network: each message sent by the `SendData()` method on the client was properly received by the `ReceiveData()` method on the server.

Using the Message Size

As you have seen in this discussion of TCP problems with message boundaries, using a fixed-size message protocol does solve the problem of separating messages—but it's an extremely clunky solution. You have to make sure that all of your messages are exactly the same length. This means having to pad shorter messages, which means wasted network bandwidth.

The simple solution to this problem is to allow variable-length messages. The only drawback to that idea is that the remote device must somehow know the size of each of the variable-length messages. This can be accomplished by sending a message size indicator within each message. Determining how to place the message size indicator within the message is somewhat of a problem.

There are many ways to include the message size within the message packet. The simplest way is to create a text representation of the message size and append it to the beginning of the message. For example, as shown in Listing 5.6, message 1 would be 9 bytes long, and it would need the text value 9 placed before the message. This would make the transmitted message look like this:

```
9message 1
```

The 9 at the front of the message indicates how many bytes are in the actual message. The receiving device can read the first byte of each message and instantly know how many bytes to read for complete the message.

It is not too hard to see where this scheme falls apart, however. With the solution now in place, both the client and server programs must know how many bytes will be used for the message size text. Obviously, one character would not be able to handle large packets. Using three or four characters would be better but would waste some bytes for smaller packets.

What's the answer? Instead of using the *text* representation of the message size, you transmit the actual *integer* value for the message size. This requires converting the integer size of the packet to a byte array and sending it before the message. The following sections describe how to use this technique to add the message size to a variable-length message.

Sending Variable-Length Messages

The SendVarData() method is a modified version of the SendData() method presented earlier. In SendVarData(), you find the size of the outbound message and add it to the beginning of the message as a 4-byte integer value. By using a set 4-byte value, any size message (up to 65KB) can be accommodated using the same coding scheme. The new method should look like this:

```
private static int SendVarData(Socket s, byte[] data)
  {
      int total = 0;
      int size = data.Length;
      int dataleft = size;
      int sent;

      byte[] datasize = new byte[4];
      datasize = BitConverter.GetBytes(size);
```

```
    sent = s.Send(datasize);

    while (total < size)
    {
        sent = s.Send(data, total, dataleft, SocketFlags.None);
        total += sent;
        dataleft -= sent;
    }
    return total;
}
```

The `SendVarData()` method first converts the integer value of the data size to 4 bytes in a byte array, using the `BitConverter` class available in the `System` namespace. The `GetBytes()` method converts the 32-bit integer value to the 4-byte array. The array is then sent to the remote system. After sending the message size, the method then attempts to send the message itself using the standard technique of looping until it knows that all of the bytes have been sent.

Receiving Variable-Length Messages

The next step is to create a method that can interpret the received message format that includes the message size bytes and the entire message. The `ReceiveData()` method must be modified to accept 4 bytes of data from the socket and convert them into the integer value that represents the size of the message. After determining the size of the message, the entire message should be read into the data buffer using the standard technique shown in `ReceiveData()`. The `ReceiveVarData()` method looks like this:

```
private static byte[] ReceiveVarData(Socket s)
{
    int total = 0;
    int recv;
    byte[] datasize = new byte[4];

    recv = s.Receive(datasize, 0, 4, 0);
    int size = BitConverter.ToInt32(datasize);
    int dataleft = size;
    byte[] data = new byte[size];

    while(total < size)
    {
        recv = s.Receive(data, total, dataleft, 0);
        if (recv == 0)
        {
            data = Encoding.ASCII.GetBytes("exit ");
            break;
        }
        total += recv;
        dataleft -= recv;
```

```
        }
        return data;
    }
```

ReceiveVarData()reads the first 4 bytes of the message and converts them to an integer value using the GetInt32() method of the BitConverter class:

```
recv = s.Receive(datasize, 0, 4, 0);
int size = BitConverter.ToInt32(datasize);
```

The long version of the Receive() method must be used to ensure that only the first 4 bytes of the message are read from the buffer. Next, the normal Receive() method loop is performed, reading data from the socket until the proper number of bytes indicated by the message size has been read.

Testing the New Methods

Now that both the SendVarData() and ReceiveVarData() methods have been determined, you can modify the bad TCP programs using the new methods. Armed with this new technique of sending and receiving variable-length messages, you can create TCP message applications that are capable of sending large text messages without worrying about messages overlapping. Listing 5.7 presents an example of a TCP server program that uses the SendVarData() and ReceiveVarData() methods.

Listing 5.7   The VarTcpSrvr.cs program

```csharp
using System;
using System.Net;
using System.Net.Sockets;
using System.Text;

class VarTcpSrvr
{
    private static int SendData(Socket s, byte[] data)
    {
        int total = 0;
        int size = data.Length;
        int dataleft = size;
        int sent;

        byte[] datasize = new byte[4];
        datasize = BitConverter.GetBytes(size);
        sent = s.Send(datasize);

        while (total < size)
        {
            sent = s.Send(data, total, dataleft, SocketFlags.None);
            total += sent;
            dataleft -= sent;
```

```
      }
      return total;
   }

   private static byte[] ReceiveVarData(Socket s)
   {
      int total = 0;
      int recv;
      byte[] datasize = new byte[4];

      recv = s.Receive(datasize, 0, 4, 0);
      int size = BitConverter.ToInt32(datasize, 0);
      int dataleft = size;
      byte[] data = new byte[size];


      while(total < size)
      {
         recv = s.Receive(data, total, dataleft, 0);
         if (recv == 0)
         {
            data = Encoding.ASCII.GetBytes("exit ");
            break;
         }
         total += recv;
         dataleft -= recv;
      }
      return data;
   }

   public static void Main()
   {
      byte[] data = new byte[1024];
      IPEndPoint ipep = new IPEndPoint(IPAddress.Any, 9050);

      Socket newsock = new Socket(AddressFamily.InterNetwork,
                    SocketType.Stream, ProtocolType.Tcp);

      newsock.Bind(ipep);
      newsock.Listen(10);
      Console.WriteLine("Waiting for a client...");

      Socket client = newsock.Accept();
      IPEndPoint newclient = (IPEndPoint)client.RemoteEndPoint;
      Console.WriteLine("Connected with {0} at port {1}",
                    newclient.Address, newclient.Port);

      string welcome = "Welcome to my test server";
      data = Encoding.ASCII.GetBytes(welcome);
      int sent = SendVarData(client, data);

      for (int i = 0; i < 5; i++)
```

```
    {
        data = ReceiveVarData(client);
        Console.WriteLine(Encoding.ASCII.GetString(data));
    }
    Console.WriteLine("Disconnected from {0}", newclient.Address);
    client.Close();
    newsock.Close();
    }
}
```

This program performs the same functionality as the original BadTcpSrvr.cs program (Listing 5.3): it sends out a banner message when a client connects and then attempts to accept five separate messages from the client before closing the connection. Of course, the difference between the bad program and VarTcpSrvr.cs is that it expects to receive each message using the new message format, which adds the 4-byte message size to the beginning of each message.

Because of the new message format, you cannot use just any TCP client program to communicate with this server. Instead, you need a special client program that can send the message size as well as the text message, using the new format. A TCP client counterpart program is shown in Listing 5.8. The client program uses the new SendVarData() method to create messages formatted with the message size to send variable length messages to the server. Once again, if you are testing this program on a network, don't forget to replace the loopback IP address with the appropriate IP address of your server machine.

Listing 5.8   The VarTcpClient.cs program

```
using System;
using System.Net;
using System.Net.Sockets;
using System.Text;

class VarTcpClient
{
    private static int SendVarData(Socket s, byte[] data)
    {
        int total = 0;
        int size = data.Length;
        int dataleft = size;
        int sent;

        byte[] datasize = new byte[4];
        datasize = BitConverter.GetBytes(size);
        sent = s.Send(datasize);

        while (total < size)
        {
```

```csharp
            sent = s.Send(data, total, dataleft, SocketFlags.None);
            total += sent;
            dataleft -= sent;
        }
        return total;
    }

    private static byte[] ReceiveVarData(Socket s)
    {
        int total = 0;
        int recv;
        byte[] datasize = new byte[4];

        recv = s.Receive(datasize, 0, 4, 0);
        int size = BitConverter.ToInt32(datasize, 0);
        int dataleft = size;
        byte[] data = new byte[size];

        while(total < size)
        {
            recv = s.Receive(data, total, dataleft, 0);
            if (recv == 0)
            {
                data = Encoding.ASCII.GetBytes("exit ");
                break;
            }
            total += recv;
            dataleft -= recv;
        }
        return data;
    }

    public static void Main()
    {
        byte[] data = new byte[1024];
        int sent;
        IPEndPoint ipep = new IPEndPoint(IPAddress.Parse("127.0.0.1"), 9050);

        Socket server = new Socket(AddressFamily.InterNetwork,
                        SocketType.Stream, ProtocolType.Tcp);

        try
        {
            server.Connect(ipep);
        } catch (SocketException e)
        {
            Console.WriteLine("Unable to connect to server.");
            Console.WriteLine(e.ToString());
            return;
        }

        data = ReceiveVarData(server);
```

```
        string stringData = Encoding.ASCII.GetString(data);
        Console.WriteLine(stringData);

        string message1 = "This is the first test";
        string message2 = "A short test";
        string message3 = "This string is an even longer test. The quick brown ➡
            fox jumps over the lazy dog.";
        string message4 = "a";
        string message5 = "The last test";
        sent = SendVarData(server, Encoding.ASCII.GetBytes(message1));
        sent = SendVarData(server, Encoding.ASCII.GetBytes(message2));
        sent = SendVarData(server, Encoding.ASCII.GetBytes(message3));
        sent = SendVarData(server, Encoding.ASCII.GetBytes(message4));
        sent = SendVarData(server, Encoding.ASCII.GetBytes(message5));
        Console.WriteLine("Disconnecting from server...");
        server.Shutdown(SocketShutdown.Both);
        server.Close();
    }
}
```

You can test the new client and server programs by starting VarTcpSrvr and then starting VarTcpClient in either a separate command prompt window, or on a separate machine on the network. The server program should output the appropriate messages:

```
C:\>VarTcpSrvr
Waiting for a client...
Connected with 127.0.0.1 at port 1044
This is the first test
A short test
This string is an even longer test. The quick brown fox jumps over the lazy dog.

a
The last test
Disconnected from 127.0.0.1

C:\>
```

You now have a complete TCP client and server program that can accurately send text messages back and forth between a client and a server.

WARNING When using the BitConverter() methods, the integer values are converted to a byte array based on the byte order of the local machine. As long as the client and server are both Intel-based Windows machines, that will work fine. If one of them is from another type of system that uses a different byte order, you can run into difficulty. Chapter 7, "Using The C# Socket Helper Classes," discusses this problem and how to solve it.

Using Message Markers

Still another way to improve control when sending TCP messages is a *message marker system*. This system separates each message by a predetermined character (or characters) to specify the end of the message. As messages are received from the socket, the data is checked character-by-character for the occurrence of the marker character(s). When a marker is detected, the preceding data is known to contain a complete message and is passed to the application as a message. The data following the marker is tagged as the start of a new message.

One of the drawbacks to using message markers is that each character received in the data stream must be checked to determine if it is the marker. For large messages, this could greatly slow down performance of the system. Also, it means that some character must be designated as a marker, and that character has to be restricted from the normal data (or things get really complicated).

Instead of creating your own message marker system, The C# language provides some classes that can be used to simplify the process. The next section describes how to use the `System.IO` namespace stream classes to easily read and write text messages in a TCP connection.

Using C# Streams with TCP

Because handling messages on a TCP connection is often a challenge for programmers, the .NET Framework supplies some extra classes to help out. This section describes the `NetworkStream` class, which provides a stream interface for sockets, as well as two additional stream classes, `StreamReader` and `StreamWriter`, that can be used to send and receive text messages using TCP.

The NetworkStream Class

As described in Chapter 1, C# uses streams to help programmers move data in large chunks. The `System.Net.Sockets` namespace contains the `NetworkStream` class, which provides a stream interface to sockets.

There are several constructors that can be used to create a `NetworkStream` object. The easiest (and most popular) way to create the `NetworkStream` object is to simply use the `Socket` object:

```
Socket newsock = new Socket(AddressFamily.InterNetwork,
                    SocketType.Stream, ProtocolType.Tcp);
NetworkStream ns = new NetworkStream(newsock);
```

This creates a new `NetworkStream` object that can then be referenced instead of the `Socket` object. After the `NetworkStream` object has been created, there are several properties and methods for augmenting the functionality of the `Socket` object, listed in Table 5.1.

TABLE 5.1: NetworkStream Class Properties

Property	Description
CanRead	Is true if the `NetworkStream` supports reading
CanSeek	Is always false for `NetworkStreams`
CanWrite	Is true if the `NetworkStream` supports writing
DataAvailable	Is true if there is data available to be read

The property most often used, `DataAvailable`, quickly checks to see if there is data waiting in the socket buffer to be read.

The `NetworkStream` class contains a healthy supply of methods for accessing data in the stream. These methods are listed in Table 5.2.

TABLE 5.2: NetworkStream Class Methods

Method	Description
BeginRead()	Starts an asynchronous `NetworkStream` read
BeginWrite()	Starts an asynchronous `NetworkStream` write
Close()	Closes the `NetworkStream` object
CreateObjRef()	Creates an object used as a proxy for the `NetworkStream`
EndRead()	Finishes an asynchronous `NetworkStream` read
EndWrite()	Finishes an asynchronous `NetworkStream` write
Equals()	Determines if two `NetworkStreams` are the same
Flush()	Flushes all data from the `NetworkStream`
GetHashCode()	Obtains a hash code for the `NetworkStream`
GetLifetimeService()	Retrieves the lifetime service object for the `NetworkStream`
GetType()	Retrieves the type of the `NetworkStream`
InitializeLifetimeService()	Obtains a lifetime service object to control the lifetime policy for the `NetworkStream`
Read()	Reads data from the `NetworkStream`
ReadByte()	Reads a single byte of data from the `NetworkStream`
ToString()	Returns a string representation
Write()	Writes data to the `NetworkStream`
WriteByte()	Writes a single byte of data to the `NetworkStream`

Use the `Read()` method to read blocks of data from the `NetworkStream`. Its format is as follows, where *buffer* is a byte array buffer to hold the read data, *offset* is the buffer location at which to start placing the data, and *size* is the number of bytes to be read.

```
int Read(byte[] buffer, int offset, int size)
```

The `Read()` method returns an integer value representing the number of bytes actually read from the `NetworkStream` and placed in the buffer.

Similarly, the `Write()` method format is as follows, where *buffer* is the buffer from which to get the data to send, *offset* is the buffer location at which to start getting data, and *size* is the number of bytes to send:

```
void Write(byte[] buffer, int offset, int size)
```

Listing 5.9 shows another version of the TCP client program that uses the `NetworkStream` object for communication with the `Socket` object.

Listing 5.9   **The NetworkStreamTcpClient.cs progam**

```csharp
using System;
using System.Net;
using System.Net.Sockets;
using System.Text;

class NetworkStreamTcpClient
{
    public static void Main()
    {
        byte[] data = new byte[1024];
        string input, stringData;
        int recv;
        IPEndPoint ipep = new IPEndPoint(
                    IPAddress.Parse("127.0.0.1"), 9050);

        Socket server = new Socket(AddressFamily.InterNetwork,
                    SocketType.Stream, ProtocolType.Tcp);

        try
        {
            server.Connect(ipep);
        } catch (SocketException e)
        {
            Console.WriteLine("Unable to connect to server.");
            Console.WriteLine(e.ToString());
            return;
        }

        NetworkStream ns = new NetworkStream(server);

        if (ns.CanRead)
```

```
      {
         recv = ns.Read(data, 0, data.Length);
         stringData = Encoding.ASCII.GetString(data, 0, recv);
         Console.WriteLine(stringData);
      }
      else
      {
         Console.WriteLine("Error: Can't read from this socket");
         ns.Close();
         server.Close();
         return;
      }

      while(true)
      {
         input = Console.ReadLine();
         if (input == "exit")
            break;
         if (ns.CanWrite)
         {
            ns.Write(Encoding.ASCII.GetBytes(input), 0, input.Length);
            ns.Flush();
         }

         recv = ns.Read(data, 0, data.Length);
         stringData = Encoding.ASCII.GetString(data, 0, recv);
         Console.WriteLine(stringData);
      }
      Console.WriteLine("Disconnecting from server...");
      ns.Close();
      server.Shutdown(SocketShutdown.Both);
      server.Close();
   }
}
```

This program creates a NetworkStream object from the Socket object:

```
NetworkStream ns = new NetworkStream(server);
```

Once the NetworkStream object has been created, the Socket object is never again referenced until it is closed at the end of the program. All communication with the remote server is done through the NetworkStream object:

```
recv = ns.Read(data, 0, data.Length);

ns.Write(Encoding.ASCII.GetBytes(input), 0, input.Length);
ns.Flush();
```

The Flush() method is used after every Write() method to ensure that the data placed in the NetworkStream will immediately be sent to the remote system rather than waiting in the TCP buffer area for more data before being sent.

Since the `NetworkStreamTcpClient` program sends and receives the same data packets, you can test it with the original `SimpleTcpSrvr` program presented at the beginning of this chapter (Listing 5.1). It should behave the same way as the SimpleTcpClient program, sending a message to the server and receiving the echoed message back.

Although the `NetworkStream` object has some additional functionality over the `Socket` object, it is still limited in how it sends and receives data from the socket. The same unprotected message boundary problems exist, as when using the plain `Socket` object to send and receive messages. The next section describes two classes that can help you have more control of the data on the socket.

The StreamReader and StreamWriter Classes

The `System.IO` namespace contains the `StreamReader` and `StreamWriter` classes that control the reading and writing of text messages on a stream. Both of these classes can be deployed with a `NetworkStream` object to help define markers for TCP messages.

The `StreamReader` class has lots of constructor formats for many applications. The simplest format to use with `NetworkStreams` is as follows:

```
public StreamReader(Stream stream)
```

The `stream` variable can reference any type of `Stream` object, including a `NetworkStream` object. You have a generous selection of properties and methods available for use with the `StreamReader` object after it is created, as described in Table 5.3.

TABLE 5.3: StreamReader Class Methods

Method	Description
Close()	Closes the `StreamReader` object
CreateObjRef()	Creates an object used as a proxy for the `StreamReader`
DiscardBufferedData()	Discards the current data in the `StreamReader`
Equals()	Determines if two `StreamReader` objects are the same
GetHashCode()	Returns a hash code for the `StreamReader` object
GetLifetimeService()	Retrieves the lifetime service object for the `StreamReader`
GetType()	Retrieves the type of the `StreamReader` object
InitializeLifetimeService()	Creates a lifetime service object for the `StreamReader`
Peek()	Returns the next available byte of data from the stream without removing it from the stream
Read()	Reads one or more bytes of data from the `StreamReader`
ReadBlock()	Reads a group of bytes from the `StreamReader` stream and places it in a specified buffer location

Continued on next page

TABLE 5.3 CONTINUED: StreamReader Class Methods

Method	Description
ReadLine()	Reads data from the StreamReader object up to and including the first line feed character
ReadToEnd()	Reads the data up to the end of the stream
ToString()	Creates a string representation of the StreamReader object

Similar to StreamReader, the StreamWriter object can be created from a NetworkStream object:

```
public StreamWriter(Stream stream)
```

StreamWriter, too, has several associated properties and methods. And, as expected, most of the common methods of the StreamReader class are also found in the StreamWriter class. Table 5.4 shows the other important methods used for StreamWriter.

TABLE 5.4: Unique StreamWriter Class Methods

Method	Description
Flush()	Sends all StreamWriter buffer data to the underlying stream
Write()	Sends one or more bytes of data to the underlying stream
WriteLine()	Sends the specified data plus a line feed character to the underlying stream

---

TIP   The most interesting StreamReader method is the ReadLine() method. It reads characters from the stream until it comes across a line feed character. This feature allows you to use the line feed character as a message marker to separate text messages. This greatly simplifies receiving text messages with TCP. You may notice that the WriteLine() method is the perfect match to the StreamReader's ReadLine() method. This was not an accident. Together, these two methods let you create message-based TCP communications using the line feed character as a message marker. This feature greatly simplifies TCP message programming—as long as you are using text messages.

The programs presented in the next two sections show you how to use the StreamReader and StreamWriter classes to modify the TCP server and client programs presented earlier to use text messages.

Stream Server

Listing 5.10 is the StreamTcpSrvr.cs program, which demonstrates using these principles in a server program.

Listing 5.10 **The StreamTcpSrvr.cs program**

```
using System;
using System.IO;
using System.Net;
using System.Net.Sockets;
using System.Text;

class StreamTcpSrvr
{
   public static void Main()
   {
      string data;
      IPEndPoint ipep = new IPEndPoint(IPAddress.Any, 9050);

      Socket newsock = new Socket(AddressFamily.InterNetwork,
                     SocketType.Stream, ProtocolType.Tcp);

      newsock.Bind(ipep);
      newsock.Listen(10);
      Console.WriteLine("Waiting for a client...");

      Socket client = newsock.Accept();
      IPEndPoint newclient = (IPEndPoint)client.RemoteEndPoint;
      Console.WriteLine("Connected with {0} at port {1}",
                     newclient.Address, newclient.Port);

      NetworkStream ns = new NetworkStream(client);
      StreamReader sr = new StreamReader(ns);
      StreamWriter sw = new StreamWriter(ns);

      string welcome = "Welcome to my test server";
      sw.WriteLine(welcome);
      sw.Flush();

      while(true)
      {
         try
         {
            data = sr.ReadLine();
         } catch (IOException)
         {
            break;
         }

         Console.WriteLine(data);
         sw.WriteLine(data);
         sw.Flush();
      }
      Console.WriteLine("Disconnected from {0}", newclient.Address);
```

```
            sw.Close();
            sr.Close();
            ns.Close();
        }
    }
```

The StreamTcpSrvr program uses the StreamWriter WriteLine() method to send text messages terminated with a line feed. As is true for the NetworkStream object, it is best to use the Flush() method after each WriteLine() call to ensure that all of the data is sent from the TCP buffer.

You may have noticed one major difference between this program and the original SimpleTcpSrvr program: the way StreamTcpSrvr knows when the remote connection is disconnected. Because the ReadLine() method works on the stream and not the socket, it cannot return a 0 when the remote connection has disconnected. Instead, if the underlying socket disappears, the ReadLine() method will produce an Exception. It is up to you to catch the Exception produced when the socket has been disconnected:

```
try
{
   data = sr.ReadLine();
} catch (IOException)
{
    break;
}
```

Stream Client

Now that you have a server that accepts messages delimited by a line feed, you need a client that can send messages in that format. Listing 5.11 shows the StreamTcpClient program that demonstrates using the StreamReader and StreamWriter objects in a TCP client application.

Listing 5.11   The StreamTcpClient.cs program

```
using System;
using System.IO;
using System.Net;
using System.Net.Sockets;
using System.Text;

class StreamTcpClient
{
    public static void Main()
```

```
    {
        string data;
        string input;
        IPEndPoint ipep = new IPEndPoint(
                        IPAddress.Parse("127.0.0.1"), 9050);

        Socket server = new Socket(AddressFamily.InterNetwork,
                        SocketType.Stream, ProtocolType.Tcp);

        try
        {
            server.Connect(ipep);
        } catch (SocketException e)
        {
            Console.WriteLine("Unable to connect to server.");
            Console.WriteLine(e.ToString());
            return;
        }


        NetworkStream ns = new NetworkStream(server);
        StreamReader sr = new StreamReader(ns);
        StreamWriter sw = new StreamWriter(ns);

        data = sr.ReadLine();
        Console.WriteLine(data);

        while(true)
        {
            input = Console.ReadLine();
            if (input == "exit")
                break;
            sw.WriteLine(input);
            sw.Flush();

            data = sr.ReadLine();
            Console.WriteLine(data);
        }
        Console.WriteLine("Disconnecting from server...");
        sr.Close();
        sw.Close();
        ns.Close();
        server.Shutdown(SocketShutdown.Both);
        server.Close();
    }
}
```

This version of the client program performs the same functions as the SimpleTcpClient program, but it sends messages terminated with a line feed. There is one important difference for you to observe. If you try using the StreamTcpClient program with the original

SimpleTcpSrvr program, it won't work. That's because the greeting banner produced by the SimpleTcpSrvr program does not include a line feed at the end of the text. Without the line feed, the ReadLine() method in the client program does not complete, and blocks the program execution, waiting for the line feed to appear. Remember this behavior whenever you use the ReadLine() stream method.

WARNING   Another point to remember when using the ReadLine() method is to ensure that the data itself does not contain a line feed character. This will create a false marker for the ReadLine() method and affect the way the data is read.

Summary

This chapter described how to send messages using a TCP socket. Because TCP sockets are connection-oriented, both ends of the connection must be established before any data can be transmitted. The data is sent to the remote device using a data stream, so message boundaries are not preserved in TCP sessions.

Message boundaries are not protected in this environment, so it is your job to create your TCP applications to recognize individual messages. This can be accomplished in various ways: by sending single messages and waiting for a response from the other end, by sending fixed-size messages, by sending messages that have the message size embedded in the message, and by sending messages that are delimited with a predetermined character. Each of these techniques presents different problems to the C# programmer, which this chapter shows how to overcome.

To simplify the transmitting of text messages using TCP, the C# library contains stream methods that allow you to use a line feed as a delimiter in the text message. The StreamReader and StreamWriter classes employ the ReadLine() and WriteLine() methods to easily send text messages across socket connections.

The next chapter discusses how to use the C# Sockets class to create connectionless network programs, which presents a whole new set of issues for your attention.

CHAPTER 6

Connectionless Sockets

- A fundamental UDP application for connectionless communication

- Using Connect() in a UDP client example

- Improved "packaging" for UDP messages

- Using a smaller buffer to prevent lost data

- Using socket time-outs to prevent lost packets

- Handling retransmission of packets

- A complete, real-world UDP application

T he preceding chapter described how to program connection-oriented sockets using TCP and the C# Socket class. Now we'll change gears and look at comparable issues for connectionless sockets. This chapter demonstrates the principles and processes for creating connectionless applications using UDP and the C# Socket class.

Connectionless sockets allow the sending of messages in self-contained packets. A single read method reads the entire message sent by a single sent method. This helps you avoid the hassle of trying to match message boundaries in packets. Unfortunately, UDP packets are not guaranteed to arrive at their destination. Many factors, such as busy networks, can prevent the packet from making it to its destination.

In this chapter, you'll first examine simple UDP server and client applications that demonstrate UDP messages at work in applications. Following that is a discussion of the problems of missing UDP packets and different UDP read buffer sizes, along with techniques for solving those problems. Then you'll see how to combine all of the application techniques into one program, and you'll study a sample UDP program that does just that.

A Simple UDP Application

As discussed in Chapter 3, "C# Network Programming Classes," UDP is a connectionless protocol. Therefore, the programmer must do only two things to make a server application ready to send or receive UDP packets:

- Create a Socket object
- Bind the socket to a local IPEndPoint

After these two actions are taken, the socket can be used to either accept incoming UDP packets on the IPEndPoint, or send outgoing UDP packets to any other device on the network. All of the TCP connection requirements are unnecessary with UDP.

NOTE   For client UDP applications that do not need to receive UDP packets on a specific UDP port, you do not have to bind the socket to a specific IPEndPoint—just create the Socket object and send data!

Because there is no connection between remote hosts, the UDP application cannot use the standard Send() and Receive() Socket methods. Instead, two new methods must be used, SendTo() and ReceiveFrom().

SendTo()   The SendTo() method specifies the data to send and the IPEndpoint of the destination machine. There are several versions of this method that can be used, based on your requirements:

```
SendTo(byte[] data, EndPoint Remote)
```

This simple version of the SendTo() method sends a byte array data to the EndPoint specified by the variable *Remote*. A slightly more complex version is as follows:

```
SendTo(byte[] data, SocketFlags Flags, EndPoint Remote)
```

This version allows you to include a SocketFlags object Flags, which specifies any special UDP socket options to use. Use the following version of SendTo()to specify the number of bytes from the byte array to send:

```
SendTo(byte[data], int Size, SocketFlags Flags, EndPoint Remote)
```

The last version of the SendTo() method, with which you can specify a specific offset within the byte array to start sending data, is as follows:

```
SendTo(byte[] data, int Offset, int Size, SocketFlags Flags, EndPoint
Remote)
```

ReceiveFrom()   The ReceiveFrom() method has the same formats as the SendTo() method, with one important difference: the way the EndPoint object is declared. The basic ReceiveFrom() method is defined as follows:

```
ReceiveFrom(byte[] data, ref EndPoint Remote)
```

As usual, a byte array is defined to accept the received data.

What's really of interest here is the second parameter, ref EndPoint. Instead of passing an EndPoint object, you must pass the *reference* to an EndPoint object. Although using references to variables is common in C and C++ programs, the structure seen here is not all that common in C# programs. The reference refers to the memory location where the variable is stored, not the value of the variable. The ReceiveFrom() method will place the EndPoint information from the remote device into the EndPoint object memory area you reference.

Both SendTo() and ReceiveFrom() are included in the simple UDP server and client examples in the following sections. These examples demonstrate the basics of connectionless communication with C# sockets.

The UDP Server

Although UDP applications aren't really servers or clients by strict definition, I will call this next application a UDP server for the sake of simplicity. It creates a Socket object and binds it to a set IPEndPoint object so it can wait for incoming packets:

```
IPEndPoint ipep = new IPEndPoint(IPAddress.Any,
                                 9050);
Socket newsock = Socket(AddressFamily.InterNetwork,
            SocketType.Dgram, ProtocolType.Udp);
newsock.Bind(ipep);
```

For connectionless communications, you must specify the Dgram SocketType, along with the Udp ProtocolType. Remember, if your application does not need to receive UDP data on a specific UDP port, you do not have to bind the socket to a specific IPEndPoint. However, if you do need to listen to specific port, such as for servers, you must use the Bind() method.

Listing 6.1, the SimpleUdpSrvr.cs program, demonstrates the basic components of a simple UDP server by binding a dedicated socket on the server for other UDP clients to connect to.

Listing 6.1   **The SimpleUdpSrvr.cs program**

```
using System;
using System.Net;
using System.Net.Sockets;
using System.Text;

class SimpleUdpSrvr
{
    public static void Main()
    {
        int recv;
        byte[] data = new byte[1024];
        IPEndPoint ipep = new IPEndPoint(IPAddress.Any, 9050);

        Socket newsock = new Socket(AddressFamily.InterNetwork,
                    SocketType.Dgram, ProtocolType.Udp);

        newsock.Bind(ipep);
        Console.WriteLine("Waiting for a client...");

        IPEndPoint sender = new IPEndPoint(IPAddress.Any, 0);
        EndPoint Remote = (EndPoint)(sender);

        recv = newsock.ReceiveFrom(data, ref Remote);

        Console.WriteLine("Message received from {0}:", Remote.ToString());
        Console.WriteLine(Encoding.ASCII.GetString(data, 0, recv));

        string welcome = "Welcome to my test server";
        data = Encoding.ASCII.GetBytes(welcome);
        newsock.SendTo(data, data.Length, SocketFlags.None, Remote);
        while(true)
        {
            data = new byte[1024];
            recv = newsock.ReceiveFrom(data, ref Remote);

            Console.WriteLine(Encoding.ASCII.GetString(data, 0, recv));
            newsock.SendTo(data, recv, SocketFlags.None, Remote);
        }
    }
}
```

As mentioned, for the UDP server program to accept incoming UDP messages, it must be bound to a specific UDP port on the local system. This is accomplished by creating an IPEndPoint object using the appropriate local IP address (or as shown here, the IPAddress.Any address to use any network interface on the system), and the appropriate UDP port:

```
IPEndPoint ipep = new IPEndPoint(IPAddress.Any, 9050);

Socket newsock = new Socket(AddressFamily.InterNetwork,
                    SocketType.Dgram, ProtocolType.Udp);
newsock.Bind(ipep);
```

The sample UDP server illustrated in the example will accept any incoming UDP packet on port 9050 from the network.

NOTE   There is not an established connection between hosts, so UDP is not picky about where the packet comes from (unlike TCP). However, because of this feature of UDP, when communicating with multiple UDP clients you must be careful to check the transmission point of the received packets.

When creating your sample UDP server, be careful that you don't choose a UDP port that is already in use by another application on your machine. You can monitor the arrangement of applications that are listening on particular UDP ports by using the netstat command at a command prompt. Here's an example of the results:

```
C:\>netstat -a

Active Connections

  Proto  Local Address          Foreign Address        State
  TCP    abednego:epmap         0.0.0.0:0              LISTENING
  TCP    abednego:microsoft-ds  0.0.0.0:0              LISTENING
  TCP    abednego:1025          0.0.0.0:0              LISTENING
  TCP    abednego:1034          0.0.0.0:0              LISTENING
  TCP    abednego:5000          0.0.0.0:0              LISTENING
  TCP    abednego:12174         0.0.0.0:0              LISTENING
  TCP    abednego:38292         0.0.0.0:0              LISTENING
  TCP    abednego:1026          0.0.0.0:0              LISTENING
  TCP    abednego:netbios-ssn   0.0.0.0:0              LISTENING
  TCP    abednego:11133         0.0.0.0:0              LISTENING
  UDP    abednego:epmap         *:*
  UDP    abednego:microsoft-ds  *:*
  UDP    abednego:isakmp        *:*
  UDP    abednego:1027          *:*
  UDP    abednego:1035          *:*
  UDP    abednego:9050          *:*
  UDP    abednego:38037         *:*
```

```
UDP        abednego:38293         *:*
UDP        abednego:ntp           *:*
UDP        abednego:1900          *:*
UDP        abednego:ntp           *:*
UDP        abednego:netbios-ns    *:*
UDP        abednego:netbios-dgm   *:*
UDP        abednego:1036          *:*
UDP        abednego:1900          *:*
UDP        abednego:12564         *:*
```

```
C:\>
```

The `netstat -a` command displays all the active TCP and UDP sessions on the system. Depending on how many network applications are configured on your system, you might see lots of output here. The first column shows the protocol type, and the second column gives you the hostname or IP address and the port number. In the third column, you get the IP hostname or address and the port number of the remote device, if the port is connected to a remote device (for TCP). The last column shows the TCP state of TCP connections.

You can select any UDP port that is not shown as being active in your netstat list. Once the `SimpleUdpSrvr` program is active, you will see an entry for the UDP port you selected, as shown in the preceding netstat output with the 9050 port number:

```
UDP        abednego:9050          *.*
```

Similar to the TCP client/server model, remote devices communicating with UDP must agree on a system to use for sending and receiving data. If both client and server are waiting for data at the same time, both devices will block and not work. To make this arrangement, the `SimpleUdpSrvr` program follows the following protocol:

- Wait to receive a message from a client

- Send a welcome banner back to the client

- Wait for additional client messages and send them back

These functions are accomplished using the `ReceiveFrom()` and `SendTo()` methods of the Socket class.

Because connectionless sockets do not establish a connection, each `SendTo()` method must include the remote device `EndPoint` information. It is imperative that you have this information available from the received message. To obtain it, a blank `EndPoint` object is created and referenced in the `ReceiveFrom()` method:

```
IPEndPoint sender = new IPEndPoint(IPAddress.Any, 0);
EndPoint Remote = (EndPoint)(sender);
recv = newsock.ReceiveFrom(data, ref Remote);
```

The `Remote` object contains the IP information for the remote device that sent the message to the server. This information identifies the incoming data and is also used if the server wants to return a message to the client:

```
string welcome = "Welcome to my test server";
data = Encoding.ASCII.GetBytes(welcome);
newsock.SendTo(data, data.Length, SocketFlags.None, Remote);
```

WARNING   As is true for the TCP server in Chapter 5, "Connection-Oriented Sockets," you must always reset the receive data buffer to its full size *before* the `ReceiveFrom()` method call occurs, or the `Length` property will reflect the length of the previously received message. This could cause some unexpected results.

Unlike the TCP server discussed in Chapter 5, the UDP server cannot be tested without an appropriate UDP client. The next section describes how to create this client.

A UDP Client

The UDP client program is similar to its partner server program.

Because the client does not need to wait on a specific UDP port for incoming data, it does not use the `Bind()` method. Instead, it employs a random UDP port assigned by the system when the data is sent, and it uses the same port to receive return messages. If you are in a production environment, you might want to specify a set UDP port for the client as well, so that both the server and client programs use the same port numbers.

WARNING   Be careful if you are using the UDP server and client programs on the same machine. You cannot `Bind()` the same UDP port number for both programs, or an error will occur. Only one application can bind to a specific port number at a time. Either select a different port number, or let the system choose a random port for the client.

Listing 6.2 shows the `SimpleUdpCLient.cs` program that demonstrates the fundamentals of a UDP setup.

Listing 6.2   The SimpleUdpClient.cs program

```
using System;
using System.Net;
using System.Net.Sockets;
using System.Text;

class SimpleUdpClient
{
```

```
public static void Main()
{
    byte[] data = new byte[1024];
    string input, stringData;
    IPEndPoint ipep = new IPEndPoint(
                    IPAddress.Parse("127.0.0.1"), 9050);

    Socket server = new Socket(AddressFamily.InterNetwork,
                    SocketType.Dgram, ProtocolType.Udp);


    string welcome = "Hello, are you there?";
    data = Encoding.ASCII.GetBytes(welcome);
    server.SendTo(data, data.Length, SocketFlags.None, ipep);

    IPEndPoint sender = new IPEndPoint(IPAddress.Any, 0);
    EndPoint Remote = (EndPoint)sender;

    data = new byte[1024];
    int recv = server.ReceiveFrom(data, ref Remote);

    Console.WriteLine("Message received from {0}:", Remote.ToString());
    Console.WriteLine(Encoding.ASCII.GetString(data, 0, recv));

    while(true)
    {
        input = Console.ReadLine();
        if (input == "exit")
            break;
        server.SendTo(Encoding.ASCII.GetBytes(input), Remote);
        data = new byte[1024];
        recv = server.ReceiveFrom(data, ref Remote);
        stringData = Encoding.ASCII.GetString(data, 0, recv);
        Console.WriteLine(stringData);
    }
    Console.WriteLine("Stopping client");
    server.Close();
}
}
```

The UDP client program first defines an IPEndPoint to which the UDP server device will send packets. If you are running the SimpleUdpSrvr program on a remote device, you must enter the appropriate IP address and UDP port number information in the IPEndPoint definition:

```
IPEndPoint ipep = new IPEndPoint(
                    IPAddress.Parse("127.0.0.1"), 9050);
```

The client program sends a quick message to the server machine to introduce itself, then waits for the welcome banner message to be sent back. Because it does not need to accept UDP messages on a specific port number, the client does not bind the Socket object. It will receive the return UDP message on the same port from which it sent the original message.

The SimpleUdpClient program reads the console input and waits for the phrase exit to appear before leaving the while loop. Once the loop is exited, the socket is closed.

Testing the Client and Server Programs

Start the SimpleUdpSrvr program on the assigned server machine you will use for your testing. When the server program starts, it displays a short message:

```
C:\>SimpleUdpSrvr
Waiting for a client...
```

Nothing too fancy here. After the server is started, you can run the SimpleUdpClient program in either a separate command-prompt window on the same machine, or on another machine on the network. (If you use a remote machine, remember to change the 127.0.0.1 IP address to the address of the server machine.)

SimpleUdpClient immediately sends a message to the server, which in turn should send its welcome banner back. On the client, it looks like this:

```
C:\>SimpleUdpClient
Message received from 127.0.0.1:9050:
Welcome to my test server
```

Notice that the EndPoint object of the remote server indicates that it is indeed sending data out from the same UDP port to which it was bound, 9050.

On the server side, you should see the connection message sent by the client:

```
C:\>SimpleUdpSrvr
Waiting for a client...
Message received from 127.0.0.1:1340:
Hello, are you there?
```

Notice that the client, because it was not bound to a specific UDP port, selected a free UDP port to use for the communication. Once the opening protocol has been completed, you can type messages into the client console and see them sent to the server and displayed, then echoed back to the client and displayed.

If you are connecting to the server from a remote client, you can use the WinDump and Analyzer programs to monitor the network traffic generated by the applications. Figure 6.1 shows a sample Analyzer output window containing output from the simple client program.

FIGURE 6.1:

Sample Analyzer output from the SimpleUdpClient program

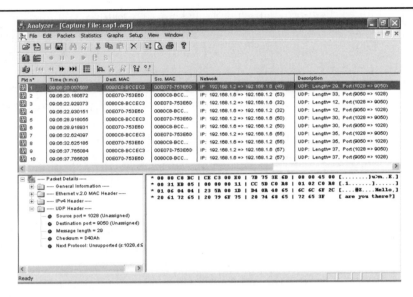

As can be seen from the network packets, each UDP message is sent in a single packet to the server, and each UDP message echoed back is sent as a single packet to the client. This is characteristic of how UDP preserves the message boundaries.

Stopping the UDP Server Program

Let's take a moment to examine an important shortfall in the sample UDP server program. When you type **exit** at the client console, the client program closes the socket and terminates. However, there is no connection per se, so the UPD server, unlike the TCP server, does not know when the remote client has closed its socket. Because it does not know that the client has stopped, the server will still wait for another packet to come in on the assigned UDP port.

You can observe this behavior by restarting the SimpleUdpClient on the same or another machine on the network, with the SimpleUdpSrvr program still running. The server program will continue to accept the greeting message sent from the client, along with any other message sent. (To stop the SimpleUdpSrvr, press Ctrl-C to halt the execution of the program.)

For real-world applications, you should program the server to watch for an external event, such as a specific command on the console, and then close the socket gracefully.

Using Connect() in a UDP Client Example

You may be wondering why the UDP client application's ReceiveFrom() and SendTo() methods are so complicated when you are only receiving and sending data to a single UDP server. Well, they don't have to be. As mentioned, the UDP methods are designed to allow the programmer to send UDP packets to any host on the network at any time. Because no prior connection is required for UDP, you must specify the destination host in each SendTo() and ReceiveFrom() method used in the program. If you're planning to send and receive data from only one host, you can take a shortcut.

After the UDP socket is created, you can use the standard Connect() method normally employed in TCP programs to specify the remote UDP server. With that in place, you can then use the Receive() and Send() methods to transfer data to the remote host. The communication still uses UDP packets, and you get to do a lot less work! This technique is demonstrated in the sample UDP client program in Listing 6.3.

Listing 6.3   **The OddUdpClient.cs program**

```
using System;
using System.Net;
using System.Net.Sockets;
using System.Text;

class OddUdpClient
{
    public static void Main()
    {
        byte[] data = new byte[1024];
        string input, stringData;
        IPEndPoint ipep = new IPEndPoint(
                    IPAddress.Parse("127.0.0.1"), 9050);

        Socket server = new Socket(AddressFamily.InterNetwork,
                    SocketType.Dgram, ProtocolType.Udp);

        server.Connect(ipep);
        string welcome = "Hello, are you there?";
        data = Encoding.ASCII.GetBytes(welcome);
        server.Send(data);

        data = new byte[1024];
        int recv = server.Receive(data);

        Console.WriteLine("Message received from {0}:", ipep.ToString());
```

```
            Console.WriteLine(Encoding.ASCII.GetString(data, 0, recv));

            while(true)
            {
                input = Console.ReadLine();
                if (input == "exit")
                    break;
                server.Send(Encoding.ASCII.GetBytes(input));
                data = new byte[1024];
                recv = server.Receive(data);
                stringData = Encoding.ASCII.GetString(data, 0, recv);
                Console.WriteLine(stringData);
            }
            Console.WriteLine("Stopping client");
            server.Close();
        }
    }
```

The OddUdpClient program behaves exactly like the SimpleUdpClient program. The only difference is that once the UDP socket is created, it is connected to a specific IPEndPoint:

```
IPEndPoint ipep = new IPEndPoint(
                        IPAddress.Parse("127.0.0.1"), 9050);

Socket server = new Socket(AddressFamily.InterNetwork,
                        SocketType.Dgram, ProtocolType.Udp);
server.Connect(ipep);
```

In this case, the Connect() method does not really do what it says. Because the socket is defined as a UDP datagram socket, no actual connection is made, but the socket information is "set" to the IPEndPoint object. All calls to the Send() and Receive() methods are now automatically referenced to the IPEndPoint object. You do not have to use the clunky SendTo() and Receive() methods to handle the data.

You can test the OddUdpClient program by starting the SimpleUdpSrvr as you normally would and using the OddUdpClient program to send messages to it. Things should work just as they did for the SimpleUdpClient program. You can even watch the traffic with WinDump or Analyzer if you don't believe that it's really sending UDP packets! Also, note that each message is sent as a single packet to the server, preserving all message boundaries, just as in the SimpleUdpClient.cs program.

Distinguishing UDP Messages

One of the best features of UDP is that it addresses the TCP difficulty of handling messages without honoring their boundaries. UDP preserves the message boundaries of all sent messages. Each ReceiveFrom() method call will read only the data sent as a result of a single SendTo() method call.

Recall that a UDP socket, once it's created, can receive messages from any UDP client. For the UDP socket to distinguish which client sent which data, it is imperative that each message be self-contained in a single packet and marked with the sending device's IP information. This allows the receiving device to identify both message and sender.

The programming for setting this up is demonstrated in the next two programs. The TestUdpClient.cs program sends multiple messages to the server, while the TestUdpSrvr.cs program attempts to read each message individually (similar to the failed TCP message test in the preceding chapter). First, let's examine TestUdpSrvr.cs in Listing 6.4.

Listing 6.4   The TestUdpSrvr.cs program

```
using System;
using System.Net;
using System.Net.Sockets;
using System.Text;

class TestUdpSrvr
{
    public static void Main()
    {
        int recv;
        byte[] data = new byte[1024];
        IPEndPoint ipep = new IPEndPoint(IPAddress.Any, 9050);

        Socket newsock = new Socket(AddressFamily.InterNetwork,
                    SocketType.Dgram, ProtocolType.Udp);

        newsock.Bind(ipep);
        Console.WriteLine("Waiting for a client...");

        IPEndPoint sender = new IPEndPoint(IPAddress.Any, 0);
        EndPoint tmpRemote = (EndPoint)(sender);

        recv = newsock.ReceiveFrom(data, ref tmpRemote);

        Console.WriteLine("Message received from {0}:", tmpRemote.ToString());
        Console.WriteLine(Encoding.ASCII.GetString(data, 0, recv));

        string welcome = "Welcome to my test server";
        data = Encoding.ASCII.GetBytes(welcome);
        newsock.SendTo(data, data.Length, SocketFlags.None, tmpRemote);

        for(int i = 0; i < 5; i++)
        {
```

```
            data = new byte[1024];
            recv = newsock.ReceiveFrom(data, ref tmpRemote);
            Console.WriteLine(Encoding.ASCII.GetString(data, 0, recv));
        }
        newsock.Close();
    }
}
```

TestUdpSrvr binds a UDP socket to the 9050 port and waits for a client to connect with
a greeting message. When this happens, the server sends back a welcome banner and then
attempts to receive five messages in a row from the client.

One nice feature of this server program is that the application protocol specifies that
after five messages the client should close its socket, so the server can likewise close its
socket.

Now take a look at the TestUdpClient.cs program (Listing 6.5), which demonstrates the
sending of multiple UDP messages to the server.

Listing 6.5   **The TestUdpClient.cs program**

```
using System;
using System.Net;
using System.Net.Sockets;
using System.Text;

class TestUdpClient
{
    public static void Main()
    {
        byte[] data = new byte[1024];
        IPEndPoint ipep = new IPEndPoint(
                        IPAddress.Parse("127.0.0.1"), 9050);

        Socket server = new Socket(AddressFamily.InterNetwork,
                        SocketType.Dgram, ProtocolType.Udp);

        string welcome = "Hello, are you there?";
        data = Encoding.ASCII.GetBytes(welcome);
        server.SendTo(data, data.Length, SocketFlags.None, ipep);

        IPEndPoint sender = new IPEndPoint(IPAddress.Any, 0);
        EndPoint tmpRemote = (EndPoint)sender;

        data = new byte[1024];
        int recv = server.ReceiveFrom(data, ref tmpRemote);

        Console.WriteLine("Message received from {0}:", tmpRemote.ToString());
```

```
            Console.WriteLine(Encoding.ASCII.GetString(data, 0, recv));


            server.SendTo(Encoding.ASCII.GetBytes("message 1"), tmpRemote);
            server.SendTo(Encoding.ASCII.GetBytes("message 2"), tmpRemote);
            server.SendTo(Encoding.ASCII.GetBytes("message 3"), tmpRemote);
            server.SendTo(Encoding.ASCII.GetBytes("message 4"), tmpRemote);
            server.SendTo(Encoding.ASCII.GetBytes("message 5"), tmpRemote);

            Console.WriteLine("Stopping client");
            server.Close();
        }
    }
```

The `TestUdpClient` program sends its greeting message to the designated server, then receives the welcome banner from the server. After it receives the welcome banner, it sends five messages in a row to the server and closes the socket.

If possible, try testing these programs on a network. When you run the test, you will see that each message is received the same way that it was sent—the UDP subsystem is guaranteed to maintain the message boundaries. You may have noticed, however, depending on your network, that some of the messages are missing. This is indicative of one of disadvantages of UDP communications. Although the messages are guaranteed to remain intact, they are not guaranteed to be delivered. The next section describes this and other problems inherent with UDP communications.

When UDP Goes Bad

While solving the message boundary problem found in TCP communications, UDP introduces some other predicaments that programmers must deal with in UDP programs:

- Lost data as a result of how the `ReceiveFrom()` method works
- Detecting and allowing for lost packets

These two UDP issues often cause unexpected dilemmas for network programmers who are more accustomed to working with TCP communications, and you must take them into consideration when creating production-quality UDP applications. This section gives you the tools you need to understand and work around these events when writing your C# network programs.

Preventing Lost Data

One of the advantages of TCP communication is the internal TCP buffer. As seen in Chapter 5, all data sent by the TCP socket is placed in an internal buffer area before being sent out on the network. Likewise, all data received on the socket is placed in the internal buffer area before being read by the `Receive()` method. When the `Receive()` method tries to read data from the buffer, if not all of the data is read, the remainder stays in the buffer and waits for the next `Receive()` call. This is not the case, however, with UDP communication.

UDP does not have to worry about packet retransmissions and therefore does not use a buffer system. All data sent from the socket to the network is immediately sent on the network. Likewise, all data received from the network is immediately forwarded to the next `ReceiveFrom()` method call. This system produces an important and potentially critical problem that is often overlooked by network programmers still learning their craft: data not immediately read from the UDP socket is lost forever.

When the `ReceiveFrom()` method is used in a program, the programmer must ensure that the data buffer specified is large enough to accept all the data from the UDP socket. If the buffer is too small, data will be lost. You can observe this unfortunate turn of events by modifying the `SimpleUDpClient` program from Listing 6.2 to use a smaller data buffer. The result is Listing 6.6, BadUdpClient.cs.

Listing 6.6   **The BadUdpClient.cs program**

```
using System;
using System.Net;
using System.Net.Sockets;
using System.Text;

class BadUdpClient
{
    public static void Main()
    {
        byte[] data = new byte[30];
        string input, stringData;
        IPEndPoint ipep = new IPEndPoint(
                    IPAddress.Parse("127.0.0.1"), 9050);

        Socket server = new Socket(AddressFamily.InterNetwork,
                    SocketType.Dgram, ProtocolType.Udp);

        string welcome = "Hello, are you there?";
        data = Encoding.ASCII.GetBytes(welcome);
        server.SendTo(data, data.Length, SocketFlags.None, ipep);

        IPEndPoint sender = new IPEndPoint(IPAddress.Any, 0);
```

```
        EndPoint tmpRemote = (EndPoint)sender;

        data = new byte[30];
        int recv = server.ReceiveFrom(data, ref tmpRemote);

        Console.WriteLine("Message received from {0}:", tmpRemote.ToString());
        Console.WriteLine(Encoding.ASCII.GetString(data, 0, recv));


        while(true)
        {
            input = Console.ReadLine();
            if (input == "exit")
                break;
            server.SendTo(Encoding.ASCII.GetBytes(input), tmpRemote);
            data = new byte[30];
            recv = server.ReceiveFrom(data, ref tmpRemote);
            stringData = Encoding.ASCII.GetString(data, 0, recv);
            Console.WriteLine(stringData);
        }
        Console.WriteLine("Stopping client");
        server.Close();
    }
}
```

The BadUdpClient program defines the data buffer as being only 30 bytes:

```
byte[] data = new byte[30];
```

After compiling the program, you can test it by running it with the SimpleUdpSrvr program. At first, things seem just fine. BadUdpClient sends the standard greeting message to the server, and receives the server's welcome banner. You can test out a few short phrases, and the program will work as expected. But try a phrase longer than 30 characters, and watch the fireworks. Take a look at the following:

```
C:\>BadUdpClient
Message received from 127.0.0.1:9050:
Welcome to my test server
test message
test message
longer test message
longer test message
This is an even longer test message

Unhandled Exception: System.Net.Sockets.SocketException: A message sent on a
datagram socket was larger than the internal message buffer or some other
```

```
network limit, or the buffer used to receive a datagram into was smaller
than the datagram itself
    at System.Net.Sockets.Socket.ReceiveFrom(Byte[] buffer, Int32 offset, Int32
      size, SocketFlags socketFlags, EndPoint& remoteEP)
    at System.Net.Sockets.Socket.ReceiveFrom(Byte[] buffer, EndPoint& remoteEP)
    at BadUdpClient.Main()
```

C:\>

When the longest test message was entered, the application produced an Exception, which of course was not accommodated in BadUdpClient and caused all sorts of difficulties. The underlying event is the ReceiveFrom() method's detecting that more data was available to read than would fit into the size of the supplied buffer. So it tried to notify the program by throwing a SocketException. This is a handy notification that more data was available than what you were able to accept, and that data is now lost.

Although you can never retrieve the original lost data, you can compensate for when this situation occurs. By placing a try-catch block around the ReceiveFrom() method, you can detect when data has been lost because of a small buffer and attempt to modify the data buffer size to accommodate the next time the application tries to receive the data. The BetterUdpClient.cs program, shown in Listing 6.7, demonstrates this technique.

Listing 6.7   **The BetterUdpClient.cs program**

```
using System;
using System.Net;
using System.Net.Sockets;
using System.Text;

class BetterdUdpClient
{
    public static void Main()
    {
        byte[] data = new byte[30];
        string input, stringData;
        IPEndPoint ipep = new IPEndPoint(
                    IPAddress.Parse("127.0.0.1"), 9050);

        Socket server = new Socket(AddressFamily.InterNetwork,
                    SocketType.Dgram, ProtocolType.Udp);

        string welcome = "Hello, are you there?";
        data = Encoding.ASCII.GetBytes(welcome);
        server.SendTo(data, data.Length, SocketFlags.None, ipep);

        IPEndPoint sender = new IPEndPoint(IPAddress.Any, 0);
```

```
        EndPoint tmpRemote = (EndPoint)sender;

        data = new byte[30];
        int recv = server.ReceiveFrom(data, ref tmpRemote);

        Console.WriteLine("Message received from {0}:", tmpRemote.ToString());
        Console.WriteLine(Encoding.ASCII.GetString(data, 0, recv));


        int i = 30;
        while(true)
        {
            input = Console.ReadLine();
            if (input == "exit")
                break;
            server.SendTo(Encoding.ASCII.GetBytes(input), tmpRemote);
            data = new byte[i];
            try
            {
                recv = server.ReceiveFrom(data, ref tmpRemote);
                stringData = Encoding.ASCII.GetString(data, 0, recv);
                Console.WriteLine(stringData);
            } catch (SocketException)
            {
                Console.WriteLine("WARNING: data lost, retry message.");
                i += 10;
            }
        }
        Console.WriteLine("Stopping client");
        server.Close();
    }
}
```

Instead of using a fixed data-buffer array size, the `BetterUdpClient` program uses a variable that can be set to a different value each time the `ReceiveFrom()` method is used:

```
data = new byte[i];
try
{
    recv = server.ReceiveFrom(data, ref tmpRemote);
    stringData = Encoding.ASCII.GetString(data, 0, recv);
    Console.WriteLine(stringData);
} catch (SocketException)
{
    Console.WriteLine("WARNING: data lost, retry message.");
    i += 10;
}
```

If a `SocketException` occurs, you know that the data overflowed the available data buffer in the `ReceiveFrom()` method. This program warns the customer of the event and increases the size of the data buffer by a set amount. All future calls to `ReceiveFrom()` will use the larger data buffer size. If another large message is received, the data buffer will be increased again. The output should look something like this:

```
C:\>BetterUdpClient
Message received from 127.0.0.1:9050:
Welcome to my test server
test
test
This is an even longer test message
WARNING: data lost, retry message.
This is an even longer test message
This is an even longer test message
This is a really, really, really long test message
WARNING: data lost, retry message.
This is a really, really, really long test message
This is a really, really, really long test message
exit
Stopping client

C:\>
```

During the test, I entered a phrase longer than the 30-byte buffer. Sure enough, the `SocketException` occurred, and the warning message was displayed. To ensure that the data buffer was increased, I retyped the same message to see if it would be accepted. As expected, it worked. This demonstrates a simple way to avoid losing data on UDP sockets.

NOTE   Most real-world applications use a geometrical technique to increase the buffer size so retransmissions are kept to a minimum. This could include doubling the buffer size with each large packet received.

In this section, we examined the importance of using a data buffer that is adequate but no larger than what is necessary to support the data in the application. This helps the program control memory usage. As an alternative, you can always use ridiculously large data buffers so that you never run out of room—but be prepared for your application to be a memory hog.

Preventing Lost Packets

The other difficult task often encountered with UDP communications is providing for the possibility of lost packets. Because UDP is a connectionless protocol, there is no way for a device to know if a packet it sends actually made it to the remote device. For some UDP applications, this is not an issue. Many games, for instance, use UDP packets to transmit positional information for players in the game. Every few seconds, a player's position and game status are transmitted to other players in the game. If a packet is lost in the network, an updated one will automatically be sent a few seconds later.

For other applications, however, packet loss can cause great difficulty. When you are trying to retrieve network management data from a device using the Simple Network Management Protocol (SNMP), you expect to get a response from the device. If you don't, you must compensate within your application.

The simplest thing to do to account for lost packets is to devise an arrangement similar to TCP's retransmission system. Packets sent successfully to a remote host should generate return packets from the remote device. If the expected return packet is not received within a specific amount of time, the original packet can be retransmitted.

There are two techniques that you can use to implement a UDP retransmission scheme:

Asynchronous sockets and a `Timer` object   This technique requires the use of an asynchronous socket that can listen for incoming packets without blocking. After the socket is set to do an asynchronous read, a `Timer` object can be set. If the `Timer` object goes off before the asynchronous read finishes, a retransmission is in order. This topic is covered in detail in Chapter 8, "Asynchronous Socket Programming."

Synchronous sockets and setting a socket time-out value   For this arrangement, you use the `SetSocketOption()` method as discussed in the next section.

Using Socket Time-outs

As seen in Chapter 3, the `ReceiveFrom()` method is a blocking function. It will block execution of the program until it receives a data packet. This is a Very Bad Thing in UDP programs because you are not guaranteed to receive a packet. If a data packet never arrives, your program is stuck forever, or at least until the customer gets aggravated and manually stops it.

By default, the `ReceiveFrom()` method blocks for infinity, waiting for data. You can control this, however, by using socket options. You can control how long `ReceiveFrom()` waits, and you can allow it to abort its wait. The `SetSocketOption()` method offers various socket options on a created `Socket` object, and one of these is the `ReceiveTimeout` option. This sets the amount of time the socket will wait for incoming data before signaling a time-out.

The format of the `SetSocketOption()` method is as follows:

```
SetSocketOption(SocketOptionLevel so, SocketOptionName sn, int value)
```

The `SocketOptionLevel` specifies what type of socket option to implement. The `SocketOptionName` defines the specific option to set, and the last parameter (`int value`) indicates the set value for the option.

To designate the `ReceiveTimeout` option, which is a socket-level option, you must use the following format:

```
server.SetSocketOption(SocketOptionLevel.Socket,
    SocketOptionName.ReceiveTimeout, 3000);
```

Because `SetSocketOption()` is a method in the `Socket` class, you can only use it on an active `Socket` object (called `server` in the preceding example). The integer parameter defines the amount of time (in milliseconds) that the socket will wait for data before triggering a time-out.

Setting the Time-out

You can see the time-out problem occur by running the `SimpleUdpClient` program without the `SimpleUdpSrvr` program running. It will wait for the server to return data—which of course won't happen. (You will have to manually stop the client program by pressing Ctrl-C.)

Let's add a few lines to the `SimpleUdpClient` program to set the time-out value. In addition to setting the socket time-out option, the Listing 6.8 also uses the `GetSocketOption()` to show that the time-out value did really change.

Listing 6.8   The TimeoutUdpClient.cs program

```
using System;
using System.Net;
using System.Net.Sockets;
using System.Text;

class TimeoutUdpClient
{
    public static void Main()
    {
        byte[] data = new byte[1024];
        string input, stringData;
        int recv;
        IPEndPoint ipep = new IPEndPoint(
                    IPAddress.Parse("127.0.0.1"), 9050);

        Socket server = new Socket(AddressFamily.InterNetwork,
                    SocketType.Dgram, ProtocolType.Udp);

        int sockopt = (int)server.GetSocketOption(SocketOptionLevel.Socket,
            SocketOptionName.ReceiveTimeout);
        Console.WriteLine("Default timeout: {0}", sockopt);
        server.SetSocketOption(SocketOptionLevel.Socket,
            SocketOptionName.ReceiveTimeout, 3000);
        sockopt = (int)server.GetSocketOption(SocketOptionLevel.Socket,
            SocketOptionName.ReceiveTimeout);
        Console.WriteLine("New timeout: {0}", sockopt);

        string welcome = "Hello, are you there?";
```

```
    data = Encoding.ASCII.GetBytes(welcome);
    server.SendTo(data, data.Length, SocketFlags.None, ipep);

    IPEndPoint sender = new IPEndPoint(IPAddress.Any, 0);
    EndPoint tmpRemote = (EndPoint)sender;

    data = new byte[1024];
    recv = server.ReceiveFrom(data, ref tmpRemote);
    Console.WriteLine("Message received from {0}:", tmpRemote.ToString());
    Console.WriteLine(Encoding.ASCII.GetString(data, 0, recv));

    while(true)
    {
        input = Console.ReadLine();
        if (input == "exit")
            break;
        server.SendTo(Encoding.ASCII.GetBytes(input), tmpRemote);
        data = new byte[1024];
        recv = server.ReceiveFrom(data, ref tmpRemote);
        stringData = Encoding.ASCII.GetString(data, 0, recv);
        Console.WriteLine(stringData);
    }
    Console.WriteLine("Stopping client");
    server.Close();
  }
}
```

The `TimeoutUdpClient` program first gets the original `ReceiveTimeout` value from the socket and displays it, then sets it to three seconds:

```
int sockopt = (int)server.GetSocketOption(SocketOptionLevel.Socket,
  SocketOptionName.ReceiveTimeout);
Console.WriteLine("Default timeout: {0}", sockopt);
server.SetSocketOption(SocketOptionLevel.Socket,
  SocketOptionName.ReceiveTimeout, 3000);
```

The `GetSocketOption()` method returns an `Object` object, so it must be typecast to an integer to see the actual value. After compiling the program, you can test it by executing it without the `SimpleUdpSrvr` program running. The output should look like this:

```
C:\>TimeoutUdpClient
Default timeout: 0
New timeout: 3000


Unhandled Exception: System.Net.Sockets.SocketException: An existing connection
was forcibly closed by the remote host
    at System.Net.Sockets.Socket.ReceiveFrom(Byte[] buffer, Int32 offset, Int32
size, SocketFlags socketFlags, EndPoint& remoteEP)
    at System.Net.Sockets.Socket.ReceiveFrom(Byte[] buffer, EndPoint& remoteEP)
```

```
    at TimeoutUdpClient.Main()

C:\>
```

As you can see, the original `ReceiveTimeout` value was set to zero, which indicates it will wait indefinitely for data. After adding the `SetSocketOption()` method to set it to 3000 milliseconds, the `GetSocketOption()` method returns 3000.

After displaying the `ReceiveTimeout` value, the program waits for incoming data for about three seconds on the `ReceiveFrom()` method. Then the program produces a `SocketException` and blows up.

The setting for the socket `ReceiveTimeout` option lasts for the duration of the socket. You can test this by starting the `SimpleUdpSrvr` program and then running the `TimeoutUdpClient` program. After the normal exchange of greetings, you can send a few test messages and then stop the `SimpleUdpSrvr` program (using Ctrl-C). Next, try and send a message from the client. Again, after about three seconds, an exception occurs.

When the `ReceiveTimeout` value has been reached, the socket stops waiting for data and produces a `SocketException`. For the time-out feature to help your program, you must write code to catch the `SocketException`. This task is described next.

Catching the Exception

Now that you know the socket will produce a `SocketException` when the time-out is reached, you need only to catch the Exception so you can gracefully inform the customer about it and allow some alternatives to the application. The `ExceptionUdpClient.cs` program (Listing 6.9) performs this function.

Listing 6.9 **The ExceptionUdpClient.cs program**

```csharp
using System;
using System.Net;
using System.Net.Sockets;
using System.Text;

class ExceptionUdpClient
{
    public static void Main()
    {
        byte[] data = new byte[1024];
        string input, stringData;
        int recv;
        IPEndPoint ipep = new IPEndPoint(
                    IPAddress.Parse("127.0.0.1"), 9050);

        Socket server = new Socket(AddressFamily.InterNetwork,
```

```
                    SocketType.Dgram, ProtocolType.Udp);
int sockopt = (int)server.GetSocketOption(SocketOptionLevel.Socket,
   SocketOptionName.ReceiveTimeout);
Console.WriteLine("Default timeout: {0}", sockopt);
server.SetSocketOption(SocketOptionLevel.Socket,
   SocketOptionName.ReceiveTimeout, 3000);
sockopt = (int)server.GetSocketOption(SocketOptionLevel.Socket,
   SocketOptionName.ReceiveTimeout);
Console.WriteLine("New timeout: {0}", sockopt);

string welcome = "Hello, are you there?";
data = Encoding.ASCII.GetBytes(welcome);
server.SendTo(data, data.Length, SocketFlags.None, ipep);

IPEndPoint sender = new IPEndPoint(IPAddress.Any, 0);
EndPoint Remote = (EndPoint)sender;

data = new byte[1024];
try
{
   recv = server.ReceiveFrom(data, ref Remote);
   Console.WriteLine("Message received from {0}:", Remote.ToString());
   Console.WriteLine(Encoding.ASCII.GetString(data, 0, recv));
} catch (SocketException)
{
   Console.WriteLine("Problem communicating with remote server");
   return;
}

while(true)
{
   input = Console.ReadLine();
   if (input == "exit")
      break;
   server.SendTo(Encoding.ASCII.GetBytes(input), ipep);
   data = new byte[1024];
   try
   {
      recv = server.ReceiveFrom(data, ref Remote);
      stringData = Encoding.ASCII.GetString(data, 0, recv);
      Console.WriteLine(stringData);
   } catch (SocketException)
   {
      Console.WriteLine("Error receiving message");
   }
}
Console.WriteLine("Stopping client");
server.Close();
      }
}
```

In ExceptionUdpClient.cs, the socket ReceiveTimeout is set to 3000 milliseconds as before. All of the ReceiveFrom() method calls are placed within a try-catch block to catch the SocketException that is raised if no data appears within the ReceiveTimeout value:

```
try
{
   recv = server.ReceiveFrom(data, ref tmpRemote);
   Console.WriteLine("Message received from {0}:", tmpRemote.ToString());
   Console.WriteLine(Encoding.ASCII.GetString(data, 0, recv));
} catch (SocketException)
{
   Console.WriteLine("Problem communicating with remote server");
   return;
}
```

If no data is received before expiration of the time-out, a SocketException occurs, and the statements in the catch block inform the customer that there was no response from the remote device. The specific behavior of the catch block depends on where in the program the error occurs. If, at the start of the communication, no packet is received from the server, it is assumed that the server is not present, and the program is terminated. During the message exchange section, a single packet gone missing is not a reason to terminate the program. Instead, a warning message is displayed on the console, and the receive loop is continued.

Running the ExceptionUdpClient program with no accompanying server program produces the following result:

```
C:\>ExceptionUdpClient
Default timeout: 0
New timeout: 3000
Problem communicating with remote server

C:\>
```

Now, that's a much kinder way to deal with the situation!

WARNING   While testing the time-out programs on a Windows XP Professional workstation, I noticed an odd behavior. When connecting to either the local IP address or the loopback address, the socket time-out value did not work properly. However, when connecting to a remote IP address, it worked as expected—yet another reason to test your network applications in a real-world environment.

If the SimpleUdpSrvr is running initially but is stopped after a few messages are passed, the output looks like this:

```
C:\>ExceptionUdpClient
Default timeout: 0
New timeout: 3000
```

```
Message received from 127.0.0.1:9050:
Welcome to my test server
test message
test message
Second test message
Second test message
Third test message
Error receiving message
Last test message
Error receiving message
exit
Stopping client

C:\>
```

In this case, the missing messages in the message loop are identified, but the customer still has control and can try sending more messages or terminate the program with the `exit` command.

This Exception-catching technique watched all the `ReceiveFrom()` methods for success and informed the customer if any of them failed. A nice feature, but it doesn't really solve the problem, which was that the original message did not make it to the destination. The preferred situation would be for the program to try resending the original message. This is the topic of the next section.

Handling Retransmissions

There are lots of reasons why a UDP packet can't make it to its destination. Many of those reasons are only temporary difficulties, and a second or third attempt at sending the same packet might be successful. These further attempts are called *retries*. Most production-quality UDP applications allow for a set number of retries before finally giving up on the communication.

If you are programming in a UDP environment where you must send a message and receive a return message, and no return message is received, you can use retries to resend the original message multiple times. When a return messagedoes eventually come, you can go on with the rest of your program. If no answer is ever received, however, you must indicate the problem to your customer and offer a solution.

Creating a Retransmission Setup

The simplest way to accomplish the retransmission arrangement is to create a separate method in the class to handle all sending and receiving of messages. The steps in this method would look something like this:

1. Send a message to a remote host.

2. Wait for an answer from the remote host.

3. If an answer is received, accept it and exit the method with the received data and the size of the data.

4. If no answer is received within a time-out value, increment a retry value.

5. Check the retry value. If it is less than the number of retries desired, go to step 1 and start over. If it is equal, abort the retransmission attempt and report the results to the customer.

Once the generic class method for sending and receiving UDP packets is created, it can be used everywhere in the program where a message is sent to a remote host and a response is expected. In C# code, the method would look like Listing 6.10.

Listing 6.10   The SndRcvData() method

```csharp
int SndRcvData(Socket s, byte[] message, EndPoint rmtdevice)
{
   int recv;
   int retry = 0;

   while (true)
   {
      Console.WriteLine("Attempt #{0}", retry);
      try
      {
         s.SendTo(message, message.Length, SocketFlags.None, rmtdevice);
         data = new byte[1024];
         recv = s.ReceiveFrom(data, ref rmtdevice);
      } catch (SocketException)
      {
         recv = 0;
      }

      if (recv > 0)
      {
         return recv;
      } else
      {
         retry++;
         if (retry > 4)
         {
            return 0;
         }
      }
   }
}
```

This method requires three parameters:

- A Socket object that has already been established by the calling program
- The data message to send to the remote host
- An EndPoint object that points to the IP address and port of the remote host

The Socket object passed to the new method should already be established as a UDP socket and have the ReceiveTimeout SocketOption value set to a reasonable amount of time to wait for an answer on the particular network.

The SndRcvData() method first attempts to send the message to the remote host using the standard SendTo() method. After sending the message, SndRcvData() blocks on the ReceiveFrom() method, waiting for a return message. If a message is received from the remote host within the ReceiveTimeout value, SndRcvData() places it in a global data buffer defined in the class as a byte array and returns the number of bytes received. The calling program can read the received message from the global data buffer, using the size returned from the SndRcvData() method.

If no message is returned by the ReceiveTimeout value, a SocketException occurs and the catch block takes effect. In the catch block, the recv value is set to zero. After the try-catch block, the recv value is tested. A positive result means a message was successfully received. A zero result means no message was received, so a retry value is incremented and then checked to see whether it has reached the desired maximum value. If it hasn't, the whole process is repeated, starting with resending the message.

If the retry value has reached its preset maximum value, the SndRcvData() method returns a zero. The calling application can then detect the zero value and act accordingly.

Using the Method in a Program
The RetryUdpClient.cs program , shown in Listing 6.11, implements the new message retransmission technique to communicate with a remote UDP echo server.

Listing 6.11   **The RetryUdpClient.cs program**

```
using System;
using System.Net;
using System.Net.Sockets;
using System.Text;

class RetryUdpClient
{
    private byte[] data = new byte[1024];
    private static IPEndPoint sender = new IPEndPoint(IPAddress.Any, 0);
    private static EndPoint Remote = (EndPoint)sender;

    private int SndRcvData(Socket s, byte[] message, EndPoint rmtdevice)
    {
        int recv;
        int retry = 0;

        while (true)
        {
```

```
            Console.WriteLine("Attempt #{0}", retry);
            try
            {
               s.SendTo(message, message.Length, SocketFlags.None, rmtdevice);
               data = new byte[1024];
               recv = s.ReceiveFrom(data, ref Remote);
            } catch (SocketException)
            {
               recv = 0;
            }

            if (recv > 0)
            {
               return recv;
            } else
            {
               retry++;
               if (retry > 4)
               {
                  return 0;
               }
            }
         }
      }

      public RetryUdpClient()
      {
         string input, stringData;
         int recv;
         IPEndPoint ipep = new IPEndPoint(
                     IPAddress.Parse("127.0.0.1"), 9050);

         Socket server = new Socket(AddressFamily.InterNetwork,
                     SocketType.Dgram, ProtocolType.Udp);

         int sockopt = (int)server.GetSocketOption(SocketOptionLevel.Socket,
            SocketOptionName.ReceiveTimeout);
         Console.WriteLine("Default timeout: {0}", sockopt);
         server.SetSocketOption(SocketOptionLevel.Socket,
            SocketOptionName.ReceiveTimeout, 3000);
         sockopt = (int)server.GetSocketOption(SocketOptionLevel.Socket,
            SocketOptionName.ReceiveTimeout);
         Console.WriteLine("New timeout: {0}", sockopt);

         string welcome = "Hello, are you there?";
         data = Encoding.ASCII.GetBytes(welcome);

         recv = SndRcvData(server, data, ipep);
         if (recv > 0)
         {
            stringData = Encoding.ASCII.GetString(data, 0, recv);
            Console.WriteLine(stringData);
```

```
        } else
        {
            Console.WriteLine("Unable to communicate with remote host");
            return;
        }

        while(true)
        {
            input = Console.ReadLine();
            if (input == "exit")
                break;
            recv = SndRcvData(server, Encoding.ASCII.GetBytes(input), ipep);
            if (recv > 0)
            {
                stringData = Encoding.ASCII.GetString(data, 0, recv);
                Console.WriteLine(stringData);
            } else
                Console.WriteLine("Did not receive an answer");
        }
        Console.WriteLine("Stopping client");
        server.Close();
    }

    public static void Main()
    {
        RetryUdpClient ruc = new RetryUdpClient();
    }
}
```

The RetryUdpClient program uses the SndRcvData() method for all communication with
the remote UDP server. As usual, a greeting message is first sent to the remote host. The
Main() method knows if a message has been received by the SndRcvData() method by testing
the returned value:

```
recv = SndRcvData(server, data, ipep);
if (recv > 0)
{
    stringData = Encoding.ASCII.GetString(data, 0, recv);
    Console.WriteLine(stringData);
} else
{
    Console.WriteLine("Unable to communicate with remote host");
    return;
}
```

If the returned value is greater than zero, it means a message has been received. The global
data buffer data contains the received message, and the returned value represents the length of
the received message. If the returned value is zero, no message was received from the remote
server, and the program acts accordingly.

The message loop uses the SndRcvData() method to send the message entered on the console and wait for the response. Here, as well, the message loop must contain code to check the return value from the SndRcvData() method and determine whether a message was received from the remote host. If not, a message informing the customer must be displayed.

Testing the Program

Now comes the fun part—testing to make sure that the newly created retransmission method will work. The first test is to see if it works with no server present at all. Run the RetryUdpClient program without the accompanying UDP server:

```
C:\>RetryUdpClient
Default timeout: 0
New timeout: 3000
Attempt #0
Attempt #1
Attempt #2
Attempt #3
Attempt #4
Unable to communicate with remote host

C:\>
```

As expected, the retry feature started and tried five times to send the greeting message to the server. After the fifth attempt, it returned a zero to the Main() method, which in turn exited the program. If you are testing this on a network, you can use WinDump or Analyzer to watch the retry packets go out. Each retry attempt generates a separate greeting packet. The time between packets should be close to the time-out value set in the program.

Next, you can test to see if the retry method works by simulating lost packets on the network. Do this by starting the RetryUdpClient program and letting it go through a couple of retry loops; then start the SimpleUdpSrvr program on the target machine. The retry loop should detect the server and pick up as if nothing ever happened:

```
C:\>RetryUdpClient
Default timeout: 0
New timeout: 3000
Attempt #0
Attempt #1
Attempt #2
Attempt #3
Attempt #4
Welcome to my test server
This is a test message.
Attempt #0
This is a test message.
Here's another message.
```

```
Attempt #0
Here's another message.
exit
Stopping client
```

`C:\>`

This test responded as expected. After four unsuccessful attempts to receive data from the server, the last attempt successfully sent the greeting message to the server and received the welcome banner in return. After that, the normal activity took place.

As a final test, you can stop the server program in the middle of the message transmissions to see what happens. Start the SimpleUdpSrvr program on the designated server machine and start the RetryUdpClient program on its designated machine. Everything should work normally (unless, of course, you have real dropped packets). After sending a couple of test messages, stop SimpleUdpSrvr by pressing Ctrl-C. Next, try to send a message from the RetryUdpClient program. You should see the following:

```
C:\>RetryUdpClient
Default timeout: 0
New timeout: 3000
Attempt #0
Welcome to my test server
First test message
Attempt #0
First test message
Second test message
Attempt #0
Second test message
Third test message
Attempt #0
Attempt #1
Attempt #2
Attempt #3
Attempt #4
Did not receive an answer
Last test message
Attempt #0
Attempt #1
Attempt #2
Attempt #3
Attempt #4
Did not receive an answer
exit
Stopping client
```

`C:\>`

Again, as expected, the client program communicated with the remote server, sending the greeting message and receiving the welcome banner. The first two messages were sent just fine, as indicated by the return message. Then, when the server program was stopped, another test message was sent. After five retries, the program gave up and displayed the designated error message. The program was still active and was able to attempt to send another message from the customer, but again it failed and another error message was displayed.

Using this retransmission technique, you can create robust UDP applications that can withstand normal network congestion problems and get data to the remote host.

A Complete UDP Application

The preceding sections have discussed several characteristics and quirks of UDP and how to program for them. Each sample program demonstrated a particular UDP programming feature. All those examples are well and good for textbook learning, but they aren't answers in themselves when you're trying to create a real-world UDP application.

This section ties together all of the UDP features we've discussed and presents a sample UDP application that deploys all the techniques described in this chapter.

Catching Multiple Exceptions by Monitoring Error Codes

So far, you have seen how to catch `SocketExceptions` when the data buffer is too small for the incoming data and when a set `ReceiveTimeout` value has expired. But what about when you want to check for both situations in the same program?

Because both events throw the same Exception, you cannot write separate `catch` blocks to perform specific functions depending on the Exception. Rather, you will have to identify which error produced the Exception. To do this, you must dive into the murky waters of socket error codes and handle them accordingly in your program code. This section describes how to determine what produced a `SocketException` and how to handle the Exception within the application program code.

When a `Socket` object throws a `SocketException`, it is because the underlying WinSock socket has produced some kind of an error condition. The exact error condition can be retrieved from the `SocketException` object using the `ErrorCode` property. The `ErrorCode` property contains the numeric WinSock error message that produced the `SocketException`. There are lots and lots of WinSock error codes. Table 6.1 lists some that you are more likely to encounter in your network programming efforts.

TABLE 6.1: WinSock Error Codes

Error Code	Description
10004	Interrupted function call
10013	Permission denied
10014	Bad address
10022	Invalid argument
10024	Too many open sockets
10035	Resource temporarily unavailable
10036	Operation now in progress
10037	Operation already in progress
10038	Socket operation on a nonsocket
10039	Destination address required
10040	Message too long
10041	Protocol wrong type for socket
10042	Bad protocol option
10043	Protocol not supported
10044	Socket type not supported
10045	Operation not supported
10046	Protocol family not supported
10047	Address family not supported by protocol family
10048	Address already in use
10049	Cannot assign requested address
10050	Network is down
10051	Network is unreachable
10052	Network dropped connection on reset
10053	Software caused connection abort
10054	Connection reset by peer
10055	No buffer space available
10056	Socket is already connected
10057	Socket is not connected
10058	Cannot send after socket shutdown
10060	Connection timed out
10061	Connection refused
10064	Host is down
10065	No route to host
10067	Too many processes

Continued on next page

TABLE 6.1 CONTINUED: WinSock Error Codes

Error Code	Description
10091	Network subsystem is unavailable
10101	Graceful shutdown in progress
10109	Class type not found
11001	Host not found

For our purposes here, you are concerned about only two of these error codes:

- 10040, when the receiving data buffer is too small
- 10054, when the `ReceiveFrom()` method times out

To create a method that can monitor both of these error conditions, you must create code for the `catch` block to check the `ErrorCode` property of the `SocketException` object created from the error, and act accordingly. It looks like this:

```
} catch (SocketException e)
{
   if (e.ErrorCode == 10054)
   {
      // statements to handle ReceiveFrom() timeout
   }
   else if (e.ErrorCode == 10040)
   {
      //statements to handle data buffer overflow
   }
}
```

By creating an instance (e) of the `SocketException` object in the `catch` filter, you can use the `ErrorCode` property of the instance to check for the exact error code that produced the `Exception`. Write whatever code is necessary to check for any or all of the specific error conditions. This example checks for the two specific error conditions discussed in this chapter: the `ReceiveFrom()` time-out and the data buffer overflow. In a real world program, you might want to check for many other things that could go wrong.

Here's a tip about running a program that produces `SocketException` errors frequently. You can use the `ErrorCode` property to help you determine the cause of the `SocketException` and code for it accordingly. You can even see a text error message of the error code by using the `Message` property:

```
} catch (SocketException e)
{
   Console.WriteLine("Socket error {0}: {1}", e.ErrorCode, e.Message)
}
```

The Complete Client Program

The BestUdpClient.cs program, Listing 6.12, utilizes the AdvSndRecvData() method, which incorporates all of the solutions discussed in this chapter.

Listing 6.12   **The BestUdpClient.cs program**

```
using System;
using System.Net;
using System.Net.Sockets;
using System.Text;

class BestUdpClient
{
    private byte[] data = new byte[1024];
    private static IPEndPoint sender = new IPEndPoint(IPAddress.Any, 0);
    private static EndPoint Remote = (EndPoint)sender;
    private static int size = 30;

    private static int AdvSndRcvData(Socket s, byte[] message,
                       EndPoint rmtdevice)
    {
        int recv = 0;
        int retry = 0;

        while (true)
        {
            Console.WriteLine("Attempt #{0}", retry);
            try
            {
                s.SendTo(message, message.Length, SocketFlags.None, rmtdevice);
                data = new byte[size];
                recv = s.ReceiveFrom(data, ref Remote);
            } catch (SocketException e)
            {
                if (e.ErrorCode == 10054)
                    recv = 0;
                else if (e.ErrorCode == 10040)
                {
                    Console.WriteLine("Error receiving packet");
                    size += 10;
                    recv = 0;
                }
            }

            if (recv > 0)
            {
                return recv;
            } else
            {
                retry++;
```

```
                if (retry > 4)
                {
                    return 0;
                }
            }
        }
    }

    public static void Main()
    {
        string input, stringData;
        int recv;
        IPEndPoint ipep = new IPEndPoint(
                        IPAddress.Parse("127.0.0.1"), 9050);

        Socket server = new Socket(AddressFamily.InterNetwork,
                        SocketType.Dgram, ProtocolType.Udp);

        int sockopt = (int)server.GetSocketOption(SocketOptionLevel.Socket,
            SocketOptionName.ReceiveTimeout);
        Console.WriteLine("Default timeout: {0}", sockopt);
        server.SetSocketOption(SocketOptionLevel.Socket,
            SocketOptionName.ReceiveTimeout, 3000);
        sockopt = (int)server.GetSocketOption(SocketOptionLevel.Socket,
            SocketOptionName.ReceiveTimeout);
        Console.WriteLine("New timeout: {0}", sockopt);

        string welcome = "Hello, are you there?";
        data = Encoding.ASCII.GetBytes(welcome);

        recv = AdvSndRcvData(server, data, ipep);
        if (recv > 0)
        {
            stringData = Encoding.ASCII.GetString(data, 0, recv);
            Console.WriteLine(stringData);
        } else
        {
            Console.WriteLine("Unable to communicate with remote host");
            return;
        }

        while(true)
        {
            input = Console.ReadLine();
            if (input == "exit")
                break;
            recv = AdvSndRcvData(server, Encoding.ASCII.GetBytes(input), ipep);
            if (recv > 0)
            {
                stringData = Encoding.ASCII.GetString(data, 0, recv);
                Console.WriteLine(stringData);
```

```
        } else
            Console.WriteLine("Did not receive an answer");
    }
    Console.WriteLine("Stopping client");
    server.Close();
    }
}
```

The AdvSndRecvDat() method accomplishes several things all in one handy method call:

- It sends a message out a UDP socket to a remote destination.

- It waits for a set time to receive a return message.

- If the return message does not arrive, it sends the message again for a set number of retries.

- If the return message is larger than the defined data buffer array, it increases the array and sends the original message again, waiting for the response.

You may have noticed that the *size* variable is now a static variable in the class and not just in the AdvSndRcvData() method. Using the *size* variable this way allows you to maintain the larger buffer size between calls to the AdvSndRcvData() method. Of course, if you think that your application would only cause one or two large packets, it would still make sense to leave the *size* parameter in the method, which resets it back to 30 every time.

You can test the BestUdpClient program with the SimpleUdpSrvr program. As I advised for the RetryUdpClient.cs program, you should try various combinations of starting and stopping the server and see how it affects the client program.

TIP   You can see from this example that it is often best to incorporate small self-contained methods to implement network functions within your programs. This allows you to create detailed methods to check for error conditions for each transmission, without having to repeat the same code every time you need to send or receive a message.

Summary

This chapter described the functions necessary to send UDP messages across the network to a remote host. To use UDP, the Socket object must use the SocketType.Dgram and ProtocolType.Udp parameters. Once the UDP Socket object is created, you can use the SendTo() and ReceiveFrom()methods to send and receive UDP packets.

Because UDP is a connectionless protocol, you must specify the destination address for each packet transmitted. Alternatively, you can use the standard Connect() method to specify the destination address one time, and then use the Receive() and Send() methods.

An important benefit of UDP communication is that it preserves message boundaries. All data sent in a SendTo() method is received in a single ReceiveFrom() method on the destination host. On the other hand, a drawback of UDP is that the data packet is not guaranteed to arrive at the destination. One way to detect dropped packets is to implement a retransmission system. Every packet sent to a destination should get a packet in return. If that doesn't happen within a set time-out period, the original packet can be retransmitted. If, after several retransmissions (retries) you do not get a response, your program should inform the customer of the network problem. The ReceiveTimeout socket option can be used to set the time-out value of the socket.

Another issue for UDP is data buffer size. When the ReceiveFrom() method reads the incoming packet, it must have a data buffer big enough to accept all of the data. Any data not accepted will be lost. You can prevent this by geometrically increasing the buffer size each time an Exception is thrown on a received packet.

You can monitor the ReceiveFrom() method for Exceptions using a try-catch block, and you can test the Exception for which socket error triggered it. The ErrorCode property of the SocketException is used to determine the underlying socket error code. If the error code is 10040, the received message was too long for the receive buffer, and the message must be resent. Error code 10054 means the remote client has disconnected from the server and the connection session can be terminated.

The next chapter describes how to use the asynchronous socket methods in network programs. This enables event-driven Windows programs to utilize network programming techniques without having to worry about blocking network function calls.

CHAPTER 7

Using The C# Sockets Helper Classes

- The `TcpClient` class: components and examples

- The `TcpListener` class: components and examples

- The `UdpClient` class: components and examples

- Moving binary data across the network

- Communicating with other host types

- Using data classes to move complex objects over the network

T he two preceding chapters described how to use the low-level Socket class to create TCP and UDP network applications. While many hard-core network programmers are familiar with this type of programming, many with less experience find the Socket class difficult and confusing to use. To make network programming tasks easier for all of us, Microsoft provides a simplified set of helper classes to assist in creating full-featured network programs.

This chapter explains how to use the helper classes in network programs. You'll also see some real-world examples of how to use them. Further into the chapter, you'll see how to use the helper classes to move data between hosts on the network.

Often application data comes in many forms, some easy to transport and some not so easy. The chapter finishes up by showing a technique that can be used to transport complex binary data across the network using the helper classes.

The TcpClient Class

The TcpClient class, located in the System.Net.Sockets namespace, was designed to facilitate the writing of TCP client applications by bypassing the need to use the Socket class TCP functions. This section describes the TcpClient class and presents a simple TCP client application that uses the TCPClient class.

The TcpClient Class Constructors

The TcpClient class allows you to create a TcpClient object using three constructor formats:

TcpClient()   The first constructor format creates a new TcpClient object, binding a socket to the local system address and a random TCP port. After the default TcpClient object is created, it must be connected to a remote device using the Connect() method, described in the upcoming section, "The TcpClient Class Methods." Here is the format for this constructor:

```
TcpClient newcon = new TcpClient();
newcon.Connect("www.ispnet.net", 8000);
```

TcpClient(IPEndPoint localEP)   The second constructor allows you to specify a specific local IP address to use, as well as a specific TCP port number. This is most often used when the device has more than one network card, and you want to specifically send packets out a particular card. Again, after the TcpClient object is created, it must be connected to a remote device using the Connect() method. Here's the format:

```
IPEndPoint iep = new IPEndPoint(IPAddress,Parse("192.168.1.6"), 8000);
TcpClient newcon = new TcpClient(iep);
newcon.Connect("www.isp.net", 8000);
```

TcpClient(String host, int port) The third constructor format is the most frequently used. It allows you to specify the remote device within the constructor, and no `Connect()` method is needed. The remote device can be specified by its address and numeric TCP port value. The address can be either a string hostname, or a string IP address. The `TcpClient` constructor will automatically resolve the string hostname into the proper IP address. The format is as follows:

```
TcpClient newcon = new TcpClient("www.isp.net", 8000);
```

Once the `TcpClient` object has been created, several properties and methods are available with which to manipulate the object and transfer data back and forth with the remote device.

The TcpClient Class Methods

The `TcpClient` class contains a helpful collection of properties and methods to assist your efforts in writing TCP client applications. Table 7.1 shows the methods available for the `TcpClient` class.

TABLE 7.1: TcpClient Methods

Method	Description
Close()	Closes the TCP connection
Connect()	Attempts to establish a TCP connection with a remote device
Equals()	Determines if two TcpClient objects are equal
GetHashCode()	Gets a hash code suitable for use in hash functions
GetStream()	Gets a Stream object that can be used to send and receive data
GetType()	Gets the Type of the current instance
ToString()	Converts the current instance to a String object

As mentioned earlier, the `Connect()` method connects the `TcpClient` object to a remote device. Once the device is connected, the `GetStream()` object assigns a `NetworkStream` object to send and receive data:

```
TcpClient newcon = new TcpClient()
newcon.Connect("www.ispnet.net", 8000);
NetworkStream ns = new NetworkStream(newcon);
```

After the `NetworkStream` object is created, you can use the `Read()` and `Write()` methods to receive and send data (this is described in Chapter 5, "Connection-Oriented Sockets").

In addition to the `TcpClient` class methods, there are several properties that can be used with the `TcpClient` object, as described in Table 7.2. These properties allow you to set low-level `Socket` object options for the `TcpClient` object.

TABLE 7.2: TcpClient Object Properties

Property	Description
LingerState	Gets or sets the socket linger time
NoDelay	Gets or sets the delay time used for sending or receiving TCP buffers that are not full
ReceiveBufferSize	Gets or sets the size of the TCP receive buffer
ReceiveTimeout	Gets or sets the receive timeout value of the socket
SendBufferSize	Gets or sets the size of the TCP send buffer
SendTimeout	Gets or sets the send timeout value of the socket

Creating a Simple Client Program

The TcpClient class was designed to make network program creation as simple as possible. You have probably already concluded from the code snippets shown so far that a basic TCP client program can be written with just a few lines of code. Listing 7.1 is a simple TCP client program that will interact with Chapter 5's SimpleTcpSrvr program.

Listing 7.1   **The TcpClientSample.cs program**

```csharp
using System;
using System.Net;
using System.Net.Sockets;
using System.Text;

class TcpClientSample
{
    public static void Main()
    {
        byte[] data = new byte[1024];
        string input, stringData;
        TcpClient server;

        try
        {
            server = new TcpClient("127.0.0.1", 9050);
        } catch (SocketException)
        {
            Console.WriteLine("Unable to connect to server");
            return;
        }
```

```
        NetworkStream ns = server.GetStream();

        int recv = ns.Read(data, 0, data.Length);
        stringData = Encoding.ASCII.GetString(data, 0, recv);
        Console.WriteLine(stringData);

        while(true)
        {
            input = Console.ReadLine();
            if (input == "exit")
                break;
            ns.Write(Encoding.ASCII.GetBytes(input), 0, input.Length);
            ns.Flush();

            data = new byte[1024];
            recv = ns.Read(data, 0, data.Length);
            stringData = Encoding.ASCII.GetString(data, 0, recv);
            Console.WriteLine(stringData);
        }
        Console.WriteLine("Disconnecting from server...");
        ns.Close();
        server.Close();
    }
}
```

Because the version of the TcpClient constructor used in this example automatically tries to connect to the specified remote server, it is a good idea to place it within a try-catch block in case the remote server is unavailable. As is true for the Socket method Connect() method, if the remote server is unavailable, a SocketException will be generated.

WARNING There is one catch to placing the TcpClient constructor within a try-catch block: variables instantiated in a try-catch block are only visible within the block. To make the TcpClient object visible outside the try-catch block, you must declare the variable outside the try-catch block, as shown in Listing 7.1 with the server TcpClient object.

After the NetworkStream object is created, you use the normal Read() and Write() methods to move the data:

```
while(true)
{
    input = Console.ReadLine();
    if (input == "exit")
        break;
    ns.Write(Encoding.ASCII.GetBytes(input), 0, input.Length);
```

```
    ns.Flush();

    data = new byte[1024];
    recv = ns.Read(data, 0, data.Length);
    stringData = Encoding.ASCII.GetString(data, 0, recv);
    Console.WriteLine(stringData);
}
```

The `Read()` method requires three parameters:

- The data-byte array in which to place the received data
- The offset location in the buffer at which you want to start placing the data
- The length of the data buffer

Like the `Socket` method `Receive()`, the object's `Read()` method will read as much data as it can fit into its buffer. If the supplied buffer is too small, the leftover data stays in the stream for the next `Read()` method call.

The `Write()` method, too, requires three parameters:

- The data-byte array to send to the stream
- The offset location in the buffer from which you want to start sending data
- The length of the data to send

NOTE It is important to remember that TCP does not preserve message boundaries. This fact also applies to the `TcpClient` class. By now you'll recognize that this method should be handled the same way as the `Receive()` method in the TCP `Socket` class, creating a loop to ensure that all of the required data is read from the stream.

Testing the Program

You can test the new `TcpClientSample` program with the original `SimpleTcpSrvr` program (Listing 5.1) presented in Chapter 5. Just start `SimpleTcpSrvr` on the designated device, and run `TcpClientSample` from either a separate command-prompt window on the same machine or from a separate machine on the network. Remember to change the IP address in the program to the correct IP address for your server machine.

The `TcpClientSample` program should behave exactly like the `NetworkStreamTcpClient` program presented in Chapter 5 (Listing 5.9). You can type phrases at the console window and watch them displayed on the server and echoed back to the client.

Use the `windump` or `analyzer` commands if you want to watch the network traffic generated from your tests. Figure 7.1 shows a sample Analyzer output from monitoring a test.

Sample Analyzer
output from the
TcpClientSample test

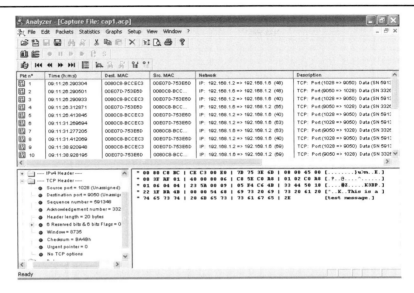

As you can see from the sample output, TcpClientSample behaves exactly the same as Chapter 5's SimpleTcpClient program, which used Socket objects. This demonstrates that you can often use the TcpClient class in place of Socket objects, saving yourself substantial programming effort.

The TcpListener Class

Like TcpClient, the TcpListener class (also located in the System.Net.Sockets namespace) provides a simplified way to create TCP server applications. This section describes the TcpListener class and shows how to use it in a simple TCP server application.

The TcpListener Class Constructors

The TcpListener class has three constructor formats:

TcpListener(int port)   This constructor binds to a specific local port number.

TcpListener(IPEndPoint ie)   This constructor binds to a specific local EndPoint object. TcpListener(IPAddress addr, int port)

TcpListener(IPAddress addr, int port)   This constructor binds to a specific local IPAddress object and port number.

Unlike `TcpClient`, the `TcpListener` class constructor requires at least one parameter: the port number on which to listen for new connections. If the server machine has multiple network cards and you want to listen on a specific one, you can use an `IPEndPoint` object to specify the IP address of the desired card, along with the desired TCP port number to listen on. The constructor described last in the list just above allows you to specify the desired IP address using an `IPAddress` object, with the port number as a separate parameter.

The TcpListener Class Methods

The `TcpListener` class methods, listed in Table 7.3, are used to perform the necessary functions on the created `TcpListener` object.

TABLE 7.3: TcpListener Class Methods

Method	Description
AcceptSocket()	Accepts an incoming connection on the port and assign it to a Socket object
AcceptTcpClient()	Accepts an incoming connection on the port and assigns it to a TcpClient object
Equals()	Determines if two TcpListener objects are equal
GetHashCode()	Gets a hash code suitable for use in hash functions
GetType()	Gets the type of the current instance
Pending()	Determines if there are pending connection requests
Start()	Starts listening for connection attempts
Stop()	Stops listening for connection attempts (closes the socket)
ToString()	Creates a string representation of the TcpListener object

The procedure to create a `TcpListener` object and listen for incoming connections goes like this:

```
TcpListener server = new TcpListener(IPAddress.Parse("127.0.0.1"), 9050);
server.Start();
TcpClient newclient = server.AcceptTcpClient();
```

The `Start()` method is similar to the combination of `Bind()` and `Listen()` used in the Socket class. `Start()` binds the socket to the endpoint defined in the `TcpListener` constructor and places the TCP port in listen mode, ready to accept new connections. The `AcceptTcpClient()` method is comparable to the `Accept()` socket method, accepting incoming connection attempts and assigning them to a `TcpClient` object.

After the `TcpClient` object is created, all communication with the remote device is performed with the new `TcpClient` object rather than the original `TcpListener` object. The `TcpListener` object can thus be used to accept other connections and pass them to other TcpClient objects. To close the TcpListener object, you must use the Stop() method:

```
server.Stop();
```

NOTE If you have any open client connections, you do not have to close them before the original TcpListener object is closed. However, you do have to remember to close the individual TcpClient objects using the Close() method.

A Simple Server Program

Now let's look at a simple example of a TCP server using the TcpListener class. This example, TcpListenerSample.cs in Listing 7.2, mimics the functionality of the original SimpleTcpSrvr program presented in Chapter 5 (Listing 5.1).

Listing 7.2   **The TcpListenerSample.cs program**

```
using System;
using System.Net;
using System.Net.Sockets;
using System.Text;

class TcpListenerSample
{
    public static void Main()
    {
        int recv;
        byte[] data = new byte[1024];

        TcpListener newsock = new TcpListener(9050);
        newsock.Start();
        Console.WriteLine("Waiting for a client...");

        TcpClient client = newsock.AcceptTcpClient();
        NetworkStream ns = client.GetStream();

        string welcome = "Welcome to my test server";
        data = Encoding.ASCII.GetBytes(welcome);
        ns.Write(data, 0, data.Length);

        while(true)
        {
            data = new byte[1024];
            recv = ns.Read(data, 0, data.Length);
            if (recv == 0)
                break;

            Console.WriteLine(
```

```
                  Encoding.ASCII.GetString(data, 0, recv));
            ns.Write(data, 0, recv);
        }
        ns.Close();
        client.Close();
        newsock.Stop();
    }
}
```

The `TcpListenerSample` program first creates a `TcpListener` object, using a UDP port of 9050, and the `Start()` method places the new object in a listening mode. Then the `AcceptTcpClient()` method waits for an incoming TCP connection and requests and assigns it to a `TcpClient` object:

```
TcpListener newsock = new TcpListener(9050);
newsock.Start();

TcpClient client = newsock.AcceptTcpClient();
NetworkStream ns = client.GetStream();
```

With the `TcpClient` object established, a `NetworkStream` object is assigned to it to communicate with the remote client. All communication is done using the `NetworkStream` object's `Read()` and `Write()` methods. Remember to place all data into a byte array for the `Write()` method. Likewise, all received data from the `Read()` method must also be assigned to a byte array.

You can test the `TcpListenerSample` program by starting it up and connecting to it with the `TcpClientSample` program from the preceding section. They should behave together exactly like the `SimpleTcpSrvr` (Listing 5.1) and `SimpleTcpClient` (Listing 5.2) programs from Chapter 5. As usual, if you are testing these programs across a network, you can use the WinDump and Analyzer programs to watch the network traffic generated by each program.

Incorporating the StreamReader and StreamWriter Classes

Because the `NetworkStream` object uses streams to transfer data among the network hosts, you will have to handle the usual problems of identifying messages in the stream. Use the standard techniques outlined in Chapter 5 to delimit messages within the stream:

• Send fixed-size messages

• Send the message size before the message

• Use message delimiter characters

After it's created from the `TcpClient` object, you can use the `NetworkStream` object to create `StreamReader` and `StreamWriter` objects. (This is demonstrated in the "Using C# Streams with

TCP" section of Chapter 5.) These objects will automatically create message delimiters to simplify moving text across the network:

```
TcpClient client = new TcpClient("127.0.0.1", 9050);
NetworkStream ns = client.GetStream();
StreamReader sr = new StreamReader(ns);
StreamWriter sw = new StreamWriter(ns);

sw.WriteLine("This is a test");
sw.Flush();
string data = sr.ReadLine();
```

The StreamReader and StreamWriter classes by default use a line feed to delimit messages, which makes it a snap to distinguish[messages in TCP communications. Because the ReadLine() and WriteLine() methods both use String objects, text messages can be created and sent using the String class objects instead of your having to mess with the bulky data-byte arrays.

The UdpClient Class

The UdpClient class was created to help make UDP network programs simpler for network programmers. This section describes the UdpClient class and its methods and walks you through creating a simple UDP server and client program using the helper class.

The UdpClient Class Constructors

The UdpClient class has four formats of constructors:

UdpClient()   This format creates a new UdpClient instance not bound to any specific address or port.

UdpClient(int port)   This constructor binds the new UdpClient object to a specific UDP port number.

UdpClient(IPEndPoint iep)   This constructor binds the new UdpClient object to a specific local IP address and port number.

UdpClient(string host, int port)   This format binds the new UdpClient object to any local IP address and port and associates it with a specific remote IP address and port.

The UdpClient constructors work like their comparable TcpClient constructors. You can either let the system choose a UDP port for the application, or you can select a specific port in the constructor. If your UDP application must accept data on a specific port, you must define that port in the UdpClient constructor.

Once the UdpClient object is created, you can manipulate the underlying socket and move data using the various methods available.

The UdpClient Class Methods

The methods of the UdpClient class provide various functionality for controlling and moving data into and out of the UDP socket. Table 7.4 describes these methods.

TABLE 7.4: The UdpClient Class Methods

Method	Description
Close()	Closes the underlying socket
Connect()	Allows you to specify a remote IP endpoint to send and receive data with
DropMulticastGroup()	Removes the socket from a UDP multicast group
Equals()	Determines if two UdpClient objects are equal
GetHashCode()	Gets a hash code for the UdpClient object
GetType()	Gets the Type of the current object
JoinMulticastGroup()	Adds the socket to a UDP multicast group
Receive()	Receives data from the socket
Send()	Sends data to a remote host from the socket
ToString()	Creates a string representation of the UdpClient object

NOTE   The JoinMulticastGroup() and DropMulticastGroup() methods allow you to program UDP applications to use IP multicasting. This feature is discussed in Chapter 10, "IP Multicasting."

Using the UdpClient Class in Programs

There are a few subtle differences between the UdpClient class's Receive() and Send() methods that make them different from the Socket methods ReceiveFrom() and SendTo().

The Receive() Method

The UdpClient class uses the Receive() method to accept UDP packets on the specified interface and port. There is only one Receive() method format:

```
byte[] Receive(ref IPEndPoint iep)
```

The Receive() method accepts UDP packets on the IP address and UDP port specified by the UdpClient constructor, either system-specified values, or values set in the constructor.

Let's take a look at how the Receive() method format differs from the ReceiveFrom() method used with standard UDP Socket objects.

For starters, the data received from the socket is not placed in a byte array within the method call. It is returned by the method. You must specify an empty byte array for the received data.

The second difference between the UdpClient method Receive() and the Socket method ReceiveFrom()is the way the remote host information is returned. ReceiveFrom()places the remote host information in an EndPoint object, whereas Receive()uses an IPEndPoint object. This makes extracting the IP address and UDP port number of the remote host a little easier for the programmer.

The following code snippet demonstrates how to use the Receive() method in a UDP application:

```
IPEndPoint ipep = new IPEndPoint(IPAddress.Any, 9050);
UdpClient newsock = new UdpClient(ipep);
byte[] data = new byte[1024];
IPEndPoint ipep2 = new IPEndPoint(IPAddress.Any, 0);
data = host.Receive(ref ipep2);
Console.WriteLine("The remote host is: {0}, port {1}",
    ipep2.Address, ipep2.Port);
Console.WriteLine(Encoding.ASCII.GetString(data));
```

In this code snippet, a UDP packet is accepted on UDP port 9050 from any network interface on the machine and is displayed on the console.

NOTE   One nice feature of the Receive() method is what happens when more data is received than the buffer size specified can accommodate. Instead of throwing a SocketException, as the Socket object does, the UdpClient returns a data buffer large enough to handle the received data. The result: a handy feature that can save you lots of extra programming effort.

The Send() Method

The Send() method has three formats that can send data to a remote host:

Send(byte[] *data*, int *sz*)   This format sends the byte array *data* of size *sz* to the default remote host. To use this format, you must specify a default remote UDP host using either UdpClient constructor, or the Connect() method:

```
UdpClient host = new UdpClient("127.0.0.1", 9050);
```

Send(byte[] *data*, int *sz*, IPEndPoint *iep*)   This format sends the byte array *data* of size *sz* to the remote host specified by *iep*.

Send(byte[] *data***, int** *sz***, string** *host***, int** *port***)**   This format sends the byte array *data* of size *sz* to the host *host* at port *port*.

If you are writing a UDP application that does not need to listen for incoming packets on a specific UDP port, you can use the UdpClient constructor that specifies the remote host information and then use the Receive() and Send() methods to move data back and forth with the remote host.

A Simple UdpClient Server Program

The UdpSrvrSample.cs program, shown in Listing 7.3, demonstrates using the UdpClient class methods in a server application environment.

Listing 7.3   **The UdpSrvrSample.cs program**

```
using System;
using System.Net;
using System.Net.Sockets;
using System.Text;

class UdpSrvrSample
{
    public static void Main()
    {
        byte[] data = new byte[1024];
        IPEndPoint ipep = new IPEndPoint(IPAddress.Any, 9050);
        UdpClient newsock = new UdpClient(ipep);

        Console.WriteLine("Waiting for a client...");

        IPEndPoint sender = new IPEndPoint(IPAddress.Any, 0);

        data = newsock.Receive(ref sender);

        Console.WriteLine("Message received from {0}:", sender.ToString());
        Console.WriteLine(Encoding.ASCII.GetString(data, 0, data.Length));

        string welcome = "Welcome to my test server";
        data = Encoding.ASCII.GetBytes(welcome);
        newsock.Send(data, data.Length, sender);

        while(true)
        {
            data = newsock.Receive(ref sender);

            Console.WriteLine(Encoding.ASCII.GetString(data, 0, data.Length));
            newsock.Send(data, data.Length, sender);
```

```
        }
    }
}
```

The `UdpSrvrSample` program creates a `UdpClient` object from an `IPEndPoint` object, specifying any IP address on the server and using UDP port 9050. The program immediately waits for an incoming UDP packet from any remote client, using the `Receive()` method:

```
IPEndPoint sender = new IPEndPoint(IPAddress.Any, 0);
data = newsock.Receive(ref sender);
```

The sender variable stores the IP information of the client, which is then used for sending messages back to the client:

```
newsock.Send(data, data.Length, sender);
```

Because the `UdpClient` object does not know the IP information of the destination host, you must specify it for each `Send()` method call.

NOTE   As seen in the UdpSrvrSample program, the data-byte array does not need to be reset to its full length after every Receive() method. This is a handy feature of the UdpClient class.

A Simple UdpClient Client Program

Here is the matching client program, `UdpClientSample.cs` (Listing 7.4), demonstrating how to use the `UdpClient` class methods in a UDP client application.

Listing 7.4   **The UdpClientSample.cs program**

```
using System;
using System.Net;
using System.Net.Sockets;
using System.Text;

class UdpClientSample
{
    public static void Main()
    {
        byte[] data = new byte[1024];
        string input, stringData;
        UdpClient server = new UdpClient("127.0.0.1", 9050);

        IPEndPoint sender = new IPEndPoint(IPAddress.Any, 0);

        string welcome = "Hello, are you there?";
        data = Encoding.ASCII.GetBytes(welcome);
        server.Send(data, data.Length);
```

```
        data = server.Receive(ref sender);

        Console.WriteLine("Message received from {0}:", sender.ToString());
        stringData = Encoding.ASCII.GetString(data, 0, data.Length);
        Console.WriteLine(stringData);

        while(true)
        {
            input = Console.ReadLine();
            if (input == "exit")
                break;

            server.Send(Encoding.ASCII.GetBytes(input), input.Length);
            data = server.Receive(ref sender);
            stringData = Encoding.ASCII.GetString(data, 0, data.Length);
            Console.WriteLine(stringData);
        }
        Console.WriteLine("Stopping client");
        server.Close();
    }
}
```

Because the UdpClientSample program does not need to listen to a specific UDP port for incoming messages, you can use the all-in-one constructor format, specifying the IP address and UDP port number of the remote host:

```
UdpClient server = new UdpClient("127.0.0.1", 9050);
```

Of course, if you are connecting to a remote UDP server, remember to place either the IP address or hostname of the remote server in the constructor instead of the loopback address.

After the UdpClient object is created, the Send() method sends the greeting message out to the server:

```
server.Send(data, data.Length);
```

Notice that because the destination host address information was already specified in the UdpClient constructor, you do not need to specify it in the Send() method.

Testing the Sample Programs

After compiling the UdpSrvrSample and UdpClientSample programs, you can test them on the same machine or on separate machines on the network.

The output looks exactly like the output from the SimpleUdpClient program (Listing 6.2) shown in Chapter 6, "Connectionless Sockets." Each message sent using the Send() method call is sent as a single UDP packet to the remote machine and read using a single Receive() method call.

Because the UdpClient class employs UDP packets to transmit messages, it suffers from one of the same problems as the UDP Socket objects, as described in Chapter 6. Specifically, there is always the possibility that sent messages will not make it to the destination device, so you must compensate for that in your UdpClient programs. This is usually accomplished by using the retry techniques demonstrated in Chapter 6.

WARNING   One problem with UDP Socket objects that is *not* found in UdpClient objects is lost data. If the data buffer supplied to the UdpClient method Receive() is too small for the incoming data, the buffer is returned to match the size of the data. No data is lost, and no SocketExceptions are thrown.

Moving Data across the Network

So far in this chapter you have seen how to move text messages efficiently from one device to another device across the network using the Socket helper classes. Certainly, for many applications this is all that is necessary; for many other applications, however, more advanced functionality is required to handle classes of data other than text such as binary data and groups of more than one type of data.

This section shows techniques for moving different types of binary data across the network. When programming to communicate with various systems, it is important that you understand how binary data is stored on a device and how it is transmitted across the network. This section also covers how to move complex datatypes, such as data elements in classes, among devices on the network.

Moving Binary Data

Whether you use TCP or UDP, sending binary data between two devices on a network is a complex topic. There are many possibilities for errors, and you must take them all into account. This section offers several suggestions for creating programs that move binary data successfully from one device to another.

Binary Data Representation

Perhaps the major issue when moving binary datatypes on a network is how they are represented. The various types of machines all represent binary datatype in their own way. You must ensure that the binary value on one machine turns out to be the same binary value on another machine.

Machines running a Microsoft Windows OS on an Intel (or compatible) processor platform store binary information using a set pattern for each datatype. It is important that you understand how this information is represented when sending binary data to a non-Windows remote host. Table 7.5 lists the binary datatypes used in C#.

TABLE 7.5: C# Binary Datatypes

Datatype	Bytes	Description
sbyte	1	Signed byte integer with values from –128 to 127
byte	1	Unsigned integer with values from 0 to 255
short	2	Signed short integer with values from –32,768 to 32,767
ushort	2	Unsigned short integer with values from 0 to 65,535
int	4	Standard integer with values from –2,147,483,648 to 2,147,483,647
uint	4	Unsigned integer with values from 0 to 4,294,967,295
long	8	Large signed integer with values from –9,223,372,036,854,775,808 to 9,223,372,036,854,775,807
ulong	8	Large unsigned integer with values from 0 to 18,446,744,073,709,551,615
float	4	A floating-point decimal number with values from 1.5×10^{-45} to $3.4 \times 1,038$, using 7-digit precision
double	8	A floating-point decimal number with values from 5.0×10^{-324} to 1.7×10^{308}, using 15–16-digit precision
decimal	16	A high-precision floating-point number with values from 1.0×10^{-28} to 7.9×10^{28}, using 28–29-digit precision

Each binary datatype must be converted into a raw byte array before it can be sent using the Send() or SendTo() methods. Fortunately, the .NET library provides a class specifically for this job: the BitConverter class.

Converting Binary Datatypes

As seen in the VarTcpClient (Listing 5.8) and VarTcpSrvr (Listing 5.7) programs in Chapter 5, the .NET System class supplies the BitConverter class to convert binary datatypes into byte arrays, and vice versa. This class is crucial to accurately sending binary datatypes across the network to remote hosts.

Sending Binary Datatypes

The BitConverter method GetBytes() converts a standard binary datatype to a byte array. For example:

```
int test = 1990;
byte[] data = BitConverter.GetBytes(test);
newsock.Send(data, data.Length);
```

This simple code snippet shows the conversion of a standard 4-byte integer value into a 4-byte byte array, which is then used in a Write() or Send() method call to forward the value to a remote device.

WARNING   If you are sending binary datatypes using TCP, you cannot use the `StreamWriter` or `StreamReader` classes because they expect data to be sent in strings, not binary. Any nulls in the binary data will damage the string conversion.

NOTE   When creating the byte array for the binary datatype, it is important that you allocate enough space in the byte array to contain all of the bytes of the binary datatype. If not all of the bytes of the converted binary datatype are sent, the receiving program will not be able to "reassemble" them back into the original datatype.

Receiving Binary Datatypes

As just stated in the preceding Note, the receiving program must be able to receive the byte array containing the binary datatype and convert it back into the original binary datatype. This is also done using `BitConverter` class methods. Table 7.6 lists the `BitConverter` class's methods for converting raw byte arrays into binary datatypes.

TABLE 7.6: BitConverter Methods for Converting Data

Method	Description
ToBoolean()	Converts a 1-byte byte array to a Boolean value
ToChar()	Converts a 2-byte byte array to a Unicode character value
ToDouble()	Converts an 8-byte byte array to a double floating-point value
ToInt16()	Converts a 2-byte byte array to a 16-bit signed integer value
ToInt32()	Converts a 4-byte byte array to a 32-bit signed integer value
ToSingle()	Converts a 4-byte byte array to a single-precision floating-point value
ToString()	Converts all bytes in the byte array to a string that represents the hexadecimal values of the binary data
ToUInt16()	Converts a 2-byte byte array to a 16-bit unsigned integer value
ToUInt32()	Converts a 4-byte byte array to a 32-bit unsigned integer value
ToUing64()	Converts an 8-byte byte array to a 64-bit unsigned integer value

All the converter methods have the same format:

```
BitConverter.ToInt16(byte[] data, int offset)
```

The byte array is the first parameter, and the second parameter is the offset location within the array where the conversion is to start. Note that the methods know how many bytes to use within the array to create the appropriate binary datatype.

Once the received byte array is converted to a binary datatype, you can use it in the program as any other value of that datatype, as shown here:

```
double total = 0.0;
byte[] data = newsock.Receive(ref sender);
double test = BitConverter.ToDouble(data, 0);
total += test;
```

Sample Programs

Sending binary information using UDP packets is fairly easy, assuming that you are sending one value per message. (We'll look at multiple-value situations in a later section.) Because UDP preserves message boundaries, you are guaranteed that if the packet arrives, there is only one data value in it. Assuming the server knows what type of binary data is in the packet, it is a snap to decode the value within the message back to its original binary value.

Listing 7.5 shows a sample UDP server program that reads binary data from the network.

Listing 7.5   **The BinaryUdpSrvr.cs program**

```csharp
using System;
using System.Net;
using System.Net.Sockets;
using System.Text;

class BinaryUdpSrvr
{
    public static void Main()
    {
        byte[] data = new byte[1024];
        IPEndPoint ipep = new IPEndPoint(IPAddress.Any, 9050);
        UdpClient newsock = new UdpClient(ipep);

        Console.WriteLine("Waiting for a client...");

        IPEndPoint sender = new IPEndPoint(IPAddress.Any, 0);

        data = newsock.Receive(ref sender);

        Console.WriteLine("Message received from {0}:", sender.ToString());
        Console.WriteLine(Encoding.ASCII.GetString(data, 0, data.Length));

        string welcome = "Welcome to my test server";
        data = Encoding.ASCII.GetBytes(welcome);
        newsock.Send(data, data.Length, sender);

        byte[] data1 = newsock.Receive(ref sender);
        int test1 = BitConverter.ToInt32(data1, 0);
        Console.WriteLine("test1 = {0}", test1);

        byte[] data2 = newsock.Receive(ref sender);
```

```
        double test2 = BitConverter.ToDouble(data2, 0);
        Console.WriteLine("test2 = {0}", test2);

        byte[] data3 = newsock.Receive(ref sender);
        int test3 = BitConverter.ToInt32(data3, 0);
        Console.WriteLine("test3 = {0}", test3);

        byte[] data4 = newsock.Receive(ref sender);
        bool test4 = BitConverter.ToBoolean(data4, 0);
        Console.WriteLine("test4 = {0}", test4.ToString());

        byte[] data5 = newsock.Receive(ref sender);
        string test5 = Encoding.ASCII.GetString(data5);
        Console.WriteLine("test5 = {0}", test5);

        newsock.Close();
    }
}
```

The BinaryUdpSrvr program uses the Receive() method to wait for a remote client to send a greeting message, then returns its welcome banner to the client.

Next, it expects to receive five test messages in a row from the remote client. Each message contains a different type of data. The order in which the messages appear is critical, because each message is decoded back into the appropriate datatype based on its position in the receipt order. Of course, with UDP, there's no guarantee that the packets will arrive at all, so this is not a good real-world example. You must be careful when using this technique with UDP messages.

One important thing to note about this program is that the BitConverter class contains methods to convert raw binary data into binary datatypes, but not into a text datatype. The BitConverter method ToString()does exist, but its role is different from what you probably expect. Rather than converting the raw binary data into a printable string, it converts the raw data into a string representation of the binary data in hexadecimal. For example, this code snippet:

```
string data = "this is a test";
string test = BitConverter.ToString(Encoding.ASCII.GetBytes(data));
Console.WriteLine("data = '{0}'", data);
Console.WriteLine("test = '{0}'", test);
```

produces these results:

```
C:\>test
data = 'this is a test'
test = '74-68-69-73-20-69-73-20-61-20-74-65-73-74'

C:\>
```

NOTE The `BitConverter` method `ToString()`is a handy way to display the hexadecimal values of a byte array, but if you want to display the actual converted text string, you must use the `Encoding.ASCII.GetString()` method, as shown in the preceding `BinaryUdpSrvr` program (Listing 7.5).

The `BinaryUdpClient` program, Listing 7.6, is the counterpart to the `BinaryUdpSrvr` program. Here it sends five types of data to the server program.

Listing 7.6   **The BinaryUdpClient.cs program**

```csharp
using System;
using System.Net;
using System.Net.Sockets;
using System.Text;

class BinaryUdpClient
{
    public static void Main()
    {
        byte[] data = new byte[1024];
        string stringData;
        UdpClient server = new UdpClient("127.0.0.1", 9050);

        IPEndPoint sender = new IPEndPoint(IPAddress.Any, 0);

        string welcome = "Hello, are you there?";
        data = Encoding.ASCII.GetBytes(welcome);
        server.Send(data, data.Length);

        data = new byte[1024];
        data = server.Receive(ref sender);

        Console.WriteLine("Message received from {0}:", sender.ToString());
        stringData = Encoding.ASCII.GetString(data, 0, data.Length);
        Console.WriteLine(stringData);

        int test1 = 45;
        double test2 = 3.14159;
        int test3 = -1234567890;
        bool test4 = false;
        string test5 = "This is a test.";

        byte[] data1 = BitConverter.GetBytes(test1);
        server.Send(data1, data1.Length);

        byte[] data2 = BitConverter.GetBytes(test2);
```

```
        server.Send(data2, data2.Length);

        byte[] data3 = BitConverter.GetBytes(test3);
        server.Send(data3, data3.Length);

        byte[] data4 = BitConverter.GetBytes(test4);
        server.Send(data4, data4.Length);

        byte[] data5 = Encoding.ASCII.GetBytes(test5);
        server.Send(data5, data5.Length);

        Console.WriteLine("Stopping client");
        server.Close();
    }
}
```

BinaryUdpClient uses the Send() method to send a greeting banner to the server (specified by an address in the UdpClient constructor) and waits for the welcome banner to be returned. Once the welcome banner is received, the program sends a series of five messages, each containing data in a different datatype.

The output from the BinaryUdpSrvr program should look like this:

```
C:\>BinaryUdpSrvr
Waiting for a client...
Message received from 127.0.0.1:1252:
Hello, are you there?
test1 = 45
test2 = 3.14159
test3 = -1234567890
test4 = False
test5 = This is a test.

C:\>
```

Each of the binary datatypes was successfully transmitted to the server program across the network and can be used in other calculations within the server program if necessary.

WinDump and Analyzer, as usual, will let you watch the actual data packets if you are testing these programs across a network.

Note how each datatype is sent within the individual packets. The packet for the integer value contains the byte array for the integer value 45. The binary data is sent as the 4-byte value 0x2D 0x00 0x00 0x00, seen in the data section of the UDP packet.

Note the order in which the binary data value is sent in the packet. This representation format is an important feature of sending binary data that is discussed in the next section.

Communicating with Other Host Types

When sending binary datatypes between two devices that are both running a Microsoft Windows OS on an Intel microprocessor platform, you do not have to worry about how the binary data is represented. Each side of the network communications channel recognizes the binary data. The byte array produced from the `BitConverter.GetBytes()` method is converted to the proper binary datatype for the other machine using the `BitConverter.ToInt32()` method.

Of course, that's not the end of the story. The C# language in your network programs is being ported to other operating systems running on other CPU platforms. So it is possible and entirely likely that the binary datatype representations of the client and server programs may not be the same. This section describes how to meet this challenge and make your C# network programs ready to accommodate the formats of various platforms.

Binary Datatype Representation

The problem of dueling binary datatypes arises from the fact that CPU platforms may store binary datatypes differently. Because multiple bytes are used for the datatype, they can be stored one of two ways:

- The least significant byte first (called *little endian*)

- The most significant byte first (called *big endian*)

It is imperative that the binary datatype is interpreted correctly on each system, sending and receiving. If the wrong datatype representation is used to convert a raw binary byte array, your programs will be working with incorrect data.

Listing 7.7 is the `BinaryDataTest.cs` program, which uses the `BitConverter.ToString()` method to demonstrate how the different binary datatypes are stored on your system.

Listing 7.7   **The BinaryDataTest.cs program**

```
using System;
using System.Net;
using System.Text;

class BinaryDataTest
{
    public static void Main()
    {
        int test1 = 45;
        double test2 = 3.14159;
        int test3 = -1234567890;
        bool test4 = false;
        byte[] data = new byte[1024];
```

```
        string output;

        data = BitConverter.GetBytes(test1);
        output = BitConverter.ToString(data);
        Console.WriteLine("test1 = {0}, string = {1}", test1, output);

        data = BitConverter.GetBytes(test2);
        output = BitConverter.ToString(data);
        Console.WriteLine("test2 = {0}, string = {1}", test2, output);

        data = BitConverter.GetBytes(test3);
        output = BitConverter.ToString(data);
        Console.WriteLine("test3 = {0}, string = {1}", test3, output);

        data = BitConverter.GetBytes(test4);
        output = BitConverter.ToString(data);
        Console.WriteLine("test4 = {0}, string = {1}", test4, output);
    }
}
```

All that happens here is that `BinaryDataTest` does some simple `BitConverter` operations on various datatypes, and it uses the `BitConverter ToString()` method to display the resulting byte array values. The output from the `BinaryDataTest` program should look like this:

```
C:\>BinaryDataTest
test1 = 45, string = 2D-00-00-00
test2 = 3.14159, string = 6E-86-1B-F0-F9-21-09-40
test3 = -1234567890, string = 2E-FD-69-B6
test4 = False, string = 00

C:\>
```

By looking at the simple integer value (test1) you can see that the standard byte representation used on this machine is little endian (the 2D value comes before the zeros). If this were a big endian system, the integer would be stored as 00-00-00-2D instead. So when sending data to a host that uses big endian data representation, errors will occur unless your program adjusts.

Converting Binary Data Representation

The problem of using different binary datatype representations is a significant issue in the Unix environment. Because so many platforms run Unix, you can never assume that the remote system will be using the same representation as yours. The Unix world has devised a solution: sending binary datatypes in a *generic* method.

The *network byte order* representation of binary datatypes was created as intermediate storage for binary data to be transmitted across the network. The idea is for each network program to convert its own local binary data into network byte order before transmitting it. On the receiving side, the system must convert the incoming data from network byte order into its own internal byte order. This ensures that the binary data will be converted to the proper representation for the destination host. Figure 7.2 illustrates the process of network-byte-order conversion.

FIGURE 7.2:

Using network byte order between hosts.

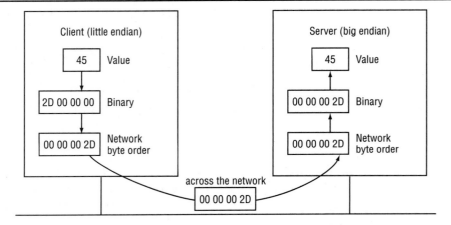

The .NET library includes methods to convert integer values to network byte order, and vice versa. These methods are included in the IPAddress class, contained in the System.Net namespace. One is HostToNetworkOrder(), which converts integer datatypes to a network byte order representation. In Listing 7.8, the BinaryNetworkByteOrder.cs program demonstrates using this method on integer datatypes.

Listing 7.8   The BinaryNetworkByteOrder.cs program

```csharp
using System;
using System.Net;
using System.Text;

class BinaryNetworkByteOrder
{
    public static void Main()
    {
        short test1 = 45;
        int test2 = 314159;
        long test3 = -123456789033452;
        byte[] data = new byte[1024];
        string output;

        data = BitConverter.GetBytes(test1);
```

```
        output = BitConverter.ToString(data);
        Console.WriteLine("test1 = {0}, string = {1}", test1, output);

        data = BitConverter.GetBytes(test2);
        output = BitConverter.ToString(data);
        Console.WriteLine("test2 = {0}, string = {1}", test2, output);

        data = BitConverter.GetBytes(test3);
        output = BitConverter.ToString(data);
        Console.WriteLine("test3 = {0}, string = {1}", test3, output);

        short test1b = IPAddress.HostToNetworkOrder(test1);
        data = BitConverter.GetBytes(test1b);
        output = BitConverter.ToString(data);
        Console.WriteLine("test1 = {0}, nbo = {1}", test1b, output);

        int test2b = IPAddress.HostToNetworkOrder(test2);
        data = BitConverter.GetBytes(test2b);
        output = BitConverter.ToString(data);
        Console.WriteLine("test2 = {0}, nbo = {1}", test2b, output);

        long test3b = IPAddress.HostToNetworkOrder(test3);
        data = BitConverter.GetBytes(test3b);
        output = BitConverter.ToString(data);
        Console.WriteLine("test3 = {0}, nbo = {1}", test3b, output);
    }
}
```

The BinaryNetworkByteOrder program creates three types of integer data values and uses the HostToNetworkOrder() method to convert them to values in network byte order. The output from the BinaryNetworkByteOrder program on my machine is as follows:

```
C:\>BinaryNetworkByteOrder
test1 = 45, string = 2D-00
test2 = 314159, string = 2F-CB-04-00
test3 = -123456789033452, string = 14-CE-F1-79-B7-8F-FF-FF
test1 = 11520, nbo = 00-2D
test2 = 801833984, nbo = 00-04-CB-2F
test3 = 1499401231033958399, nbo = FF-FF-8F-B7-79-F1-CE-14

C:\>
```

You may notice something odd here. Notice that HostToNetworkOrder() returns the value in the same datatype as the original value. The byte values within the datatype are now placed in network byte order, ready for sending out on the network. Unfortunately, if the network byte order is not in the same binary representation as the local host, those data values will not be the same. For example, the value assigned to the test1 variable is 45. When test1 is converted to network byte order, it is assigned to the variable *test1b*. Now, the variable *test1b* is still a valid short integer variable, but has the value 11520. This is obviously not the same as the original value of 45. When *test1b* is transmitted across the network, it must be converted back to the local host order to get the original value of 45.

WARNING   Remember that when data is converted to network byte order, it may not have the same value as the original data value. The network byte order is only used for transporting the data across the network.

Before the destination host can use the data received, it must convert the data to the local binary datatype representation of the host.

Reading Data in Network Byte Order

After the integer values are converted to network byte order and sent to the remote system, they must be converted back to the host byte order representation so their original values can be used in the program. The NetworkToHostOrder() method of the IPAddress class converts data received in network byte order back to the appropriate byte order of the system running the program. Similar to HostToNetworkOrder(), the NetworkToHostOrder() method converts an integer value in network byte order to an integer value in the local host's byte order. It is possible that both orders are the same and no conversion will be necessary, but to be on the safe side, it is always best to include this method.

Sample Programs

Listing 7.9 is the NetworkOrderClient.cs program, which demonstrates how to use the HostToNetworkOrder() and NetworkToHostOrder() methods to transmit data across the network.

Listing 7.9   **The NetworkOrderClient.cs program**

```
using System;
using System.Net;
using System.Net.Sockets;
using System.Text;

class NetworkOrderClient
{
    public static void Main()
    {
        byte[] data = new byte[1024];
        string stringData;
        TcpClient server;

        try
```

```
    {
        server = new TcpClient("127.0.0.1", 9050);
    } catch (SocketException)
    {
        Console.WriteLine("Unable to connect to server");
        return;
    }
    NetworkStream ns = server.GetStream();

    int recv = ns.Read(data, 0, data.Length);
    stringData = Encoding.ASCII.GetString(data, 0, recv);
    Console.WriteLine(stringData);

    short test1 = 45;
    int test2 = 314159;
    long test3 = -123456789033452;

    short test1b = IPAddress.HostToNetworkOrder(test1);
    data = BitConverter.GetBytes(test1b);
    Console.WriteLine("sending test1 = {0}", test1);
    ns.Write(data, 0, data.Length);
    ns.Flush();

    int test2b = IPAddress.HostToNetworkOrder(test2);
    data = BitConverter.GetBytes(test2b);
    Console.WriteLine("sending test2 = {0}", test2);
    ns.Write(data, 0, data.Length);
    ns.Flush();

    long test3b = IPAddress.HostToNetworkOrder(test3);
    data = BitConverter.GetBytes(test3b);
    Console.WriteLine("sending test3 = {0}", test3);
    ns.Write(data, 0, data.Length);
    ns.Flush();

    ns.Close();
    server.Close();
    }
}
```

The NetworkOrderClient program uses the TcpClient class to create a TCP connection to a server. It then creates a NetworkStream object to send and receive data with the remote server. Once the connection is established, it sets values for three integer datatypes and sends them in network byte order to the server.

The NetworkOrderSrvr.cs program, shown in Listing 7.10, is used to receive the data and convert it back to host byte order.

Listing 7.10   **The NetworkOrderSrvr.cs program**

```
using System;
using System.Net;
using System.Net.Sockets;
using System.Text;

class NetworkOrderSrvr
{
    public static void Main()
    {
        int recv;
        byte[] data = new byte[1024];

        TcpListener server = new TcpListener(9050);
        server.Start();
        Console.WriteLine("waiting for a client...");

        TcpClient client = server.AcceptTcpClient();
        NetworkStream ns = client.GetStream();

        string welcome = "Welcome to my test server";
        data = Encoding.ASCII.GetBytes(welcome);
        ns.Write(data, 0, data.Length);
        ns.Flush();

        data = new byte[2];
        recv = ns.Read(data, 0, data.Length);
        short test1t = BitConverter.ToInt16(data, 0);
        short test1 = IPAddress.NetworkToHostOrder(test1t);
        Console.WriteLine("received test1 = {0}", test1);

        data = new byte[4];
        recv = ns.Read(data, 0, data.Length);
        int test2t = BitConverter.ToInt32(data, 0);
        int test2 = IPAddress.NetworkToHostOrder(test2t);
        Console.WriteLine("received test2 = {0}", test2);

        data = new byte[8];
        recv = ns.Read(data, 0, data.Length);
        long test3t = BitConverter.ToInt64(data, 0);
        long test3 = IPAddress.NetworkToHostOrder(test3t);
        Console.WriteLine("received test3 = {0}", test3);

        ns.Close();
        client.Close();
        server.Stop();
    }
}
```

The `NetworkOrderSrvr` program uses the `TcpListener` class to listen on TCP port 9050 for incoming connection attempts. When a connection attempt is received, the program creates a `TcpClient` object. It then uses the `GetStream()` method to create a `NetworkStream` object for sending and receiving data from the remote host.

After the network connection is established and a welcome banner message is sent, the `NetworkOrderSrvr` expects to receive three integer datatypes from the remote host. Keep in mind that TCP is a stream-oriented communications channel and thus there is no guarantee that the three datatypes will be sent in three separate messages. To compensate for this, the `NetworkOrderSrvr` reads a set number of bytes from the `NetworkStream` for each datatype. This ensures that no matter how the data is received, it will be read from the TCP buffer in the right sizes.

Once the data is read from the TCP buffer, it is converted to the appropriate binary datatype using the `BitConverter` methods:

```
data = new byte[2];
recv = ns.Read(data, 0, data.Length);
short test1t = BitConverter.ToInt16(data, 0);
```

Remember, because you are not sure if the network byte order is correct for the system, the converted value should not be directly used; it is just temporary. To create the correct value, you must convert it to the host byte order:

```
short test1 = IPAddress.NetworkToHostOrder(test1t);
```

This ensures that the data value is in the correct binary representation for the host system on which the program is running.

The output from the `NetworkOrderClient` and `NetworkOrderSrvr` programs should be similar. The output from the client program should look like this:

```
C:\>NetworkOrderClient
Welcome to my test server
sending test1 = 45
sending test2 = 314159
sending test3 = -123456789033452

C:\>
```

And the output from the `NetworkOrderSrvr` program should be as follows:

```
C:\>NetworkOrderSrvr
waiting for a client...
received test1 = 45
received test2 = 314159
received test3 = -123456789033452

C:\>
```

The binary data values shown from the server program should be the same as those sent from the client program, showing that the data bytes were converted, sent, and reconverted to the proper order.

As usual, if you are running this program across the network, you can use the WinDump or Analyzer programs to watch the individual packets. By comparing the packet data bytes in network byte order from the BinaryNetworkOrder program against the Analyzer trace packets, you can see what data values are sent in which packets.

In my sample trace, the TCP data bytes show that the network byte order values test2 (00 04 CB 2F) and test3 (FF FF 8F B7 79 F1 CE 14) were sent in the same TCP packet. (Compare these values to those in the Listing 7.8 Binary Network ByteOrder output.) When these values are received, they are converted back to host byte order to retrieve the original values.

Moving Complex Objects

Now that you can send individual binary data values to a remote host, you may be wondering about the next step: sending groups of values across the network to a remote host. This section describes how to send groups of data as a single element to a remote device and how to decode the data back and retrieve the proper data values on the other end.

Creating a Collective Data Class

One common way to move groups of multiple data values between systems on a network is to create a class that contains all the data, along with a specific method for converting the data into a byte array. The basic class contains variables for the data elements used in the communication. For example:

```
class Employee
{
    public int EmployeeID;
    public string LastName;
    public string FirstName;
    public int YearsService;
    public double Salary;

    public int LastNameSize;
    public int FirstNameSize;
    public int size;
}
```

Here, the class Employee can be considered similar to a record, with the variables representing the fields in the record. Each instance of the class represents a record in the database.

Because the two string elements can have variable lengths, you should include additional elements to define the size of those elements. This is comparable to the variable text field methods shown in Chapter 5.

Eventually, a data element is created to hold the size of the total byte representation of the class instance—again a necessity because the class instance itself will be a variable length.

The GetBytes() Method

With the "collective" data class in place, you create a GetBytes() method for the class to help in converting all of the elements into a single byte array, suitable for sending out on the network. It looks like this:

```
public byte[] GetBytes()
{
   byte[] data = new byte[1024];
   int place = 0;
   Buffer.BlockCopy(BitConverter.GetBytes(EmployeeID), 0, data, place, 4);
   place += 4;
   Buffer.BlockCopy(BitConverter.GetBytes(LastName.Length), 0, data, place, 4);
   place += 4;
   Buffer.BlockCopy(Encoding.ASCII.GetBytes(LastName), 0,
      data, place, LastName.Length);
   place += LastName.Length;
   Buffer.BlockCopy(BitConverter.GetBytes(FirstName.Length),
      0, data, place, 4);
   place += 4;
   Buffer.BlockCopy(Encoding.ASCII.GetBytes(FirstName), 0,
      data, place, FirstName.Length);
   place += FirstName.Length;
   Buffer.BlockCopy(BitConverter.GetBytes(YearsService), 0, data, place, 4);
   place += 4;
   Buffer.BlockCopy(BitConverter.GetBytes(Salary), 0, data, place, 8);
   place += 8;
   size = place;
   return data;
}
```

The GetBytes() method performs three functions:

- It converts each element of the class to a byte array.

- It places all of the individual byte arrays into a single-byte array.

- It calculates the total size of the byte array.

By now you are familiar with the BitConverter methods to convert the various binary datatypes to byte arrays. What you may not be familiar with is the Buffer class's BlockCopy()

method. The `BlockCopy()` method allows you to copy an entire byte array into a location within another byte array. Here is the format of this method:

```
BlockCopy(byte[] array1, int start, byte[] array2, int offset, int size)
```

The *array1* parameter is the array to copy to *array2*. The starting location of the copy within *array1* is always the first byte. The `offset` within the second array changes after each item is added to the array. Each short integer value added takes up 2 bytes, and the double floating-point value takes up 8 bytes.

The unknowns are the two variable-length string values. This is where string-size elements from the class come in handy. Because you know how long the string instance is, you can use that value when placing it in the byte array, as illustrated in Figure 7.3.

FIGURE 7.3:

Placing data values within a byte array

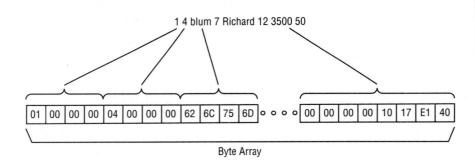

The idea is to drop each byte array into its proper place in the data array. Care must be taken when calculating the location to ensure that each value is placed in the correct order in the byte array. Once the byte array is completed, it is ready to be sent across the network.

The Constructors

There should be two constructor formats for the data class. One is the default constructor, used to manually enter values into the data elements. The other reads a byte array produced from the `GetBytes()` method and converts it back into a class instance:

```
public Employee()
{
}

public Employee(byte[] data)
```

```
{
    int place = 0;
    EmployeeID = BitConverter.ToInt32(data, place);
    place += 4;
    LastNameSize = BitConverter.ToInt32(data, place);
    place += 4;
    LastName = Encoding.ASCII.GetString(data, place, LastNameSize);
    place = place + LastNameSize;
    FirstNameSize = BitConverter.ToInt32(data, place);
    place += 4;
    FirstName = Encoding.ASCII.GetString(data, place, FirstNameSize);
    place += FirstNameSize;
    YearsService = BitConverter.ToInt32(data, place);
    place += 4;
    Salary = BitConverter.ToDouble(data, place);
}
```

The default constructor allows you to manually specify each of the data elements for a class instance, storing values in the instance. The second constructor format walks through the byte array and extracts each data element value. The variable-length string fields require the size parameters to help determine how many bytes are allocated for each string. Because the sizes were embedded into the byte array by the GetBytes() method, it is important to read each one and extract the proper number of bytes for the string.

The Whole Class Program
Putting all of the elements and methods together produces the Employee class file, Employee.cs, shown in Listing 7.11.

Listing 7.11   **The Employee.cs program**

```
using System;
using System.Text;

class Employee
{
    public int EmployeeID;
    private int LastNameSize;
    public string LastName;
    private int FirstNameSize;
    public string FirstName;
    public int YearsService;
    public double Salary;
    public int size;

    public Employee()
```

```csharp
    {
    }

    public Employee(byte[] data)
    {

        int place = 0;
        EmployeeID = BitConverter.ToInt32(data, place);
        place += 4;
        LastNameSize = BitConverter.ToInt32(data, place);
        place += 4;
        LastName = Encoding.ASCII.GetString(data, place, LastNameSize);
        place = place + LastNameSize;
        FirstNameSize = BitConverter.ToInt32(data, place);
        place += 4;
        FirstName = Encoding.ASCII.GetString(data, place, FirstNameSize);
        place += FirstNameSize;
        YearsService = BitConverter.ToInt32(data, place);
        place += 4;
        Salary = BitConverter.ToDouble(data, place);

    }

    public byte[] GetBytes()
    {

        byte[] data = new byte[1024];
        int place = 0;
        Buffer.BlockCopy(BitConverter.GetBytes(EmployeeID), 0, data, place, 4);
        place += 4;
        Buffer.BlockCopy(BitConverter.GetBytes(
            LastName.Length), 0, data, place, 4);
        place += 4;
        Buffer.BlockCopy(Encoding.ASCII.GetBytes(
            LastName), 0, data, place, LastName.Length);
        place += LastName.Length;
        Buffer.BlockCopy(BitConverter.GetBytes(
            FirstName.Length), 0, data, place, 4);
        place += 4;
        Buffer.BlockCopy(Encoding.ASCII.GetBytes(
            FirstName), 0, data, place, FirstName.Length);
        place += FirstName.Length;
        Buffer.BlockCopy(BitConverter.GetBytes(YearsService), 0, data, place, 4);
        place += 4;
        Buffer.BlockCopy(BitConverter.GetBytes(Salary), 0, data, place, 8);
        place += 8;
        size = place;
        return data;
    }
}
```

Because it is just a data container and can't run by itself, the `Employee.cs` program does not contain a `Main()` method. You can't compile the `Employee.cs` program by itself with the `csc` command. Instead, it must be compiled along with whatever programs use the `Employee` class.

Using Data Classes

Once the `Employee.cs` program is created, it's a snap to put it to work in client and server programs. Listing 7.12 shows a sample TCP client program that uses the `Employee` class to send employee information to the server.

Listing 7.12   The EmployeeClient.cs program

```
using System;
using System.Net;
using System.Net.Sockets;


class EmployeeClient
{
    public static void Main()
    {
        Employee emp1 = new Employee();
        Employee emp2 = new Employee();
        TcpClient client;

        emp1.EmployeeID = 1;
        emp1.LastName = "Blum";
        emp1.FirstName = "Katie Jane";
        emp1.YearsService = 12;
        emp1.Salary = 35000.50;

        emp2.EmployeeID = 2;
        emp2.LastName = "Blum";
        emp2.FirstName = "Jessica";
        emp2.YearsService = 9;
        emp2.Salary = 23700.30;

        try
        {
            client = new TcpClient("127.0.0.1", 9050);
        } catch (SocketException)
        {
            Console.WriteLine("Unable to connect to server");
            return;
        }
        NetworkStream ns = client.GetStream();

        byte[] data = emp1.GetBytes();
```

```
        int size = emp1.size;
        byte[] packsize = new byte[2];
        Console.WriteLine("packet size = {0}", size);
        packsize = BitConverter.GetBytes(size);
        ns.Write(packsize, 0, 2);
        ns.Write(data, 0, size);
        ns.Flush();

        data = emp2.GetBytes();
        size = emp2.size;
        packsize = new byte[2];
        Console.WriteLine("packet size = {0}", size);
        packsize = BitConverter.GetBytes(size);
        ns.Write(packsize, 0, 2);
        ns.Write(data, 0, size);
        ns.Flush();

        ns.Close();
        client.Close();
    }
  }
```

After two instances of the `Employee` class are created, data is entered into the data elements. The `GetByte()` method then converts the data into a byte array to send to the server. Before the byte array is sent, the size of the array is sent so the server knows how many bytes of data to read to complete the data package.

Similarly, the `EmployeeSrvr.cs` program, Listing 7.13, performs the server function using the `Employee` class.

Listing 7.13   **The EmployeeSrvr.cs program**

```
using System;
using System.Net;
using System.Net.Sockets;

class EmployeeSrvr
{
    public static void Main()
    {
        byte[] data = new byte[1024];
        TcpListener server = new TcpListener(9050);

        server.Start();
        TcpClient client = server.AcceptTcpClient();
        NetworkStream ns = client.GetStream();

        byte[] size = new byte[2];
        int recv = ns.Read(size, 0, 2);
        int packsize = BitConverter.ToInt16(size, 0);
```

```
Console.WriteLine("packet size = {0}", packsize);
recv = ns.Read(data, 0, packsize);

Employee emp1 = new Employee(data);
Console.WriteLine("emp1.EmployeeID = {0}", emp1.EmployeeID);
Console.WriteLine("emp1.LastName = {0}", emp1.LastName);
Console.WriteLine("emp1.FirstName = {0}", emp1.FirstName);
Console.WriteLine("emp1.YearsService = {0}", emp1.YearsService);
Console.WriteLine("emp1.Salary = {0}\n", emp1.Salary);

size = new byte[2];
recv = ns.Read(size, 0, 2);
packsize = BitConverter.ToInt16(size, 0);
data = new byte[packsize];
Console.WriteLine("packet size = {0}", packsize);
recv = ns.Read(data, 0, packsize);

Employee emp2 = new Employee(data);
Console.WriteLine("emp2.EmployeeID = {0}", emp2.EmployeeID);
Console.WriteLine("emp2.LastName = {0}", emp2.LastName);
Console.WriteLine("emp2.FirstName = {0}", emp2.FirstName);
Console.WriteLine("emp2.YearsService = {0}", emp2.YearsService);
Console.WriteLine("emp2.Salary = {0}", emp2.Salary);

ns.Close();
client.Close();
server.Stop();

    }
}
```

The EmployeeSrvr program reads 2 bytes from the network, then converts them into an integer size value. The size value represents how many bytes to read for the data package. Once the data package is read, it can be converted to an Employee class instance using the Employee constructor.

To compile both the EmployeeClient.cs and EmployeeSrvr.cs programs, you must also include the Employee.cs file:

```
csc EmployeeClient.cs Employee.cs
csc EmployeeSrvr.cs Employee.cs
```

After compiling the two programs, you can test them out by starting EmployeeSrvr in a command-prompt window and EmployeeClient program in either a separate command-prompt window or on a separate network client. The output from the EmployeeSrvr program should look like this:

```
C:\>EmployeeSrvr
packet size = 30
```

```
emp1.EmployeeID = 1
emp1.LastName = Blum
emp1.FirstName = Katie Jane
emp1.YearsService = 12
emp1.Salary = 35000.5

packet size = 27
emp2.EmployeeID = 2
emp2.LastName = Blum
emp2.FirstName = Jessica
emp2.YearsService = 9
emp2.Salary = 23700.3

C:\>
```

The client program successfully transferred the employee data for each instance to the server program.

NOTE You may have noticed that the Employee examples did not use the network byte order to transfer the data values. These programs will only work on like machines on the network. You can experiment with converting the byte values to network byte order in order to make the examples run on any platform on the network.

NOTE Note: What we just wrote is a *serializer*—it serializes a class into a binary stream. .NET offers its own serializers, and we'll cover them in Chapter 16, "Using .NET Remoting."

Summary

In this chapter, you explored the .NET helper classes that are used in creating network programs. Whereas the Socket class allows you to manually create network programs using traditional Unix network programming methods, the three classes in this chapter—TcpClient, TcpListener, and UdpClient—help you produce network programs with a minimum amount of coding. The TcpClient and TcpListener classes are used for creating TCP network programs, and the UDPClient class for UDP programs.

You must be able to make the sent data intelligible to the receiving system. Text data is usually not a problem, but there are particular challenges to sending binary data. The C# language offers many types of binary data that must be converted to a byte array before sending to a remote system. The BitConverter class does this work. Once the data is converted to a byte array, it can be transmitted across the network to a remote system using one of the network classes.

Not all systems use the same method of representing binary data. The order in which bytes of multibyte values are stored is crucial to interpreting the data. Systems that use the big endian storage method cannot immediately interpret data from systems that use the little endian method. Communicating the binary data accurately requires conversion to a generic network byte order before sending the data. On the remote system, the converted data must be decoded from network byte order to the local system's byte order.

Transmitting complex data classes across the network can also be difficult. The simplest method is to convert each data element individually into a byte array and combine the byte arrays into a single large-byte array for transmission. After the array is received, it must be reassembled back into the original data class.

CHAPTER 8

Asynchronous Sockets

- Windows event programming

- Working with events and delegates

- Using asynchronous sockets

- Using non-blocking sockets

- The Poll() method

- The Select() method

S o far, you have seen how to create network programs using sockets in blocking mode. Sockets in blocking mode will wait forever to complete their functions, holding up other functions within the application program until they complete. Many programs can work quite competently in this mode, but for applications that work in the Windows programming environment, this can be a problem.

Chapter 3, "C# Network Programming Classes," introduced the concept of asynchronous programming. Non-blocking programming is implemented with the asynchronous Socket methods, allowing a network program to continue rather than waiting for a network operation to be performed. In addition, you got a taste of asynchronous programming with the asynchronous DNS class methods in Chapter 4, "DNS and C#."

In this chapter, we'll look at asynchronous sockets in greater detail. We'll begin with a brief description of the Windows programming environment. You'll see how Windows event programming changes the way network programs operate. We'll discuss two ways to avoid using blocking sockets in your network applications:

- Using .NET asynchronous sockets
- Using traditional non-blocking socket methods

Each of these models has its own set of pros and cons to consider in terms of a Windows network application. The following sections describe the methods and processes used in both models, along with tips for employing them within your C# network programs.

Windows Event Programming

So far in this book, all but one of the network programming examples have used the console mode in .NET. Windows console-mode programming uses a traditional *structured programming* model. In structured programming, program flow is controlled within the program itself. Each method within the class is called in turn by the functions as they occur in the program execution. The customer does not have options for changing the program execution other than what is allowed by the program. By contrast, Windows programming uses an *event programming model*.

Windows event programming bases program flow on events. As events occur within the program, specific methods are called and performed based on the events, as illustrated in Figure 8.1. This does not work well with blocking network functions, however. When an application presents a graphical interface to a customer, it will wait for events from the customer to determine what functions to perform. Event programming assumes that while other functions are processing (such as network access), the customer will still have control over the graphical interface. This allows the customer to perform other functions while waiting for a network response, or even abort network connections if necessary. However, if the blocking network functions were used, program execution would wait while the function was performed, and the customer would have control over neither the interface nor the program.

FIGURE 8.1:

The Windows event programming model

Program Code

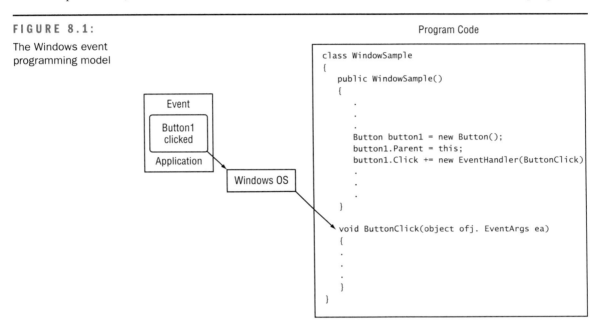

```
class WindowSample
{
    public WindowSample()
    {
        .
        .
        .
        Button button1 = new Button();
        button1.Parent = this;
        button1.Click += new EventHandler(ButtonClick)
        .
        .
        .
    }

    void ButtonClick(object ofj. EventArgs ea)
    {
        .
        .
        .
        .
    }
}
```

This section describes how Windows event programming is accomplished using C# constructs and how the .NET asynchronous network methods work within the Windows event programming model.

Using Events and Delegates

The .NET programming environment is closely tied to the Windows environment, so it is not surprising that .NET fully supports the event programming model. In .NET event programming, the two key constructs are the *events* and *delegates*.

An *event* is a message sent by an object that represents an action that has taken place. The message identifies the action and gives any useful data related to the action. Events can be anything from the customer clicking a button (where the message represents the button name), to a packet being received on a socket (where the message represents the socket that received the data). The event sender does not necessarily know what object will handle the event message once it is sent through the Windows system. It is up to the event receiver to register with the Windows system and inform it of what types of events the receiver wants to receive. Figure 8.2 demonstrates this function.

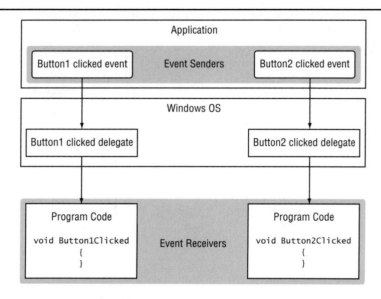

FIGURE 8.2:

Windows event senders and receivers

The event receiver is identified within the Windows system by a pointer class called a *delegate*. The delegate is a class that holds a reference to a method that can handle the received event. When Windows receives an event, it checks to see if any delegates are registered to handle it. If any delegates are registered to handle the event, the event message is passed to the methods defined by the delegates. After the methods complete, the Windows system processes the next event that occurs, until an event signals the end of the program.

Sample Event Program

Successful event programming is, of course, vital to writing successful Windows programs. Every object produced in a Windows graphical program can generate one or more events based on what the customer is doing with the object. The .NET Framework System.Windows.Forms namespace contains classes for all the Windows objects necessary to create full-featured graphical programs in the Windows environment. These include the following:

- Buttons
- Text boxes
- List boxes
- Combo boxes
- Check boxes
- Text labels

- Scroll bars
- Window menus

It's easy to create professional-quality network programs using these Windows objects. As each object is added to a Window form, you must register the method that will be used for its event handler. When the event is generated, Windows passes control of the program to the event handler method. Listing 8.1 demonstrates a simple Windows Forms program that uses some simple Windows objects.

Listing 8.1   **The WindowSample.cs program**

```
using System;
using System.Drawing;
using System.Windows.Forms;


class WindowSample  : Form:
{
   private TextBox data;
   private ListBox results;


   public WindowSample()
   {
      Text = "Sample Window Program";
      Size = new Size(400, 380);

      Label label1 = new Label();
      label1.Parent = this;
      label1.Text = "Enter text string:";
      label1.AutoSize = true;
      label1.Location = new Point(10, 10);

      data = new TextBox();
      data.Parent = this;
      data.Size = new Size(200, 2 * Font.Height);
      data.Location = new Point(10, 35);

      results = new ListBox();
      results.Parent = this;
      results.Location = new Point(10, 65);
      results.Size = new Size(350, 20 * Font.Height);

      Button checkit = new Button();
      checkit.Parent = this;
      checkit.Text = "test";
      checkit.Location = new Point(235,32);
      checkit.Size = new Size(7 * Font.Height, 2 * Font.Height);
      checkit.Click += new
```

```
            EventHandler(checkit_OnClick);

    }

    void checkit_OnClick(object obj, EventArgs ea)
    {
       results.Items.Add(data.Text);
       data.Clear();
    }

    public static void Main()
    {
       Application.Run(new WindowSample());
    }
 }
```

This sample program is pretty simplistic from the Forms point of view so you can focus on what it teaches you about event programming. First, remember that all Windows Forms programs must use the System.Windows.Forms namespace, along with the System.Drawing namespace, to help position objects in the window:

```
using System.Drawing;
using System.Windows.Forms;
```

Because the application creates a window, it must inherit the standard window Form class:

```
class WindowSample : Form
```

The constructor for the class must define all the graphical objects that are used in the form. First, the standard values for the Windows header and default size are defined:

```
Text = "Sample Window Program";
Size = new Size(400, 380);
```

Next, each object that will appear in the window is defined, along with its own properties. This example creates the following objects:

- A Label object to display an instructional text string

- A TextBox object to allow the customer to enter data

- A ListBox object to easily display output to the customer

- A Button object to allow the customer to control when the action will occur

The key to the action in this program is the EventHandler registered for the Button object, which registers the method ButtonOnClick() with a click event on the Button object checkit:

```
checkit.Click += new EventHandler(ButtonOnClick);
```

When the customer clicks the button, the program control moves to the `ButtonOnClick()` method:

```
void ButtonOnClick(object obj, EventArgs ea)
{
    results.Items.Add(data.Text);
    data.Clear();
}
```

This simple method performs only two functions. First it extracts the text string entered in the `TextBox` object and writes it to the `ListBox` object. Next, it clears the text in the `TextBox`. Each time the customer clicks the `Button` object, a new text string is placed in the `ListBox` as a new line. These simple Windows Forms programming objects will be utilized in a network programming example in the "Sample Programs Using Asynchronous Sockets" section later in this chapter.

NOTE When compiling a Windows Forms program, you should use the `csc` command compiler `/t:winexe` option, as follows: `csc /t:winexe WindowSample.cs`. This creates a Windows executable program, which does not needlessly open a command prompt window when it is run.

The AsyncCallback Class

Just as events can trigger delegates, .NET also provides a way for methods to trigger delegates. The .NET `AsyncCallback` class allows methods to start an asynchronous function and supply a delegate method to call when the asynchronous function completes.

This process is different from standard event programming in that the event is not generated from a Windows object, but rather from another method in the program. This method itself registers an `AsyncCallback` delegate to call when the method completes its function. As soon as this occurs and the method indicates its completion to the Windows OS, an event is triggered to transfer the program control to the method defined in the registered `AsyncCallback` delegate.

The `Socket` class utilizes the method defined in the `AsyncCallback` to allow network functions to operate asynchronously in background processing. It signals the OS when the network functions have completed and passes program control to the `AsyncCallback` method to finish the network function. In a Windows programming environment, these methods often help avoid the occurrence of an application lock-up while waiting for network functions to complete.

Using Asynchronous Sockets

The Socket object contains methods that utilize the AsyncCallback class to call completion methods when the network functions are finished. This allows the application to continue processing other events while waiting for network operations to complete their work.

The Socket asynchronous methods split common network programming functions into two pieces:

- A Begin method that starts the network function and registers the AsyncCallback method
- An End method that completes the function when the AsyncCallback method is called

Table 8.1 shows the asynchronous methods that are available to use with Socket objects. Each Begin method has an associated End method to complete the function.

TABLE 8.1:   .Net asynchronous Socket methods

Requests Started By...	Description of Request	Requests Ended BY...
BeginAccept()	To accept an incoming connection	EndAccept()
BeginConnect()	To connect to a remote host	EndConnect()
BeginReceive()	To retrieve data from a socket	EndReceive()
BeginReceiveFrom()	To retrieve data from a specific remote host	EndReceiveFrom()
BeginSend()	To send data from a socket	EndSend()
BeginSendTo()	To send data to a specific remote host	EndSendTo()

NOTE   Notice that these methods apply only to Socket objects. In .NET Framework release 1, the TcpClient, TcpListener, and UdpClient classes do not include asynchronous methods.

In this section, we'll walk through the process of using each of the asynchronous Socket methods to process network functions. Then we'll look at a couple of sample programs that put it all together.

Establishing the Connection

The method used to establish a connection with a remote host depends on whether the program is acting as a server (waiting for clients to connect to it) or a client (attempting to connect to a remote server). For servers, the BeginAccept() method should be used; for clients, the BeginConnect() method is used.

The BeginAccept() and EndAccept() Methods

To accept an incoming connection attempt from a remote client, you must use the BeginAccept() method. Its format is as follows:

```
IAsyncResult BeginAccept(AsyncCallback callback, object state)
```

The BeginAccept() method takes two parameters: the name of the AsyncCallback method used to complete the function, and a generic state object that can pass information between the asynchronous methods.

This is how the BeginAccept() method is typically used:

```
Socket sock = new Socket(AddressFamily.InterNetwork, SocketType.Stream,
    ProtocolType.Tcp);
IPEndPoint  iep = new IPEndPoint(IPAddress.Any, 9050);
sock.Bind(iep);
sock.Listen(5);
sock.BeginAccept(new AsyncCallback(CallAccept), sock);
```

This code snippet creates a Socket object and assigns it to a local IP address and TCP port to listen for incoming connections. The BeginAccpet() method defines the method used as the delegate to be used when a connection attempt is detected on the socket. The last parameter passed to the BeginAccept() method is the original Socket object created.

After the BeginAccept() method is finished, the AsyncCallback method defined will be called when a connection attempt occurs. The AsyncCallback method must include the EndAccept() method to finish the socket accept. Here is the format of the EndAccept() method:

```
Socket EndAccept(IAsyncResult iar);
```

The IAsyncResult object parameter passes the IAsyncResult value from the associated BeginAccept() method to the EndAccept() method—this is how the BeginAccept() and EndAccept() pairs are matched.

Similar to the synchronous Accept() method, the EndAccept() method returns a Socket object that is used for the new connection with the client. All further communication with the remote client should be done using this Socket object. A sample section from an EndAccept() AsyncCallback method would look like this:

```
private static void CallAccept(IAsyncResult iar)
{
    Socket server = (Socket)iar.AsyncState;
    Socket client = server.EndAccept(iar);
    .
    .
    .
}
```

The name of the `AsyncCallback` method must match the name used in the `BeginAccept()` method parameter. The first step in the method is to retrieve the original server socket. This is done using the `AsyncState` property of the `IAsyncResult` class. This property passes the original object placed in the `BeginAccept()` object parameter. Because it is defined as a generic object, it must be typecast into a `Socket` object.

After the original `Socket` object is retrieved, the `EndAccept()` method can obtain a new `Socket` object for the client connection. The `IAsyncResult` object parameter should be the same as that passed to the `AsyncCallback` method.

The client `Socket` object, once created, can be used just like any other `Socket` object, using either synchronous or asynchronous methods to read and write data to the socket.

In the end, the `BeginAccept()`/`EndAccept()` asynchronous pair produce the same results as the `Accept()` synchronous method. You will find that this is true of all the asynchronous `Begin()` and `End()` methods. This allows them to be used as direct replacements for the synchronous method calls in network programs that need asynchronous behavior.

The BeginConnect() and EndConnect() Methods

For a client application to connect to a remote server using asynchronous methods, you must use the `BeginConnect()` method. Its format is as follows:

```
IAsyncResult BeginConnect(EndPoint ep, AsyncCallback callback, Object state)
```

The first parameter passed to the `BeginConnect()` method is the `EndPoint` value of the remote host to connect to. Like the `BeginAccept()` method, the `BeginConnect()` method specifies the `AsyncCallback` method name of the delegate method to call when the connection is ready for completion. The last parameter is a state object that can be passed to the `EndConnect()` method to transfer necessary data.

Here is an example of `BeginConnect()` code:

```
Socket newsock = new Socket(AddressFamily.InterNetwork, SocketType.Stream,
    ProtocolType.Tcp);
IPEndPoint iep = new IPEndPoint(IPAddress.Parse("127.0.0.1"), 9050);
newsock.BeginConnect(iep, new AsyncCallback(Connected), newsock);
```

This code snippet creates a `Socket` object `newsock` and an `IPEndPoint` object `iep` for the remote host. The `BeginConnect()` method references the `AsyncCallback` method (`Connected`) and passes the original `Socket` object `newsock` to the `AsyncCallback` method.

When the connection is completed, the `AsyncCallback` method that was declared is called. The `AsyncCallback` method uses the `EndConnect()` method to complete the connection.

The format of the `EndConnect()` method is as follows:

```
EndConnect(IAsyncResult iar)
```

Here again, the IAsyncResult object specified pass the object value from the BeginConnect() method. It will be instantiated with the IAsyncResult object returned by the BeginConnect() method. A sample method to use this would look like the following:

```
public static void Connected(IAsyncResult iar)
{
    Socket sock = (Socket)iar.AsyncState;
    try
    {
       sock.EndConnect(iar);
    } catch (SocketException)
    {
       Console.WriteLine("Unable to connect to host");
    }
}
```

The first statement in the AsyncCallback method retrieves the original socket used for the BeginConnect() method call, using the AsyncState property of the IAsyncResult object passed to the AsyncCallback method.

After the original socket is recreated, the EndConnect() method is called, using the IAsyncResult object to point it back to the original BeginConnect() method. Because it is possible that the remote host will not be available, it is good practice to place the EndConnect() method in a try-catch block. If the EndConnect() method is unsuccessful, it will throw a SocketException error.

Sending and Receiving Data

After a connection is established, you will most likely want to send and receive data with the remote host. Asynchronous methods can also be used to do this.

The BeginSend() and EndSend() Methods

The BeginSend() method sends data to a connected socket. The format of this method is as follows:

```
IAsyncResult BeginSend(byte[] buffer, int offset, int size,
    SocketFlags sockflag, AsyncCallback callback, object state)
```

As you can see, there are plenty of parameters to use with the BeginSend() method. You may notice that most of them are similar to the synchronous Send() method. Walking through them, the first one is the byte array that contains the data you want sent. The offset parameter points to the location within the buffer parameter from which to start sending data, and the size parameter specifies how many bytes from the buffer parameter to send. Next, the sockflag parameter specifies any special socket flags that you want set for the communication. Finally, the AsyncCallback callback and state objects are specified, defining the method to call when the `BeginSend()` method succeeds and a state object to send information to the `EndSend()` method.

A sample `BeginSend()` method would look like this:

```
sock.BeginSend(data, 0, data.Length, SocketFlags.None,
   new AsyncCallback(SendData), sock);
```

This example sends the entire *data* buffer and calls the `SendData()` method when the socket is ready to send the data. The *sock* Socket object is passed to the `AsynCallback()` method.

The `EndSend()` method completes the sending of the data. The format for this method is as follows, where the `IAsyncResult` parameter defines an empty object that references the result of the `BeginSend()` method call:

```
int EndSend(IAsyncResult iar)
```

The `EndSend()` method returns the number of bytes successfully sent from the socket.

Here's an example of the `EndSend()` `AsyncCallback` method:

```
private static void SendData(IAsyncResult iar)
{
   Socket server = (Socket)iar.AsyncState;
   int sent = server.EndSend(iar);
}
```

The original *sock* socket is re-created using the `AsyncState` property of the `IAsyncResult` object passed to the `AsyncCallback` method. Again, this relates to the state object specified in the `BeginSend()` method.

The BeginSendTo() and EndSendTo() Methods

The `BeginSendTo()` method is used with connectionless sockets to start an asynchronous data transmission to a remote host. The format of the `BeginSendTo()` method is as follows:

```
IAsyncResult BeginSendTo(byte[] buffer, int offset, int size,
   SocketFlags sockflag, EndPoint ep, AsyncCallback callback, object state)
```

As you can see, for the most part the `BeginSendTo()` method format is similar to the `SendTo()` method format, with the asynchronous features of the `BeginSend()` method added. The `BeginSendTo()` method allows you to specify the `EndPoint` object of the remote host to which to send the message.

Sample s`BeginSendTo()` code would look like this:

```
IPEndPoint iep = new IPEndPoint(IPAddress.Parse("192.168.1.6"), 9050);
sock.BeginSendTo(data, 0, data.Length, SocketFlags.None, iep,
   new AsynCallback(SendDataTo), sock);
```

Again, the only difference between this call and the `BeginSend()` call is the `IPEndPoint` of the remote host added to the parameters.

The `EndSendTo()` method uses the standard format of End methods:

```
int EndSendTo(IAsyncResult iar)
```

As always, the `IAsyncResult` parameter accepts the `IAsyncResult` value returned by the `BeginSendTo()` method. The `EndSendTo()` method returns the number of bytes sent out from the socket.

The BeginReceive() and EndReceive() Methods

The `BeginReceive()` method accepts data from a remote host on a socket. The format for this method is as follows:

```
IAsyncResult BeginReceive(byte[] buffer, int offset, int size,
    SocketFlags sockflag, AsyncCallback callback, object state)
```

The first parameter is a byte array that accepts the incoming data. The *offset* and *size* parameters are used to specify where in the buffer to start placing the data, and how large the buffer is. The *sockflags* parameter sets any needed socket flags for the communication. The *callback* and *state* parameters allows you to pass information to the `EndReceive()` method.

Here's a sample `BeginReceive()` method call:

```
sock.BeginReceive(data, 0, data.Length, SocketFlags.None,
    new AsyncCallback(ReceivedData), sock);
```

The `BeginReceive()` method passes the original socket to the `EndReceive()` method so that it can re-create the socket for the `AsyncCallback` method. The `AsyncCallback` method used for the `EndReceive()` method would look like this:

```
void ReceivedData(IAsyncResult iar)
{
    Socket remote = (Socket)iar.AsyncState;
    int recv = remote.EndReceive(iar);
    string receivedData = Encoding.ASCII.GetString(data, 0, recv);
    Console.WriteLine(stringData);
}
```

You see the same `AsyncCallback` behavior again: the first statement recreates the original socket from the `IAsyncResult` object. The second statement uses the socket to finish the socket receive, via the `EndReceive()` method call. Incoming data is placed in the data buffer specified in the corresponding `BeginReceive()` method call. To access the data buffer from the `AsyncCallback` method, you must ensure that it is accessible from both methods (such as using a global variable or data class).

The BeginReceiveFrom() and EndReceiveFrom() Methods

The `BeginReceiveFrom()` method accepts data from any remote host on a connectionless socket. Here is the format:

```
IAsyncResult BeginReceiveFrom(byte[] buffer, int offset, int size,
    SocketFlags sockflag, ref EndPoint ep, AsyncCallback callback, object state)
```

Notice that the `BeginReceiveFrom()` method is similar to the `BeginReceive()` method, except that it specifies a reference to an `EndPoint` object. The `EndPoint` object defines the remote host IP address and port number that sent the data.

> **WARNING** Remember that the `BeginReceiveFrom()` method uses a reference to an `EndPoint` object, not the object itself. It's easy to forget that `ref` keyword and thus have a problem on your hands.

A sample `BeginReceiveFrom()` method would look like this:

```
sock.BeginReceive(data, 0, data.Length, SocketFlags.None, ref iep, new
AsyncCallback(ReceiveData), sock);
```

The corresponding `EndReceiveFrom()` method is placed in the appropriate `AsyncCallback` method:

```
void ReceiveData(IasyncResult iar)
{
    Socket remote = (Socket)iar.AsyncState;
    int recv = remote.EndReceiveFrom(iar);
    string stringData = Encoding.ASCII.GetString(data, 0, recv);
    Console.WriteLine(stringData);
}
```

The `EndReceiveFrom()` method returns the number of bytes read from the socket and places the received data in the data buffer defined in the `BeginReceiveFrom()` method. Again, if you need to access this data within the `AsyncCallback` method, you should ensure that the data buffer is accessible from both methods.

Sample Programs Using Asynchronous Sockets

Now that you have studied all the pieces, it's time to put them together and create a set of real Windows asynchronous network programs. The following two programs recreate the `SimpleTcpSrvr` and `SimpleTcpClient` programs (Listings 5.1 and 5.2, respectively) introduced in Chapter 5, "Connection-Oriented Sockets," but this time they use asynchronous network methods.

The Client Program

The `AsyncTcpClient.cs` program (Listing 8.2) uses the .NET Windows Forms library to create a Windows GUI environment for a simple TCP client. In a Windows environment, it is important that the program respond to Windows events from the user, as well as from the network

Listing 8.2   **The AsyncTcpClient.cs program**

```csharp
using System;
using System.Drawing;
using System.Net;
using System.Net.Sockets;
using System.Text;
using System.Windows.Forms;


class AsyncTcpClient  :  Form:
{
    private TextBox newText;
    private TextBox conStatus;
    private ListBox results;
    private Socket client;
    private byte[] data = new byte[1024];
    private int size = 1024;

    public AsyncTcpClient()
    {
        Text = "Asynchronous TCP Client";
        Size = new Size(400, 380);

        Label label1 = new Label();
        label1.Parent = this;
        label1.Text = "Enter text string:";
        label1.AutoSize = true;
        label1.Location = new Point(10, 30);

        newText = new TextBox();
        newText.Parent = this;
        newText.Size = new Size(200, 2 * Font.Height);
        newText.Location = new Point(10, 55);

        results = new ListBox();
        results.Parent = this;
        results.Location = new Point(10, 85);
        results.Size = new Size(360, 18 * Font.Height);

        Label label2 = new Label();
```

```
    label2.Parent = this;
    label2.Text = "Connection Status:";
    label2.AutoSize = true;
    label2.Location = new Point(10, 330);

    conStatus = new TextBox();
    conStatus.Parent = this;
    conStatus.Text = "Disconnected";
    conStatus.Size = new Size(200, 2 * Font.Height);
    conStatus.Location = new Point(110, 325);

    Button sendit = new Button();
    sendit.Parent = this;
    sendit.Text = "Send";
    sendit.Location = new Point(220,52);
    sendit.Size = new Size(5 * Font.Height, 2 * Font.Height);
    sendit.Click += new EventHandler(ButtonSendOnClick);

    Button connect = new Button();
    connect.Parent = this;
    connect.Text = "Connect";
    connect.Location = new Point(295, 20);
    connect.Size = new Size(6 * Font.Height, 2 * Font.Height);
    connect.Click += new EventHandler(ButtonConnectOnClick);

    Button discon = new Button();
    discon.Parent = this;
    discon.Text = "Disconnect";
    discon.Location = new Point(295,52);
    discon.Size = new Size(6 * Font.Height, 2 * Font.Height);
    discon.Click += new EventHandler(ButtonDisconOnClick);
}

void ButtonConnectOnClick(object obj, EventArgs ea)
{
    conStatus.Text = "Connecting...";
    Socket newsock = new Socket(AddressFamily.InterNetwork,
                         SocketType.Stream, ProtocolType.Tcp);
    IPEndPoint iep = new IPEndPoint(IPAddress.Parse("127.0.0.1"), 9050);
    newsock.BeginConnect(iep, new AsyncCallback(Connected), newsock);
}

void ButtonSendOnClick(object obj, EventArgs ea)
{
    byte[] message = Encoding.ASCII.GetBytes(newText.Text);
    newText.Clear();
    client.BeginSend(message, 0, message.Length, SocketFlags.None,
             new AsyncCallback(SendData), client);
}

void ButtonDisconOnClick(object obj, EventArgs ea)
{
    client.Close();
```

```
      conStatus.Text = "Disconnected";
   }

   void Connected(IAsyncResult iar)
   {
      client = (Socket)iar.AsyncState;
      try
      {
         client.EndConnect(iar);
         conStatus.Text = "Connected to: " + client.RemoteEndPoint.ToString();
         client.BeginReceive(data, 0, size, SocketFlags.None,
                     new AsyncCallback(ReceiveData), client);
      } catch (SocketException)
      {
         conStatus.Text = "Error connecting";
      }
   }

   void ReceiveData(IAsyncResult iar)
   {
      Socket remote = (Socket)iar.AsyncState;
      int recv = remote.EndReceive(iar);
      string stringData = Encoding.ASCII.GetString(data, 0, recv);
      results.Items.Add(stringData);
   }

   void SendData(IAsyncResult iar)
   {
      Socket remote = (Socket)iar.AsyncState;
      int sent = remote.EndSend(iar);
      remote.BeginReceive(data, 0, size, SocketFlags.None,
                  new AsyncCallback(ReceiveData), remote);
   }

   public static void Main()
   {
      Application.Run(new AsyncTcpClient());
   }
}
```

The class constructor creates the window objects for the program. For this simple client program, the following objects are created:

- A Label object and a TextBox object; these allow the customer to input text messages to send to the remote host

- A ListBox object to display the messages returned by the remote host

- A Label object and a TextBox object to display the connection status of the client program

- Three Button objects; one for establishing a new TCP connection to a remote host, one for sending the text message and receiving a reply, and one for disconnecting the TCP session.

Each object is placed using the `Point` class and sized using the `Size` class; both of these classes are from the `System.Drawing` namespace. You can experiment with these values to get a feel for manually locating the objects on the Window form.

> **NOTE** If you have one of the Microsoft Visual products, such as Visual Studio or Visual C#, you can place all the Window objects using the graphical editing environment and allow the Form code to be generated automatically for you.

The Client Program Flow

You may notice that there is no network programming code at all in the class constructor. All of the network functions happen within `EventHandler()` methods. To get the `AsyncTcpClient` program to perform the same way as the original `SimpleTcpClient` program, you must first determine how to link the program protocol with the asynchronous events that will be triggered in the program. Then you must program them into the Windows event code methods. The diagram in Figure 8.3 shows each of the required methods and how they interact with the Windows event code. The following paragraphs describe the steps accomplished by the sample client program: connecting, receiving, sending, and disconnecting.

FIGURE 8.3:

Diagramming the asynchronous events

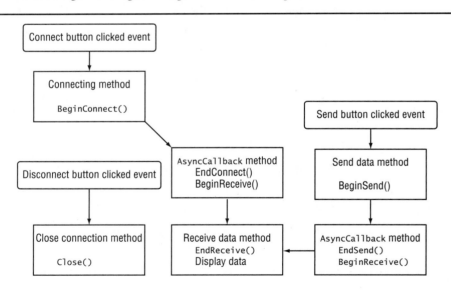

Connecting

As seen in the figure, when the customer clicks the Connect button, the method used to start the connection is performed. In the program code, this is the `ButtonConnectOnClick()` method:

```
void ButtonConnectOnClick(object obj, EventArgs ea)
```

```
{
    conStatus.Text = "Connecting...";
    Socket newsock = new Socket(AddressFamily.InterNetwork, SocketType.Stream,
        ProtocolType.Tcp);
    IPEndPoint iep = new IPEndPoint(IPAddress.Parse("127.0.0.1"), 9050);
    newsock.BeginConnect(iep, new AsyncCallback(Connected), newsock);
}
```

The `ButtonConnectOnClick()` method creates a new `Socket` object for the communication. Then it starts the `BeginConnect()` method with the address information of the remote host, the name of the associated `AsyncCallback` method, and the newly created `Socket` object. When this method finishes processing, Windows waits for the `BeginConnect()` method to trigger its event, which indicates that a connection is established with the remote host. When this occurs, program control is passed to the `Connected()` method:

```
void Connected(IAsyncResult iar)
{
    client = (Socket)iar.AsyncState;
    try
    {
        client.EndConnect(iar);
        conStatus.Text = "Connected to: " + client.RemoteEndPoint.ToString();
        client.BeginReceive(data, 0, size, SocketFlags.None,
            new AsyncCallback(ReceiveData), client);
    } catch (SocketException)
    {
        conStatus.Text = "Error connecting";
    }
}
```

The first thing that must be done in the `Connected()` method is to retrieve the original `Socket` object used for the connection. The `AsyncState` property of the `IAsyncResult` class returns the object passed to the `AsyncCallback` method, which in the case of the `BeginConnect()` method was the newly created `Socket` object.

After the `Socket` object is recreated, the `EndConnect()` method can be performed. Because it is possible that the `EndConnect()` method could fail (for instance, if the remote host is unavailable), it is a good idea to place it in a `try-catch` block. Should `EndConnect()` fail, you can notify the customer through the *conStatus* TextBox object.

In this program protocol, the first thing the server does after the connection is established is to send a welcome banner. To accommodate this, the `AsyncTcpClient` program must be prepared to accept an incoming message immediately after establishing the connection. This is done by using a `BeginReceive()` method call at the end of the `Connected()` method.

Receiving Data

After a new connection, and after every sent message, a `ReceiveData()` method is performed. The `BeginReceive()` method declares the `ReceiveData()` method, the `AsyncCallback` method that's used when the data is received:

```
void ReceiveData(IAsyncResult iar)
{
    Socket remote = (Socket)iar.AsyncState;
    int recv = remote.EndReceive(iar);
    string stringData = Encoding.ASCII.GetString(data, 0, recv);
    results.Items.Add(stringData);
}
```

Again, the first statement recreates the communication socket. After the original socket is recreated, the `EndReceive()` method is used, referencing the original `IAsyncResult` object, which pairs it with the original `BeginReceive()` method call. When the message is received from the remote host, it is placed in the data buffer referenced in the `BeginReceive()` method call. Because the data variable was defined as a global variable, it is used within this method to place the message in the *results* ListBox.

Sending Data

After entering a message in the `TextBox` object to send to the remote host, the customer clicks the Send button, and the `SendData()` method is performed. The `EventHandler` for the button points to the `ButtonSendOnClick()` method:

```
void ButtonSendOnClick(object obj, EventArgs ea)
{
    byte[] message = Encoding.ASCII.GetBytes(newText.Text);
    newText.Clear();
    client.BeginSend(message, 0, message.Length, SocketFlags.None,
      new AsyncCallback(SendData), client);
}
```

The message is extracted from the `TextBox` object, converted to a byte array, and sent out the socket. Because the `ButtonSendOnClick()` method does not have the original `Socket` object passed to it, it needs to use a class member to reference the connected socket. The `BeginSend()` method is used on the connected socket. It specifies the message and the `AsyncCallback` method to call when the `BeginSend()` function is ready to complete, along with an object to pass to the `EndSend()` method. In this case, it is the connected socket.

The `AsyncCallback` method, `SendData()`, is triggered when the socket indicates it is ready to send the message:

```
void SendData(IAsyncResult iar)
{
    Socket remote = (Socket)iar.AsyncState;
    int sent = remote.EndSend(iar);
```

```
        remote.BeginReceive(data, 0, size, SocketFlags.None,
          new AsyncCallback(ReceiveData), remote);
    }
```

Once again, you see the familiar behavior: the original connected socket is recreated using the `AsyncState` of the state object passed from the `BeginSend()` method. When the original socket is recreated, the `EndSend()` method completes the data transmission. The `IAsyncResult` object pairs the `EndSend()`to the original `BeginSend()` and `EndSend()`returns the number of bytes that were actually sent out from the socket.

In this application, after a message is sent, the server is expected to echo it back. Knowing this, the `BeginReceive()` method is called to start the receiving process. `BeginReceive()`again calls the same `ReadData()` method, just as it did to receive the original connection's welcome banner.

Disconnecting

Now that you have the wonders of event programming at your disposal, you can finally create a button to control the disconnect from the remote host (rather than having to define a control word to stop the client). Here's how that works:

```
void ButtonDisconOnClick(object obj, EventArgs ea)
{
    client.Close();
    conStatus.Text = "Disconnected";
}
```

By issuing the `Close()` method for the client socket, the connection is disconnected. To establish a new connection, the customer can click the Connect button.

WARNING There are lots of things that can go wrong with this simple client example, including the customer's clicking the wrong button at the wrong time. A real-world production application should check each time a button is clicked to ensure that the function can be performed.

Testing the Asynchronous Client

Because the `AsyncTcpClient` program followed the same protocol model as the `SimpleTcpClient` program in Chapter 5, you can use the `SimpleTcpSrvr` program to test the new asynchronous version.

1. Start `SimpleTcpSrvr` in a command-prompt window on the appropriate server.

2. Start the `AsyncTcpClient` program, either in a separate command prompt window or on another network device.

3. Click the Connect button. The status window should show that the client has connected to the server, and the server's welcome banner should be echoed back to the list box, as shown in Figure 8.4.

The `AsyncTcpClient`
program, with server's
welcome banner
showing in the list box

4. After the original connection, try sending messages from the text box to the server program by clicking the Send button. Each message will be displayed in the `SimpleTcpSrvr` console on the server and echoed in the list box in the `AsyncTcpClient` program.

5. To stop the connection, click the Disconnect button. The `SimpleTcpSrvr` program will properly terminate, and the status text box in the `AsyncTcpClient` program will show that the client is disconnected from the server.

The Server Program

Now that you have moved the client program into the Windows world, it is time to tackle the server program. Listing 8.3 shows the `AsyncTcpSrvr.cs` program, which mimics the functionality of the `SimpleTcpSrvr` program (Listing 5.1) from Chapter 5 but uses a Windows Forms environment and asynchronous sockets.

Listing 8.3   The AsyncTcpSrvr.cs program

```
using System;
using System.Drawing;
using System.Net;
using System.Net.Sockets;
using System.Text;
```

```csharp
using System.Windows.Forms;


class AsyncTcpSrvr : Form
{
    private TextBox conStatus;
    private ListBox results;
    private byte[] data = new byte[1024];
    private int size = 1024;
    private Socket server;


    public AsyncTcpSrvr()
    {
        Text = "Asynchronous TCP Server";
        Size = new Size(400, 380);

        results = new ListBox();
        results.Parent = this;
        results.Location = new Point(10, 65);
        results.Size = new Size(350, 20 * Font.Height);

        Label label1 = new Label();
        label1.Parent = this;
        label1.Text = "Text received from client:";
        label1.AutoSize = true;
        label1.Location = new Point(10, 45);

        Label label2 = new Label();
        label2.Parent = this;
        label2.Text = "Connection Status:";
        label2.AutoSize = true;
        label2.Location = new Point(10, 330);

        conStatus = new TextBox();
        conStatus.Parent = this;
        conStatus.Text = "Waiting for client...";
        conStatus.Size = new Size(200, 2 * Font.Height);
        conStatus.Location = new Point(110, 325);

        Button stopServer = new Button();
        stopServer.Parent = this;
        stopServer.Text = "Stop Server";
        stopServer.Location = new Point(260,32);
        stopServer.Size = new Size(7 * Font.Height, 2 * Font.Height);
        stopServer.Click += new EventHandler(ButtonStopOnClick);

        server = new Socket(AddressFamily.InterNetwork,
                    SocketType.Stream, ProtocolType.Tcp);
        IPEndPoint iep = new IPEndPoint(IPAddress.Any, 9050);
        server.Bind(iep);
        server.Listen(5);
```

```
        server.BeginAccept(new AsyncCallback(AcceptConn), server);
    }

    void ButtonStopOnClick(object obj, EventArgs ea)
    {
        Close();
    }

    void AcceptConn(IAsyncResult iar)
    {
        Socket oldserver = (Socket)iar.AsyncState;
        Socket client = oldserver.EndAccept(iar);
        conStatus.Text = "Connected to: " + client.RemoteEndPoint.ToString();
        string stringData = "Welcome to my server";
        byte[] message1 = Encoding.ASCII.GetBytes(stringData);
        client.BeginSend(message1, 0, message1.Length, SocketFlags.None,
                new AsyncCallback(SendData), client);
    }

    void SendData(IAsyncResult iar)
    {
        Socket client = (Socket)iar.AsyncState;
        int sent = client.EndSend(iar);
        client.BeginReceive(data, 0, size, SocketFlags.None,
                new AsyncCallback(ReceiveData), client);
    }

    void ReceiveData(IAsyncResult iar)
    {
        Socket client = (Socket)iar.AsyncState;
        int recv = client.EndReceive(iar);
        if (recv == 0)
        {
            client.Close();
            conStatus.Text = "Waiting for client...";
            server.BeginAccept(new AsyncCallback(AcceptConn), server);
            return;
        }
        string receivedData = Encoding.ASCII.GetString(data, 0, recv);
        results.Items.Add(receivedData);
        byte[] message2 = Encoding.ASCII.GetBytes(receivedData);
        client.BeginSend(message2, 0, message2.Length, SocketFlags.None,
                new AsyncCallback(SendData), client);
    }

    public static void Main()
    {
        Application.Run(new AsyncTcpSrvr());
    }
}
```

Just as the client program does, the AsyncTcpSrvr program uses basic Windows Forms objects to create the customer graphical environment:

- A Label object and a ListBox object to identify the data received from the connected client
- A Label object and a TextBox object to display the status of the socket and the connected client
- A Button object to allow the customer to stop the server and exit the program

After creating the customer interface, you must code the network programming part. Unlike the client program, the AsyncTcpSrvr program includes network programming code that must be done in the class constructor.

The Server Program Flow

Like its counterpart SimpleTcpSrvr in Chapter 5, the AsyncTcpSrvr program must follow a set procedure for communicating with remote clients. Figure 8.5 diagrams the steps required for the server.

FIGURE 8.5:

The AsyncTcpSrvr
processes

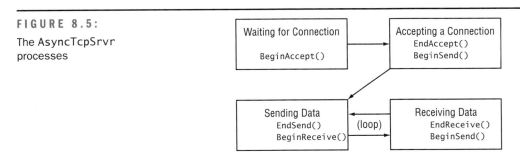

Waiting for New Client Connections

Because you know that the server must immediately listen for incoming connections, the required network programming code is added to the class constructor after the Forms objects have been created:

```
server = new Socket(AddressFamily.InterNetwork, SocketType.Stream,
    ProtocolType.Tcp);
IPEndPoint iep = new IPEndPoint(IPAddress.Any, 9050);
server.Bind(iep);
server.Listen(5);
server.BeginAccept(new AsyncCallback(AcceptConn), server);
```

By now, you should recognize this as standard server socket code: creating a new Socket object, binding it to a local IPEndPoint object, and listening for new connection attempts.

The `BeginAccept()` method specifies the `AsyncCallback` method to use when a connection is received, and the object to pass to the `AsyncCallback` method.

When a connection attempt is detected, the `AsyncCallback` method registered with the `BeginAccept()` method is performed:

```
void AcceptConn(IAsyncResult iar)
{
    Socket oldserver = (Socket)iar.AsyncState;
    Socket client = oldserver.EndAccept(iar);
    conStatus.Text = "Connected to: " + client.RemoteEndPoint.ToString();
    string stringData = "Welcome to my server";
    byte[] message1 = Encoding.ASCII.GetBytes(stringData);
    client.BeginSend(message1, 0, message1.Length, SocketFlags.None,
        new AsyncCallback(SendData), client);
}
```

The `AsyncCallback` method recreates the original `Socket` object using the `AsyncState` property of the `IAsyncResult` object. When the `EndAccept()` method is called, it uses the `IAsyncResult` object to pair it up with the calling `BeginAccept()` method. The `EndAccept()` method returns a new `Socket` object to be used for all communication with the remote client.

As reflected in the program flow diagram, the next step for the server is to send a welcome banner to the client. This requires the `BeginSend()` method, which registers an `AsyncCallback` method to complete the send operation when the socket is ready to send out data.

WARNING Note that the Socket object passed to the `AsyncCallback` method is the newly created client socket, not the original server socket. This is the socket that is connected to the remote client, and it should be used for all communications with that client.

Sending Data

The `EndSend()` method is found in the `AsyncCallback` method registered in the `BeginSend()` method:

```
void SendData(IAsyncResult iar)
{
    Socket client = (Socket)iar.AsyncState;
    int sent = client.EndSend(iar);
    client.BeginReceive(data, 0, size, SocketFlags.None,
        new AsyncCallback(ReceiveData), client);
}
```

This sample program uses the standard `EndSend()` format. A good-quality production program would also compare this value with the original byte count of the sent message and perform the `BeginSend()` method again if some of the message were not properly sent.

The server program flow model specifies that after the welcome banner is sent, the server should wait for an incoming message from the client. This is accomplished with the BeginReceive() method, which specifies a data buffer in which to place the received data, along with the AsyncCallback method to call when the data is received.

Receiving Data

The EndReceive() method is placed in the AsyncCallback method for the BeginReceive() method:

```
void ReceiveData(IAsyncResult iar)
{
    Socket client = (Socket)iar.AsyncState;
    int recv = client.EndReceive(iar);
    if (recv == 0)
    {
        client.Close();
        conStatus.Text = "Waiting for client...";
        server.BeginAccept(new AsyncCallback(AcceptConn), server);
        return;
    }
    string receivedData = Encoding.ASCII.GetString(data, 0, recv);
    results.Items.Add(receivedData);
    byte[] message2 = Encoding.ASCII.GetBytes(receivedData);
    client.BeginSend(message2, 0, message2.Length, SocketFlags.None, new
AsyncCallback(SendData), client);
}
```

The ReceiveData() method is a little lengthier than the others because it has to accommodate two scenarios in the program flow. First, as always, the client socket is recreated using the standard AsyncState property. Next, the EndReceive() method is called using the IAsyncResult object to pair it up with the appropriate BeginReceive() method. EndReceive()returns the number of bytes received from the socket. As stated earlier, a real-time production program would check the number of bytes received against an expected message size.

If the received message size is zero bytes, it is assumed that the remote client has disconnected the TCP session. In that case, the client socket is closed, and the server can start listening for a new client connection by using the BeginAccept() method and starting the whole program flow all over again.

If a message has been received from the remote client, it must be displayed in the ListBox object and echoed back to the client. This is done by using the BeginSend() method again. Because the program flow now duplicates the original flow from sending the welcome banner, the original SendData() method is used for this AsyncCallback method as well.

Testing the Programs Together

The AsyncTcpSrvr program can be tested with either the AsyncTcpClient program or the original SimpleTcpClient program from Chapter 5:

1. Start both the AsyncTcpClient and SimpleTcpClient programs, either from command-prompt windows or from Windows Explorer.

2. When AsyncTcpClient starts, click the Connect button. Both the server and client programs will indicate that a connection has been established and show the address of the remote host. Figure 8.6 shows the output window of AsyncTcpSrvr after a client has connected.

FIGURE 8.6:

The AsyncTcpSrvr program window

3. Send a message from the AsyncTcpClient. Each time a message is sent using the AsyncTcpClient program, it should appear in the AsyncTcpSrvr list box and be echoed back to the AsyncClient list box.

4. To close the connection, click the Disconnect button on the client program. Immediately after disconnecting the current client, the AsyncTcpSrvr program waits for a new client connection attempt.

Using Non-blocking Socket Methods

Asynchronous sockets have been created specifically for the Windows environment. As explained in Chapter 3, traditional Unix network programming does not use asynchronous sockets. Instead, programs contain non-blocking socket *methods* that check a socket without actually committing to a blocking function. This allows the program to continue executing even if the network operation would normally block the program. If the socket is determined to be ready for the network function, the blocking function is performed.

The .NET Sockets library includes non-blocking socket methods found in the Unix socket library. This allows network programmers to easily port Unix network programs to the Windows environment. This section describes the Poll() and Select() methods that are used to determine whether a network function would block and to help network applications avoid getting stuck on a blocking network function.

The Poll() Method

Often, when you're attempting to perform a blocking network function such as a Receive() command, you need to have the capability of checking the socket before committing to the command.

The Socket method Poll() gives you just that. It checks a Socket object to see whether a network method call would block or be successfully completed. If the poll indicates that the method would execute without blocking, you're home free. Otherwise, you can perform some other functions and check again at a later time.

The format of the Poll() method is simple:

```
bool Poll(int microseconds, SelectMode mode);
```

It returns a simple boolean value: true if the action would complete, or false if the action would block.

The *int* parameter allows you to set the amount of time (in microseconds) the Poll() method will wait and watch the socket for the indicated events. Use the *SelectMode* parameter to specify what type of action to watch for. The SelectMode class enumerates three possible events for the Poll() method to monitor:

SelectRead   The SelectRead value for SelectMode will cause the Poll()to return a true value under the following conditions:

- If an Accept() method call would succeed
- If data is available on the socket
- If the connection has been closed

SelectWrite   The `SelectWrite` value for `SelectMode` will cause the `Poll()`to return a true value under the following conditions:

- If a `Connect()` method call has succeeded
- If data can be sent on the socket

SelectError   The `SelectError` value for `SelectMode` will cause the `Poll()` method to return a `true` value under the following conditions:

- If a `Connect()` method call has failed
- If out-of-band data is available *and* the `Socket OutOfBandInline` property has not been set.

You can check the return value of the `Poll()` method to determine if a socket is ready for a blocking function or not, based on the `SelectMode` value set. The resulting `Poll()` method call would look like this:

```
result = sock.Poll(1000000, SelectMode.SelectRead);
```

The `Socket` object, `sock`, would be checked for 1,000,000 microseconds (one second) to determine if data is present on the socket. If the return value is `true`, a `Receive()` method will complete successfully without blocking.

A Sample Poll() Program

The `TcpPollSrvr.cs` program, Listing 8.4, demonstrates the `Poll()` method at work in a server program.

Listing 8.4   **The TcpPollSrvr.cs program**

```
using System;
using System.Net;
using System.Net.Sockets;
using System.Text;

class TcpPollSrvr
{
    public static void Main()
    {
        int recv;
        byte[] data = new byte[1024];
        IPEndPoint ipep = new IPEndPoint(IPAddress.Any,
                            9050);

        Socket newsock = new
            Socket(AddressFamily.InterNetwork,
                    SocketType.Stream, ProtocolType.Tcp);

        newsock.Bind(ipep);
```

```csharp
newsock.Listen(10);
Console.WriteLine("Waiting for a client...");
bool result;
int i = 0;
while(true)
{
    i++;
    Console.WriteLine("polling for accept#{0}...", i);
    result = newsock.Poll(1000000, SelectMode.SelectRead);
    if (result)
    {
        break;
    }
}
Socket client = newsock.Accept();

IPEndPoint newclient =
            (IPEndPoint)client.RemoteEndPoint;
Console.WriteLine("Connected with {0} at port {1}",
              newclient.Address, newclient.Port);

string welcome = "Welcome to my test server";
data = Encoding.ASCII.GetBytes(welcome);
client.Send(data, data.Length,
                SocketFlags.None);

i = 0;
while(true)
{
    Console.WriteLine("polling for receive #{0}...", i);
    i++;
    result = client.Poll(3000000, SelectMode.SelectRead);
    if(result)
    {
        data = new byte[1024];
        i = 0;
        recv = client.Receive(data);
        if (recv == 0)
            break;

        Console.WriteLine(
            Encoding.ASCII.GetString(data, 0, recv));
        client.Send(data, recv, 0);
    }
}

Console.WriteLine("Disconnected from {0}",
                newclient.Address);
client.Close();
newsock.Close();
    }
}
```

After the server socket is created, it is bound to a local IPEndPoint object and placed in listen mode using the standard Bind() and Listen() Socket methods. In a normal blocking program, the next step would be to use the Accept() method to wait for an incoming connection attempt from a client. This would cause the program to wait at that point and prevent it from doing any other work until an incoming connection is received.

Instead, in this example, the non-blocking Poll() method polls the socket to determine if an incoming connection is available:

```
while(true)
{
    Console.WriteLine("polling for receive #{0}...", i

    i++;
    result = client.Poll(3000000, SelectMode.SelectRead);
    if(result)
    {
        data = new byte[1024];
        i = 0;
        recv = client.Receive(data);
        if (recv == 0)
            break;

        Console.WriteLine(
            Encoding.ASCII.GetString(data, 0, recv));
        client.Send(data, recv, 0);
    }
}
```

Here, a while() loop is created to continuously loop, checking the socket for the SelectRead attribute. If the SelectRead attribute is set, the Poll() method returns a value of true. An incoming connection is then available and the Accept() method can be safely called without blocking. The Poll() method is set to wait one second each time.

Between calls to the Poll() method, the program can perform any other function, including calls to other methods. This program merely increments a counter and displays it on the console to inform you that the program is still running while it is polling.

After an incoming connection attempt is connected, another poll loop is created to wait for incoming data for the Receive() method. Again, between Poll() calls, the program can perform any other operation that is needed.

Testing the Poll() Method

You can test this program by running it from the command prompt, watching it poll, and waiting for a client connection. Either the SimpleTcpClient program, shown in Chapter 5, or the fancy `AsyncTcpClient` program created earlier in this chapter, can connect to `TcpPollSrvr`. After running `TcpPollSrvr` for a few seconds, start the client program to establish a connection. Once the connection attempt is detected, `Poll()`returns a true value and the program continues, sending the welcome banner to the client and then entering another loop to receive data.

Following is sample output from this test:

```
C:\>TcpPollSrvr
Waiting for a client...
polling for accept#1...
polling for accept#2...
polling for accept#3...
polling for accept#4...
polling for accept#5...
polling for accept#6...
polling for accept#7...
Connected with 192.168.1.2 at port 1985
polling for receive #0...
polling for receive #1...
polling for receive #2...
polling for receive #3...
This is a test message.
polling for receive #0...
polling for receive #1...
polling for receive #2...
This is another test message.
polling for receive #0...
Disconnected from 192.168.1.2

C:\>
```

As you can see, the program polls and waits for a client connection. Once the connection is established, the program polls again, waiting for data. As each new message is received, a new poll loop is started, waiting again for data. When the remote client closes the connection, `Poll()`detects the closure and returns a `true` value. Because the return value was `true`, the `Receive()` method is called and a zero value is returned.

NOTE   Unlike the `Accept()` or `Receive()` methods, the `Connect()` method must be started before the `Poll()` method can be used. Therefore, to ensure that the socket will not block, you must manually use the non-blocking socket option.

The `Poll()` method works well for watching a single socket for activity but can get extremely complex if you are trying to monitor multiple sockets. For that situation you can use the `Select()` method.

The Select() Method

The Select() method of the Socket class polls one or more sockets for blocking functions. As sockets become available for reading or writing, the Select() method can determine which ones are ready to use and which ones would block if used.

The Select() Format

Because the Select() method is declared as a static method, it cannot be used on an instance of a Socket object. Instead, you must use it from a generic Socket declaration: Here's the format:

```
Socket.Select(IList checkRead, IList checkWrite, IList checkError, int
microseconds)
```

The three IList objects represent three categories to monitor for socket activity:

- *checkRead* monitors the specified sockets for the ability to read data from the socket.

- *checkWrite* monitors the specified sockets for the ability to write data to the socket.

- *checkError* monitors the specified sockets for error conditions.

The IList object represents a collection of objects that can be individually accessed by an index value. When the Select() method exits, each IList object will be modified to only contain Socket objects that meet the criteria of the position (read, write, or error).

The IList object must allow the Select() method to manipulate the entries in the list, because sockets are added and removed as data becomes available. The easiest way to create an IList object that can be manipulated is to use an ArrayList object. The ArrayList class can be found in the System.Collections namespace. In the case of the Select() method, an ArrayList of Socket objects is used. The *microseconds* parameter determines how long the Select() method will monitor the sockets before returning to the program (similar to the Poll() method).

For example, the following code snippet creates three separate sockets and monitors them for new connections:

```
IPEndPoint iep1 = new IPEndPoint(IPAddress.Any, 9050);

Socket sock = new Socket(AddressFamily.InterNetwork, SocketType.Stream,
ProtocolType.Tcp);

sock.Bind(iep1);
sock.Listen(5);

Socket newsock1 = sock.Accept();
Socket newsock2 = sock.Accept();
```

```
Socket newsock3 = sock.Accept();

ArrayList socketList = new ArrayList(3);
socketList.Add(newsock1);
socketList.Add(newsock2);
socketList.Add(newsock3);

Socket.Select(sockList, null, null, 10000000);
for(int I = 0; I < sockList.Count; i++)
{
    client = (Socket)sockList[i];
    data = new byte[1024];
    recv = client.Receive(data);
}
```

This code snippet demonstrates the placing of three separate sockets in an ArrayList and passing it to the Select() method for monitoring. The three sockets are the result of client connections to a single socket placed in listen mode. The Select() method waits ten seconds and then exits. The result is that the *sockList* ArrayList will now contain any sockets that have data waiting to be read.

WARNING It is very important to remember that the ArrayList passed to the Select() method will be modified. On return, it will only contain the sockets that pass the Select filter. If you need to use the original ArrayList of sockets, make a copy of it before passing it to the Select() method.

After the Select() method returns, the individual sockets within the ArrayList can be extracted and the data read.

A Sample Select() Program

This section demonstrates how to use the Select() method to monitor more than one socket at a time in a program. This technique is especially useful for server programs that must service multiple clients simultaneously.

The Select() Server Program

The SelectTcpSrvr.cs program (Listing 8.5) uses the Select() method to monitor two separate clients at the same time. It creates a single socket, places it in listen mode, and then waits for two clients to connect to the socket. Each client generates its own separate socket, which is placed in an ArrayList. The ArrayList of sockets is then monitored using the Select() method for incoming data. When data is detected on a socket, it is echoed back to the same client.

Listing 8.5   **The SelectTcpSrvr.cs program**

```
using System;
using System.Collections;
using System.Net;
using System.Net.Sockets;
using System.Text;

class SelectTcpSrvr
{
   public static void Main()
   {
      ArrayList sockList = new ArrayList(2);
      ArrayList copyList = new ArrayList(2);
      Socket main = new Socket(AddressFamily.InterNetwork,
                       SocketType.Stream, ProtocolType.Tcp);

      IPEndPoint iep = new IPEndPoint(IPAddress.Any, 9050);
      byte[] data = new byte[1024];
      string stringData;
      int recv;

      main.Bind(iep);
      main.Listen(2);

      Console.WriteLine("Waiting for 2 clients...");
      Socket client1 = main.Accept();
      IPEndPoint iep1 = (IPEndPoint)client1.RemoteEndPoint;
      client1.Send(Encoding.ASCII.GetBytes("Welcome to my server"));
      Console.WriteLine("Connected to {0}", iep1.ToString());
      sockList.Add(client1);

      Console.WriteLine("Waiting for 1 more client...");
      Socket client2 = main.Accept();
      IPEndPoint iep2 = (IPEndPoint)client2.RemoteEndPoint;
      client2.Send(Encoding.ASCII.GetBytes("Welcome to my server"));
      Console.WriteLine("Connected to {0}", iep2.ToString());
      sockList.Add(client2);
      main.Close();

      while(true)
      {
         copyList = new ArrayList(sockList);
         Console.WriteLine("Monitoring {0} sockets...", copyList.Count);
         Socket.Select(copyList, null, null, 10000000);

         foreach(Socket client in copyList)
         {

            data = new byte[1024];
```

```
            recv = client.Receive(data);
            stringData = Encoding.ASCII.GetString(data, 0, recv);
            Console.WriteLine("Received: {0}", stringData);
            if (recv == 0)
            {
                iep = (IPEndPoint)client.RemoteEndPoint;
                Console.WriteLine("Client {0} disconnected.", iep.ToString());
                client.Close();
                sockList.Remove(client);
                if (sockList.Count == 0)
                {
                    Console.WriteLine("Last client disconnected, bye");
                    return;
                }
            }
            else
                client.Send(data, recv, SocketFlags.None);
        }
    }
  }
}
```

The SelectTcpSrvr program starts off simply enough by creating a TCP socket to listen for incoming connections. It then waits for two clients to connect to the server by using two separate Accept() method calls. Each client connection is saved in a separate Socket object, and each Socket object is added to the ArrayList *sockList* to be used by the Select() method.

After the ArrayList object is created, the program enters a loop checking the ArrayList sockets for incoming data using the Select() method. To allow for the fact that the ArrayList used in the Select() method will be destroyed, a copy is created to use on each iteration:

```
copyList = new ArrayList(sockList);
Console.WriteLine("Monitoring {0} sockets...", copyList.Count);
Socket.Select(copyList, null, null, 10000000);
```

After either one of the sockets receives data, or 10 seconds elapse (whichever comes first), the Select() method exits. The *copyList* ArrayList object will contain any sockets that have received data. The for loop iterates through all of the sockets returned in the *copyList* array.

The first step in the for loop is to get the socket that has received data. The Socket object contained in the *copyList* ArrayList is copied to the *client* Socket object. Then it can be used as any normal socket, using the Receive() method to receive the waiting data:

```
client = (Socket)copyList[i];
data = new byte[1024];
recv = client.Receive(data);
```

The return value from the Receive() method has to be examined to see if the remote client disconnected from the session. This can be determined by detecting a zero return value. If the remote client disconnected, you must close the socket and remove it from the ArrayList. This is easily done using the Remove() method:

```
if (recv == 0)
{
    iep = (IPEndPoint)client.RemoteEndPoint;
    Console.WriteLine("Client {0} disconnected.", iep.ToString());
    client.Close();
    sockList.Remove(client);
    if (sockList.Count == 0)
    {
        Console.WriteLine("Last client disconnected, bye");
        return;
    }
}
```

WARNING When no more sockets are left in the ArrayList, be sure to terminate the Select() loop, or you will get an Exception error.

Finally, if the socket did receive actual data, it is echoed back to the originating client using the standard Send() method. After the for loop completes, the whole process can start over again (after the original ArrayList of sockets has been recopied back into the working copy).

The Select() Client Program

The SelectTcpClient.cs program (Listing 8.6) is a simple client program that connects to the specified server and waits for the customer to enter a text message on the console. The message is sent to the SelectTcpSrvr program, which echoes it back to the client. The message is displayed on the console, and the program waits for another message to be entered. The SelectTcpClient program itself does not need to use the Select() method because it only connects with one server.

Listing 8.6   **The SelectTcpClient.cs program**

```
using System;
using System.Collections;
using System.Net;
using System.Net.Sockets;
using System.Text;

class SelectTcpClient
{
    public static void Main()
    {
        Socket sock = new Socket(AddressFamily.InterNetwork,
                        SocketType.Stream, ProtocolType.Tcp);
        IPEndPoint iep = new IPEndPoint(IPAddress.Parse("127.0.0.1"), 9050);
```

```
        byte[] data = new byte[1024];
        string stringData;
        int recv;

        sock.Connect(iep);
        Console.WriteLine("Connected to server");
        recv = sock.Receive(data);
        stringData = Encoding.ASCII.GetString(data, 0, recv);
        Console.WriteLine("Received: {0}", stringData);

        while(true)
        {
            stringData = Console.ReadLine();
            if (stringData == "exit")
                break;
            data = Encoding.ASCII.GetBytes(stringData);
            sock.Send(data, data.Length, SocketFlags.None);
            data = new byte[1024];
            recv = sock.Receive(data);
            stringData = Encoding.ASCII.GetString(data, 0, recv);
            Console.WriteLine("Received: {0}", stringData);
        }
        sock.Close();
    }
}
```

Testing the SelectTcpClient.cs Program

To test this setup, you need to have three command-prompt windows open—one for the
SelectTcpSrvr program and two others for the SelectTcpClient program. You can run
the SelectTcpClient programs from other workstations on the network if you want; just
remember to set the IPEndPoint value to the server address.

When you start the SelectTcpSrvr program, it waits for two connections from clients.
The first client that connects to the server will block, waiting for the second connection
to complete. After both clients are connected to the server, either one can send messages to
the server at any time.

The server program monitors both sockets for incoming data. The Console.WriteLine()
method displays status information so you can see what is happening on the server at any
time. Here's what the output from the server should look like:

```
C:\>SelectTcpSrvr
Waiting for 2 clients...
Connected to 127.0.0.1:1893
Waiting for 1 more client...
Connected to 127.0.0.1:1894
Monitoring 2 sockets...
```

```
Monitoring 2 sockets...
Received: This is a test message
Monitoring 2 sockets...
Received: This is another test message
Monitoring 2 sockets...
Received:
Client 127.0.0.1:1894 disconnected.
Monitoring 1 sockets...
Received: This is a final test message
Monitoring 1 sockets...
Received:
Client 127.0.0.1:1893 disconnected.
Last client disconnected, bye

C:\>
```

The server accepts two client connections and goes into the `while` loop to monitor the sockets for incoming data. As each client sends a message to the server, it is processed and echoed back to the proper client. Figure 8.7 shows Analyzer output from monitoring the two clients and the server.

FIGURE 8.7:

Monitoring the SelectTcpSrvr program with the Analyzer program

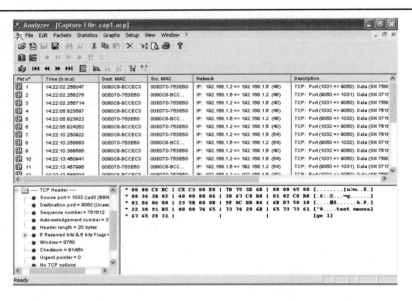

The trace shows two client connections, one using port 1031 and the other using port 1032. The server handles each client TCP session independently. When one client disconnects from the server, the other client can still send messages to the server for processing. When the last client disconnects, the server stops processing sockets and exits.

TIP   Although the example shown in this section manually creates two client connections, the Select() method can also be used to accept many clients for a single server. The main socket can be polled for new connection attempts and passed to an Accept() method, which will assign each connection a separate socket and place it in the ArrayList to be monitored.

Summary

This chapter discusses how to use network functions in the Windows graphically oriented programs—an environment that is different from the traditional Unix programming environment because it supports an event programming model. Event programming puts control of program execution in the hands of the customer. The program does not follow a normal program flow. Instead, it responds to events that occur in the course of the customer's interaction with the program (clicking buttons, double-clicking list items, selecting menu items, and so on). Program control jumps around from method to method, reacting to events generated both by the customer and by the network.

The .NET network classes include asynchronous Socket methods that can interact within a Windows event program. These asynchronous functions do not block program execution waiting for network events. Instead, the asynchronous methods register a method from the AsyncCallback class that completes the network function when it is ready for processing. For instance, instead of a function's blocking on a Receive() method, a BeginReceive() method registers an AsyncCallback method to run when data is available on the socket. When the data is available, the registered method is called, and the EndReceive() method reads it.

The .NET network library also supports the traditional Unix method of using non-blocking sockets. The Socket method Poll() allows a programmer to check a socket for network availability—either the availability of data if it is ready for writing, or whether an error has occurred. If the socket is not ready, the Poll() method indicates this, and the program can avoid the network function. Most programmers use a loop to check the Poll() method on a regular basis while performing other functions in between.

Another traditional non-blocking socket method is the Socket method Select(), which monitors multiple Socket objects for network availability. Similar to the Poll() method, Select() checks for the availability of data if the socket is ready for writing, or whether any errors have occurred. The ArrayList of Socket objects sent to the Select() method is monitored for a predetermined amount of time. If an event occurs on one or more of the sockets, then Select()returns with the ArrayList modified to contain only the sockets that are ready for the network action. If the time limit expires before any of the sockets are ready, the ArrayList is returned empty.

The Select() method is often used in server applications where a large number of client sockets must be monitored for activity. Each of the active sockets is placed in an ArrayList object and monitored by the Select() method for incoming data. When incoming data is detected on a group of sockets, they are passed to a method to read the data and act accordingly. As each client disconnects from the server, its Socket object is dropped from the ArrayList and no longer monitored.

The asynchronous Socket methods do all their work using threads running in background from the main application. The next chapter, "Using Threads," tells you how you can manually use threads in your own network programs to perform network functions separately from the main application.

CHAPTER 9

Using Threads

- Accessing information on system processes from C# programs

- Threads and the `ProcessThread` class

- Creating threads in a program

- Using threads in a server

- Using threads for sending and receiving data

- Thread pools

In this chapter, you'll continue your study of accomplishing network programming for Windows systems using C#. The preceding chapter discussed using asynchronous socket methods in Windows programs to perform all network socket routines in background; the main part of the program continues while the socket function waits to complete. Behind the scenes, the .NET Framework utilizes *threads* to perform this duty. Instead of asynchronous socket methods, you can utilize threads manually within your own network programs. By running separate threads, you can program your server to communicate simultaneously with many clients.

This chapter defines threads and how they are created and used in C# programs. We'll explore the use of threads in network programs and look at some examples in various types of network programs. We'll close by examining *thread pools* and their role in a network program.

How Applications Run in Windows

As you run programs on a Windows system, the underlying operating system software must know how to manipulate the programs to ensure that they all have a chance to get time on the CPU and access memory and I/O devices. To do this, the OS handles each program as a self-contained *process*. A process represents a single instance of a program. If another copy of the program is running at the same time, each instance of the program creates a new process. You can use the Task Manager to watch the separate processes running on the Windows system. Figure 9.1 shows the various processes running on a Windows XP Professional workstation. (On Windows 95 or 98 systems, press Ctrl-Alt-Del to see a listing of running processes.)

FIGURE 9.1:

The Task Manager Processes window for a Windows XP Professional workstation

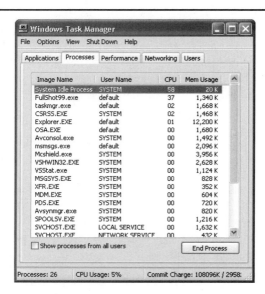

As you can see in Figure 9.1, each process running on the system is identified by a unique process ID value. The Task Manager also shows the current CPU time used by the process and the current memory used to store execution code and data. As in the Windows 95 and 98 process list, you can highlight a single process and terminate it by clicking the End Process button.

Although Windows appears to run multiple processes simultaneously, in reality the CPU can run only one process at a time. Each process must have a turn using the CPU cycles on the system. The information for each process is swapped into the CPU area to execute, then swapped out when the process is idle. For systems with multiple CPUs, two situations can exist: one process can be run for each CPU at the same time, or a single process can be split between the CPUs, as discussed in this chapter's later sections on threads.

Allotment of CPU time for individual processes is determined by the *process priority*. The Windows system uses two categories of process priorities:

- A priority class that defines a base priority for the process
- A specific priority level within the priority class to "fine-tune" the process priority

Table 9.1 describes the priority classes that can be assigned to a process.

TABLE 9.1: The Process Priority Classes

Class	Description
Idle	The process runs only when the system is idle
BelowNormal	The process has less than normal priority but greater than idle priority
Normal	The default priority class for all processes
AboveNormal	The process has above-normal priority but less than high priority
High	The process has time-critical tasks that must be run immediately
RealTime	Preempts all other processes, including system processes

The priority classes are enumerated in the `ProcessPriorityClass` class. You can use the enumeration when defining a new priority level for a process:

```
proc.PriorityClass = ProcessPriorityClass.High;
```

Finding Process Information Using C#

The .NET library contains classes for allowing your C# programs to access the process information on the system. You can use this information to determine the status of your program as it is running, or you can get information about other programs running on the system at the same time as your program.

The .NET Process Class

The System.Diagnostics namespace includes the Process class, which is used within a C# program to retrieve and set information for individual processes running on the system. The Process class can start, stop, control, and monitor processes, all from within your program.

NOTE When trying to start or stop processes, be aware of the system privileges assigned to your program (that is, the user ID under which it is running). Normal user accounts cannot stop processes started by another user. Accounts with Administrator privileges can manipulate most of the processes on the system; some system processes cannot be stopped by anyone.

The most useful elements of the Process class are the class properties, listed in Table 9.2. They are used to get or set the information about the running processes.

TABLE 9.2: The Process Class Properties

Property	Description
BasePriority	Gets the base priority of the process
Container	Gets the Icontainer object of the process
EnableRaisingEvents	Gets or sets whether the Exited event should be raised when the process terminates
ExitCode	Gets the value the process specified when it terminated
ExitTime	Gets the time the process terminated
Handle	Get the native handle of the process
HandleCount	Gets the number of handles opened by the process
HasExited	Gets a value indicating whether the process has terminated
Id	Gets the assigned process identifier for the process
MachineName	Gets the name of the computer the process is running on
MainModule	Gets the main module for the process
MainWindowHandle	Gets the window handle of the main window of the process
MainWindowTitle	Gets the window title of the main window of the process
MaxWorkingSet	Gets or sets the maximum allowable working set size for the process
MinWorkingSet	Gets or sets the minimum allowable working set size for the process
Modules	Gets the modules that have been loaded by the process
NonpagedSytemMemorySize	Gets the nonpaged system memory size allocated to the process
PagedMemorySize	Gets the paged memory size allocated to the process
PagedSystemMemorySize	Gets the paged system memory size allocated to the process
PeakPagedMemorySize	Gets the peak paged memory size for the process
PeakVirtualMemorySize	Gets the peak virtual memory size for the process
PeakWorkingSet	Gets the peak working set size for the process

Continued on next page

TABLE 9.2 CONTINUED: The Process Class Properties

Property	Description
PriorityBoostEnabled	Gets or sets a value indicating whether the process priority should be boosted when the main window has the focus
PriorityClass	Gets or sets the overall priority category for the process
PrivateMemorySize	Gets the amount of private memory used by the process
PrivilegedProcessorTime	Gets the privileged processor time used by the process
ProcessName	Gets the name of the process
ProcessorAffinity	Gets or sets the processors on which the process threads will run
Responding	Gets a value indicating if the user interface of the process is responding
Site	Gets or sets the ISite component
StandardError	Gets a StreamReader object through which to read error output from the process
StandardInput	Gets a StreamWriter object through which to write input to the process
StandardOutput	Gets a StreamReader object through which to read output from the process
StartInfo	Gets or sets the properties passed to the process Start() method
StartTime	Gets the time that the process was started
SynchronizingObject	Gets or sets the object used to marshal event handler calls issued as a result of the process exiting
Threads	Gets the list of threads running in the process
TotalProcessorTime	Gets the total amount of processor time for this process
UserProcessorTime	Gets the amount of user processor time for this process
VirtualMemorySize	Gets the size of the virtual memory used by the process
WorkingSet	Gets the amount of physical memory usage of the process

As you can see from Table 9.2, you can gather lots of information about a running process. Typically, you'll be most interested in the process name, ID, processor time, and memory usage.

NOTE Don't be surprised by the MachineName property. If the process is running on the local machine, the MachineName is set to a period (.), not the actual machine name. If the process is running on a remote machine, the machine name will be the hostname of the remote host.

The methods of the Process class contain several static methods that are used for obtaining information about processes on the system in general and are not necessarily related to a specific Process instance. There are also lots of methods that are used on specific Process instances. Table 9.3 shows the Process methods used on Process instances.

TABLE 9.3: The Process Class Methods

Method	Description
Close()	Frees all components associated with the process
CloseMainWindow()	Closes the process by sending a close message to the main window
CreateObjRef()	Creates a proxy object used to communicate with a remote process object
Dispose()	Releases the resources used by the process
Equals()	Determines if two Process objects are the same
GetHashCode()	Gets a unique hash code for the process
GetLifetimeService()	Gets the current lifetime service object that controls the lifetime policy for the process
GetType()	Gets the object type of the process
InitializeLifetimeService()	Obtains a lifetime service object to control the lifetime policy of the process
Kill()	Immediately stops the process
Refresh()	Removes any information about the process from the process object cache
Start()	Starts a process and associates it with a Process() object
ToString()	Gets a string representation of the process
WaitForExit()	Sets a period of time to wait for the process to exit and blocks the current thread until the time has elapsed or the process exits
WaitForInputIdle()	Causes the Process object to wait for the process to enter the idle state

Each of these Process class methods can be used on a Process instance, modifying its behavior or obtaining information about it. The Process static methods are used to obtain generic information about processes on the system. Table 9.4 shows these methods.

TABLE 9.4: The Process Static Methods

Method	Description
EnterDebugMode()	Allows a Process object to interact with operating system processes that run in a special mode
GetCurrentProcess()	Creates a new Process object and associates it with the currently active process
GetProcessById()	Creates a new Process object and associates it with the process identified by its process ID
GetProcesses()	Creates an array of Process objects and associates them with the processes currently running on the system

Continued on next page

TABLE 9.4 CONTINUED: The Process Static Methods

Method	Description
GetProcessByName()	Creates a new `Process` object and associates it with the process identified by its process name
LeaveDebugMode()	Stops a `Process` object from interacting with operating system processes that run in a special mode

If you are interested in finding a particular process, you can use the `GetProccessById()` or `GetProcessByName()` methods to retrieve information based on either the process ID or process name. If you do not know what processes are running on the system, you can use the `GetProcesses()` method to retrieve all the processes to an array and then iterate through the array, obtaining information for each process.

Information for the Current Process

To determine process information for the current program, create a `Process` object using the `GetCurrentProcess()` method and poke around at some of the properties. Listing 9.1 shows the `GetProc.cs` program, which does just that.

Listing 9.1   The GetProc.cs program

```
using System;
using System.Diagnostics;

class GetProc
{
    public static void Main()
    {
        Process thisProc = Process.GetCurrentProcess();

        string procName = thisProc.ProcessName;
        DateTime started = thisProc.StartTime;
        int procID = thisProc.Id;
        int memory = thisProc.VirtualMemorySize;
        int priMemory = thisProc.PrivateMemorySize;
        int physMemory = thisProc.WorkingSet;
        int priority = thisProc.BasePriority;
        ProcessPriorityClass priClass = thisProc.PriorityClass;
        TimeSpan cpuTime = thisProc.TotalProcessorTime;


        Console.WriteLine("Process: {0}, ID: {1}", procName, procID);
        Console.WriteLine("    started: {0}", started.ToString());
        Console.WriteLine("    CPU time: {0}", cpuTime.ToString());
        Console.WriteLine(
            "    priority class: {0}  priority: {1}", priClass, priority);
```

```
        Console.WriteLine("    virtual memory: {0}", memory);
        Console.WriteLine("    private memory: {0}", priMemory);
        Console.WriteLine("    physical memory: {0}", physMemory);

        Console.WriteLine("\n   trying to change priority...");
        thisProc.PriorityClass = ProcessPriorityClass.High;
        priClass = thisProc.PriorityClass;
        Console.WriteLine("    new priority class: {0}", priClass);
    }
}
```

The GetProc program uses the GetCurrentProcess() method to retrieve several Process properties for the program's process. You can experiment by trying other properties as well. A sample output from my system looks like this:

```
C:\>GetProc
Process: GetProc, ID: 313
    started: 7/17/02 8:09:54 PM
    CPU time: 00:00:00.7911376
    priority class: Normal  priority: 8
    virtual memory: 70676480
    private memory: 3981312
    physical memory: 5636096

    trying to change priority...
    new priority class: High

C:\>
```

As shown in the sample output, the process was successful in changing its process priority on the system. Any other operations performed by the program after the priority change would have privileged access to CPU time on the system.

Information for All Processes

As stated earlier, you can use Task Manager to manually display process information for all processes running on the system. The GetProcesses() method does the same task in your C# program. Listing 9.2, the ListProcs.cs program, lists all the processes running on the system, along with some useful information for each process.

Listing 9.2   **The ListProcs.cs program**

```
using System;
using System.Diagnostics;

class ListProcs
{
    public static void Main()
```

```
        {
            int totMemory = 0;
            Console.WriteLine("Info for all processes:");

            Process[] allProcs = Process.GetProcesses();
            foreach(Process thisProc in allProcs)
            {
                string procName = thisProc.ProcessName;
                DateTime started = thisProc.StartTime;
                int procID = thisProc.Id;
                int memory = thisProc.VirtualMemorySize;
                int priMemory = thisProc.PrivateMemorySize;
                int physMemory = thisProc.WorkingSet;
                totMemory += physMemory;
                int priority = thisProc.BasePriority;
                TimeSpan cpuTime = thisProc.TotalProcessorTime;

                Console.WriteLine("Process: {0}, ID: {1}", procName, procID);
                Console.WriteLine("    started: {0}", started.ToString());
                Console.WriteLine("    CPU time: {0}", cpuTime.ToString());
                Console.WriteLine("    virtual memory: {0}", memory);
                Console.WriteLine("    private memory: {0}", priMemory);
                Console.WriteLine("    physical memory: {0}", physMemory);
            }

            Console.WriteLine("\nTotal physical memory used: {0}", totMemory);
        }
    }
```

After the GetProcesses() method places the process information in an array of Process objects, you can use the handy foreach function to iterate through the array, assigning each Process array item to a single Process object and extracting the pertinent information. Depending on what is running on your system, the resulting output could be quite lengthy. Here's a partial output from my system:

```
C:\>ListProcs
Info for all processes:
Process: winword, ID: 318
    started: 7/18/02 7:38:58 PM
    CPU time: 00:00:11.3363008
    virtual memory: 59056128
    private memory: 4009984
    physical memory: 9977856
Process: drvmgr, ID: 94
    started: 7/18/02 6:48:49 PM
    CPU time: 00:00:00.0701008
    virtual memory: 25489408
    private memory: 1691648
    physical memory: 204800
```

```
Process: CMD, ID: 307
    started: 7/18/02 7:46:13 PM
    CPU time: 00:00:00.2303312
    virtual memory: 18448384
    private memory: 471040
    physical memory: 1810432
Process: spoolss, ID: 82
    started: 7/18/02 6:48:46 PM
    CPU time: 00:00:00.5307632
    virtual memory: 62898176
    private memory: 4313088
    physical memory: 1732608
.
.
.

Process: SysTray, ID: 62
    started: 7/18/02 7:36:50 PM
    CPU time: 00:00:00.0701008
    virtual memory: 25239552
    private memory: 1642496
    physical memory: 1413120
Process: MsgSys, ID: 167
    started: 7/18/02 6:49:05 PM
    CPU time: 00:00:00.0901296
    virtual memory: 30765056
    private memory: 921600
    physical memory: 77824
Process: ListProcs, ID: 365
    started: 7/18/02 7:47:19 PM
    CPU time: 00:00:00.7510800
    virtual memory: 70676480
    private memory: 4001792
    physical memory: 5619712
Process: OUTLOOK, ID: 356
    started: 7/18/02 7:38:31 PM
    CPU time: 00:00:01.1516560
    virtual memory: 57663488
    private memory: 2883584
    physical memory: 5099520
Process: System, ID: 2
    started: 7/18/02 6:48:16 PM
    CPU time: 00:00:31.4151728
    virtual memory: 544768
    private memory: 36864
```

```
      physical memory: 204800
Process: Idle, ID: 0
      started: 7/18/02 6:48:16 PM
      CPU time: 00:51:37.8344672
      virtual memory: 0
      private memory: 0
      physical memory: 16384

Total physical memory used: 75292672


C:\>
```

Examine the sample output, and you'll see some familiar process names—`winword`, `outlook`, and of course, `ListProc`. Also, notice the various system processes that, while not visible on the system desktop, are running on the system, performing functions in the background. You can also compare the CPU times of each of the processes to see which applications have been using the most time on your system.

Threads

Processes are made up of one or more *threads*. A thread is defined as a single flow of operation within a program. When a program executes on the CPU, it traverses the program statements in a single thread until the thread is complete. A *multithreaded* application distributes functions among multiple program flows, allowing two or more paths of execution to occur. Each path of execution is a separate thread.

Multithreaded programs create their own threads that can be executed separately from the main thread of the program. All threads created by the primary thread share the same memory address space as the primary thread. Often the secondary threads are used to perform computationally intensive functions, allowing the main thread to continue responding to Windows events. Without the secondary threads, the user could not select anything from the menu or click any buttons while an application computed a mathematical function.

The thread is the basic unit of execution on the Windows operating system. Each process is scheduled to run on the CPU by its threads. On a multiprocessor system, more than one thread can run at a time, allowing the operating system to schedule multiple threads either from the same process, or from separate processes to run simultaneously.

Threads have several operational states, which are enumerated using the .NET `ThreadState` enumeration, found in the `System.Threading` namespace. Table 9.5 lists the possible thread states available in the Windows OS.

TABLE 9.5: The ThreadState Enumeration

ThreadState	Description
Initialized	The thread has been initialized but not started.
Ready	The thread is waiting for a processor.
Running	The thread is currently using the processor.
Standby	The thread is about to use the processor.
Terminated	The thread is finished and is ready to exit.
Transition	The thread is waiting for a resource other than the processor.
Unknown	The system is unable to determine the thread state.
Wait	The thread is not ready to use the processor.

An individual thread may change states several times during its lifetime, toggling between the Running state and the Standby, Transition, or Wait states. The operating system itself can place a running thread into another state to preempt it with the thread of a high-priority process.

The .NET Framework's ProcessThread Class

The .NET ProcessThread class in the System.Diagnostics namespace allows you to access the threads within a process from your C# program. Similar to the Process class, the ProcessThread class contains many properties and methods used to obtain information regarding the threads in a process. Table 9.6 defines the ProcessThread properties available to obtain information regarding the operation of the thread.

TABLE 9.6: The ProcessThread Properties

Property	Description
BasePriority	Gets the base priority of the thread
Container	Gets the IContainer that contains the thread object
CurrentPriority	Gets the current priority of the thread
Id	Gets the unique thread identifier of the thread
IdealProcessor	Sets the preferred processor for the thread to run on
PriorityBoostEnabled	Gets or sets a value indicating whether the operating system should temporarily boost the priority of the thread when its main window has the focus
PriorityLevel	Gets or sets the priority level of the thread
PrivilegedProcessorTime	Gets the amount of time the thread has spent running code in the operating system core
ProcessorAffinity	Sets the processors that the thread can run on

Continued on next page

TABLE 9.6 CONTINUED: The ProcessThread Properties

Property	Description
Site	Gets or sets the ISite of the thread object
StartAddress	Gets the memory address of the function used to start the thread
ThreadState	Gets the current state of the thread
TotalProcessorTime	Gets the total amount of time the thread has spent using the processor
UserProcessorTime	Gets the amount of time the thread has spent running code in the application
WaitReason	Gets the reason the thread is in the Wait state

NOTE   The Id property creates a unique number to identify the thread on the system. No two threads active on the system have the same thread Id. The IdealProcessor and ProcessorAffinity properties allow you to manipulate the running of a thread on a multiprocessor machine.

Determining the Threads in a Process

It is a snap to write a quick program to display the threads of the current program. Listing 9.3 shows an example of a simple program to get thread information.

Listing 9.3   **The GetThreads.cs program**

```
using System;
using System.Diagnostics;

class GetThreads
{
    public static void Main()
    {

        Process thisProc = Process.GetCurrentProcess();
        ProcessThreadCollection myThreads = thisProc.Threads;

        foreach(ProcessThread pt in myThreads)
        {
            DateTime startTime = pt.StartTime;
            TimeSpan cpuTime = pt.TotalProcessorTime;
            int priority = pt.BasePriority;
            ThreadState ts = pt.ThreadState;

            Console.WriteLine("thread: {0}", pt.Id);
            Console.WriteLine("    started: {0}", startTime.ToString());
            Console.WriteLine("    CPU time: {0}", cpuTime);
            Console.WriteLine("    priority: {0}", priority);
```

```
            Console.WriteLine("    thread state: {0}", ts.ToString());
        }
    }
}
```

The `ProcessThreadCollection` class contains information from all threads returned from the `Threads()` method of the `Process` class. The example in Listing 9.3 uses the `foreach` function to iterate through each thread in the `ProcessThreadCollection`, extracting property information from each thread.

Running the `GetThreads` program may produce an unexpected result:

```
C:\>GetThreads
thread:  263
    started: 7/18/02 11:25:45 PM
    CPU time: 00:00:00.8211808
    priority: 8
    thread state: Running
thread:  382
    started: 7/18/02 11:25:45 PM
    CPU time: 00:00:00
    priority: 8
    thread state: Wait
thread:  378
    started: 7/18/02 11:25:45 PM
    CPU time: 00:00:00
    priority: 10
    thread state: Ready

C:\>
```

As you can see in this output, the `GetThreads` program shows three separate threads running for this process. There was only one path of execution in the program, so you may be wondering where the other two threads came from. You can find the answer in the .NET Framework. As explained in Chapter 1, "The C# Language," the program is not a fully executable program; it is compiled to the Microsoft Intermediate Language (MSIL). As each MSIL program is run, the just-in-time (JIT) compiler must also run, processing each statement in the MSIL code—thus the multiple threads for a single program.

NOTE   The foregoing thread example was run on a machine with just the .NET Framework runtime installed. On machines with the full SDK installed, even more threads are used for a single process.

Another thing to notice in this output is the status of the three threads. Because this program was run on a single processor system, only one thread can be in a Running state at a time. The last thread is in a Ready state, indicating that it is waiting for its turn on the processor. The middle thread in the program is not ready to be run yet.

Seeing Threads in All Processes

You can now put the ProcList and GetThreads programs together, getting a listing of all threads for all processes. Listing 9.4, the ListThreads.cs program, displays thread information for all the threads running on the system.

Listing 9.4   **The ListThreads.cs program**

```
using System;
using System.Diagnostics;

class ListThreads
{
    public static void Main()
    {

        Process[] allProcs = Process.GetProcesses();

        foreach(Process proc in allProcs)
        {
            ProcessThreadCollection myThreads = proc.Threads;
            Console.WriteLine("process: {0},  id: {1}", proc.ProcessName, proc.Id);

            foreach(ProcessThread pt in myThreads)
            {
                DateTime startTime = pt.StartTime;
                TimeSpan cpuTime = pt.TotalProcessorTime;
                int priority = pt.BasePriority;
                ThreadState ts = pt.ThreadState;

                Console.WriteLine("  thread:  {0}", pt.Id);
                Console.WriteLine("     started: {0}", startTime.ToString());
                Console.WriteLine("     CPU time: {0}", cpuTime);
                Console.WriteLine("     priority: {0}", priority);
                Console.WriteLine("     thread state: {0}", ts.ToString());
            }
        }
    }
}
```

The ListThreads program uses the GetProcesses() method to obtain an array of all the running processes on the system. Then, each process is taken individually, and the Threads() method creates a ProcessThreadCollection object. From there, each individual thread in the process is extracted into a ProcessThread object. After the ProcessThread object is created, you can extract any thread property that you require.

Depending on how busy your particular system is, the output from the ListThreads program can be pretty large. A *small* sample of an output looks like this:

```
C:\>ListThreads
process: ListThreads,  id: 318
  thread:  327
    started: 7/18/02 11:42:22 AM
    CPU time: 00:00:00.7711088
    priority: 8
    thread state: Running
  thread:  371
    started: 7/18/02 11:42:22 AM
    CPU time: 00:00:00
    priority: 8
    thread state: Wait
  thread:  377
    started: 7/18/02 11:42:22 AM
    CPU time: 00:00:00
    priority: 10
    thread state: Ready
process: SysTray,  id: 62
  thread:  330
    started: 7/18/02 7:36:50 AM
    CPU time: 00:00:00.1001440
    priority: 8
    thread state: Wait
  thread:  351
    started: 7/18/02 7:36:51 AM
    CPU time: 00:00:00.0200288
    priority: 10
    thread state: Wait
process: winword,  id: 374
  thread:  264
    started: 7/18/02 10:51:48 AM
    CPU time: 00:01:40.3943600
    priority: 8
    thread state: Wait
  thread:  381
    started: 7/18/02 10:51:49 AM
    CPU time: 00:00:00
    priority: 8
    thread state: Wait
  thread:  155
    started: 7/18/02 10:53:24 AM
    CPU time: 00:00:00.0100144
    priority: 10
    thread state: Wait
```

```
   thread:  376
     started: 7/18/02 10:57:50 AM
     CPU time: 00:00:00
     priority: 8
     thread state: Wait
 process: Explorer,  id: 350
   thread:  277
     started: 7/18/02 7:36:46 AM
     CPU time: 00:00:05.1173584
     priority: 9
     thread state: Wait
   thread:  363
     started: 7/18/02 7:36:47 AM
     CPU time: 00:00:00.1301872
     priority: 8
     thread state: Wait
   thread:  317
     started: 7/18/02 7:36:54 AM
     CPU time: 00:00:00.0100144
     priority: 8
     thread state: Wait
   thread:  294
     started: 7/18/02 7:42:55 AM
     CPU time: 00:00:00
     priority: 8
     thread state: Wait
   thread:  296
     started: 7/18/02 9:27:43 AM
     CPU time: 00:00:03.4048960
     priority: 8
 process: notepad,  id: 337
   thread:  378
     started: 7/18/02 11:38:40 AM
     CPU time: 00:00:00.0901296
     priority: 8
     thread state: Wait
 process: Idle,  id: 0


C:\>
```

You'll learn a few things by going through the output from the ListThreads program. If you are using a single processor system, only one thread in the list will be in the Running state—the primary thread from your ListThreads program. If you have a multiprocessor system, you should see the same number of Running threads as the number of processors you have.

Notice how many threads each process uses. Simpler programs like Notepad use only one thread, while more complex programs such as Winword and Explorer use many. Obviously, complex programs such as Winword are doing a lot of background work, creating new threads to do the work so the main user interface is not affected.

Creating Threads in a Program

Now that you have seen how a program can contain multiple threads, it's time to learn how to create C# programs that utilize multiple threads. The C# language provides the System.Threading namespace, which includes classes for creating and controlling threads within a program. This section describes how to use these classes in a C# program.

The Thread Class

Use the Thread class to create a new Thread object, which produces a new thread within the current process. The format of the Thread constructor is as follows, where start is a ThreadStart delegate:

```
Thread(ThreadStart start)
```

The ThreadStart delegate points to the method that will be performed within the new thread.

Here's an abbreviated example of creating a new thread:

```
    .
    .
    .
Thread newThread = new Thread(new ThreadStart(newMethod));
    .
    .
}

void newMethod()
{
    .
    .
}
```

The *newMethod* parameter defines a method that is performed in the thread when it receives time on a processor. In this example, the method was contained within the same class as the Thread object. You can also run methods defined in other classes.

After the Thread object is created, it can be controlled using various Thread class methods, which are described in Table 9.7.

TABLE 9.7: The Thread Class Methods

Method	Description
Abort()	Terminates the thread
Equals()	Determines whether two Thread objects are the same
GetHashCode()	Gets a unique representation for the thread
GetType()	Gets the type of the current thread
Interrupt()	Interrupts a thread that is in the Wait thread state
Join()	Blocks the calling thread until the thread terminates
Resume()	Resumes a thread that has been suspended
Start()	Causes the operating system to change the thread state to Running
Suspend()	Suspends the execution of the thread
ToString()	Gets a string representation of the Thread object

After the Thread object is created, the Start() method must be used to get it going.

WARNING It is important to remember that a Thread object does not begin processing until the Start() method has been invoked.

After the thread starts, it can be manipulated using the Abort(), Interrupt(), Resume() or Suspend() methods.

Using the Thread Class

The best way to learn about threads is to see them in action. Listing 9.5 presents a simple program that demonstrates threads.

Listing 9.5 **The ThreadSample.cs program**

```
using System;
using System.Threading;

class ThreadSample
{
    public static void Main()
    {
        ThreadSample ts = new ThreadSample();
    }

    public ThreadSample()
    {
```

```
        int i;
        Thread newCounter = new Thread(new ThreadStart(Counter));
        Thread newCounter2 = new Thread(new ThreadStart(Counter2));

        newCounter.Start();
        newCounter2.Start();

        for(i = 0; i < 10; i++)
        {
            Console.WriteLine("main: {0}", i);
            Thread.Sleep(1000);
        }
    }

    void Counter()
    {
        int i;
        for (i = 0; i < 10; i++)
        {
            Console.WriteLine("  thread: {0}", i);
            Thread.Sleep(2000);
        }
    }

    void Counter2()
    {
        int i;
        for (i = 0; i < 10; i++)
        {
            Console.WriteLine("    thread2: {0}", i);
            Thread.Sleep(3000);
        }
    }
}
```

The `ThreadSample.cs` program creates two separate threads from the main program thread, using the `Thread` constructor (along with the `ThreadStart` constructor). The main program performs a `for` loop, displaying a counter value every second and using the `Sleep()` static method of the `Thread` class. The second thread does the same thing but uses a two-second delay; and the third thread uses a three-second delay. Again, remember that the threads start running only when the `Start()` method is used, not when the constructor finishes.

You can run the `ThreadSample` program to see how the output behaves:

```
C:\>ThreadSample
main: 0
  thread: 0
    thread2: 0
main: 1
  thread: 1
```

```
main: 2
    thread2: 1
main: 3
  thread: 2
main: 4
main: 5
    thread2: 2
  thread: 3
main: 6
main: 7
  thread: 4
main: 8
    thread2: 3
main: 9
  thread: 5
    thread2: 4
  thread: 6
  thread: 7
    thread2: 5
  thread: 8
    thread2: 6
  thread: 9
    thread2: 7
    thread2: 8
    thread2: 9
```

C:\>

There are a few interesting things to note in the program output. First, notice that the program does not exit until the last thread is finished processing, even after the main thread has finished its tasks. This is an important feature of threads. Also, you can see at the beginning of the program that the spacing of the thread outputs is not consistent with what you might expect. This is due to the extra time required to set up and start each new thread. Once the threads are running, the time spacing of the outputs becomes consistent with the delay values.

All these facts bear out a very important characteristic of threads: *creating new threads is a very CPU-intensive operation.*

Later in this chapter (in the "Thread Pool" section) you'll explore some tricks that can help reduce the effect of thread creation on your program, such as creating thread pools.

WARNING When writing programs that use multiple threads, be very careful about how the threads interoperate. Multiple threads can produce problems such as deadlocks (when two threads stop responding, waiting for each other to complete) and race conditions (when erroneous results occur due to unexpected timing flaws between two or more threads). Good quality production programs must always take these events into consideration.

Using Threads in a Server

Now that you have the power of threads at your disposal, let's see how a network program can benefit from them. One of the biggest challenges of network server design is accommodating multiple clients. Up until Chapter 8, "Asynchronous Socket Programming," where the Select() method was introduced, all of this book's examples allowed only one client at a time to access the server.

A problem with using the Select() method to handle multiple clients is that the code can become convoluted and confusing. Trying to accommodate multiple clients as they send and receive data at different intervals can be quite a programming chore. Also, when using the Select() method, only one client can be serviced at a time, effectively blocking access to any other clients. It would be nice if instead you could split off each client into its own world and deal with its data separately from the rest of the clients. Threads allow you to do just that.

Creating a Threaded Server

The key to creating a threaded server is to map out its handling of each client individually and then extrapolate to hundreds (or thousands) of clients. Figure 9.2 diagrams how our sample threaded server program will operate.

FIGURE 9.2:

The threaded
server's operation

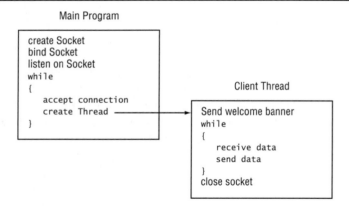

The key to the threaded server is to create the main server Socket object in the main program. As each client connects to the server, the main program creates a separate Thread object to handle the connection. Because the Socket Accept() method creates a new Socket object for the connection, the new object is passed to the delegate method and used for all communication with the client from the new thread. The original Socket object is then free to accept more client connections.

After you have determined how the new server program will create threads to handle new clients, it's easy to program the model with C#. Listing 9.6 is a sample threaded TCP server that can be used to communicate with multiple clients.

Listing 9.6   **The ThreadedTcpSrvr.cs program**

```csharp
using System;
using System.Net;
using System.Net.Sockets;
using System.Text;
using System.Threading;

class ThreadedTcpSrvr
{
    private TcpListener client;

    public ThreadedTcpSrvr()
    {
        client = new TcpListener(9050);
        client.Start();

        Console.WriteLine("Waiting for clients...");
        while(true)
        {
            while (!client.Pending())
            {
                Thread.Sleep(1000);
            }

            ConnectionThread newconnection = new ConnectionThread();
            newconnection.threadListener = this.client;
            Thread newthread = new Thread(new
                    ThreadStart(newconnection.HandleConnection));
            newthread.Start();
        }
    }

    public static void Main()
    {
        ThreadedTcpSrvr server = new ThreadedTcpSrvr();
    }
}

class ConnectionThread
{
    public TcpListener threadListener;
    private static int connections = 0;

    public void HandleConnection()
```

```
    {
        int recv;
        byte[] data = new byte[1024];

        TcpClient client = threadListener.AcceptTcpClient();
        NetworkStream ns = client.GetStream();
        connections++;
        Console.WriteLine("New client accepted: {0} active connections",
                          connections);

        string welcome = "Welcome to my test server";
        data = Encoding.ASCII.GetBytes(welcome);
        ns.Write(data, 0, data.Length);

        while(true)
        {
            data = new byte[1024];
            recv = ns.Read(data, 0, data.Length);
            if (recv == 0)
                break;

            ns.Write(data, 0, recv);
        }
        ns.Close();
        client.Close();
        connections-;
        Console.WriteLine("Client disconnected: {0} active connections",
                          connections);
    }
}
```

ThreadedTcpSrvr.cs starts off much like the other TCP server programs presented so far in this book. It uses the TcpListener class to listen for incoming TCP connections on a standard port (9050), and it uses the Start() method to begin waiting for new clients. The difference with this example is in how it accepts new clients:

```
while(true)
{
    while (!client.Pending())
    {
        Thread.Sleep(1000);
    }

    ConnectionThread newconnection = new ConnectionThread();
    newconnection.threadListener = this.client;
    Thread newthread = new Thread(new
        ThreadStart(newconnection.HandleConnection));
    newthread.Start();
}
```

The server's main program goes into an infinite loop, checking once every second to see if a client has connected and, if it has, creating a new thread to accept the connection. A separate class handles the actual communication with the client. The `TcpListener` object for the class is set to the original `TcpListener` object from the client connection.

This technique will create as many threads as there are clients wanting to connect to the server. (Under extreme conditions, of course, this may not be a good idea. Depending on the CPU power of the server, you may have to restrict the number of active clients to a reasonable number.)

Testing the Server

After starting the `ThreadedTcpSrvr` program, you can run as many client programs as you like to connect to the server. The easiest method may be to use the `AsyncTcpClient` program described in Chapter 8 because you can launch many clients from a single command-prompt window.

As the server accepts the connection from each client, it creates a separate socket and passes it to a new thread. Each thread is self-contained and performs the standard server functions without having to pass the connection back to the main program.

Each client program can operate completely independently. You can send messages from clients at will, receiving the correct message back for each client. Also, each client can terminate the connection without affecting the other clients.

Watching the Threads

You can watch the threads created for each client by using the `ListThreads` program while the server is running. If you redirect the output of the `ListThreads` program to a file, you can use the Notepad program to search for the `ThreadedTcpSrvr` process and see the threads in action:

```
process: ThreadedTcpSrvr,  id: 944
  thread:  1480
    started: 7/21/2002 9:22:54 PM
    CPU time: 00:00:00.3404896
    priority: 8
    thread state: Wait
  thread:  3648
    started: 7/21/2002 9:22:55 PM
    CPU time: 00:00:00
    priority: 8
    thread state: Wait
  thread:  1012
    started: 7/21/2002 9:22:55 PM
```

```
    CPU time: 00:00:00
    priority: 10
    thread state: Wait
thread:  1612
    started: 7/21/2002 9:25:29 PM
    CPU time: 00:00:00
    priority: 8
    thread state: Wait
thread:  2340
    started: 7/21/2002 9:25:32 PM
    CPU time: 00:00:00
    priority: 8
    thread state: Wait
```

When no clients are connected to the ThreadedTcpSrvr program, it uses three threads. When two clients are connected, it has five threads. As expected, an additional thread is created in the ThreadedTcpSrvr process as each client connects. When each client disconnects, the thread is terminated.

Using Threads for Sending and Receiving Data

In addition to supporting multiple clients, threads can also be used in network programs when there is no clear protocol model to use.

In the sample programs thus far in the book, a consistent model was defined so that both the client and server knew when to expect data to be received and when they should send data. This is not always the case in network programs, however. An example is the common chat program, which allows two people to communicate via a message-board system, where text entered on one system is displayed on the remote system, and vice-versa. The problem is that either person can decide to send a message at any time during the connection—this would cause havoc on a network protocol model.

Fortunately, threads can come to the rescue. A secondary thread can be created apart from the main program and used to block on a Receive() method, so any incoming data at any time is displayed on the message board. This concept is diagrammed in Figure 9.3. The chat participant that chooses to be the chat server places the program in a listen mode, waiting to accept a new chat client. When the client connects, the server creates a separate thread to wait for any incoming data.

Likewise, when the chat client connects to the server, it too creates a separate thread to wait for incoming data from the server. Because the secondary thread is always listening for incoming data, the primary thread has to worry only about when the local person wants to send a message to the remote host.

FIGURE 9.3:

Using threads for a
network chat program

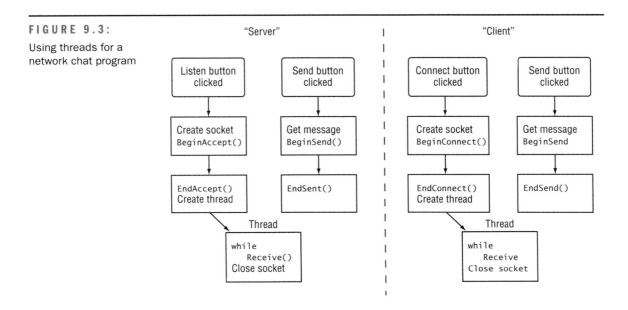

The TcpChat Program

Now that the application has been diagrammed, you'll find it fairly simple to understand and
follow the C# program in Listing 9.7, the TcpChat.cs program, which demonstrates a simple
network chat program.

Listing 9.7   **The TcpChat.cs program**

```
using System;
using System.Drawing;
using System.Net;
using System.Net.Sockets;
using System.Text;
using System.Threading;
using System.Windows.Forms;


class TcpChat  :  Form
{
    private static TextBox newText;
    private static ListBox results;
    private static Socket client;
    private static byte[] data = new byte[1024];

    public TcpChat()
```

```
        {
            Text = "TCP Chat Program";
            Size = new Size(400, 380);

            Label label1 = new Label();
            label1.Parent = this;
            label1.Text = "Enter text string:";
            label1.AutoSize = true;
            label1.Location = new Point(10, 30);

            newText = new TextBox();
            newText.Parent = this;
            newText.Size = new Size(200, 2 * Font.Height);
            newText.Location = new Point(10, 55);

            results = new ListBox();
            results.Parent = this;
            results.Location = new Point(10, 85);
            results.Size = new Size(360, 18 * Font.Height);

            Button sendit = new Button();
            sendit.Parent = this;
            sendit.Text = "Send";
            sendit.Location = new Point(220,52);
            sendit.Size = new Size(5 * Font.Height, 2 * Font.Height);
            sendit.Click += new EventHandler(ButtonSendOnClick);

            Button connect = new Button();
            connect.Parent = this;
            connect.Text = "Connect";
            connect.Location = new Point(295, 20);
            connect.Size = new Size(6 * Font.Height, 2 * Font.Height);
            connect.Click += new EventHandler(ButtonConnectOnClick);

            Button listen = new Button();
            listen.Parent = this;
            listen.Text = "Listen";
            listen.Location = new Point(295,52);
            listen.Size = new Size(6 * Font.Height, 2 * Font.Height);
            listen.Click += new EventHandler(ButtonListenOnClick);
        }

        void ButtonListenOnClick(object obj, EventArgs ea)
        {
            results.Items.Add("Listening for a client...");
            Socket newsock = new Socket(AddressFamily.InterNetwork, SocketType.Stream,
                ProtocolType.Tcp);
            IPEndPoint iep = new IPEndPoint(IPAddress.Any, 9050);
            newsock.Bind(iep);
            newsock.Listen(5);
            newsock.BeginAccept(new AsyncCallback(AcceptConn), newsock);
```

```
}

void ButtonConnectOnClick(object obj, EventArgs ea)
{
    results.Items.Add("Connecting...");
    client = new Socket(AddressFamily.InterNetwork, SocketType.Stream,
      ProtocolType.Tcp);
    IPEndPoint iep = new IPEndPoint(IPAddress.Parse("127.0.0.1"), 9050);
    client.BeginConnect(iep, new AsyncCallback(Connected), client);
}

void ButtonSendOnClick(object obj, EventArgs ea)
{
    byte[] message = Encoding.ASCII.GetBytes(newText.Text);
    newText.Clear();
    client.BeginSend(message, 0, message.Length, 0,
      new AsyncCallback(SendData), client);
}

void AcceptConn(IAsyncResult iar)
{
    Socket oldserver = (Socket)iar.AsyncState;
    client = oldserver.EndAccept(iar);
    results.Items.Add("Connection from: " + client.RemoteEndPoint.ToString());
    Thread receiver = new Thread(new ThreadStart(ReceiveData));
    receiver.Start();
}

void Connected(IAsyncResult iar)
{
    try
    {
        client.EndConnect(iar);
        results.Items.Add("Connected to: " + client.RemoteEndPoint.ToString());
        Thread receiver = new Thread(new ThreadStart(ReceiveData));
        receiver.Start();

    } catch (SocketException)
    {
        results.Items.Add("Error connecting");
    }
}

void SendData(IAsyncResult iar)
{
    Socket remote = (Socket)iar.AsyncState;
    int sent = remote.EndSend(iar);
}

void ReceiveData()
{
```

```
        int recv;
        string stringData;
        while (true)
        {
            recv = client.Receive(data);
            stringData = Encoding.ASCII.GetString(data, 0, recv);
            if (stringData == "bye")
                break;
            results.Items.Add(stringData);
        }
        stringData = "bye";
        byte[] message = Encoding.ASCII.GetBytes(stringData);
        client.Send(message);
        client.Close();
        results.Items.Add("Connection stopped");
        return;
    }

    public static void Main()
    {
        Application.Run(new TcpChat());
    }
}
```

Because the `TcpChat` program must be used as both the client and server, it must be multifunctional. The main program creates the Windows Form, which includes the following objects:

- A Listen button for placing the program in listen mode
- A Connect button for connecting to a remote chat partner
- A Send button for sending messages entered into a `TextBox` item to the remote partner
- A `ListBox` object for displaying status information and messages received from the remote partner

If the customer clicks the Listen button, a socket is created and listens for an incoming connection using the `BeginAccept()` method:

```
void ButtonListenOnClick(object obj, EventArgs ea)
{
    results.Items.Add("Listening for a client...");
    Socket newsock = new Socket(AddressFamily.InterNetwork, SocketType.Stream,
        ProtocolType.Tcp);
    IPEndPoint iep = new IPEndPoint(IPAddress.Any, 9050);
    newsock.Bind(iep);
    newsock.Listen(5);
    newsock.BeginAccept(new AsyncCallback(AcceptConn), newsock);
}
```

When the other chat program connects, the `AcceptConn()` method creates a separate socket for the client, passing it off to the secondary thread.

If the customer clicks the Connect button, a socket is created and attempts to connect to the remote host, using the `BeginConnect()` method. After the remote host accepts the connection, the socket is passed off to the secondary thread. The sole purpose of the secondary thread is to wait for incoming data, and post it to the list box:

```
void ReceiveData()
{
    int recv;
    string stringData;
    while (true)
    {
        recv = client.Receive(data);
        stringData = Encoding.ASCII.GetString(data, 0, recv);
        if (stringData == "bye")
            break;
        results.Items.Add(stringData);
    }
    stringData = "bye";
    byte[] message = Encoding.ASCII.GetBytes(stringData);
    client.Send(message);
    client.Close();
    results.Items.Add("Connection stopped");
    return;
}
```

If the received data consists of the string `"bye"`, the program replies to the string with the same message and then closes the socket. Both chat programs thus realize the conversation is over and properly close the TCP connection.

Because the secondary thread is separate from the main program thread, it can use standard blocking network methods such as `Receive()`; the secondary thread won't impede the operation of the Windows Form.

Meanwhile, back on the main program, when the customer clicks the Send button, the text entered into the text box is sent to the remote chat host.

Testing the Chat Program and Watching the Threads

To test the program, you must have two copies of it running at the same time. If you choose to test this over a network, the proper IP addresses of the remote hosts should be entered into the `IPEndPoint` object for each program.

Place one copy of `TcpChat` in listen mode by clicking the Listen button. The other copy can then connect to the remote host by clicking the Connect button. After the connection is established, messages can be sent back and forth between the two hosts. To terminate the session, the "bye" phrase must be sent to the remote chat partner. Figure 9.4 illustrates one of the TcpChat programs as it communicates with the remote copy.

FIGURE 9.4:

The TcpChat
program in action

As you did with the ThreadedTcpSrvr program, you can use the ListThreads program to see how the secondary threads are created during the connection. Each TcpChat program will create a separate thread for receiving data. After the remote TcpChat host disconnects, the secondary thread terminates and is no longer listed as an active thread. The main program still runs, however, and must be manually terminated.

Thread Pools

As you've observed in the "Using the Thread Class" section, there is a fair amount of overhead involved with having your program create new threads. The .NET library provides a way to avoid some of this overhead. The Windows OS allows you to maintain a pool of "prebuilt" threads; this *thread pool* supplies worker threads for assignment to specific methods in the application as needed. One thread controls the operation of the thread pool, and the application can assign additional threads to processes. By default, there are 25 threads per processor in the thread pool, so this method does not work well for large-scale applications.

NOTE You access the thread pool via the .NET ThreadPool class.

The ThreadPool Class

The System.Threading namespace contains the ThreadPool class, which assigns delegates to threads in the thread pool. All of the methods in the ThreadPool class are static, so no constructor is ever used to make an instance of a ThreadPool object. Instead, once a ThreadPool method is called, the operating system automatically creates a thread pool, and the static ThreadPool methods are used to manipulate the worker threads within the pool.

Table 9.8 defines the static methods used in the ThreadPool class.

TABLE 9.8: The ThreadPool Static Methods

Method	Description
BindHandle()	Binds an operating system handle to the thread pool
GetAvailableThreads()	Gets the number of worker threads available for use in the thread pool
GetMaxThreads()	Gets the maximum number of worker threads available in the thread pool
QueueUserWorkItem()	Queues a user delegate to the thread pool
RegisterWaitForSingleObject()	Registers a delegate waiting for a WaitHandle object
UnsafeQueueUserWorkItem()	Queues an unsafe user delegate to the thread pool but does not propagate the calling stack onto the worker thread
UnsafeRegisterWaitForSingleObject()	Registers an unsafe delegate waiting for a WaitHandle object

To register a delegate for use in a thread pool's thread, use the following format:

```
ThreadPool.QueueUserWorkItem(new WaitCallback(Counter));
```

The *Counter* parameter is a delegate for the method run in the thread.

Unlike Thread objects, once the delegate is placed in the thread pool queue, it will be processed; no other methods are required to start it.

WARNING When the main program thread exits, all thread-pool threads are aborted. The main thread does not wait for them to finish.

A Sample ThreadPool Program

Again, the best way to learn about the thread pool is to see it in action. The ThreadPoolSample.cs program in Listing 9.8 demonstrates the creation of two threads in the thread pool to process a method apart from the main program thread.

Listing 9.8   **The ThreadPoolSample.cs program**

```
using System;
using System.Threading;

class ThreadPoolSample
{

   public static void Main()
   {
      ThreadPoolSample tps = new ThreadPoolSample();
   }

   public ThreadPoolSample()
   {
      int i;

      ThreadPool.QueueUserWorkItem(new WaitCallback(Counter));
      ThreadPool.QueueUserWorkItem(new WaitCallback(Counter2));

      for(i = 0; i < 10; i++)
      {
         Console.WriteLine("main: {0}", i);
         Thread.Sleep(1000);
      }
   }

   void Counter(object state)
   {
      int i;
      for (i = 0; i < 10; i++)
      {
         Console.WriteLine("  thread: {0}", i);
         Thread.Sleep(2000);
      }
   }

   void Counter2(object state)
   {
      int i;
      for (i = 0; i < 10; i++)
      {
         Console.WriteLine("    thread2: {0}", i);
         Thread.Sleep(3000);
```

```
        }
      }
    }
```

There is not much to this example—the main program places two method calls in the thread pool queue and then proceeds to perform its own function, counting from zero to nine, with a one-second delay between counts.

Similar to the `ThreadSample` program, each of the separate methods performs the same task but with a different delay interval.

Testing the Program and Watching the Threads

When you run the `ThreadPoolSample` program, watch how the output from the various methods work. Notice how the program stops after the main thread finishes its loop. As mentioned, the application will not wait for a thread-pool thread to finish. After the main program thread is done, it will abort any running thread-pool threads, as demonstrated in this example:

```
C:\>ThreadPoolSample
main: 0
  thread: 0
    thread2: 0
main: 1
  thread: 1
main: 2
main: 3
    thread2: 1
  thread: 2
main: 4
main: 5
  thread: 3
main: 6
    thread2: 2
main: 7
  thread: 4
main: 8
main: 9
    thread2: 3
  thread: 5

C:\>
```

Use the `ListThreads` program created earlier to watch the threads generated by `ThreadPoolSample`. Start `ThreadPoolSample` from one command-prompt window and then run `ListThreads` in another. To make it easier to see the threads for the

ThreadPoolSample process, you can redirect the output from the ListThreads program to a file, and examine the file in Notepad:

```
C:\>ListThreads > threads.txt
C:\>notepad threads.txt
```

You should see several threads being used by the ThreadPoolSample program:

```
process: ThreadPoolSample,  id: 2676
  thread:  2632
    started: 7/23/2002 11:57:31 PM
    CPU time: 00:00:00.1502160
    priority: 8
    thread state: Wait
  thread:  2620
    started: 7/23/2002 11:57:31 PM
    CPU time: 00:00:00
    priority: 8
    thread state: Wait
  thread:  2508
    started: 7/23/2002 11:57:31 PM
    CPU time: 00:00:00
    priority: 10
    thread state: Wait
  thread:  3032
    started: 7/23/2002 11:57:31 PM
    CPU time: 00:00:00.0200288
    priority: 8
    thread state: Wait
  thread:  3036
    started: 7/23/2002 11:57:31 PM
    CPU time: 00:00:00
    priority: 8
    thread state: Wait
  thread:  2888
    started: 7/23/2002 11:57:32 PM
    CPU time: 00:00:00
    priority: 8
    thread state: Wait
  thread:  3040
    started: 7/23/2002 11:57:32 PM
    CPU time: 00:00:00
    priority: 8
    thread state: Wait
```

NOTE   You may be wondering why so many threads appear in the list when only two additional threads were created. The answer is that the thread pool must create its own thread when two or more thread-pool threads are being used. This "overhead" thread controls the running threads of the thread pool. You will not see this control thread if only one thread-pool thread is created.

Using Thread Pools in a Server

For servers that service only a few clients (less than the thread pool maximum of 25 threads), the ThreadPool class can quickly service clients in separate threads *without* the overhead of creating separate Thread objects. Each client can be assigned to the user work item and processed by an available thread pool's thread.

NOTE   Keep in mind that the main program must remain active for as long as each of the ThreadPool objects is active, or the connection will be terminated. Once the main program is terminated, each of the thread pool's threads will also terminate, possibly killing an active connection and sending the client into a tailspin—but of course, you will have programmed the client to accommodate such an unruly situation.

A ThreadPool Server

The ThreadPoolTcpSrvr.cs program demonstrates the standard TCP server model used in this book with a ThreadPool object. As each client connects to the server, a separate ThreadPool user work item is created to handle the socket. Listing 9.9 shows the ThreadPoolTcpSrvr.cs program.

Listing 9.9   **The ThreadPoolTcpSrvr.cs program**

```
using System;
using System.Net;
using System.Net.Sockets;
using System.Text;
using System.Threading;

class ThreadPoolTcpSrvr
{
```

```
    private TcpListener client;

    public ThreadPoolTcpSrvr()
    {
        client = new TcpListener(9050);
        client.Start();

        Console.WriteLine("Waiting for clients...");
        while(true)
        {
            while (!client.Pending())
            {
                Thread.Sleep(1000);
            }
            ConnectionThread newconnection = new ConnectionThread();
            newconnection.threadListener = this.client;
            ThreadPool.QueueUserWorkItem(new
                        WaitCallback(newconnection.HandleConnection));
        }
    }

    public static void Main()
    {
        ThreadPoolTcpSrvr tpts = new ThreadPoolTcpSrvr();
    }
}

class ConnectionThread
{
    public TcpListener threadListener;
    private static int connections = 0;

    public void HandleConnection(object state)
    {
        int recv;
        byte[] data = new byte[1024];

        TcpClient client = threadListener.AcceptTcpClient();
        NetworkStream ns = client.GetStream();
        connections++;
        Console.WriteLine("New client accepted: {0} active connections",
                        connections);

        string welcome = "Welcome to my test server";
        data = Encoding.ASCII.GetBytes(welcome);
        ns.Write(data, 0, data.Length);

        while(true)
        {
            data = new byte[1024];
            recv = ns.Read(data, 0, data.Length);
            if (recv == 0)
```

```
            break;

        ns.Write(data, 0, recv);
    }
    ns.Close();
    client.Close();
    connections-;
    Console.WriteLine("Client disconnected: {0} active connections",
                    connections);
    }
}
```

Similar to all of the other TCP server programs presented in this book, the ThreadPoolTcpSrvr program creates a socket to listen for new connections. In this situation, the TcpListener class creates the socket and listen for incoming connections. When a connection is detected, a new instance of the ConnectionThread class is created, and the TcpListener object is copied to the class to continue the communication. The HandleConnection() method is passed to the QueueUserWorkItem() method to start a new ThreadPool thread with the new connection.

When the connection is terminated, the socket is closed and the thread-pool thread terminates. Because the main program is in an endless loop waiting for new clients, there is no risk of terminating active connections unless the main program is manually aborted.

Testing the Program and Watching the Threads

The ThreadPoolTcpSrvr program can be tested with any of the TCP clients used in this book. First, start the ThreadPoolTcpSrvr program from a command prompt, and then start as many TCP clients (such as the AsyncTcpClient program from Chapter 8) as you like.

Each client creates a new socket, which is passed off to a new user work item in the thread pool. The user work item is then assigned to a new thread and processed as normal. Each client can disconnect without affecting the session of any of the other clients. Because the server is running in an endless loop waiting for new clients, you must manually stop it by pressing Ctrl-C. (If you do this while any connections are active, the connections will abort and the clients will receive an Exception.)

You can use the ListThreads program to see the threads being used by the ThreadPoolTcpSrvr program. First, obtain a list of the threads being used before any connections are accepted:

```
process: ThreadPoolTcpSrvr,  id: 1876
  thread:  980
    started: 7/23/2002 11:23:10 PM
    CPU time: 00:00:00.4306192
    priority: 8
    thread state: Wait
```

```
thread:  1544
  started: 7/23/2002 11:23:11 PM
  CPU time: 00:00:00
  priority: 8
  thread state: Wait
thread:  536
  started: 7/23/2002 11:23:11 PM
  CPU time: 00:00:00
  priority: 10
  thread state: Wait
```

This shows that the standard three threads are being used in the program. Next, use a TCP client program to connect to the server, and then get another snapshot of the threads in use:

```
process: ThreadPoolTcpSrvr,  id: 1876
  thread:  980
    started: 7/23/2002 11:23:09 PM
    CPU time: 00:00:00.4806912
    priority: 8
    thread state: Wait
  thread:  1544
    started: 7/23/2002 11:23:10 PM
    CPU time: 00:00:00
    priority: 8
    thread state: Wait
  thread:  536
    started: 7/23/2002 11:23:10 PM
    CPU time: 00:00:00
    priority: 10
    thread state: Wait
  thread:  1184
    started: 7/23/2002 11:25:53 PM
    CPU time: 00:00:00.0400576
    priority: 8
    thread state: Wait
```

As you can see from the ListThreads output for the ThreadPoolTcpSrvr process, the thread-pool thread is counted as a new thread, processing the client connection for the main program. This becomes interesting when a second client connects to the server. When the second client connects to the server, again take a snapshot of the running threads for the program. Instead of the five threads you might expect, you will see seven. That's because, as soon as a second thread-pool thread is created, the thread pool itself creates another thread to manage the existing threads.

Summary

This chapter demonstrates processes and threads in C# network programs. Processes are controlled by the OS based on a process priority. Each process gets a turn to use the system CPU and memory based on its priority in the system.

The .NET library's Process class allows you to control processes from within a C# program. The current process is obtained with the GetCurrentProcess() method. Other processes can be obtained by using the process name or ID. Once a Process object is created, the methods of the Process class can be used to control it. Characteristics of the process can be displayed using properties of the Process class.

Each process comprises one or more threads, which are individual flows of operation within a program. Many programs only have one flow of operation, from the start of the program to the end. These programs contain only one thread. Others may create secondary threads to process information in a background mode while the main application continues in the foreground.

The .NET library's Thread class allows you to create and modify Thread objects. Each Thread object creates a new thread for the system to process. Once a process's threads are obtained from the Process class Threads() method, they can be added to a ProcessThreadCollection object. Each thread can then be extracted from the ProcessThreadCollection object to retrieve information regarding the thread state and system usage.

C# network programs can create secondary threads to process multiple client connections. As each new connection attempt is received, it can be passed off to a new thread. Each thread is independent of the main program, which continues to wait for new connection attempts. The new threads can then process the incoming data from the client.

Although creating new threads is useful, it also demands extensive CPU resources. Creating many new threads may cause a significant performance problem as the overhead of creating the new threads is processed. An alternative is to use the ThreadPool object, which lets you use threads from the system thread pool to process new client connections. These threads have already been created and are waiting to be assigned something to do. This technique lessens the overhead of creating new threads for each new client.

In the next chapter, you'll study IP multicasting, which allows a single device to communicate with multiple remote clients by sending a single packet. This can greatly reduce network bandwidth requirements for programs that send duplicate information to multiple hosts.

## CHAPTER 10

IP Multicasting

- Broadcasting, local versus global

- Broadcasting with C#

- Using broadcast packets

- How multicasting works

- C# socket multicasting

- C# `UdpClient` multicasting

- A sample multicast application

All of the programming examples in the preceding chapters have one thing in common (other than being written in C#): they were designed to send messages to one remote device at a time. When there were multiple clients involved, each message was sent to each client separately.

This chapter changes that pattern by introducing the ideas *IP broadcasting*, which sends information to all devices on a subnet at the same time, and *IP multicasting*, which sends information to multiple devices on the network at the same time. Implementing either or both of these IP communication techniques will decrease the amount of network bandwidth used by an application, because you use a single packet to send the same information to a collection of devices.

We'll start with an overview of IP broadcasting and show how to implement it in some example C# network programs. In the process, we'll improve that clunky chat program (Listing 9.7, `TcpChat.cs`) we studied in Chapter 9. Then we'll move on to the concepts of IP multicasting. We'll examine the two ways to control multicast sessions: a peer-to-peer network, and a central server that communicates with group clients. The section on C# implementation of IP multicast support covers how to create multicast packets using both `Socket` and `UdpClient` objects and how to incorporate them into network programs.

What Is Broadcasting?

IP broadcasting is used by network devices to send a single packet of information that can be accessible by every device on the network. Because TCP communication requires that two devices have a dedicated connection, it is not possible to send broadcast messages in a strictly TCP environment. Instead, UDP packets must be used because that protocol has the capability of sending messages without a specific connection being defined.

Local versus Global Broadcasts

Broadcast messages contain a special destination IP address. The IP address format allows for two types of broadcast message addresses: local broadcasts and global broadcasts.

Network programmers use the *local broadcast address* to send a broadcast message destined for all devices on a particular subnet. The idea is to localize a broadcast message so that other networks are not affected by the broadcast.

As discussed in Chapter 2, "IP Programming Basics," an IP address is divided into two parts, a network address and a host address. The standard network address part makes up the first part of the local broadcast address, and all 1s are used for the host part of the address (which is the decimal value 255 in the address octet). This is demonstrated in Figure 10.1. Thus, for the class B network 192.168.0.0, using a subnet mask of 255.255.0.0, the local broadcast address would be 192.168.255.255.

FIGURE 10.1:

The IP network and host address parts of a local broadcast address

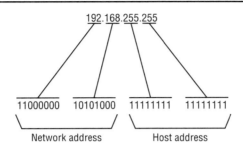

Similarly, if the subnet is further divided using a subnet mask of 255.255.255.0, each subnet would have its own local broadcast address. The subnet 192.168.1.0 would have a broadcast address of 192.168.1.255, and so on up to the subnet 192.168.254.0, which would have the broadcast address 192.168.254.255.

The *global broadcast* was originally intended to allow a device to send a packet to all devices on an internetwork. It uses all 1s in the IP address, creating an address of 255.255.255.255. This special broadcast address indicates that the destination of the packet is all devices on all networks accessible from the device sending the message.

The vast size and burgeoning popularity of the Internet, of course, meant that this behavior had to be modified. Otherwise, it would be easy for a rogue programmer to create a stream of global broadcasts that would propagate to all networks on the Internet, effectively clogging the worldwide system with bogus broadcasts and stopping normal traffic. To eliminate this possibility, routers do not send global IP broadcasts to other networks unless specifically configured to do so (which is practically never). Instead, they silently ignore global broadcasts, effectively turning them into local broadcasts that are seen only on the local network over which they were sent.

Implementing Broadcasting with C#

The .NET network library contains elements for sending and receiving broadcast packets. This section describes the techniques necessary to handle broadcast packets in your network application programs.

Sending Broadcast Packets

By default, sockets are not allowed to send broadcast messages. You can test this by running the simple program shown in Listing 10.1.

Listing 10.1 **The BadBroadcast.cs program**

```csharp
using System;
using System.Net;
using System.Net.Sockets;
using System.Text;

class BadBroadcast
{
    public static void Main()
    {
        Socket sock = new Socket(AddressFamily.InterNetwork, SocketType.Dgram,
                            ProtocolType.Udp);
        IPEndPoint iep = new IPEndPoint(IPAddress.Broadcast, 9050);

        byte[] data = Encoding.ASCII.GetBytes("This is a test message");
        sock.SendTo(data, iep);
        sock.Close();
    }
}
```

When you try to run this program, you will get an Exception message:

C:\>**BadBroadcast**

```
Unhandled Exception: System.Net.Sockets.SocketException: An attempt was made to
access a socket in a way forbidden by its access permissions
    at System.Net.Sockets.Socket.SendTo(Byte[] buffer, Int32 offset, Int32 size,
SocketFlags socketFlags, EndPoint remoteEP)
    at System.Net.Sockets.Socket.SendTo(Byte[] buffer, EndPoint remoteEP)
    at BadBroadcast.Main()
```

C:\>

The BadBroadcast.cs program seems simple enough, but when it runs, the .NET environment doesn't allow the SendTo() method to send the message. As seen, if you attempt to send a broadcast message from a default UDP socket, you will get a SocketException error.

For a C# application to send broadcast packets, the broadcast socket option must be set on the created socket using the SetSocketOption() method of the Socket class. (The SetSocketOption was discussed in Chapter 3, "C# Network Programming Classes.") Here is a code snippet for using the SetSocketOption() method in this way:

```csharp
Socket sock = new Socket(AddressFamily.InterNetwork,
                SocketType.Dgram, ProtocolType.Udp);
sock.SetSocketOption(SocketOptionLevel.Socket, SocketOptionName.Broadcast, 1);
```

Note that the SocketType must be set to Dgram for broadcast messages. The SocketOption-Name.Broadcast option is a Socket level option, so the SocketOptionLevel parameter must be set to Socket.

Because the SetSocketOption() method does not allow boolean values for the data parameter, you must set the value parameter to any non-zero value to represent the true boolean value. Zero represents the false boolean value.

After the socket option is set, you specify a broadcast address and port to use for the broadcast and use the SendTo() method to send a message on that address:

```
IPEndPoint iep = new IPEndPoint(IPAddress.Broadcast, 9050);
byte[] data = Encoding.Ascii.GetBytes("test message");
sock.SendTo(data, iep);
```

Using the Broadcast property of the IPAddress class as a destination address, the program will send the broadcast message out to all network interfaces configured on the device. To limit the broadcast to a specific interface, you must manually supply a local broadcast address to use for the destination address. Listing 10.2 demonstrates using both the IPAddress.Broadcast address and a local broadcast address in a sample C# program, Broadcst.cs.

Listing 10.2   **The Broadcst.cs program**

```
using System;
using System.Net;
using System.Net.Sockets;
using System.Text;

class Broadcst
{
    public static void Main()
    {
        Socket sock = new Socket(AddressFamily.InterNetwork, SocketType.Dgram,
                            ProtocolType.Udp);
        IPEndPoint iep1 = new IPEndPoint(IPAddress.Broadcast, 9050);
        IPEndPoint iep2 = new IPEndPoint(IPAddress.Parse("192.168.1.255"), 9050);

        string hostname = Dns.GetHostName();
        byte[] data = Encoding.ASCII.GetBytes(hostname);

        sock.SetSocketOption(SocketOptionLevel.Socket,
                            SocketOptionName.Broadcast, 1);
        sock.SendTo(data, iep1);
        sock.SendTo(data, iep2);
        sock.Close();
    }
}
```

The `Broadcst` program creates two separate `IPEndPoint` objects, one using the `IPAddress.Broadcast` address and one using a local broadcast address 192.168.1.255. Next, the local hostname of the device is determined using the standard `Dns GetHostName()` method, and it is sent out in two separate broadcast messages.

As you've done throughout this book, you can use WinDump or Analyzer to monitor the network for the broadcast messages. Figure 10.2 illustrates the output of the `Broadcst` program in Analyzer.

FIGURE 10.2:

The Analyzer output from the `Broadcst` program

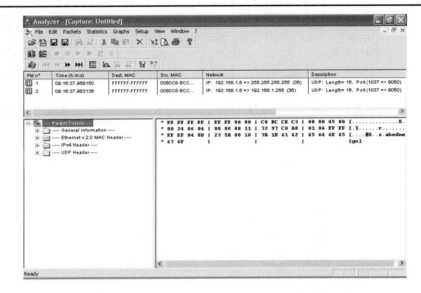

The Analyzer program captured two separate broadcast packets sent out on the network. The first packet was sent to the 255.255.255.255. global broadcast address, which resulted from setting the destination address to `IPAddress.Broadcast`. The second broadcast packet was sent to the local 192.168.1.255 address, the manually specified local broadcast address in the program.

Receiving Broadcast Packets

Receiving broadcast packets is a little less complex than sending them. By default, no special options are required for a socket to receive a broadcast message. If a socket is listening on a specified UDP port, it will accept any message destined for either a broadcast address or the local IP address of the device. The `RecvBroadcst.cs` program in Listing 10.3 demonstrates this by creating a socket to listen for packets on UDP port 9050, the same port from which the `Broadcst` program is sending broadcast messages.

Listing 10.3   **The RecvBroadcst.cs program**

```csharp
using System;
using System.Net;
using System.Net.Sockets;
using System.Text;

class RecvBroadcst
{
    public static void Main()
    {
        Socket sock = new Socket(AddressFamily.InterNetwork,
                        SocketType.Dgram, ProtocolType.Udp);
        IPEndPoint iep = new IPEndPoint(IPAddress.Any, 9050);
        sock.Bind(iep);
        EndPoint ep = (EndPoint)iep;
        Console.WriteLine("Ready to receive…");


        byte[] data = new byte[1024];
        int recv = sock.ReceiveFrom(data, ref ep);
        string stringData = Encoding.ASCII.GetString(data, 0, recv);
        Console.WriteLine("received: {0}  from: {1}",
                            stringData, ep.ToString());

        data = new byte[1024];
        recv = sock.ReceiveFrom(data, ref ep);
        stringData = Encoding.ASCII.GetString(data, 0, recv);
        Console.WriteLine("received: {0}  from: {1}",
                            stringData, ep.ToString());
        sock.Close();
    }
}
```

The RecvBroadcst program is a simple UDP program that creates a socket and binds it to all network interfaces on the device, using port 9050, the same port that the Broadcst program uses to send its broadcast messages. After binding the socket to the UDP port, the program attempts to receive two messages sent to the port and displays the message and the sending host address information.

You can start the RecvBroadcst program in a command prompt window, and then run the Broadcst program from either another command prompt window on the same device, or from another device on the same subnet. A sample output from the RecvBroadcst program is as follows:

```
C:\>RecvBroadcst
received: abednego  from: 192.168.1.6:1042
```

```
received: abednego  from: 192.168.1.6:1042

C:\>
```

As expected, the RecvBroadcst program received both forms of the broadcast message that were sent by the Broadcst program.

WARNING When testing broadcast programs, remember to use devices on the same subnet.

Using Broadcast Packets to Advertise a Server

One of the most common uses for broadcast packets is to advertise the presence of a server on the network. By repeatedly sending out a broadcast packet containing information regarding the server at a predetermined time interval, you make it possible for clients to easily detect the presence of the server on the local subnet. This technique is used for many types of applications, from Windows application servers to network printers.

This section shows you a simple way to add broadcast advertising to the TcpChat program (Listing 9.7) presented in Chapter 9, "Using Threads." This version allows clients to know when another chat program is running on the same subnet.

The Advertising Loop

The easiest way to add advertising to a network application is to create a background thread that repeatedly broadcasts the server information at a set time interval. The trick is to repeat the broadcast often enough that new clients can quickly find the broadcasting server, but not so often that the local network gets flooded with broadcast packets. Often a one-minute interval is chosen as a compromise.

The advertising thread should be self-contained, creating its own socket and sending the broadcast packet at the predetermined interval. It should be created as a background thread and assigned a lower priority than the main program thread. This ensures that the advertising thread does not take away from the main program's processing time and affect the program's overall response.

The Advertise.cs program in Listing 10.4 creates a background thread that sends out a broadcast packet every minute with the hostname of the device running the application.

Listing 10.4   **The Advertise.cs program**

```
using System;
using System.Net;
```

```
using System.Net.Sockets;
using System.Text;
using System.Threading;

class Advertise
{
    public static void Main()
    {
        Advertise server = new Advertise();
    }

    public Advertise()
    {
        Thread advert = new Thread(new ThreadStart(sendPackets));
        advert.IsBackground = true;
        advert.Start();
        Console.Write("Press Enter to stop");
        string data = Console.ReadLine();
    }

    void sendPackets()
    {
        Socket sock = new Socket(AddressFamily.InterNetwork,
                        SocketType.Dgram, ProtocolType.Udp);
        sock.SetSocketOption(SocketOptionLevel.Socket,
                            SocketOptionName.Broadcast, 1);
        IPEndPoint iep = new IPEndPoint(IPAddress.Broadcast, 9050);

        string hostname = Dns.GetHostName();
        byte[] data = Encoding.ASCII.GetBytes(hostname);
        while (true)
        {
            sock.SendTo(data, iep);
            Thread.Sleep(60000);
        }
    }
}
```

The Advertise.cs program creates a new Thread object using the sendPackets() method, which generates a Socket object for the broadcast address and broadcasts the hostname every 60 seconds. The Thread.Sleep() method puts the thread in idle mode between broadcasts. The broadcast thread is placed in background mode by means of the IsBackground property of the Thread class.

Because the main part of the application does nothing but create the background thread, it must wait, or the background thread will be terminated. This is set up using the Console.ReadLine() method to wait for input from the console before terminating the main program.

You can watch the `Advertise.cs` program by running the `RecvBroadcst` program, which will show the first two broadcast messages. You can use the WinDump or Analyzer programs to watch how the broadcast messages are sent on the network. As expected, the program sends out a broadcast packet every 60 seconds identifying itself on the network. Any clients listening to broadcasts on port 9051 will receive the messages and know that the server is available on the network.

The `TcpChat` program (Listing 9.7) presented in Chapter 9 had one major drawback: for it to communicate properly, you had to manually compile the address of the remote host into the program—obviously not a good way to do business in a production application. With broadcast messages at your disposal, you can fix the `TcpChat` program to be more user-friendly.

There are two pieces that need to be added to the original `TcpChat` program to accomplish this goal:

- A background thread that broadcasts an identification message on the subnet
- A way to listen for broadcast messages and detect another chat application running on the subnet

As seen in the `Advertise.cs` program, the first part is easy; you just create a background thread using the `Thread` class to broadcast a message using a UDP port that's separate from the one used for the chat communication. The second piece—the listener—is a little trickier to implement.

First, the program must listen for broadcast messages from possible chat clients on the subnet. This can be done by another background thread that listens for broadcasts on the network. As broadcast messages from other chat clients are detected, their information will be listed for the customer's selection. A problem with creating this list is that each client is sending its information out every minute. You cannot simply add any message detected to the list, or a single chat client will appear multiple times. A production-quality application must keep track of each client added to the list and not duplicate it. For this simple example, you can handle that issue by having the program get only the first advertising chat program it sees and place its information in the `ListBox`.

The second part of this process is to enable the customer's selection of the desired client information from the list box (which for this example will be only one entry). Then the customer needs to click the Connect button to chat with the selected client. The hostname and address for the remote client are taken from the information gathered from the broadcast packet, and the chat connection is created.

The NewTcpChat Program

All of these features are demonstrated in the `NewTcpChat.cs` program, shown in Listing 10.5.

Listing 10.5   **The NewTcpChat.cs program**

```csharp
using System;
using System.Drawing;
using System.Net;
using System.Net.Sockets;
using System.Text;
using System.Threading;
using System.Windows.Forms;


class NewTcpChat : Form
{
    private static TextBox newText;
    private static ListBox results;
    private static ListBox hosts;
    private static Socket client;
    private static byte[] data = new byte[1024];

    public NewTcpChat()
    {
        Text = "New TCP Chat Program";
        Size = new Size(400, 380);

        Label label1 = new Label();
        label1.Parent = this;
        label1.Text = "Enter text string:";
        label1.AutoSize = true;
        label1.Location = new Point(10, 30);

        newText = new TextBox();
        newText.Parent = this;
        newText.Size = new Size(200, 2 * Font.Height);
        newText.Location = new Point(10, 55);

        results = new ListBox();
        results.Parent = this;
        results.Location = new Point(10, 85);
        results.Size = new Size(360, 10 * Font.Height);

        Label label2 = new Label();
        label2.Parent = this;
        label2.Text = "Active hosts";
        label2.AutoSize = true;
        label2.Location = new Point(10, 240);

        hosts = new ListBox();
        hosts.Parent = this;
        hosts.Location = new Point(10, 255);
```

```
            hosts.Size = new Size(360, 5 * Font.Height);

            Button sendit = new Button();
            sendit.Parent = this;
            sendit.Text = "Send";
            sendit.Location = new Point(220,52);
            sendit.Size = new Size(5 * Font.Height, 2 * Font.Height);
            sendit.Click += new EventHandler(ButtonSendOnClick);

            Button connect = new Button();
            connect.Parent = this;
            connect.Text = "Connect";
            connect.Location = new Point(295, 20);
            connect.Size = new Size(6 * Font.Height, 2 * Font.Height);
            connect.Click += new EventHandler(ButtonConnectOnClick);

            Button listen = new Button();
            listen.Parent = this;
            listen.Text = "Listen";
            listen.Location = new Point(295,52);
            listen.Size = new Size(6 * Font.Height, 2 * Font.Height);
            listen.Click += new EventHandler(ButtonListenOnClick);

            Thread fh = new Thread(new ThreadStart(findHosts));
            fh.IsBackground = true;
            fh.Start();
        }

        void ButtonListenOnClick(object obj, EventArgs ea)
        {
            results.Items.Add("Listening for a client...");
            Socket newsock = new Socket
              (AddressFamily.InterNetwork, SocketType.Stream, ProtocolType.Tcp);
            IPEndPoint iep = new IPEndPoint(IPAddress.Any, 9050);
            newsock.Bind(iep);
            newsock.Listen(5);
            newsock.BeginAccept(new AsyncCallback(AcceptConn), newsock);
            Thread advertise = new Thread(new ThreadStart(srvrAdvertise));
            advertise.IsBackground = true;
            advertise.Start();
        }

        void ButtonConnectOnClick(object obj, EventArgs ea)
        {
            results.Items.Add("Connecting...");
            client = new Socket
              (AddressFamily.InterNetwork, SocketType.Stream, ProtocolType.Tcp);
            string selectedhost = (string)hosts.SelectedItem;
            string[] hostarray = selectedhost.Split(':');
            IPEndPoint iep = new IPEndPoint(IPAddress.Parse(hostarray[1]), 9050);
            client.BeginConnect(iep, new AsyncCallback(Connected), client);
        }

        void ButtonSendOnClick(object obj, EventArgs ea)
```

```
{
   byte[] message = Encoding.ASCII.GetBytes(newText.Text);
   newText.Clear();
   client.BeginSend(message, 0, message.Length, 0,
                    new AsyncCallback(SendData), client);
}

void AcceptConn(IAsyncResult iar)
{
   Socket oldserver = (Socket)iar.AsyncState;
   client = oldserver.EndAccept(iar);
   results.Items.Add("Connection from: " + client.RemoteEndPoint.ToString());
   Thread receiver = new Thread(new ThreadStart(ReceiveData));
   receiver.IsBackground = true;
   receiver.Start();
}

void Connected(IAsyncResult iar)
{
   try
   {
      client.EndConnect(iar);
      results.Items.Add("Connected to: " + client.RemoteEndPoint.ToString());
      Thread receiver = new Thread(new ThreadStart(ReceiveData));
      receiver.IsBackground = true;
      receiver.Start();

   } catch (SocketException)
   {
      results.Items.Add("Error connecting");
   }
}

void SendData(IAsyncResult iar)
{
   Socket remote = (Socket)iar.AsyncState;
   int sent = remote.EndSend(iar);
}

void ReceiveData()
{
   int recv;
   string stringData;
   while (true)
   {
      recv = client.Receive(data);
      stringData = Encoding.ASCII.GetString(data, 0, recv);
      if (stringData == "bye")
         break;
      results.Items.Add(stringData);
   }
   stringData = "bye";
   byte[] message = Encoding.ASCII.GetBytes(stringData);
   client.Send(message);
```

```
        client.Close();
        results.Items.Add("Connection stopped");
        return;
    }

    void srvrAdvertise()
    {
        Socket server = new Socket(AddressFamily.InterNetwork,
                            SocketType.Dgram, ProtocolType.Udp);
        server.SetSocketOption(SocketOptionLevel.Socket,
                            SocketOptionName.Broadcast, 1);
        IPEndPoint iep = new IPEndPoint(IPAddress.Broadcast, 9051);
        byte[] hostname = Encoding.ASCII.GetBytes(Dns.GetHostName());
        while (true)
        {
            server.SendTo(hostname, iep);
            Thread.Sleep(60000);
        }
    }

    void findHosts()
    {
        while (true)
        {
            Socket remoteHosts = new Socket(AddressFamily.InterNetwork,
                                SocketType.Dgram, ProtocolType.Udp);
            IPEndPoint iep = new IPEndPoint(IPAddress.Any, 9051);
            EndPoint ep = (EndPoint)iep;
            remoteHosts.Bind(iep);
            byte[] data = new byte[1024];
            int recv = remoteHosts.ReceiveFrom(data, ref ep);
            string stringData = Encoding.ASCII.GetString(data, 0, recv);
            string entry = stringData + ":" + ep.ToString();
            if (!hosts.Items.Contains(entry))
                hosts.Items.Add(""entry);
        }
    }
    public static void Main()
    {
        Application.Run(new NewTcpChat());
    }
}
```

The NewTcpChat program uses the basic form of the old TcpChat program, but it adds the new required pieces for broadcasting. When the Listen button is clicked to put the program in listen mode, a background thread starts. The srvrAdvertise() method implements a broadcast advertising program to announce the name of the system on which the chat program is running. This ensures that only chat clients in the listen mode will be advertised on the network.

The second enhancement in NewTcpChat is a new method, findHosts(),which listens for broadcasts on the UDP 9051 port. Because this method must be run in a background thread when the application starts, it is placed in the main program section.

Finally, notice that the Connect button method has been modified. Instead of connecting to a predetermined address, the selected entry from the host's list box is retrieved and parsed to find the destination IP address, which is used in the connection attempt.

Testing the New Application

Unfortunately, because the NewTcpChat program automatically listens for broadcasts on UDP port 9051, you can only run one instance of the program on a machine. (Remember, only one program at a time can bind to a port). To test this program you must have two machines on the same subnet.

Start the NewTcpChat program in the command prompt window on two separate machines. On one, click the Listen button to place it in listen mode. The other program should eventually see the broadcast from the listening program and display that machine's hostname along with the IP address and port number in the list box. Figure 10.3 shows what this should look like.

FIGURE 10.3:

The NewTcpChat program after it detects a remote chat program

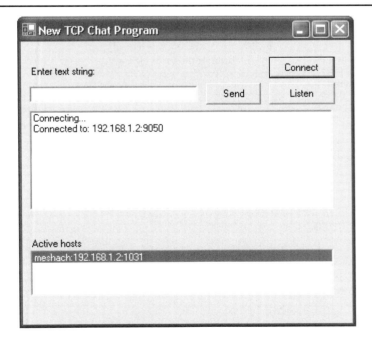

When you see the host information in the list box, click once to select the information, and then click the Connect button. This should establish the chat connection with the remote chat program, and you can begin sending text messages.

What Is Multicasting?

Broadcasting is an excellent way to send information to all devices on a subnet, but it does have a drawback: the broadcast packets are restricted to the local subnet. *IP multicasting* was devised to allow an application to send a single packet to a select subset of devices both on the local subnet and across network boundaries. This feature allows an application to join a multicast group to participate in a wide-area conference.

Just like broadcasting, IP multicasting uses special IP addresses. The IP multicasting scheme uses a particular range of IP addresses to designate different *multicast groups*. Each multicast group consists of a group of devices listening to the same IP address. As packets are sent out destined for the multicast group address, each device listening to the address receives them.

The IP address range 224.0.0.1 through 239.255.255.255 represents multicast groups. According to Internet Request For Comments (RFC) 3171, the groups are divided as shown in Table 10.1.

TABLE 10.1: IP Multicast Address Assignments

Range	Assignment
224.0.0.0–224.0.0.255	Local network control block
224.0.1.0–224.0.1.255	Internetwork control block
224.0.2.0–224.0.255.0	AD-HOC block
224.1.0.0–224.1.255.255	ST multicast groups
224.2.0.0–224.2.255.255	SDP/SAP block
224.252.0.0–224.255.255.255	DIS transient block
225.0.0.0–231.255.255.255	Reserved
232.0.0.0–232.255.255.255	Source-specific multicast block
233.0.0.0–233.255.255.255	GLOP block
234.0.0.0–238.255.255.255	Reserved
239.0.0.0–239.255.255.255	Administratively scoped block

Within each of these address blocks, individual IP addresses are assigned to specific projects. For example, addresses 224.0.0.1 and 224.0.0.2 are reserved for routers to communicate multicast group information between themselves. You should avoid using multicast group addresses that occur within these blocks.

Multicast Techniques

There are two techniques used to control multicast sessions:

- A peer-to-peer technique, in which all clients can send messages to all other clients in the group

- A central server that sends messages to group clients

Peer-to-Peer Technique

In a peer-to-peer multicast group (Figure 10.4), all of the clients in the multicast group have equal rights in the group. Any client in the group has the capability to exchange messages with any other client in the group.

FIGURE 10.4:

In a peer-to-peer multicast group, all clients can exchange messages with any client in the group.

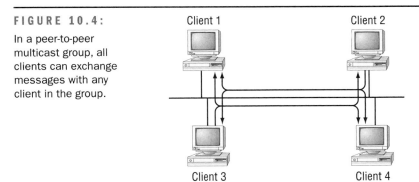

Client 1   Client 2

Client 3   Client 4

The IP system supports peer-to-peer multicast groups by allowing any device on the network to accept and send packets destined for the multicast group IP address. By default, there are no restrictions on which clients can join a multicast group. Some implementations use encryption to prevent unauthorized clients from interpreting the data received in the multicast group, but there is still no way to block the clients' receipt of the data.

Central Server

The other multicast system employs a central server, a single device on the network that controls all multicast group activity. An individual client wanting to join the multicast group must ask permission from the central server. If the central server denies the client access to that multicast group, no multicast packets will be forwarded to the requesting client. This technique is shown in Figure 10.5.

FIGURE 10.5:

The central server setup for controlling multicast groups

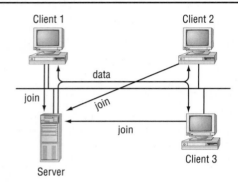

NOTE The central server multicast group system is not supported by IP. Currently, Asynchronous Transfer Mode (ATM) networks are the only networks capable of supporting central server multicast groups.

Sending Multicast Packets through Routers

Although multicast packets can be passed across network boundaries, making this happen requires some effort on the part of the network routers. By default, most routers do not pass multicast packets through to other subnets. If a router passed every received multicast packet to every interface, it would put the network at risk of being flooded with multicast packets. Instead, a system has been developed to allow selective forwarding of multicast packets.

The Internet Group Management Protocol (IGMP) was developed to aid in notifying routers when multicast packets should to be passed to various subnets. When a network device wants to join a multicast group, it sends an IGMP packet to the local router on its subnet. The IGMP packet registers the network device and the multicast group address from which that device must receive messages. This enables the router to know that it must forward any received multicast messages for that group to the subnet of the specified network device. Figure 10.6 demonstrates the principle of multicast group registration.

FIGURE 10.6:

Network devices
registering multicast
group memberships
on a router

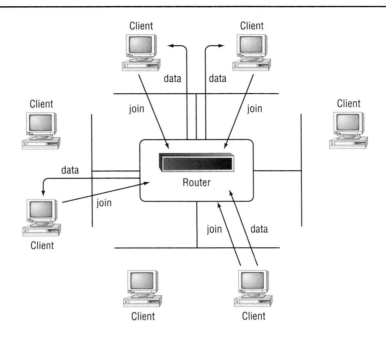

As shown in Figure 10.6, when each network device registers its intention to receive packets for the multicast group, the router must forward any received multicast packets to each interface that contains a registered host. Interfaces that do not contain registered hosts do not need to receive the multicast packet.

Similarly, when a network host leaves the multicast group, another IGMP packet is sent to the router, notifying it that the host no longer needs to have packets for that multicast group forwarded. When the last network host on a specific router interface leaves the group, the router can stop forwarding multicast packets to that interface.

C# IP Multicast Support

The .NET network library supports IP multicasting by using Socket options. Once a Socket object is created, it can be set to join a multicast group or to leave a multicast group that it has previously joined. This technique is used for UdpClient objects, as well.

C# Socket Multicasting

The Socket class supports IP multicasting by using the SetSocketOption() method of the socket, but in a different way than with broadcasting.

There are two socket options that can be used for multicasting:

- Adding the socket to a multicast group
- Removing the socket from a multicast group

Both of these options are defined by IP-level Socket option names, AddMembership and DropMembership.

The value parameter of the SetSocketOption() method is not a normal data value. Instead, it uses the MulticastOption class.

The MulticastOption class defines the multicast group that the socket will be added to or removed from. These two constructors are used for the MulticastOption class:

```
MulticastOption(IPAddress)
MulticastOption(IPAddress,IPAddress)
```

The firsts constructor format defines the IP multicast address used in the SetSocketOption. The default behavior of this constructor is to allow all interfaces on the system to be affected by the SetSocketOption() method. If you want to limit the action to an individual network interface on the system, the second constructor allows specification of an IPAddress value to represent the interface.

For example, if you wanted to add a socket to the multicast group 224.100.0.1, you would use the following statement:

```
sock.SetSocketOption(SocketOptionLevel.IP, SocketOptionName.AddMembership,
    new MulticastOption(IPAddress.Parse("224.100.0.1"));
```

This sets the socket to join the multicast group for all interfaces on the system.

Receiving Multicast Packets

The MultiRecv.cs program in Listing 10.6 sets a socket to receive multicast packets destined for the 224.100.0.1 multicast group.

Listing 10.6   The MultiRecv.cs program

```
using System;
using System.Net;
using System.Net.Sockets;
using System.Text;

class MultiRecv
```

```csharp
{
    public static void Main()
    {

        Socket sock = new Socket(AddressFamily.InterNetwork,
                            SocketType.Dgram, ProtocolType.Udp);
        Console.WriteLine("Ready to receive...");

        IPEndPoint iep = new IPEndPoint(IPAddress.Any, 9050);
        EndPoint ep = (EndPoint)iep;
        sock.Bind(iep);
        sock.SetSocketOption(SocketOptionLevel.IP, ➡
        SocketOptionName.AddMembership, ➡
        new MulticastOption(IPAddress.Parse("224.100.0.1")));

        byte[] data = new byte[1024];
        int recv = sock.ReceiveFrom(data, ref ep);
        string stringData = Encoding.ASCII.GetString(data, 0, recv);
        Console.WriteLine("received: {0}  from: {1}", stringData, ep.ToString());
        sock.Close();
    }
}
```

The MultiRecv program creates a UDP socket in the normal way, using the standard Socket class methods. After being added to the multicast group, the socket blocks on a ReceiveFrom() method call, waiting for data to arrive.

Some Cautions about Multicast Sockets

There are two very important points to remember about using multicast sockets:

First, the SetSocketOption() method call must be made after the Bind() method call for the socket. This enables the multicast group to be set for a specific IPEndPoint address on the socket.

Second, once the socket has been added to a multicast group, the ReceiveFrom() method will accept packets destined for the following:

- The IPEndPoint address and port specified in the Bind() method
- The multicast group IP address specified in the MulticastOption constructor and the port specified in the IPEndPoint object
- Broadcast packets for the specified IPEndPoint port

Many novice network programmers forget the second item, especially. When a ReceiveFrom() method is performed, you are not guaranteed to receive packets destined just for the multicast group. So be careful of extraneous packets sent from other sources. You will not be able to easily distinguish those packets.

Sending Multicast Packets

Sending multicast packets is easy. Nothing special must be done to send the packets to members in the multicast group; you just specify the multicast group IP address as the destination address of the packet. Listing 10.7 demonstrates this with the MultiSend.cs program.

Listing 10.7   **The MultiSend.cs program**

```
using System;
using System.Net;
using System.Net.Sockets;
using System.Text;

class MultiSend
{
    public static void Main()
    {
        Socket server = new Socket(AddressFamily.InterNetwork,
                        SocketType.Dgram, ProtocolType.Udp);
        IPEndPoint iep = new IPEndPoint(IPAddress.Parse("224.100.0.1"), 9050);

        byte[] data = Encoding.ASCII.GetBytes("This is a test message");
        server.SendTo(data, iep);
        server.Close();
    }
}
```

Note that nowhere is the SetSocketOption() used on the socket. It is unnecessary if the socket will only send packets to the multicast group on the local subnet. As you will see later, if you want to forward multicast packets to other networks, you will have to use the SetSocketOption(). Also, if the socket needs to receive multicast packets, the SetSocketOption() must be used with the appropriate MulticastOption constructor for the multicast group.

Watching the Programs

You can test these programs on your system and watch the network traffic using WinDump or Analyzer. In this case, because the MulticastOption constructor did not specify an interface, you can watch the network packets even if both the sender and receiver are running on the same machine.

First, start the MultiRecv program in a command prompt window. Then run the MultiSend program in a second command prompt window. You should see the following text, along with the address of the sending machine, displayed in the MultiRecv console:

```
C:\>MultiRecv
received: This is a test message  from: 192.168.1.6:1294

C:\>
```

What is even more interesting is the trace file from running `MultiSend` and `MultiRecv`. Listing 10.8 shows a sample output from the WinDump program.

Listing 10.8   **Sample WinDump output from the multicast test**

```
C:\>windump -X ip host 158.18.125.32
windump    listening on\Device\Packet_E190x1
09:05:20.776334 158.18.125.32 > 224.100.0.1: 158.18.125.32 > 224.100.0.1: igmp v
2 report 224.100.0.1 [ttl 1]
0x0000   4600 0020 f613 0000 0102 332c 9e12 7d20        F.........3,..}.
0x0010   e064 0001 9404 0000 1600 099a e064 0001        .d...........d..
09:05:24.357183 158.18.125.32 > 224.100.0.1: 158.18.125.32 > 224.100.0.1: igmp v
2 report 224.100.0.1 [ttl 1]
0x0000   4600 0020 fc13 0000 0102 2d2c 9e12 7d20        F.........-,..}.
0x0010   e064 0001 9404 0000 1600 099a e064 0001        .d...........d..
09:05:28.433814 158.18.125.32.1502 > 224.100.0.1.9050:  udp 22 [ttl 1]
0x0000   4500 0032 0114 0000 0111 bd0f 9e12 7d20        E..2..........}.
0x0010   e064 0001 05de 235a 001e dfda 5468 6973        .d....#Z....This
0x0020   2069 7320 6120 7465 7374 206d 6573 7361        .is.a.test.messa
0x0030   6765                                           ge
09:05:28.435433 158.18.125.32 > ALL-ROUTERS.MCAST.NET: 158.18.125.32 > ALL-ROUTE
RS.MCAST.NET: igmp leave 224.100.0.1 [ttl 1]
0x0000   4600 0020 0214 0000 0102 278f 9e12 7d20        F.........'...}.
0x0010   e000 0002 9404 0000 1700 089a e064 0001        .............d..

289 packets received by filter
0 packets dropped by kernel

C:\>
```

When the `MultiRecv` program started, it sent two IGMP packets on the network destined for the multicast group address. These were not sent as part of the program methods. They were automatically sent by the .NET network library functions.

The IGMP packets are intended to notify any routers on the network that the device intends to join the multicast group, and that any packets with that multicast group address should be forwarded to the subnet. After the IGMP packets go out, the `MultiSend` program sends its UDP packet with the test message, as expected, using the multicast group address as the destination.

When the `MultiRecv` program closes the `Socket` object, another IGMP packet is sent on the network to indicate the device is leaving the multicast group. You may notice that this packet is not sent to the multicast group address but is instead sent to an address specified as `ALL-ROUTERS.MCAST.NET`. This is the multicast address 224.0.0.2, which is a special router control multicast group. This packet informs any routers on the local network that they no longer have to forward multicast group packets for this device.

The Multicast TTL Value

If you look closely at the multicast packet sent out from the MultiSend program, you may notice that it has a TTL value of 1. With this value, the TCP packet will not be allowed to be forwarded by a router. This indicates that the Socket class by default allows the socket to send messages to the multicast group, but it restricts it to the local subnet. To send multicast packets that can traverse multiple routers, you must increase the TTL value of the multicast packet. This can be done with the SetSocketOption() method, but things get considerably more complicated.

As with receiving multicast sockets, to use the SetSocketOption() method you must bind the socket to a local IPEndPoint object, indicate that the socket will be used for multicasting, and then set the new TTL value. It looks like this:

```
Socket sock = new Socket(AddressFamily.InterNetwork,
                         SocketType.Dgram, ProtocolType.Udp);
IPEndPoint iep = new IPEndPoint(IPAddress.Any, 9050);
sock.Bind(iep);
sock.SetSocketOption(SocketOptionLevel.IP, SocketOptionName.AddMembership,
    new MulticastOption(IPAddress.Parse("224.100.0.1")));
sock.SetSocketOption(SocketOptionLevel.IP,
    SocketOptionName.MulticastTimeToLive, 50);
```

Now the socket is added to the multicast group, and its TTL value is changed to 50 hops.

Using this concept, the NewMultiSend.cs program in Listing 10.9 is created to send multicast packets across network boundaries.

Listing 10.9   The NewMultiSend.cs program

```
using System;
using System.Net;
using System.Net.Sockets;
using System.Text;

class NewMultiSend
{
    public static void Main()
    {
        Socket server = new Socket(AddressFamily.InterNetwork,
                                   SocketType.Dgram, ProtocolType.Udp);
        IPEndPoint iep = new IPEndPoint(IPAddress.Any, 9051);

        IPEndPoint iep2 = new IPEndPoint(IPAddress.Parse("224.100.0.1"), 9050);
        server.Bind(iep);

        byte[] data = Encoding.ASCII.GetBytes("This is a test message");
```

```
        server.SetSocketOption(SocketOptionLevel.IP,
SocketOptionName.AddMembership,
                           new
MulticastOption(IPAddress.Parse("224.100.0.1")));
        server.SetSocketOption(SocketOptionLevel.IP,

        SocketOptionName.MulticastTimeToLive, 50);
        server.SendTo(data, iep2);
        server.Close();
    }
}
```

Now when the multicast packet is sent out, it has a TTL value of 50, allowing it to traverse up to 50 hops before it is terminated. You can use the MultiRecv program to watch the multicast packet go out on the network. You can also view the packet using the WinDump or Analyzer programs.

C# UdpClient Multicasting

The .NET UdpClient class also supports IP multicast group addresses. The UdpClient class uses specific methods to allow the socket to join a multicast group or be removed from a multicast group. The following two methods are used:

- JoinMulticastGroup()
- DropMulticastGroup()

As you'd expect, the JoinMulticastGroup() method allows the socket to receive messages destined for a particular multicast group address. This method can be created using one of two formats:

```
JoinMulticastGroup(IPAddress)
JoinMulticastGroup(IPAddress, int)
```

The first constructor allows the socket to join the multicast group specified by the IPAddress object. The second constructor format lets you include a TTL value to the socket, enabling it to receive multicast packets sent from more distant hosts.

Here's an example code snippet using the UdpClient multicast methods:

```
UdpClient uc = new UdpClient(9050);
uc.JoinMulticastGroup(IPAddress.Parse("224.100.0.1"));
```

WARNING   Remember to use a default UDP port number in the UdpClient constructor. If you do not include a port number, the JoinMulticastGroup() method will fail because it does not know for what port to accept multicast messages.

UdpClient Multicast Receiver

The UdpClientMultiRecv program in Listing 10.10 demonstrates the programming for joining a UdpClient object to a multicast group and receiving packets from the group.

Listing 10.10   The UdpClientMultiRecv.cs program

```
using System;
using System.Net;
using System.Net.Sockets;
using System.Text;

class UdpClientMultiRecv
{
   public static void Main()
   {
      UdpClient sock = new UdpClient(9050);
      Console.WriteLine("Ready to receive…");
      sock.JoinMulticastGroup(IPAddress.Parse("224.100.0.1"), 50);
      IPEndPoint iep = new IPEndPoint(IPAddress.Any, 0);
      byte[] data = sock.Receive(ref iep);
      string stringData = Encoding.ASCII.GetString(data, 0, data.Length);
      Console.WriteLine("received: {0}  from: {1}", stringData, iep.ToString());
      sock.Close();
   }
}
```

Nothing too fancy here. You're just creating a simple UdpClient object and using the JoinMulticastGroup() method to allow it to accept messages destined for the 224.100.0.1 multicast group address. After the first message is received, the socket is closed and the program terminates.

UdpClient Multicast Sender

Similar to the Socket class, the UdpClient class does not need any special methods to send packets to a multicast group address. Just follow the standard UdpClient procedures to send a message to the specific IP address. Listing 10.11 shows the UdpClientMultiSend.cs program, which demonstrates sending a message to a multicast group address using the UdpClient class.

Listing 10.11   The UdpClientMultiSend.cs program

```
using System;
using System.Net;
using System.Net.Sockets;
using System.Text;

class UdpClientMultiSend
{
```

```
public static void Main()
{
    UdpClient sock = new UdpClient();
    IPEndPoint iep = new IPEndPoint(IPAddress.Parse("224.100.0.1"), 9050);
    byte[] data = Encoding.ASCII.GetBytes("This is a test message");
    sock.Send(data, data.Length, iep);
    sock.Close();
}
}
```

Testing the Programs

Like the Socket versions of the multicasting programs, you can test the UdpClient versions by first starting the UdpClientMultiRecv program in a command prompt window and then running the UdpClientMultiSend program. You should see the test message appear in the UdpClientMultiRecv program's console.

Because the traffic is sent out all the interfaces, you can monitor it using WinDump or Analyzer. Listing 10.12 shows the output from the WinDump trace. Just like the Socket class, the UdpClient class sends out two IGMP packets to inform local routers that the device wants to join the multicast group. The rest of the behavior of the program is exactly the same as the Socket version.

Listing 10.12   **The WinDump output from the UdpClient multicast test**

```
C:\>windump -X ip host 158.18.125.32
windump     listening on\Device\Packet_El90x1
10:52:19.653155 158.18.125.32 > 224.100.0.1: 158.18.125.32 > 224.100.0.1: igmp v
2 report 224.100.0.1 [ttl 1]
0x0000    4600 0020 f922 0000 0102 301d 9e12 7d20      F...."....0...}.
0x0010    e064 0001 9404 0000 1600 099a e064 0001      .d..........d..
10:52:21.615597 158.18.125.32 > 224.100.0.1: 158.18.125.32 > 224.100.0.1: igmp v
2 report 224.100.0.1 [ttl 1]
0x0000    4600 0020 fc22 0000 0102 2d1d 9e12 7d20      F...."....-...}.
0x0010    e064 0001 9404 0000 1600 099a e064 0001      .d..........d..
10:52:23.101905 158.18.125.32.1718 > 224.100.0.1.9050:  udp 22 [ttl 1]
0x0000    4500 0032 fe22 0000 0111 c000 9e12 7d20      E..2."........}.
0x0010    e064 0001 06b6 235a 001e df02 5468 6973      .d....#Z....This
0x0020    2069 7320 6120 7465 7374 206d 6573 7361      .is.a.test.messa
0x0030    6765                                         ge
10:52:23.104539 158.18.125.32 > ALL-ROUTERS.MCAST.NET: 158.18.125.32 > ALL-ROUTE
RS.MCAST.NET: igmp leave 224.100.0.1 [ttl 1]
0x0000    4600 0020 ff22 0000 0102 2a80 9e12 7d20      F...."....*...}.
0x0010    e000 0002 9404 0000 1700 089a e064 0001      ............d..

329 packets received by filter
0 packets dropped by kernel

C:\>
```

Sample Multicast Application

Multicast applications come in handy when a device needs to send information to multiple remote devices without having to maintain a connection to each device or send out multiple packets (one for each device). This section demonstrates a simple multicast whiteboard/chat system, in which any client that joins the multicast group can forward messages to all devices in the multicast group and can receive messages from all the other devices in the group. This is a common application for multicast communication. By allowing anyone on the network to join the multicast group chat, you create an environment where everyone can post comments to the group and see the posts from everyone else.

The basic format for this program will be the TcpChat program (Listing 9.7) introduced in Chapter 9. Instead of sending packets to an individual device, the chat program sends packets to the 224.100.0.1 multicast IP address. Any clients listening to that multicast group will receive the messages. Similarly, the TcpChat program will be modified to listen to the same multicast group address and display messages received from other chat clients on the network.

The easiest way to modify the existing TcpChat program is to create a new Thread object, which monitors the multicast group address. As messages are received on the address, they are displayed in the list box. The message-sending function can remain the same, with the exception that the multicast group IP address must now be used. Listing 10.13 is the multicast chat program that uses this concept.

Listing 10.13   **The MulticastChat.cs program**

```
using System;
using System.Drawing;
using System.Net;
using System.Net.Sockets;
using System.Text;
using System.Threading;
using System.Windows.Forms;

class MulticastChat : Form
{
    TextBox newText;
    ListBox results;
    Socket sock;
    Thread receiver;
    IPEndPoint multiep = new IPEndPoint(IPAddress.Parse("224.100.0.1"), 9050);

    public MulticastChat()
    {
        Text = "Multicast Chat Program";
        Size = new Size(400, 380);

        Label label1 = new Label();
```

```
      label1.Parent = this;
      label1.Text = "Enter text string:";
      label1.AutoSize = true;
      label1.Location = new Point(10, 30);

      newText = new TextBox();
      newText.Parent = this;
      newText.Size = new Size(200, 2 * Font.Height);
      newText.Location = new Point(10, 55);

      results = new ListBox();
      results.Parent = this;
      results.Location = new Point(10, 85);
      results.Size = new Size(360, 18 * Font.Height);

      Button sendit = new Button();
      sendit.Parent = this;
      sendit.Text = "Send";
      sendit.Location = new Point(220,52);
      sendit.Size = new Size(5 * Font.Height, 2 * Font.Height);
      sendit.Click += new EventHandler(ButtonSendOnClick);

      Button closeit = new Button();
      closeit.Parent = this;
      closeit.Text = "Close";
      closeit.Location = new Point(290, 52);
      closeit.Size = new Size(5 * Font.Height, 2 * Font.Height);
      closeit.Click += new EventHandler(ButtonCloseOnClick);

      sock = new Socket(AddressFamily.InterNetwork, SocketType.Dgram,
                     ProtocolType.Udp);
      IPEndPoint iep = new IPEndPoint(IPAddress.Any, 9050);
      sock.Bind(iep);
      sock.SetSocketOption(SocketOptionLevel.IP, SocketOptionName.AddMembership,
                        new MulticastOption(IPAddress.Parse("224.100.0.1")));
      receiver = new Thread(new ThreadStart(packetReceive));
      receiver.IsBackground = true;
      receiver.Start();
   }

void ButtonSendOnClick(object obj, EventArgs ea)
{
   byte[] message = Encoding.ASCII.GetBytes(newText.Text);
   newText.Clear();
   sock.SendTo(message, SocketFlags.None, multiep);
}

void ButtonCloseOnClick(object obj, EventArgs ea)
{
   receiver.Abort();
   sock.Close();
   Close();
```

```
    }
    void packetReceive()
    {
        EndPoint ep = (EndPoint)multiep;
        byte[] data = new byte[1024];
        string stringData;
        int recv;
        while (true)
        {
            recv = sock.ReceiveFrom(data, ref ep);
            stringData = Encoding.ASCII.GetString(data, 0, recv);
            results.Items.Add("from " + ep.ToString() + ":  " + stringData);
        }
    }

    public static void Main()
    {
        Application.Run(new MulticastChat());
    }
}
```

The MulticastChat program is not unlike the other chat programs presented in this book. The main difference is that it creates a Socket object to receive and send data out the 224.100.0.1 multicast group address:

```
sock = new Socket(AddressFamily.InterNetwork,
            SocketType.Dgram, ProtocolType.Udp);
IPEndPoint iep = new IPEndPoint(IPAddress.Any, 9050);
sock.Bind(iep);
sock.SetSocketOption(SocketOptionLevel.IP, SocketOptionName.AddMembership,
        new MulticastOption(IPAddress.Parse("224.100.0.1")));
```

Because the socket joins the multicast group using the SetSocketOption() method, it must use the Bind() method to bind it to a specific port. For the sake of simplicity, it is bound to the same port that the multicast group uses.

A Thread object is then created to listen for messages on the multicast group address using the packetReceive() method. The packetReceive() method enters a continuous loop, waiting for messages from the multicast group and displaying them in the results ListBox object:

```
void packetReceive()
{
    EndPoint ep = (EndPoint)multiep;
    byte[] data = new byte[1024];
    string stringData;
    int recv;
    while (true)
```

```
        {
            recv = sock.ReceiveFrom(data, ref ep);
            stringData = Encoding.ASCII.GetString(data, 0, recv);
            results.Items.Add("from " + ep.ToString() + ":  " + stringData);
        }
    }
```

Because the multicast chat program is a connectionless application, you must tell it when to stop and close the socket. When the Close button is clicked, the receiver thread is terminated, the created socket is properly closed on the system, and the window form is closed:

```
void ButtonCloseOnClick(object obj, EventArgs ea)
{
    receiver.Abort();
    sock.Close();
    Close();
}
```

Testing the Multicast Chat Program

Because it is a Windows forms program, when you compile `MulticastChat.cm`, you will most likely want to use the `/t` compiler option to make it a Windows executable:

```
csc /t:winexe MulticastChat.cs
```

After the compile finishes, you can run the program by either double-clicking the program name in the Windows Explorer window, or running it from a command prompt window.

WARNING   Because the `MulticastChat` program binds to a specific UDP port, only one instance can be run on a machine.

When the program starts, the chat window should be displayed, and it should be ready to accept messages from the multicast group. To check this out, you can first see if the UDP port appears in the `netstat` output:

```
C:\>netstat -a

Active Connections

Proto  Local Address          Foreign Address        State
.
.
UDP    abednego:9050          *:*
.
.

C:\>
```

Sure enough, the system has created a socket on UDP port 9050. You can also use WinDump or Analyzer to monitor the network traffic generated by the `MulticastChat` program. You should see the standard IGMP packets sent out when the program starts:

```
C:\>windump igmp
windump: listening on\Device\Packet_E190x1
07:24:09.950210 192.168.1.6 > 224.100.0.1: 192.168.1.6 > 224.100.0.1: igmp v2
report 224.100.0.1 [ttl 1]
07:24:14.799582 192.168.1.6 > 224.100.0.1: 192.168.1.6 > 224.100.0.1: igmp v2
report 224.100.0.1 [ttl 1]

1237 packets received by filter
0 packets dropped by kernel

C:\>
```

After starting the program, you can enter a text message in the text box and click the Send button. Because the application itself is listening to the multicast group address, the message will appear in the list box. If you have a network with multiple Windows devices, you can experiment by running the application on multiple devices at the same time. Each instance of the application should display the message sent by another other device on the subnet.

NOTE   Remember that if your network uses routers, they must be configured to allow multicast traffic to be forwarded for this program to work across subnets.

Summary

This chapter describes techniques that can be used to communicate simultaneously with multiple network hosts using broadcast and multicast packets. Because both IP broadcasting and multicasting are connectionless communications, they can only be done using UDP sockets.

The C# programming language supports broadcast packets by providing `SetSocketOption()` method's `Broadcast` option. By default, any socket is allowed to accept broadcast messages that are received for a defined UDP port. However, to send broadcast messages, the `SetSocketOption()` method must be used to enable the `Broadcast` option for the socket.

Many server applications broadcast a server service at a regular time interval. Clients can thus detect the server's presence on the network and know how to communicate with the service. This broadcasting is often done using a background thread, continuously looping to repeat a broadcast message at the set interval.

The C# programming language also supports IP multicast groups by providing the MulticastOption class used in the SetSocketOption() method. The AddMembership and DropMembership socket options allow a socket to either join or leave a multicast group. The MulticastOption class defines the IP address of the multicast group. Once the socket joins a multicast group, it will receive any message destined for the multicast group IP address. Similarly, the UdpClient class provides the JoinMulticastGroup() and DropMulticastGroup() methods. These methods provide the functionality of joining and leaving multicast groups for UdpClient objects.

C# network applications can utilize IP multicast groups to communicate with a select subset of network devices. The simple network chat program presented in this chapter demonstrates simultaneous communication among multiple devices on the network without having to send duplicate packets for every message.

This is the last chapter of Part II, in which you've examined many network layer programming techniques in the C# environment. The remaining chapters, in Part III, introduce examples of programming specific network applications using C#. The first two, Chapter 11, "ICMP," and Chapter 12, "SNMP," show how to use raw sockets to communicate with remote network devices. The remaining chapters discuss specific application layer programming, such as SMTP and HTTP, as well as using Active Directory, remoting, and security features in network programs.

PART III

Application Layer Programming Examples

Chapter 11: ICMP

Chapter 12: SNMP

Chapter 13: SMTP

Chapter 14: HTTP

Chapter 15: Active Directory

Chapter 16: Using .NET Remoting

Chapter 17: Using Network Security Features

CHAPTER 11

ICMP

- The ICMP protocol

- Using raw sockets

- Creating a C# ICMP class

- A simple ping program

- An advanced ping program

- A traceroute program

- A find subnet mask program

So far, this book has explained the fundamentals of network programming using the C# programming language. Here in Part III, you'll start building some real-world applications that utilize the C# network classes. This chapter walks you through the steps of creating some network utilities that use the *Internet Control Message Protocol (ICMP)* to communicate with remote hosts on the network. Many popular network utilities, such as ping and traceroute, are based on ICMP.

After a discussion of ICMP, you'll create a separate ICMP class to demonstrate how to encapsulate a protocol in a class. Finally, three separate ICMP utility programs are presented to demonstrate use of the ICMP class in C# network programs.

The ICMP Protocol

ICMP was defined in RFC 792 to allow network devices to report errors in datagram processing. Since its inception, ICMP has undergone some additions, making it a more robust means of communicating errors and network information among hosts.

ICMP uses IP to communicate across the network. Although it uses IP, ICMP is a completely separate protocol from TCP or UDP. As explained in Chapter 2, "IP Programming Basics," IP packets identify the next layer protocol contained in the data section using the protocol Type field. ICMP packets are identified by IP protocol Type 1. The entire ICMP packet is then contained within the data section of the IP packet. Figure 11.1 shows how the ICMP packet fields are placed in an IP packet.

FIGURE 11.1:

The IP and ICMP packet formats

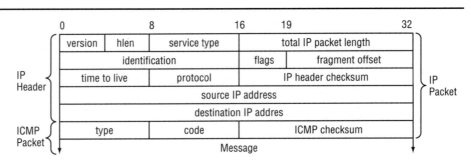

ICMP Packet Format

Similar to TCP and UDP, ICMP uses a specific packet format to identify information in the packet. As seen in Figure 11.1, the ICMP packet contains the following fields:

Type   The 1-byte Type element defines what kind of ICMP message is in the packet. Many types of ICMP packets are used to send control request messages to remote hosts. Each message type has its own format and data requirements.

Code   The 1-byte Code element further defines the Type field. The various ICMP message types require specific control and data options. These options are defined in the Code field.

Checksum   The 2-byte Checksum element ensures that the ICMP packet has arrived without corruption or tampering. The checksum is computed on only the ICMP portion of the packet, using a specific algorithm defined in RFC 792. When computing the checksum value, the Checksum field is set to zero.

Message   The multibyte Message element contains various other data elements that are unique to each ICMP message type. The Message data fields are often used to contain information sent to and from the remote host. Many of the ICMP message types define the first two fields in the Message element as an Identifier and a Sequence number. Both of these fields are used to uniquely identify the ICMP packet to the hosts.

ICMP Packet Types

There are many types of ICMP packets. Each type of ICMP packet is defined by the 1-byte value in the Type element. Table 11.1 lists the ICMP types as originally defined in RFC 792.

TABLE 11.1: The ICMP Packet Types

Type Code	Description
0	Echo reply
3	Destination unreachable
4	Source quench
5	Redirect
8	Echo request
11	Time exceeded
12	Parameter problem
13	Timestamp request
14	Timestamp reply
15	Information request
16	Information reply

Since the release of RFC 792 in September 1981, many new ICMP types have been created. ICMP packets are used for everything from a simple echo test to complex network error reporting. Following are descriptions of some commonly used ICMP packets.

Echo Request and Echo Reply Packets

Two of the ICMP packets used most often are the Echo Request and Echo Reply. These packets allow a device to request an ICMP response from a remote device on the network—the core of the ping utility that has become a universal staple for network administration.

The Echo Request packet uses ICMP Type 8, with a Code value of 0. The Message data area contains three elements:

- A 1-byte Identifier that uniquely identifies the Echo Request packet
- A 1-byte Sequence number providing additional identification for the ICMP packet in a stream of ping packets
- A multibyte data element containing data that should be returned by the receiving host

When a device receives an Echo Request packet, it must respond with an Echo Reply packet, ICMP Type 0. The Echo Reply packet must contain the same Identifier and Sequence number values as the Echo Request packet to which it is responding. Also, the data element value must be the same as received in the Echo Request packet.

Destination Unreachable Packet

The Destination Unreachable ICMP packet (Type 3) is usually returned by a router device after it receives an IP packet that it cannot forward to the appropriate destination. The data portion of the Destination Unreachable packet contains the IP header plus the first 64 bits of the datagram.

In this packet, the Code field identifies the reason the packet could not be forwarded by the router. See Table 11.2 for a list of Code values that may be encountered.

TABLE 11.2: The Destination Unreachable Code Values

Code	Description
0	Network unreachable
1	Host unreachable
2	Protocol unreachable
3	Port unreachable
4	Fragmentation needed and DF flag set
5	Source route failed
6	Destination network unknown
7	Destination host unknown
8	Source host isolated
9	Communication with destination network prohibited
10	Communication with destination host prohibited
11	Network unreachable for type of service
12	Host unreachable for type of service

NOTE   RFC 792, the original RFC describing ICMP, specifies only Destination Unreachable Codes 0 through 5. Subsequent RFCs have expanded on this, defining the 13 codes shown in Table 11.2.

Time Exceeded Packet

The Time Exceeded (ICMP Type 11) packet has become an important tool that is used for network troubleshooting. It reports that an IP packet has exceeded the time to live (TTL) value defined in the IP header.

Each time an IP packet traverses a network router, the TTL value is decreased by 1. If the TTL value reaches 0 before the IP packet reaches the intended destination, the last receiving router must send a Time Exceeded ICMP packet to the sending host. As you will see, this procedure is exploited in the traceroute program.

Using Raw Sockets

Because ICMP packets do not use either TCP or UDP, you cannot use either of the socket helper classes, TcpClient or UdpClient. Instead, you have to use what are called *raw sockets*, which are a feature of the Socket class. Raw sockets allow you to define your own network packet above the IP layer. Of course, this means that you must do all the work of manually creating all the individual fields in the ICMP packet, rather than having the .NET library create the packet for you, as it does with TCP and UDP.

Raw Sockets Format

To create a raw socket, you must use the SocketType.Raw socket type when the socket is created. There are several ProtocolType values that you can use to match with the raw socket type; they're listed in Table 11.3.

TABLE 11.3: The Raw Socket ProtocolType Values

Value	Description
Ggp	Gateway-to-Gateway Protocol
Icmp	Internet Control Message Protocol
Idp	IDP Protocol
Igmp	Internet Group Management Protocol
IP	A raw IP packet

Continued on next page

TABLE 11.3 CONTINUED: The Raw Socket ProtocolType Values

Value	Description
Ipx	Novell IPX Protocol
ND	Net Disk Protocol
Pup	Xerox PARC Universal Protocol (PUP)
Raw	A raw IP packet
Spx	Novell SPX Protocol
SpxII	Novell SPX Version 2 Protocol
Unknown	An unknown protocol
Unspecified	An unspecified protocol

The specific protocols listed for a raw socket allows the .NET library to properly create the underlying IP packet. By using the ProtocolType.Icmp value, the IP packet created by the socket defines the next layer protocol as ICMP (IP value Type 1). This allows the remote host to immediately identify the packet as an ICMP packet, and process it accordingly.

Obviously, for the applications in this chapter, you will use the ProtocolType.Icmp value. Here's the command to create a socket for ICMP packets:

```
Socket sock = new Socket(AddressFamily.InterNetwork, SocketType.Raw,
    ProtocolType.Icmp);
```

Sending Raw Packets

Because ICMP is a connectionless protocol, you do not have to bind the socket to a specific local port to send a packet or use the Connect() method to connect it to a specific remote host. You must use the SendTo() method to specify the IPEndPoint object of the destination address. ICMP does not use ports, so the value of the port property of the IPEndPoint object is not important. The following creates an IPEndPoint destination object with no port and sends a packet to it:

```
IPEndPoint iep = new IPEndPoint(IPAddress.Parse("192.168.1.2"), 0);
sock.SendTo(packet, iep);
```

> **WARNING** Remember that because the raw socket does not format the data, whatever value entered in the *packet* byte array will be forwarded "as-is" to the remote host. This means you must manually create the ICMP packet in the byte array and then send it to the remote host. Any mistakes in creating the packet will result in an error on the receiving host, and most likely you will not get a return ICMP packet.

Receiving Raw Packets

Receiving data from a raw socket is trickier than sending data in a raw socket. To receive data from the raw socket, you must use the `ReceiveFrom()` method. Because the raw socket does not identify a higher-layer protocol, the data returned from a `ReceiveFrom()` method call contains the entire IP packet contents. You must extract the data from the raw IP packet information to create the ICMP packet elements. As you can see in Figure 11.1, the IP packet data starts at byte 20. Therefore, to extract the ICMP packet data and header, you start reading the byte array at the 20th position in the received data packet.

WARNING Because the `ReceiveFrom()` method returns the entire IP packet, you must remember to declare the receiving buffer size to be at least 20 bytes larger than your expected data.

Creating an ICMP Class

As just mentioned, the raw socket does not automatically format your ICMP packet, so you must do this yourself. C# is an object-oriented language. It makes sense to create a C# ICMP class that you can use to format an ICMP packet and manipulate the packet contents as necessary. This allows you to use the ICMP class in any of your network applications that use ICMP packets.

The ICMP Class Constructors

The ICMP class should define a data variable for each element in the ICMP packet. Table 11.4 shows the data variables to be defined to represent a generic ICMP packet.

TABLE 11.4: The ICMP Class Generic Data Elements

Data Variable	Size	Type
Type	1 byte	Byte
Code	1 byte	Byte
Checksum	2 bytes	Unsigned 16-bit integer
Message	multibyte	Byte array

The Default Constructor

The default ICMP constructor creates an instance of the ICMP class but does not assign any values to the data variables. These can be assigned within the ICMP application program when you are ready to create the ICMP packet.

Here is the format for the ICMP class default constructor:

```
class ICMP
{
    public byte Type;
    public byte Code;
    public UInt16 Checksum;
    public int MessageSize;
    public byte[] Message = new byte[1024];

    public ICMP()
    {
    }
}
```

Although it is not part of the ICMP packet, the *MessageSize* variable is added to portray the actual size of the variable-length *Message* variable. You will understand why this is necessary when you see it in action, coming up.

To construct a new ICMP packet, the application need only create a new ICMP object and assign the appropriate values to the data elements, like this:

```
ICMP packet = new ICMP();
packet.Type = 0x08;
packet.Code = 0x00;
packet.Checksum = 0;
```

This code snippet shows an example of creating the first part of an Echo Request ICMP packet. The Echo Request packet demonstrates a common scenario that you will run into when creating an ICMP packet. Since the Echo Request packet defines fields within the ICMP Message element (the Identifier and the Sequence fields), you must decide how you are going to build the Message element. You have two options for accomplishing this:

- Create another class specifically for the unique Echo Request fields, and retrieve the byte array of the class.

- Convert the Message fields separately into byte arrays and place them in the data element.

If you are planning to create a lot of Echo Request packets, creating a Ping class that defines the individual Echo Request fields may be the way to go. Otherwise, for just a few Echo Request packets, it won't be too big a task to convert the values into individual byte arrays and add them to the Message element:

```
Buffer.BlockCopy(BitConverter.GetBytes((short)1), 0, packet.Message, 0, 2);
Buffer.BlockCopy(BitConverter.GetBytes((short)1), 0, packet.Message, 2, 2);
byte[] data = Encoding.ASCII.GetBytes("test packet");
Buffer.BlockCopy(data, 0, packet.Message, 4, data.Length);
packet.MessageSize = data.Length + 4;
```

Here the Identifier and Sequence fields for the Echo Reply packet are each converted into byte arrays and placed in the proper place in the Message element.

Rebuilding an ICMP Object

After sending an ICMP packet, most likely you will get an ICMP packet returned from the remote device. To make it easier to decipher the contents of the packet, you should create another ICMP class constructor that can take a raw ICMP byte array and place the values into the appropriate data elements in the class:

```
public ICMP(byte[] data, int size)
{
   Type = data[20];
   Code = data[21];
   Checksum = BitConverter.ToUInt16(data, 22);
   MessageSize = size - 24;
   Buffer.BlockCopy(data, 24, Message, 0, MessageSize);

}
```

Remember that raw socket returns the entire IP packet. This means you must skip the IP header information before you can extract the ICMP packet information. So the start of the ICMP information, the Type element, is in the 20th position in the byte array. The individual data elements within the ICMP packet are then extracted byte by byte into the appropriate ICMP element.

After creating the new ICMP object with the received packet data, you can reference the data elements individually:

```
int recv = ReceiveFrom(data, ref ep);
ICMP response = new ICMP(data, recv);
Console.WriteLine("Received ICMP packet:");
Console.WriteLine("  Type {0}", response.Type);
Console.WriteLine("  Code: {0}", response.Code);
Int16 Identifier = BitConverter.ToInt16(response.Message, 0);
Int16 Sequence = BitConverter.ToInt16(response.Message, 2);
Console.WriteLine("  Identifier: {0}", Identifier);
Console.WriteLine("  Sequence: {0}", Sequence);
stringData = Encoding.ASCII.GetString(response.Message, 4,
          response.MessageSize - 4);
Console.WriteLine("  data: {0}", stringData);
```

Obtaining the first two data elements of the received ICMP packet is easy; all you have to do is read their values from the ICMP class elements. Extracting the data fields from the Message element is a little trickier. Because you know that the first 2 bytes constitute the unsigned integer Identifier field, and the second 2 bytes are the unsigned integer Sequence field, you can use the BitConverter class to assign those values from the appropriate bytes. The remainder of the Message element is assigned to the Message field of the Echo Reply packet.

From this code snippet, it is now easy to see why the MessageSize data element was added to the ICMP class. Without it, it would be difficult to determine how to reconstruct the Message element from the received packet.

The ICMP Packet Creator

After a new ICMP object is created and the packet data elements have been defined, you will want to send the packet to a remote network device. Unfortunately, you cannot directly send the ICMP object in a SendTo() method; it must be turned into a byte array.

As discussed in Chapter 7, "Using the C# Sockets Helper Classes," the easiest way to send a complex class object across the network is to create a method that converts each data element into a byte array and concatenate the byte arrays into a single large byte array. This was done using the Buffer.BlockCopy() method:

```
public byte[] getBytes()
{
    byte[] data = new byte[MessageSize + 9];
    Buffer.BlockCopy(BitConverter.GetBytes(Type), 0, data, 0, 1);
    Buffer.BlockCopy(BitConverter.GetBytes(Code), 0, data, 1, 1);
    Buffer.BlockCopy(BitConverter.GetBytes(Checksum), 0, data, 2, 2);
    Buffer.BlockCopy(Message, 0, data, 4, MessageSize);
    return data;
}
```

Let's see what is happening here. A data byte array is created to hold the newly converted data elements of the ICMP object. Each data element is converted to a byte array using the appropriate BitConverter class method and placed in the data byte array for the getBytes() method. When all of the data elements have been converted to the byte array, it contains a properly formatted ICMP packet, which can be sent to a remote network device:

```
IPEndPoint iep = new IPEndPoint(IPAddress.Parse("192.168.1.2"), 0);
sock.SendTo(packet.getBytes(), iep);
```

Remember that because ICMP does not use ports, you can use a zero value for the port parameter when creating the IPEndPoint object for the destination address.

> **NOTE**   You may have noticed that the Identifier and Sequence values were not converted to network byte order before being placed in the byte array. This is because the remote device will return the exact same packet for you to decode, you know that they will be in the same format when you get them back.

The ICMP Checksum Method

Perhaps the most dreaded part of creating an ICMP packet is calculating the checksum value of the packet (unless, of course, you enjoy binary math). The easiest way to do this task is to create a self-contained method for calculating the checksum and place it in the ICMP class to be used by the ICMP application program.

The ICMP RFC defines the Checksum element as "the 16-bit one's complement of the one's complement sum of the ICMP message, starting with the ICMP type. For computing the checksum, the Checksum element should be set to zero."

Fortunately for us non–math majors, there are quite a few examples of checksum utilities available in the public domain. Listing 11.1 shows the checksum method I chose to implement in the ICMP class.

Listing 11.1 **The getChecksum() ICMP method**

```
public UInt16 getChecksum()
    {
        UInt32 chcksm = 0;

        byte[] data = getBytes();
        int packetsize = MessageSize + 8;

        int index = 0;

        while ( index < packetsize)
        {
            chcksm += Convert.ToUInt32(BitConverter.ToUInt16(data, index));
            index += 2;
        }

        chcksm = (chcksm >> 16) + (chcksm & 0xffff);
        chcksm += (chcksm >> 16);
        return (UInt16)(~chcksm);
    }
```

Because the ICMP checksum value uses 16-bit arithmetic, this algorithm reads 2-byte chunks of the ICMP packet at a time (using the ToUInt16() method of the BitConverter class) and performs the necessary arithmetic operations on the bytes. The return value is a 16-bit unsigned integer value.

To use the checksum value in an ICMP application program, first fill in all the data elements, setting the Checksum element to zero. Next, call the getChecksum() method to calculate the checksum of the ICMP packet, and then place the result in the Checksum element of the packet:

```
packet.Checksum = 0;
packet.Checksum = packet.getChecksum();
```

After the Checksum element is calculated, the packet is ready to be sent out to the destination host using the SendTo() method.

In a production application, when an ICMP packet is received from a remote host, you should extract the Checksum element value and compare it to the calculated value for the packet. If the two values do not match, an error has occurred and the packet should be retransmitted.

Putting It All Together

Now that you have seen all of the individual elements of the ICMP class, we can look at the entire class as defined in the C# code. Listing 11.2 is the ICMP.cs program, which implements the ICMP class to assist you in creating and reading ICMP packets.

Listing 11.2   The ICMP.cs program

```csharp
using System;
using System.Net;
using System.Text;

class ICMP
{
    public byte Type;
    public byte Code;
    public UInt16 Checksum;
    public int MessageSize;
    public byte[] Message = new byte[1024];

    public ICMP()
    {
    }

    public ICMP(byte[] data, int size)
    {
        Type = data[20];
        Code = data[21];
        Checksum = BitConverter.ToUInt16(data, 22);
        MessageSize = size - 24;
        Buffer.BlockCopy(data, 24, Message, 0, MessageSize);
    }

    public byte[] getBytes()
    {
        byte[] data = new byte[MessageSize + 9];
        Buffer.BlockCopy(BitConverter.GetBytes(Type), 0, data, 0, 1);
        Buffer.BlockCopy(BitConverter.GetBytes(Code), 0, data, 1, 1);
        Buffer.BlockCopy(BitConverter.GetBytes(Checksum), 0, data, 2, 2);
        Buffer.BlockCopy(Message, 0, data, 4, MessageSize);
        return data;
    }

    public UInt16 getChecksum()
    {
```

```
            UInt32 chcksm = 0;
            byte[] data = getBytes();
            int packetsize = MessageSize + 8;

            int index = 0;

            while ( index < packetsize)
            {
                chcksm += Convert.ToUInt32(BitConverter.ToUInt16(data, index));
                index += 2;
            }
            chcksm = (chcksm >> 16) + (chcksm & 0xffff);
            chcksm += (chcksm >> 16);
            return (UInt16)(~chcksm);
        }
    }
```

Something to keep in mind: do not try and compile the ICMP.cs class by itself. It does not include a Main() method and so cannot create an executable program on its own. Instead, the class supports ICMP network applications, allowing you to easily create, send, and interpret ICMP packets. The rest of the programs in this chapter use this class to build ICMP packets.

A Simple Ping Program

The first ICMP application program discussed is a simple version of the ping program that is found on almost all network devices. Ping is an important and fundamental diagnostic tool that tells you whether a network device has network connectivity and can connect to a particular remote device on the network. The ping program uses the ICMP Echo Request packet (Type 8) to send a simple message to a remote host. When the remote host receives the message, it replies with an ICMP Echo Reply packet (Type 0), which contains the original message. Figure 11.2 demonstrates this transaction.

FIGURE 11.2:

The ICMP control messages behind the ping program

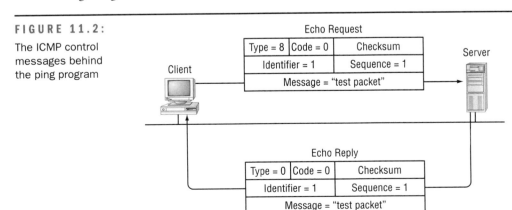

Because you now have the ICMP class, implementing a simple ping program is a snap. Listing 11.3 is the SimplePing.cs program, which uses ICMP to ping a remote host on the network.

Listing 11.3 **The SimplePing.cs program**

```
using System;
using System.Net;
using System.Net.Sockets;
using System.Text;

class SimplePing
{
   public static void Main (string[] argv)
   {
      byte[] data = new byte[1024];
      int recv;
      Socket host = new Socket(AddressFamily.InterNetwork, SocketType.Raw,
                  ProtocolType.Icmp);
      IPEndPoint iep = new IPEndPoint(IPAddress.Parse(argv[0]), 0);
      EndPoint ep = (EndPoint)iep;
      ICMP packet = new ICMP();

      packet.Type = 0x08;
      packet.Code = 0x00;
      packet.Checksum = 0;
      Buffer.BlockCopy(
          BitConverter.GetBytes((short)1), 0, packet.Message, 0, 2);
      Buffer.BlockCopy(
          BitConverter.GetBytes((short)1), 0, packet.Message, 2, 2);
      data = Encoding.ASCII.GetBytes("test packet");
      Buffer.BlockCopy(data, 0, packet.Message, 4, data.Length);
      packet.MessageSize = data.Length + 4;
      int packetsize = packet.MessageSize + 4;

      UInt16 chcksum = packet.getChecksum();
      packet.Checksum = chcksum;

      host.SetSocketOption(SocketOptionLevel.Socket,
                      SocketOptionName.ReceiveTimeout, 3000);
      host.SendTo(packet.getBytes(), packetsize, SocketFlags.None, iep);
      try
      {
         data = new byte[1024];
         recv = host.ReceiveFrom(data, ref ep);
      } catch (SocketException)
      {
         Console.WriteLine("No response from remote host");
         return;
      }
      ICMP response = new ICMP(data, recv);
      Console.WriteLine("response from: {0}", ep.ToString());
```

```
            Console.WriteLine("  Type {0}", response.Type);
            Console.WriteLine("  Code: {0}", response.Code);
            int Identifier = BitConverter.ToInt16(response.Message, 0);
            int Sequence = BitConverter.ToInt16(response.Message, 2);
            Console.WriteLine("  Identifier: {0}", Identifier);
            Console.WriteLine("  Sequence: {0}", Sequence);
            string stringData = Encoding.ASCII.GetString(response.Message,
             4, response.MessageSize - 4);
            Console.WriteLine("  data: {0}", stringData);

            host.Close();
        }
    }
```

This simple program doesn't include any of the bells and whistles you may expect from real ping programs. For starters, `SimplePing` requires that an IP address be used on the command line of the program. (If desired, you can use the `Dns.Resolve()` method instead of the `IPAddress.Parse()` method to allow hostnames as well as IP addresses.)

In the first part of the program, an ICMP packet is created, defining the ICMP Type element as 8 and the Code element as 0. This creates an Echo Request packet that uses the Identifier and Sequence elements to track the individual ping packet, and allows you to enter any text into the data element.

Similar to connectionless UDP programs, a time-out value is set for the socket using the `SetSocketOption()` method. If no ICMP packet is received from the remote host in three seconds, an Exception is thrown and the program exits.

The returned ICMP packet (if one is returned) creates a new `ICMP` object, which can then be used to determine if the received packet is the match for the sent ICMP packet. The Identifier, Sequence, and data elements of the received packet should match the same values of the sent ICMP packet. If not, you've intercepted an ICMP packet from another application running on the same device, and you need to listen for your ICMP packet to be returned.

To compile the `SimplePing` program, you must include the `ICMP.cs` program on the `csc` command line:

```
csc SimplePing.cs ICMP.cs
```

Because the `Main()` method is defined in the `SimplePing.cs` program, the compiler creates a `SimplePing.exe` executable file that executes the program.

Testing SimplePing

You can test the `SimplePing` program by starting a command-prompt window and pinging the local device address. The output shows that you were indeed able to successfully ping yourself:

```
C:\>SimplePing 127.0.0.1
response from: 127.0.0.1:0
```

```
    Type 0
    Code: 0
    Identifier: 1
    Sequence: 1
    data: test packet

C:\>
```

The next test is to try and ping a nonexistent IP address. This should force the socket time-out feature to kick in and throw an Exception:

```
C:\>SimplePing 192.168.1.111
No response from remote host

C:\>
```

So far, so good. The last test is to ensure that the ping packets can successfully traverse the network. You can do this by pinging either a device on the Internet or a remote device on your local network:

```
C:\>SimplePing 192.168.1.2
response from: 192.168.1.2:0
    Type 0
    Code: 0
    Identifier: 1
    Sequence: 1
    data: test packet

C:\>
```

WARNING   In these days of high network security, do not be surprised if a ping to a remote device fails. Many sites use firewalls to protect their networks from ping attacks.

You can use WinDump or Analyzer to watch the ping packets go out and (if all goes well) come back. Each ping packet appears in the trace as a separate ICMP packet on the network.

An Advanced Ping Program

SimplePing was designed to demonstrate the basics of using the ICMP Echo Request/Reply sequence to ping a remote host. If you have used commercial ping products, you know that several features of such programs were not implemented here. The unsophisticated SimplePing has the following limitations:

- The destination address had to be entered as an IP address.

- Only one ping message was sent and received.

- The size of the ping data was not configurable.
- The elapsed time for the ping to process was not recorded.

This section shows how to create a more advanced version of the ping program that implements features to remove these limitations.

AdvPing.cs is a Windows-based ping program that implements some of the features of more sophisticated ping utilities.

To allow the customer to enter either IP addresses or hostnames in the query text box, the Dns.Resolve() method is used. You learned in Chapter 4, "DNS and C#," that the Dns.Resolve() method will resolve either a text hostname or a text IP address into an IPHostEntry array. The IPHostEntry array contains all of the IP addresses associated with the hostname or IP address. Because the ping program needs to worry about only one address, it takes the first one in the list:

```
IPHostEntry iphe = Dns.Resolve(hostbox.Text);
IPEndPoint iep = new IPEndPoint(iphe.AddressList[0], 0);
```

You want to allow multiple ping packets, so AdvPing uses a separate thread to handle the actual ping function. When the customer clicks the Start button, a new thread is started. The new thread contains a loop that continually pings the remote host until the thread is aborted. To do this, the customer interface includes a button that the customer can click to stop the pinging.

Each separate pinging ICMP packet sent from the program is assigned a sequential Sequence number, to help identify the individual pings. Because the Sequence number changes for each ping packet, the ICMP checksum value needs to be recomputed for each packet.

Listing 11.4 is the AdvPing.cs program.

Listing 11.4   The AdvPing.cs program

```
using System;
using System.Drawing;
using System.Net;
using System.Net.Sockets;
using System.Text;
using System.Threading;
using System.Windows.Forms;

class AdvPing  :  Form
{
    private static int pingstart, pingstop, elapsedtime;
    private static TextBox hostbox, databox;
    private static ListBox results;
    private static Thread pinger;
```

```
private static Socket sock;

public AdvPing()
{
    Text = "Advanced Ping Program";
    Size = new Size(400, 380);

    Label label1 = new Label();
    label1.Parent = this;
    label1.Text = "Enter host to ping:";
    label1.AutoSize = true;
    label1.Location = new Point(10, 30);

    hostbox = new TextBox();
    hostbox.Parent = this;
    hostbox.Size = new Size(200, 2 * Font.Height);
    hostbox.Location = new Point(10, 55);

    results = new ListBox();
    results.Parent = this;
    results.Location = new Point(10, 85);
    results.Size = new Size(360, 18 * Font.Height);

    Label label2 = new Label();
    label2.Parent = this;
    label2.Text = "Packet data:";
    label2.AutoSize = true;
    label2.Location = new Point(10, 330);

    databox = new TextBox();
    databox.Parent = this;
    databox.Text = "test packet";
    databox.Size = new Size(200, 2 * Font.Height);
    databox.Location = new Point(80, 325);

    Button sendit = new Button();
    sendit.Parent = this;
    sendit.Text = "Start";
    sendit.Location = new Point(220,52);
    sendit.Size = new Size(5 * Font.Height, 2 * Font.Height);
    sendit.Click += new EventHandler(ButtonSendOnClick);

    Button stopit = new Button();
    stopit.Parent = this;
    stopit.Text = "Stop";
    stopit.Location = new Point(295,52);
    stopit.Size = new Size(5 * Font.Height, 2 * Font.Height);
    stopit.Click += new EventHandler(ButtonStopOnClick);

    Button closeit = new Button();
    closeit.Parent = this;
    closeit.Text = "Close";
    closeit.Location = new Point(300, 320);
```

```
      closeit.Size = new Size(5 * Font.Height, 2 * Font.Height);
      closeit.Click += new EventHandler(ButtonCloseOnClick);

      sock = new Socket(AddressFamily.InterNetwork,
               SocketType.Raw, ProtocolType.Icmp);
      sock.SetSocketOption(SocketOptionLevel.Socket,
               SocketOptionName.ReceiveTimeout, 3000);
   }

   void ButtonSendOnClick(object obj, EventArgs ea)
   {
      pinger = new Thread(new ThreadStart(sendPing));
      pinger.IsBackground = true;

      pinger.Start();
   }

   void ButtonStopOnClick(object obj, EventArgs ea)
   {
      pinger.Abort();
      results.Items.Add("Ping stopped");
   }

   void ButtonCloseOnClick(object obj, EventArgs ea)
   {
      sock.Close();
      Close();
   }

   void sendPing()
   {
      IPHostEntry iphe = Dns.Resolve(hostbox.Text);
      IPEndPoint iep = new IPEndPoint(iphe.AddressList[0], 0);
      EndPoint ep = (EndPoint)iep;
      ICMP packet = new ICMP();
      int recv, i = 1;

      packet.Type = 0x08;
      packet.Code = 0x00;
      Buffer.BlockCopy(BitConverter.GetBytes(1), 0, packet.Message, 0, 2);
      byte[] data = Encoding.ASCII.GetBytes(databox.Text);
      Buffer.BlockCopy(data, 0, packet.Message, 4, data.Length);
      packet.MessageSize = data.Length + 4;
      int packetsize = packet.MessageSize + 4;

      results.Items.Add("Pinging " + hostbox.Text);
      while(true)
      {
         packet.Checksum = 0;
         Buffer.BlockCopy(BitConverter.GetBytes(i), 0, packet.Message, 2, 2)
         UInt16 chcksum = packet.getChecksum();
         packet.Checksum = chcksum;

         pingstart = Environment.TickCount;
```

```
            sock.SendTo(packet.getBytes(), packetsize, SocketFlags.None, iep);
            try
            {
               data = new byte[1024];
               recv = sock.ReceiveFrom(data, ref ep);
               pingstop = Environment.TickCount;
               elapsedtime = pingstop - pingstart;
               results.Items.Add("reply from: " + ep.ToString() + ", seq: " + i +
                        ", time = " + elapsedtime + "ms");
            } catch (SocketException)
            {
               results.Items.Add("no reply from host");
            }
            i++;
            Thread.Sleep(3000);
         }
      }

      public static void Main()
      {
         Application.Run(new AdvPing());
      }
   }
}
```

In the AdvPing class constructor, the Windows form is created. It presents the customer with an interface to enter the hostname or IP address to ping, a ListBox object to display ping results, and two buttons to stop and start the ping thread. The Socket object used for the ICMP connection is also created, and a ReceiveTimeout value of 3 seconds is set:

```
sock = new Socket(AddressFamily.InterNetwork,
         SocketType.Raw, ProtocolType.Icmp);
sock.SetSocketOption(SocketOptionLevel.Socket,
         SocketOptionName.ReceiveTimeout, 3000);
```

After the customer enters a hostname or IP address in the text box and clicks the Start button, a separate thread is created to handle the ping process. The sendPing() method is similar to the SimplePing program, except that sendPing() performs an endless loop of pinging the remote destination.

The Environment.TickCount property tracks the amount of time it takes to send and receive the ping packets. Each TickCount value represents the length of time (in milliseconds) the system has been operating. By subtracting the value taken before the first packet is sent and the value when the return packet is received, the program determines the time it takes for the ping process to run.

When the customer clicks the Stop button, the ping thread is aborted, but the socket is left open. This enables the customer to choose another hostname or IP address to ping and click the Start button. When the Close button is clicked, the Socket object is closed and the program is terminated.

Similar to the SimplePing program, the AdvPing program must be compiled with the ICMP.cs class file:

```
csc /t:winexe AdvPing.cs ICMP.cs
```

The /t:winexe parameter is also used on the compiler command line to create a windows executable program.

Testing AdvPing

You can test the AdvPing program by starting it from Windows Explorer, or by opening a command-prompt window and running the program there. When the program starts, you'll see the customer interface (Figure 11.3). After entering a hostname or IP address, along with the data text you would like sent in the message, click the Start button to start the ping. Each ping attempt is recorded in the central list box.

FIGURE 11.3:

The AdvPing customer interface window

The TraceRoute.cs Program

A close cousin to ping is traceroute. The traceroute program sends an ICMP Echo Request to a remote host, but with a twist. To determine what routers the ICMP packet travels through to reach its destination, traceroute exploits another ICMP message packet.

By setting the IP packet TTL (time to live) to increasing values, the traceroute program can force the ICMP packet to die at different points along its path to the destination host. Each time the TTL value expires, the last receiving network router sends an ICMP Time Exceeded (Type 11) packet back to the sending host. By starting off with a TTL of 1 and increasing it by 1 after each attempt, the traceroute program forces each router along the network path to return an ICMP Time Exceeded packet. By displaying the sending address of each packet, you can watch each router along the path of the ping packet.

The traceroute operation can be implemented by using the SetSocketOption() method call and the IPTimeToLive socket option to manipulate the TTL value in the IP packet. Again, the newly created ICMP class will be used, creating an Echo Request packet to send to the remote host. Because only the IP TTL value is changed, the ICMP packet can be created once and used for all of the attempts.

The TraceRoute.cs program, Listing 11.5, implements these features.

Listing 11.5   The TraceRoute.cs program

```
using System;
using System.Net;
using System.Net.Sockets;
using System.Text;

class TraceRoute
{
    public static void Main (string[] argv)
    {
        byte[] data = new byte[1024];
        int recv, timestart, timestop;
        Socket host = new Socket(AddressFamily.InterNetwork,
                    SocketType.Raw, ProtocolType.Icmp);
        IPHostEntry iphe = Dns.Resolve(argv[0]);
        IPEndPoint iep = new IPEndPoint(iphe.AddressList[0], 0);
        EndPoint ep = (EndPoint)iep;
        ICMP packet = new ICMP();

        packet.Type = 0x08;
        packet.Code = 0x00;
        packet.Checksum = 0;
        Buffer.BlockCopy(BitConverter.GetBytes(1), 0, packet.Message, 0, 2);
        Buffer.BlockCopy(BitConverter.GetBytes(1), 0, packet.Message, 2, 2);
        data = Encoding.ASCII.GetBytes("test packet");
        Buffer.BlockCopy(data, 0, packet.Message, 4, data.Length);
```

```
        packet.MessageSize = data.Length + 4;
        int packetsize = packet.MessageSize + 4;

        UInt16 chcksum = packet.getCchecksum();
        packet.Checksum = chcksum;

        host.SetSocketOption(SocketOptionLevel.Socket,
                         SocketOptionName.ReceiveTimeout, 3000);

        int badcount = 0;
        for (int i = 1; i < 50; i++)
        {
            host.SetSocketOption(SocketOptionLevel.IP,
                        SocketOptionName.IpTimeToLive, i);
            timestart = Environment.TickCount;
            host.SendTo(packet.getBytes(), packetsize, SocketFlags.None, iep);
            try
            {
                data = new byte[1024];
                recv = host.ReceiveFrom(data, ref ep);
                timestop = Environment.TickCount;
                ICMP response = new ICMP(data, recv);
                if (response.Type == 11)
                    Console.WriteLine("hop {0}: response from {1}, {2}ms",
                            i, ep.ToString(), timestop-timestart);
                if (response.Type == 0)
                {
                    Console.WriteLine("{0} reached in {1} hops, {2}ms.",
                            ep.ToString(), i, timestop-timestart);
                    break;
                }
                badcount = 0;
            } catch (SocketException)
            {
                Console.WriteLine("hop {0}: No response from remote host", i);
                badcount++;
                if (badcount == 5)
                {
                    Console.WriteLine("Unable to contact remote host");
                    break;
                }
            }
        }

        host.Close();
    }
}
```

The TraceRoute.cs program creates a normal ICMP Echo Request packet and then enters a loop, setting the IP TTL value to increasing values until the destination host is reached:

```
for (int i = 1; i < 50; i++)
{
```

```
host.SetSocketOption(SocketOptionLevel.IP,
          SocketOptionName.IpTimeToLive, i);
timestart = Environment.TickCount;
host.SendTo(packet.getBytes(), packetsize, SocketFlags.None, iep);
```

Each time an Echo Request packet is sent out, the program waits for a response. The Type element of the return packet is examined to determine if the packet made it to the destination. Two types of ICMP packets will be returned:

- Time Exceeded (Type 11) packets sent from routers when the TTL value expires

- Echo Reply (Type 0) packets sent from the destination host when the Echo Request packet is received

By examining the source of the Time Exceeded packets, you can see what routers are in the network path to the destination device. It is possible that some routers in the network path are configured to ignore ICMP packets. They will produce the "no response from host" error message, but the TTL value will be increased and the next router will be queried. Typically, you'll run across several routers in a network path that ignore ICMP packets. However, it is also possible that the destination host either won't respond to the ICMP packet or won't even be active. In that case, to prevent an endless loop of packets, after five no responses, the program assumes that the remote host cannot be reached.

Also, similar to the AdvPing program, the Environment.TickCount property value measures the time it takes for the response to the Echo Request packet for each router.

Here, too, you must compile the TraceRoute.cs program with the ICMP.cs file included on the compiler command line:

```
csc TraceRoute.cs ICMP.cs
```

Testing TraceRoute.cs

You can test the TraceRoute.cs program by running it from a command-prompt window, using a known host that responds to pings:

```
C:\>TraceRoute www.cisco.com
hop 1: No response from remote host
hop 2: response from 206.148.207.106:0, 220ms
hop 3: response from 65.123.106.113:0, 140ms
hop 4: response from 205.171.20.125:0, 141ms
hop 5: response from 205.171.20.142:0, 140ms
hop 6: response from 205.171.1.162:0, 130ms
hop 7: response from 144.232.26.54:0, 130ms
hop 8: response from 144.232.8.117:0, 191ms
hop 9: response from 144.232.3.138:0, 190ms
hop 10: response from 144.228.44.14:0, 190ms
hop 11: response from 128.107.239.89:0, 190ms
```

```
hop 12: response from 128.107.239.102:0, 191ms
198.133.219.25:0 reached in 13 hops, 180ms.

C:\>
```

As you can see, it took 13 hops to get from my workstation connected to an ISP, to the www.cisco.com host. From the hops, you can see the IP addresses of the individual routers that pass the packet on to the destination address. The first router in the path did not send an ICMP packet back when the TTL value expired.

Notice the different response times for each router along the path. The response times do not necessarily get longer as the hops get larger because some networks and equipment are faster than others.

Sometimes it is interesting to watch the routes for several remote network addresses. Often networks out on the Internet route traffic to various sites through vastly different paths. You can often see how your ISP connects to the Internet by tracing the routes to remote sites.

The FindMask Program

The FindMask program uses another ICMP message type to automatically discover the subnet mask of the subnet the device is connected to. This section describes the ICMP Subnet Request packet type, along with the FindMask.cs program, which can determine the subnet mask of the local network.

The Subnet Request Packet

One of the extended ICMP types is the Subnet Request packet (ICMP Type 17). It can query devices on a network to determine what the network subnet mask is. Figure 11.4 shows the layout of the Subnet Request packet. Its Identifier and Sequence fields are similar to the Echo Request packet. Each packet must have unique Identifier and Sequence values to distinguish it from other Subnet Request packets sent out by the device.

FIGURE 11.4:

The ICMP Subnet Request packet format

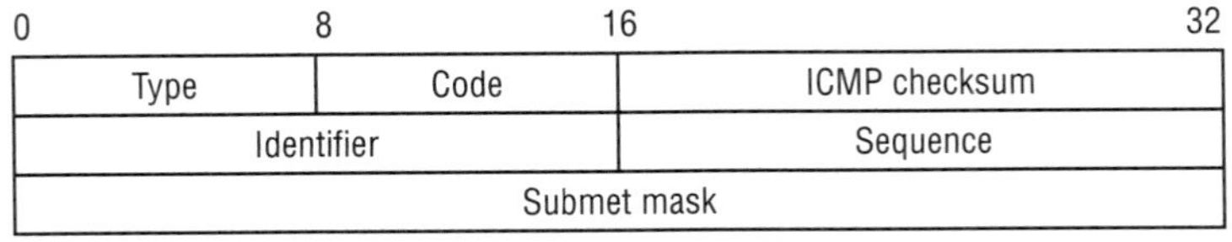

	0	8	16	32
	Type	Code	ICMP checksum	
	Identifier		Sequence	
	Submet mask			

After the Identifier and Sequence field comes a 4-byte integer field that identifies the subnet. The Subnet Request packet places all zeros in this field. A responding device on the network will replace the zeros with the appropriate value for the subnet. Because the value is returned as a long integer, you will want to convert it to an IPAddress object for easier reading. The IPAddress constructor can do this:

```
ICMP response = new ICMP(data, recv);
long answer = BitConverter.ToUInt32(response.Data, 4);
IPAddress netmask = new IPAddress(answer);
```

The BitConverter class extracts the 4-byte value from the received ICMP packet and convert it to a long integer value. The long integer value can create a new IPAddress object.

Listing 11.6, the FindMask.cs program broadcasts a Subnet Request ICMP packet on the local subnet. If there are any devices configured to respond to the ICMP packet, they should return an answer.

Listing 11.6   The FindMask.cs program

```
using System;
using System.Net;
using System.Net.Sockets;
using System.Text;

class FindMask
{
    public static void Main ()
    {
        byte[] data = new byte[1024];
        int recv;
        Socket host = new Socket(AddressFamily.InterNetwork,
                SocketType.Raw, ProtocolType.Icmp);
        IPEndPoint iep = new IPEndPoint(IPAddress.Broadcast, 0);
        EndPoint ep = (EndPoint)iep;
        ICMP packet = new ICMP();

        packet.Type = 0x11;
        packet.Code = 0x00;
        packet.Checksum = 0;
        Buffer.BlockCopy(BitConverter.GetBytes(1), 0, packet.Message, 0, 2);
        Buffer.BlockCopy(BitConverter.GetBytes(1), 0, packet.Message, 2, 2);
        Buffer.BlockCopy(BitConverter.GetBytes(0), 0, packet.Message, 4, 4);
        packet.MessageSize = 8;
        int packetsize = packet.MessageSize + 4;

        UInt16 chksm = packet.getChecksum();
        packet.Checksum = chksm;

        host.SetSocketOption(SocketOptionLevel.Socket,
                        SocketOptionName.ReceiveTimeout, 3000);
        host.SetSocketOption(SocketOptionLevel.Socket,
                        SocketOptionName.Broadcast, 1);
        host.SendTo(packet.getBytes(), packetsize, SocketFlags.None, iep);
        try
```

```
    {
        data = new byte[1024];
        recv = host.ReceiveFrom(data, ref ep);
    } catch (SocketException)
    {
        Console.WriteLine("Unable to determine subnet mask for this subnet");
        return;
    }
    ICMP response = new ICMP(data, recv);
    Console.WriteLine("Received an ICMP type {0} packet", response.Type);
    long answer = BitConverter.ToUInt32(response.Message, 4);
    IPAddress netmask = new IPAddress(answer);
    Console.WriteLine("The subnet mask for this subnet is: {0}",
        netmask.ToString());
    }
}
```

Similar to the other ICMP programs presented in this chapter, the FindMask.cs program must be compiled with the ICMP.cs class file:

```
csc FindMask.cs ICMP.cs
```

The FindMask program first builds an ICMP Subnet Request packet by creating an ICMP object and filling in the appropriate elements in the class. The subnet field is set to zero for the request and will be filled in by the responding network device.

Because you will want the program to terminate cleanly if no response is received, the ReceiveTimeout socket option is set to a reasonable value. Also, this program is using IP broadcasting to send the request out to all devices on the subnet, so the Broadcast socket option must also be set:

```
host.SetSocketOption(SocketOptionLevel.Socket,
        SocketOptionName.ReceiveTimeout, 3000);
host.SetSocketOption(SocketOptionLevel.Socket, SocketOptionName.Broadcast, 1);
```

After the broadcast packet is sent, the ReceiveFrom() method is called, waiting for a response from a device on the network. When a response is received, the subnet mask address is extracted and converted to an IPAddress object.

Testing FindMask.cs

To test the FindMask program, just open a command-prompt window and run the program. If one or more devices on your subnet respond to the request, you will see the result displayed:

```
C:\>FindMask
Received an ICMP type 18 packet
The subnet mask for this subnet is: 255.255.252.0

C:\>
```

It's possible that there aren't any devices on your network that will respond to the Type 17 ICMP packet. It's also possible that a network device may respond to your ICMP packet with an ICMP error packet of a different type. If you receive anything other than a type 18 packet, a device on the network is sending you a different ICMP packet.

What's more interesting than the output is watching what happens behind the scenes on the network. You can use WinDump or Analyzer to watch how many (if any) devices respond to your request. Listing 11.7 shows a sample output from the WinDump program when running the FindMask program.

Listing 11.7   The WinDump output from the FindMask program

```
C:\>windump -X icmp
windump     listening on\Device\Packet_E190x1
13:21:49.576074 192.168.1.32 > 255.255.255.255: icmp: address mask request
0x0000    4500 0020 b355 0000 8001 6c55 c0a8 0120         E....U....lU..}.
0x0010    ffff ffff 1100 ecff 0100 0100 0000 0000         ...............
13:21:49.576203 192.168.1.149 > 192.168.1.32: icmp: address mask is 0xfffffc00

0x0000    4500 0020 6103 0000 ff01 23ff c0a8 0195         E...a.....#...}.
0x0010    c0a8 0120 1200 effe 0100 0100 ffff fc00         ..}............
0x0020    0000 0000 0000 0000 0000 0000 0000              ...............
13:21:49.576236 192.168.1.143 > 192.168.1.32: icmp: address mask is 0xfffffc00

0x0000    4500 0020 8db8 0000 ff01 f74f c0a8 018f         E.........O..}.
0x0010    c0a8 0120 1200 effe 0100 0100 ffff fc00         ..}............
0x0020    0000 0000 0000 0000 0000 0000 0000              ...............
13:21:49.576320 192.168.1.5 > 192.168.1.32: icmp: address mask is 0xfffffc00
0x0000    4500 0020 de96 0000 3c01 6afc c0a8 0105         E.......<.j...|.
0x0010    c0a8 0120 1200 effe 0100 0100 ffff fc00         ..}............
0x0020    0000 0000 0000 0000 0000 0000 0000 0000         ...............
0x0030    0000 0000 0000                                  ......
408 packets received by filter
0 packets dropped by kernel

C:\>
```

On this particular subnet, three separate devices responded to the Subnet Request broadcast. As expected, they all returned the same subnet mask value.

Summary

This chapter shows how to create programs that utilize the Internet Control Message Protocol (ICMP). ICMP allows a network device to quickly send queries and error messages to other network devices. Many types of ICMP packets can be used on the network, the most common of which is the Echo Request packet. When an Echo Request packet is sent to a device, the device responds with an Echo Reply packet. This procedure is the basis for the popular ping program, which tests whether a network device is reachable and how long it takes to send packets to the device.

Programmers can send non-TCP and non-UDP packets with the Socket class, which contains the SocketType.Raw property. This allows raw IP packets to be created and sent on the network. The ProtocolType.Icmp property formats the IP packet used with an ICMP data packet. When working with the raw socket type, you must be careful handling received messages. The received message will include the complete IP packet information, including the IP header fields. You must ensure that your code compensates for the added IP packet information in the returned data by allocating a larger buffer, as well as starting at the right position in the buffer when decoding the ICMP portion of the packet.

To simplify ICMP programs, an ICMP class is established to handle the packet details for ICMP packets. An application program that needs to create or read ICMP packets can create an instance of an ICMP object and place the required data into the data variables of the class. The class also includes a method that allows you to retrieve the raw bytes of the packet so it can be sent using the SendTo() method. When an ICMP packet is received, a separate ICMP class constructor places the raw data from the ICMP packet into the ICMP class variables for easier access.

Several ICMP utility programs are presented in this chapter, including simplified and advanced versions of a ping program. A traceroute program is also created, which exploits how routers handle packets that have an expired IP time to live (TTL) value. When the router receives a packet whose TTL value will expire on the next route, it sends an ICMP Time Exceeded packet back to the packet sender. By starting out with a small TTL value and increasing it, you can track what routers are handling the packet on its way to its final destination. Finally, the ICMP Subnet Request packet type queries network devices to determine the configured subnet mask for a network.

CHAPTER 12

SNMP

- SNMP commands

- Community names

- The Common Management Information Base (CMIB)

- Creating SNMP packets

- Creating a simple SNMP class

- A sample SNMP program: `SimpleSNMP`

- Vendor MIBs

- Using GetNextRequest queries

A popular protocol used in network management is the Simple Network Management Protocol (SNMP). SNMP is used to query and control network devices from a central management station.

SNMP behaves quite differently from other network protocols. Rather than following a set byte-by-byte protocol layout, the SNMP layout changes depending on the type of the query and the type of data queried. This makes for an interesting exercise in learning how to build a network program.

This chapter gives you a foundation in SNMP principles and all the pieces necessary to communicate with SNMP-enabled devices on the network. I'll demonstrate several types of SNMP programs. As you work through these programs, you'll see how to communicate with various network devices and retrieve various types of SNMP information from network devices. If you are responsible for network management, you can create your own SNMP programs to monitor and control devices on your network.

Understanding SNMP

When the Internet was in its infant stage, designers realized the critical need for an easy way to monitoring network devices. Many types of monitoring protocols have been developed over the years, presenting a real challenge to those who would standardize network monitoring. Eventually, SNMP emerged as the most robust and widely accepted way to monitoring network devices.

The principle behind SNMP is simple. Each network device maintains a database of network statistics that can be queried from a remote device. The core database is called the *Management Information Base* (MIB), defined in RFC 1155. Every network device that implements SNMP contains the same core MIB structure. The MIB contains records for simple network statistics such as these:

- The network name of the device
- The number of network interfaces on the device
- The in and out packet counts of each interface
- Error rates of each network interface
- Protocol-specific counts such as TCP and UDP packets

SNMP contains techniques for querying and setting values in the database. Because of this versatility, many vendors of network equipment use the SNMP database to store network device configuration settings, as well. This allows a network management station to retrieve and change the configuration settings for all devices on the network from a single location. This makes SNMP more versatile in the network environment, but it also makes the SNMP database more complex.

Before you can start writing SNMP network programs, you must understand how SNMP works and how it uses network packets to query and retrieve network data. This section describes these concepts.

SNMP and MIB Versions

SNMP has progressed from the original management protocol described in RFC 1157 in May 1990 to a full-blown implementation, currently in version 3. New versions of SNMP do not make the earlier versions obsolete, they just add new functionality (such as authentication and encryption). Therefore, all SNMP-capable network devices must still respond to the original SNMP version 1 requests. The same is true for the original MIB database. Many network management software packages still use the SNMP version 1 protocol to access MIB information from network devices.

This chapter describes the fundamental concepts of working with SNMP and does not get into authentication and encryption, and the programs offered here use SNMP version 1 requests to access MIB information. You should be careful when using SNMP version 1 in a working network environment, because it does send device information across the network in plain text.

SNMP Commands

Instead of using a large set of commands to control network devices, SNMP uses the MIB database to do all of the work. Each controllable feature of the network device is allocated a record in the database. Controlling the feature is as simple as setting the proper value in the database. This means SNMP only has to worry about retrieving and setting database values, rather than having to interpret lots of individual commands to perform actions on the network device.

For example, instead of having a specific SNMP command to shut down a network interface on a device, the device contains a database record related to the state of the interface. If the record is set to a value representing an "off" condition, the device shuts down the interface. This allows any network management station to send an SNMP command to modify the database value and shut down the interface.

Using the MIB database reduces the complexity of the SNMP packets. Each SNMP command is called a *protocol data unit* (PDU). In SNMP version 1, there are only five types of PDUs that used to retrieve and set database values on network devices:

GetRequest   The GetRequest PDU queries the remote SNMP device for a single data value in the MIB database.

GetNextRequest   The GetNextRequest PDU queries the remote SNMP device for a series of data values starting at a specified point in the MIB. As each data value is returned, the next MIB object in the series is also returned to point the querying device to the next related object in the query. This enables an SNMP client to traverse an entire table of MIB database entries on the remote SNMP device.

GetResponse   The GetResponse PDU returns the information that was requested in a GetRequest or GetNextRequest query.

SetRequest   The SetRequest PDU attempts to set a value in the MIB database on the remote SNMP device. The sending device must have the proper access authority to write to the remote device MIB database.

Trap   The Trap PDU sends an unsolicited data value to a remote SNMP management station. The Trap PDU is used for allowing devices to report error conditions automatically to a central management station on the network without having to be constantly queried.

Community Names

Because of the control that SNMP can have over a device, unauthorized users must be prevented from modifying a network device's MIB database. SNMP provides a method of authentication through the *community name* system.

An SNMP application running on a network device contains an individual MIB database. A community name is the password that grants a particular access level to particular area in the MIB database (called a view). Community names can grant access levels to various MIB views. SNMP allows two access modes to the MIB database elements: read-only and read-write.

The pairing of an SNMP access mode with an SNMP MIB view is called a *community profile*. The pairing of a community name with a community profile is called an SNMP *access policy*. Many network devices allow you to create a large number of access policies, while some only allow two (one for reading the entire MIB database, and one for reading and writing to the entire MIB database).

The community name is defined as a byte string. There are no length limitations to the string. Two of the most popular community names (often used as default values on network devices) are public, for read-only access, and private, for read-write access. Obviously, if you are configuring an SNMP access policy on a network device, you will not want to use either of these well-known values.

Common Management Information Base

The Common MIB is the default standard database used for SNMP implementations on network devices. It is defined in RFC 1155 and provides for a set database format for network devices. Since its initial creation, a second version has been approved (MIB-II) and is used as the current standard.

MIB Structure

The MIB structure is one of the most confusing parts of SNMP. The MIB uses a treelike hierarchical database structure that defines data records as *objects*. Each object is referenced by an *object identifier* and has an *object value*.

The object identifier follows the Abstract Syntax Notation, version 1 (called ASN.1) naming convention. This standard syntax assigns a numerical value to each object and references objects in the tree based on a hierarchical naming convention. The naming convention is similar to the way DNS names are referenced, with dots separating name levels, except that for SNMP the root node is specified first.

For SNMP, the root object is named iso, for the International Organization for Standardization, and is assigned an object identifier of 1. All MIB entries are located under this object. The iso object contains a child node, named org, that can be referenced by name (iso.org) or by its object identifier (1.3). The third-level object, dod, has an object identifier of 1.3.6.

All of the MIB-II database entries are located under the internet object, which is a child node of the dod object and has an object identifier of 1.3.6.1.

You may see the official ASN.1 syntax name for objects in the MIB database. The ASN.1 syntax defines the object with the set of higher-level objects that it is derived from. Thus, for the internet object, the ASN.1 syntax is defined as follows:

```
internet ::= { iso(1) org(3) dod(6) 1 }
```

This syntax defines the exact location of the internet object in the MIB database structure. The object can also be referenced by name, iso.org.dod.internet, but referencing the object identifier is much more common.

> **NOTE**   The Internet Activities Board (IAB) is responsible for assigning all MIB object identifiers under the internet object.

Each child node under an object is assigned a unique object identifier. To reference an individual object, you must list each object identifier for each object level, starting at the top level. There are four child nodes located under the internet object, illustrated in Figure 12.1.

FIGURE 12.1:

The iso.org.dod
.internet objects

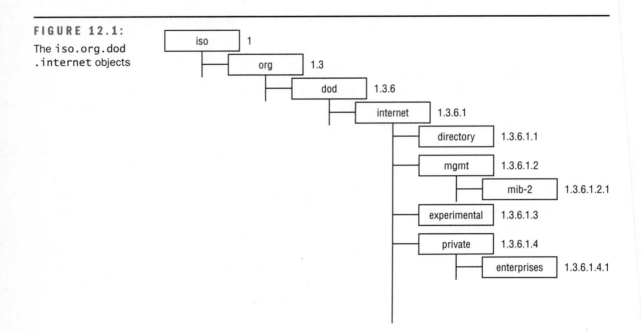

As seen in Figure 12.1, the mgmt object contains the mib-2 object (1.3.6.1.2.1), which contains the MIB-II database objects. These mib-2 objects contain many network statistics objects, which allow you to query network devices for performance and monitoring. The mib-2 objects are listed in Table 12.1.

TABLE 12.1: The mib-2 Objects Used for Network Statistics

object	Node identifier	Description
System	1	System-specific values
Interfaces	2	Network interface statistics
At	3	Address translation table
Ip	4	IP statistics
Icmp	5	ICMP statistics
Tcp	6	TCP statistics
Udp	7	UDP statistics
Egp	8	EGP statistics
Transmission	10	Transmission statistics
Snmp	11	SNMP statistics

Each `mib-2` object contains yet more child nodes that represent database values for the network device. For example, the `system` object contains the following objects:

sysDescr (1)   A description of the network device

sysObjectID (2)   A unique vendor identifier for the object

sysUpTime (3)   The time since the network management portion of the system was initialized (in hundredths of a second)

sysContact (4)   A point-of-contact for the network device

sysName (5)   The administratively assigned name for the device

sysLocation (6)   A descriptive location of the network device

sysServices (7)   A value describing the services the device provides

Each system child node is assigned a unique node identifier (shown in parenthesis) and is referenced by the object identifier in ASN.1 syntax. For example, to see the system description of a network device, you would query for the 1.3.6.1.2.1.1.1 object identifier.

NOTE   When specifying an individual instance of an object in a GetRequest SNMP command, it is required that a trailing zero be placed at the end of the object identifier. This references the single instance value associated with the object. An instance of the sysDescr object would then be referenced as 1.3.6.1.2.1.1.1.0 in the GetRequest packet.

MIB Object Values

Once you find the object identifier of the information you need, you must be able to use the data retrieved. To do this, you need to know how the information is stored in the database. There are many datatypes for MIB objects; some of the more common datatype assignments are as follows:

Integer	type 2
Byte string	type 4
Null	type 5
Object Identifier	type 6
Sequence	type 48 (used in the example programs in this chapter)
TimeTick	type 67

For example, the `sysDescr` object (1.3.6.1.2.1.1.1.0) holds data as a `byte string` (type 4). The `byte string` can be read and stored as a C# string variable and displayed as the description of the system.

The Integer datatype can be especially difficult to work with because it has no set length. It can be as short as 1 byte or as long as 4 bytes. The length is always specified in the received SNMP packet. While this makes the SNMP packet more flexible in handling small and large values, it makes decoding received SNMP packets more challenging for the network programmer.

Working with SNMP Packets

Now that you have seen what constitutes the SNMP system, let's discuss how to place those pieces in a packet to send to the remote device. This section describes the process of creating SNMP packets and how C# can be used to create and send them.

SNMP Packet Format

Each SNMP packet is defined as a *sequence*. The sequence consists of three basic parts:

- The SNMP version number
- The community name used in the query
- The SNMP *PDU (protocol data unit)*

Version and Community Name

The first section of the SNMP packet is standard for all PDU types. For SNMP version 1 packets, the version number is always set to zero (strange, but true). The second section, the community name, is also standard in each of the PDU types. Each character in the community name is placed in a byte in the packet. If the community name passed in the SNMP packet is invalid, no response is returned from the network device.

PDU

The final part of the packet sequence is the PDU. It contains information specific to the PDU type of the packet. Each SNMP packet contains only one PDU section, which can contain only one PDU type.

The five PDU types of SNMP version 1 all have their own formats, but three of them (GetRequest, GetNextRequest, and GetResponse) all use the same PDU format, making things a little bit easier. Let's look under the hood of these PDU types. Their common format contains the following fields, which define the PDU information passed to the SNMP device:

- PDU type
- Request-ID

- Error status
- Error index
- One or more variable bindings

PDU Type

The PDU type is a 1-byte value that identifies which PDU format the SNMP packet is using. The values for the PDU types are as follows:

GetRequest	0xA0
GetNextRequest	0xA1
GetResponse	0xA2
SetRequest	0xA3
Trap	0xA4

Request-ID

The request-ID is a 4-byte integer value that uniquely identifies each query sent to a device. The response from the device must contain a matching request-ID.

Error Status and Error Index

The error status and error index fields are both 1-byte integers. They contain a zero for the GetRequest. The GetResponse packet contains values that indicate whether an error has occurred in the SNMP transaction, and what kind of error it was, as listed in Table 12.2. The error index further defines the specific error condition within the error status of the SNMP transaction.

TABLE 12.2: SNMP Error Status Values

Error Status	Name	Description
0	No error	No errors are present in the transaction.
1	tooBig	The SNMP packet is too large.
2	noSuchName	The MIB object does not exist.
3	badValue	The MIB object value is not the proper datatype or is not in the proper range.
4	readOnly	A SetRequest message is attempting to modify a MIB entry with read-only privileges.
5	genErr	Generic error condition.

Variable Binding

A *variable binding* represents a single object identifier/object value pair in the SNMP packet. For example, the following is a valid variable binding for the sysName MIB object:

```
1.3.6.1.2.1.1.5.0Jessica's workstation
```

In this example, the object identifier 1.3.6.1.2.1.1.5.0 is the sysName object, and the object value is Jessica's workstation.

For GetRequest and GetNextRequest PDUs, the object value is obviously not known (since it is querying the remote device for the value); in these cases it is set to null. The GetResponse packet returned by the remote device will have the object value set to the database value of the object queried.

A single SNMP packet can contain multiple variable bindings. The variable bindings are separated by a sequence identifier (described in the SNMP Packet Layout section). There is no limit on the number of variable bindings that can be in an SNMP packet. The GetResponse packet should contain information for each variable binding sent by the querying device.

SNMP Packet Layout

The tricky part of running SNMP is placing all the SNMP information into a packet. There are plenty of rules for these packets, and if anything is not right the remote host will silently ignore the SNMP packet. Because SNMP uses UDP, you can never be sure whether the SNMP query was lost on the network or if something was actually wrong and made the remote device ignore the packet. That makes for fun troubleshooting.

The easiest way to study the SNMP packet layout is to show a sample SNMP packet and walk through it byte by byte. Take a look at Figure 12.2.

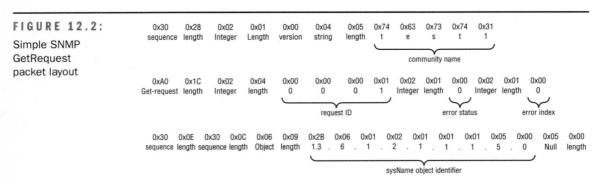

FIGURE 12.2:

Simple SNMP GetRequest packet layout

The SNMP packet starts with a sequence byte (0x30) to indicate the start of an SNMP transaction.

Next comes the length of the entire SNMP packet (0x28) so the remote device can determine whether the packet was received in its entirety.

After the length byte, each remaining data value in the SNMP packet is preceded by a 2-byte sequence. Within that sequence, the first byte represents the SNMP datatype of the object value. The second byte represents the length of the value. Here are the contents of these 2-byte values, as illustrated in Figure 12.2:

SNMP version number   An Integer datatype (0x02) with a length of 1 (0x01). The version number value itself is zero (0x00), which is used for SNMP version 1 packets (go figure).

Community name   Starts with two bytes, then the string object datatype (0x04) and the length of the community name string (0x05). After the length comes the community name bytes.

SNMP PDU type   A single byte. Because the value here is 0xA0, this is a GetRequest PDU packet.

Length of the PDU area of the packet   A single byte (0x1c).

Request ID   An Integer datatype (0x02), a length of 4 bytes (0x04), and the actual request ID. The request ID can be any value and is matched with the GetResponse Request ID value. In this example, the value is 1 (0x00 0x00 0x00 0x01).

Error information   This includes error status and error index values with their respective datatypes and lengths. This is a GetRequest packet, so the error status and error index values are set to zero.

Variable bindings section   Because there can be more than one variable binding, it is encapsulated with a Sequence byte (0x30), along with the size of the entire variable bindings section (0x0e). After that, each individual variable binding will be preceded with Sequence and length bytes for the variable binding. This SNMP packet contains a single variable binding, with a length of 0x0c.

Object identifier/object value pair in the variable binding   The object identifier has a datatype showing that it is an Object Identifier (0x06). Following the datatype is the length of the object identifier (0x09), followed by the object identifier itself.

Note that there is an oddity with how the object identifier is placed in the SNMP packet. Each of the individual object identifier node values are converted to a single-byte value with two exceptions:

- The first two objects in the object identifier (1.3) are converted to a single-byte value of 0x2B
- Node values over 127 are converted to a 2-byte signed integer value

The object identifier seen in the example is 1.3.6.1.2.1.1.5.0. This represents a single instance of the sysName object.

Object value   This is a GetRequest packet, so the object value is set to null, identified by the null datatype (0x05) and the length of zero (0x00).

SNMP Communication

SNMP packets use UDP to communicate with remote devices. Because UDP is a connectionless protocol, your SNMP programs should be formulated to be capable of accounting for typical UDP problems, as described in Chapter 6, "Connectionless Sockets." The biggest problem encountered when sending and receiving SNMP packets is packets that get lost in the network and are never received.

SNMP uses two separate UDP ports for communications: port 161 for GetRequest, GetNextRequest, and SetRequest PDUs, and port 162 for Trap PDUs.

Individual SNMP packets are created by placing the appropriate data into the SNMP byte array. When the entire packet is assembled, the byte array is sent to the remote network device using the appropriate UDP port. Devices that accept GetRequest, GetNextRequest, and SetRequest queries must listen to port 161, while SNMP management stations must listen to port 162 for Trap packets being sent from SNMP devices.

Creating a Simple SNMP Class

The process of creating an SNMP class is different from creating the ICMP class (which was covered in Chapter 11, "ICMP"). Because there is no set byte format for SNMP packets, you must create the SNMP packet as you go, adding the appropriate values as necessary.

This makes creating a class constructor somewhat difficult, because it must be versatile enough to accommodate the changing field sizes and PDU types. I find it easier to instead implement the SNMP packet creation within a class method, which allows you to create the packet on-the-fly and directly send and receive the SNMP packets within the methods themselves. Thus you can quickly send and receive multiple SNMP packets without having to create new instances of the class for every packet.

Three pieces of information are needed to create the SNMP packet:

- The PDU type of the packet
- The MIB object identifier to query
- A valid community name to gain access to the MIB database

Each of these values can be passed to the class method and built into the SNMP packet on-the-fly. After the packet is returned, the method can either return the raw SNMP packet to the application, or attempt to decode it and place it into data values in the class.

The SNMP Class Program

The `SNMP.cs` program in Listing 12.1 defines an SNMP class with a default constructor and one method. The `get()` method is used as a catch-all method to create either a GetRequest or a GetNextRequest PDU packet and send it to a specified remote host. The response packet received from the remote host is then passed directly to the calling application. The single method defined creates the required SNMP packet byte by byte, as explained earlier in "SNMP Packet Layout."

Listing 12.1   **The SNMP.cs program**

```
using System;
using System.Net;
using System.Net.Sockets;
using System.Text;

class SNMP
{
    public SNMP()
    {

    }

    public byte[] get(string request, string host, string community, string
    mibstring)
    {
        byte[] packet = new byte[1024];
        byte[] mib = new byte[1024];
        int snmplen;
        int comlen = community.Length;
        string[] mibvals = mibstring.Split('.');
        int miblen = mibvals.Length;
        int cnt = 0, temp, i;
        int orgmiblen = miblen;
        int pos = 0;

        // Convert the string MIB into a byte array of integer values
        // Unfortunately, values over 128 require multiple bytes
        // which also increases the MIB length
        for (i = 0; i < orgmiblen; i++)
        {
            temp = Convert.ToInt16(mibvals[i]);
            if (temp > 127)
            {
                mib[cnt] = Convert.ToByte(128 + (temp / 128));
                mib[cnt + 1] = Convert.ToByte(temp - ((temp / 128) * 128));
                cnt += 2;
                miblen++;
            } else
```

```
            {
                mib[cnt] = Convert.ToByte(temp);
                cnt++;
            }
        }
        snmplen = 29 + comlen + miblen - 1;   //Length of entire SNMP packet

        //The SNMP sequence start
        packet[pos++] = 0x30; //Sequence start
        packet[pos++] = Convert.ToByte(snmplen - 2);   //sequence size

        //SNMP version
        packet[pos++] = 0x02; //Integer type
        packet[pos++] = 0x01; //length
        packet[pos++] = 0x00; //SNMP version 1

        //Community name
        packet[pos++] = 0x04; // String type
        packet[pos++] = Convert.ToByte(comlen); //length
        //Convert community name to byte array
        byte[] data = Encoding.ASCII.GetBytes(community);
        for (i = 0; i < data.Length; i++)
        {
            packet[pos++] = data[i];
        }

        //Add GetRequest or GetNextRequest value
        if (request == "get")
            packet[pos++] = 0xA0;
        else
            packet[pos++] = 0xA1;

        packet[pos++] = Convert.ToByte(20 + miblen - 1); //Size of total MIB

        //Request ID
        packet[pos++] = 0x02; //Integer type
        packet[pos++] = 0x04; //length
        packet[pos++] = 0x00; //SNMP request ID
        packet[pos++] = 0x00;
        packet[pos++] = 0x00;
        packet[pos++] = 0x01;

        //Error status
        packet[pos++] = 0x02; //Integer type
        packet[pos++] = 0x01; //length
        packet[pos++] = 0x00; //SNMP error status

        //Error index
        packet[pos++] = 0x02; //Integer type
        packet[pos++] = 0x01; //length
        packet[pos++] = 0x00; //SNMP error index

        //Start of variable bindings
```

```
        packet[pos++] = 0x30; //Start of variable bindings sequence

        packet[pos++] = Convert.ToByte(6 + miblen - 1); // Size of variable
binding

        packet[pos++] = 0x30; //Start of first variable bindings sequence
        packet[pos++] = Convert.ToByte(6 + miblen - 1 - 2); // size
        packet[pos++] = 0x06; //Object type
        packet[pos++] = Convert.ToByte(miblen - 1); //length

        //Start of MIB
        packet[pos++] = 0x2b;
        //Place MIB array in packet
        for(i = 2; i < miblen; i++)
            packet[pos++] = Convert.ToByte(mib[i]);
        packet[pos++] = 0x05; //Null object value
        packet[pos++] = 0x00; //Null

        //Send packet to destination
        Socket sock = new Socket(AddressFamily.InterNetwork, SocketType.Dgram,
                        ProtocolType.Udp);
        sock.SetSocketOption(SocketOptionLevel.Socket,
                        SocketOptionName.ReceiveTimeout, 5000);
        IPHostEntry ihe = Dns.Resolve(host);
        IPEndPoint iep = new IPEndPoint(ihe.AddressList[0], 161);
        EndPoint ep = (EndPoint)iep;
        sock.SendTo(packet, snmplen, SocketFlags.None, iep);

        //Receive response from packet
        try
        {
            int recv = sock.ReceiveFrom(packet, ref ep);
        } catch (SocketException)
        {
            packet[0] = 0xff;
        }
        return packet;
    }
}
```

Walking through the Class

When you look at the SNMP class, you can understand why SNMP programming gets pretty complex. Manually creating an SNMP packet is not for the weak of heart.

Converting the MIB

First, the MIB object identifier is converted into a byte array:

```
byte[] mib = new byte[1024];
string[] mibvals = mibstring.Split('.');
int miblen = mibvals.Length;
```

```
int cnt = 0, temp, i;
int orgmiblen = miblen
for (i = 0; i < orgmiblen; i++)
{
    temp = Convert.ToInt16(mibvals[i]);
    if (temp > 127)
    {
        mib[cnt] = Convert.ToByte(128 + (temp / 128));
        mib[cnt + 1] = Convert.ToByte(temp - ((temp / 128) * 128));
        cnt += 2;
        miblen++;
    } else
    {
        mib[cnt] = Convert.ToByte(temp);
        cnt++;
    }
}
```

The object identifier is extracted from the MIB into a string array containing only the numerical values (still stored as strings) using the string Split() method. Next, each identifier is converted to an integer value. SNMP makes this task a little challenging.

The integer MIB value is converted into a 16-bit (2-byte) signed integer, although there are never any negative identifier values. If the value fits into a single byte, it is placed in the byte array as is. If the value requires two bytes (that is, it's larger than 127), the high byte is placed first in the packet, followed by the low byte. When the value requires two bytes, the total MIB length value miblength is increased by one to accommodate for the extra byte. This value is important when creating the actual SNMP packet. The resulting byte array mib[] contains the bytes of the MIB object identifier for the PDU.

Creating the Packet

After the MIB is converted to a byte array, the entire SNMP packet can be created. Each piece of the SNMP packet is added individually to the packet byte array. The community name is converted from its string value to a byte array and placed piece-by-piece into the array using a for loop. The MIB byte array is also placed in the packet using the same technique.

The only difference between SNMP GetRequest and GetNextRequest packets is the PDU type value. A GetRequest packet has a value of 0xA0, while a GetNextRequest packet has a value of 0xA1. Because the class get() method can be used for both types of packets, depending on the calling program, it must provide a way for the calling application to indicate which PDU type to use. This is done using a simple string value. When the value is equal to "get", the GetRequest PDU type is used; otherwise, the GetNextRequest PDU type is used.

Sending the Packet

When the packet is created, a Socket object is created to connect to the remote device SNMP port (UDP port 161):

```
Socket sock = new Socket(AddressFamily.InterNetwork,
  SocketType.Dgram,
 ProtocolType.Udp);
sock.SetSocketOption(SocketOptionLevel.Socket,
  SocketOptionName.ReceiveTimeout, 5000);
IPHostEntry ihe = Dns.Resolve(host);
IPEndPoint iep = new IPEndPoint(ihe.AddressList[0], 161);
EndPoint ep = (EndPoint)iep;
sock.SendTo(packet, iep);
```

The SetSocketOption() method sets the ReceiveTimeout socket option to a reasonable value to wait for the response from the remote device.

Receiving a Response

After the packet is sent, a Receive() method waits for the response:

```
try
{
   int recv = sock.ReceiveFrom(packet, ref ep);
} catch (SocketException)
{
   packet[0] = 0xff;
}
return packet;
```

If no response is received from the remote device in five seconds, the first byte of the returned packet is set to 0xff. The calling program can check this value to determine if a valid SNMP packet has been received.

The SimpleSNMP Program

The system object identifiers are often used to track and identify devices on the network. They are also used to help network administrators track information from a central network management station. For your first simple SNMP program, you'll start out by querying a network device for its system information from the MIB database. Table 12.3 shows the system object values that will be queried from the sample program.

TABLE 12.3: System Object Values Used in SimpleSNMP.cs

Object	Object Identifier	Datatype	Description
sysUptime	1.3.6.1.2.1.1.3.0	Integer	How long a device has been powered on (in hundredths of seconds)
sysContact	1.3.6.1.2.1.1.4.0	String	The person responsible for the device
sysName	1.3.6.1.2.1.1.5.0	String	The network name of the device
sysLocation	1.3.6.1.2.1.1.6.0	String	The location of the device

NOTE   This program requires that you have an existing network device with SNMP capabilities and a valid community name to query data values in the device. This can include a Windows NT or 2000 server with the SNMP service running.

The SimpleSNMP.cs program, Listing 12.2, is a simple network program used to retrieve the system objects from a remote network device using the SNMP class. To compile the SimpleSNMP.cs program, you must include the SNMP.cs class file on the compiler command line:

```
csc SimpleSNMP.cs SNMP.cs
```

Listing 12.2   **The SimpleSNMP.cs program**

```csharp
using System;
using System.Text;

class SimpleSNMP
{
    public static void Main(string[] argv)
    {
        int commlength, miblength, datatype, datalength, datastart;
        int uptime = 0;
        string output;
        SNMP conn = new SNMP();
        byte[] response = new byte[1024];

        Console.WriteLine("Device SNMP information:");

        // Send sysName SNMP request and get the response
        response = conn.get("get", argv[0], argv[1], "1.3.6.1.2.1.1.5.0");
        if (response[0] == 0xff)
        {
            Console.WriteLine("No response from {0}", argv[0]);
            return;
        }

        // Get the community name and MIB lengths from the packet
        commlength = Convert.ToInt16(response[6]);
```

```
miblength = Convert.ToInt16(response[23 + commlength]);

// Extract the MIB data from the SNMP response
datatype = Convert.ToInt16(response[24 + commlength + miblength]);
datalength = Convert.ToInt16(response[25 + commlength + miblength]);
datastart = 26 + commlength + miblength;
output = Encoding.ASCII.GetString(response, datastart, datalength);
Console.WriteLine("  sysName - Datatype: {0}, Value: {1}",
        datatype, output);

// Send a sysLocation SNMP request
response = conn.get("get", argv[0], argv[1], "1.3.6.1.2.1.1.6.0");
if (response[0] == 0xff)
{
    Console.WriteLine("No response from {0}", argv[0]);
    return;
}

// Get the community name and MIB lengths from the response
commlength = Convert.ToInt16(response[6]);
miblength = Convert.ToInt16(response[23 + commlength]);

// Extract the MIB data from the SNMP response
datatype = Convert.ToInt16(response[24 + commlength + miblength]);
datalength = Convert.ToInt16(response[25 + commlength + miblength]);
datastart = 26 + commlength + miblength;
output = Encoding.ASCII.GetString(response, datastart, datalength);
Console.WriteLine("  sysLocation - Datatype: {0}, Value: {1}",
     datatype, output);

// Send a sysContact SNMP request
response = conn.get("get", argv[0], argv[1], "1.3.6.1.2.1.1.4.0");
if (response[0] == 0xff)
{
    Console.WriteLine("No response from {0}", argv[0]);
    return;
}

// Get the community and MIB lengths
commlength = Convert.ToInt16(response[6]);
miblength = Convert.ToInt16(response[23 + commlength]);

// Extract the MIB data from the SNMP response
datatype = Convert.ToInt16(response[24 + commlength + miblength]);
datalength = Convert.ToInt16(response[25 + commlength + miblength]);
datastart = 26 + commlength + miblength;
output = Encoding.ASCII.GetString(response, datastart, datalength);
Console.WriteLine("  sysContact - Datatype: {0}, Value: {1}",
        datatype, output);

// Send a SysUptime SNMP request
response = conn.get("get", argv[0], argv[1], "1.3.6.1.2.1.1.3.0");
if (response[0] == 0xff)
```

```
    {
        Console.WriteLine("No response from {0}", argv[0]);
        return;
    }

    // Get the community and MIB lengths of the response
    commlength = Convert.ToInt16(response[6]);
    miblength = Convert.ToInt16(response[23 + commlength]);

    // Extract the MIB data from the SNMp response
    datatype = Convert.ToInt16(response[24 + commlength + miblength]);
    datalength = Convert.ToInt16(response[25 + commlength + miblength]);
    datastart = 26 + commlength + miblength;

    // The sysUptime value may by a multi-byte integer
    // Each byte read must be shifted to the higher byte order
    while(datalength > 0)
    {
        uptime = (uptime << 8) + response[datastart++];
        datalength-;
    }
    Console.WriteLine("  sysUptime - Datatype: {0}, Value: {1}",
            datatype, uptime);

    }
}
```

The SimpleSNMP program uses the get() method from the SNMP class to send each
GetRequest packet to the remote network device. As each GetResponse packet is received,
it is decoded from the SNMP packet.

This is an excellent opportunity to use the WinDump or Analyzer programs. After sending
a test SNMP request packet, you should see the response packet returned by the SNMP
device. You must decode the SNMP response packet to determine where in the packet
structure the variables you are interested in are located. The numbers used to reference
variables in these examples are taken from counting byte locations in test SNMP
response packets.

First, the community name length and MIB length are computed from their locations in
the returned packet:

```
int commlength = Convert.ToInt16(response[6]);
int miblength = Convert.ToInt16(response[23 + commlength]);
```

The community length is easy, as it is always located in the same spot in the packet. The
miblength byte location depends on the length of the community name.

After the community name and MIB lengths, you determine the datatype of the returned object value, its start and length. When you know the location and length of the byte string, you can extract it from the packet:

```
int datatype = Convert.ToInt16(response[24 + commlength + miblength]);
int datalength = Convert.ToInt16(response[25 + commlength + miblength]);
int datastart = 26 + commlength + miblength;
string output = Encoding.ASCII.GetString(response, datastart, datalength);
Console.WriteLine("response:");
Console.WriteLine("  Datatype: {0}, length: {1}", datatype, datalength);
Console.WriteLine("  data: {0}", output);
```

The sysName MIB object is represented as a string value, so it's easy to find the location of the string within the SNMP packet (knowing how the packet is formatted and knowing the community name and MIB lengths).

The sysUptime value can be a little tricky to decode. There is no way of knowing ahead of time how many bytes it will be. You must program for each possibility, from 1 byte to 5 bytes. The datalength value indicates how many bytes are used in the value. As each byte is read, it is added to a total. When another byte is read, the preceding bytes are shifted 8 bits over to make the high byte value.

Testing the Program

You can test the SimpleSNMP program with any SNMP-capable device on your network, as long as you have access to at least a read-only community name. Many network hubs and switches, as well as Windows NT and 2000 servers, have the SNMP service installed and can be used for this test:

```
C:\>SimpleSNMP 192.168.1.100 test1
Device SNMP information:
  sysName - Datatype: 4, Value: Rich's workstation
  sysLocation - Datatype: 4, Value: The office
  sysContact - Datatype: 4, Value: Rich Blum
  sysUptime - Datatype: 67, Value: 4906397

C:\>
```

For this example, the remote device is located at IP address 192.168.1.100 and is using a read-only community name of test1. If you have created the SNMP packet properly and have used a valid community name, you should get an SNMP response back from the network device. If you do not get a response, you can use WinDump or Analyzer to watch the SNMP packet get sent and see if it is formatted properly.

NOTE The Windows 2000 Server does not include the SNMP service by default. You must manually install the SNMP service and configure the system information. The default read community name is "public".

Watching the Packets

More interesting than watching the output of this program is watching the packets that are generated. The easiest way to understand the SNMP packet format is to watch a live SNMP transaction on the network. Listing 12.3 shows the SNMP GetRequest and GetResponse packets that resulted from the sysName SNMP query in the SimpleSNMP program.

Listing 12.3 **The SimpleSNMP program network trace (WinDump)**

```
C:\>windump -X udp port 161
windump     listening on\Device\Packet_E190x1
10:19:22.728534 192.168.1.6.1450 > 192.168.1.100.161:  [12 extra after iSEQ]C=te
st1 GetRequest(28) system.sysName.0
0x0000    4500 041c fb1f 0000 8011 0667 c0a8 0106     E.........g..}.
0x0010    c0a8 0164 05aa 00a1 0408 5f8b 3028 0201     ..|......._.0(..
0x0020    0004 0574 6373 7431 a01c 0204 0000 0001     ...test1........
0x0030    0201 0002 0100 300e 300c 0608 2b06 0102     ......0.0...+...
0x0040    0101 0500 0500 0000 0000 0000 0000 0000     ..............
0x0050    0000                                        ..
10:19:22.731609 192.168.1.100 > 192.168.1.6.1450:  C=test1 GetResponse(40)
system.sysName.0="Rich's workstat"
0x0000    4500 005b 755e 0000 1e11 f1e9 c0a8 0164     E..[u^........|.
0x0010    c0a8 0106 00a1 05aa 0047 f69e 303d 0201     ..}......G..0=..
0x0020    0004 0574 6373 7431 a231 0201 0102 0100     ...test1.1......
0x0030    0201 0030 2630 2406 082b 0601 0201 0105     ...0&0$..+......
0x0040    0004 1252 6964 6827 7320 776F 726b 7374     ...Rich's workst
0x0050    6274                                        at

551 packets received by filter
0 packets dropped by kernel

C:\>
```

The WinDump program recognized the SNMP packet and did some of the decoding work for us. The packet headers show the pertinent information for each SNMP packet:

```
10:19:22.728534 192.168.1.6.1450 > 192.168.1.100.161:  [12 extra after iSEQ]C=te
st1 GetRequest(28) system.sysName.0
```

This packet is a GetRequest packet, and it queries for the sysName object, located under the mib-2 system object. Note that the community name used also appears in the WinDump header (C=test1).

The raw packet dump contains both the IP and UDP packet headers, as well as the SNMP packet information. The SNMP packet starts at location 0x001c with the 0x30 `sequence` byte. You should recognize the bytes in the packet (you helped create them). The community name and MIB object identifier are contained within the packet as expected.

WinDump also decoded the important information in the SNMP GetResponse packet that was returned by the remote device:

```
10:19:22.731609 192.168.1.100 > 192.168.1.6.1450:  C=test1 GetResponse(40)
system.sysName.0="Rich's workstat"
```

Note that the object value was truncated because of the default capture size of the WinDump program. If you want to see the entire GetResponse packet, you can use the `-s` option to increase the capture buffer size to a larger value.

Using Vendor MIBs

Most network device vendors utilize the enterprise MIB object (1.3.6.1.4.1) to add their own device configurations and statistics to augment the standard MIB-II statistics. The IAB assigns child node values to vendors under this object. When writing real-world SNMP network applications, you often have to use enterprise database objects to control network devices and extract useful information.

This section describes how to interpret vendor MIB data and how to create an SNMP program to query information from a network device based on objects from the vendor MIB. This is done using an SNMP application, CiscoRouter, that has come in handy for me as a network administrator. With several Cisco brand routers on the network, it is nice to see how each one is working throughout the day without having to manually Telnet to each router and watch statistics. One useful statistic to monitor on Cisco routers is the CPU utilization. By watching the CPU utilization of a router you can often tell when network segments are being overloaded, or when strange things are happening on the network.

The CiscoRouter program presented in this section sends an SNMP packet to a Cisco router using a Cisco vendor MIB to query the 5-minute CPU utilization average on the router.

The Cisco CPU MIB

The first step to writing the SNMP application is to obtain the vendor's MIB data for the device you want to monitor.

Fortunately, Cisco offers a large variety of MIB files for all its network devices, freely available to download from `ftp://ftp.cisco.com/pub/mibs/v1/`. Various MIB categories and devices are defined in specific MIB files. Usually a quick search on the Cisco web page (`http:///www.cisco.com`) produces the MIB filename that contains the data you are looking for. The MIB information for router CPU utilization is contained in the `OLD-CISCO-CPU-MIB.my` file, which defines the MIBs used for monitoring CPU statistics on Cisco devices.

NOTE   There is a newer MIB file available to obtain CPU statistics, but this MIB is not guaranteed to be compatible with all of the Cisco router models. The `OLD-CISCO-CPU-MIB.my` file is usable with all models of Cisco routers.

The MIB file uses ASN.1 syntax to define each of the separate MIB objects and object identifiers. The top of the MIB file lists each of the high-level objects on which these MIBs are based. Depending on how often you want to monitor CPU utilization on your router, you can use one of three MIB objects, shown in Table 12.4.

NOTE   Some vendor MIBs (such as Cisco) employ a Unix text format rather than a DOS text format. So each line ends in only a linefeed character instead of both a carriage control and a linefeed. This will make the text look odd if you're viewing it with Notepad. You can correct it by using an advanced editor such as Microsoft Word to view the MIB.

TABLE 12.4: The Cisco CPU Utilization MIBs

MIB Object	Description
busyPer	The 5-second CPU utilization average
avgbusy1	The 1-minute CPU utilization average
avgbusy5	The 5-minute CPU utilization average

Each MIB object has its own unique object identifier to use to obtain the values stored in the device database. The ASN.1 definitions of the objects show the node value for the object, but not the whole object identifier to use. Listing 12.4 shows the three MIB values that can be used.

Listing 12.4   **Cisco CPU Utilization MIBs**

```
busyPer OBJECT-TYPE
    SYNTAX   INTEGER
    ACCESS   read-only
    STATUS   mandatory
    DESCRIPTION
            "CPU busy percentage in the last 5 second
            period. Not the last 5 realtime seconds but
            the last 5 second period in the scheduler."
    ::= { lcpu 56 }

avgBusy1 OBJECT-TYPE
```

```
        SYNTAX  INTEGER
        ACCESS  read-only
        STATUS  mandatory
        DESCRIPTION
                "1 minute exponentially-decayed moving
                average of the CPU busy percentage."
        ::= { lcpu 57 }

avgBusy5 OBJECT-TYPE
        SYNTAX  INTEGER
        ACCESS  read-only
        STATUS  mandatory
        DESCRIPTION
                "5 minute exponentially-decayed moving
                average of the CPU busy percentage."
        ::= { lcpu 58 }
```

The ASN.1 notation defines five separate values:

- The datatype (called SYNTAX)

- The access mode

- Whether the object is optional or mandatory in each device

- A text description of the object

- The ASN.1 definition of the object identifier

The MIB indicates that the avgBusy5 object has a node value of 58 and is a child node of the lcpu object. This in itself does not give you enough information to define the object identifier for the object. You must do some legwork to determine the complete object identifier.

To find the complete object identifier for the object, you must backtrack through the MIBs to find each object's identifier in the chain. The lcpu object is defined in the same MIB file. It is defined as follows:

```
lcpu      OBJECT IDENTIFIER ::= { local 1 }
```

The lcpu object is defined as node 1 under the local object. So now you at least know that the avgBusy5 object identifier ends with 1.58.

Unfortunately, the local object is not defined in this MIB file. However, in the comments of the MIB file you see that the local object is referenced as coming from the CISCO-SMI MIB file. To find the rest of the MIB object identifier, you must also download the CISCO-SMI-V1SMI.my MIB file from the Cisco ftp site. In that MIB file, the local object is defined as follows:

```
local OBJECT IDENTIFIER ::= { cisco 2 }
```

The local object is child node 2 under the cisco object.

The cisco object is also defined in the same MIB file as follows:

```
cisco OBJECT IDENTIFIER ::= { enterprises 9 }
```

OK, now you're getting somewhere. The cisco object is child node 9 under the enterprises object. The enterprises object is one of the standard MIB objects, with an object identifier of 1.3.6.1.4.1.

Putting all of the pieces together, the whole object identifier for the avgBusy5 object instance is 1.3.6.1.4.1.9.2.1.58.0. Now that you know what MIB object to query, you can write an SNMP program to query the router for the avgBusy5 MIB object at 5-minute intervals.

The CiscoRouter Program

The CiscoRouter.cs program shown in Listing 12.5 uses the avgBusy5 MIB object to get the 5-minute CPU utilization average for a router. The value is retrieved every five minutes, allowing you to see the router CPU utilization over a period of time. The program displays the information in a window and also logs the information in a log file for future reference.

Listing 12.5   **The CiscoRouter.cs program**

```
using System;
using System.Drawing;
using System.IO;
using System.Threading;
using System.Windows.Forms;

class CiscoRouter  :  Form
{

    private TextBox host;
    private TextBox community;
    private ListBox results;
    private Thread monitor;
    private FileStream fs;
    private StreamWriter sw;

    public CiscoRouter()
    {
        Text = "Cisco Router Utilization";
        Size = new Size(400, 380);

        Label label1 = new Label();
        label1.Parent = this;
        label1.Text = "Host:";
        label1.AutoSize = true;
        label1.Location = new Point(10, 30);

        host = new TextBox();
        host.Parent = this;
```

```
      host.Size = new Size(170, 2 * Font.Height);
      host.Location = new Point(40, 27);

      Label label2 = new Label();
      label2.Parent = this;
      label2.Text = "Community:";
      label2.AutoSize = true;
      label2.Location = new Point(10, 60);

      community = new TextBox();
      community.Parent = this;
      community.Size = new Size(170, 2 * Font.Height);
      community.Location = new Point(75, 57);

      results = new ListBox();
      results.Parent = this;
      results.Location = new Point(10, 85);
      results.Size = new Size(360, 18 * Font.Height);

      Button start = new Button();
      start.Parent = this;
      start.Text = "Start";
      start.Location = new Point(250, 52);
      start.Size = new Size(5 * Font.Height, 2 * Font.Height);
      start.Click += new EventHandler(ButtonStartOnClick);

      Button stop = new Button();
      stop.Parent = this;
      stop.Text = "Stop";
      stop.Location = new Point(320, 52);
      stop.Size = new Size(5 * Font.Height, 2 * Font.Height);
      stop.Click += new EventHandler(ButtonStopOnClick);
   }

   void ButtonStartOnClick(Object obj, EventArgs ea)
   {
      monitor = new Thread(new ThreadStart(checkRouter));
      monitor.IsBackground = true;
      monitor.Start();
   }

   void ButtonStopOnClick(Object obj, EventArgs ea)
   {
      monitor.Abort();
      sw.Close();
      fs.Close();
   }

   void checkRouter()
   {
```

```
int commlength, miblength, datastart, cpuUtil;
SNMP conn = new SNMP();
byte[] response = new byte[1024];
DateTime time;
string logFile = "routerlog.txt";
fs = new FileStream(logFile, FileMode.OpenOrCreate,
        FileAccess.ReadWrite);
sw = new StreamWriter(fs);

while (true)
{
    response = conn.get("get", host.Text,
        community.Text, "1.3.6.1.4.1.9.2.1.58.0");
    if (response[0] == 0xff)
    {
        results.Items.Add("No reponse from host");
        sw.WriteLine("No response from host");
        sw.Flush();
        break;
    }
    commlength = Convert.ToInt16(response[6]);
    miblength = Convert.ToInt16(response[23 + commlength]);
    datastart = 26 + commlength + miblength;

    cpuUtil = Convert.ToInt16(response[datastart]);
    time = DateTime.Now;
    results.Items.Add(time + " CPU Utilization: " + cpuUtil + "%");
    sw.WriteLine("{0} CPU Utilization: {1}%", time, cpuUtil);
    sw.Flush();
    Thread.Sleep(5 * 60000);
}
}

public static void Main()
{
    Application.Run(new CiscoRouter());
}
}
```

The CiscoRouter program uses two TextBox objects to allow the customer to enter the hostname (or address) of the remote device and an appropriate community name for read-only access. After the information is entered, the Start button is pressed. Next, a new Thread object is created, which creates the SNMP object and creates the SNMP packet with the avgBusy5 object identifier. The returned packet contains the CPU utilization value. Because this value will never be above 100, you know that it will be contained in a single byte in the SNMP packet and can be converted to an integer value. The current date and time, along with the CPU utilization value, are then displayed in the ListBox and written to the log file. Figure 12.3 shows a sample running of the CiscoRouter application.

FIGURE 12.3:

The CiscoRouter application

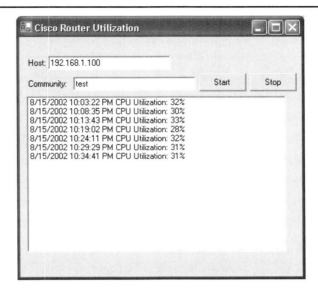

Using GetNextRequest Queries

As can be seen from the SimpleSNMP and CiscoRouter programs, writing GetRequest programs using the SNMP class is a snap. The next step is to experiment with the SNMP GetNextRequest queries. These queries behave a little bit differently from the GetRequest queries we've looked at so far.

Extracting the Next MIB

A GetNextResponse PDU is used when you need to retrieve a series of data from the network device. The data in the series is usually related in some way, such as a series of network interfaces installed on the device, or a series of statistics taken of a period of time.

The data series is stored in the MIB using separate objects, each one located beneath the original object. For example, the interface object may have several child nodes below it, one for each interface on the device. Figure 12.4 shows what this would look like.

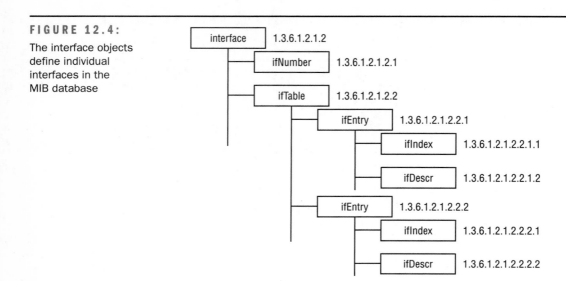

FIGURE 12.4:

The interface objects
define individual
interfaces in the
MIB database

The MIB database contains an object for the interface table (ifTable) at object identifier 1.3.6.1.2.1.2.2. In order for a device to query each of the interface objects in the series, it must start at the ifTable object and "walk" through the related child nodes in the database. This is done with the help of the SNMP device.

When a GetNextRequest packet is sent to a network device, the device responds with a standard GetResponse packet. The difference is that it changes the value of the MIB entry in the packet. The new MIB entry is the next MIB that should be queried to continue in the series of information.

To follow the series, you must extract the new MIB value from the GetResponse packet and use it as the MIB value in the next GetNextRequest query. This continues until the remote SNMP device returns an error status, or you determine you have finished collecting all of the data in the series.

The getnextMIB() Method

Because extracting the next MIB in the GetResponse packet is a common function, it would be best to create a new method in the SNMP class. Any SNMP application program that needs to walk through a data series can call the new method. Listing 12.6 shows the getnextMIB() method that should be added to the SNMP.cs class file, after the get() method.

Listing 12.6   The getnextMIB() method of the SNMP class

```
public string getnextMIB(byte[] mibin)
{
   string output = "1.3";
   int commlength = mibin[6];
   int mibstart = 6 + commlength + 17; //find the start of the mib section
   //The MIB length is the length defined in the SNMP packet
   // minus 1 to remove the ending .0, which is not used
   int miblength = mibin[mibstart] - 1;
   mibstart += 2; //skip over the length and 0x2b values
   int mibvalue;

   for(int i = mibstart; i < mibstart + miblength; i++)
   {
      mibvalue = Convert.ToInt16(mibin[i]);
      if (mibvalue > 128)
      {
         mibvalue = (mibvalue/128)*128 + Convert.ToInt16(mibin[i+1]);
         i++;
      }
      output += "." + mibvalue;
   }
   return output;
}
```

The getnextMIB() method is basically the opposite operation to what was done by the get() method. This method takes a byte array representing the MIB and converts it to a string value. The only tricky part is remembering to watch for object node values that are larger than 128 and thus occupy 2 bytes instead of the usual 1 byte.

After the MIB is converted to a string, it is returned to the calling application. The application can then display the new MIB and use it in another get() method call to determine the object value for the MIB.

The MAC Address Program

There are quite a few applications that need to step through a series of data on a network device. One application that I find myself using quite often is determining the active MAC addresses on Cisco switches. The Cisco switch keeps track of all active MAC addresses for each configured VLAN on the switch in a table accessible from a common MIB under the interfaces object. Using the SNMP class, it is easy to write an application that walks through the table, retrieving all of the active MAC addresses on the VLAN.

Listing 12.7 shows the `MacAddress.cs` program, which queries a Cisco switch for all the active MAC addresses.

Listing 12.7   **The MacAddress.cs program**

```
using System;

class MacAddress
{
    public static void Main(string[] argv)
    {
        int commlength, miblength, datastart, datalength;
        string nextmib, value;
        SNMP conn = new SNMP();
        string mib = "1.3.6.1.2.1.17.4.3.1.1";
        int orgmiblength = mib.Length;
        byte[] response = new byte[1024];

        nextmib = mib;

        while (true)
        {
            response = conn.get("getnext", argv[0], argv[1], nextmib);
            commlength = Convert.ToInt16(response[6]);
            miblength = Convert.ToInt16(response[23 + commlength]);
            datalength = Convert.ToInt16(response[25 + commlength + miblength]);
            datastart = 26 + commlength + miblength;
            value = BitConverter.ToString(response, datastart, datalength);
            nextmib = conn.getnextMIB(response);

            if (!(nextmib.Substring(0, orgmiblength) == mib))
                break;

            Console.WriteLine("{0} = {1}", nextmib, value);

        }
    }
}
```

With the help of the SNMP class file, it is amazing how small the application program can be. The only tricky part to the application is knowing when to stop walking the MIB objects.

The Cisco switch uses the `dot1netTable` (1.3.6.1.2.1.17.4.3.1.1) object, located in the `mib-2` database (1.3.6.1.2.1) to access the MAC address table. Once you reference the base object of the table, the Cisco switch will direct you to the individual values with the returned MIBs.

The switch will continually walk down the child nodes from the MIB you specify, but when it runs out, it attempts to go to the next MIB object on the same level. To prevent this, you must keep a copy of the original MIB object identifier and compare it to the new MIB returned in the GetResponse packets. Each child node will have more node values in the object identifier, so all you need to compare is the length of the original MIB to the new MIB. When the new MIB changes within the length of the original MIB, you know that a new object on the same level has been returned, and you can stop walking.

For example, the original MIB value is as follows:

```
1.3.6.1.2.1.17.4.3.1.1
```

The first data object in this table has the following MIB value:

```
1.3.6.1.2.1.17.4.3.1.1.0.0.12.7.172.124
```

The subsequent values use a depth-first approach within the table: the lower MIB places are expanded until they are exhausted, then the next higher MIB place is expanded, and so on up until the base MIB value changes to the following:

```
1.3.6.1.2.1.17.4.3.1.2
```

When the base MIB value changes, the program detects this and halts the search.

Because MAC addresses are usually presented in their hexadecimal values, you can use the BitConverter class's ToString() method to produce a string version of the hexadecimal values of the MAC address.

Testing the Program

After compiling the MacAddress program (with the new version of the SNMP class file), you can run it with a Cisco switch. One oddity of Cisco equipment is the way it handles community names.

Cisco uses a system called *indexed community names*. A general community name, such as the word test, provides access to only the general switch information. To access information for a particular VLAN, you must add the VLAN number to the community name. For example, to access the MAC address table for VLAN 100, you would use the community name test@100.

Listing 12.8 shows a partial output from running the MacAddress program on a busy Cisco switch.

Listing 12.8   Sample MacAddress program output

```
C:\>MacAddress 192.168.1.5 horse@100
1.3.6.1.2.1.17.4.3.1.1.0.0.12.7.172.124 = 00-00-0C-07-AC-7C
1.3.6.1.2.1.17.4.3.1.1.0.0.170.91.20.67 = 00-00-AA-5B-14-43
1.3.6.1.2.1.17.4.3.1.1.0.0.170.91.23.14 = 00-00-AA-5B-17-0E
1.3.6.1.2.1.17.4.3.1.1.0.0.170.91.24.202 = 00-00-AA-5B-18-CA
1.3.6.1.2.1.17.4.3.1.1.0.1.3.190.158.77 = 00-01-03-BE-9E-4D
1.3.6.1.2.1.17.4.3.1.1.0.1.230.77.209.187 = 00-01-E6-4D-D1-BB
1.3.6.1.2.1.17.4.3.1.1.0.1.230.84.119.202 = 00-01-E6-54-77-CA
1.3.6.1.2.1.17.4.3.1.1.0.4.0.248.44.12 = 00-04-00-F8-2C-0C
1.3.6.1.2.1.17.4.3.1.1.0.6.91.52.17.87 = 00-06-5B-34-11-57
1.3.6.1.2.1.17.4.3.1.1.0.6.91.52.108.108 = 00-06-5B-34-6C-6C
```

```
1.3.6.1.2.1.17.4.3.1.1.0.6.91.129.249.64 = 00-06-5B-81-F9-40
1.3.6.1.2.1.17.4.3.1.1.0.6.91.130.3.112 = 00-06-5B-82-03-70
1.3.6.1.2.1.17.4.3.1.1.0.6.91.166.250.231 = 00-06-5B-A6-FA-E7
1.3.6.1.2.1.17.4.3.1.1.0.16.131.13.143.121 = 00-10-83-0D-8F-79
1.3.6.1.2.1.17.4.3.1.1.0.80.218.16.120.6 = 00-50-DA-10-78-06
.
.
.
1.3.6.1.2.1.17.4.3.1.1.0.224.41.146.58.140 = 00-E0-29-92-3A-8C
1.3.6.1.2.1.17.4.3.1.1.8.0.9.216.30.170 = 08-00-09-D8-1E-AA
1.3.6.1.2.1.17.4.3.1.1.8.0.32.117.204.112 = 08-00-20-75-CC-70

C:\>
```

The returned MIBs from the Cisco switch show some interesting values. Notice how there is no particular order to the returned MIB values. Only Cisco knows what these individual node values mean—all we poor programmers know is that each one represents a MAC address value.

The other feature to notice is that the program stopped when the returned MIB's object identifier differed from the original MIB object identifier sent to the device.

Summary

The Simple Network Management Protocol (SNMP) presents true challenges to programmers writing applications that use it. Because of its complexity, many novice network programmers avoid using the protocol altogether. This chapter gives you a look under the hood of SNMP and how to build C# network programs that use SNMP to query network devices

SNMP allows network devices to maintain a database of network statistics and configuration settings. The database can be queried and manipulated using the SNMP network protocol from a remote device on the network. Each SNMP device must implement the Common Management Information Base (called MIB-II) that tracks network statistics for interfaces on the device. In addition to the common MIB, many vendors implement their own database objects to make controlling the network device from a remote workstation easy.

SNMP uses five types of command packets. The GetRequest and GetNextRequest packets are used to obtain either a single value or a series of values from the device. The GetResponse packet returns information requested in a query. The SetRequestpacket changes the value of database objects. The Trap packet is used by a network device to send an unsolicited network information packet to a central network monitoring station.

Each SNMP device uses security based on access modes and profiles. A community name is assigned access privileges in the MIB database. A remote device uses the community name as a password to query and update values in the database.

SNMP packets are difficult to create because they contain variable length information. Both the community name and MIB object included in the SNMP packet can vary in length. The SNMP commands are contained in Protocol Data Units (PDUs) that are encapsulated in the SNMP packet. Each PDU represents a single query but can contain multiple MIB objects and object values.

In this chapter, an SNMP class is created to allow programmers a single method for creating SNMP packets and sending them to remote devices. The returned response packets are forwarded to the applications for decoding.

You studied three sample network applications: a simple SNMP application to obtain system information from a network device, an application to monitor the CPU utilization of a Cisco router, and an application to obtain the MAC address table of a Cisco switch.

Next, we'll move forward to the tricky business of Internet e-mail. The .NET network library provides a class to help the network programmer integrate Internet e-mail in network applications. Chapter 13, "SMTP," shows how to use the .NET Mail class to send e-mail across the Internet from your program.

CHAPTER 13

SMTP

- E-mail basics

- SMTP and Windows

- The `SmtpMail` class

- Using expanded mail message formats

- The `MailMessage` class

- Mail attachments

- The `MailAttachment` class

- A POP3 client

The preceding two chapters demonstrated network application programming by showing how to code specific network applications using the standard C# network library classes. This chapter switches gears a little and introduces a separate C# network namespace that includes classes used specifically for a single network application.

The System.Web.Mail namespace contains classes that are used for creating and sending e-mail messages to remote hosts. This is done using either the default Windows Simple Mail Transfer Protocol (SMTP) service on Windows 2000 and XP machines, or an external mail server.

This chapter describes how Internet e-mail works and how mail messages are formatted to transfer both text and binary data to a remote host. It then discusses how to use the .NET e-mail classes to incorporate e-mail messaging into your C# network programs. We'll take a look at an e-mail client protocol, the Post Office Protocol (POP) and study an example program that demonstrates the coding of e-mail client functionality in C# network programs.

E-mail Basics

Almost all Internet e-mail packages use the Unix e-mail model to implement electronic messaging with remote hosts. This model has become the most popular and widely implemented technique of delivering messages both to local customers and to remote host customers.

The Unix e-mail model divides the e-mail functions into three parts:

- The Message Transfer Agent (MTA)
- The Message Delivery Agent (MDA)
- The Message User Agent (MUA)

Each of these parts performs a specific function in the e-mail process of sending, delivering, and displaying messages. Figure 13.1 shows how these pieces interact.

The MTA Process

The MTA process handles both incoming and outgoing mail messages. This obviously includes two separate functions:

- Determining where and how to deliver outgoing mail
- Determining where to deliver incoming mail

Each of these functions requires different processing capabilities within the MTA process.

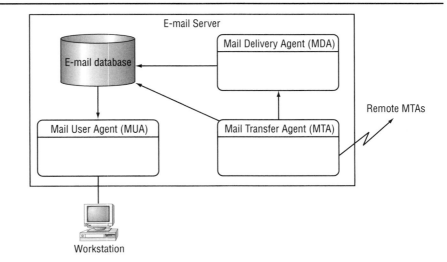

FIGURE 13.1:
The Unix e-mail model

Sending Outgoing Mail

For each outgoing mail message, the MTA must determine the destination of the recipient addresses. If the destination is the local system, the MTA process can either deliver the message directly to the local mailbox system, or pass the message off to the MDA process for delivery.

However, if the destination is a remote domain, the MTA process must perform two functions:

- Determine the responsible mail server for the domain using the MX entry in DNS

- Establish a communication link with the remote mail server and transfer the message

The communication link that is established with the remote mail server almost always uses the Simple Mail Transfer Protocol (SMTP). This standard protocol provides a common communication technique to move messages between various types of systems on the Internet.

Receiving Incoming Mail

The MTA process is responsible for accepting incoming messages from both local system users and remote host users. Many variables are associated with this seemingly simple function. Destination addresses in the mail message must be examined closely, and a decision must be made as to whether the message can in fact be delivered by the local system.

There are three categories of destination addresses that can be used in a mail message: local system accounts, local alias accounts, and remote user accounts.

Local system accounts   Every mail system, whether Windows, Unix, or even Macintosh, has its own set of configured local user accounts that have access to the system. The MTA must recognize messages destined for the user accounts and forward them either directly to the user's mailbox, or to a separate MDA process for delivery.

Local alias accounts   Many MTA programs allow for user alias names to be created. The alias name itself cannot store mail messages. Instead, it is used as a pointer to one or more actual system user accounts where the messages are stored. Once the MTA determines that the alias name is valid, it converts the destination address to the actual system user account name and either delivers the message or passes it to an MDA process.

Remote user accounts   Many MTA processes also accept incoming messages destined for user accounts not on the local system. This is the trickiest of the delivery categories. There have been many debates and arguments over how MTA programs handle mail destined for remote user accounts.

This technique is called mail *relaying*. A mail server accepts a message destined for a remote host user and automatically forwards it to the destination remote host. For many ISPs, this feature is a necessity because dial-up customers do not have the capability to send Internet mail messages directly to remote hosts. Instead, they must send messages to the ISP mail server, which in turn passes them off (relays them) to the remote destination.

Unfortunately, mail relaying can be exploited. Unscrupulous individuals can use relay mail servers to help hide their original host addresses when forwarding mass mail advertisements to remote e-mail users. Whether it's called Unsolicited Commercial E-mail (UCE), Unsolicited Bulk E-mail (UBE), or just plain old spam, this mail is annoying and must be stopped by the mail administrator.

> **NOTE**   In case you were wondering, the term *spam* originated from the old Monty Python send-up of Hormel's canned meat product. The Hormel Corporation has agreed that its trademark is not violated by the term *spam* in relation to UCE, as long as the word is not printed in all capital letters (see `http://www.spam.com/ci/ci_in.htm`).

To help stop spam, most ISPs now use selective relaying, allowing only a set of IP addresses or authenticated users associated with their dial-up customers to forward mail through their mail servers and blocking any other host from forwarding mail through the server.

The MDA Process

The primary function of the MDA process is to deliver mail messages destined for local system user accounts. To do this, the MDA must know the type and location of the individual user mailboxes. Most e-mail systems use some type of database system to track the e-mail messages stored for local users. The MDA process must have access to each user's mailbox to insert incoming messages.

Many MDA processes also perform advanced techniques in addition to just delivering mail messages:

Automatic mail filtering   Possibly the most helpful and popular feature of the MDA process is enabling the filtering of incoming mail messages. For users who get a lot of e-mail messages, this feature can be a lifesaver. Messages can be automatically sorted into separate e-mail folders based on a subject header value, or even just one word contained in the subject header.

Most MDA programs also allow the mail administrator to configure a global filter that can help block spam and well-known virus mail messages. This is done using standard text wildcard expressions. Each expression can be matched against incoming message subject headers, and the messages that match the expression are dropped and not delivered.

Automatic mail replying   Many MDA programs allow the customer to configure an auto-reply message for e-mail messages. Some auto-reply messages can be configured to reply to all mail messages received by a user, such as an out-of-office message indicator. Other auto-reply messages can be set up to reply to specific text found in the message subject header, much like the mail filter. When a message matches the text expression, a specific auto-reply message is automatically sent.

Automatic Program Initialization   The ability to start system programs based on incoming mail messages is another feature found in MDA programs. Certainly there must be controls in place to prevent misuse, but when used safely this feature is a handy tool. Administrators can use it to start server processes remotely, or to change configuration values from a machine other than the server.

The MUA Process

The MUA process allows customers who are located remotely from their mail server to access mailboxes. One common misconception about MUA programs is that they send mail messages. The MUA process itself is only responsible for *reading* mailbox messages; it does not receive or send new messages. The misconception comes from the fact that many MUA programs include a small MTA process that offers the convenience of *relaying* new messages to the mail server.

There are two philosophies underlying MUA programs, both dealing with how incoming messages are read and stored.

Storing Messages on the Client

Many ISPs prefer to have customers download their messages directly to their workstations. Once the message is downloaded, it is removed from the mail server. This helps the mail administrator maintain the disk space on the server and prevent messages from clogging up the disk system.

The access protocol used for this type of message access is the Post Office Protocol (POP, often called POP3 for version 3). The POP3 MUA program allows a customer to connect to the server and download all the messages in the mailbox to the workstation. This is demonstrated in Figure 13.2.

FIGURE 13.2:

Downloading messages using POP3 software

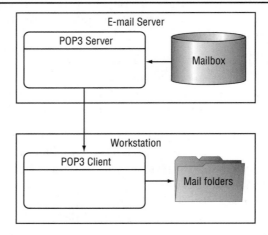

The drawback to using POP3 is that the messages are stored on the workstation with which the customer connected to the mail server. If the customer connects using multiple workstations, the messages may end up being split between workstations, making it harder for the customer to access messages after they are downloaded.

NOTE Some ISPs may allow you to download mail messages using POP3 without deleting them from the mailbox. This convenience is not the norm, however. Don't confuse this feature with the IMAP feature described next.

Storing Messages on the Server

As an alternative to the POP3 access method, the Interactive Mail Access Protocol (IMAP, or IMAPrev4 for version 4) was created. IMAP allows the customer to build folders on the mail server and store messages in the folders instead of downloading them to the workstation. This is demonstrated in Figure 13.3. Because the messages are stored on the server, the customer can connect from as many workstations as necessary and still see the same mail messages in the folders.

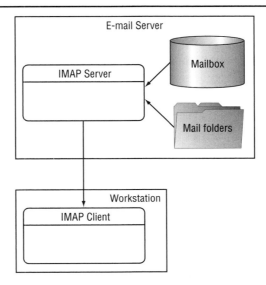

The drawback to this system is that the mail administrator has the added concern of disk space consumption on the server. It does not take long for today's mail messages and attachments to fill up system disks.

SMTP and Windows

The .NET mail library uses the Microsoft CDOSYS message component to send messages to remote hosts using SMTP. One significant area of confusion is when and how Windows OSes provide support for CDOSYS and how the CDOSYS relates to .NET. This section will shed some light on this topic, in addition to answering questions about CDOSYS.

Collaboration Data Objects (CDO)

Microsoft has had quite a history of supporting Internet messaging on various platforms. To understand the problems associated with .NET mail support, you need to know the history of Microsoft mail support. It started with the Microsoft Exchange 5 mail system and the Active Messaging library (OLEMSG32.DLL). This library allowed programmers to write code that utilized the Exchange messaging system to send messages to individual user mailboxes, as well as to other remote Exchange hosts in the Exchange network.

With the release of Exchange 5.5, a new messaging system was introduced, Collaboration Data Objects (CDO). Unlike Active Messaging, CDO used the Message Application Program Interface (MAPI) standard to provide programmers a simplified way to send messages. CDO survived for many years, with many upgrades, including versions 1.1, 1.2, and 1.2.1. With the Microsoft NT Server platform came the CDO NT Server library (CDONTS). This library broke away from the MAPI standards used in the other CDO versions and started using Internet standards, such as SMTP, to transfer messages to remote hosts.

The current version of CDO (CDO 2, also known as CDO for Windows 2000) was released with the Windows 2000 platform and is used on the Windows XP platform as well. It expands the work done with the CDONTS library in using Internet standards to provide mail and news service libraries to programmers. Other new items in CDO 2 are the ability to process multipart mail attachments and various mail protocol events. These features help programmers create full-featured mail server code with minimal effort. CDO 2 greatly expanded the Internet mail functionality provided to programmers and is the library that .NET uses to support its Internet mail features.

In Windows 2000 and XP, the CDO 2 library is the file CDOSYS.DLL. This file must be present for all .NET mail library functions to work. Because CDO 2 is completely different from the CDO 1.*x* versions, both libraries can be present on the same machine if necessary. Unfortunately, the CDO 2 library is not backward compatible with older Windows platforms.

WARNING   The System.Web.Mail classes will not work on any Windows platform that does not include the CDOSYS.DLL file. These platforms include Windows 95, 98, Me, and NT workstation.

SMTP Mail Service

Both Windows 2000 and XP provide a basic SMTP server service that supports both sending and receiving mail messages using the SMTP protocol. This functionality is included as part of the Internet Information Services (IIS) package. The .NET mail classes can utilize the IIS SMTP server to send outgoing messages directly to remote mail servers.

Windows XP systems include IIS version 5.1, which among other things includes the SMTP service. Before you can use the SMTP service, it must be configured to work properly in your Internet mail environment. Configuration is done from the Computer Management window.

Here are the steps to access the Default SMTP Virtual Server Properties window:

1. Right-click the My Computer item in the Start menu, and select the Manage menu item.

2. When the Computer Management window appears, expand Services and Applications and then Internet Information Services.

3. Right-click Default SMTP Virtual Server and select Properties.

The Properties window is where you'll configure the settings for the SMTP service.

In the General tab, select the network interface(s) that should allow incoming SMTP connections and the number of concurrent SMTP connections allowed. Also, you can enable/disable logging for the SMTP service.

In the Delivery tab (Figure 13.4), configure delivery retry times. The Advanced button reveals settings for a smart host for the mail server. This is important if your ISP does not allow you to directly communicate via SMTP to remote hosts. Often you must use your ISP mail server as a mail relay to reach remote mail servers. To do this, you must enter the ISP mail server address as the smart host, and the SMTP service will forward all outgoing messages through that mail server.

FIGURE 13.4:

The Default SMTP Virtual Server Properties dialog box is where you configure SMTP settings.

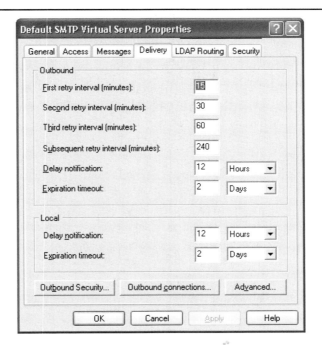

The SmtpMail Class

The SmtpMail class, found in the System.Web.Mail namespace, allows you to send SMTP messages in your C# network programs. This section discusses the methods and properties of the SmtpMail class and shows some examples of typical uses in C# programs.

Class Methods and Properties

The `SmtpMail` class provides a .NET interface to the `CDOSYS` mail library on Windows 2000 and XP systems. It does not use a constructor to create an instance of the class. Instead, you must use the static class methods and properties to pass information to the `CDOSYS` library.

The `SmtpMail` class does contain the standard `Equals()`, `GetHashCode()`, and `ToString()` methods, but they're rarely (if ever) used. The `Send()` method, on the other hand, gets plenty of use. The `Send()` method is overloaded, using two separate formats:

```
Send(MailMessage message)
Send(string from, string to, string subject, string body)
```

The first format allows you to send a `MailMessage` object. The `MailMessage` class is a self-contained e-mail message, created by populating the properties of the class with information related to the message, and the destination address(es). This process will be covered a little later in the section on the `MailMessage` class.

The second format allows you to send a raw message, manually specifying the typical e-mail message header fields:

- `From` specifies the e-mail address of the sender.

- `To` specifies the e-mail address of one or more recipients, separated by commas.

- `Subject` specifies the topic of the e-mail message.

The final parameter of the `Send()` method is the actual body of the message. The body can be in either a plain text or HTML format.

The sole property of the `SmtpMail` class is `SmtpServer`. It's a static property that specifies the address of a mail relay server to use for forwarding outgoing mail messages. By default, the `SmtpServer` property is set to the IIS SMTP service if it is installed. If IIS is not installed, the `SmtpServer` property is set to a null value and will produce an error when you attempt to send a message.

If you are using a relay mail server, you must set the `SmtpServer` property before you attempt to send messages:

```
SmtpMail.SmtpServer = "mailsrvr.myisp.net";
```

When this value is set, all outgoing mail messages will be relayed through this mail server. Of course, you must ensure that you are allowed to relay mail messages through the server, or they will be rejected.

Using the SmtpMail Class

The `MailTest.cs` program in Listing 13.1, demonstrates how to create a simple mail message and send it through a remote mail relay to the recipient.

Listing 13.1   The MailTest.cs program

```csharp
using System;
using System.Net;
using System.Web.Mail;

class MailTest
{
    public static void Main()
    {
        string from = "jessica@myisp.net";
        string to = "katie@anotherisp.net";
        string subject = "This is a test mail message";
        string body = "Hi Katie, I hope things are going well today.";

        SmtpMail.SmtpServer = "192.168.1.150";
        SmtpMail.Send(from, to, subject, body);
    }
}
```

The `MailTest` program is about as simple as they come. All it does is define the relay mail server using the `SmtpServer` property, define each of the required string fields, and use the `Send()` method to send the message. If all goes well, the intended recipient should receive the message in their mailbox.

If you try to run this on a Windows platform that does not use the CDO 2 library, you will get an `Exception` message. The exact message will vary, depending on which platform you run it on. On my Windows NT 4 workstation, it looks like this:

```
C:\>MailTest

Unhandled Exception: System.Web.HttpException: Could not create 'CDONTS.NewMail'
  object.
    at System.Web.Mail.LateBoundAccessHelper.get_LateBoundType()
    at System.Web.Mail.CdoNtsHelper.Send(String from, String to, String subject,
String messageText)
    at System.Web.Mail.SmtpMail.Send(String from, String to, String subject, Stri
ng messageText)
```

```
    at MailTest.Main()

C:\>
```

As you can see from the Exception message, the SmtpMail class tried to use the CDONTS library on the NT system but was unsuccessful. If you are writing code that will be run on more than one Windows platform, it is best to catch this Exception and produce your own informational message:

```
try
{
    SmtpMail.SmtpServer = "192.168.1.150";
    SmtpMail.Send(from, to, subject, body);
} catch (System.Web.HttpException)
{
    Console.WriteLine("Sorry, this application only works
                       on Windows 2000 and XP platforms.");
}
```

This simple program used the form of the Send() method that only sets the From:, To:, and Subject: header fields in the message. There are lots more header fields that can be defined and used in e-mail messages. The next section describes these fields and how you can use them in your mail messages.

Using Expanded Mail Message Formats

With the popularity of e-mail came compatibility problems. Many e-mail systems had their own way of formatting mail messages. It wasn't long before a standard e-mail message format was created, allowing the various e-mail systems to communicate and interpret each other's mail messages. RFC 2822 defines the standard formatting of an e-mail message. The .NET MailMessage class offers a standard way for you to create RFC2882 messages to send to remote customers.

The RFC2822 Mail Format

RFC 2822 specifies that each message should consist of two separate sections:

- A header that contains message information
- A body that contains the text of the message

The header of an RFC2822 standard mail message contains separate data fields that supply additional information in the message (see Figure 13.5). Each header field is on a separate line in the message and contains data in text format. The format of each header line is as follows (note the colon separating the header tag from the data value):

```
header: text data
```

Individual header fields do not need to be specified in any particular order in the message. The header fields must also appear before the body of the message and must be separated by a single blank line.

FIGURE 13.5:

The RFC2822
message format

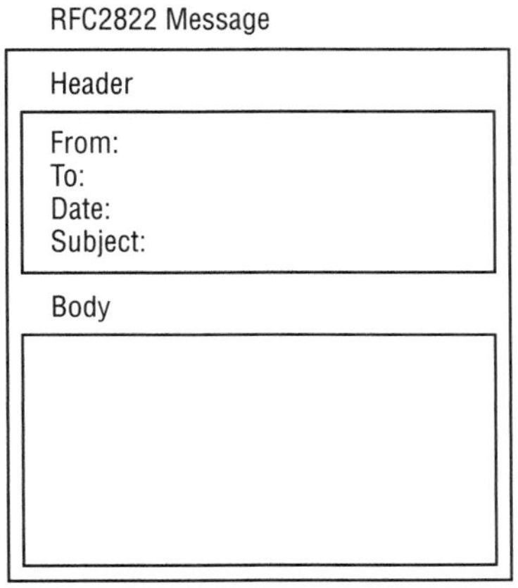

The Origination Date Field

The origination date field identifies the date and time the message was originally sent. It consists of the keyword `Date:`, followed by the appropriate date and time value:

```
Date: Wed, 21 Aug 2002 18:30:00 -0500
```

It is important that the origination date identify the time zone of the sending host so the receiving customer can determine the actual time the message was sent.

The Originator Fields

Three separate originator fields identify where the message originated:

```
From: mailbox-list
Sender: mailbox
Reply-To: mailbox-list
```

At least one of the three originator fields must be present in a mail message. The `mailbox-list` value can contain either a single mail address or multiple mail addresses separated by commas.

The From field identifies the specific person who originated the message, while the Sender field identifies the person who actually sent the message (the two don't necessarily have to be the same). If the Reply-To field is present, it represents the return address where the message originator intends replies to be sent.

The Destination Address Fields

Three destination address fields identify where the message should be sent:

```
To: address-list
Cc: address-list
Bcc: address-list
```

The destination address fields can each specify one or more addresses in the `address-list` fields, using commas to separate multiple addresses.

The To field identifies primary recipients of the mail message, and the Cc field contains addresses of others who are to receive the message though it wasn't directed toward them.

The Bcc field contains addresses of recipients who are not disclosed in the mail message. The Bcc field is different from the other destination address fields; although the sending message may contain a Bcc field, it must be stripped off before sending to the intended destination addresses.

The Identification Fields

The identification fields help uniquely identify the message, both to the mail system and to the recipients. There are quite a few identification fields available, but these are the most common:

```
Message-ID: msg-id
In-Reply-To: msg-id
References: msg-id
```

The Message-ID field provides a unique tracking number to the mail message. Each message sent by an MTA should contain a Message-ID field, assigned by the MTA, that uniquely identifies the message from all others. The `msg-id` value can contain any combination of letters and numbers to uniquely identify the message.

The In-Reply-To and References fields are used to relate one message to a previous message. Often, a message sent in reply to a previous message will contain the Message-ID field of the previous message in the In-Reply-To field.

The Informational Fields

The informational fields are optional; they help recipients identify and possibly filter mail messages. The informational fields are as follows:

```
Subject: subject-text
Comments: comment-text
Keywords: phrase-text
```

The Subject field is the most common field. It identifies the message with a short string describing the topic of the message. The Comments field can present a longer string further describing the body of the message. The Keywords field specifies short phrases, separated by commas, that identify the message content. The Keywords field can be used in MDA filtering software to sort incoming messages.

The MailMessage Class Properties

The .NET `MailMessage` class easily creates RFC2822-formatted messages to send using the `SmtpMail` class. This allows you to add more useful header field information than what the generic `SmtpMail.Send()` method allows. You construct the e-mail message piece by piece and specify formatting options for the message.

The default constructor for the `MailMessage` class is not very difficult:

```
MailMessage newmessage = new MailMessage();
```

That's it—no fancy parameters to remember. All of the work is done in the properties of the class. Table 13.1 lists the properties that can be used.

TABLE 13.1: The MailMessage Class Properties

Property	Description
Attachments	Specifies a list of file attachments to add to the message
Bcc	Gets or sets a semicolon-delimited list of addresses to use in the Bcc: header field
Body	Gets or sets the body of the e-mail message
BodyEncoding	Gets or sets the encoding type of the message body
BodyFormat	Gets or sets the content type of the message body
Cc	Gets or sets a semicolon-delimited list of addresses to use in the Cc: header field
From	Gets or sets the address to use in the From: header field
Headers	Sets custom header fields and values for the message
Priority	Gets or sets the priority of the message
Subject	Gets or sets the text string used in the Subject: header field
To	Gets or sets the semicolon-delimited list of addresses used in the To: header field
UrlContentBase	Gets or sets the Content-Base HTTP header value
UrlContentLocation	Gets or sets the Content-Location HTTP header value

The easy properties to use are the typical To, From, Cc, and Bcc values. You can specify additional header fields using the Header property, although this is done a little differently.

The Header Property

The `Header` property uses the `IDictionary` class to store the header field and value pair. The easiest way to do this is to use the `Add()` method:

```
newmessage.Header.Add("Reply-To", "testing@myisp.net");
```

You can specify any valid RFC2822 header field using the `Header` property and it will be included in the message header fields. You can easily add a Date field to your messages using the format:

```
DateTime mydate = DateTime.Now;
newmessage.Header.Add("Date", mydate.ToString());
```

The Body Properties

The `Body` property, the `BodyEncoding`, and `BodyFormat` properties specify both the content and the format of the message body. The text of the message is assigned to the `Body` property. How it looks to the remote mail server is controlled by the `BodyEncoding` and `BodyFormat` properties.

The `BodyEncoding` property uses the `System.Text.Encoding` classes to specify the type of text used for the message. The possible values are ASCII, Unicode, UTF-7, and UTF-8. The default is the default system encoding type (which is ASCII in the United States).

In contrast to the text encoding, the `BodyFormat` property specifies how the text will be presented in the mail message. The possible values are defined in the `MailFormat` enumeration:

MailFormat.Html   Uses hypertext markup language formatting

MailFormat.Text   Uses plain text formatting

By default, the `Text` value is used. This ensures that any e-mail client can read the message. Alternatively, you can use the `Html` value to incorporate special text formatting within the message.

The Priority Property

The `Priority` property allows you to set the Priority header field. Though it's not a standard header field, many mail clients recognize the Priority field as indicating the importance of a mail message. The `System.Web.Mail` namespace includes the `MailPriority` enumeration that specifies this value. The possible values are as follows:

MailPriority.High   Important messages that require immediate attention

MailPriority.Normal   Regular mail messages

MailPriority.Low   Extraneous mail messages, such as advertisements

To set the priority of a message, just assign the appropriate value to the `Priority` property:

```
newmessage.Priority = MailPriority.High;
```

The Attachment Property

The `Attachment` property specifies files you want to include as attachments to the mail message. You can specify one or more `MailAttachment` class objects as attachments using the following format:

```
MailAttachment ma = new MailAttachment("c:\\tempfile.bmp");
newmessage.Attachment.Add(ma);
```

The file specified in the `MailAttachment` object is encoded and added to the message, as explained in the later section "Mail Attachments."

Using the MailMessage Class

The `FancyMailTest.cs` program in Listing 13.2 uses the `MailMessage` class to produce a fancier mail message to send to the recipient.

Listing 13.2   The FancyMailTest.cs program

```csharp
using System;
using System.Web.Mail;

class FancyMailTest
{
    public static void Main()
    {
        MailMessage mm = new MailMessage();
        mm.From = "haley@myisp.net";
        mm.To = "riley@yourisp.net;rich@shadrach.ispnet1.net";
        mm.Cc = "matthew@anotherisp.net;chris@hisisp.net";
        mm.Bcc = "katie@herisp.net;jessica@herisp.net";
        mm.Subject = "This is a fancy test message";
        mm.Headers.Add("Reply-To", "haley@myisp.net");
        mm.Headers.Add("Comments", "This is a test HTML message");
        mm.Priority = MailPriority.High;
        mm.BodyFormat = MailFormat.Html;
        mm.Body = "<html><body><h1>This is a test message</h1><h2>This message ➡
            should have HTML-type formatting</h2>Please use an HTML-capable
viewer.";

        try
        {
            SmtpMail.Send(mm);
        } catch (System.Web.HttpException)
        {
            Console.WriteLine("This device is unable to send Internet messages");
        }
    }
}
```

The `FancyMailtest` program creates a `MailMessage` object and assigns values to the various properties. Multiple recipients are added to the `To`, `Cc`, and `Bcc` properties, each one separated by a semicolon. Message priority is set to `High`, and two additional header lines are added to the mail message.

Because the `BodyFormat` type is set to `Html`, you can use any valid HTML syntax in the body text to format the message. Figure 13.6 demonstrates how this message looks when viewed with a Microsoft Outlook Express mail client.

FIGURE 13.6:

Reading the FancyMailTest mail message using Outlook Express

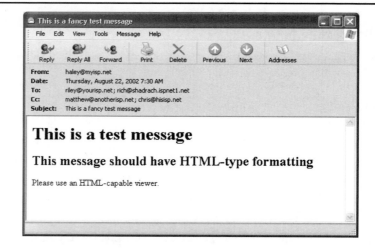

Mail Attachments

You may have noticed that the `Body` property allows you only to enter text, and a separate property is used to include file attachments. This arrangement is the result of how SMTP works and how mail servers must handle binary data.

SMTP transfers only text messages between systems on the Internet. To compensate for this, mail clients must convert any binary data (such as file attachments) into an ASCII text message before passing the message to the mail server. Then, of course, the recipient's mail client must be able to convert the text message back into the original binary data.

There are two popular techniques that can convert binary data into text: the uuencode format and the Multipurpose Internet Mail Extensions (MIME) format. Most mail systems allow you to use either technique, although there are still some that require a particular format.

uuencode

Many years before the Internet became popular, Unix administrators were sending binary data across modem lines by converting it to ASCII text and embedding it in mail messages. The program they used to convert binary data into ASCII text was called *uuencode*. The uu stands for Unix-to-Unix, part of the Unix-to-Unix Copy Protocol (UUCP) that's used to send messages between Unix hosts via modem.

The uuencode program uses a 3-to-4 encoding scheme, in which 3 bytes of binary data are converted to 4 bytes of ASCII characters. This scheme significantly increases the size of the converted file but ensures that the encoded file can be safely decoded back into the original binary data.

Because of its popularity, many mail systems still support the uuencode method of encoding binary data. However, a newer Internet standard for encoding binary data has been developed: MIME.

MIME

The MIME format (Multipurpose Internet Mail Extensions) is defined in RFCs 2045 and 2046. MIME is more versatile than uuencode in that it includes additional information about the binary file within the converted file. The decoder can thus automatically detect and decode various types of binary files.

The MIME standard also provides a way for the MIME-encoded binary data to be directly incorporated into a standard RFC2822 message. Five new header fields (see Table 13.2) were defined to identify binary data types embedded in the mail message. E-mail clients that can handle MIME messages must be able to process these five new header fields. The fields are added immediately after the RFC2822 header fields, and before the message body. Any MIME attachments are added after the message body, as illustrated in Figure 13.7.

TABLE 13.2: The MIME Message Header Fields

Field	Description
MIME-Version	Specifies the version of MIME used in the encoding
Content-Transfer-Encoding	Specifies the encoding scheme used to encode the binary data into ASCII
Content-ID	Specifies a unique identifier for the message section
Content-Description	A short description identifying the message section
Content-Type	Specifies the type of content contained in the encoded data

FIGURE 13.7:

The MIME message
format

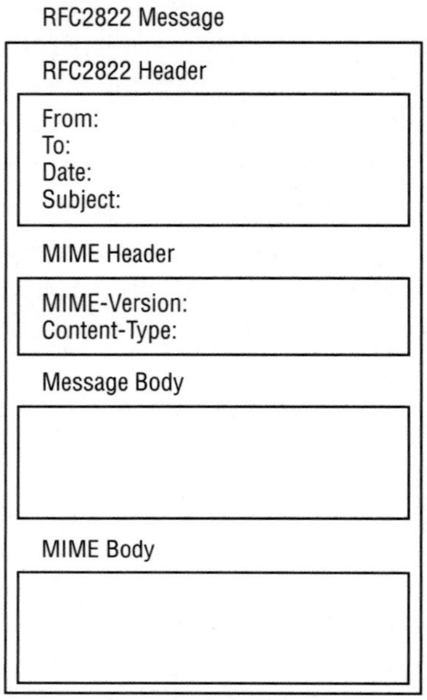

RFC2822 Message

RFC2822 Header

From:
To:
Date:
Subject:

MIME Header

MIME-Version:
Content-Type:

Message Body

MIME Body

The MIME-Version Field

The MIME-Version field identifies the MIME encoding version that the sender used to encode the message:

```
MIME-Version: 1.0
```

Alternatively, some software packages add text after the version number to identify additional vendor version information:

```
MIME-Version: 1.0 (software test 2.3a)
```

The MIME decoding software of the receiving mail server ignores the additional text.

The Content-Transfer-Encoding Field

The Content-Transfer-Encoding field identifies how the binary data in the message is encoded. There are currently seven methods defined for MIME, listed in Table 13.3. Note that the first three methods define no encoding of the data. The 7-bit encoding method assumes that the encoded data is already 7-bit ASCII text characters, not binary data. This is the default used if no Content-Transfer-Encoding field is present.

TABLE 13.3: MIME Encoding Methods

Method	Description
7-bit	Standard 7-bit ASCII text
8-bit	Standard 8-bit ASCII text
binary	Raw binary data
quoted-printable	Encodes binary data to printable characters in the U.S.-ASCII character set
base64	Encodes 6 bits of binary data into an 8-bit printable character
ietf-token	Extension token encoding defined in RFC 2045
x-token	Two characters, X- or x-, followed (with no intervening space) by any token

Base64 is the most common method used for encoding binary data. This scheme encodes binary data by mapping 6-bit blocks of binary data to an 8-bit byte of ASCII text. There is less "wasted space" in the encoded file than with the uuencode method, and it often results in a smaller encoded file.

The Content-ID Field

The Content-ID field identifies MIME sections with a unique identification code. One MIME content section can refer to another MIME message by using this unique field value.

The Content-Description Field

The Content-Description field is an ASCII text description of the data to help identify it in the e-mail message. The text can be any ASCII text of any length.

The Content-Type Field

The Content-Type field is where all the action is. This field identifies the data enclosed in the MIME message. Two separate values, a type and a subtype, identify the data. Here's the field format:

```
Content-Type: type/subtype
```

Following are descriptions of the seven basic types of Content-Type identified in MIME:

text   The text Content-Type identifies data that is in ASCII text format. The subtypes for the text Content-Type can be in one of three formats:

   plain   For unformatted ASCII text

html   For text formatted with HTML tags

enriched   For text formatted with rich text format (RTF) tags

The text Content-Type also specifies the character set used to encode the data with the charset parameter:

```
Content-Type: text/plain; charset=us-ascii
```

This line identifies the MIME section as being plain text, using the U.S. ASCII encoding system.

message   The message Content-Type identifies multiple RFC2822-formatted messages contained within a single message. It has three subtypes:

rfc822   Specifies a normal embedded RFC 822-formatted message

partial   Specifies one section of a long message that was broken up into separate sections

external-body   Specifies a pointer to an object that is not within the e-mail message

image   The image Content-Type defines embedded binary data that represents a graphic image. Currently two subtypes are defined: the JPEG format and the GIF format.

video   The video Content-Type defines embedded binary data that represents video data. The only subtype defined is the MPEG format.

audio   The audio Content-Type defines embedded binary data that represents audio data. The only subtype for this is the basic format, which defines a single-channel Integrated Services Digital Network (ISDN) mu-law encoding at an 8KHz sample rate.

application   The application Content-Type identifies embedded binary data that represents application data, such as spreadsheets, word processing documents, and other applications. There are two formal subtypes defined: the postscript format for Postscript-formatted print documents, and the octet-stream format, which defines messages containing arbitrary binary data. The octet-stream subtype represents most application-specific data, such as Microsoft Word documents and Microsoft Excel spreadsheets.

multipart   The multipart Content-Type is a special type. It identifies messages that contain multiple data content types combined into one message. This format is common in e-mail packages that can present a message in a variety of ways, such as plain ASCII text and HTML, or in messages that contain multiple attachments. There are four subtypes used:

Mixed   Specifies that each of the separate parts are independent of one another and should all be presented to the end customer in the order they are received.

Parallel   Specifies that each of the separate parts are independent of one another but can be presented to the end customer in any order.

Alternative   Specifies that each of the separate parts represents different ways of presenting the same information. Only one part should be presented to the end customer.

Digest   Identifies the same method as the mixed subtype but specifies that the body of the message is always in RFC822-format.

NOTE   There are lots more Content-Types in addition to the basic seven shown here. Many e-mail packages even define their own types. As long as the mail server and the mail client understand the ContentType, it can be used. Be careful, though, when using non-standard Content-Types: other mail client packages may not recognize them.

The MailAttachment Class

To simplify e-mail attachments, the .NET library includes the `MailAttachment` class. This class specifies the content and format of any attachments that are included in the mail message.

There are two constructors that can create a new mail attachment:

```
MailAttachment(string filename);
MailAttachment(string filename, MailEncoding encodetype);
```

The first constructor format creates a new mail attachment using the file specified in the filename path and encodes it using the UUEncode encoding type. The second constructor format allows you to specify an alternative encoding type, such as the `Base64` encoding type used for MIME messages.

The `System.Web.Mail` namespace includes the `MailEncoding` enumeration that defines the two separate encoding types:

MailEncoding.Base64   For base64 MIME encoding

MailEncoding.UUEncode   For uuencode encoding

You can query the encoding and filename properties of the `MailAttachment` object using the `Encoding` and `Filename` properties:

```
MailAttachment newfile = new
    MailAttachment("c:\\testfile.bmp", MailEncoding.Base64);
string filename = newfile.Filename;
if (newfile.Encoding == MailEncoding.Base64)
    Console.WriteLine("{0} is a MIME encoded file", filename);
```

When the `MailAttachment` object is created, it can be included in a `MailMessage` object using the `Attachments` property:

```
MailMessage newmessage = new MailMessage();
MailAttachment newfile = new MailAttachment("c:\\testfile.bmp");
newmessage.Attachments.Add(newfile);
newmessage.From = "frank@myisp.net";
```

```
newmessage.To = "melanie@myisp.net;nicholas@myisp.net";
newmessage.Body = "Here's my picture!!";
SmtpMail.Send(newmessage);
```

The `MailAttachTest.cs` program in Listing 13.3 demonstrates how to include file attachments with your e-mail messages.

Listing 13.3   **The MailAttachTest.cs program**

```
using System;
using System.Web.Mail;

class MailAttachTest
{
    public static void Main()
    {

        MailAttachment myattach =
            new MailAttachment("c:\\temp\\MailAttachTest.exe",
                MailEncoding.Base64);
        MailMessage newmessage = new MailMessage();
        newmessage.From = "barbara@shadrach.ispnet1.net";
        newmessage.To = "rich@shadrach.ispnet1.net";
        newmessage.Subject = "A test mail attachment message";
        newmessage.Priority = MailPriority.High;
        newmessage.Headers.Add("Comments",
                    "This message attempts to send a binary attachment");
        newmessage.Attachments.Add(myattach);
        newmessage.Body = "Here's a test file for you to try";

        try
        {
            SmtpMail.SmtpServer = "192.168.1.100";
            SmtpMail.Send(newmessage);
        } catch (System.Web.HttpException)
        {
            Console.WriteLine("This device cannot send Internet messages");
        }
    }
}
```

The `MailAttachTest` program creates a `MailAttachment` object, using the `Base64` encoding scheme. Next a normal `MailMessage` object is created, and the `MailAttachment` object is added as an attachment:

```
newmessage.Attachments.Add(myattach);
```

This example also uses a remote SMTP mail relay server to forward the message to the intended recipients.

A POP3 Client

Now that you know everything there is to know about sending SMTP messages using C#, you might want to know how to retrieve messages from mailboxes.

As mentioned in the "E-mail Basics" section, the MUA program is responsible for allowing remote clients to read messages stored in their mailboxes. The most common network protocol used to retrieve messages from remote mail servers is the Post Office Protocol, version 3 (POP3).

This section describes how POP3 works and then presents a sample program that allows a customer to read mail messages stored on a remote mail server.

The POP3 Protocol

POP3 is a command-based protocol. Once the client establishes a connection with the server, it issues simple text commands, and the server responds with the appropriate information. You need to know which commands are used, and in what order, to properly retrieve messages from the server.

POP3 servers listen to TCP port 110 for incoming connection attempts. When a new connection is established, the POP3 server sends a welcome banner and waits for the client to send commands.

Authentication Commands

The first step (after the connection is established) is to log in to the POP3 server, using one of these methods:

- Sending a plain text user ID and password
- Sending an encrypted authentication token

Using the encrypted authentication token method is the more secure way of connecting to the server, but that technique is way beyond the scope of this simple example—unless you know how to easily implement the MD-5 encryption algorithm! For this example, we will use the plain text user ID and password method. This is done using the USER and PASS commands:

```
USER username
PASS password
```

Each command is entered separately and should receive a response from the server. All POP3 server responses are preceded with either +OK for a positive acknowledgement, or -ERR for a negative acknowledgement.

You can manually test the login sequence with a POP3 server by telnetting to port 110 and entering the appropriate commands:

```
C:\>telnet 192.168.1.100 110
+OK QPOP (version 2.53) at shadrach.ispnet1.net starting.
<6352.1030035698@shadrach.ispnet1.net>
USER rich
+OK Password required for rich.
PASS myaccount1
+OK rich has 2 messages (889 octets).
QUIT
+OK Pop server at shadrach.ispnet1.net signing off.

C:\>
```

In this case, each command received a positive response from the POP3 server. When the PASS command was acknowledged, the response message also included the number of messages in the mailbox. Unfortunately, this text is specific to POP3 server software and cannot be relied upon to check for the number of messages available.

Information Commands

The STAT and LIST commands can retrieve information about the mailbox. The STAT command response looks like this:

```
+OK n mmm
```

This response includes the number of messages contained in the mailbox (*n*), and the total size (in bytes) of the messages (*mmm*).

The LIST command retrieves an individual listing of the messages, along with the size of each message. Here's what these commands look like:

```
STAT
+OK 2 889
LIST
+OK 2 messages (889 octets)
1 464
2 425
.
```

Note that the end of the LIST response is a single period on a line by itself. This indicates the end of the listing has been reached.

Retrieving Messages

Two commands are useful in retrieving message text from the mailbox: TOP and RETR.

Although the TOP command is an optional command, it is supported by most e-mail servers. It can retrieve the message header and a selected number of text lines from the message body. The format of the TOP command is as follows, where *n* is the message number (as shown in the LIST command results) and *mm* is the number of body text lines to display:

```
TOP n mm
```

If you only need to retrieve the message header, you can specify 0 as the second parameter:

```
TOP 1 0
+OK 464 octets
Return-Path: rich
Received: (from root@localhost)
        by shadrach.ispnet1.net (8.9.3/8.9.3) id KAA06215
        for rich; Thu, 22 Aug 2002 10:32:34 -0500 (EST)
        (envelope-from rich)
Date: Thu, 22 Aug 2002 10:32:34 -0500 (EST)
From: Rich Blum <rich>
Message-Id: <200208221532.KAA06215@shadrach.ispnet1.net>
To: rich
Subject: Another test message
X-UIDL: 5291f9ae56f2e88b4f7acdc5511c4ae9
Status: RO
.
```

First, the POP3 server returns with a positive acknowledgement statement (+OK). Most servers also return the number of bytes in the mail message. Next the headers for the mail message are returned. Again, a period delineates the end of the response text.

To retrieve the entire message, you use the RETR command. The RETR command uses one parameter, the number of the message to retrieve:

```
RETR 1
+OK 464 octets
Return-Path: rich
Received: (from root@localhost)
    by shadrach.ispnet1.net (8.9.3/8.9.3) id KAA06215
    for rich; Thu, 22 Aug 2002 10:32:34 -0500 (EST)
    (envelope-from rich)
Date: Thu, 22 Aug 2002 10:32:34 -0500 (EST)
From: Rich Blum <rich>
Message-Id: <200208221532.KAA06215@shadrach.ispnet1.net>
To: rich
```

```
Subject: Another test message
X-UIDL: 5291f9ae56f2e88b4f7acdc5511c4ae9
Status: RO


This is a test message to test the popcheck program with.

.
```

Similar to the TOP command, the RETR command returns the total number of bytes in the mail message and the text of the entire mail message.

When the POP3 session is finished, you should send the QUIT command to the server to properly terminate the session, and close the mailbox.

WARNING   Be careful when retrieving messages that contain binary attachments. The message will be returned in its original text format, including the text encoding of the binary attachment.

Writing a POP3 Client

Now that you are armed with the POP3 information, you can write a simple network client program to check a remote POP3 mailbox and retrieve some information about the messages in it. Listing 13.4 is the PopCheck.cs program, which demonstrates some of these basic principles.

Listing 13.4   **The PopCheck.cs program**

```csharp
using System;
using System.Drawing;
using System.IO;
using System.Net;
using System.Net.Sockets;
using System.Text;
using System.Threading;
using System.Windows.Forms;

class PopCheck  :  Form
{
    private TextBox hostname;
    private TextBox username;
    private TextBox password;
    private TextBox status;
    private ListBox messages;

    private TcpClient mailclient;
    private NetworkStream ns;
    private StreamReader sr;
```

```
private StreamWriter sw;

public PopCheck()
{
    Text = "popcheck - A POP3 e-mail checker";
    Size = new Size(400, 380);

    Label label1 = new Label();
    label1.Parent = this;
    label1.Text = "Hostname:";
    label1.AutoSize = true;
    label1.Location = new Point(10, 33);

    hostname = new TextBox();
    hostname.Parent = this;
    hostname.Size = new Size(200, 2 * Font.Height);
    hostname.Location = new Point(75, 30);

    Label label2 = new Label();
    label2.Parent = this;
    label2.Text = "User name:";
    label2.AutoSize = true;
    label2.Location = new Point(10, 53);

    username = new TextBox();
    username.Parent = this;
    username.Size = new Size(200, 2 * Font.Height);
    username.Location = new Point(75, 50);

    Label label3 = new Label();
    label3.Parent = this;
    label3.Text = "Password:";
    label3.AutoSize = true;
    label3.Location = new Point(10, 73);

    password = new TextBox();
    password.Parent = this;
    password.PasswordChar = '*';
    password.Size = new Size(200, 2 * Font.Height);
    password.Location = new Point(75, 70);

    Label label4 = new Label();
    label4.Parent = this;
    label4.Text = "Status:";
    label4.AutoSize = true;
    label4.Location = new Point(10, 325);

    status = new TextBox();
    status.Parent = this;
    status.Text = "Not connected";
    status.Size = new Size(200, 2 * Font.Height);
```

```
      status.Location = new Point(50, 322);

      messages = new ListBox();
      messages.Parent = this;
      messages.Location = new Point(10, 108);
      messages.Size = new Size(360, 16 * Font.Height);
      messages.DoubleClick += new EventHandler(getmessagesDoubleClick);

      Button login = new Button();
      login.Parent = this;
      login.Text = "Login";
      login.Location = new Point(295, 32);
      login.Size = new Size(5 * Font.Height, 2 * Font.Height);
      login.Click += new EventHandler(ButtonloginOnClick);

      Button close = new Button();
      close.Parent = this;
      close.Text = "Close";
      close.Location = new Point(295, 62);
      close.Size = new Size(5 * Font.Height, 2 * Font.Height);
      close.Click += new EventHandler(ButtoncloseOnClick);
   }

void ButtonloginOnClick(object obj, EventArgs ea)
{
   status.Text = "Checking for messages...";
   Thread startlogin = new Thread(new ThreadStart(loginandretr));
   startlogin.IsBackground = true;
   startlogin.Start();
}

void ButtoncloseOnClick(object obj, EventArgs ea)
{
   if (ns != null)
   {
      sw.Close();
      sr.Close();
      ns.Close();
      mailclient.Close();
   }
   Close();
}

void loginandretr()
{
   string response;
   string from = null;
   string subject = null;
   int totmessages;

   try
   {
      mailclient = new TcpClient(hostname.Text, 110);
   } catch (SocketException)
```

```
{
   status.Text = "Unable to connect to server";
   return;
}

ns = mailclient.GetStream();
sr = new StreamReader(ns);
sw = new StreamWriter(ns);

response = sr.ReadLine(); //Get opening POP3 banner

sw.WriteLine("User " + username.Text); //Send username
sw.Flush();

response = sr.ReadLine();
if (response.Substring(0,3) == "-ER")
{
   status.Text = "Unable to log into server";
   return;
}

sw.WriteLine("Pass " + password.Text);  //Send password
sw.Flush();

try
{
   response = sr.ReadLine();
} catch (IOException)
{
   status.Text = "Unable to log into server";
   return;
}
if (response.Substring(0,4) == "-ERR")
{
   status.Text = "Unable to log into server";
   return;
}

sw.WriteLine("stat"); //Send stat command to get number of messages
sw.Flush();

response = sr.ReadLine();
string[] nummess = response.Split(' ');
totmessages = Convert.ToInt16(nummess[1]);
if (totmessages > 0)
{
   status.Text = "you have " + totmessages + " messages";
} else
{
   status.Text = "You have no messages" ;
}

for (int i = 1; i <= totmessages; i++)
{
```

```
        sw.WriteLine("top " + i + " 0"); //read header of each message
        sw.Flush();
        response = sr.ReadLine();

        while (true)
        {
            response = sr.ReadLine();
            if (response == ".")
                break;
            if (response.Length > 4)
            {
                if (response.Substring(0, 5) == "From:")
                    from = response;
                if (response.Substring(0, 8) == "Subject:")
                    subject = response;
            }
        }
        messages.Items.Add(i + "   " + from + "   " + subject);
    }

}

void getmessagesDoubleClick(object obj, EventArgs ea)
{
    string text = (string)messages.SelectedItem;
    string[] textarray = text.Split(' ');
    ShowMessage sm = new ShowMessage(ns, textarray[0]);
    sm.ShowDialog();
}

public static void Main()
{
    Application.Run(new PopCheck());
}
}

class ShowMessage : Form
{
    public ShowMessage(NetworkStream ns, string messnumber)
    {
        StreamReader sr = new StreamReader(ns);
        StreamWriter sw = new StreamWriter(ns);
        string response;

        Text = "Message " + messnumber;
        Size = new Size(400, 380);
        ShowInTaskbar = false;

        TextBox display = new TextBox();
        display.Parent = this;
        display.Multiline = true;
```

```
            display.Dock = DockStyle.Fill;
            display.ScrollBars = ScrollBars.Both;

            sw.WriteLine("retr " + messnumber); //Retrieve entire message
            sw.Flush();
            response = sr.ReadLine();

            while (true)
            {
                response = sr.ReadLine();
                if (response == ".")
                    break;
                display.Text += response + "\r\n";
            }
        }
    }
```

The PopCheck program implements many of the network programming techniques demonstrated in previous chapters. Figure 13.8 shows what the PopCheck window should look like in action.

FIGURE 13.8:

The PopCheck
program interface

After the customer enters a hostname, username, and password in the appropriate text boxes, they click the Login button. This starts a Thread object that uses the loginandretr() method to log in to the specified remote POP3 server with the designated username and password. After the user is logged in, the STAT command determines the number of messages in the mailbox, and the TOP command retrieves the header information for each message.

The message number, along with the From and Subject header field information, is placed in the list box. The customer can then click an individual message listed in the list box to display the entire message.

PopCheck.cs is a little different from other programs presented so far, in that it includes a second class definition in the same source file. This second class defines a DialogBox window that displays the retrieved message text. The main program passes the connected NetworkStream object, along with the desired message number, to the DialogBox class. This information is used to send a RETR command to the POP3 server and retrieve the message text. Because the already-connected NetworkStream object is passed, the DialogBox does not need to create a new connection to the server.

Summary

This chapter tells you how to create network programs that handle network mail. Most network mail systems divide the mail function into three parts: the Mail Transfer Agent (MTA) delivers messages to local and remote users using the Simple Mail Transfer Protocol (SMTP). The Mail Delivery Agent (MDA) delivers mail to local users but contains special functions such as mail filtering. The Mail User Agent (MUA) allows remote users to read messages in their mailboxes.

Windows 2000 and XP platforms contain the Collaborative Data Object (CDO) library, which can be used by programs to deliver mail using SMTP, as well as other network mail and news functions. The .NET mail library utilizes CDO to support the System.Web.Mail mail functions. Windows 2000 and XP platforms also allow customers to install the Internet Information Server (IIS) package, which includes an internal SMTP mail server that can forward and receive messages from the CDO library.

The SmtpMail class is used for sending e-mail messages using either the internal SMTP server, or an external mail relay server. Messages can be created using the MailMessage class to include fancy formatting of text and special mail headers. The MailAttachment class is used to include binary attachments to mail messages sent by the SmtpMail class. This allows the network program to create full-featured mail programs with minimal effort.

Also covered in this chapter is the Post Office Protocol (POP3) and how to construct a simple POP3 mail client program to retrieve messages from a remote mail server.

Next to e-mail, the World Wide Web (WWW) is possibly the most influential application used on the Internet. It is no surprise that the .NET library contains many classes that support web programming. The next chapter discusses the many classes used for web programming in C#.

CHAPTER 14

HTTP

- The WebClient class for downloading and uploading web data

- Using credentials

- Advanced classes HttpWebRequest and HttpWebResponse

- Implementing web services

Web programming today is among the truly hot topics, so it is no surprise that Microsoft has incorporated many web features into the .NET network library to assist programmers in creating web-aware network programs.

This chapter presents the .NET `WebClient` class—the easiest way to communicate via HTTP from your C# programs. A discussion of the `WebRequest` and `WebResponse` classes talks about the many features available to help you create full-featured web programs, and a complete example walks you through the steps of creating a web program. Finally, we'll touch on the more advanced topic of Web Services, .NET's new way of allowing C# programs to directly communicate with web servers to send and retrieve information.

The WebClient Class

The easiest way to communicate with websites from a C# network program is to use the `WebClient` class, found in the `System.Net` namespace. This class provides methods to send requests and receive responses from a web server within your program, making it easy to incorporate web functionality in your programs.

Downloading Web Data

The `WebClient` class provides three methods that can download information from a web server:

DownloadData()   Downloads data to a byte array from a specified URI

DownloadFile()   Downloads data to a local file from a specified URI

OpenRead()   Opens a read-only stream to download data from a specified URI.

Each of the download methods requires that a URI parameter be entered to specify the website location. The URI must follow the standard HTTP URI specifications.

The DownloadData() Method

The `DownloadData()` method can retrieve the raw HTML response from an HTTP request and place it in a byte array. Once the message is in the byte array, you can process the HTML, looking for keywords and values within the web page. Listing 14.1 shows the `DownloadDataTest.cs` program, a simple example of downloading a web page from a website and displaying the results.

Listing 14.1   The DownloadDataTest.cs program

```
using System;
using System.Net;
using System.Text;

class DownloadDataTest
{
```

```
      public static void Main (string[] argv)
      {
         WebClient wc = new WebClient();
         byte[] response = wc.DownloadData(argv[0]);

      Console.WriteLine(Encoding.ASCII.GetString(response));
      }
   }
```

The DownloadDataTest program will display the HTTP web page that's entered on the command prompt line:

```
C:\>DownloadDataTest http://localhost/test.htm
<html>
<title>This is a test web page</title>
<body>
<h1>This is a test web page</h1>
</body>
</html>

C:\ >
```

The complete HTML text of the web page is returned and displayed in text mode on the console.

The DownloadFile() Method

Instead of downloading the returned web page into a byte array, you can just as easily download it directly into a file on the local device using the DownloadFile() method. Listing 14.2, DownloadFileTest.cs program, is an example of how to download a web page into a local file.

Listing 14.2   **The DownloadFileTest.cs program**

```
using System;
using System.Net;

class DownloadFileTest
{
   public static void Main (string[] argv)
   {
      WebClient wc = new WebClient();
      string filename = "webpage.htm";
```

```
        wc.DownloadFile(argv[0], filename);
        Console.WriteLine("file downloaded");
    }
}
```

The DownloadFileTest program stores the retrieved web page in the local file webpage.htm:

```
C:\>DownloadFileTest http://localhost/test.htm
file downloaded

C:\>type webpage.htm
<html>
<title>This is a test web page</title>
<body>
<h1>This is a test web page</h1>
</body>
</html>

C:\>
```

The OpenRead() Method

The OpenRead() method extracts the web page into a Stream object, which can then be used in a StreamReader object to easily retrieve data from the web server. Listing 14.3 demonstrates this with the OpenReadTest.cs program.

Listing 14.3   The OpenReadTest.cs program

```
using System;
using System.IO;
using System.Net;

class OpenReadTest
{
    public static void Main (string[] argv)
    {
        WebClient wc = new WebClient();
        string response;

        Stream strm = wc.OpenRead(argv[0]);

        StreamReader sr = new StreamReader(strm);

        while(sr.Peek() > -1)
        {
            response = sr.ReadLine();
            Console.WriteLine(response);
        }
        sr.Close();
    }
}
```

The output from the `OpenReadTest` program is exactly the same as from the `DownloadDataTest` program—the raw HTML text of the web page. The `OpenRead()` method allows you to use special features such as the `StreamReader.Peek()` method. It works with the HTTP message as it is being downloaded from the web server, providing additional flexibility in manipulating and using the retrieved code.

Viewing HTTP Headers

The `WebClient` class also contains the `ResponseHeaders` property, which allows you to retrieve the HTTP header fields used in the HTTP communication with the web server. These header fields don't appear in the web page itself, but they often provide useful information about the HTTP communication. The `ResponseHeadersTest.cs` program in Listing 14.4 demonstrates how these can be used.

Listing 14.4　　　**The ResponseHeadersTest.cs program**

```csharp
using System;
using System.Collections.Specialized;
using System.Net;

class ResponseHeadersTest
{
    public static void Main (string[] argv)
    {
        WebClient wc = new WebClient();

        byte[] response = wc.DownloadData(argv[0]);
        WebHeaderCollection whc = wc.ResponseHeaders;
        Console.WriteLine("header count = {0}", whc.Count);
        for (int i = 0; i < whc.Count; i++)
        {
            Console.WriteLine(whc.GetKey(i) + " = " + whc.Get(i));
        }
    }
}
```

The `ResponseHeaders` property returns a `WebHeaderCollection` object. Like all collections in .NET, you can access the item names (header fields) in the object by using the `GetKey()` method and the values by using the `Get()` method. Here's a sample output from the `ResponseHeadersTest` program. Each of the HTTP header fields from the original HTTP response message is displayed, along with its value.

```
C:\>ResponseHeadersTest http://www.microsoft.com
header count = 10
Date = Tue, 27 Aug 2002 04:06:34 GMT
Server = Microsoft-IIS/6.0
P3P = CP='ALL IND DSP COR ADM CONo CUR CUSo IVAo IVDo PSA PSD TAI TELo OUR SAMo
CNT COM INT NAV ONL PHY PRE PUR UNI'
```

```
Content-Length = 31257
Content-Type = text/html
Expires = Tue, 27 Aug 2002 18:06:34 GMT
Cache-Control = private
Age = 0
X-Cache = MISS from proxy.ispnet.net
Proxy-Connection = keep-alive

C:\ >
```

Uploading Web Data

The WebClient class provides four ways to upload information to the web server:

OpenWrite()   Sends a stream of data to the web server

UploadData()   Sends a byte array of data to the web server

UploadFile()   Sends a local file to the web server

UploadValues()   Sends a NameValueCollection of data names and values to the web server

Similar to the download methods, the upload methods all must have a valid URI to upload information to. The URI must be specified in standard format.

WARNING   For any of the data upload methods to work, you must have proper access privileges for uploading data to the web server.

The OpenWrite() Method

The OpenWrite() method creates a Stream object that can send data to the web server. The OpenWrite() method uses two constructor formats:

```
OpenWrite(string URI);
OpenWrite(string URI, string method);
```

The first constructor uses the HTTP POST method to send the data from the stream to the web server. The second constructor allows you to specify the HTTP method to use to send the data to the server.

Once the Stream object is created, a StreamWriter object can be created to simplify sending text in HTML format to the web server. Listing 14.5 shows the OpenWriteTest.cs program, which demonstrates this technique. The OpenWriteTest program uses the HTTP POST method to post the data to the URI specified in the command line.

Listing 14.5   **The OpenWriteTest.cs program**

```
using System;
using System.IO;
```

```
using System.Net;

class OpenWriteTest
{
   public static void Main (string[] argv)
   {
      WebClient wc = new WebClient();
      string data = "Data up upload to server";

      Stream strm = wc.OpenWrite(argv[0]);
      StreamWriter sw = new StreamWriter(strm);

      sw.WriteLine(data);
      sw.Close();
      strm.Close();
   }
}
```

The UploadData() Method

The UploadData() method uploads information from a byte array to a specified URI location.
Similar to the OpenWrite() method, the UploadData() method uses two constructor formats:

```
UploadData(string URI, byte[] array);
UploadData(string URI, string method, byte[] array);
```

By default, the UploadData() method uses the HTTP POST method to move the data to the
web server. You can specify an alternative HTTP method using the second constructor.

Listing 14.6 shows UploadDataTest.cs, which demonstrates using the UploadData() method
to post data to a web server.

Listing 14.6   The UploadDataTest.cs program

```
using System;
using System.Net;
using System.Text;

class UploadDataTest
{
   public static void Main (string[] argv)
   {
      WebClient wc = new WebClient();

      string data = "This is the data to post";
      byte[] dataarray = Encoding.ASCII.GetBytes(data);

      wc.UploadData(argv[0], dataarray);
   }
}
```

The UploadFile() Method

The UploadFile() method uploads a file to the web server in a single method call. The UploadFile() method uses two constructors:

```
UploadFile(string URI, string filename);
UploadFile(string URI, string method, string filename);
```

Both the URI location and the filename must be specified in the UploadFile() method. The second constructor allows you to also specify the HTTP method to use for the upload (the default is POST).

The UploadValues() Method

Unlike the other upload methods, the UploadValues() method does not upload data to the web server. Instead, the UploadValues() method sends data name/value pairs to the web server, similar to how the query portion of the URI specifies data. An ampersand sign separates each data name/value pair:

```
?lastname=Blum&firstname=Rich
```

The UploadValues() method uses a NameValueCollection object to pair the data names and values:

```
NameValueCollection nvc = new NameValueCollection();
nvc.Add("lastname", "Blum");
nvc.Add("firstname", "Rich");
byte[] response = wc.UploadValues(uri, "POST", nvc);
```

The second parameter in the UploadValues() method defines the HTTP request method used to upload the data. Most web pages use either the GET or POST request method to upload data values.

Listing 14.7 shows the UploadValuesTest.cs program, which sends data names and values to a test web page. The program creates a NameValueCollection that is used as the data to send to the web server specified in the *uri* variable.

NOTE   The web page specified points to a form that requires data to be entered. To run this example, you must have a web page that can accept HTML form data.

Listing 14.7   The UploadValuesTest.cs program

```
using System;
using System.Collections.Specialized;
using System.Net;
using System.Text;

class UploadValuesTest
{
    public static void Main (string[] argv)
```

```
    {
        WebClient wc = new WebClient();
        string uri = "http://localhost/testform.aspx";   //

        NameValueCollection nvc = new NameValueCollection();

        nvc.Add("lastname", "Blum");
        nvc.Add("firstname", "Rich");

        byte[] response = wc.UploadValues(uri, nvc);

    Console.WriteLine(Encoding.ASCII.GetString(response));
    }
}
```

Using Credentials

Another property of the WebClient class is the Credentials property. The Credentials property allows you to send username and password information to the web server for web pages that require authentication. The Credentials property must be set to one of two types of special credential classes - NetworkCredential or CredentialCache.

The NetworkCredential Class

The NetworkCredential class (found in the System.Net namespace) authenticates a client to the web server using a simple username/password combination (and a specified domain name for Windows web servers). The NetworkCredential object is created using one of three constructor formats:

```
NetworkCredential()
NetworkCredential(string username, string password)
NetworkCredential(string username, string password, string domain)
```

The first constructor creates an empty NetworkCredential object that can be set using the UserName, Password, and Domain properties. The second and third constructors are used to assign these values immediately when the object is created.

Listing 14.8 shows the CredTest.cs program, which uses a NetworkCredential object to supply a username and password for a website. The program creates a NetworkCredential object that specifies a valid username and password pair used to authenticate the client to the web server. If the authentication was successful, the web page will be returned and stored as a byte array. If the authentication was not successful, a WebException will be thrown.

Listing 14.8   The CredTest.cs program

```
using System;
using System.Net;
```

```
using System.Text;

class CredTest
{
    public static void Main()
    {
        WebClient wc = new WebClient();

        NetworkCredential nc = new NetworkCredential("alex", "mypassword");

        wc.Credentials = nc;

        byte[] response = wc.DownloadData("http://localhost/testlogin");

        Console.WriteLine(Encoding.ASCII.GetString(response));
    }
}
```

The CredentialCache Class

If you write a network program that must connect to several websites that require authentication, it could be a nightmare trying to keep all of the proper NetworkCredential objects straight with the proper websites. The .NET network library offers a simple solution: the CredentialCache class, found in the System.Net namespace. It allows you to keep a cache of frequently used NetworkCredential objects. Each NetworkCredential object is paired with a URI object and an authentication method. Each time a NetworkCredential is required to access a website, you can provide the entire CredentialCache object. The proper NetworkCredential that matches the URI and authentication method will automatically be used.

The CredentialCache constructor creates a new CredentialCache object but does not add any NetworkCredential objects. These objects are added using the Add() method:

```
Add(URI website, string authtype, NetworkCredential cred)
```

The website must be specified as a URI object, created using the URI class. The authentication type is a string representing the HTTP authentication method used. Currently two types of authentication methods are possible:

Basic   Sends the username and password in plain text

Digest   Uses the MD-5 encryption method to send the username and password

Listing 14.9 shows the CredCacheTest.cs program, which creates a CredentialCache for three separate URI sites. The CredentialCache object *cc* contains the NetworkCredential objects for all three websites. Instead of having to specify the proper NetworkCredential object for each website, all that is done is specify the single `CredentialCache` object. The `WebClient` object then uses the proper credential for each website.

Listing 14.9   The CredCacheTest.cs program

```csharp
using System;
using System.Net;
using System.Text;

class CredCacheTest
{
    public static void Main()
    {
        WebClient wc = new WebClient();
        string website1 = "http://remote1.ispnet.net";
        string website2 = "http://remote2.ispnet.net";
        string website3 = "http://remote3.ispnet.net/login";

        NetworkCredential nc1 = new NetworkCredential("mike", "guitars");
        NetworkCredential nc2 = new NetworkCredential
                                ("evonne", "singing", "home");
        NetworkCredential nc3 = new NetworkCredential("alex", "drums");

        CredentialCache cc = new CredentialCache();
        cc.Add(new Uri(website1), "Basic", nc1);
        cc.Add(new Uri(website2), "Basic", nc2);
        cc.Add(new Uri(website3), "Digest", nc3);

        wc.Credentials = cc;

        wc.DownloadFile(website1, "website1.htm");
        wc.DownloadFile(website2, "website2.htm");
        wc.DownloadFile(website3, "website3.htm");
    }
}
```

Advanced Web Classes

In addition to the `WebClient` class, the .NET library also includes the `WebRequest` and `WebResponse` classes. Both of these classes are contained in the `System.Net` namespace and provide advanced functionality for the network programmer. `WebRequest` and `WebResponse` are abstract base classes. That means they should not be used directly as objects in programs. Instead, they should be used by descendant classes once the objects are created. The descendant class used depends on the URI prefix specified in the URI parameter.

For http and https URIs, the HttpWebRequest and HttpWebResponse classes are used to handle the HTTP communication with the web server. These classes contain more advanced HTTP-specific functions than the WebClient class provides. For file URIs (accessing local HTML pages), the FileWebRequest and FileWebResponse classes are used. These classes provide the same functionality as the HTTP versions.

The HttpWebRequest Class

The HttpWebRequest class provides many advanced features for retrieving web pages using HTTP from the web server. To create an HttpWebRequest object, you must typecast the result of the WebRequest.Create() static method. For example:

```
HttpWebRequest hwr =
    (HttpWebRequest)WebRequest.Create("http://remotehost/webpage.htm");
```

Because the WebRequest class method is typecast to an HttpWebRequest object, the returned object is an HttpWebRequest object. After the HttpWebRequest object is created, you can set many of the HTTP header fields using the many HttpWebRequest class properties.

Using a Web Proxy

In today's world of hackers, many corporations use firewalls between their local networks and the Internet. The firewalls block access for certain types of traffic, including direct web traffic.

Often, to pass web data through a firewall, a *web proxy* server is used. Any web request from the local network must be sent to the web proxy server, which then passes it to the proper destination on the Internet. The web client software on the network device must know to pass HTTP messages to the web proxy server instead of directly to the intended destination.

The HttpWebRequest class allows you to specify a web proxy server to use for all HTTP communication. The Proxy property defines the URI of the web proxy server. The WebProxy class must be used to specify the value for the Proxy property.

The WebProxy class has many constructors for specifying features for the web proxy server, including adding login credentials and whether or not local websites will be accessed through the web proxy server. The simplest way to define a WebProxy object is to specify just the web proxy server's URI as a string:

```
HttpWebRequest hwr = (HttpWebRequest)WebRequest.Create(
        "http://remote1.ispnet2.net);
WebProxy proxysrv = new WebProxy("http://proxy1.ispnet.net:2000");
hwr.Proxy = proxysrv;
```

After the web proxy server is defined, you can send and receive HTTP messages as if there were no web proxy servers between the client and the web server.

Sending Data

To send data to the web server, you must use the GetRequestStream() method, as shown here:

```
HttpWebrequest hwr = (HttpWebRequest)WebRequest.Create("http://localhost");
Stream strm = hwr.GetRequestStream();
StreamWriter sw = new StreamWriter(strm);
sw.WriteLine(data);
```

This method returns a Stream object that can send data directly to the web server.

WARNING   The Stream object returned by the GetRequestStream() method can only be used for writing data to the server. It cannot be used for retrieving data.

Retrieving Data

There are two ways to retrieve the response from a HttpWebRequest object:

GetResponse()   Places the response from the web server in an HttpWebResponse object.

BeginGetResponse()   Uses an asynchronous function call to place the response from the web server in an HttpWebResponse object. This method uses the asynchronous method of returning the server response. For more information on asynchronous calls, see Chapter 8, "Asynchronous Socket Programming."

Both of these methods return the server response as an HttpWebResponse object.

The HttpWebResponse Class

The HttpWebResponse class is a descendant of the WebResponse class and was created specifically for handling HTTP responses from web servers. It includes many methods and properties for extracting the information from the received web page.

Retrieving HTTP Header Fields

The HttpWebResponse class contains separate properties for most of the common HTTP header fields. This allows you to easily access the information in the header fields of the HTTP response message. Table 14.1 lists the properties that can be used with an HttpWebResponse object.

TABLE 14.1: The HttpWebResponse Class Properties

Property	Gets
CharacterSet	The character set used in the response
ContentEncoding	The encoding method used in the response

Continued on next page

TABLE 14.1 CONTINUED: The HttpWebResponse Class Properties

Property	Gets
ContentLength	The length of the content returned in the response
ContentType	The content type of the response
Cookies	(Or sets) the cookies associated with the response
Headers	The HTTP headers in the response
LastModified	The date and time the contents of the response were modified
Method	The HTTP method used in the response
ProtocolVersion	The HTTP version used for the response
ResponseUri	The URI of the server that responded to the request
Server	The name of the server that sent the response
StatusCode	The HTTP status code of the response
StatusDescription	The HTTP text status phrase used in the response

You can use the individual header field properties to extract the header information for specific header fields, or you can use the Header property to create a WebHeaderCollection object. This object contains all of the headers contained in the HTTP response message, just like the WebClient ResponseHeader property.

Retrieving an Uncommon Header Field

Even though the HttpWebResponse class provides lots of properties for retrieving common HTTP header information, there are still plenty of other header fields that can be present in the response. To retrieve the information for these fields, use the GetResponseHeader() method. It specifies a single text value of a header field, and returns the value as a string:

```
string header = hwr.GetResponseHeader("X-Cache");
```

This example retrieves the special X-Cache: HTTP header field, which specifies whether the HTTP proxy server found the URI in its cache or from the actual website.

Retrieving Data

When an HttpWebRequest object uses the GetResponse() method, it returns an HttpWebResponse object. To retrieve the information from the HTTP response, use the GetResponseStream() method. It returns a Stream object that reads data from the HTTP response message. After the Stream object is created, you can also create a StreamReader object to easily retrieve each line of the HTML code in the HTTP response message.

Using Cookies

The Cookie property allows you to see all of the cookies that the web server sent in the response message. Cookies are used to store static information from the web server on the client machine.

They can be read from the web server to determine and track static state information about the client. An example of this is an Internet shopping site that needs to track the contents of a virtual shopping cart during the web session.

There are two steps to retrieving cookies in an HTTP session:

1. Define an empty `CookieContainer` class object in the `HttpWebRequest` class `CookieContainer` property before the HTTP request is sent:

```
HttpWebRequest hwr =
(HttpWebRequest)WebRequest.Create("http://www.amazon.com");
hwr.CookieContainer = new CookieContainer();
```

2. Use the `HttpWebResponse` class as usual to retrieve the web page from the web server. Then you must assign the `Cookie` property of the `HttpWebResponse` object to the original `CookieContainer` object in the `HttpWebRequest` object:

```
HttpWebResponse hwrsp = (HttpWebResponse)hwr.GetResponse();
hwrsp.Cookies = hwr.CookieContainer.GetCookies(hwr.RequestUri);
```

Now the `Cookies` property of the `HttpWebResponse` object contain all of the cookies associated with the HTTP session. You can iterate through the cookies using a `foreach` statement:

```
foreach(Cookie cky in hwrsp.Cookies)
{
    Console.WriteLine(cky.Name + " = " + cky.Value);
}
```

Advanced Web Client Example

Now that you have seen all of the advanced web features that the .NET library has to offer, let's create a simple program that sends a request to a website and dissects the response. The `WebGet.cs` program in Listing 14.10 demonstrates how to use the `HttpWebRequest` and `HttpWebResponse` classes to communicate with a web server and retrieve all of the header fields, cookies, and of course, the HTML web page.

Listing 14.10   **The WebGet.cs program**

```
using System;
using System.Drawing;
using System.IO;
using System.Net;
using System.Windows.Forms;

class WebGet         Form
{
    private TextBox uribox;
    private ListBox headers;
    private ListBox cookies;
```

```
private ListBox response;

public WebGet()
{
   Text = "WebGet - a web page retriever";
   Size = new Size(500, 450);

   Label label1 = new Label();
   label1.Parent = this;
   label1.Text = "URI:";
   label1.AutoSize = true;
   label1.Location = new Point(10, 23);

   uribox = new TextBox();
   uribox.Parent = this;
   uribox.Size = new Size(200, 2 * Font.Height);
   uribox.Location = new Point(35, 20);

   Label label2 = new Label();
   label2.Parent = this;
   label2.Text = "Headers:";
   label2.AutoSize = true;
   label2.Location = new Point(10, 46);

   headers = new ListBox();
   headers.Parent = this;
   headers.HorizontalScrollbar = true;
   headers.Location = new Point(10, 65);
   headers.Size = new Size(450, 6 * Font.Height);

   Label label3 = new Label();
   label3.Parent = this;
   label3.Text = "Cookies:";
   label3.AutoSize = true;
   label3.Location = new Point(10, 70 + 6 * Font.Height);

   cookies = new ListBox();
   cookies.Parent = this;
   cookies.HorizontalScrollbar = true;
   cookies.Location = new Point(10, 70 + 7 * Font.Height);
   cookies.Size = new Size(450, 6 * Font.Height);

   Label label4 = new Label();
   label4.Parent = this;
   label4.Text = "HTML:";
   label4.AutoSize = true;
   label4.Location = new Point(10, 70 + 13 * Font.Height);

   response = new ListBox();
   response.Parent = this;
```

```
        response.HorizontalScrollbar = true;
        response.Location = new Point(10, 70 + 14 * Font.Height);
        response.Size = new Size(450, 12 * Font.Height);


        Button sendit = new Button();
        sendit.Parent = this;
        sendit.Text = "GetIt";
        sendit.Location = new Point(275, 18);
        sendit.Size = new Size(7 * Font.Height, 2 * Font.Height);
        sendit.Click += new EventHandler(ButtongetitOnClick);
    }

    void ButtongetitOnClick(object obj, EventArgs ea)
    {
        headers.Items.Clear();
        cookies.Items.Clear();
        response.Items.Clear();

        HttpWebRequest hwr = (HttpWebRequest)WebRequest.Create(uribox.Text);
        hwr.CookieContainer = new CookieContainer();
        HttpWebResponse hwrsp = (HttpWebResponse)hwr.GetResponse();
        WebHeaderCollection whc = hwrsp.Headers;
        for (int i = 0; i < whc.Count; i++)
        {
            headers.Items.Add(whc.GetKey(i) + " = " + whc.Get(i));
        }

        hwrsp.Cookies = hwr.CookieContainer.GetCookies(hwr.RequestUri);
        foreach(Cookie cky in hwrsp.Cookies)
        {
            cookies.Items.Add(cky.Name + " = " + cky.Value);
        }

        Stream strm = hwrsp.GetResponseStream();
        StreamReader sr = new StreamReader(strm);

        while (sr.Peek() > -1)
        {
            response.Items.Add(sr.ReadLine());
        }
        sr.Close();
        strm.Close();
    }

    public static void Main()
    {
        Application.Run(new WebGet());
    }
}
```

The WebGet program creates a simple window that contains three ListBox objects: one for showing the HTTP headers in the response, one for showing any cookies returned by the response, and one for showing the raw HTML text from the response.

All of the web code is in the ButtongetitOnClick() method. It uses a WebHeaderContainer object to hold the HTTP header fields that are returned and a CookieContainer object to hold any cookie information returned from the website. Figure 14.1 shows a sample WebGet output from the website www.amazon.com.

FIGURE 14.1:

The WebGet program output

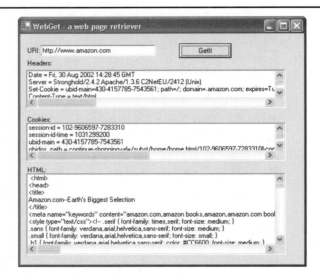

Web Services

One of the new and exciting features facilitated by the .NET Framework is *web services*. Web services allow a web server to advertise specific methods that can be consumed by remote applications on the network. This can be a way to incorporate distributed computing techniques for programmers. One company can provide information via a web service to remote customers running web service client programs. The clients can write their own application programs that use the remote web service server to obtain information from the company.

NOTE   This section describes using the web services feature of ASP.NET on a Microsoft Internet Information Services (IIS) server. To perform the examples in this section, you must have IIS installed on your development machine with the .NET Framework package, or have access to an existing web service server on the Internet.

The .NET web services feature utilizes ASP.NET technology to publish C# methods from web pages. The C# methods can be advertised to remote clients so they can access the methods and process information through them. Data is transferred to the web service using the Simple Object Access Protocol (SOAP). SOAP utilizes a standard HTTP connection along with the eXtensible Markup Language (XML) to format all data and transfer it to and from the web server. Because all of the data is transferred using HTTP, applications can easily communicate across firewalls and other network obstacles.

As illustrated in Figure 14.2, the three parts to a web service application:

The web service server   The web service server provides one or more application methods via a standard IIS web server running the ASP.NET software. The application methods receive data from remote clients using SOAP, process the data, and send the results back to the clients, also using SOAP. All of the returned data is in XML format.

The proxy object   The proxy object is created to allow the remote client to pass data to and from the web service server. The proxy object is created from the data definitions of the web service methods.

The client application   The client application consumes the web service methods located on the server. This application can be written as a local Windows application that obtains information from the web service server.

FIGURE 14.2:

The web service diagram

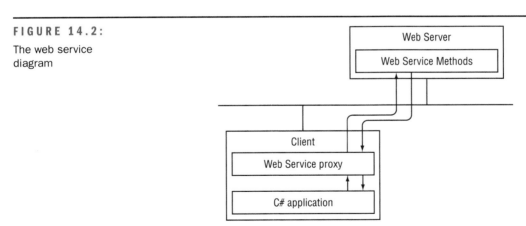

Creating the Web Service Server

To create a web service you must write C# methods that can be run from the IIS server. This is done by incorporating C# methods within an ASP.NET web page. Web service pages always must have an `.asmx` extension. Listing 14.11 shows the `MathService.asmx` program, which provides some simple math functions in a web service.

Listing 14.11 **The MathService.asmx program**

```csharp
<%@ WebService Language="c#" Class="MathService"%>

using System;
using System.Web.Services;

[WebService(Namespace="http://localhost/test")]
public class MathService : WebService
{
    [WebMethod]
    public int Add(int a, int b)
    {
      int answer;
      answer = a + b;
      return answer;
    }

    [WebMethod]
    public int Subtract(int a, int b)
    {
        int answer;
        answer = a - b;
        return answer;
    }

    [WebMethod]
    public int Multiply(int a, int b)
    {
        int answer;
        answer = a * b;
        return answer;
    }

    [WebMethod]
    public int Divide(int a, int b)
    {
        int answer;
        if (b != 0)
        {
            answer = a / b;
            return answer;
        } else
            return 0;
    }
}
```

The MathService program looks similar to a regular C# program, with just a few exceptions. To identify it as a web service program, the first line must declare the type of program, the language used (in case you are interested in using Visual Basic instead of C#), and the class name of the service:

```
<%@ WebService Language="c#" Class="MathService"%>
```

After the web service is declared, you must define the namespace that will contain and uniquely identify the methods. Most often the URI of the server where the web service is located is used. If no namespace is designated, a global namespace value of http://tempuri.org is assigned:

```
[WebService(Namespace="http://localhost/test")]
```

For this simple example, the local host value identifies the web service methods. In a real-world situation, you would use a real URI for the web server.

After declaring the namespace, you are ready to declare the individual methods for the web service. Each method must be preceded with a WebMethod tag to identify it as a web service method. Then the normal C# method is declared, including any parameters used to pass information into the method and the return datatype and value used to return any results.

Testing the Web Service

After creating the MathService.asmx file, you must place it under the wwwroot directory on the IIS server. You can create a subdirectory to separate it from other web pages on the server. On my Windows XP Professional workstation with IIS 5.1, I created the test directory:

```
C:\Inetpub\wwwroot\test\MathService.asmx
```

After saving the web service file, you can access it using Internet Explorer using the appropriate URI value (http://localhost/test/MathService.asmx for this example). A web page showing the web service methods available will appear, as seen in Figure 14.3.

FIGURE 14.3:

The main
MathService
web service page

Click any of the methods available and you'll see the web services helper page for the method. Each method can be tested using the helper page for the method. Figure 14.4 shows the helper page for the `Multiply()` method. You can test the method by entering parameter values for both parameters and clicking the Invoke button. If all is well, a separate Internet Explorer window should appear with the XML page for the response. Notice how the XML shows the answer, along with the datatype information to properly handle the answer. That is the beauty of XML.

FIGURE 14.4:

The `Multiply()` method helper page

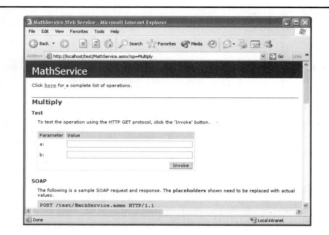

Creating the Web Service Proxy

After testing the web service server, you must create a proxy library for use by any C# clients. This is done using the `wsdl` program in the .NET Framework SDK. This program connects to the web service and create a `.cs` file that defines the web service methods available on the web service. By default, the `wsdl` program creates a .cs file with the name of the class name of the web service. The following command produces the file `MathService.cs`:

```
C:\>wsdl http://localhost/test/MathService.asmx
```

You can look at this file and see how `wsdl` automatically generated the methods needed to contact the web service server and pass the appropriate parameters to the methods.

After the `MathService.cs` file is generated, you can add it to your compile line when you create the client application, or you can create a DLL library file from it:

```
csc /t:library MathService.cs
```

This creates the `MathService.dll` file that creates C# client programs that utilize the web service. The new file includes the methods required to access the web service using both synchronous and asynchronous methods.

Creating a C# Web Service Client

Now that the web service server is running and a proxy library has been created, it's time to work on a client program that can use the web service. Listing 14.12 shows the ServiceTest.cs program, which does just that.

Listing 14.12   **The ServiceTest.cs program**

```csharp
using System;

class ServiceTest
{
    public static void Main (string[] argv)
    {
        MathService ms = new MathService();

        int x = Convert.ToInt16(argv[0]);
        int y = Convert.ToInt16(argv[1]);

        int sum = ms.Add(x, y);
        int sub = ms.Subtract(x, y);
        int mult = ms.Multiply(x, y);
        int div = ms.Divide(x, y);
        Console.WriteLine("The answers are:");
        Console.WriteLine("  {0} + {1} = {2}", x, y, sum);
        Console.WriteLine("  {0} - {1} = {2}", x, y, sub);
        Console.WriteLine("  {0} * {1} = {2}", x, y, mult);
        Console.WriteLine("  {0} / {1} = {2}", x, y, div);
    }
}
```

As you can see, once the web service is created, using it is simple. Just create an instance of the web service class and start using the class methods as you would any other class method.

To compile the program, you must use the MathService.dll library as a resource:

```
csc /r:MathService.dll ServiceTest.cs
```

The resulting program can then be run from any device on the network:

```
C:\>ServiceTest 100 50
The answers are:
  100 + 50 = 150
  100 - 50 = 50
  100 * 50 = 5000
  100 / 50 = 2

C:\>
```

Summary

This chapter focuses on using web resources in your C# network programs. HTTP has provided a means for data to shared to a vast number of people in a simple and easy-to-access manner.

HTTP uses two types of message formats, a request message and a response message. A client uses the request message to request a web resource from a web server. The Universal Resource Identifier (URI) specifies the protocol, host, and filename of the resource to access. Web servers use response messages to send information back to the client. The response message contains a status code, to indicate if the request was accepted or if an error occurred. If the request was accepted, the response usually contains a message body that includes the Hypertext Markup Language (HTML) text web page.

The .NET network library includes many classes that assist you in creating full-featured web programs. The WebClient class provides simple web access methods for making simple network programs. Most basic web functionality can be found in the WebClient class. The WebRequest and WebResponse class descendants are available for more advanced web programs. These abstract base classes contain additional properties and methods based on the specific protocol used. For HTTP communications, the HttpWebRequest and HttpWebResponse descendant classes are used. These classes provide additional features of handling header fields and cookies.

Finally, the chapter discusses the .NET concept of web services. A web service provides access to class methods in an HTTP environment. Remote clients can use the Simple Object Access Protocol (SOAP) to access class methods on remote machines. All data used in the web service transaction is in the eXtensible Markup Language (XML) format. This provides a way for dissimilar computers to share information in complex datatypes.

The next chapter turns to the subject of network directories. If you are writing Windows network applications, most likely you are doing it in a Windows network environment. The Microsoft Active Directory system controls access and information for many network resources, including usernames and passwords. With C#, it is easy to tap into an Active Directory and retrieve user information.

CHAPTER 15

Active Directory

- Network directory basics

- Working with Active Directory

- Using C# to access a network directory

- Modifying directory data

- Searching the network directory

So far in Part III you have seen how to use the .NET network library to communicate with remote network devices using standard network protocols. This chapter departs from that a little by discussing a different type of network communication process. Microsoft's Active Directory (AD) is used in Windows 2000 Server environments to manage network resources, including server shares, network printers, usernames, and passwords. If you are writing network programs that are used in a Windows 2000 Server environment, you can take advantage of the AD database to look up, add, and modify entries for users and systems on the network. The .NET library includes special classes that assist you in using the AD database to access network data, such as user information.

This chapter first presents an overview of network directory services in general, describing the Lightweight Directory Access Protocol (LDAP) for network directory service. You'll see how AD is used in Windows network environments to control network information. Next, an in-depth discussion of the .NET AD classes is presented, showing how to use each class in a network directory environment.

Network Directory Basics

The technology of *network directory services* has become one of the biggest crazes of computer networks. It allows multiple hosts on a network to share information about applications, resources, and users from a common database on the network. Novell's Netware Directory Service and Microsoft's AD are just two examples of network directory services. Many other vendors are experimenting with this technology to handle network resources.

The Internet community has developed a standard network directory service protocol that can be utilized by any host or client on a TCP/IP network to access information in a directory service database. The Lightweight Directory Access Protocol (LDAP) is defined by several Internet Request for Comments (RFCs) posted to the public domain. Any client that uses LDAP can access any network services database using LDAP. Microsoft's AD is based on the LDAP model and is more easily understood after seeing how LDAP works.

The LDAP System

An LDAP database is based on a hierarchical database design, similar to how the DNS database stores domain names. Hierarchical databases are often used in databases that match organizational constructs because they can easily represent the hierarchies of a company. They are known for their fast access times, but slow write times. The hierarchical method assumes that once an object is written to the database, it will be accessed many times by various network clients. This is true for most network directory situations, in which a username and password are created once in the database and network servers access the record each time the user attempts to use a network resource on the server.

The objects in an LDAP database are connected to one another in a tree-like fashion, as demonstrated in Figure 15.1. Each LDAP tree must have a root object, with other objects connected in sequence. Objects connect to one another by reference, similar to the DNS naming system.

FIGURE 15.1:

A sample LDAP database

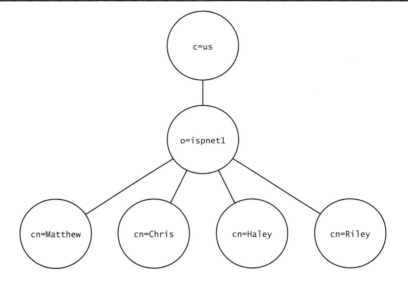

Because the LDAP database is so similar to the DNS structure, many LDAP designs (including AD) incorporate the DNS system into the LDAP database. This is accomplished by naming objects within the database structure the same as the various domain and subdomain names used in an organization.

LDAP Objects and Attributes

An LDAP tree references each object in the database using an LDAP *type* and a *value*. The LDAP type describes the type of object that it represents in the database. Various object types have been defined for LDAP database objects. Most are derived from the standard X.500 network naming convention, shown in Table 15.1.

TABLE 15.1: The X.500 Object Types

Object Type	Description
C	A Country object
O	An Organization object
OU	An Organizational Unit object

Continued on next page

TABLE 15.1 CONTINUED: The X.500 Object Types

Object Type	Description
CN	A Common Name object
DC	A Directory Context object

An object's type and value identify it in the database. For example, the term o=ispnet1 represents the Organization object ispnet1. In addition to this, the LDAP database must be able to uniquely identify each object in the database. Individual objects are uniquely referenced by their *distinguished name (dn)*. The dn incorporates all the LDAP tree objects used from the object back to the root of the tree. From the example shown in Figure 15.1, the ispnet1 organization uses a dn of o=ispnet1, c=us. This ensures that no other object under the c=us object can have the value ispnet1.

However, instead of using organization and country types to identify the object, most companies use Directory Context objects to reference their DNS domain objects within the database. For example, the following dn refers to the object containing information regarding the username rmullen in the engineering Organizational Unit of the ispnet1.net domain:

    cn=rmullen, ou=engineering, dc=ispnet1, dc=net

Directory Context and Organizational Unit objects are called *container* objects because they can contain other objects, such as other DC and OU objects. Common Name objects are typically used to define user objects and can be contained within any type of container object.

Each object in the LDAP database represents an entity on the network. Objects in the LDAP database contain two elements that define the object stored in the database: a defined objectClass name with an associated set of attributes. The objectClass defines what kind of information the object represents.

There are lots of objectClasses used in LDAP. Table 15.2 shows just a few of the more common ones.

TABLE 15.2: Common LDAP objectClasses

objectClass	Description
country	Represents a country object
locality	Represents a city, county, or state object
organization	Represents an organization or business
organizationalPerson	Represents a person within the organization
organizationalRole	Represents a person with a specific role within the organization (such as an administrator)

Continued on next page

TABLE 15.2 CONTINUED: Common LDAP objectClasses

objectClass	Description
organizationalUnit	Represents an entity within an organization
person	Represents a generic person entity
residentialPerson	Represents a person's private information, such as address and telephone number
applicationEntity	Represents an application accessed via the network

Each objectClass contains attributes that store information about the object. For example, the person objectClass contains attributes cn (common name) to represent the person's name (such as Rich Blum), sn (surname) to represent the person's last name (such as Blum), and telephoneNumber to store phone contact information for the person. A person querying the LDAP database for the cn=rblum, dc=engineering, dc=ispnet1, dc=net object can view the attributes associated with the object to find information about the person.

NOTE   Note that the cn property value is not the same as the CN common name object type.

Working with Active Directory

The Microsoft Active Directory (AD) system replaces the older Windows NT domain system. With the release of Windows 2000 Server, Microsoft converted the domain system to an LDAP database model. Instead of holding domain information in a flat database, a hierarchical network directory service system allows a more robust network configuration. AD databases contain objects that represent all the network resources that were previously maintained in the domain database. Object attributes are used to track specific information for each object, such as usernames, passwords, login times, and personal information.

Network administrators use AD to store server, workstation, and network printer information for each item in the domain within the network directory database.

Parts of an Active Directory

The AD system comprises several pieces that are used to store and retrieve the network objects for the domain.

Domains

The AD concept of a domain is similar to the original Windows NT concept. An AD domain contains a group of network resources sharing the same database structure and security policy. In the AD system, network administrators use a hierarchical database to organize network resources within directory contexts in the domain. This makes domain management much simpler than the Windows NT domain method.

In most AD networks, the organization's DNS name is used as the domain name. An organization with a single DNS domain name can be configured within a single AD domain. Figure 15.2 shows how this works.

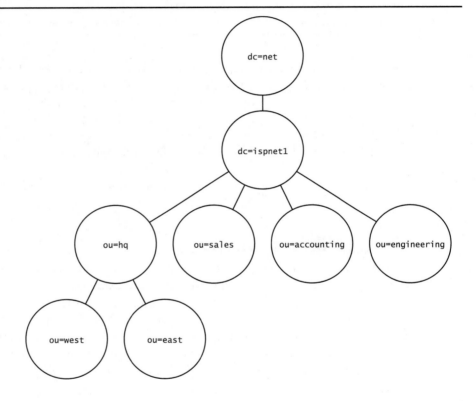

Organizational Units

Domains themselves can be subdivided into smaller entities. *Organizational Units (OUs)* are the containers within the domain used to group related objects (similar to the directory context in LDAP). Often the OU is based on the business structure of the organization, keeping network resource objects in each business unit (or division) in its own OU container.

One nice feature of OUs is that AD allows the network administrator to delegate local administrators at that level. You can assign a user from a local OU to manage all of the resources within the organizational unit, without having to worry about granting them security privileges to other parts of the AD database.

Trees

In the Windows NT domain system, accessing network resources located in another domain meant having the network administrator arrange a complicated configuration of domain security rules. Each domain that required access to resources in another domain had to establish a *trust relationship* with the remote domain.

A trust relationship is the set of rules configured in a domain that allows users (or other network objects) from one domain to access network resources in another domain. For an organization with multiple domains to allow each domain access to resources in all of the other domains, a trust relationship has to be created between every combination of domains. This can quickly grow into a huge administration nightmare.

To solve this problem, the AD system created the concept of *trees*. A tree is an interconnection of separate domains, all within the control of a single AD database. One domain is designated as the main domain in the tree (called the *root domain*), and all other domains are configured as objects under the root domain (similar to the basic LDAP structure). All of the domains in the tree share the common naming space of the root domain.

For organizations that use DNS domains and subdomains, it is easy to configure an AD tree for each subdomain on the network. Figure 15.3 shows a sample of how a simple subdomain system can be configured in an AD tree. Each triangle represents a self-contained AD domain, as was shown in Figure 15.2. The root domain, ispnet1.net, contains objects used to control the entire tree (the domain administrator user and the main AD servers). Each subdomain is a self-contained domain, including local domain user and server objects.

FIGURE 15.3:

An AD tree structure

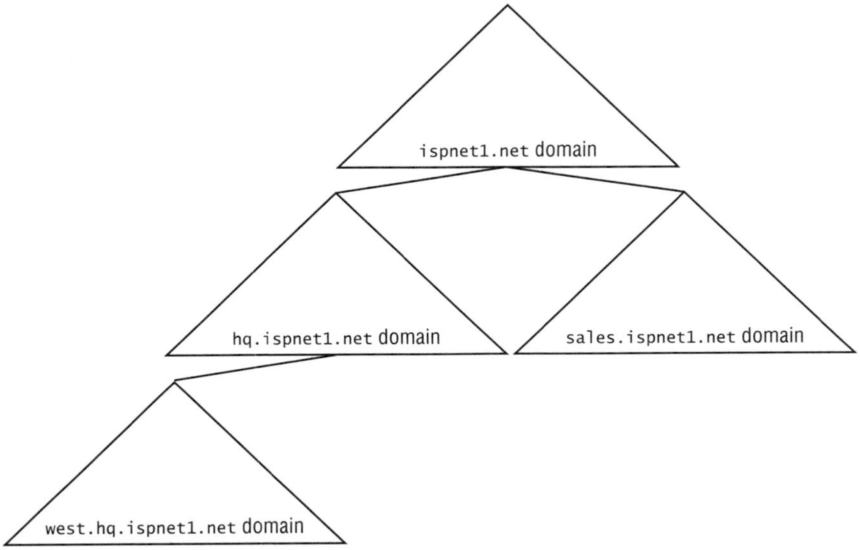

Forests

While the concept of trees allows an organization to connect contiguous domains within the organization to a single AD database, situations may (and often do) occur where an organization contains two or more trees that must be managed. To help with this situation, AD was designed to incorporate the concept of a *forest*. The forest is a collection of two or more trees that incorporate the same AD database. Although the trees use the same database, they do not use the same namespace, that is, each tree still maintains its own root object, and objects within the tree are referenced based on the tree root object. Figure 15.4 shows an example of this arrangement.

FIGURE 15.4:

An AD forest structure with two trees

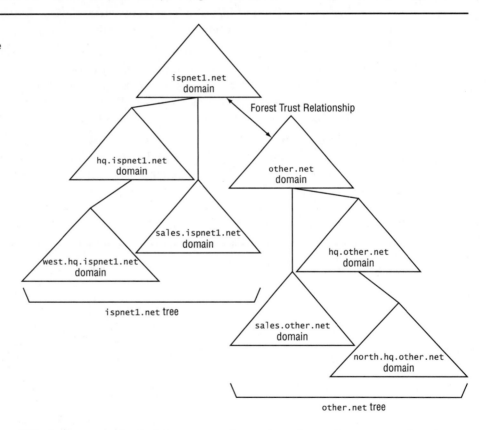

It is often difficult for network administrators to determine when to incorporate domains within trees and forests. One important item to remember is that within a forest, each tree must maintain trust relationships between any other tree that it needs access to network resources from (similar to the old NT domain trust relationship model). For organizations that merge and share substantial resources, it may be easier to bite the bullet and merge the separate trees into a single tree rather than create a forest and deal with the trust relationships.

Active Directory Objects

The AD system is similar to LDAP but uses some different terminology and concepts. The basic item within the directory structure is still called an object. The object represents a single entity in the network, such as a server, workstation, printer, or user. Each object is defined with a class, also called an object class. This is similar to the LDAP concept of the `objectClass`. Each object class consists of specific attributes that are used to hold information about the object.

Connecting to an Active Directory Server

To connect to a Windows 2000 AD Server, the workstation must be running the AD Services Interface (ADSI). All communication with an AD server, whether it is from the operating system or from a user program on the system, is done through the ADSI. The .NET AD library uses the ADSI for all of its AD functions.

For a network device to work in AD, the ADSI software library must be loaded. All Windows 2000 Professional Workstation and Server devices, as well as Windows XP Professional workstations, include the ADSI to operate with an AD server. Windows 98, Me, and NT systems do not include ADSI. You can download an ADSI client package from Microsoft for these systems (as well as any AD programs running on these systems) to operate in an AD environment.

Using C# to Access a Network Directory

The main .NET class for working with network directory services objects is the `DirectoryEntry` class, found in the `System.DirectoryServices` namespace. The `DirectoryEntry` class allows you to bind to a directory object and perform operations to retrieve, add, delete, and modify information about the object.

The `DirectoryEntry` class has many constructor formats, depending on your requirements within the database.

NOTE   To perform the examples in this chapter, you will need access to some type of LDAP database system, either a Windows 2000 Active Directory server or an LDAP server. These examples were done using an OpenLDAP server, but the programming principles discussed here apply equally, no matter what type of LDAP server you are using.

Anonymous Directory Login

Many network directory services allow either all or some database objects to be read by anyone on the network, regardless of network permissions. This allows network users to look up resources on the network, such as a user phone number and address, without requiring advanced privileges on the directory server.

To create a `DirectoryEntry` instance to reference a directory object without using privileges, you use the following constructor format:

```
DirectyoryEntry(string ldappath)
```

The *ldappath* parameter is a string value that represents the location of the database object. The object must be referenced using a URI-like syntax, which includes the access method, the network directory service server address, and the distinguished name of the object.

The ADSI library offers various access methods for connecting to different types of network directory services. Each access method is specified in a URI format. Table 15.3 lists the access methods available to use.

WARNING   The access methods are case sensitive, so be careful when declaring them.

TABLE 15.3: The ADSI Access Methods

Access Method	Accesses
WinNT	Windows NT domains
IIS	A Microsoft Internet Information Services server
LDAP	Any LDAP-compliant network directory (including Active Directory)
NDS	Novell Netware Directory Service server
NWCOMPAT	Novell Netware 3.x bindary service

For AD access, you should use the LDAP access method because it offers the most robust access method, including searching capabilities (described in the "Searching the Network Directory" section).

After the access method, the address of the desired directory server should be specified, along with the full distinguished name of the object to reference. A few examples of proper LDAP paths would be:

```
LDAP://server1.ispnet1.net/dc=ispnet1, dc=net
LDAP://server1.ispnet1.net/cn=kblum, ou=sales, dc=ispnet1, dc=net
LDAP://192.168.1.100/ou=accounting, dc=ispnet1, dc=net
```

Listing 15.1 shows the `BindObject.cs` program, which binds a variable to a directory object and displays the LDAP path associated with the object.

Listing 15.1   The BindObject.cs program

```
using System;
using System.DirectoryServices;

class BindObject
{
```

```
    public static void Main()
    {
        DirectoryEntry de = new DirectoryEntry(
            "LDAP://192.168.1.100/dc=ispnet1, dc=net");

        string ldappath = de.Path;
        Console.WriteLine("The LDAP path is: {0}", ldappath);
        de.Close();
    }
}
```

While the `BindObject` program is extremely trivial (seeing as you need to know the LDAP path to bind to the object anyway) it shows the basic steps required to bind a variable to a directory services object. The `Path` property retrieves the LDAP path of the object as a string value, which can be used in a `DirectoryEntry` instance to bind to the object. This will be used later in the "Searching the Network Directory" section to iterate through objects in a directory service.

The output from this example is simple. If you were successful in binding to the directory service object, the LDAP path should display on the console. This entry should be the same as what you used to create the `DirectoryEntry` object. If the program was not able to bind to the directory services object, an `Exception` will be thrown, stating the reason for the error. One of the most common errors is that the directory services server requires that you authenticate yourself before binding to an object.

NOTE   You may notice that many of the errors produced from AD code are COM `Exceptions`. The ADSI library uses the COM interface of Windows to access the AD environment.

Logging In to a Directory

For database actions that require user authentication, two formats can be used. The following constructor allows you to specify a username and password to use to login into the directory service:

```
DirectoryEntry(string ldappath, string username, string password)
```

Once the connection is authenticated, you can perform the actions that the username specified is allowed to perform, including adding, deleting, or modifying objects.

The second constructor allows you to specify a specific authentication type used for the login:

```
DirectoryEntry(string ldappath, string username, string password,
        AuthenticationTypes authtype)
```

The `AuthenticationTypes` enumerator specifies the authentication type used for logging into the directory service server.

Table 15.4 shows the authentication types that are available.

TABLE 15.4: AuthenticationTypes

AuthenticationType	Description
Anonymous	No authentication is performed (not supported under Windows NT)
Delegation	Enables the ADSI to delegate the user's security context
Encryption	Uses encryption for all data exchanged with the server
FastBind	Does not attempt to query the objectClass property, exposing only the base interfaces supported by ADSI
None	Used as a null reference
ReadonlyServer	Indicates that read-only access is required to the server
Sealing	Encrypts data using Kerberos encryption
Secure	Requests secure authentication.
SecureSocketsLayer	Uses the Secure Sockets Layer (SSL) encryption with a known certificate
ServerBind	Used to log the session into a specific server when a server is specified in the LDAP path
Signing	Signs all packets to verify data integrity

An example of using authentication to access a directory object is:

```
DirectoryEntry de = DirectoryEntry("LDAP://192.168.1.100/dc=ispnet1, dc=net",
    "rich", "password", AuthenticationTypes.ServerBind);
```

This example uses the server username "rich" and the appropriate password to log into the directory services server.

> **NOTE** Almost all network directory services require a user to log in before administrative functions (such as adding, deleting, and modifying objects) can be performed.

Modifying Directory Data

After you bind a variable to the network directory service object, you can use the DirectoryEntry properties and methods to retrieve and manipulate either the object itself or its attributes.

> **WARNING** Within the .NET ADSI libraries, object attributes are referred to as properties. Don't get confused by this change in terminology.

Working with Object Properties

The Properties property of a DirectoryEntry object accesses all the properties associated with the object. The Properties property returns a PropertyCollection class object, which can be manipulated to work with the various object properties.

Listing Object Properties

The `PropertyCollection` class contains the `PropertyNames` and `Values` properties, which get the existing object properties and their values:

```
DirectoryEntry de = new DirectoryEntry(
        "LDAP://192.168.1.100/dc=ispnet1, dc=net");
PropertyCollection pc = de.Properties
foreach(string propName in pc.PropertyNames)
        Console.WriteLine("property: {0}", propName);
```

To obtain the value of the `objectClass` property, use the `Properties` property. Using the property name as an array index retrieves each value. The following statement retrieves the `objectClass` property of the object:

```
string value = de.Properties["objectClass"];
```

Listing 15.2, `GetProperties.cs`, is a brief example of how to iterate through all of the properties of an object and display the values of each property.

Listing 15.2	The GetProperties.cs program

```
using System;
using System.DirectoryServices;

class GetProperties
{
    public static void Main()
    {
        DirectoryEntry de = new DirectoryEntry(
            "LDAP://192.168.1.100/cn=kblum, ou=sales, dc=ispnet1, dc=net");
        Console.WriteLine("object: {0}", de.Path);
        PropertyCollection pc = de.Properties;
        foreach(string propName in pc.PropertyNames)
        {
            foreach(object value in de.Properties[propName])
                Console.WriteLine("   property = {0}    value = {1}",
                    propName, value);
        }
    }
}
```

The first `foreach` statement iterates through the `PropertyCollection`, finding all the property names associated with the object. The second `foreach` statement then extracts the property value(s) associated with each property name. Here's the output from this example:

```
C:\>GetProperties
object: LDAP://192.168.1.100/cn=kblum, ou=sales, dc=ispnet1, dc=net
   property = objectClass    value = person
   property = cn    value = Katie Blum
```

```
   property = sn    value = Blum
```

C:\>

The output shows that the object cn=kblum, ou=sales, dc=ispnet1, dc=net is a person objectClass and has two additional properties, a common name of Katie Blum, and a surname of Blum.

Modifying Properties

After you have the property name, you can use it to modify the value assigned to the property. There is only one catch to this: the database information may be cached on your system.

The ADSI system contains a mechanism for caching information that is retrieved from the directory service server. Any operation performed on this data is done in the system cache. There are two ways to get the data changes to take affect on the actual directory services database:

- Use the CommitChanges() method to force any changes made to the cache to the directory services server

- Set the UsePropertyCache property to false, ensuring that any database changes are immediately sent to the server

Either way of saving database changes will work in the AD environment. If you are making database changes over a period of time, you may want to use the UsePropertyCache property to ensure that all of the changes are being made in case of a system failure. On the other hand, if you are making lots of changes in a short period of time, it will be faster to make them in the cache and commit the changes all at once using the CommitChanges() method.

Listing 15.3 shows the ModifyProperty.cs program, which demonstrates how to modify a property value of an object in the directory services database.

Listing 15.3   The ModifyProperty.cs program

```
using System;
using System.DirectoryServices;

class ModifyProperty
{
   public static void Main()
   {
      DirectoryEntry de = new DirectoryEntry(
         "LDAP://192.168.1.100/cn=kblum, ou=sales, dc=ispnet1, dc=net",
         "cn=Administrator, dc=ispnet1, dc=net", "password",
         AuthenticationTypes.ServerBind);

      de.Properties["sn"][0] = "Mullen";
      de.CommitChanges();
```

```
        Console.WriteLine("New property value: {0}", de.Properties["sn"][0]);
        de.Close();
    }
}
```

Because the object property in the database is being modified, you will probably have to include a username and password (and possibly an AuthenticationTypes value) for the directory services server.

Note that the property value itself must be referenced using a two-dimensional array. The first element of the array is the property name, and the second element is the property value index. This shows that properties may have more than one value associated with them, although this is not often the case.

Adding Properties

To add a new property to an object, you must use the Add() method of the PropertyCollection class. The property to add must be a valid property of the object's objectClass. The directory service schema contains the formal definitions of all objectClass types, along with what properties can be used with each objectClass.

The easiest way to add a new property is to reference the new property using the property name as the Properties array index and then use the Add() method:

```
de.Properties["telephoneNumber"].Add("(111)222-3333");
```

This statement adds the telephoneNumber property to the DirectoryEntry object de and assigns a value to it, as demonstrated in Listing 15.4, AddProperty.cs.

Listing 15.4   The AddProperty.cs program

```
using System;
using System.DirectoryServices;

class AddProperty
{
    public static void Main()
    {
        DirectoryEntry de = new DirectoryEntry(
            "LDAP://192.168.1.100/cn=kblum, ou=sales, dc=ispnet1, dc=net",
            "cn=Administrator, dc=ispnet1, dc=net","password",
            AuthenticationTypes.ServerBind);

        de.Properties["telephoneNumber"].Add("(111)222-3333");
        de.Properties["telephoneNumber"].Add("(444)555-6666");
        de.CommitChanges();
        de.Close();
    }
}
```

After compiling and running the `AddProperty` program, you can use the `GetProperties` program to see if the additional properties were added:

```
C:\>GetProperties
object: LDAP://192.168.1.100/cn=kblum, ou=sales, dc=ispnet1, dc=net
   property = objectClass    value = person
   property = cn    value = Katie Blum
   property = sn    value = Blum
   property = telephoneNumber    value = (111)222-3333
   property = telephoneNumber    value = (444)555-6666

C:\>
```

<table>
<tr><td>**NOTE**</td><td>This example also demonstrates that you can often have multiple instances of a single property for an object. This feature can lead to incomplete information if you do not write your AD programs to take this into account. Remember to retrieve all instances of a property, not just the first value.</td></tr>
</table>

Working with Objects

Within the network directory service tree, any directory container object can have other objects as children (this is how the tree gets its structure). You can use the `Children` property to both add and remove children objects of an object.

Listing Child Objects

The `Children` property returns a `DirectoryEntries` object, which contains all of the children objects of the object as `DirectoryEntry` objects. However, the `DirectoryEntries` class is an `IEnumerator`-type class, so you can simply use a `foreach` statement to extract each `DirectoryEntry` object from the `DirectoryEntries` object.

Listing 15.5 shows the `ListObjects.cs` program, which lists all the child objects of a base object.

Listing 15.5   The ListObjects.cs program

```
using System;
using System.Collections;
using System.DirectoryServices;

class ListObjects
{
    public static void Main()
    {

        DirectoryEntry de = new DirectoryEntry(
```

```
        "LDAP://192.168.1.100/dc=ispnet1, dc=net");

        Console.WriteLine(de.Path);
        DirectoryEntries des = de.Children;
        foreach(DirectoryEntry entry in des)
        {
            Console.WriteLine("  child: " + entry.Name);
        }

    }
}
```

The `ListObjects` program binds a `DirectoryEntry` object to the object in the directory services database from which to begin listing objects. The `Children` property obtains the `DirectoryEntries` object, which is then enumerated to find each of the individual child objects. The output of the program looks like this:

```
C:\>ListObjects
LDAP://192.168.1.100/dc=ispnet1, dc=net
  child: cn=Administrator
  child: ou=accounting
  child: ou=engineering
  child: ou=sales
  child: ou=hq

C:\>
```

Note that all objects, no matter what object type they are, appear as child objects of the base object.

Adding a Child Object

You can use the `Add()` method of the `Children` property to add new children objects and use the `CommitChanges()` method to ensure the new objects are stored in the directory service database. The `Add()` method format is as follows:

```
Add(string objectname, string schemaclassname)
```

To add a new object you must know the intended schema `objectClass` for the new object. Often you can copy this value from a similar object in the directory service database. Listing 15.6 is the `AddObject.cs` program, which demonstrates how to add a new `organizationalUnit` object under an existing directory context.

NOTE In this example, I obtain the schema `objectClass` from a similar object already in the directory. You can use the same technique, or you can create new `objectClass` objects using other schemas.

Listing 15.6   **The AddObject.cs program**

```csharp
using System;
using System.DirectoryServices;

class AddObject
{
    public static void Main()
    {
        DirectoryEntry de = new DirectoryEntry(
            "LDAP://192.168.1.100/ou=accounting, dc=ispnet1, dc=net",
            "cn=Administrator, dc=ispnet1, dc=net", "password",
            AuthenticationTypes.ServerBind);

        DirectoryEntries children = de.Children;
        DirectoryEntry newchild = children.Add("ou=auditing", de.SchemaClassName);
        newchild.Properties["ou"].Add("Auditing Department");
        newchild.CommitChanges();
        newchild.Close();
        de.Close();

        DirectoryEntry de2 = new DirectoryEntry(
            "LDAP://192.168.1.100/ou=auditing, dc=accounting, dc=ispnet1, dc=net");
        string newpath = de2.Path;
        Console.WriteLine("new path: {0}", newpath);
        de2.Close();
    }
}
```

The AddObject program first binds to the parent of the new object and creates a DirectoryEntries object from the Children property of the parent object. The Add() method is used on the DirectoryEntries object, specifying both the name of the new object and the objectClass to use. (In this case, the objectClass is copied from the parent object, as the new object is also an organizationalUnit object.)

Remember that the new object's distinguished name will still include the parent name (ou=auditing, ou=accounting, dc=ispnet1, dc=net, for this example).

WARNING   Remember to log in to the directory services database as a user with permissions to add new objects. For Windows 2000 Active Directory Server, you may have to use the AuthenticationType.Secure technique to bind to the DirectoryEntry object.

Removing Child Objects

Only empty child objects can be removed from the AD. There are two ways to remove objects from the directory services database:

- Using the `DirectoryEntries` `Find()` and `Remove()` methods
- Using the `DirectoryEntry` `DeleteTree()` method

Using DirectoryEntries Methods

The first technique uses the `Find()` and `Remove()` methods of the `DirectoryEntries` class to first locate and then remove the desired object. In the following code snippet, you can see how you find an object given its name, create a `DirectoryEntry` object referencing the object, and use the `Remove()` method to remove it from the directory:

```
DirectoryEntries children = de.Children;
DirectoryEntry badObject = children.Find("auditing");
if (badObject != null)
    children.Remove(badObject);
children.CommitChanges();
```

Of course, the final step is to ensure that the change is propagated to the actual directory services server.

Listing 15.7 shows the `RemoveObject.cs` program, which uses this technique to remove a child object. The program binds a variable to the parent of the object to remove, then uses the `Find()` method to bind a `DirectoryEntry` object to the object to remove. Next, the `Remove()` method is used, using the `DirectoryEntry` variable of the object to remove.

> **Listing 15.7   The RemoveObject.cs program**

```
using System;
using System.DirectoryServices;

class RemoveObject
{
    public static void Main()
    {
        DirectoryEntry de = new DirectoryEntry(
          "LDAP://192.168.1.100/ou=accounting, dc=ispnet1, dc=net",
          "cn=Administrator, dc=ispnet1, dc=net", "password",
          AuthenticationTypes.ServerBind);

        DirectoryEntries children = de.Children;
        try
```

```
    {
        DirectoryEntry badObject = children.Find("ou=auditing");
        children.Remove(badObject);
        de.CommitChanges();
        Console.WriteLine("the object was removed");
    } catch (Exception)
    {
        Console.WriteLine("the object was not found");
    }
    }
  }
```

Using the DeleteTree() Method

The DiretoryEntry class includes the DeleteTree() method, which can be used for removing a bound object from the directory services database.

WARNING The DeleteTree() method can only be used on DirectoryEntry objects that are not bound, or an Exception will be thrown.

Listing 15.8 shows the DeleteObject.cs program, which demonstrates using the DeleteTree() method.

Listing 15.8   **The DeleteObject.cs program**

```
using System;
using System.DirectoryServices;

class DeleteObject
{
    public static void Main()
    {
        DirectoryEntry de = new DirectoryEntry(
          "LDAP://192.168.1.100/ou=accounting, dc=ispnet1, dc=net",
          "cn=Administrator, dc=ispnet1, dc=net", "password",
          AuthenticationTypes.ServerBind);

        DirectoryEntries children = de.Children;
        try
        {
          DirectoryEntry badObject = children.Find("ou=auditing");
          badObject.DeleteTree();
          de.CommitChanges();
          Console.WriteLine("the object has been deleted");
        } catch (Exception e)
        {
          Console.WriteLine("the object was not found or deleted:");
```

```
            Console.WriteLine(e.ToString());
        }
    }
}
```

When using the DeleteTree() method, you cannot delete an object that you are currently bound to. Instead, as seen in this example, you must bind to the parent object, and find the desired child object using the Find() method.

WARNING The DeleteTree() method does not allow you to delete objects that are not containers of other objects.

Renaming Child Objects

The Rename() method renames directory objects. The single parameter in the Rename() method is the new name assigned to the object:

```
de.Rename("cn=testing");
```

WARNING Use the Rename() method with caution. It affects not just the object that you rename, but also the distinguished names of any objects below that object in the directory tree.

The RenameObject.cs program in Listing 15.9 demonstrates how to rename a person object using the Rename() method.

Listing 15.9   **The RenameObject.cs program**

```
using System;
using System.DirectoryServices;

class RenameObject
{
    public static void Main()
    {
        DirectoryEntry de = new DirectoryEntry(
            "LDAP://192.168.1.100/ou=auditing, ou=accounting, dc=ispnet1, dc=net",
            "cn=Administrator, dc=ispnet1, dc=net", "password",
            AuthenticationTypes.ServerBind);

        DirectoryEntries des = de.Children;
        DirectoryEntry badObject = des.Find("cn=test");
        badObject.Rename("cn=testing");
        de.CommitChanges();
        de.Close();
    }
}
```

Searching the Network Directory

One of the most frequently used functions within network directory services is searching for information. To help make this job easier, the .NET library includes the `DirectorySearcher` class, which provides a substantial number of properties to help you define the search and retrieve the results.

Step 1: Defining the Search Properties

Four properties of the `DirectorySearcher` class control how the search is performed:

SearchRoot

The `SearchRoot` property defines where in the directory structure the search will begin. The `SearchRoot` value can be specified using the standard URI technique to define a `DirectoryEntry` object:

```
SearchRoot = "LDAP://192.168.1.100/dc=ispnet1, dc=net";
```

For some network directory services (including AD), a special name is assigned to the root object. The `RootDSE` object can reference the root object in the directory:

```
SearchRoot = "LDAP://192.168.1.100/RootDSE";
```

If no value is set for the `SearchRoot` property, the search will attempt to find the root object and start there.

Filter

By default, the `DirectorySearcher` object will return all objects in the directory services database. The `Filter` property can define what objects will be returned in the search results.

The `Filter` property is a string value and must be enclosed in parentheses. The default filter value is as follows:

```
(objectClass=*)
```

This value returns all `objectClass` objects in the database (filter values can use wildcard characters). Alternatively, you can choose to filter on any `objectClass` or any object property that is defined in the database. For example:

(objectClass=person)   Returns all objects that have an `objectClass` of `person`

(sn=Bl*)   Returns all objects that have a surname value that starts with Bl

(sn>=Blum)   Returns all objects that have a surname value that are alphabetically equal or greater than Blum

The last example shows that any type of mathematical expression can be used within the filter value. You can also specify multiple filter values, along with a `boolean` operation to use.

For example, the following returns the object that has an `objectClass` of `person` and the `sn` value of Blum:

```
(&(objectClass=person)(sn=Blum))
```

Likewise, you can use multiple `boolean` operations:

```
(&(objectClass=person)(|(sn=Blum)(sn=Pierce)))
```

This hodgepodge returns all objects that are `objectClass` of `person` and have a surname value of either Blum or Pierce.

PropertiesToLoad

By default, the `DirectorySearcher` object returns all the properties associated with an object. For some objects, this returns a lot of data. If you are only interested in a few properties, you can tell the `DirectorySearcher` which properties to return, saving time and network bandwidth. The `PropertiesToLoad` property is a `StringCollection` object, which adds each property name to retrieve in the collection using the `Add()` method:

```
ds.PropertiesToLoad.Add("cn");
ds.PropertiesToLoad.Add("sn");
```

The return result set (see the "Extracting the Search Results" section) will only contain the object properties that you specified in the `PropertiesToLoad` property.

SearchScope

By default, the `DirectorySearcher` object will search the entire tree under the `SearchRoot` object. You can define the search depth using the `SearchScope` property. It can be one of three values:

SearchScope.Base   Limits the search to only the base object defined in the `SearchRoot` property

SearchScope.OneLevel   Limits the search to only the immediate children of the base object defined in the `SearchRoot` property

SearchScope.Subtree   Searches the entire tree under the base object defined in the `SearchRoot` property

Step 2: Retrieving the Search Results

Once the `DirectorySearcher` parameters have been determined, you can start the search and retrieve the results. Use either `FindOne()` or `FindAll()` to retrieve results from a search.

FindOne()

The `FindOne()` method returns only one result of the defined search in a `SearchResult` class object. If more than one item is found in the result, only the first item is returned.

The SearchResult class is similar to the DirectoryEntry object but only refers to a database object by reference and cannot access the object. The SearchResult object includes the Path and Properties properties that can extract information about the database object, such as its location in the database, and the names and values of its properties.

The Path property can create a DirectoryEntry object, which can then directly access the object to modify or delete the object or any properties of the object.

FindAll()

The FindAll() method returns all of the results of a search in a SearchResultCollection class object. The SearchResultCollection object is a collection of SearchResult objects, one object for each result from the search.

You can iterate through the SearchResultCollection object using the foreach statement, extracting each individual SearchResult object.

Step 3: Extracting the Search Results

Once the SearchResult or SearchResultCollection object is retrieved from the search, you can extract the individual database object information using the Properties property:

```
SearchResult sr = ds.FindOne();
string user = sr.Properties["cn"][0];
```

This code snippet finds the first result from the search and extracts the common name (cn) property value.

Alternatively, you can use the Path property to create a DirectoryEntry object to use for further manipulation:

```
SearchResult sr = ds.FindOne();
string newpath = sr.Path;
DirectoryEntry de = new DirectoryEntry(newpath);
```

Here, after the DirectoryEntry object is created, it can extract, modify, or delete any property of the object, or the object itself, as shown in the "Modifying Directory Data" section.

Performing a Search

Listing 15.10, the SimpleSearch.cs program, demonstrates how to perform a simple network directory services search for all of the items in the database.

Listing 15.10   **The SimpleSearch.cs program**

```
using System;
using System.DirectoryServices;

class SimpleSearch
{
```

```
public static void Main()
{
    DirectoryEntry root = new DirectoryEntry(
      "LDAP://192.168.1.100/DC=ispnet1,DC=net",
      "cn=Administrator, dc=ispnet1, dc=net", "password",
      AuthenticationTypes.ServerBind);

    DirectorySearcher searcher = new DirectorySearcher(root);
    searcher.Filter = "(&(objectClass=person)(sn=Blum))";
    searcher.PropertiesToLoad.Add("cn");
    searcher.PropertiesToLoad.Add("telephoneNumber");
    SearchResultCollection results = searcher.FindAll();

    foreach(SearchResult result in results)
    {
        string searchpath = result.Path;
        Console.WriteLine("path: {0}", searchpath);
        ResultPropertyCollection rpc = result.Properties;
        foreach(string property in rpc.PropertyNames)
        {
            foreach(object value in rpc[property])
                Console.WriteLine("  property = {0}  value = {1}",
                                                property, value);
        }
    }
}
```

The SimpleSearch program uses a filter to specify retrieving only objects that use the person objectClass and have a surname of Blum. The results are stored in a SearchResultCollection and extracted using a foreach statement.

For each result, the properties are extracted using the ResultPropertyCollection object and the PropertyNames property. The resulting output should contain the desired objects. For instance, in the following output, you can see that the only properties that were returned by the search were the properties specified in the PropertiesToLoad Add() methods:

```
C:\>SimpleSearch
path: LDAP://192.168.1.100/cn=kblum, ou=sales, dc=ispnet1, dc=net
  property= cn   value = Katie Blum
  property= telephonenumber   value = (111)222-3333
  property= telephonenumber   value = (444)555-6666
  property= adspath   value = LDAP://192.168.1.100/cn=kblum, ou=sales, ➥
dc=ispnet1, dc=net
path: LDAP://192.168.1.100/cn=jblum, ou=accounting, dc=ispnet1, dc=net
  property= cn   value = Jessica Blum
  property= adspath   value = LDAP://192.168.1.100/cn=jblum, ou=accounting, ➥
dc=ispnet1, dc=net

C:\>
```

You may notice that both objects contained an extra property, the adspath. This is an internal property that is used for the network directory service and cannot be modified or removed by you.

Advanced Search Features

The DirectorySearcher class also provides some advanced functions that can help the searching process, in terms of both the searching process and the results returned.

Using Server Referrals

If you are running your AD programs in an AD tree environment, multiple domains can be accessed. If you specify a server address within your DirectorySearcher object, it is possible that the actual database object may be contained on a different server. If this is the case, the server you attempt to bind to will send you a server referral notice, which informs the program of the proper server to use to bind to the database object.

By default, the DirectorySearcher object will produce an exception when it receives a server referral. You can change this behavior by using the ReferralChasing property to define the DirectorySearcher object reaction when it receives a server referral notice from the server. Four options can be specified, each one enumerated by the ReferralChasingOption enumerator:

None   Specifies that the program does not follow server referrals and will throw an Exception.

Subordinate   Specifies that the program will follow server referrals for servers that contain subordinate objects in the directory tree.

External   Specifies that the program will follow server referrals for servers that are external to the local network.

All   Specifies that the program will follow all server referrals received by network directory service servers.

Limiting Searches

For searches on large network directory service databases, you may have to place limits on how much data is returned to prevent having applications appear to "lock-up" during a search. Use the following properties in the DirectorySearcher class to specify search limitations:

ClientTimeout   Allows you to set the amount of time (in seconds) to wait for an answer from the server before timing out and throwing an Exception.

PageSize Defines the maximum number of objects to return in a search. The default value is 0, which defines an unlimited number of objects.

If the `PageSize` property is set to a value larger than 0, and more objects are present in the returned results, the next search will pick up where the initial search left off. This allows an application to retrieve as many objects as necessary and continue the search until the proper object is found.

PropertyNamesOnly A `boolean` value. If it is set to `true`, the `DirectorySearcher` object returns only the names of the object properties without any data values. The default value is `false`.

ServerPageTimeLimit Allows the program to specify how long the server should spend (in seconds) looking for search results for an individual page (see the `PageSize` property definition). If the search exceeds the time limit, the server should return the results obtained up to the time limit, along with information about where to resume searching. The default value is -1, which defines no page time limit.

ServerTimeLimit Defines the total amount of time (in seconds) the server should spend processing a search query. If the time limit is exceeded, the server should return the results obtained up to the time limit, along with information about where to resume the search. The default value for this property is -1, indicating no server time limit.

SizeLimit Sets a total number of objects the server should return for a search. If more results are available, the server should disregard them. There is no way to continue searching from the `SizeLimit` point. Each network directory service server has its own set `SizeLimit` value. If the `SizeLimit` property is set to exceed the server default value, the server value will be used.

Summary

This chapter describes how to use the classes in the `System.DirectoryServices` namespace to access AD and other network directory service servers from your C# applications.

The Lightweight Directory Access Protocol (LDAP) defines network resources in a hierarchical network database. An object in the database represents each network resource, and each object contains attributes that define values for the resource. Devices on the network can access the database and retrieve information about each network resource.

Microsoft's AD, used in Windows 2000 Server networks, employs the LDAP model to store information about network resources in the domain. Information from multiple domains can be combined to form a tree, while multiple trees can be combined to form a forest. Network devices on the network access the AD database to retrieve information regarding users, passwords, printers, servers, and other network resources. AD uses the AD Services Interface (ADSI) to allow client workstations access to the AD server.

The .NET library includes the `DirectoryEntry` and `DirectorySearcher` classes to implement ADSI functionality from C# programs. The `DirectoryEntry` class binds a variable to a network directory object. Once the variable is bound to the object, you can use the variable to retrieve object and attribute information (called *properties* in .NET).

The `DirectorySearcher` class is used to form complex searches within the network directory to help extract information about network resources. The `Filter` property narrows the number of objects returned in a search, while the `PropertiesToLoad` property limits the number of object properties that are returned.

CHAPTER 16

Remoting

- Moving data, revisited

- Using a serialization class

- Problems with serialization

- What is remoting?

- Using remoting

- Creating a remote class proxy

- Creating the remoting server program

- Creating the remoting client program

One of the most exciting features of the .NET Framework is the ability to easily communicate with applications distributed across multiple computers, located on separate networks. *Remoting*, as supported by the .NET Framework, allows applications to share class data and methods among computers on the network, similar to the concept of web services, introduced in Chapter 14, "HTTP." With remoting, class methods can be hosted on a network device and called from any C# program, without the use of a Microsoft IIS server running on the device.

Remoting relies on data *serialization*, which was introduced back in Chapter 7, "Using the C# Sockets Helper Classes." Serialization allows class data elements of any datatype to be transmitted across a stream and reassembled. For remoting, the stream that transmits the data is, of course, a NetworkStream object.

This chapter begins by describing serialization and how you can use serialization without remoting to send data between network applications on network devices. Next, you'll examine the elements of .NET remoting and how they interact to provide a distributed computing environment for your C# network programs. Finally, you'll walk through an example of implementing remoting in your network programs.

Moving Data, Revisited

In Chapter 7 you learned how to convert complex C# classes into binary arrays that could be sent across the network to a remote system. As mentioned then, the .NET library contains classes that can do some of that work for you.

This section describes two classes that serialize data for transmission across a network, the BinaryFormatter and SoapFormatter classes. These classes can be used to easily convert class instances into a serial stream of bytes that can be sent across the network to a remote system and converted back into the original data.

Using a Serialization Class

There are three steps that are required to serialize a class and send it across the network:

1. Create a library object for the serialized class.

2. Write a sender program that creates instances of the serialized class and send it to a stream.

3. Write a receiver program to read data from the stream and re-create the original serialized class data.

Creating the Serialized Class

Each data class that transports data across the network must be tagged with the [Serializable] attribute in the source code file. This indicates that, by default, all of the data elements in the class will be serialized for transit. Listing 16.1 shows how to create a serialized version of the Employee class introduced in Chapter 7.

Listing 16.1   **The SerialEmployee.cs program**

```
using System;

[Serializable]
public class SerialEmployee
{
    public int EmployeeID;
    public string LastName;
    public string FirstName;
    public int YearsService;
    public double Salary;

    public SerialEmployee()
    {
        EmployeeID = 0;
        LastName = null;
        FirstName = null;
        YearsService = 0;
        Salary = 0.0;
    }
}
```

The SerialEmployee.cs file contains a class definition for the SerialEmployee class. The class contains the data elements used to track basic employee information, along with a simple default constructor for the class. Positioned before the class definition, the [Serializable] attribute indicates that the class can be converted to a serial stream of bytes using one of the formatter classes.

To use this class to transport employee data, you must first create a library file that can be compiled into application programs:

```
csc /t:library SerialEmployee.cs
```

The output from this command will be the SerialEmployee.dll file. This file must be included as a resource in any program that uses the SerialEmployee class.

WARNING In serialization, it is extremely important to remember that all applications that use the serialized data class *must* use the same data library file. When .NET creates the serialized data to send, the data stream includes the class name that defines the data. If the class name does not match when the data is read, the program will not be able to deserialize the stream into the original data class.

Creating a Sender Program

After you create the data class, you can build an application that uses instances of the new class and performs the serialization of the new data to a stream. As mentioned, the BinaryFormatter and SoapFormatter classes serialize the data.

BinaryFormatter serializes the data into a binary stream, much like the GetBytes() method of the Employee.cs program in Listing 7.11. In addition to the actual data, additional information, such as the class name and a version number, are added to the serialized data.

Alternatively, you can use the SoapFormatter class to pass the data using the XML format, similar to the technique used by the web service programs described in Chapter 14. The benefit of using XML is that it is portable between any system or application that recognizes the XML format.

First, you must create an instance of a Stream class to send the data across. This can be any type of stream, including a FileStream, MemoryStream, or of course, a NetworkStream. Next, you create an instance of the appropriate serialization class and use the Serialize() method to send the data across the Stream object:

```
Stream str = new FileStream(
    "testfile.bin", FileMode.Create, FileAccess.ReadWrite);
IFormatter formatter = new BinaryFormatter();
formatter.Serialize(str, data);
```

The IFormatter class creates an instance of the desired serialization class (either BinaryFormatter or SoapFormatter), and the data is serialized using the Serialize() method of the formatter.

To see what information is passed on the network in a serialized data class, you can use a FileStream object to save the output to a file and view the file. Listing 16.2 shows the SoapTest.cs program, which serializes two instances of the SerialEmployee class in a file using the SoapFormatter.

Listing 16.2   **The SoapTest.cs program**

```
using System;
using System.IO;
using System.Runtime.Serialization;
using System.Runtime.Serialization.Formatters.Soap;

class SoapTest
{
    public static void Main()
    {
        SerialEmployee emp1 = new SerialEmployee();
        SerialEmployee emp2 = new SerialEmployee();

        emp1.EmployeeID = 1;
        emp1.LastName = "Blum";
```

```
        emp1.FirstName = "Katie Jane";
        emp1.YearsService = 12;
        emp1.Salary = 35000.50;

        emp2.EmployeeID = 2;
        emp2.LastName = "Blum";
        emp2.FirstName = "Jessica";
        emp2.YearsService = 9;
        emp2.Salary = 23700.30;

        Stream str = new FileStream("soaptest.xml", FileMode.Create,
          FileAccess.ReadWrite);
        IFormatter formatter = new SoapFormatter();

        formatter.Serialize(str, emp1);
        formatter.Serialize(str, emp2);
        str.Close();
    }
}
```

The `SoapFormatter` class is found in the `System.Runtime.Serialization.Formatters.Soap`
namespace, so it must be declared with a `using` statement. If you want to use the `BinaryFormatter`
class instead, that is found in the `System.Runtime.Serialization.Formatters.Binary` namespace. The `IFormatter` interface is in the `System.Runtime.Serialization` namespace, so that
must also be included. After creating two instances of the `SerialEmployee` class, the program
generates a `FileStream` object pointing to a file to store the output in, and then uses the
`Serialize()` method to save the two instances to the stream.

To compile the program, remember to include the `SerialEmployee.dll` file as a resource:

```
csc /r:SerialEmployee.dll SoapTest.cs
```

After running the `SoapTest.exe` program, you can examine the `soaptest.xml` file that is
generated (Listing 16.3).

Listing 16.3   The soaptest.xml file

```
<SOAP-ENV:Envelope xmlns:xsi="http://www.w3.org/2001/XMLSchema-instance" ➥
xmlns:xsd="http://www.w3.org/2001/XMLSchema" xmlns:SOAP-ENC= ➥
"http://schemas.xmlsoap.org/soap/encoding/" xmlns:SOAP-ENV= ➥
"http://schemas.xmlsoap.org/soap/envelope/" xmlns:clr= ➥
"http://schemas.microsoft.com/soap/encoding/clr/1.0" SOAP-ENV:encodingStyle= ➥
"http://schemas.xmlsoap.org/soap/encoding/">
<SOAP-ENV:Body>
<a1:SerialEmployee id="ref-1" xmlns:a1= ➥
"http://schemas.microsoft.com/clr/assem/SerialEmployee%2C%20Version%3D0.➥
0.0.0%2C%20Culture%3Dneutral%2C%20PublicKeyToken%3Dnull">
<EmployeeID>1</EmployeeID>
<LastName id="ref-3">Blum</LastName>
<FirstName id="ref-4">Katie Jane</FirstName>
<YearsService>12</YearsService>
```

```
<Salary>35000.5</Salary>
</a1:SerialEmployee>
</SOAP-ENV:Body>
</SOAP-ENV:Envelope>
<SOAP-ENV:Envelope xmlns:xsi="http://www.w3.org/2001/XMLSchema-instance" ➡
xmlns:xsd="http://www.w3.org/2001/XMLSchema" xmlns:SOAP-ENC= ➡
"http://schemas.xmlsoap.org/soap/encoding/" xmlns:SOAP-ENV= ➡
"http://schemas.xmlsoap.org/soap/envelope/" xmlns:clr= ➡
"http://schemas.microsoft.com/soap/encoding/clr/1.0" SOAP-ENV:encodingStyle= ➡
"http://schemas.xmlsoap.org/soap/encoding/">
<SOAP-ENV:Body>
<a1:SerialEmployee id="ref-1" xmlns:a1= ➡
"http://schemas.microsoft.com/clr/assem/SerialEmployee%2C%20Version%3D0.➡
0.0.0%2C%20Culture%3Dneutral%2C%20PublicKeyToken%3Dnull">
<EmployeeID>2</EmployeeID>
<LastName id="ref-3">Blum</LastName>
<FirstName id="ref-4">Jessica</FirstName>
<YearsService>9</YearsService>
<Salary>23700.3</Salary>
</a1:SerialEmployee>
</SOAP-ENV:Body>
</SOAP-ENV:Envelope>
```

By looking over the `soaptest.xml` file, you can see how SOAP defines each data element in the serialized class. One important feature of the XML data to notice are the following lines:

```
<a1:SerialEmployee id="ref-1" xmlns:a1= ➡
"http://schemas.microsoft.com/clr/assem/SerialEmployee%2C%20Version%3D0.➡
0.0.0.%2C%20Culture%3Dneutral%2C%20PublicKeyToken%3Dnull">
```

Here, the actual class name for the serialized data class is used within the XML definition data. This is important If the receiving program uses a different class name to define the same data class, it will not match with the XML data read from the stream. The classes must match or the read will fail.

NOTE   As demonstrated in Listing 16.3, though the `SoapFormatter` adds the ability to communicate class information with other systems, it can greatly increase the amount of data sent in the transmission.

Now that you have seen how the data is serialized, you can write a network application that serializes the class data and sends it to a program running on a remote device. Listing 16.4 shows the `BinaryDataSender.cs` program, which uses the `BinaryFormatter` class to send the `SerialEmployee` data.

⟳ **Listing 16.4**   **The BinaryDataSender.cs program**

```
using System;
using System.Net;
```

```
using System.Net.Sockets;
using System.Runtime.Serialization;
using System.Runtime.Serialization.Formatters.Binary;

class BinaryDataSender
{
    public static void Main()
    {
        SerialEmployee emp1 = new SerialEmployee();
        SerialEmployee emp2 = new SerialEmployee();

        emp1.EmployeeID = 1;
        emp1.LastName = "Blum";
        emp1.FirstName = "Katie Jane";
        emp1.YearsService = 12;
        emp1.Salary = 35000.50;

        emp2.EmployeeID = 2;
        emp2.LastName = "Blum";
        emp2.FirstName = "Jessica";
        emp2.YearsService = 9;
        emp2.Salary = 23700.30;

        TcpClient client = new TcpClient("127.0.0.1", 9050);
        IFormatter formatter = new BinaryFormatter();
        NetworkStream strm = client.GetStream();

        formatter.Serialize(strm, emp1);
        formatter.Serialize(strm, emp2);
        strm.Close();
        client.Close();
    }
}
```

The BinaryDataSender program uses the BinaryFormatter to serialize two instances of the SerialEmployee class and sends it to a remote device specified in the TcpClient object. After the two instances are sent, both the Stream and the TcpClient objects are closed.

NOTE   Because both the BinaryFormatter and SoapFormatter classes require a Stream object to send the serialized data, you must use either a TCP Socket object, or a TcpClient object to send the data. You cannot directly use UDP with the serializers.

Creating a Receiver Program

The third and final step in moving the class data across the network is to build a program that can read the data from the stream and assemble it back into the original class data elements. Again, this is done using either the BinaryFormatter or SoapFormatter classes. Obviously, you must use the same class that was used to serialize the data on the sender.

When the formatter classes deserialize the data, the data elements are extracted into a generic `Object` object. You must typecast the output to the appropriate class to extract the data elements:

```
IFormatter formatter = new BinaryFormatter();
SerialEmployee emp1 = (SerialEmployee)formatter.Deserialize(str);
```

When the data is received from the stream, it is reassembled into the appropriate data class elements. You should take care to ensure that the proper amount of data is present to reconstruct the data class.

Listing 16.5 shows the `BinaryDataRcvr.cs` program, which accepts the serialized data from the `BinaryDataSender` program and re-creates the original data classes.

Listing 16.5   The BinaryDataRcvr.cs program

```csharp
using System;
using System.Net;
using System.Net.Sockets;
using System.Runtime.Serialization;
using System.Runtime.Serialization.Formatters.Binary;

class BinaryDataRcvr
{
    public static void Main()
    {
        TcpListener server = new TcpListener(9050);
        server.Start();
        TcpClient client = server.AcceptTcpClient();
        NetworkStream strm = client.GetStream();
        IFormatter formatter = new BinaryFormatter();

        SerialEmployee emp1 = (SerialEmployee)formatter.Deserialize(strm);
        Console.WriteLine("emp1.EmployeeID = {0}", emp1.EmployeeID);
        Console.WriteLine("emp1.LastName = {0}", emp1.LastName);
        Console.WriteLine("emp1.FirstName = {0}", emp1.FirstName);
        Console.WriteLine("emp1.YearsService = {0}", emp1.YearsService);
        Console.WriteLine("emp1.Salary = {0}\n", emp1.Salary);

        SerialEmployee emp2 = (SerialEmployee)formatter.Deserialize(strm);
        Console.WriteLine("emp2.EmployeeID = {0}", emp2.EmployeeID);
        Console.WriteLine("emp2.LastName = {0}", emp2.LastName);
        Console.WriteLine("emp2.FirstName = {0}", emp2.FirstName);
        Console.WriteLine("emp2.YearsService = {0}", emp2.YearsService);
        Console.WriteLine("emp2.Salary = {0}", emp2.Salary);
        strm.Close();
        server.Stop();
    }
}
```

The `BinaryDataRcvr` program creates a `TcpListener` object bound to a specific port and waits for a connection attempt from the `BinaryDataSender` program. When the connection is established, the `Deserialize()` method converts the received data stream back into the original data class.

This example used simple datatypes, but you can easily modify it to add more complex datatypes, such as an employee start date. Just add the new data elements to the `SerialEmployee.cs` file, re-create the DLL library file, and rebuild the sender and receiver programs.

Problems with Serialization

While the serializing examples so far show a simple technique for serializing and transmitting complex data classes, in the real world, on real networks, it is not often this easy. You may have noticed that the `BinaryDataSender` and `BinaryDataRcvr` programs assumed one important thing: they both expected all of the data to arrive at the receiver for the `BinaryFormatter` to deserialize the stream into the original class data. As you probably know by now, this is not necessarily what occurs on a real network.

If not all of the data is received on the stream before the `Deserialize()` method is performed, there will be a problem. When the `Deserialize()` method does not have enough bytes to complete the reassembly, it produces an `Exception`, and the data class is not properly created. The solution to this is to use a hybrid technique, combining the serialization classes presented here with the data sizing methods demonstrated back in Chapter 7. If you send the size of each serialized data object before the actual object, the receiver can determine how many bytes of data to receive before attempting to deserialize the data.

The easiest way to do this is to serialize the data coming from the stream into a `MemoryStream` object. The `MemoryStream` object holds all of the serialized data in a memory buffer. It allows you to easily determine the total size of the serialized data. When the size of the data stream is determined, both the size value and the serialized data buffer can be sent out the `NetworkStream` to the remote device.

Listing 16.6 shows the `BetterDataSender.cs` program, which uses this technique to transmit two instances of the `SerialEmployee` data class to a remote device.

Listing 16.6   The BetterDataSender.cs program

```
using System;
using System.IO;
using System.Net;
using System.Net.Sockets;
```

```
using System.Runtime.Serialization;
using System.Runtime.Serialization.Formatters.Soap;

class BetterDataSender
{
   public void SendData (NetworkStream strm, SerialEmployee emp)
   {
      IFormatter formatter = new SoapFormatter();
      MemoryStream memstrm = new MemoryStream();

      formatter.Serialize(memstrm, emp);
      byte[] data = memstrm.GetBuffer();
      int memsize = (int)memstrm.Length;
      byte[] size = BitConverter.GetBytes(memsize);
      strm.Write(size, 0, 4);
      strm.Write(data, 0, memsize);
      strm.Flush();
      memstrm.Close();
   }

   public BetterDataSender()
   {
      SerialEmployee emp1 = new SerialEmployee();
      SerialEmployee emp2 = new SerialEmployee();

      emp1.EmployeeID = 1;
      emp1.LastName = "Blum";
      emp1.FirstName = "Katie Jane";
      emp1.YearsService = 12;
      emp1.Salary = 35000.50;

      emp2.EmployeeID = 2;
      emp2.LastName = "Blum";
      emp2.FirstName = "Jessica";
      emp2.YearsService = 9;
      emp2.Salary = 23700.30;

      TcpClient client = new TcpClient("127.0.0.1", 9050);
      NetworkStream strm = client.GetStream();

      SendData(strm, emp1);
      SendData(strm, emp2);
      strm.Close();
      client.Close();
   }

   public static void Main()
   {
      BetterDataSender bds = new BetterDataSender();
   }
}
```

The BetterDataSender program uses the SendData() method to create a MemoryStream object with the serialized data to send to the remote device. From the MemoryStream object, the size of the data is determined and sent to the remote receiver. Then the serialized data MemoryStream buffer is sent to the remote receiver.

Now take a look at the BetterDataRcvr.cs program, Listing 16.7, which demonstrates how to reassemble the received data size and serialized data from the sender.

Listing 16.7   The BetterDataRcvr.cs program

```
using System;
using System.IO;
using System.Net;
using System.Net.Sockets;
using System.Runtime.Serialization;
using System.Runtime.Serialization.Formatters.Soap;

class BetterDataRcvr
{
    private SerialEmployee RecvData (NetworkStream strm)
    {
        MemoryStream memstrm = new MemoryStream();
        byte[] data = new byte[4];
        int recv = strm.Read(data, 0, 4);
        int size = BitConverter.ToInt32(data, 0);
        int offset = 0;
        while(size > 0)
        {
            data = new byte[1024];
            recv = strm.Read(data, 0, size);
            memstrm.Write(data, offset, recv);
            offset += recv;
            size -= recv;
        }
        IFormatter formatter = new SoapFormatter();
        memstrm.Position = 0;
        SerialEmployee emp = (SerialEmployee)formatter.Deserialize(memstrm);
        memstrm.Close();
        return emp;
    }

    public BetterDataRcvr()
    {
        TcpListener server = new TcpListener(9050);
        server.Start();
        TcpClient client = server.AcceptTcpClient();
        NetworkStream strm = client.GetStream();

        SerialEmployee emp1 = RecvData(strm);
        Console.WriteLine("emp1.EmployeeID = {0}", emp1.EmployeeID);
```

```
        Console.WriteLine("emp1.LastName = {0}", emp1.LastName);
        Console.WriteLine("emp1.FirstName = {0}", emp1.FirstName);
        Console.WriteLine("emp1.YearsService = {0}", emp1.YearsService);
        Console.WriteLine("emp1.Salary = {0}\n", emp1.Salary);

        SerialEmployee emp2 = RecvData(strm);
        Console.WriteLine("emp2.EmployeeID = {0}", emp2.EmployeeID);
        Console.WriteLine("emp2.LastName = {0}", emp2.LastName);
        Console.WriteLine("emp2.FirstName = {0}", emp2.FirstName);
        Console.WriteLine("emp2.YearsService = {0}", emp2.YearsService);
        Console.WriteLine("emp2.Salary = {0}", emp2.Salary);
        strm.Close();
        server.Stop();
    }

    public static void Main()
    {
        BetterDataRcvr bdr = new BetterDataRcvr();
    }
}
```

The BetterDataRcvr program uses the RecvData() method to obtain the incoming data from the sender. First, a 4-byte size value come in. This value indicates how many bytes to expect in the serialized data portion of the transmission. The RecvData() method then goes into a loop until all of the expected bytes are received from the NetworkStream. As the bytes arrive, they are added to a MemoryStream object. When all of the bytes have been received, the MemoryStream object creates the data class instance.

WARNING It is important to remember that the MemoryStream object must be reset to point to the start of the stream before being used in the Deserialize() method.

To test the BetterDataSender and BetterDataRcvr programs, you must compile them with the same SerialEmployee.dll file.

NOTE The BinaryFormatter and SoapFormatter take care of any network byte order issues when transferring the data to the remote host.

An Overview of Remoting

In addition to sending class data among network devices, the .NET architecture provides a technique for sending entire class method information across the network. Similar to web services, which was introduced in Chapter 14, remoting allows you to share C# class methods between machines on a network. Unlike web services, remoting does not require any additional server software to process incoming requests. It is easy to use .NET remoting to incorporate distributed computing in your network applications.

The idea behind remoting is to utilize computing resources on other systems on the network. Remoting enables you to write applications that provide application services to anyone on the network. You'll need five elements to build a .NET remoting application:

- A remoting class that provides C# methods used by client applications on the network.

- A remoting server, which hosts the remoting class, allowing network clients to connect and process method calls.

- A communication channel that passes method calls from the network client to the remoting server and returns the results back to the network client.

- A *proxy class*, which runs on the client machine. The proxy class accepts method calls from the client and passes them through the communication channel to the remote class.

- A client application, which passes method calls to the proxy class, and interprets information returned from the remoting class through the proxy class.

Figure 16.1 shows how the .NET remoting pieces fit together.

FIGURE 16.1:

The .NET remoting framework

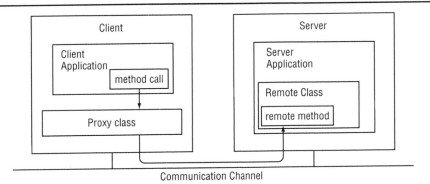

The Remote Class

The remote class used in .NET remoting provides the data elements and methods advertised by the remoting server to clients. Until now, all of the programs were contained in a single *application domain*. An application domain is defined as an area where all of the applications share the same memory space. Any class that is outside of the application domain of a client is considered a remote class. This is shown in Figure 16.2.

FIGURE 16.2:

The application
domain of a client

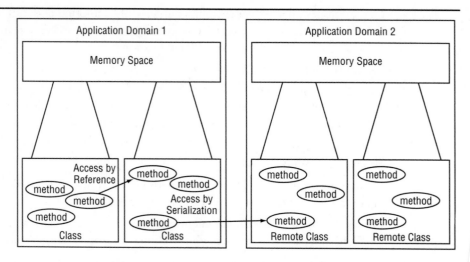

Also bear in mind that remote classes don't necessarily have to be on remote devices. A single workstation can contain multiple application domains. Instead of a physical barrier between the domains (such as a network), a security barrier is present, with the operating system's security rules providing the separation between the application domains. When classes are outside the application domain, they cannot directly access each other by reference (there is no shared memory area). Instead, each class instance must be serialized and passed through a communication channel to the other client application.

The Remoting Server

The remoting server is a C# application program that interfaces with the .NET remoting system and the remote class. It does this by registering the remote class in the application domain on the machine and listening for incoming requests on a specific communication channel. There are two techniques with which the remoting server can process incoming requests on the remote class:

SingleCall object mode   The SingleCall mode creates a new instance of the remote class object for each incoming client request. When the client connection is terminated, the class instance is deleted. No state information can be shared between client requests. The SingleCall object mode is used when it is important to separate information between class instances.

Singleton object mode   In contrast, the Singleton mode uses one instance of the remote class object to handle all incoming requests. Singleton mode allows you to build server applications that have persistent data between client connections on the server. The Singleton mode object has a set lifetime to hold the remote class state information. When the lifetime expires, the remote class object is deleted. If a new client request is received, a new remote class object is created. The Singleton object mode is used when it is important to share class instances for performance reasons.

The Communication Channel

The .NET remoting system relies heavily on communication channels to pass remote class information to clients. As each client accesses a remote class, information about the class methods, method parameters, and method return values must be passed between the devices. This can occur via raw TCP communication, which passes serialized class information directly using TCP on a designated port. Or an HTTP communication channel can be used, which provides a standard communication technique for passing data between the client and the remote class.

WARNING   When using multiple remoting classes on a single device, you must remember that only one communication per port per channel can be used.

The Proxy Class

The proxy class on the client machine represents the remote class methods that can be accessed on the remoting server. The proxy class offers an interface for the client programs to access the remote classes running on the remote server.

It is the responsibility of the proxy class to serialize the data and pass it to the remote class server. Conversely, it is also the proxy class's responsibility to deserialize any incoming data and place it in the proper class data elements for the client programs.

Without the proxy class, the client application would not know how the class data elements are formatted, or what datatypes to use for the data elements.

The Client Program

For a client program to use the class methods in the remote class, the client must know what methods are available and how to access them. The client program must be compiled with a proxy class to determine the format of the remote class methods. All references to the remote class methods are passed to the proxy class for processing.

The client program has two options for contacting the remote class methods, to register a communication channel to use for the remote class itself and handle all communication with the remote class, using the proxy class for the remote class method information, or to allow the proxy class to register the communication channel and handle all of the communication.

Both techniques have their pros and cons. If you allow the proxy class to handle all of the communication channel requirements, the client program becomes less complicated, but it is tied to one specific communication channel. On the other hand, if the client program handles the communication channel, it can be changed as necessary if the remote class moves to a different server.

Using Remoting

There are three separate programs that must be created to build an application that uses remoting:

- A remote class that allows clients to access and use the methods contained in the class.
- A server program that advertises and hosts the server class on a machine
- A client program that uses the server class methods

This section describes how to configure each of these parts so you can create C# network programs that utilize remoting.

Creating the Remote Class Proxy

Each remoting application requires a set of methods that can be accessed by clients on a network. Like serialization classes, these methods must be contained in a special class and compiled into a proxy library object that is used in the server and client programs.

To identify a class as a remote class, it must be derived from the `MarshalByRefObject` class. This allows clients to access the remote class methods by reference through a proxy. Listing 16.8 is the `MathClass.cs` program, which defines a class to use as a remote class in the example programs.

Listing 16.8   **The MathClass.cs program**

```
using System;

public class MathClass       MarshalByRefObject
{
    public int Add(int a, int b)
    {
      int c = a + b;
      return c;
    }

    public int Subtract(int a, int b)
    {
       int c = a - b;
       return c;
    }

    public int Multiply(int a, int b)
    {
       int c = a * b;
       return c;
    }

    public int Divide(int a, int b)
```

```
    {
        int c;
        if (b != 0)
            c = a / b;
        else
            c = 0;
        return c;
    }
}
```

The `MathClass` class is derived from the `MarshalByRegObject` class, which means it can be a remote class in a server program. It defines four common math functions that can be called by remote network clients. Each function receives two parameters from the client and returns the corresponding value, which will be sent back to the client.

Similar to the serialization technique, you must make a library DLL file from the remote class program. This is done using the `/t:library` option of the `csc` compiler:

```
csc /t:library MathClass.cs
```

The `MathClass.dll` file contains all the information necessary for the server and client applications to access the data elements and methods in the remote class.

WARNING   Also similar to the serialization technique, you must ensure that the same proxy class library file defines the remote class for both the server and client programs. If a different proxy class library is used for each program, the serialization will not work, and the remoting function will fail. Also remember that the proxy class library is referenced by class name, not filename. Make sure that the class library references the proper class name.

Creating the Server Program

The server program hosts the remote class on the network, accepting requests from clients and passing them to the remote class. The server program must register a channel to support the communication with the remote class and then register the remote class as a service in the .NET remoting server.

There are three steps to building the server program for the remote class:

1. Create a communication channel to support access to the remote class.

2. Register the communication channel with the remoting channel services.

3. Register the remote class as a service with the remoting services.

Create a Communication Channel

First, a communication channel must be defined. .NET remoting has two separate classes for the two types of communication channels used for network access: `TcpChannel` and `HttpChannel`.

TcpChannel   The TcpChannel class, defined in the System.Runtime.Remoting .Channels.Tcp namespace, receives and sends data in a binary format within TCP packets for the remote class. The TcpChannel class instance is created using the TCP port that will listen for incoming requests for the remote class:

```
TcpChannel chan = new TcpChannel(9050);
```

By default, the TcpChannel class uses the BinaryFormatter class to serialize all data sent and received on the channel.

HttpChannel   The HttpChannel class, defined in the System.Runtime.Remoting .Channels.Http namespace, sends data using the SOAP format within an HTTP session for the remote class. The HttpChannel instance also uses a TCP port number to accept HTTP requests on for the remote class:

```
HttpChannel chan = new HttpChannel(9050);
```

By default, the Httpchannel class uses the SoapFormatter class to serialize all data received and sent on the channel.

Register the Communication Channel

After you create either the TcpChannel or HttpChannel object, it must be registered with the system before it can receive network messages. The RegisterChannel() method of the ChannelServices class registers new channels on the system. The ChannelServices class is found in the System.Runtime.Remoting.Channels namespace:

```
ChannelServices.RegisterChannel(chan);
```

The sole parameter *(chan)* identifies the channel to register, which can be either a TcpChannel or a HttpChannel object:

Register the Remote Class Service

After the communication channel is created and registered, the server program must register the remote class as a service on the system. The System.Runtime.Remoting namespace contains the RemotingConfiguration class, which configures a new service for the remoting system. This class specifies the configuration parameters used when registering the service with the remoting service. The parameters that must be specified are shown in Table 16.1.

TABLE 16.1: The RemotingConfiguration Parameters

Parameter	Description
type	The full type name of the remote class object, along with the assembly filename where the class is defined
objectUri	The URI of the remote class object
mode	How the server will handle calls to the remote class object

The `type` parameter specifies both the class name and the DLL filename where the remote class definition can be found. Because the `MathClass` example used the same name for the DLL filename as the class name, it would be defined as the following:

```
type="MathClass, MathClass"
```

The `objectUri` parameter defines a unique URI value to represent the remote class on the server. This value does not have to be related to the remote class name in any way, but to avoid confusion on servers with multiple remote classes, it often helps to make it somewhat related to the class name used.

You must also specify whether to use the `SingleCall` or `Singleton` object mode to handle incoming requests for the remote class. This is done with the mode option:

```
mode = "SingleCall"
```

After determining the `RemotingConfiguration` parameters necessary for defining the remote class on the remoting server, you must declare them in the server program. There are two ways to do this, either using a separate configuration file (using XML format), or through statements within the server program.

Using a Separate Configuration File
When you use a configuration file, it contains XML tags to identify the required parameters for the `RemotingConfigutation` object. Listing 16.9 shows a sample configuration file for defining the `MathClass` remote class on the server.

Listing 16.9   The server.xml configuration file]

```
<configuration>
    <system.runtime.remoting>
        <application>
            <service>
                <wellknown
                    type="MathClass, MathClass"
                    objectUri="MyMathServer"
                    mode="SingleCall"
                />
            </service>
        </application>
    </system.runtime.remoting>
</configuration>
```

After the configuration file is created, you must use the `Configure()` method to read the parameters from the file. The following example assumes that the `server.xml` file is located in the same directory as the server program:

```
RemotingConfiguration.Configure("server.xml");
```

If that is not the case, a full path name must reference the configuration file.

Using Program Statements

Instead of using a separate configuration file, the `RegisterWellKnownServiceType()` method can define the properties of the remote class within the application program:

```
RemotingConfiguration.RegisterWellknownServiceType(
    Type.GetType("MathClass, MathClass"), "MyMathServer",
    WellKnownObjectMode.SingleCall);
```

The same parameters in the configuration file are defined within the `RegisterWellknownServiceType()` method.

The drawback to defining the parameters in the program statements is that they are not easily changeable in dynamic environments. If your application is in an environment that will not change, defining the parameters using the `RegisterWellknownServiceType()` method may perform better.

The Full Server Program

Putting all of the pieces together, the `MathServer.cs` program (Listing 16.10) demonstrates how to create a remoting server program that hosts the remote class object.

Listing 16.10   The MathServer.cs program

```
using System;
using System.Runtime.Remoting;
using System.Runtime.Remoting.Channels;
using System.Runtime.Remoting.Channels.Http;


public class MathServer
{
   public static int Main()
   {
      HttpChannel chan = new HttpChannel(9050);
      ChannelServices.RegisterChannel(chan);
      RemotingConfiguration.RegisterWellKnownServiceType(
         Type.GetType("MathClass, MathClass"), "MyMathServer",
         WellKnownObjectMode.SingleCall);
      Console.WriteLine("Hit <enter> to exit...");
      Console.ReadLine();
      return 0;
   }
}
```

The `MathServer` program creates and registers an `HttpChannel` using port 9050 to receive requests for the `MathClass` remote class object. Once the information is registered, the server program must stay active for the service to accept incoming requests. Once the program exits, the service will be removed from the remoting system. To ensure the server program remains active, a simple `Console.ReadLine()` method waits for an Enter key from the keyboard.

The server program must be compiled with the `MathClass.dll` file so it knows about the `MathClass` remote class definitions:

```
csc /r:MathClass.dll MathServer.cs
```

Creating the Client Program

The client program connects to the server program and utilizes the methods hosted in the remote class object. Similar to the server program, the client program must create a communication channel (the same type the server uses), and must register the channel with the local remoting system on the client machine:

```
HttpChannel chan = new HttpChannel();
ChannelServices.RegisterChannel(chan);
```

Because the client program does not need to listen to a specific port, it does not need to specify a port number in the `HttpChannel` constructor.

After the channel is created and registered, you can instantiate the proxy class to create an object of the remote class. This proxy class mimics the functionality of the remote class for local calls. When the proxy receives a call to a method for the remote class, it passes the call via the established communication channel to the server. The server receives the call and passes it to the remote class, which processes the call and passes any return information through the server program back to the proxy class.

There are two ways of creating the proxy object in the client program:

- Registering the remote class as a client type in the remoting system and creating a new instance of the remote class for the proxy class

- Using the `Activator` class to register the remote class information for the proxy class

Registering the Remote Class Proxy Object

Similar to the server program registering the remote class, the client program can also use the `RemotingConfiguration` class to register the information needed to make a proxy object that contacts the remote class server. The `Activator` class in the `System` namespace is used for this. This class creates proxy objects that pass method calls from an application to the appropriate location, either within the local program, or in the case of remoting, to the appropriate remote URI location of the remote class. The `GetObject()` method defines the location of the remote class for the proxy object.

The `GetObject()` method requires two parameters, the type of the remote class and the URI to which to pass requests:

```
Activator.GetObject(Type objecttype, string uri)
```

The *objecttype* parameter defines the remote class name that is used, while the *uri* parameter defines where to access the remote class.

The Full Client Program

The `MathClient.cs` program in Listing 16.11 demonstrates how to create a client program that can access the remote class methods hosted by the server.

Listing 16.11   The MathClient.cs program

```
using System;
using System.Runtime.Remoting;
using System.Runtime.Remoting.Channels;
using System.Runtime.Remoting.Channels.Http;

public class MathClient
{
    public static int Main (string[] argv)
    {

        HttpChannel chan = new HttpChannel();
        ChannelServices.RegisterChannel(chan);
        MathClass obj = (MathClass)Activator.GetObject(
            typeof(MathClass), "http://127.0.0.1:9050/MyMathServer");
        if (obj == null)
            System.Console.WriteLine("Could not locate server");
        else
        {
            int a = Convert.ToInt32(argv[0]);
            int b = Convert.ToInt32(argv[1]);
            int c = obj.Add(a, b);
            Console.WriteLine("a + b = {0}", c);
            c = obj.Subtract(a, b);
            Console.WriteLine("a - b = {0}", c);
            c = obj.Multiply(a, b);
            Console.WriteLine("a * b = {0}", c);
            c = obj.Divide(a, b);
            Console.WriteLine("a / b = {0}", c);
        }
        return 0;
    }
}
```

After the proxy object is created, the `MathClient` program proceeds to use the various class methods defined in the `MathClass` class to process data. Each time a class method is called, the proxy class forwards the data across the network to the server program, which processes the data and returns the result to the proxy class.

You can test the programs out and see that the `MathClient` functions work as advertised:

```
C:\>MathClient 1 5
a + b = 6
```

```
a - b = -4
a * b = 5
a / b = 0

C:\>MathClient 100 50
a + b = 150
a - b = 50
a * b = 5000
a / b = 2

C:\>
```

If you are using separate devices to run the MathServer and MathClient programs (assuming you changed the URL in the client program), you can use the WinDump or Analyzer programs to watch the transactions as they cross the network. Because an HttpChannel channel was used for communication, all of the transactions will be in XML format, which makes it easier to read.

Creating a Proxy Class Using soapsuds

The remoting example shown in this chapter assumed one important fact - that you were in control of both the remoting server and the client application. In the real world, this may not be (and often is not) the case. You may run into a situation where you are asked to write a client application that uses the methods hosted by a remoting server without much (if any) knowledge of how the remote class is defined. This section describes how you can build a remoting client application even if you don't have the original remote class file used to create the client.

Viewing the Remote Class Interfaces

When the HttpChannel is used for communication with the remoting server, the remote class definition can be viewed using a normal web browser. The URI registered for the remoting server represents how the remote class is accessed via the web. To see the class interfaces, you must add the tag ?wsdl to the end of the URI:

```
http://192.168.1.100:9050/MyMathServer?wsdl
```

This URI produces the standard SOAP web page that defines the MathClass class in Listing 16.8. Each of the individual methods in the class is defined within the Web Services Definition Language (WSDL) page, along with definitions for each of the parameters and return values. Figure 16.3 illustrates part of the WSDL definition.

FIGURE 16.3:

The `MathClass` WSDL definition

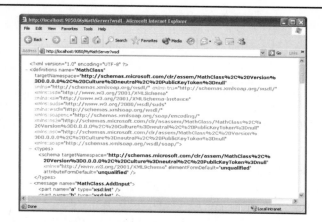

Instead of manually creating the library DLL file for the remoting proxy class, you can do it with the WSDL definition and the `soapsuds` program.

The soapsuds Program

The .NET Framework SDK package contains the `soapsuds` program, which extracts class information from remote classes (you may remember this function from the `wsdl` program, which was discussed in the "Web Services" section in Chapter 14). The extracted information forms the DLL proxy file necessary to communicate with the remote class from a client application.

The `soapsuds` program offers a healthy collection of command-line options that produce many features, as described in Table 16.2.

TABLE 16.2:   The soapsuds Command-Line Options

Option	Specifies
`-d:domain`	The domain name to use when connecting to a server
`-gc`	To generate C# code for the connected server
`-hpn:name`	An HTTP proxy server to use to connect to the server
`-hpp:port`	An HTTP proxy port to use to connect to the server
`-ia:file`	An input assembly file
`-id:dir`	Location of the input DLL files
`-is:file`	The input XML schema file
`-nowp`	Not to create a wrapped proxy
`-oa:file`	The file to save the output information
`-od:dir`	The directory of the output file

Continued on next page

TABLE 16.2 CONTINUED: The soapsuds Command-Line Options

Option	Specifies
-os:file	The file to save the XML schema information
-p:password	A password to use to connect to the server
-pn:namespace	The proxy namespace for the code in the generated proxy file
-sdl	To generate Service Description Language (SDL) formatted files
-se:url	The URL for the service endpoint to place in the output file
-sn:file	The file that contains the key pair used to sign the assembly
-types:info	The input type list
-url:url	The URL of the service from which to retrieve the XML schema
-u:username	The user name that connects to the server
-wp	To create a wrapped proxy
-wsdl	To generate Web Services Description Language (WSDL) formatted files

Of all these command-line options, the most common are the -url option (to specify the remote class URI), and the -oa option (to specify the DLL file to store the information).

Building the Proxy Class

The following command creates a basic DLL proxy file to replace the original remote class file:

```
soapsuds -url:http://192.168.1.100:9050/MyMathServer?wsdl
 -oa:MathClass.dll -nowp
```

The resulting MathClass.dll file then creates the client application; this is just like the original class file that was manually created (see Listing 16.8). You can also add the -gc command-line option to generate the C# code that created the DLL file (see Listing 16.13).

Listing 16.13   **The soapsuds-generated MathClass.cs file**

```
using System;
using System.Runtime.Remoting.Messaging;
using System.Runtime.Remoting.Metadata;
using System.Runtime.Remoting.Metadata.W3cXsd2001;
[Serializable, SoapType(XmlNamespace=@"http://schemas.microsoft.com/clr/assem/
➥ MathClass%2C%20Version%3D0.0.0.0%2C%20Culture%3Dneutral%2C%20PublicKeyToken%3
➥ Dnull", %3D0.0.0.0%2C%20Culture%3Dneutral%2C%20PublicKeyToken%3Dnull")]
public class MathClass : System.MarshalByRefObject
{
    [SoapMethod(SoapAction=@"http://schemas.microsoft.com/clr/nsassem/
    ➥ MathClass/MathClass#Add")]
    public Int32 Add(Int32 a, Int32 b)
    {
        return((Int32) (Object) null);
```

```
    }
[SoapMethod(SoapAction=@"http://schemas.microsoft.com/clr/nsassem/
➡ MathClass/MathClass#Subtract")]
public Int32 Subtract(Int32 a, Int32 b)
{
    return((Int32) (Object) null);
}
[SoapMethod(SoapAction=@"http://schemas.microsoft.com/clr/nsassem/
➡ MathClass/MathClass#Multiply")]
public Int32 Multiply(Int32 a, Int32 b)
{
    return((Int32) (Object) null);
}
[SoapMethod(SoapAction=@"http://schemas.microsoft.com/clr/nsassem/
➡ MathClass/MathClass#Divide")]
public Int32 Divide(Int32 a, Int32 b)
{
    return((Int32) (Object) null);
}

}
```

The proxy class file generated by `soapsuds` reproduces the code for the remote class, showing how each class method is defined and what parameters are within the class. After `soapsuds` creates the DLL file, you can write the client program, just you did when the DLL file was manually created:

```
csc /r:MathClass.dll MathClient.cs
```

The `MathClient.exe` file generated by this compile behaves exactly as the executable generated from the original proxy class file in Listing 16.11.

Using Wrapped Proxies

In the previous `soapsuds` example, which generated Listing 16.13, the -nowp option produced the generic code to access the remote class. This allows the client to access the remote class from whatever remoting server the class is hosted on. The `RemotingConfiguration` information is compiled into the client application to determine from where the remote class will be accessed.

Alternatively, if you do not include the -nowp option on the `soapsuds` command line, `soapsuds` creates a *wrapped proxy*, which handles all of the remoting communication configuration features. This includes building a constructor of the remote class, indicating how to connect to the URI specified in the soapsuds command. If you use the -gc command-line option, you can see the class constructor section:

```
// Constructor
    public MathClass()
    {
        base.ConfigureProxy(this.GetType(), @"http://192.168.1.100:9050/ ➥
MyMathServer");
    }
```

When using the wrapped proxy option, the class constructor created specifies exactly where the remote class can be accessed, so no RemotingConfiguration section is needed in the client application. All the client needs to create is an instance of the remote class; the remoting system automatically knows how to access the class methods. Listing 16.14 shows the NewMathClient.cs program, which uses this technique to access the remote class.

Listing 16.14   The NewMathClient.cs program

```
using System;
using System.Runtime.Remoting;
using System.Runtime.Remoting.Channels;
using System.Runtime.Remoting.Channels.Http;

public class NewMathClient
{
    public static int Main(string[] argv)
    {
        HttpChannel chan = new HttpChannel();
        ChannelServices.RegisterChannel(chan);
        MathClass obj = new MathClass();
        if (obj == null)
            System.Console.WriteLine("Could not locate server");
        else
        {
            int a = Convert.ToInt32(argv[0]);
            int b = Convert.ToInt32(argv[1]);
            int c = obj.Add(a, b);
            Console.WriteLine("a + b = {0}", c);
            c = obj.Subtract(a, b);
            Console.WriteLine("a - b = {0}", c);
            c = obj.Multiply(a, b);
            Console.WriteLine("a * b = {0}", c);
            c = obj.Divide(a, b);
            Console.WriteLine("a / b = {0}", c);
        }
        return 0;
    }
}
```

Notice that using the wrapped proxy DLL makes the actual client code cleaner. All you need to do is create a new `MathClass` object using the default constructor, and the proxy wrapper does the rest. However, as discussed, the network address information of the remote class server is hard-coded into the proxy class. If the remote class server changes, the proxy class must be re-created.

Performance Considerations

There are lots of remoting combinations: any combination of the two communication channels (TCP and HTTP) and two serialization formats (`BinaryFormatter` and `SoapFormatter`) can be used. If you are developing a brand new application, you may be confused about which combination would work best in your environment. Many developers assume that using standard protocols such as the HTTP channel and `SoapFormatter` work best in all situations. In tests published by Microsoft, however, it was found that using a TCP channel with `BinaryFormatter` has the highest throughput rate, significantly outperforming the HTTP/SOAP solution. If cross-platform compatibility is not an issue for your application, it may be best to use the TCP channel and `BinaryFormatter`.

Summary

The .NET Framework incorporates the concept of remoting, which allows applications to share methods between application domains, either on the same computer, or between separate computers on a network.

An important feature of remoting is the ability of a client to serialize class instances and pass them to a different application domain. The .NET library includes two serialization formatting classes, the `BinaryFormatter` and the `SoapFormatter`. Each of these classes can be used apart from remoting to help serialize data for transmission across a network connection.

While the `BinaryFormatter` and `SoapFormatter` classes help in the job of serializing data elements, you must still ensure all the data is properly sent across the network from the client to the server machines. You can incorporate techniques learned in Chapter 7 along with the serialization classes to ensure the data is properly delivered to the remote machine. By creating a separate buffer for the serialized data and sending the buffer size along with the buffer, you can ensure that the server receives the complete serialized data before attempting to deserialize the information.

The .NET remoting classes allow you to create a remote class whose methods can be accessed by any client on the network. The remote class must be derived from the `MarshalByRefObject` class to allow classes in remote application domains to access its methods and data elements.

For the client application to access the remote class, a proxy class must be created to accept method calls from the client, and pass them off to the remote class. The proxy class can be created either by the original data library of the remote class, or by interrogating the remote class using the `soapsuds` program. The `soapsuds` program allows you to determine the remote class interfaces necessary to properly access class methods without the original data class file.

The remote class must be registered in an application domain by a remoting server program. The remoting server registers the remote class within the .NET remoting system, along with a specific communication channel that can access the remote class. After all the pieces of the remoting system are in place, the client application can access methods in the remote class as if they were in the same application domain.

The next chapter dives into the sticky world of security within the .NET Framework. With the current emphasis on application security, Microsoft incorporated lots of security features with the .NET Framework that can be used in your C# network programs.

CHAPTER 17

Security

- Application security basics, including policies, groups, and permissions

- Tools for setting security policies: the `caspol` and `mscorcfg` programs

- Declarative and imperative socket permissions

- Implementing declarative socket permissions

- Protecting network data using encryption

With more and more hacking occurring on both the Internet and in local corporate networks, security has become a hot topic for most programmers. Network programming is no exception. Keeping your programs and data safe in a network environment is almost a fulltime job.

This chapter describes some of the .NET security features that you can implement to keep your network programs secure against tampering and hacking. The first section describes the .NET security features for applications running in the CLR, and how you can use those features to help control who can and cannot use your programs. The next section describes how to use socket permissions to prevent server programs from accessing unauthorized sockets, or keeping client programs from accessing unauthorized servers. The .NET concept of declarative and imperative socket permissions is discussed, and an example of using declarative permissions is presented. Finally, you'll examine the .NET cryptography libraries and study examples that demonstrate how you can implement protective cryptography in your network programs.

Application Security: What's Involved?

The .NET Framework offers a robust security model for dealing with application security. Each application that runs (or attempts to run) on the system must pass the security system. You must understand how this security model works before you distribute your C# network programs to customers. It would not be a good thing at all if your fancy network programs were prevented from running in your customers' security environments!

This section discusses the .NET application security model and how to apply it within your network applications.

Security Policies

The .Net Framework controls applications in the Common Language Runtime (CLR) with strict security policies. These policies determine how applications are allowed to run and access resources within the CLR.

The *CLR security policy* is the set of rules, configured by the system administrator, that matches permissions with system resources. All managed code within the CLR is governed by the security policies. There are four levels of security policy in the CLR:

- Enterprise-level policies
- Machine-level policies
- User-level policies
- Application domain policies

The security policy levels are hierarchical, that is, security rights flow downhill from the enterprise-level policies on top. Lower-level policies cannot increase permissions set at higher levels, but they can decrease permissions. By default, the user-level and application domain policies are less restrictive than the higher-level policies.

Enterprise-level policies   Enterprise-level policies are the highest level of security policies that govern applications in the CLR. They can only be set by the system administrator (or a user within the Administrators group), and they affect all applications running in the enterprise domain.

Machine-level policies   Machine-level security policies define the security rules for all applications running on an individual computer system. This is the level at which application policies for a system are most commonly set. All applications running on the system are controlled by the machine-level policies.

User-level policies   User-level policies define the security rules applied to individual user accounts on the computer system. Individual users can be restricted from accessing resources on the system based on user-level policies.

Application domain policies   Application domain policies define the security rules applied to all applications running in a set application domain. There may be more than one application domain running on a single system at a time, so an individual application can be affected by several application domain policies.

Security Groups

Security groups are defined to control what policies are applicable for a set of applications. Groups are defined based on characteristics of the applications, such as the application creator or the original location of the application.

Group memberships can overlap. An individual application can be a member of multiple groups. The security policies assigned to each group are implemented on the individual application. Table 17.1 shows the CLR security groups that classify applications. Each group can have multiple instances. For example, there can be multiple site membership groups, each group containing applications from a single HTTP site.

TABLE 17.1: The CLR Application Groups

Group	Membership Based on Affects
All code	All applications on the system
Application directory	The application's installation directory
Cryptographic hash	The application's cryptographic hash value

Continued on next page

TABLE 17.1 CONTINUED: The CLR Application Groups

Group	Membership Based on Affects
Software publisher	The originator of the application, based on a digital signature
Site membership	The HTTP, HTTPS, or FTP site from which the code originates
Strong name	The cryptographically strong name of the application
URL	The URL path where the code originates
Zone	The zone where the code originates

The Zone group defines the general location of the application and includes the following values:

Internet   Applications loaded from Internet sites

Intranet   Applications loaded from an internal network server

MyComputer   Applications that exist on the local system

NoZone   Applications that do not have a zone specified

Trusted   Applications from sites that are trusted by the administrator

Untrusted   Applications from sites that are not trusted by the administrator

Each zone is assigned different access privileges for accessing system resources. Applications running from the `Internet` zone are restricted from accessing many of the system resources. Applications in the `MyComputer` zone are allowed full access to all system resources.

Security Permissions

Applications can be configured to request the proper permissions before attempting to access the restricted resources. The request is granted or denied based on the CLR security policy settings.

Permission Types

The decision to grant or deny permissions is determined by rules configured in the CLR security settings by the system administrator of the system the application is running on. The .NET Framework provides three separate types of permissions:

Code access permissions   Code access permissions grant applications permissions based on the individual application. As each application runs in the CLR, its functions are checked to see what resources are being accessed. If any restricted resources are accessed, the CLR throws a security `Exception`, and the application is halted.

Identity permissions   Identity permissions are granted based on a set of credentials presented to the CLR by the application. The credentials are presented to the CLR as an Identity object, which is established when the user logs in to the system.

Role-based permissions   Role-based permissions are granted based on the user running the application and the function that is attempted. Permissions can be granted to individual users to perform individual functions, or to groups of users to perform multiple functions.

Permission Sets

A permission set identifies a group of policies that are implemented on a security group. Table 17.2 shows the seven permission sets in the CLR.

TABLE 17.2: The CLR Permission Sets

Permission Set	Description
Nothing	No permissions are granted.
Execution	The application can be run but does not have access to use protected resources.
Internet	Provides access to run with limited access to resources. A default permission set for applications from unknown locations.
LocalIntranet	Provides access to run with extended access to resources. The default permission set for applications within an Enterprise.
SkipVerification	The application is not verified for any groups and granted all permissions.
Everything	All standard permissions are granted except for skip verification.
FullTrust	Provides full access to all resources on the system.

The permission sets are matched with each individual security group to represent a security policy on the system. For example, the MyComputer group zone in the machine-level policies can have the FullTrust permission set. This allows all applications in the MyComputer zone complete access to all system resources.

Security Tools

The .NET Framework supplies two separate tools—the caspol and mscorcfg programs—for setting a system's CLR security policies. Once a security policy is set, it remains in effect until changed or reset by the system administrator.

The caspol Program

The caspol program is a console application that views and sets CLR security policies on the system. Table 17.3 lists the generous supply of options and parameters that can be used with caspol.

TABLE 17.3: The caspol Options

Option	Description
-af	Adds an assembly that implements a custom security object
-ag	Adds a new code group to the group hierarchy
-ap	Adds a new permission set to the permission sets
-all	Specifies that all options following on the command line are applied to all policies
-cg	Changes a code group's membership condition
-cp	Changes a permission set's permissions
-ca	Specifies that all options following on the command line are applied to the specified custom user policies
-cu	Specifies a custom user policy to apply changes to
-e	Enables or disables the check for the permission to execute the code
-en	Specifies that all permissions are applied to the enterprise-level policy
-f	Forces a policy change, even it if means that caspol will not be able to run
-h	Displays the help screen
-l	Lists the current code groups and permission sets
-listdescription	Lists all code group descriptions for the specified policy level
-lf	Lists the full trust assembly list for the policy level
-lg	Lists the code groups and their permissions
-lp	Lists the permission sets
-m	Specifies that all permissions are applied to the machine-level policy
-pp	Enables or disables the prompt that is displayed when a policy level changes
-r	Recovers a policy from a backup file
-rf	Removes an assembly from the full trust permission set
-rg	Removes a code group
-rp	Removes a permission set
-rs	Resets policies to the default
-rsg	Displays all groups that an assembly belongs to
-rsp	Displays all the permission sets that would be granted to an assembly
-s	Turns CLR security on or off
-u	Specifies that all permissions are applied to the user-level policy

Listing Group Permissions

You can see all of the group permissions currently assigned to your system by using the -lg option:

```
C:\>caspol -lg
Microsoft (R) .NET Framework CasPol 1.0.3705.288
```

```
Copyright (C) Microsoft Corporation 1998-2001. All rights reserved.

Security is ON
Execution checking is ON
Policy change prompt is ON

Level = Machine

Code Groups:

1.  All code: Nothing
     1.1.  Zone - MyComputer: FullTrust
          1.1.1.  StrongName - 436518206DC093344D5AD293: FullTrust
          1.1.2.  StrongName - 00000000000000000400000000000000: FullTrust
     1.2.  Zone - Intranet: LocalIntranet
          1.2.1.  All code: Same site Web.
          1.2.2.  All code: Same directory FileIO - Read, PathDiscovery
     1.3.  Zone - Internet: Nothing
     1.4.  Zone - Untrusted: Nothing
     1.5.  Zone - Trusted: Internet
          1.5.1.  All code: Same site Web.
Success

C:\>
```

The first three items listed indicate the overall security settings for the system. The CLR security is set to the on mode, enabling all security policies. If you want to disable security on the system, you can use the -s option:

```
C:\>caspol -s off
Microsoft (R) .NET Framework CasPol 1.0.3705.288
Copyright (C) Microsoft Corporation 1998-2001. All rights reserved.

Success

C:\ >
```

Not much fanfare here, but this command did something quite significant: it disabled all security functions on the system, allowing any .NET application from anywhere to have full privileges on the system. You can turn the security back on by using the -s on option.

WARNING   Turning off all CLR security settings opens your system to possible attacks, especially if you connect to Internet sites. If you are experiencing security policy problems, don't try to fix them by just turning off security altogether. Find out what policies need to be implemented and implement the least amount of permissions possible.

Returning to the group listing, notice that it continues on, indicating the policy level that is being displayed. In this case it is the machine-level policies. If no other policy levels are set, the levels will not be displayed in the output.

Next, each group that is assigned policies is displayed in outline format. The top-level group, All Code, is assigned to the Nothing permission set. This ensures that by default, any application running on the machine is denied access to all resources—a safe thing to do. Following the All Code top-level group are the individual zones that are under the group:

- The first zone listed is the MyComputer zone. Applications within this zone are assigned to the FullTrust permission set, allowing them to access all resources on the system. This is the policy that allows your C# programs residing on your system to access things like the disk and the network.

- The MyComputer zone also has two subzones that are similar but separate. Both are zones that include applications using a *strong name*, or a cryptographically signed application. The first strong name (which was shortened for the output listing) belongs to Microsoft. This policy assigns any application signed by Microsoft to the FullTrust permission set, granting them full access to system resources. The second strong name belongs to the ECMA.

- Next, the LocalIntranet zone is defined, allowing specific permissions for all applications located either on the same website or in the same application directory.

- The next two zones, the Internet and Untrusted networks, are assigned to the Nothing permission set, and refuses both access to all resources on the system.

- Finally, the Trusted zone is defined, assigning applications marked as trusted to the Internet permission set.

Listing Application Permissions

If you have an application that you distribute to a customer who does not work within their security policies, they may have to specifically assign the application group to a different permission set. A common example of this is applications that are run from network shares on Microsoft networks.

When an application is located on a network share drive, it is considered to be in either the Internet or the Intranet zone, depending on whether the remote file server is considered to be on the corporate intranet. If you do not know how .NET will classify the file server your applications are located on, you can use the caspol -resolvegroup option to determine what zone .NET thinks the application is in:

```
Z:\>caspol -resolvegroup NewTcpChat.exe
Microsoft (R) .NET Framework CasPol 1.0.3705.288
```

```
Level = Enterprise

Code Groups:

1.  All code: FullTrust


Level = Machine

Code Groups:

1.  All code: Nothing
    1.1.  Zone - Intranet: LocalIntranet
        1.1.1.  All code: Same site Web.
        1.1.2.  All code: Same directory FileIO - Read, PathDiscovery


Level = User

Code Groups:

1.  All code: FullTrust

Success

Z:\>
```

This application is located on a remote file server that is considered to be on the Intranet (the machine-level policy notes the zone name) and is assigned to the LocalIntranet permission set. The application can run, but with limited access to local resources.

Unfortunately for network programmers, sockets are one of the local resources that is restricted. For your network application to work properly, you must increase the permission set for the Intranet zone to allow access to the sockets.

Changing Permissions

You can use the caspol program to change the permission set for a security group to allow applications to function within your environment. From the caspol -lg command performed earlier, you saw that the Intranet group was in the LocalIntranet permission set. To enable network programs to work from a shared network drive, they must be in either the FullTrust or Everything permission set. You can assign it to the Everything permission set, which grants enough privileges to the zone without giving away the entire store.

To change the permission set for the group, use the `caspol -cg` option. Because this setting is for a machine-level policy, you must also include the -m option. You reference the security group by the security group number assigned to it, as seen in the -lg output. For the Intranet zone, the security group number is 1.2.

The following shows output from the `caspol` command to change the permission set of the Intranet zone on the machine-level policies:

```
C:\>caspol -m -cg 1.2 Everything
Microsoft (R) .NET Framework CasPol 1.0.3705.288
Copyright (C) Microsoft Corporation 1998-2001. All rights reserved.

The operation you are performing will alter security policy.
Are you sure you want to perform this operation? (yes/no)
y
Changed code group permission set to "Everything" in the Machine level.
Success

C:\>
```

You can verify that the permission set has changed by looking at the output of the -lg command. The following line tells you that the permission set for the Intranet group has now been changed to Everything:

```
1.2.  Zone - Intranet: Everything
```

Now your network application can be run from a shared drive on a server within your network.

The mscorcfg Program

For Windows 2000 and XP systems, you can utilize a .NET plug-in for the Microsoft Management Console (mmc.exe) to help you view and change security policies. The `mscorcfg.msc` program is a graphical way of viewing and changing the security policies in the CLR system. This program is located in the .NET application directory, usually found in the Microsoft.NET subdirectory of the system's Windows or Winnt directory.

After you double-click the application, the main `mscorcfg` screen appears. In the left frame, you should see options you can configure for the .NET Framework. One of those options is the Runtime Security Policy. Expanding this item reveals the three main policy levels: Enterprise, Machine, and User. Expand the Machine policy level to see the code groups and permission sets assigned for the policy level, as seen in Figure 17.1.

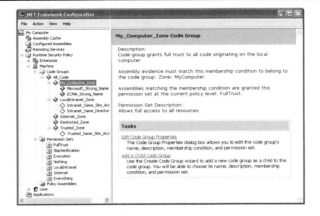

The `mscorcfg`
Runtime Security
Policy screen

By expanding each of the items, you can see all of the code groups under the `All Code` group and see what the defined permission sets are for each group. This information is located in the right frame of the application window, along with links to perform common policy administration functions. The information you see with the `mscorcfg` program is exactly the same as the `caspol` program, but in a graphical form.

Similar to the `caspol` program, you can modify security settings within each of the policy levels, using the links in the right frame of the application window.

Socket Permissions

One common feature of network applications is the ability to allow or deny access to the application from specific clients on the network. This feature allows the application administrator to provide a basic level of security to keep unwanted customers out of the application.

You can add this functionality to your C# network applications using the `SocketPermission` and `SocketPermissionAttribute` classes, found in the `System.Net` namespace. These classes provide techniques that allow you to control access to and from your C# network applications based on client network addresses. The two classes implement either declarative or imperative security on the `Socket` object.

Declarative security   Defines security attributes within the application using the SocketPermissionAttribute class. This technique uses metadata within the application code to define security restrictions for the application. Each restriction is defined as an attribute, using the SocketPermissionAttribute class to define the attribute properties.

Imperative security   Creates a SocketPermission object within the application to control access. With imperative security, you must create a SocketPermission object and assign a list of security permissions to it.

By far, declarative security is the easiest and most-used technique of the two. Imperative security requires creating a new SocketPermission object, and assigning the proper permissions for the proper objects. This technique is more complex than declarative security, and beyond the scope of this chapter. The following section describes how to easily use declarative security in your network programs.

Implementing Declarative Security

Using declarative security in your network applications is simple. All you need is to add a separate attribute line to your source code for each security attribute you want to include.

The attribute line must be formatted properly for the security attribute. The attribute is placed in the application code using square brackets ([]). This is exactly what you saw in Chapter 16, "Remoting," with the [Serializable] attribute.

The SocketPermissionAttribute class properties are defined within the class constructor:

```
[SocketPermission(SecurityAction act, Access=acc, Host=host,
    Port=port, Transport=trans)]
```

Each property in the constructor defines an element that is checked for the security attribute. All elements in the attribute must be satisfied for the attribute to take effect. Following are definitions for the five parameters in the class:

The SecurityAction object   The SecurityAction object defines the specific security action that is performed by the attribute. Table 17.4 lists the possible SecurityAction values. The most common values are SecurityAction.Assert, which allows access to the resource, and SecurityAction.Deny, which denies access to the resource.

TABLE 17.4: The SecurityAction Members

member	Description
Assert	The object can access the resource even if calls higher in the attributes deny access.
Demand	All calls to this class higher in the stack must have granted the permission.

Continued on next page

TABLE 17.4 CONTINUED: The SecurityAction Members

member	Description
Deny	The ability to access the resource specified is denied.
InheritanceDemand	The derived class inheriting this class is required to have been granted permission.
LinkDemand	The immediate caller is required to have been granted permission.
PermitOnly	Only the resources specified in this action can be accessed.
RequestMinimum	The request for the minimum permissions required for the code to run.
RequestOptional	The request for additional permissions that are optional.
RequestRefuse	The request that permissions that might be misused will not be granted.

Access property   The Access property defines the network access method allowed by the security attribute. Only two values can be used:

Accept   For allowing (or denying) binding to specific sockets

Connect   For allowing (or denying) connecting to specific remote sockets

WARNING   Be careful of the Accept Access property. The name makes it sound like you can limit incoming connections by remote address. This is not the case. Instead, it specifies a local socket address that will be restricted from binding.

The Host property   The Host property defines the hostname or address in the security attribute. The value is specified as either a hostname string or an IP address octet string. Wildcards can also define more than one address on a network:

    Host="192.168.1.*"

The Port property   The Port property defines the TCP or UDP port in the security attribute. The value is specified as either an individual port number or the special value All, to represent all ports for the given transport and host.

The Transport property   The Transport property defines the type of socket in the security attribute. The value is specified as one of the following string values:

All   All transport types

Connectionless   Connectionless transports, such as UDP

ConnectionOriented   Connection-oriented transports, such as TCP

Tcp   The TCP transport

Udp   The UDP transport

Attributes are listed within the application code in the order in which they should be implemented. Each attribute is tested individually against the object attempting to access the application. As soon as one attribute denies access, the object is denied access to the application.

Using Declarative Security

Using declarative security in network applications is easy—just add the attribute statements within the class file and compile the program as normal. When the application is run, the socket permissions configured in the attribute lines will affect how the program is allowed to connect or bind to local sockets.

A Client Program

Listing 17.1 is the PickyTcpClient.cs program, which modifies the TcpClientSample.cs program from Listing 7.1 to incorporate declarative security restrictions that restrict what remote hosts the client can connect to.

Listing 17.1   The PickyTcpClient.cs program

```
using System;
using System.Net;
using System.Net.Sockets;
using System.Security;
using System.Security.Permissions;
using System.Text;

[SocketPermission(SecurityAction.Deny, Access="Connect", Host="127.0.0.1",
[SocketPermission(SecurityAction.Deny, Access="Connect", Host="192.168.0.2",
    Port="All", Transport="All")]
[SocketPermission(SecurityAction.Deny, Access="Connect", Host="192.168.1.100",
    Port="80", Transport="All")]


class PickyTcpClient
{
   public static void Main()
   {
      byte[] data = new byte[1024];
      string input, stringData;
      TcpClient server = null;

      Console.Write("Enter a host to connect to: ");
      string stringHost = Console.ReadLine();

      try
      {
         server = new TcpClient(stringHost, 9050);
      } catch (SocketException)
      {
         Console.WriteLine("Unable to connect to server");
```

```
            return;
        } catch (SecurityException)
        {
            Console.WriteLine(
                "Sorry, you are restricted from connecting to this server");
            return;
        }
        NetworkStream ns = server.GetStream();

        int recv = ns.Read(data, 0, data.Length);
        stringData = Encoding.ASCII.GetString(data, 0, recv);
        Console.WriteLine(stringData);

        while(true)
        {
            input = Console.ReadLine();
            if (input == "exit")
                break;
            ns.Write(Encoding.ASCII.GetBytes(input), 0, input.Length);
            ns.Flush();

            data = new byte[1024];
            recv = ns.Read(data, 0, data.Length);
            stringData = Encoding.ASCII.GetString(data, 0, recv);
            Console.WriteLine(stringData);
        }
        Console.WriteLine("Disconnecting from server...");
        ns.Close();
        server.Close();
    }
}
```

As you can see, the network program code itself is the same as the original TcpClientSample.cs program—the difference is in the metadata defined at the start of the program. The security attributes specified at the beginning define which sockets are restricted from being accessed by the client. The following is a sample attribute:

```
[SocketPermission(SecurityAction.Deny, Access="Connect", Host="127.0.0.1",
    Port="All", Transport="All")]
```

This attribute restricts the client program from connecting to any port on host 127.0.0.1 (the local machine).

A SecurityException is thrown when a socket permission attribute is triggered. An additional catch statement captures the Exception and produces a customer-friendly error message to the user:

```
try
{
    server = new TcpClient(stringHost, 9050);
} catch (SocketException)
{
```

```
    Console.WriteLine("Unable to connect to server");
    return;
} catch (SecurityException)
{
    Console.WriteLine(
        "Sorry, you are restricted from connecting to this server");
    return;
}
```

The output from this program should look like:

```
C:\>PickyTcpCLient
Enter a host to connect to: 127.0.0.1
Sorry, you are restricted from connecting to this server

C:\>
```

As expected, the connection attempt was denied, and the SecurityException was thrown.

A Server Program

The declarative security feature also works for servers, but in a slightly different manner. The security attributes defined for the server program restrict access to the local socket. Address and port pairs defined in the security attribute relate to the local address and ports on the server.

If the address and port pair are configured to be restricted, the application program cannot perform a Bind() method on that socket. An example of a server security attribute would be the following:

```
[SocketPermission(SecurityAction.Deny, Access="Accept", Host="0.0.0.0",
    Port="9050", Transport="All")]
```

This security attribute prevents the application from binding to TCP port 9050 on the local machine.

> **NOTE** Be careful when specifying the host part for Accept security attributes. If you use the machine's internal loopback IP address, the application may still be able to bind to the external IP address. The special IP address IPAddress.Any (0.0.0.0) can represent all addresses for the interface.

Listing 17.2 shows the PickyTcpListener.cs program, which uses the original TcpListenerSample.cs program from Listing 7.2 and adds socket permission attributes.

Listing 17.2   The PickyTcpListener.cs program

```
using System;
using System.Net;
using System.Net.Sockets;
using System.Security;
```

```
using System.Security.Permissions;
using System.Text;

[SocketPermission(SecurityAction.Deny, Access="Accept", Host="0.0.0.0",
[SocketPermission(SecurityAction.Deny, Access="Accept", Host="0.0.0.0",
    Port="9051", Transport="All")]
[SocketPermission(SecurityAction.Deny, Access="Accept", Host="0.0.0.0",
    Port="9052", Transport="All")]

class PickyTcpListener
{
    public static void Main()
    {
        int recv;
        TcpListener newsock = null;
        byte[] data = new byte[1024];

        Console.Write("Enter port number to use: ");
        string stringPort = Console.ReadLine();
        int port = Convert.ToInt32(stringPort);

        try
        {
            newsock = new TcpListener(port);
            newsock.Start();
        } catch (SecurityException)
        {
            Console.WriteLine("Sorry, that port is unavailable");
            return;
        }
        Console.WriteLine("Waiting for a client...");

        TcpClient client = newsock.AcceptTcpClient();
        NetworkStream ns = client.GetStream();

        string welcome = "Welcome to my test server";
        data = Encoding.ASCII.GetBytes(welcome);
        ns.Write(data, 0, data.Length);

        while(true)
        {
            data = new byte[1024];
            recv = ns.Read(data, 0, data.Length);
            if (recv == 0)
                break;

            Console.WriteLine(
                    Encoding.ASCII.GetString(data, 0, recv));
            ns.Write(data, 0, recv);
        }
        ns.Close();
        client.Close();
```

```
        newsock.Stop();
    }
  }
```

The `PickyTcpListener.cs` program restricts the application from accessing three separate ports (actually, six, if you count three for the TCP transport and three for the UDP transport). If the application attempts to access one of the restricted ports, a `SecurityException` is thrown, and an error message is produced.

Protecting Network Data

Sending data across the Internet can be a risky business. There are lots of prying eyes looking at your packets as they traverse nodes on the Internet. Many applications that send data across networks incorporate some type of encryption system to encrypt data. While encrypting data is not 100 percent fool-proof, it adds a basic level of data protection to your applications. The .NET Framework includes several encryption classes to help protect your data as it travels across the network.

WARNING Encrypted data is not totally safe from prying eyes. No matter how complex the encryption method, it can still be broken. The key is to use an encryption method that would take so long to break, the data would not be useful anymore.

Data Encryption

When you are sending data over the network, anyone can intercept your packets and look at their contents. If the data you are sending is sensitive (or even if it isn't) you can encrypt it before sending out in the packets.

The .NET library's `System.Security.Cryptography` namespace includes lots of classes for encrypting data. Many encryption algorithms are in use, and trying to differentiate between them can be difficult. Basically, they fall into two encryption/decryption schemes: symmetric encryption and asymmetric encryption.

Symmetric Encryption

Symmetric encryption algorithms use a single key to both encrypt and decrypt a message. The same key must be shared between both parties involved on the encrypted data transaction. Because of this arrangement, symmetric encryption is often referred to as *private key* encryption. A single private key performs all of the encrypting and decrypting tasks.

Symmetric encryption algorithms encrypt data in blocks, often padding data to ensure the same block sizes are used for each block. Each block of encrypted data is chained together with the previously encrypted blocks (called *cipher block chaining*). Thus symmetric encryption can support data streams, which makes it an ideal way to encrypt network data.

To ensure that each block of encrypted data is unique (so a hacker cannot detect patterns within the data), a second known data value, called an *initialization vector (IV)* is used along with the private key. The key and IV combination define how the data is encrypted, and both are required to decrypt the data back into its original form.

The .NET library includes several symmetric encryption algorithm classes, described in Table 17.5.

TABLE 17.5: The .NET Symmetric Encryption Classes

Class	Description
DESCryptoServiceProvider	Implements the DES encryption algorithm
RC2CryptoServiceProvider	Implements the RC2 encryption algorithm
RijndaelManaged	Implements the Rijndael Managed encryption algorithm
TripleDESCryptoServiceProvider	Implements the triple DES encryption algorithm

Asymmetric Encryption

Asymmetric encryption allows you to provide a key to other users to encrypt data (called a *public key*). You maintain a private version of the key that is able to decrypt data encrypted with the public key. This technique is called *public key encryption*.

While the public key can encrypt data, only the private key can decrypt the data. A person with a copy of the public key cannot decrypt messages, only encrypt them. This makes asymmetric encryption ideal for someone who needs to receive data from multiple people doesn't want to worry about their messages being decrypted by others.

The asymmetric encryption algorithms use a fixed block encryption technique, and the blocks of encrypted data cannot be chained together. Unfortunately this feature makes asymmetric encryption difficult to use in a network environment, and this chapter does not provide an example of its use.

NOTE   One common technique is to use symmetric encryption to encrypt network data and use asymmetric encryption to encrypt the symmetric private key as it is sent to the remote customer.

The .NET library offers two asymmetric encryption classes to encrypt data with private and public keys:

- DSACryptoServiceProvider
- RSACryptoServiceProvider

Using Data Encryption

Using symmetric encryption within network programs can be somewhat tricky. Encrypting data and sending it out on the network is a multistep task, with plenty of opportunity for things to go wrong.

Encrypting Data

The .NET symmetric encryption classes pass data in streams. The tricky part is dealing with data in the stream. All of the standard problems of handling data in a stream apply.

For this example, the `TripleDESCryptoServiceProvider` class will provide the encryption functionality using the triple DES encryption algorithm. The `CryptoStream` class passes the blocks of encrypted data through to a `Stream` object. The stream can be anything including `FileStreams`, `MemoryStreams`, and `NetworkStreams`.

The `CryptoStream` constructor requires three parameters:

```
CryptoStream(Stream stream, ICryptoTransform transform, CryptoStreamMode mode)
```

The first parameter, *stream*, represents the external `Stream` object that the encrypted data will be passed to (or read from).

The second parameter, *transform*, represents the encryption algorithm. To create this value, you must use the `CreateEncryptor()` method of the `TripleDESCryptoServiceProvider` class, where the *key* parameter is the private key value and the *iv* parameter is the initialization vector:

```
CreateEncryptor(Key key, IV iv)
```

Both of these values are 16-byte byte arrays, which must be the same for both sides of the encryption transaction.

The final parameter of the constructor, *mode*, defines whether the stream will read (`CryptoStreamMode.Read`) or write (`CryptoStreamMode.Write`). Unfortunately, the same `CryptoStream` object cannot both read and write.

A code snippet for encrypting data with symmetric encryption looks something like this:

```
FileStream fs = new FileStream("test.enc",
  FileAccess.Create);
TripleDESCryptoServiceProvider tdes = new TripleDESCryptoServiceProvider();
CryptoStream csw = new CryptoStream(fs,
    Tdes.CreateEncryptor(key, iv), CryptoStreamMode.Write);

byte[] data = Encoding.ASCII.GetBytes("Phrase to encrypt");
csw.Write(data, 0, data.Length);
csw.Close();
fs.Close();
```

Once the `CryptoStream` object is created, any data written to the stream is encrypted and passed to the underlying stream defined in the constructor (the `FileStream` object in this example).

Decrypting Data

The decryption process works similar to the encryption process: data is passed through the decryptor to a specified stream object. The decryptor stream is created using the `CreateDecryptor()` method of the `TripleDESCryptoServiceProvider` class:

```
CryptoStream csr = new CryptoStream(memstrm,
tdes.CreateDecryptor(key, iv), CryptoStreamMode.Read);
```

WARNING   It is imperative that you use the same key and initialization vector values to decrypt the data that encrypted it. Often these values can be transferred in a secure snail-mail message or via a separate encrypted message.

A simple example of symmetric decryption looks like this:

```
FileStream fs = new FileStream("test.enc", FileAccess.Open);
TripleDESCryptoServiceProvider tdes = new TripleDESCryptoServiceProvider();
CryptoStream csr = new CryptoStream(fs,
tdes.CreateDecryptor(key, iv), CryptoStreamMode.Read);
byte[] data = new byte[1024];
int recv = csr.Read(data, 0, data.Length);
string phrase = Encoding.ASCII.GetString(data, 0, recv);
csr.Close();
fs.Close();
```

The `CryptoStream` again points to the `FileStream` object, but this time defines a decryptor and uses `CryptoStreamMode.Read` to enable reading data from the stream. As data is read from the stream, it is automatically decrypted back to the original text.

Sample Encryption/Decryption Program

To see the encryption technique in action, here's a simple program that encrypts a text phrase and then decrypts it back to the original text. Listing 17.3, the `CryptoTest.cs` program, is a simple example of how the encryption functions work in a C# program.

Listing 17.3   **The CryptoTest.cs program**

```
using System;
using System.IO;
using System.Security;
using System.Security.Cryptography;
using System.Text;

class CryptoTest
{
...public static void Main()
    {
        Console.Write("Enter phrase to encrypt: ");
        string phrase = Console.ReadLine();
```

```
        MemoryStream memstrm = new MemoryStream();

        byte[] Key = {0x01, 0x02, 0x03, 0x04, 0x05, 0x06, 0x07, 0x08, 0x09,
                      0x10, 0x11, 0x12, 0x13, 0x14, 0x15, 0x16};
        byte[] IV = {0x01, 0x02, 0x03, 0x04, 0x05, 0x06, 0x07, 0x08, 0x09,
                      0x10, 0x11, 0x12, 0x13, 0x14, 0x15, 0x16};

        TripleDESCryptoServiceProvider tdes = new
    TripleDESCryptoServiceProvider();
        CryptoStream csw = new CryptoStream(memstrm,
                    tdes.CreateEncryptor(Key, IV), CryptoStreamMode.Write);

        csw.Write(Encoding.ASCII.GetBytes(phrase), 0, phrase.Length);
        csw.FlushFinalBlock();
        byte[] cryptdata = memstrm.GetBuffer();
        Console.WriteLine("Encrypted: {0}",
                Encoding.ASCII.GetString(cryptdata, 0, (int)memstrm.Length));

        memstrm.Position = 0;
        byte[] data = new byte[1024];
        CryptoStream csr = new CryptoStream(memstrm,
                    tdes.CreateDecryptor(Key, IV),
        CryptoStreamMode.Read);
        int recv = csr.Read(data, 0, data.Length);
        string newphrase = Encoding.ASCII.GetString(data, 0, recv);
        Console.WriteLine("Decrypted: {0}", newphrase);
        csr.Close();
        csw.Close();
        memstrm.Close();
    }
  }
```

The CryptoTest.cs program uses a MemoryStream to hold the encrypted data. The key and IV values are hard-coded into the program, using phony 16-byte values for each. For a real encryption application you should determine real values for these parameters and keep them secret.

After the string phrase is converted to a byte array, encrypted, and stored in the MemoryStream, the FlushFinalBlock() method is called. This method ensures that all of the encrypted blocks have been sent out to the stream, and none are sitting in the encryption class buffer space.

After the phrase is encrypted, the MemoryStream contents are converted into a byte array and displayed on the console as a string. (Because the encrypted value will contain non-ASCII text characters, you may see some interesting results.) The idea is to see that the data really was encrypted.

After the encrypted data is displayed, the MemoryStream object place pointer is reset back to the beginning of the stream, and the decryptor method converts the encrypted text back into the original string phrase. Here's a sample output from the program:

```
C:\>CryptoTest
Enter phrase to encrypt: A test phrase.
Encrypted: ~/@'F?p{=.$g=R2U
Decrypted: A test phrase.

C:\>
```

Network Data Encryption

Although it is convenient to use the `CryptoStream` class with `FileStream` and `MemoryStream` objects, it is often difficult to use it with `NetworkStream` objects. The downside to using the `CryptoStream` class with `NetworkStream` objects is the same old issue of determining data boundaries within the data stream. When data is encrypted and passed directly to a `NetworkStream` object, there is no easy way of determining when the receiver has received the end of the encrypted data. If the decryptor attempts to decrypt the data before the end of the stream has arrived, an error will occur.

Handling Encrypted Data

The solution to the data boundary issue is to deploy one of the common stream data handling techniques discussed in Chapter 7, "Using the C# Sockets Helper Classes." As described in Chapter 7, to handle stream data you can either use fixed-length messages, send the message size in the stream before the message, or use message boundary markers.

The easiest technique to use with encrypted messages is to determine the size of each encrypted message and send it in the stream before the actual message. The receiving program can extract the message size from the `NetworkStream` and will know exactly how many bytes of data to read from the network to properly form the encrypted message. The receiving program can then forward the entire encrypted message to the appropriate decryptor to extract the original data.

To determine the size of each encrypted message, the message must be stored in a buffer after being encrypted and before being sent out on the `NetworkStream`. Once the encrypted message is in the buffer, it's easy to determine the size of the message and send both the message size and the message out on the `NetworkStream`. A simple solution is to use the `MemoryStream` class, as demonstrated in the `CryptoTest.cs` program. By forwarding the `CryptoStream` output to a `MemoryStream`, you can use the `GetBuffer()` method to create a byte array with the encrypted message. The array can then be sent out on the network just like any other byte array of data.

On the receiver side, the opposite steps are performed. Data read from the `NetworkStream` is fed for decryption into the `CryptoStream` object, which points to a `MemoryStream` object. Once the entire decrypted message is in the `MemoryStream` object, it can be extracted using the `GetBuffer()` method.

Figure 17.2 illustrates both the sender and receiver processes in network data encryption.

FIGURE 17.2:

Encrypting data for the network

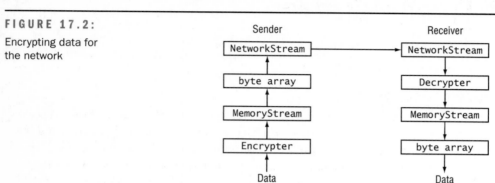

The CryptoDataSender Program

The CryptoDataSender.cs program, Listing 17.4, demonstrates encryption of complex data for sending on the network. CryptoDataSender takes the original BetterDataSender.cs program (Listing 16.6) and adds triple DES encryption to secure the data being sent.

> **NOTE**　Just like the original program, the CryptoDataSender program must be compiled with the SerialEmployee.dll file created in Chapter 16 using the /r: compiler option: csc /r:SerialEmployee.dll CryptoDataSender.cs.

Listing 17.4　　**The CryptoDataSender.cs program**

```
using System;
using System.IO;
using System.Net;
using System.Net.Sockets;
using System.Runtime.Serialization;
using System.Runtime.Serialization.Formatters.Soap;
using System.Security;
using System.Security.Cryptography;
using System.Text;

class CryptoDataSender
{
    private void SendData (NetworkStream strm, SerialEmployee emp)
    {
        IFormatter formatter = new SoapFormatter();
        MemoryStream memstrm = new MemoryStream();

        byte[] Key = {0x01, 0x02, 0x03, 0x04, 0x05, 0x06, 0x07, 0x08, 0x09, 0x10,
0x11, 0x12, 0x13, 0x14, 0x15, 0x16};
```

```
    byte[] IV = {0x01, 0x02, 0x03, 0x04, 0x05, 0x06, 0x07, 0x08, 0x09, 0x10,
0x11, 0x12, 0x13, 0x14, 0x15, 0x16};

    TripleDESCryptoServiceProvider tdes = new
TripleDESCryptoServiceProvider();
    CryptoStream csw = new CryptoStream(memstrm, tdes.CreateEncryptor(Key,
IV), CryptoStreamMode.Write);

    formatter.Serialize(csw, emp);
    csw.FlushFinalBlock();
    byte[] data = memstrm.GetBuffer();
    int memsize = (int)memstrm.Length;
    byte[] size = BitConverter.GetBytes(memsize);
    strm.Write(size, 0, 4);
    strm.Write(data, 0, (int)memsize);
    strm.Flush();
    csw.Close();
    memstrm.Close();
}

public CryptoDataSender()
{
    SerialEmployee emp1 = new SerialEmployee();
    SerialEmployee emp2 = new SerialEmployee();

    emp1.EmployeeID = 1;
    emp1.LastName = "Blum";
    emp1.FirstName = "Katie Jane";
    emp1.YearsService = 12;
    emp1.Salary = 35000.50;

    emp2.EmployeeID = 2;
    emp2.LastName = "Blum";
    emp2.FirstName = "Jessica";
    emp2.YearsService = 9;
    emp2.Salary = 23700.30;

    TcpClient client = new TcpClient("127.0.0.1", 9050);
    NetworkStream strm = client.GetStream();

    SendData(strm, emp1);
    SendData(strm, emp2);
    strm.Close();
    client.Close();
}

public static void Main()
{
    CryptoDataSender cds = new CryptoDataSender();
}
}
```

If you remember, the `BetterDataSender` program used SOAP serialization to serialize an employee data object for sending to a remote device across the network. Because the `SOAPFormatter` was used, all of the data was sent in text mode across the network. Should that data include sensitive information such as a Social Security number, anyone viewing the packet would see the information. You don't want this to happen, of course, in your applications.

The `CryptoDataSender` program creates the same SOAP serialization of the data, but then it runs it through the `CryptoStream` object to encrypt the information before sending it out:

```
formatter.Serialize(csw, emp);
csw.FlushFinalBlock();
byte[] data = memstrm.GetBuffer();
int memsize = (int)memstrm.Length;
byte[] size = BitConverter.GetBytes(memsize);
strm.Write(size, 0, 4);
strm.Write(data, 0, (int)memsize);
```

The `SOAPFormatter Serialize()` method serializes the employee data object to a stream but uses the `CryptoStream` stream object instead of the `NetworkStream`. The `FlushFinalBlock()` method ensures that all of the encrypted blocks are flushed out of the buffer. Because the `CryptoStream` object pointed to a `MemoryStream` object, that object contains the entire encrypted, SOAP-serialized, `SerialEmployee` data object. The `MemoryStream` object is then converted to a byte array, the size of the data is determined, and both are sent out on the `NetworkStream` object to the remote receiver.

The CryptoDataRcvr Program

Now let's look at the receiving program. The `CryptoDataRcvr.cs` program, Listing 17.5, demonstrates how to read and decrypt data from a `NetworkStream`. As expected, the `CryptoDataRcvr.cs` program mimics the `BetterDataRcvr` program of Listing 16.7.

> **NOTE** Again, the CryptoDataRcvr program must be compiled with the SerialEmployee.dll file from Chapter 16 using the /r: option: csc /r:SerialEmployee.dll CryptoDataRcvr.cs.

Listing 17.5   **The CryptoDataRcvr.cs program**

```
using System;
using System.IO;
using System.Net;
using System.Net.Sockets;
using System.Runtime.Serialization;
using System.Runtime.Serialization.Formatters.Soap;
using System.Security;
using System.Security.Cryptography;
using System.Text;

class CryptoDataRcvr
```

```
{
   private SerialEmployee RecvData (NetworkStream strm)
   {
      MemoryStream memstrm = new MemoryStream();

      byte[] Key = {0x01, 0x02, 0x03, 0x04, 0x05, 0x06, 0x07, 0x08, 0x09,
                    0x10, 0x11, 0x12, 0x13, 0x14, 0x15, 0x16};
      byte[] IV = {0x01, 0x02, 0x03, 0x04, 0x05, 0x06, 0x07, 0x08, 0x09,
                    0x10, 0x11, 0x12, 0x13, 0x14, 0x15, 0x16};

      TripleDESCryptoServiceProvider tdes = new
TripleDESCryptoServiceProvider();
      CryptoStream csw = new CryptoStream(memstrm, tdes.CreateDecryptor(Key,
IV),
                         CryptoStreamMode.Write);

      byte[] data = new byte[2048];
      int recv = strm.Read(data, 0, 4);
      int size = BitConverter.ToInt32(data, 0);
      int offset = 0;
      while(size > 0)
      {

         recv = strm.Read(data, 0, size);
         csw.Write(data, offset, recv);
         offset += recv;
         size -= recv;
      }
      csw.FlushFinalBlock();
      IFormatter formatter = new SoapFormatter();
      memstrm.Position = 0;
      SerialEmployee emp = (SerialEmployee)formatter.Deserialize(memstrm);
      memstrm.Close();
      return emp;
   }

   public CryptoDataRcvr()
   {
      TcpListener server = new TcpListener(9050);
      server.Start();
      Console.WriteLine("Waiting for a client...");
      TcpClient client = server.AcceptTcpClient();
      NetworkStream strm = client.GetStream();

      SerialEmployee emp1 = RecvData(strm);
      Console.WriteLine("emp1.EmployeeID = {0}", emp1.EmployeeID);
      Console.WriteLine("emp1.LastName = {0}", emp1.LastName);
      Console.WriteLine("emp1.FirstName = {0}", emp1.FirstName);
      Console.WriteLine("emp1.YearsService = {0}", emp1.YearsService);
      Console.WriteLine("emp1.Salary = {0}\n", emp1.Salary);

      SerialEmployee emp2 = RecvData(strm);
      Console.WriteLine("emp2.EmployeeID = {0}", emp2.EmployeeID);
      Console.WriteLine("emp2.LastName = {0}", emp2.LastName);
```

```
            Console.WriteLine("emp2.FirstName = {0}", emp2.FirstName);
            Console.WriteLine("emp2.YearsService = {0}", emp2.YearsService);
            Console.WriteLine("emp2.Salary = {0}", emp2.Salary);
            strm.Close();
            server.Stop();
        }

        public static void Main()
        {
            CryptoDataRcvr cdr = new CryptoDataRcvr();
        }
    }
```

In Chapter 16's BetterDataRcvr program, the data was read from the NetworkStream and fed directly into the SOAP Deserialize() method. Here in the CryptoDataRcvr program, however, there is obviously another step involved. Because the new data is encrypted, it must be decrypted before it can be deserialized.

First, the size of the encrypted data array is read from the NetworkStream. Knowing the size of the data array to expect, a while loop ensures that all of the encrypted data is read from the network:

```
while(size > 0)
{
    data = new byte[2048];
    recv = strm.Read(data, 0, size);
    csw.Write(data, offset, recv);
    offset += recv;
    size -= recv;
}
csw.FlushFinalBlock();
```

As each block of data is read from the network, it is fed to the CryptoStream stream, which decrypts the data and stores it in the created MemoryStream object. When all of the data has been received from the network, the FlushFinalBlock() method ensures that all of the decrypted data blocks have been sent to the MemoryStream.

After all of the decrypted data is placed in the MemoryStream object, the pointer is reset, and the MemoryStream object is used in the Deserializer() method to produce the original employee data object.

Testing the Programs

After compiling both the CryptoDataSender.cs and CryptoDataRcvr.cs programs (using the SerialEmployee.dll file), you can test them out on your network. The final result should be the complete data for both employee records:

```
C:\>CryptoDataRcvr
```

```
Waiting for a client...
emp1.EmployeeID = 1
emp1.LastName = Blum
emp1.FirstName = Katie Jane
emp1.YearsService = 12
emp1.Salary = 35000.5

emp2.EmployeeID = 2
emp2.LastName = Blum
emp2.FirstName = Jessica
emp2.YearsService = 9
emp2.Salary = 23700.3

C:\>
```

As shown in the output, both employee data objects sent by the sender were successfully received by the receiver. However, this does not prove that the encryption really did take place. The only way to see this is to watch the packets as they are sent across the network. If you are testing these applications on separate devices on a network, you can use the WinDump or Analyzer programs to watch the packets on the network. Figure 17.3 shows one packet in the Analyzer program. You can see that the data contained in the packets has indeed been encrypted, preventing the casual network snooper from seeing your data.

FIGURE 17.3:

Displaying a data packet in the Analyzer program

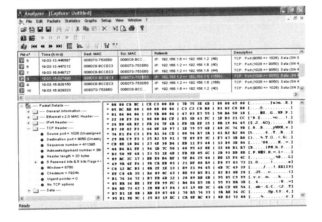

Summary

With today's constant worries about security, you need to know how to incorporate security features in your C# network programs. This chapter presented various .NET security features that can be easily used in programs.

The .NET CLR uses security policies to determine how (and if) applications run on the system. Each application is a member of a security group based on characteristics of the application (such as the location or the author of the application). The CLR system uses security permission sets to determine each security group's permissions for local system resources such as files and network sockets.

You can use the caspol program, included in .NET, to determine the security settings for a machine and to modify security settings to grant your applications the appropriate permissions to access network sockets. Often, if applications are run from a remote file server disk share, they will not have sufficient permissions to access network sockets on the system. To solve this problem, you can add the appropriate group (usually intranet) to the Everything permission set.

The .NET network library also includes classes for securing the network sockets that applications can access. The SocketPermissionAttribute class allows you to define attribute commands within your C# network programs to block customers from using specified sockets or IP addresses. Each metadata command defines a security attribute that is implemented on the application. If a security attribute specifies to deny access to a specific network port, the application will throw a SecurityException if the port is accessed.

Sending data across the network to a remote network host is dangerous. Depending on the network, there can be many prying eyes watching at data packets as they traverse the network. To protect your data, it is a good idea to implement some type of encryption technique before sending it out on the network. The .NET library includes several excellent encryption classes to assist you in this task.

The easiest way to implement encryption in a network program is to use a symmetric encryption class. Symmetric encryption allows the data to be encrypted in variable-length blocks, which can be chained together to form a stream. The encrypted data stream can then be passed to any other type of stream, including a NetworkStream. Often though, it is easier to handle the data by placing it in a MemoryStream and creating a byte array from the stream data. The byte array can then be safely sent across the NetworkStream as normal, using standard network stream techniques. When the data is received on the other end, it must be decrypted back to the original data using the same key pair that was used to encrypt it.

Over the past 17 chapters, we have covered lots of networking topics. I hope you have enjoyed your experience in learning network programming and that you're ready to go off and create your own network applications. With the advent of new networking technologies, there is always something new to learn in the area of network programming. It is a good idea to stay in touch with the current network trends by browsing networking newsgroups and keeping up with the latest RFCs. Happy networking.

Index

Note to the Reader: Throughout this index **boldfaced** page numbers indicate primary discussions of a topic. *Italicized* page numbers indicate illustrations.

A

-a option
 in netstat, 214
 in WinDump, 44
A (Address) records, **134**, 137
Abort method, 351
AboveNormal class, 335
Abstract Syntax Notation, version 1 (ASN.1) naming
 convention, 445, 464–465
accept method, 93, 114
 for asynchronous sockets, 322–323, 327
 for connection-oriented sockets, 168, 170
 in Winsock, 99
Accept value, 605
AcceptConn method
 in AsyncTcpSrvr, 314, 316
 in NewTcpChat, 387
 in TcpChat, 361
AcceptSocket method, 122, 256
AcceptTcpClient method, 122–123, 256
access policies, 444
Access property, 605
accounts, e-mail, 480
ACK flag, 66–67, *67*
acknowledgements
 in POP3, 502–503
 in TCP, 65
Activator class, 583
Active Directory, **536**. *See also* network directories
 connecting to, **543**
 domains in, **539–540**, *540*
 forests in, **542**, *542*
 objects in, **543**
 Organizational Units in, **540**
 trees in, **541**, *541*
Active Messaging, 483–484
AD Services Interface (ADSI), 543–544
Add method
 in Children, 551–552

 in Header, 492
 in MathClass, 578, 587–588
 in MathService, 530
 in NetworkCredentials, 520
 in PropertyCollection, 549
addem method, 13–15
AddMembership option, 394
AddObject.cs program, 551–552
AddProperty.cs program, 549–550
address fields
 in A records, 134
 in IP layer, **58–59**
address-list fields, 490
address parameter, 114
Address property, 107, 170
Address (A) records, **134**, 137
addresses
 broadcast, 376–377, *377*
 Ethernet, **53–55**
 IP. *See* IP addresses
 MAC
  in Ethernet packets, 52
  tracking, **471–474**
  in Win32_NetworkAdapterConfiguration, 81
 network, **91–92**
AddressFamily property
 in IPEndPoint, 107
 in Socket, 110
AddressList property, 84, 105
AddressSample.cs program, 104–106
ADSI (AD Services Interface), 543–544
adspath property, 560
Advertise.cs program, 382–384
advertising servers, **382–390**, *389*
AdvPing.cs program, 427–431, *431*
AdvSndRecvData method, 245–247
.aero domain, 128
-af option in caspol, 598
-ag option in caspol, 598
aliases for e-mail, 480
All code security group, 595, 600

-all option in caspol, 598
/all switch in ipconfig, 73
All value in Transport, 605
Alternative MIME subtype, 499
Analyzer program, 43
    operation of, **48–51**, *48–50*
    for TCP servers, **172–173**, *173*
Anonymous AuthenticationType, 546
anonymous logins, **543–545**
Any field, 104
-ap option in caspol, 598
APIs (Application Program Interfaces), 4
application Content-Type, 498
Application directory security group, 595
application domain policies, **595**
application domains, 575–576, *576*
Application Program Interfaces (APIs), 4
applicationEntity objectClass, 539
applications
    permissions for, **600–601**
    ports for, **63–65**, *63*
ArrayList class, 324–325, 327
arrays
    for directory objects, 549
    for ICMP packets, 420
ASCII output in Analyzer, 51
ASCII property, 171
ASN.1 (Abstract Syntax Notation, version 1) naming
        convention, 445, 464–465
Assert member, 604
asymmetric encryption, **611**
AsyncCallback class, 159–160, **297**
AsyncCallback method, 316
asynchronous DNS methods, **159–164**, *163*
asynchronous sockets, **118, 292, 298**
    connections for, **298–301, 308–309, 315–316**
    event programming for, **292–293**, *293*
        AsyncCallback class for, **297**
        events and delegates in, **293–294**, *294*
        sample programs, **294–297**
    non-blocking methods for, **319**
        poll, **319–323**
        select, **324–331**, *330*
    receiving data with, **303–304, 310, 317**
    sample programs
        client, **305–312**, *308, 312*
        server, **312–318**, *315, 318*
    sending data with, **301–303, 310–311, 316–317**
Asynchronous Transfer Mode (ATM) networks, 392
AsyncResolve.cs program, 160–163
AsyncState property, 309
AsyncTcpClient.cs program, 305–312, *312*
AsyncTcpSrvr.cs program, 312–318, *315*
ATM (Asynchronous Transfer Mode) networks, 392

Attachment property, 491, **493**
attachments, **493–494**
    MailAttachment class for, **499–501**
    MIME for, **495–499**, *496*
    uuencode for, **495**
audio Content-Type, 498
authentication
    in HTTP, 520
    in POP3 client, **501–502**
AuthenticationTypes enumerator, 545–546
auto-reply messages, 481
Available property, 110
avgBusy5 object, 465

B

-B option in WinDump, 44
backlog parameter, 114
backslashes (\) in Registry, 74
BadBroadcast.cs program, 378
BadError.cs program, 36–37
BadTcpClient.cs program, 182–183
BadTcpSrvr.cs program, 181–182
BadUdpClient.cs program, 224–226
Base value in SearchScope, 557
Base64 MIME encoding type, 497, 499–500
BasePriority property
    in Process, 336
    in ProcessThread, 344
Basic authentication, 520
Bcc field, 490
Bcc property, 491
BeginAccept method
    for asynchronous sockets, **299–300**, 316
    in TcpChat, 362
BeginConnect method
    for asynchronous sockets, **300–301**, 309
    in TcpChat, 363
BeginGetHostByName method, 159
BeginGetResponse method, 523
BeginRead method, 199
BeginReceive method, 118, 309–311, 317
BeginReceiveFrom method, **303–304**
BeginResolve method, 159, 162
BeginSend method, **301–302**, 311, 316–317
BeginSendTo method, **302–303**
BeginWrite method, 199
BelowNormal class, 335
BestUdpClient.cs program, 245–247
BetterDataRcvr.cs program, 573–574
BetterDataSender.cs program, 571–573
BetterUdpClient.cs program, 226–228
big endian data representation, 272–273

binary data
    converting, **266–267**, **273–276**, *274*
    representing, **265–266**, **272–273**
    sample programs, **268–272**
binary MIME encoding method, 497
BinaryDataRcvr.cs program, 570–571
BinaryDataSender.cs program, 568–569
BinaryDataTest.cs program, 272–273
BinaryFormatter class, 564–565
BinaryNetworkByteOrder.cs program, 274–276, 280
BinaryUdpClient.cs program, 270–271
BinaryUdpSrvr.cs program, 268–269
Bind method, 94
    with declarative security, 608
    operation of, 92–93
    for server sockets, 114, 117, 170, 322
    in Winsock, 99
BindHandle method, 365
binding SNMP variables, **450**
BindObject.cs program, 544–545
BitConverter class, 197, 266, 269–270, 273
.biz domain, 128
BlockCopy method
    for byte arrays, 281–282, *282*
    for ICMP packets, 420
blocking functions, 95
Blocking property, 110–111
Body property, **491–492**
BodyEncoding property, 491–492
BodyFormat property, 491–492
boundaries in TCP messages, 71, **180–184**, *180*
break command, 21
broadcast addresses
    in Ethernet, 54
    in IPAddress, 104, 379–380
broadcasts, **376**
    for advertising loops, **382–390**, *389*
    local vs. global, **376–377**, *377*
    receiving packets in, **380–382**
    sending packets in, **377–380**, *380*
Broadcst.cs program, 379–380, *380*
buffers
    for asynchronous sockets, 301–303
    overflows in, 28, 228
    in TCP, 70–71, *70*, **177–180**, *179*
Button class, 162, 296–297
ButtonCloseOnClick method
    in AdvPing, 429
    in MulticastChat, 403–405
    in PopCheck, 506
ButtonConnectOnClick method
    in AsyncTcpClient, 306, 308–309
    in NewTcpChat, 386
    in TcpChat, 361
ButtonDisconOnClick method, 306–307, 311

ButtongetitOnClick method, 527–528
ButtonListenOnClick method
    in NewTcpChat, 386
    in TcpChat, 360–362
ButtonloginOnClick method, 506
ButtonOnClick method, 296–297
ButtonResolveOnClick method, 161–163
ButtonSendOnClick method
    in AdvPing, 429
    in AsyncTcpClient, 306, 310
    in MulticastChat, 403
    in NewTcpChat, 386–387
    in TcpChat, 361
ButtonStartOnClick method, 467
ButtonStopOnClick method
    in AdvPing, 429
    in AsyncTcpSrvr, 314
    in CiscoRouter, 467
byte datatype, 266

C

C object type in LDAP, 537
-c option in WinDump, 44
.ca domain, 128
-ca option in caspol, 598
Canonical Name (CNAME) records, **134**, 137
CanRead property, 199
CanSeek property, 199
CanWrite property, 199
capacity of strings, 31–32
Capture in Progress window, 50
capturing network packets, **48–50**
CardGrab.cs program, 77–79
caspol program
    options for, **597–598**
    permissions in
        application, **600–601**
        changing, **601–602**
        group, **598–600**
CatchError.cs program, 38–39
Cc field, 490
Cc property, 491
CDO (Collaboration Data Objects), **483–484**
CDO 2, 484
CDO NT Server library (CDONTS), 484
CDOSYS.DLL file, 484
CDOSYS message component, 483
-cg option in caspol, 598, 602
ChannelServices class, 580
CharacterSet property, 523
chat programs
    MulticastChat.cs, 402–406
    NewTcpChat.cs, **384–390**

TcpChat.cs, **359–364**, *364*
checkError object, 324
checkit_OnClick method, 296
checkRead object, 324
checkRouter method, 467–468
checksums
    in Ethernet packets, 52
    in ICMP, 413, 417, **420–422**
checkWrite object, 324
child objects in network directories
    listing, **550–551**
    removing, **553–555**
    renaming, **555**
Children property, 550–551
cipher block chaining, 611
Cisco CPU MIB, **463–469**, *469*
cisco object, 466
CISCO-SMI MIB file, 465
CISCO-SMI-V1SMI.my MIB file, 465
CiscoRouter.cs program, 463, 466–469, *469*
class field
    in A records, 134
    in HINFO records, 135
    in MX records, 136
    in NS records, 134
    in PTR records, 135
    in SOA records, 133
classes, 14
    for complex objects, 280
        collection, **280–285**, *282*
        data, **285–288**
    names for, 24–26
    of network addresses, 58–59
clients
    in asynchronous sockets, **305–312**, *308*, *312*
    in connection-oriented sockets, **94**, **116**
    in declarative security, **606–608**
    POP3, **501**
        authentication commands in, **501–502**
        information commands in, **502**
        retrieving messages in, **503–504**
        writing, **504–510**, *509*
    in remoting, **577**, **583–585**
    for storing e-mail, 481
    stream, **205–207**
    TCP. *See* TCP (Transmission Control Protocol)
    UDP. *See* UDP (User Datagram Protocol)
    Web, **525–528**, *528*, **533**
ClientTimeout property, 560
Clone method, 29
close method, 257
    for asynchronous sockets, 311
    for connection-oriented sockets, 94, 116, 122, 172
    for connectionless sockets, 95
    in NetworkStream, 199

in Process, 338
in StreamReader, 202
in TcpClient, 251
in UdpClient, 260
CLOSED connection state, 67
CloseMainWindow method, 338
closing connections, **94**
CLR (Common Language Routine) environment, **4–5**, *5*
    security groups in, **595–596**
    security policy in, **594–595**
CN object type, 538
CNAME (Canonical Name) records, **134**, 137
code access permissions, **596**
Code element, 413–414, 417
Collaboration Data Objects (CDO), **483–484**
collection classes, **280–285**, *282*
.com domain, 128
command-line parameters
    in Main, 14
    in WinDump, **44–45**
command/response method in UDP, 72
commands
    in POP3, **501–502**
    in SNMP, **443–444**
commas (,) in variable lists, 15
comment-text value, 490
Comments field, 490–491
CommitChanges method, 548, 551
Common Language Routine (CLR) environment, **4–5**, *5*
    security groups in, **595–596**
    security policy in, **594–595**
common MIB, **445–448**, *446*
Common Name objects, 538
communication channels for remoting, **577**, **579–580**
community names, **444–445**, **448**, 451, 473
community profiles, 444
Compare method, 29
CompareTo method, 29
compiling programs
    with namespaces, **26–28**
    process, **15–16**
completion ports, **102–103**
complex objects, classes for, **280**
    collection, **280–285**, *282*
    data, **285–288**
Computer Management window, 484
computer names, **126**
Concat method, 29
configuration files for remote services, **581–582**
Configure method, 581
Connect method
    for asynchronous sockets, 323
    for connection-oriented sockets, 94, 116
    for connectionless sockets, 95, 117
    for ICMP raw sockets, 416

in Socket, 174–176
for TCP clients, 251
for UDP clients, **219–220**, 260
in Winsock, 99
Connect value in Access, 605
Connected method
in AsyncTcpClient, 307, 309
in NewTcpChat, 387
in TcpChat, 361
Connected property, 110
connection-oriented protocols, 62, 70
connection-oriented sockets, **168**
programming, **92–94**, *92*, **113–116**
TCP. *See* TCP (Transmission Control Protocol)
connection states in TCP, 66–68
connectionless protocols, 68
connectionless sockets, **210**
programming, **94–95**, *95*, **117**
testing, **217–218**, *218*
UDP. *See* UDP (User Datagram Protocol)
Connectionless value, 605
ConnectionOriented value, 605
connections
for Active Directory servers, **543**
for asynchronous sockets, **298–301**, **308–309**, **315–316**
with hosts, **272**
converting data in, **273–276**, *274*
representing data in, **272–273**
sample programs, **276–280**
ConnectionThread class, 355–356, 370–371
constructors, 14–15
container objects, 538
Container property
in Process, 336
in ProcessThread, 344
Content-Description field, **497**
Content-ID field, **497**
Content-Transfer-Encoding field, **496–497**
Content-Type field, **497–499**
ContentEncoding property, 523
ContentLength property, 524
ContentType property, 524
control threads, 369
converting
binary data, **266–268**, **273–276**, *274*
MIB, **456–457**
CookieContainer property, 525
cookies, **524–525**
Cookies property, 524–525
.coop domain, 128
Copy method, 29
CopyTo method, 29
cordbg program, **19–22**
Counter method, 366
Counter2 method, 366–367

country codes in DNS, 128
Country objects in LDAP, 537–538
-cp option in caspol, 598
CPU time, displaying, 335
Create method
in IPEndPoint, 106
in WebRequest, 522
CreateDecryptor method, 613
CreateEncryptor method, 612
CreateObjRef method
in NetworkStream, 199
in Process, 338
in StreamReader, 202
CredCacheTest.cs program, 520–521
CredentialCache class, **520–521**
Credentials property, **519–521**
CredTest.cs program, 519–520
CryptoDataRcvr.cs program, 618–620
CryptoDataSender.cs program, **616–618**
Cryptographic hash security group, 595
CryptoStream class, 612, 618
CryptoTest.cs program, 613–614
csc.exe program
command line switches for, 15
compiling with, 11–12
csc.rsp file, 27–28
-cu option in caspol, 598
current process, information on, **339–340**
CurrentPriority property, 344

D

-d option in soapsuds, 586
-D option in WinDump, 44
data buffers
for asynchronous sockets, 301–303
overflows in, 28
in TCP, 70–71, *70*, **177–180**, *179*
data classes for complex objects, **285–288**
data encryption, **610**
asymmetric, **611**
decryption, **613**
network data, **615–621**, *616*, *621*
process, **612**
sample program, **613–615**
symmetric, **610–611**
data items in Registry, 74
data payloads in Ethernet packets, 52
DataAvailable property, 199
DatabasePath value, 141
databases
DNS, **131–137**
LDAP, 536

DataClass class, 13–15
datalength value, 461
dates in RFC2822, 489
dbgclr program, **18–19**, *19*
DC object type, 538
.de domain, 128
deadlocks, 353
debug option in nslookup, **149–151**
/debug switch in csc, 15
debugging, **17–18**
    with cordbg, **19–22**
    with dbgclr, **18–19**, *19*
    MSIL code, **22–23**, *22–23*
decimal datatype, 266
declarative security, **604–606**
    client program for, **606–608**
    server program for, **608–610**
decryption, **613**
default queries in hostname resolution, **144–146**
Default SMTP Virtual Server Properties window, 484–485,
    485
DefaultGateway name, 75
DefaultIPGateway field, 80
delegates in event programming, **293–294**, *294*
Delegation AuthenticationType, 546
DeleteObject.cs program, 554–555
DeleteTree method, **554–555**
deleting child objects, **553–555**
Delivery tab, 485, *485*
Demand member, 604
Deny member, 605
Description field, 80
DESCryptoServiceProvider class, 611
Deserialize method, 574
    in encryption, 620
    exceptions with, 571
destination address fields
    in IP, 57
    in RFC2822 format, **490**
Destination Unreachable packets, **414–415**
development environment, **6–8**
Dgram socket type, 109
DHCP, 140, 142
DHCPEnabled field, 80
DHCPServer field, 81
Digest authentication, 520
Digest MIME subtype, 499
Directory Context objects, 538
DirectoryEntries class, 550, 553
DirectoryEntry class, 543–546, 550
DirectorySearcher class, **556–557**, 560
DiscardBufferedData method, 202
Dispose method, 338
distinguished names (dns), 538
divide-by-zero errors, 36–37

Divide method
    in MathClass, 578–579, 588
    in MathService, 530
dividing strings, 143–144, 456
DLLs, referencing, 26–28
DNS (Domain Name System), **126–127**
    asynchronous methods in, **159–164**, *163*
    configuration, **138–144**, *140–141*
    database for, **131–137**
    hostnames in, **130–131**, *130*
        advanced queries for, **148–153**
        default queries for, **144–146**
        watching queries for, **146–148**
    for IP addresses, **83–84**
    structure of, **127–129**, *127, 129*
    synchronous methods in, **153–158**
DNSHostName field, 81
DNSName.cs program, 83–84
domain dump option in nslookup, **152–153**
Domain Name System. *See* DNS (Domain Name System)
Domain value for DNS servers, 141
domains
    in Active Directory, **539–540**, *540*
    in DNS, **127–131**, *127, 129*
    names of, **129**, 540
    in NS records, 134
    in SOA records, 133
    in socket function, 89
DontRoute SocketFlag value, 115
dot1netTable object, 472
dotetfx.exe file, 11
dotnetredist.exe file, 11
dotted decimal notation, 58–59
double datatype, 266
DownloadData method, **512–513**
DownloadDataTest.cs program, 512–513
DownloadFile method, **513–514**
DownloadFileTest.cs program, 513–514
downloading
    .NET Framework SDK, **8–9**
    runtime environment, **11**
    Web data, **512–515**
DropMembership option, 394
DropMulticastGroup method, 260, 399
DSACryptoServiceProvider class, 611

E

e-mail, **478**
    attachments in, **493–494**
        MailAttachment class for, **499–501**
        MIME for, **495–499**, *496*
        uuencode for, **495**

filtering, 481
MDA process in, **480–481**
MTA process in, **478–480**, *479*
MUA process in, **481–483**, *482–483*
POP3 clients for, **501**
      authentication commands in, **501–502**
      information commands in, **502**
      retrieving messages in, **503–504**
      writing, **504–510**, *509*
SMTP for. *See* SMTP (Simple Mail Transfer Protocol)
-e option
      in caspol, 598
      in WinDump, 45
Echo Reply packets, **413–414**, 418, 423, *423*, 434
Echo Request packets, **413–414**, 418, 423, *423*, 425,
      432–434
echo servers, 171
editing network directory objects, **548–549**
editors, 12–13
.edu domain, 128
8-bit MIME encoding method, 497
Employee.cs program, 283–285
EmployeeClient.cs program, 285–286
EmployeeSrvr.cs program, 286–287
-en option in caspol, 598
EnableRaisingEvents property, 336
Encoding class, 171
encoding in MIME, 497, 499–500
encryption, **610**
      asymmetric, **611**
      CryptoDataRcvr.cs program for, 618–621, *621*
      CryptoDataSender.cs program for, 616–618
      decryption, **613**
      handling data in, **615–616**, *616*
      in POP3 authentication, 501
      process, **612**
      sample program, **613–615**
      symmetric, **610–611**
Encryption AuthenticationType, 546
EndAccept method, **299–300**, 316
EndConnect method, **300–301**, 309
EndGetHostByName method, 159
EndPoint class, 121
EndRead method, 199
EndReceive method, 118, 310, 317
EndReceiveFrom method, **303–304**
EndResolve method, 159–160, 163
EndSend method, **301–302**, 311, 316
EndSendTo method, **302–303**
EndsWith method, 29
EndWrite method, 199
enriched MIME subtype, 498
EnterDebugMode method, 338
enterprise-level policies, **595**
enterprises object, 466

Equals method
      in IPAddress, 103
      in IPEndPoint, 106
      in NetworkStream, 199
      in Process, 338
      in SMTPMail, 486
      in StreamReader, 202
      in String, 29
      in TcpClient, 251
      in TcpListener, 256
      in Thread, 351
      in UdpClient, 260
error codes and fields
      in SNMP, **449**, 451
      in UDP, **242–244**
ErrorCode property, 242–244
errors, compiler, 16
ESTABLISHED connection state, 67
Ethernet, **51–53**, *52*
      addresses, **53–55**
      protocol types, **56**
event object handles, 102
event programming, **292–293**, *293*
      AsyncCallback class for, **297**
      events and delegates in, **293–294**, *294*
      sample programs, **294–297**
      in Windows, **100–101**
EventHandler class, 162, 296
Everything permission, 597
exceptfds parameter, 97
exceptions
      handling, **36–39**
      in socket programming, **119–120**
      in UDP, **232–235**, **242–244**
ExceptionUdpClient.cs program, 232–234
Execution permission, 597
exit command
      in nslookup, 148
      in UDP, 218
ExitCode property, 336
ExitTime property, 336
expire field, 133
Extensible Markup Language (XML), 529, 532
external-body MIME subtype, 498
External option, 560

F

-f option in caspol, 598
-F option in WinDump, 45
FancyMailTest.cs program, 493–494, *494*
FastBind AuthenticationType, 546
fcntl function, 96, 100

FD_ event types, 101
FD_CLR function, 97
FD_ISSET function, 97
FD_SET function, 97
FD_ZERO function, 97
file descriptors, 88
FileStream class, 34–35
    in decryption, 613
    in encryption, 615
Filter property, **556–557**
Filter Selection window, 49, *49*
filters
    in Analyzer, **49–50**, *49–50*
    in catch statements, 37
    in directory searches, **556–557**
    in e-mail, 481
    in WinDump, **45–46**
FIN flag, 66–67, *67*
FIN-WAIT-1 connection state, 67
FIN-WAIT-2 connection state, 68
finally blocks, 37
Find method, 553
FindAll method, 558
FindDNSServers.cs program, 142–144
findHosts method, 388–389
FindMask.cs program, **435–438**, *435*
FindOne method, 557
Finger command, 148
fixed-size TCP messages, **184–190**
FixedTcpClient.cs program, 188–190
FixedTcpSrvr.cs program, 187–188
Flags field
    in IP, 57
    in TCP, 66
float datatype, 266
Flush method
    in NetworkStream, 199, 201
    in StreamWriter, 203
FlushFinalBlock method, 614, 618, 620
foreach function, 83–84
forests in Active Directory, **542**, *542*
Form class, 296
FQDNs (fully-qualified domain names), 153
Fragment offset field, 57, 60
fragmentation flags, **59–60**
From field, 489
From property, 491
FullTrust permission, 597
fully-qualified domain names (FQDNs), 153

General tab, 485
get method
    for HTTP headers, 515
    in SNMP, 453–456, 460
GetAvailableThreads method, 365
GetBuffer method, 615
GetBytes method
    for collective classes, **281–286**, *282*
    for converting binary datatypes, 266–267, 272
    in ICMP, 420, 422
    in TCP, 171, 192
getChecksum method, 421–423
GetCurrentProcess method, 338–340
GetDNSAddressInfo.cs program, 156–157
GetDNSHostInfo.cs program, 154–155
GetHashCode method
    in IPAddress, 103
    in IPEndPoint, 106
    in NetworkStream, 199
    in Process, 338
    in SMTPMail, 486
    in StreamReader, 202
    in TcpClient, 251
    in TcpListener, 256
    in Thread, 351
    in UdpClient, 260
GetHostByAddress method, **155–157**
GetHostByName method, 83, 105, **154–155**
GetHostName method, 83, 105, **153**, 380
GetKey method, 515
GetLifetimeService method
    in NetworkStream, 199
    in Process, 338
    in StreamReader, 202
GetMaxThreads method, 365
getmessagesDoubleClick method, 508
getnextMIB method, **470–471**
GetNextRequest PDUs, 444, 449
    vs. GetRequest, 456–457
    ports for, 452
    queries with, **469–474**, *470*
    in variable binding, 450
GetObject method, 583
GetProc.cs program, 339–340
GetProcessById method, 338–339
GetProcessByName method, 339
GetProcesses method, 338–341, 347
GetProperties.cs program, 547–548
GetRequest PDUs, 444
    in error status and error index fields, 449
    vs. GetNextRequest, 456–457
    monitoring, 462
    object identifiers in, 447, 452
    ports for, 452
    in variable binding, 450

G

-gc option in soapsuds, 586, 589

GetRequestStream method, 523
GetResolveInfo.cs program, 157–158
GetResponse method in HttpWebResponse, 523
GetResponse PDUs, 444
    in error status and error index fields, 449
    monitoring, 462–463
    queries with, 470
GetSocketOption method, 230–232
GetStream method, 121, 123, 251
GetString method, 171, 178–179, 270
GetSubKeyNames method, 79
GetThreads.cs program, 345–347
GetType method
    in IPAddress, 103
    in IPEndPoint, 106
    in NetworkStream, 199
    in Process, 338
    in StreamReader, 202
    in TcpClient, 251
    in TcpListener, 256
    in Thread, 351
    in UdpClient, 260
GetValue method, 77, 79
Ggp ProtocolType value, 415
global broadcasts, **376–377**, *377*
global namespaces, 24
.gov domain, 128
groups
    multicast, 390
    permissions for, **598–600**
    for security, **595–596**

H

-h option in caspol, 598
Handle property
    in Process, 336
    in Socket, 110
HandleConnection method, 355–356, 370–371
HandleCount property, 336
handshakes in TCP, 66–67, *67*
hardware field, 135
HasExited property, 336
Header Checksum field, 57
Header Length field, 57
Header property, **492**
headers, HTTP
    retrieving, **523–525**
    viewing, **515–516**
Headers property
    in HttpWebResponse, 524
    in MailMessage, 491
Help command, 148

helper classes
    TcpClient, **120–122**, **250**
        constructors for, **250–251**
        in ICMP, 415
        methods in, **251–252**
        sample program, **252–255**, *255*
    TcpListener, **122–123**, **255**
        constructors for, **255–256**
        methods for, **256–257**
        sample program, **257–258**
    UdpClient, **123–124**, **259**
        constructors for, **259–260**
        in ICMP, 415
        methods for, **260**
        for multicasting, **399–401**
        in programs, **260–262**
        sample programs, 262–264
hexadecimal output in Analyzer, 51
hierarchical databases, 536
high bits in IP addresses, 58
High class, 335
HINFO (Host Information) records, **135**
HKEY_ prefix, 74
host field
    in A records, 134
    in HINFO records, 135
    in MX records, 136
Host Information (HINFO) records, **135**
host part of addresses, 376–377, *377*
Host property, 605
Hostname value, 142
hostnames
    local domain, **130**, *130*
    remote domain, **130–131**
    resolving
        advanced queries in, **148–153**
        default queries in, **144–146**
        watching queries in, **146–148**
hosts, communicating with, **272**
    converting data in, **273–276**, *274*
    representing data in, **272–273**
    sample programs, **276–280**
hosts file, **138–139**
HostToNetworkOrder method, 103, 274–275
-hpn option in soapsuds, 586
-hpp option in soapsuds, 586
html MIME subtype, 498
HTTP, **512**
    headers for
        retrieving, **523–525**
        viewing, **515–516**
    HttpWebRequest class, **522–523**
    HttpWebResponse class, **523–525**
    Web client example, **525–528**, *528*
    Web services, **528–533**, *529*, *531–532*

WebClient class, **512**
  Credentials property, **519–521**
  for downloading Web data, **512–515**
  for uploading Web data, **516–519**
  for viewing HTTP headers, **515–516**
  WebRequest and WebResponse classes, **521–522**
HttpChannel class, **579–580**, 585
HttpWebRequest class, **522–523**
HttpWebResponse class, **523–525**

I

-i option in WinDump, 45
-ia option in soapsuds, 586
IAB (Internet Activities Board), 445
IANA (Internet Assigned Numbers Authority), 53
IAsyncResult class, 160, 163, 299–301
ICANN (Internet Corporation for Assigned Names and
    Numbers), 129
ICMP (Internet Control Message Protocol), 412
  checksums in, 413, 417, **420–422**
  example class, **422–423**
  FindMask program for, **435–438**, *435*
  packets in
    creator for, **420**
    format of, **412–413**, *412*
    types of, **413–415**
  ping program for
    advanced, **426–431**, *431*
    simple, **423–426**, *423*
  raw sockets in, **415–417**
  traceroute program for, **432–435**
ICMP class, **417–419**
ICMP.cs program, 422–423
Icmp ProtocolType value, 415–416
-id option in soapsuds, 586
Id property
  in Process, 336
  in ProcessThread, 344–345
IDE (Integrated Development Environment), 7
IdealProcessor property, 344–345
Identification field
  in IP, 57, 60
  in RFC2822 format, **490**
Identifier field
  in Echo Reply packets, 418
  in Echo Request packets, 414, 418
  in Subnet Request packets, 435
identifiers in MIB, 445
identity permissions, **597**
IDictionary class, 492
Idle class, 335
Idp ProtocolType value, 415

IFormatter class, 566–567
ifTable object, 470
IGMP (Internet Group Management Protocol), 392–393,
    393, 397
Igmp ProtocolType value, 415
IIS (Internet Information Services) package, **484–485**, *485*
IIS access method, 544
IL DASM (Intermediate Language Disassembler), 22, *22*
IList class, 324
image Content-Type, 498
IMAP (Interactive Mail Access Protocol), 482–483, *483*
immutable strings, 31
imperative security, 604
IN-ADDR name field, 135
In-Reply-To field, 490
indexed community names, 473
IndexOf method, 29
.info domain, 128
information commands in POP3 client, **502**
information fields in RFC2822 format, **490–491**
InheritanceDemand member, 605
initialization of programs, e-mail for, 481
initialization vectors (IVs), 611
Initialized state, 344
InitializeLifetimeService method
  in NetworkStream, 199
  in Process, 338
  in StreamReader, 202
Insert method, 29
Install Options screen, 10, *10*
installing
  .NET Framework SDK, **9–10**, *10*
  runtime environment, **11**
  WinPcap programs, **43**
int datatype, 266
Integrated Development Environment (IDE), 7
Interactive Mail Access Protocol (IMAP), 482–483, *483*
interface objects, 469–471, *470*
Intermediate Language Disassembler (IL DASM), 22, *22*
Intern method, 29
Internet Activities Board (IAB), 445
Internet Assigned Numbers Authority (IANA), 53
Internet Control Message Protocol (ICMP). *See* ICMP
    (Internet Control Message Protocol)
Internet Corporation for Assigned Names and Numbers
    (ICANN), 129
Internet Group Management Protocol (IGMP), 392–393,
    393, 397
Internet Information Services (IIS) package, **484–485**, *485*
internet object, 445, *446*
Internet permission, 597
Internet Protocol. *See* IP (Internet Protocol)
Internet Protocol Properties window, 139, 141
Internet value, 596, 600
Internic Corporation, 129

Interprocess Communication (IPC) pipes, 89
Interrupt method, 351
Intranet value, 596, 601
ioctlsocket function, 100
IP (Internet Protocol), 42, **56–58**, *57*
  address fields in, **58–59**
  fragmentation flags in, **59–60**
  protocol field in, **61**
  Type of Service field in, **60–61**
IP addresses
  in declarative security, 608
  DNS for. *See* DNS (Domain Name System)
  ipconfig for, **72–74**
  Registry for, **74–79**
  in socket programming, **103–108**
  WMI for, **80–83**
IP broadcasting, **376**
  for advertising loops, **382–390**, *389*
  local vs. global, **376–377**, *377*
  receiving packets in, **380–382**
  sending packets in, **377–380**, *380*
IP endpoints, 64
IP multicasting, **376**, **390–391**
  peer-to-peer, **391**, *391*
  receiving packets in, **394–395**, **400**
  sample program, **402–406**
  sending packets in, **392–393**, *393*, **395**, **398–401**
  servers for, **392**, *392*
  sockets for, **393–399**
  TTL value for, **398–399**
  UdpClient, **399–401**
IP ProtocolType value, 415
IPAddress class, **103–106**, 379–380
IPAddress field
  in Registry, 75
  in Win32_NetworkAdapterConfiguration, 81
IPC (Interprocess Communication) pipes, 89
ipconfig tool, **72–74**
IPEnabled field, 81
IPEndPoint class, **106–108**, 170, 175, 210–211
IPEndPointSample.cs program, 107–108
IPHostEntry class, 84, 105
IPMask name, 75
IPSubnet field, 81
Ipx ProtocolType value, 416
-is option in soapsuds, 586
IsBackground property, 383
IsLoopBack method, 104
iso object, 445
IVs (initialization vectors), 611

J

JIT (just-in-time) compiler, 5, 346

JITTracking flag, 17
Join method
  in String, 29
  in Thread, 351
JoinMulticastGroup method, 260, 399–400
just-in-time (JIT) compiler, 5, 346

K

keys
  encryption, 610–611
  Registry, 74–75
Keywords field, 491
Kill method, 338

L

-l option in caspol, 598
Label class, 296
LAST-ACK connection state, 68
LastIndexOf method, 30
LastModified property, 524
LDAP (Lightweight Directory Access Protocol), **536–539**, *537*
LDAP access method, 544
least significant bytes in datatype representation, 272
LeaveDebugMode method, 339
left-token encoding method, 497
Length of PDU area field, 451
Length property, 32
-lf option in caspol, 598
-lg option in caspol, 598, 601–602
libraries, namespaces for, 26–28
Lightweight Directory Access Protocol (LDAP), **536–539**, *537*
line numbers with compiler, 16
LingerState property, 252
LinkDemand member, 605
LIST command, 502
ListBox class, 296–297
-listdescription option in caspol, 598
LISTEN connection state, 67
Listen method
  operation of, 93
  for server sockets, 114, 117, 170, 322
  in Winsock, 99
listing
  in network directories
    child objects, **550–551**
    properties, **547–548**
  permissions
    application, **600–601**

group, **598–600**
threads, **347–350**, **357–358**
ListObjects.cs program, 550–551
ListProcs.cs program, 340–341
ListThreads.cs program, 347–350, 357–358, 364, 367–368, 371–372
little endian data representation, 272–273
local alias e-mail accounts, 480
local broadcasts, **376–377**, *377*
local buffers in TCP, 70, *70*
local domain hostnames, **130**, *130*
local system e-mail accounts, 480
LocalEndPoint property, 110
localhost hostname, 139
LocalIntranet group, 600–601
LocalIntranet permission, 597
locality objectClass, 538
Locals tab, 19, *19*
loginandretr method, 506–509
logins to network directories, **543–546**
long datatype, 266
loopback addresses, 139
Loopback field, 104
lost packets in UDP
    exceptions in, **232–235**, **242–244**
    preventing, **223–229**
    retransmissions in, **235–242**
    socket time-outs in, 229–232
-lp option in caspol, 598
ls command, 148, **152–153**
Lserver command, 148

M

-m option in caspol, 598, 602
MAC (Media Access Card) addresses
    in Ethernet packets, 52
    tracking, **471–474**
    in Win32_NetworkAdapterConfiguration, 81
MAC identifiers, 53–54
MacAddress.cs program, 471–474
MACAddress field, 81
machine-level policies, **595**
MachineName property, 336–337
mail. *See* e-mail; SMTP (Simple Mail Transfer Protocol)
Mail Exchange (MX) records, **135–137**
MailAttachment class, 493, **499–501**
MailAttachTest.cs program, 500–501
mailbox-list value, 489
MailFormat enumeration, 492
MailMessage class, **491–494**, *494*
MailPriority enumeration, 492
MailTest.cs program, 487–488

Main() method, 14, 17
/main switch in csc, 15, 17
MainModule property, 336
MainWindowHandle property, 336
MainWindowTitle property, 336
Management Information Base (MIB), 442–443
    converting, **456–457**
    extracting, **469–470**
    object values in, 445, **447–448**, 452
    structure of, **445–447**, *446*
    vendor, **463–469**, *469*
ManagementObject class, 81, 83
ManagementObjectiveCollection class, 81, 83
ManagementObjectiveSearcher class, 81–82
MAPI (Message Application Program Interface) standard, 484
markers for TCP messages, **198**
MarshalByRefObject class, 578–579
MathClass class, 585–586, *586*
MathClass.cs program
    for remoting, 578–579
    soapsuds-generated, 587–588
MathClass.dll file, 579, 583
MathClient.cs program, 584–585
MathServer.cs program, 582
MathService.asmx program, 529–531, *531–532*
MathService.cs file, 532
MathService.dll file, 532–533
MaxIOVectorLength value, 115
MaxPort field, 107
MaxWorkingSet property, 336
MD-5 encryption, 520
MDA (Message Delivery Agent) process, **480–481**
Media Access Card (MAC) addresses
    in Ethernet packets, 52
    tracking, **471–474**
    in Win32_NetworkAdapterConfiguration, 81
memory for strings, 31
MemoryStream class
    in encryption, 614–615, 618, 620
    in serialization, 571, 574
Message Application Program Interface (MAPI) standard, 484
message Content-Type, 498
Message data variable, 417
Message Delivery Agent (MDA) process, **480–481**
Message element in ICMP, 413, 418–419
Message-ID field, 490
Message Transfer Agent (MTA) process, **478–480**, *479*
Message User Agent (MUA) process, **481–483**, *482–483*
messages
    mail. *See* e-mail; SMTP (Simple Mail Transfer Protocol)
    in TCP, **180**
        fixed-size, **184–190**
        markers for, **198**

unprotected boundaries in, **180–184**, *180*
variable-length, **190–197**
in UDP, **220–223**
MessageSize data element, 419
Method property, 524
methods, referencing, 26
mgmt object, 446
MIB (Management Information Base), 442–443
converting, **456–457**
extracting, **469–470**
object values in, 445, **447–448**, 452
structure of, **445–447**, *446*
vendor, **463–469**, *469*
mib-2 objects, 446–447
Microsoft Intermediate Language (MSIL), **4–6**, *6*
debugging, **22–23**, *22–23*
for threads, 346
Microsoft.Win32 namespace, 25
Microsoft.Win32.Registry namespace, 77
Microsoft.Win32.RegistryKey namespace, 77
.mil domain, 128
MIME (Multipurpose Internet Mail Extensions), **495–500**, *496*
MIME-Version field, **496**
minimum field, 133
MinPort field, 107
MinWorkingSet property, 336
Mixed MIME subtype, 498
mode parameter
in CryptoStream, 612
in RemotingConfiguration, **580–581**
ModifyProperty.cs program, 548–549
Modules property, 336
most significant bytes in datatype representation, 272
moving data
across networks
binary data, **265–271**
complex objects, **280–288**, *282*
serialized class for, **564–574**
mscorcfg program, **602–603**, *603*
msg-id value, 490
MSIL (Microsoft Intermediate Language), **4–6**, *6*
debugging, **22–23**, *22–23*
for threads, 346
MTA (Message Transfer Agent) process, **478–480**, *479*
MUA (Message User Agent) process, **481–483**, *482–483*
multicast addresses, 55
multicast groups, 390
MulticastChat.cs program, 402–406
multicasting. *See* IP multicasting
MulticastOption class, 394
multipart Content-Type, 498
multiple source files, **16–17**
multiplexed sockets, **96–98**, 100–101, 118

Multiply method
in MathClass, 578, 588
in MathService, 530, 532, *532*
Multipurpose Internet Mail Extensions (MIME), **495–500**, *496*
MultiRecv.cs program, 394–397
MultiSend.cs program, 396
multithreaded applications, 343
.museum domain, 128
MX (Mail Exchange) records, **135–137**
MyComputer value, 596, 600

N

-n option in WinDump, 45
-N option in WinDump, 45
NAME command, 148
.name domain, 128
Name Server (NS) records, **134**, 137
names
for child objects, **555**
for classes, 24–26
community, **444–445**, 448, 451, 473
for computers, **126**
for domains, **129**, 540
in MX records, 135
in PTR records, 135
in SNMP, **448**
NameServer value, 142
namespace directive, 24
namespaces, **24–25**
compiling programs with, **26–28**
.NET Framework, **25**
in programs, **26**
ND ProtocolType value, 416
NDS access method, 544
.NET, **4**
CLR in, **4–5**, *5*
MSIL code in, **5–6**, *6*
.net domain, 128
.NET Framework, **8**
downloading, **8–9**
installing, **9–10**, *10*
namespaces in, **25**
netmon program, 42
netstat command, 213–214
network addresses, **91–92**
network analyzers, 42
network byte order
converting to, 273–274
reading data in, **276–280**
network cards, promiscuous mode in, 43

network data security, encryption for, **610**
    asymmetric, **611**
    CryptoDataRcvr.cs program for, 618–621, *621*
    CryptoDataSender.cs program for, 616–618
    decryption, **613**
    handling data in, **615–616**, *616*
    in POP3 authentication, 501
    process, **612**
    sample program, **613–615**
    symmetric, **610–611**
network directories, **536**
    child objects in
        adding, **551–553**
        listing, **550–551**
        removing, **553–555**
        renaming, **555**
    LDAP system for, **536–539**, *537*
    logins to, **543–546**
    object properties in, **546–550**
    searching in, **556–561**
network packets. *See* packets
network traffic, monitoring, **42**
    Analyzer program for, 43
        operation of, **48–51**, *48–50*
        for TCP servers, **172–173**, *173*
    WinDump program for, 43
        command-line options in, **44–45**
        filter expressions in, **45–46**
        with nslookup, **146–148**
        running, **46–47**
NetworkCredentials class, **519–520**
NetworkOrderClient.cs program, 276–277
NetworkOrderSrvr.cs program, 277–279
NetworkStream class, 121, 123, **198–202**, 258, 564
NetworkStreamTcpClient.cs program, 200–202
NetworkToHostOrder method, 104, 276
NewMathClient.cs program, 589–590
NewMultiSend.cs program, 398–399
NewTcpChat.cs program, **384–390**, *389*
NoDelay property, *252*
non-blocking methods
    for asynchronous sockets, **319**
        poll, **319–323**
        select, **324–331**, *330*
    in socket programming, **95–98**, **117–118**
None AuthenticationType, 546
None SocketFlag value, 115
NonpagedSystemMemorySize property, 336
Normal class, 335
Nothing permission, 597
-nowp option in soapsuds, 586, 588
NoZone value, 596
NS (Name Server) records, **134**, 137
nslookup
    debug option in, **149–151**

    for hostname resolution, **144–153**
    ls option in, **152–153**
    querytype option in, **151–152**
    Set command in, 148–149
NWCOMPAT access method, 544

O

O object type in LDAP, 537
-oa option in soapsuds, 586
object identifiers
    in MIB, 445, 465
    in SNMP packets, 451
object properties and values
    in MIB, 445, **447–448**, 452
    in network directories, **546–550**
objectClasses in LDAP, 538–539, 549
objectUri parameter, **580–581**
-od option in soapsuds, 586
OddUdpClient.cs program, 219–220
offset values for buffers, 301, 303
OLEMSG32.DLL library, 483
OneLevel value, 557
OpenRead method, **514–515**
OpenReadTest.cs program, 514–515
OpenSubKey method, 77, 143
OpenWrite method, **516–517**
OpenWriteTest.cs program, 516–517
operational states of threads, 343–344
Options field, 57
.org domain, 128
Organization objects, 537–538
Organizational Units (OUs)
    in Active Directory, **540**
    in LDAP, 537
Organizationally Unique Identifiers (OUIs), 53
organizationalPerson objectClass, 538
organizationalRole objectClass, 538
organizationalUnit objectClass, 539
origin field, 133
origination date field, **489**
-os option in soapsuds, 587
OU object type, 537
OUIs (Organizationally Unique Identifiers), 53
OUs (Organizational Units)
    in Active Directory, **540**
    in LDAP, 537
/out switch in csc, 15, 17
OutOfBand SocketFlag value, 115
overflows, buffer, 28, 228
overlapped I/O, **102**

P

p command in cordbg, 21
-p option in soapsuds, 587
Packet details section, 50
Packet index section, 50
packetReceive method, 404–405
packets, **51**, *51*
    capturing, **48–50**
    Ethernet, **51–56**, *52*
    in ICMP
        creator for, **420**
        format of, **412–413**, *412*
        types of, **413–415**
    IP, **56–61**, *57*
    in SNMP
        format of, **448–450**
        layout of, **450–452**, *450*
        receiving, **457**
        sending, **457**
    in TCP, **61–68**, *62–63*, *67*
    in UDP, **68–69**, *68*
        exceptions for, **232–235**, **242–244**
        lost, preventing, **223–229**
        retransmissions of, **235–242**
        socket time-outs in, **229–232**
PadLeft method, 30
PadRight method, 30
PagedMemorySize property, 336
PageSize property, 561
Parallel MIME subtype, 498
parentheses() in catch statements, 37
Parse method
    in ICMP, 425
    in IPAddress, 104
partial MIME subtype, 498
Partial SocketFlag value, 115
PASS command, 501–502
passwords in POP3, 501–502
Path property, 545, 558
PDB (programmer database) files, 17–18
PDUs (protocol data units), 444, **448–449**
PeakPagedMemorySize property, 336
PeakVirtualMemorySize property, 336
PeakWorkingSet property, 336
Peek method, 202, 515
Peek SocketFlag value, 115
peer-to-peer multicasting, **391**, *391*
Pending method, 256
performance in serialization, 590
periods (.) for machine names, 337
permissions, **596–597**
    application, **600–601**
    changing, **601–602**
    group, **598–600**
    socket, **603–610**
PermitOnly member, 605
person field, 133
person objectClass, 539
PF_ domains, 89–90
phrase-text value, 490
PickyTcpClient.cs program, 606–607
PickyTcpListener.cs program, 608–610
ping program for ICMP
    advanced, **426–431**, *431*
    simple, **423–426**, *423*
plain MIME subtype, 497
-pn option in soapsuds, 587
Point class, 308
Pointer (PTR) records, **135**, 137
policies
    for security, **594–595**
    in SNMP, 444
Poll method, **319–323**
pools of threads, **364**
    sample programs, **366–369**
    in servers, **369–372**
    ThreadPool class for, **365**
POP (Post Office Protocol), 482, *482*
POP3 clients, **501**
    authentication commands in, **501–502**
    information commands in, **502**
    retrieving messages in, **503–504**
    writing, **504–510**, *509*
PopCheck.cs program, 504–510, *509*
Port property
    in IPEndPoint, 107, 170
    in SocketPermissionAttribute, 605
ports
    in sockets programming, **102–103**
    in TCP, **63–65**, *63*
    in UDP, 69, 399
Post Office Protocol (POP), 482, *482*. *See also* POP3 clients
-pp option in caspol, 598
PPP connections
    IP information for, 73
    monitoring, 49
preference field, 136
primitives in filter expressions, 45
priority
    of e-mail, **492**
    in IP packets, 60–61
    of processes, 335
priority field, 60–61
Priority property, **491–492**
PriorityBoostEnabled property
    in Process, 337
    in ProcessThread, 344
PriorityClass property, 337

PriorityLevel property, 344
private key encryption, 610
PrivateMemorySize property, 337
PrivilegedProcessorTime property
    in Process, 337
    in ProcessThread, 344
pro command, 21
.pro domain, 128
Process class, **336–339**, 341
process IDs, 335
processes, **334–335**, *334. See also* threads
    information on, **335**, **339–343**
    Process class for, **336–339**
ProcessName property, 337
ProcessorAffinity property
    in Process, 337
    in ProcessThread, 344–345
ProcessPriorityClass class, 335
ProcessThread class, 344–345, 347
ProcessThreadCollection class, 346–347
profiles, community, 444
program initialization, e-mail for, 481
programmer database (PDB) files, 17–18
programs
    compiling and running, **15–16**
    creating, **12–15**
    debugging, **17–22**, *19*
    initialization of, e-mail for, 481
    multiple source files for, **16–17**
    namespaces in, **26–28**
promiscuous mode in network cards, 43, 49
Promiscuous Mode option, 49
Properties property, *546*, 558
PropertiesToLoad property, **557**
PropertyCollection class, 546–547, 549
PropertyNames property, 547, 559
PropertyNamesOnly property, 561
protocol data units (PDUs), 444, **448–449**
Protocol field, 57, **61**
protocols
    connection-oriented, 62, 70
    connectionless, 68
    Ethernet, 52, **56**
    in IP, 57, **61**
    in socket, 90
ProtocolType property and value
    in ICMP, 415–416
    in Socket, 110
ProtocolVersion property, 524
proxies
    for remoting, **577–579**, **585–590**, *586*
    web, **522**, 529, *529*, **532**
    wrapped, **588–590**
PTR (Pointer) records, **135**, 137

public key encryption, 611
Pup ProtocolType value, 416

Q

-q option in WinDump, 45
qualifiers in filter expressions, 45–46
Quality of Service (QoS) type, 60
queries
    in DNS
        advanced, **148–153**
        default, **144–146**
        watching, **146–148**
    in WMI, **81–83**
querytype option, **151–152**
QueueUserWorkItem method, 365, 371
QUIT command, 504
quoted-printable MIME encoding method, 497

R

-r option
    in caspol, 598
    in WinDump, 45
race conditions, 353
RAD (rapid application development), 7
Raw ProtocolType value, 416
raw sockets, 109, **415–417**
RC2CryptoServiceProvider class, 611
Read method
    in NetworkStream, 199–200
    in StreamReader, 202
    in TcpClient, 254
ReadBlock method, 202
ReadByte method, 199
ReadData method, 311
readfds parameter, 97
reading
    data in network byte order, **276–280**
    e-mail, 481
ReadLine method, 202–207
ReadonlyServer AuthenticationType, 546
ReadToEnd method, 203
Ready state, 344, 347
RealTime class, 335
Receive method
    for clients, 116
    for connectionless sockets, 117
    in non-blocking programming, 118, 323, 327–328
    for servers, 115–116
    for SNMP, 457

in Socket, 170
for TCP
    buffers, 177–180, *179*
    clients, 176, 254
    with fixed-size messages, 185–186
    servers, **171–172**
    with unprotected message boundaries, 181–184
for UDP clients, 123, 219–220, **260–261**
ReceiveBufferSize property, 252
ReceiveData method
    in AsyncTcpClient, 307, 310
    in AsyncTcpSrvr, 314, 317
    for connection-oriented sockets, 192
    in NewTcpChat, 387–388
    for TCP fixed-size messages, 186–189
    in TcpChat, 361–363
ReceiveFrom method
    for connectionless sockets, 117
    for ICMP, 417, 437
    for multicasts, 395
    for UDP, **210–211**, 214, 221, 224–229, 232–235, 244
ReceiveTimeout property and option
    for ICMP, 437
    in TcpClient, 252
    for UDP, 230
ReceiveVarData method, 193–194, 196
receiving data
    with asynchronous sockets, **303–304**, **310**, **317**
    binary, **267–268**
    e-mail, **479–480**
    with ICMP sockets, **417**
    packets
        broadcast, **380–382**
        multicast, **394–395**, **400**
        SNMP, **457**
    with serialized class, **569–571**
    TCP messages
        fixed-size, **186–187**
        variable-length, **192–193**
    threads for, **358**, *359*
recv function, 93–96
RecvBroadcst.cs program, 380–382
RecvData method
    in BetterDataRcvr, 573–574
    in CryptoDataRcvr, 619
recvfrom function, 95
Redistributable package, 11–12
ref keyword, 117
References field, 490
referencing
    DLLs, 26–28
    methods, 26
    variables, 211
ReferralChasing property, 560
ReferralChasingOption enumerator, 560

refresh field, 133
Refresh method, 338
reg command, 21
RegisterChannel method, 580
registering remote class services, **580–581**, **583**
RegisterWaitForSingleObject method, 365
RegisterWellKnownServiceType method, 582
Registry
    for DNS, 141–142
    for IP addresses, **74–79**
    searching, **76–79**
RegistryKey class, 143
relationships in Active Directory, 541
relaying e-mail, 480–481
reliability in TCP layer, **65**
Remote class, 215, **575–576**, *576*
remote DNS servers, **139–140**, *140–141*
remote domain hostnames, **130–131**
remote hosts, 121
remote user e-mail accounts, 480
RemoteEndPoint property, 110, 170
remoting, **574–575**, *575*
    client program for, **577**, **583–585**
    communication channels for, **577**, **579–580**
    proxy class for, **577–579**, **585–590**, *586*
    server for, **576–577**, **579–583**
    soapsuds program for, **585–590**, *586*
RemotingConfiguration class, **580–581**, 583
Remove method
    in DirectoryEntries, 553
    in String, 30
RemoveObject.cs program, 553–554
removing child objects, **553–555**
Rename method, 555
RenameObject.cs program, 555–556
renaming child objects, **555**
Replace method, 30
Reply-To field, 489
Request For Comments (RFC) documents, 53
request-ID field, **449**, 451
RequestMinimum member, 605
RequestOptional member, 605
RequestRefuse member, 605
residentialPerson objectClass, 539
Resolve method
    for DNS, **157–158**
    for ICMP, 425, 427
Resolved method, 160–163
-resolvegroup option, 600
resource records (RRs) in DNS, **131–132**
    A, **134**
    CNAME, **134**
    HINFO, **135**
    MX, **135–136**
    NS, **134**

PTR, **135**
SOA, **132–133**
/resource switch in csc, 15, 27
Responding property, 337
ResponseHeaders property, 515
ResponseHeaderTest.cs program, 515–516
ResponseUri property, 524
ResultPropertyCollection class, 559
Resume method, 351
RETR command, 503–504, 510
retransmissions in UDP, **235–242**
retries in UDP, 235
retrieving
    in HTTP
        data, **523**
        headers, **523–525**
    POP3 messages, **503–504**
retry counts in UDP, 72
retry field in SOA records, 133
RetryUdpClient.cs program, 237–241
-rf option in caspol, 598
rfc822 MIME subtype, 498
RFC2822 mail format, **488–491**, *489*
-rg option in caspol, 598
RijndaelManaged class, 611
role-based permissions, **597**
Root command, 148
root DNS servers, 131
root domains, 541
root nodes in DNS, 127, *127*
root objects in LDAP, 537, *537*
Rotor project, 5
routers for multicast packets, **392–393**, *393*
-rp option in caspol, 598
RRs (resource records) in DNS, **131–132**
    A, **134**
    CNAME, **134**
    HINFO, **135**
    MX, **135–136**
    NS, **134**
    PTR, **135**
    SOA, **132–133**
-rs option in caspol, 598
RSACryptoServiceProvider class, 611
-rsg option in caspol, 598
-rsp option in caspol, 598
run command, 21
running programs, **15–16**
Running state, 344
runtime environment, **10–11**
    developing with, **11–12**
    downloading and installing, **11**
Runtime Security Policy, 602–603, *603*

S

s command in cordbg, 21
-s option
    in caspol, 598–599
    in WinDump, 45, 47, 147
-S option in WinDump, 45
sa_data element, 91
sa_family element, 91
SampleBuilder.cs program, 32–33
SampleClass.cs program, 13–16
sbyte datatype, 266
-sdl option in soapsuds, 587
-se option in soapsuds, 587
Sealing AuthenticationType, 546
searching
    network directories, **556–561**
    Registry, **76–79**
SearchList value, 142
SearchResultCollection class, 558–559
SearchRoot property, 556
SearchScope property, **557**
Secure AuthenticationType, 546
SecureSocketsLayer AuthenticationType, 546
security, **594**
    caspol program for, **597–602**
    groups for, **595–596**
    mscorcfg program for, **602–603**, *603*
    for network data. *See* encryption
    permissions for, **596–597**
        application, **600–601**
        changing, **601–602**
        group, **598–600**
        socket, **603–610**
    policies for, **594–595**
SecurityAction class, **604–605**
SecurityException exceptions, 607
Select method
    for asynchronous sockets, **324–331**
    for multiple clients, 354
    for multiplexed sockets, **96–98**, 100–101, 118
SelectError value, 320
SelectMode class, 319–320
SelectRead value, 319
SelectTcpClient.cs program, 328–331
SelectTcpSrvr.cs program, 326–331, *330*
SelectWrite value, 320
Send method, 93–95, 123–124
    for connectionless sockets, 117
    for servers, 115–116
    in SMTPMail, 486–488, 491
    in Socket, 170
    for TCP
        clients, 176

with fixed-size messages, 185–186
with unprotected message boundaries, 180–184, *180*
for UDP clients, 123–124, 219–220, **260–262**
SendBufferSize property, 252
SendData method
in AsyncTcpClient, 307, 310
in AsyncTcpSrvr, 314, 316
in BetterDataSender, 572
in CryptoDataSender, 616–617
in NewTcpChat, 387
for TCP fixed-size messages, 187–189
in TcpChat, 361
Sender field, 489
sending data
with asynchronous sockets, **301–303**, **310–311**,
   316–317
binary, **266–267**, **273–276**, *274*
e-mail, **479**
in HTTP, **523**
ICMP raw sockets, **416**
packets
broadcast, **377–380**, *380*
multicast, **392–393**, *393*, **395**, **398–401**
SNMP, **457**
with serialized class, **566–569**
TCP messages
fixed-size, **185–186**
variable-length, **191–192**
threads for, **358**, *359*
sendPackets method, 383
sendPing method, 429–430
SendTimeout property, 252
SendTo method
for broadcasts, 379
for connectionless sockets, 95, 117
for ICMP, 416, 421
for UDP, **210–211**, 214, 221
SendVarData method, 191–193, 195
sequence field
in SNMP packets, 450
in Subnet Request packets, 435
in TCP, 65
Sequence number
in Echo Reply packets, 418
in Echo Request packets, 414, 418
sequences in SNMP, 448
serial numbers
in Ethernet addresses, 53
in SOA records, 133
SerialEmployee.cs program, 565
SerialEmployee.dll file, 567
Serialize method, 566
in IPEndPoint, 106
in SOAPFormatter, 618

serialized class, **564**
creating, **565**
problems with, **571–574**
receiver program for, **569–571**
sender program for, **566–569**
serializers, 288
Server command, 148
server field, 134
Server property, 524
server.xml configuration file, 581
ServerBind AuthenticationType, 546
ServerPageTimeLimit property, 561
servers
Active Directory, connecting to, **543**
advertising, **382–390**, *389*
asynchronous sockets, **312–318**, *315*, *318*
with connection-oriented sockets, **92–93**, **114–116**
for declarative security, **608–610**
DNS, **139–142**, *140–141*
for multicasting, **392**, *392*
in NS records, 134
for remoting, **576–577**, **579–583**
for storing e-mail, **482–483**, *483*
stream, **203–205**
for TCP. *See* TCP (Transmission Control Protocol)
thread pools in, **369–372**
threaded, **354–358**, *354*
for UDP. *See* UDP (User Datagram Protocol)
for Web services, **529–532**, *531–532*
ServerTimeLimit property, 561
Services Registry key, 76
ServiceTest.cs program, 533
sessions in TCP, **66–68**, *67*
Set command, 148–149
SetRequest PDUs, 444, 449, 452
SetSocketOption method
for broadcasts, 378–379
for ICMP, 425, 432
for multicasts, 394–396, 398, 404
options in, 111–112
for SNMP, 457
for time-outs, 229–232
setsockopt function, 91
setup.bat file, 9
7-bit MIME encoding method, 497
sh command in cordbg, 21
Shared Source Common Language Interface project, 5
short datatype, 266
ShowMessage class, 508–509
shutdown method, 94–95, 116, 172
si command in cordbg, 21
Signing AuthenticationType, 546
Simple Mail Transfer Protocol. *See* SMTP (Simple Mail
   Transfer Protocol)

Simple Network Management Protocol. *See* SNMP (Simple Network Management Protocol)
Simple Object Access Protocol (SOAP), 529
SimplePing.cs program, 423–426, *423*
SimpleSearch.cs program, 558–559
SimpleSNMP.cs program, **457–463**
SimpleTcpClient.cs program, 174–176
SimpleTcpSrvr.cs program, 168–171
SimpleUdpClient.cs program, 215–218
SimpleUdpSrvr.cs program, 212–213, 217–218, 240–241
simplified socket helper classes, 120
sin_ elements, 91–92
SingleCall object mode, 576, 581
Singleton object mode, 576–577, 581
Site membership security group, 596
Site property
    in Process, 337
    in ProcessThread, 345
Size class, 308
SizeLimit property, 561
SkipVerification permission, 597
Sleep method, 352, 383
sliding windows in TCP, 65
SMTP (Simple Mail Transfer Protocol), **478**. *See also* e-mail
    attachments in, **493–494**
        MailAttachment class for, **499–501**
        MIME for, **495–499**, *496*
        uuencode for, **495**
    CDO in, **483–484**
    expanded message formats in, **488–491**, *489*
    mail service, **484–485**, *485*
    MailMessage class for, **491–494**, *494*
SMTPMail class, **485**
    methods and properties in, **486**
    working with, **487–488**
SmtpServer property, 486
-sn option in soapsuds, 587
SndRcvData method, 236–240
SNMP (Simple Network Management Protocol), **442–443**
    class for, **452–457**
    commands in, **443–444**
    communication in, **452**
    community names in, **444–445**
    GetNextRequest queries in, **469–474**, *470*
    MIB in. *See* MIB (Management Information Base)
    packets in
        format of, **448–450**
        layout of, **450–452**, *450*
        receiving, **457**
        sending, **457**
    SimpleSNMP program, **457–463**
    with UDP, 229
SNMP.cs program, 453–457
SNMP PDU type field, 451
so command in cordbg, 21

SOA (Start of Authority) records, **132–133**, 137
SOAP (Simple Object Access Protocol), 529
SoapFormatter class, 564–568
soapsuds program, **585–590**, *586*
SoapTest.cs program, 566–567
soaptest.xml file, 567–568
SOCK_ values, 90
sockaddr structure, 91, 93
socket flags, 301
socket function
    parameters for, **89–90**, 93
    in Winsock, 99
SocketAddress class, 106–107
SocketExcept.cs program, 119–120
SocketException exception, 119
    from buffer overflow, 228
    error codes for, 242–244
    from time-outs, 232, 234, 237
SocketFlag values, 115
SocketOptionNames values, **112–113**
SocketPermission class, 603–604
SocketPermissionAttribute class, 603–604
sockets and Socket class
    for ICMP, **415–417**
    for IP multicasts, **393–399**
    permissions for, **603–610**
    programming, **88**
        asynchronous, **118**. *See also* asynchronous sockets
        completion ports in, **102–103**
        connection-oriented sockets in, **92–94**, *92*, **113–116**. *See also* TCP (Transmission Control Protocol)
        connectionless sockets in, **94–95**, *95*, **117**. *See also* UDP (User Datagram Protocol)
        exceptions in, **119–120**
        helper classes in, **120–124**
        IP addresses in, **103–108**
        network addresses in, **91–92**
        non-blocking programming in, **95–98**, **117–118**
        overlapped I/O in, **102**
        socket construction in, **109–111**
        socket options in, **91**, **111–113**
        sockets in, **88–90**, *89*
        in Windows, **98–102**, *100*
    for TCP, **168–170**, 174
    time-outs in, 229–232
    for UDP, 210, 229–232
SocketType property, 110
SockProp.cs program, 110–111
software field, 135
Software publisher application group, 596
Solution Explorer, 18, *19*
Source Address field, 57
source code window, 18, *19*
source files, multiple, **16–17**

spam, 480
Split method, 30, 143–144, 456
Spx ProtocolType value, 416
SpxII ProtocolType value, 416
SQL statements, 81
srvrAdvertise method, 388
ss command in cordbg, 21
StandardError property, 337
StandardInput property, 337
StandardOutput property, 337
Standby state, 344
Start method
    in Process, 338
    in TcpListener, 122, 256, 258
    in Thread, 351–352, 356
Start of Authority (SOA) records, **132–133**, 137
StartAddress property, 345
StartInfo property, 337
StartsWith method, 30
StartTime property, 337
STAT command, 502, 509
StatusCode property, 524
StatusDescription property, 524
Step Into function, 19
Stop method, 123, 256–257
stopping UDP servers, **218**
storing e-mail, **481–483**, *482–483*
stream parameter, 612
Stream socket type, 109
StreamReader class, 35, **202–203**, 258–259
streams, **33–35**
    in CryptoStream, 612
    with TCP, **198**
        NetworkStream class, **198–202**
        StreamReader and StreamWriter classes, **202–203**
        StreamTcpClient.cs program, 205–207
        StreamTcpSrvr.cs program, 203–205
StreamWriter class, 34–35, **202–203**, 258–259
String class, **28–31**
StringBuilder class, **31–33**
strings, **28**
    dividing, 143–144, 456
    String class, **28–31**
    StringBuilder class, **31–33**
StringTest.cs program, 30–31
strong names, 596, 600
structured programming model, 292
stub programs, 5
Subject field, 490
Subject property, 491
subject-text value, 490
subkeys in Registry, 74–76
subnet masks, 59, **435–438**, *435*
Subnet Request packets, **435–437**
subnets, 59

Subordinate option, 560
Subtract method
    in MathClass, 578, 588
    in MathService, 530
Subtree value, 557
Suspend method, 351
symmetric encryption, **610–611**
SYN flag, 66, *67*
SYN-RECEIVED connection state, 67
SYN-SENT connection state, 67
SynchronizingObject property, 337
synchronous DNS methods, **153–158**
sysContact object, 447
sysDescr object, 447
sysLocation object, 447
sysName object, 447, 461–462
sysObjectID object, 447
sysServices object, 447
System namespaces, 25
System.NET.Sockets namespace, 108–109
system object, 447, 457–458
sysUptime object, 461

T

-t option in WinDump, 45
/target switch in csc, 15
Task Manager, 334–335, *334*
TCP (Transmission Control Protocol), 42, **61–62**, *62*
    application ports in, **63–65**, *63*
    buffers in, 70–71, *70*, **177–180**, *179*
    clients, 173
        AsyncTcpClient.cs program, 305–312, *312*
        BadTcpClient.cs program, 182–183
        creating, **174–176**
        FixedTcpClient.cs program, 188–190
        NetworkStreamTcpClient.cs program, 200–202
        PickyTcpClient.cs program, 606–607
        SelectTcpClient.cs program, 328–331
        SimpleTcpClient.cs program, 174–176
        StreamTcpClient.cs program, 205–207
        TcpClientSample.cs program, 252–255, *255*, 607
        testing, **176–177**
        VarTcpClient.cs program, 195–197
    messages in, **180**
        fixed-size, **184–190**
        markers for, **198**
        unprotected boundaries in, **180–184**, *180*
        variable-length, **190–197**
    programming features for, **70–71**, *70*
    reliability in, **65**
    servers, **168**
        AsyncTcpSrvr.cs program, 312–318, *315*

BadTcpSrvr.cs program, 181–182
creating, **168–171**
FixedTcpSrvr.cs program, 187–188
Receive method for, **171–172**
SelectTcpSrvr.cs program, 326–331, *330*
SimpleTcpSrvr.cs program, 168–171
StreamTcpSrvr.cs program, 203–205
testing, **172**
ThreadedTcpSrvr.cs program, 355–357
ThreadPoolTcpSrvr.cs program, 369–371
VarTcpSrvr.cs program, 193–195
watching, **172–173**, *173*
sessions in, **66–68**, *67*
streams with, **198**
NetworkStream class, **198–202**
StreamReader and StreamWriter classes, **202–203**
StreamTcpClient.cs program, 205–207
StreamTcpSrvr.cs program, 203–205
Tcp value, 605
TcpChannel class, **579–580**
TcpChat.cs program, 359–364, *364*
TcpClient class, **120–122**, **250**
constructors for, **250–251**
in ICMP, 415
methods in, **251–252**
sample program, 252–255, *255*
TcpClientSample.cs program, 252–255, *255*, 607
TcpListener class, **122–123**, **255**
constructors for, **255–256**
methods for, **256–257**
sample program, 257–258
TcpListenerSample.cs program, 257–258
TcpPollSrvr.cs program, 320–323
Terminated state, 344
testing
asynchronous sockets
clients, **301–312**, *312*
servers, **318**, *318*
connectionless sockets, **217–218**, *218*
TCP
clients, **176–177**
servers, **172**
UDP
clients, 222–223
servers, 221–222
TestLog.cs program, 34–35
TestUdpClient.cs program, 222–223
TestUdpSrvr.cs program, 221–222
text Content-Type, 497
text editors, 12–13
text mode, 13
TextBox class, 296–297
Thread class, **350–353**
ThreadedTcpSrvr.cs program, 355–357
Threading namespace, 350

ThreadPool class, **365**
ThreadPoolSample.cs program, 366–367
ThreadPoolTcpSrvr.cs program, 369–371
threads, **334**, **343–344**
creating, **350–353**
determining, **345–347**
listing, **347–350**, **357–358**
pools of, **364**
sample programs, **366–369**
in servers, **369–372**
ThreadPool class for, **365**
and processes, **334–335**, *334*
information on, **335**, **339–343**
Process class for, **336–339**
ProcessThread class for, **344–345**
for sending and receiving data, **358**, *359*
in servers, **354–358**, *354*
Threads method, 346
Threads property, 337
ThreadSample.cs program, 351–353
ThreadStart delegate, 350
ThreadState enumeration, 343–344
ThreadState property, 345
three-way handshakes in TCP, 66
TickCount property, 430, 434
Time Exceeded packets, **415**, 434
time-outs, socket, **229–232**
time to live (TTL)
in A records, 134
in DNS, 131
in HINFO records, 135
in ICMP, 415, 432
in IP, 57, **398–399**
in MX records, 136
in NS records, 134
in PTR records, 135
in SOA records, 133
time value in RFC2822, 489
TIME-WAIT connection state, 68
TimeoutUdpClient.cs program, 230–231
Timer class, 229
timers in UDP, 72, 229
To field, 490
To property, 491
ToBoolean method, 267
ToChar method, 267
ToCharArray method, 30
ToDouble method, 267
ToInt16 method, 267
ToInt32 method, 267, 272
ToLower method, 30
TOP command, 503
top-level domains, 128–129
ToS (Type of Service) field, 57, **60–61**
ToSingle method, 267

ToString method
    in BitConverter, 267, 269–270, 272–273
    in IPAddress, 104
    in IPEndPoint, 106
    in NetworkStream, 199
    in Process, 338
    in SMTPMail, 486
    in StreamReader, 203
    in String, 30
    in TcpClient, 251
    in TcpListener, 256
    in Thread, 351
    in UdpClient, 260
Total Length field, 57
TotalProcessorTime property
    in Process, 337
    in ProcessThread, 345
ToUing64 method, 267
ToUInt16 method, 267
ToUInt32 method, 267
ToUpper method, 30
TraceRoute.cs program, 432–435
transform parameter, 612
Transition state, 344
Transmission Control Protocol. *See* TCP (Transmission
    Control Protocol)
Transport property, 605
Trap PDUs, 444, 449, 452
trees in Active Directory, **541**, *541*
Trim method, 30
TrimEnd method, 30
TrimStart method, 30
TripleDESCryptoServiceProvider class, 611–613
trust relationships, 541
Trusted value, 596, 600
try-catch blocks, 37–39, 119, 253
TTL (time to live)
    in A records, 134
    in DNS, 131
    in HINFO records, 135
    in ICMP, 415, 432
    in IP, 57, **398–399**
    in MX records, 136
    in NS records, 134
    in PTR records, 135
    in SOA records, 133
Type element in ICMP, **412–415**, 417
Type of Service (ToS) field, 57, **60–61**
type parameter
    in RemotingConfiguration, **580–581**
    in socket, 90
types, LDAP, 537–538
-types option in soapsuds, 587

U

-u option
    in caspol, 598
    in soapsuds, 587
UCE (Unsolicited Commercial E-mail), 480
UDP (User Datagram Protocol), 42, **210–211**
    clients
        BadUdpClient.cs program, 224–226
        BestUdpClient.cs program, 245–247
        BinaryUdpClient.cs program, 270–271
        ExceptionUdpClient.cs program, 232–234
        OddUdpClient.cs program, 219–220
        RetryUdpClient.cs program, 237–241
        SimpleUdpClient.cs program, 215–218
        TestUdpClient.cs program, 222–223
        TimeoutUdpClient.cs program, 230–231
        UdpClientMultiRecv.cs program, 400
        UdpClientMultiSend.cs program, 400–401
        UdpClientSample.cs program, 263–264
    lost packets in
        exceptions in, **232–235**, **242–244**
        preventing, **223–229**
        retransmissions in, **235–242**
        socket time-outs in, 229–232
    messages in, **220–223**
    in network packets, **68–69**, *68*
    programming features for, **71–72**, *71*
    servers, **211–215**, **217–218**
        BinaryUdpSrvr.cs program, 268–269
        SimpleUdpSrvr.cs program, 212–213, 217–218,
          240–241
        TestUdpSrvr.cs program, 221–222
        UdpSrvrSample.cs program, 262–264
    for SNMP, 452
Udp value, 605
UdpClient class, **123–124**, **259**
    constructors for, **259–260**
    in ICMP, 415
    methods for, **260**
    for multicasting, **399–401**
    in programs, **260–262**
    sample programs, 262–264
UdpClientMultiRecv.cs program, 400
UdpClientMultiSend.cs program, 400–401
UdpClientSample.cs program, 263–264
UdpSrvrSample.cs program, 262–264
uint datatype, 266
ulong datatype, 266
Unknown ProtocolType value, 416
Unknown state, 344
unprotected TCP message boundaries, **180–184**, *180*
UnsafeQueueUserWorkItem method, 365
UnsafeRegisterWaitForSingleObject method, 365

Unsolicited Commercial E-mail (UCE), 480
Unspecified ProtocolType value, 416
Untrusted value, 596, 600
UploadData method, **517**
UploadDataTest.cs program, 517
UploadFile method, **518**
uploading Web data, **516–519**
UploadValues method, **518–519**
UploadValuesTest.cs program, 518–519
URL application group, 596
-url option in soapsuds, 587
UrlContentBase property, 491
UrlContentLocation property, 491
.us domain, 128
UsePropertyCache property, 548
USER command, 501
User Datagram Protocol. *See* UDP (User Datagram
    Protocol)
user-level policies, **595**
UserProcessorTime property
    in Process, 337
    in ProcessThread, 345
ushort datatype, 266
using directive, 26
UUEncode encoding type, 499
uuencode program, **495**

V

values
    LDAP, 537–538
    MIB, 445, **447–448**, 452
    Registry, 74
Values property, 547
variable-length TCP messages, **190–197**
variables, 15
    binding in SNMP, **450–451**
    in debugging, 19, *19*
    references to, 211
VarTcpClient.cs program, 195–197
VarTcpSrvr.cs program, 193–195
vendor identifiers in Ethernet addresses, 53
vendor MIBs, **463–469**, *469*
versions
    in IP, 57
    in SNMP, **448**, 451
video Content-Type, 498
View command, 148
views in MIB, 444
VirtualMemorySize property, 337
Visual C# .NET development environment, **8**
Visual Studio .NET development environment, **7**

W

-w option in WinDump, 45
Wait state, 344
WaitForExit method, 338
WaitForInputIdle method, 338
WaitReason property, 345
warnings, compiler, 16
Web-Based Enterprise Management (WBEM), 80
Web client example, **525–528**, *528*
Web data
    downloading, **512–515**
    uploading, **516–519**
web proxies, **522**, 529, *529*, **532**
Web services, **528–529**, *529*
    clients for, **533**
    proxies for, **532**
    servers for, **529–532**, *531–532*
Web Services Definition Language (WSDL), 585–586, *586*
WebClient class, **512**
    Credentials property, **519–521**
    for downloading Web data, **512–515**
    for uploading Web data, **516–519**
    for viewing HTTP headers, **515–516**
WebGet.cs program, 525–528, *528*
WebHeaderCollection class, 515, 524
WebProxy class, 522
WebRequest class, **521–522**
WebResponse class, **521–522**
well-known ports
    in TCP, 64
    in UDP, 69
whiteboard/chat system, 402
Win32_NetworkAdapterConfiguration table, 80–81
Windows
    Registry for IP address information in, **75–76**
    socket programming in, **98–102**, *100*
Windows Management Instrumentation (WMI), **80–83**
WindowSample.cs program, 295–297
WinDump program, 43
    command-line options in, **44–45**
    filter expressions in, **45–46**
    with nslookup, **146–148**
    running, **46–47**
WinNT access method, 544
WinPcap programs, **43**
winsock functions, **99–103**, *100*, 118
WMI (Windows Management Instrumentation), **80–83**
WMICardGrab.cs program, 81–83
WorkingSet property, 337
-wp option in soapsuds, 587
wrapped proxies, **588–590**
Write method
    in NetworkStream, 199–201

in StreamWriter, 203
in TcpClient, 254
WriteByte method, 199
writefds parameter, 97
WriteLine method, 203
WSAAsyncSelect function, **100–101**
WSACleanup function, **99**
WSACreateEvent function, 102
WSAEventSelect function, **102**
WSARecv function, 99–100, 102
WSASend function, 102
WSAStartup function, **99**
WSDL (Web Services Definition Language), 585–586, *586*
-wsdl option in soapsuds, 587
wsdl program, 532

X

-x option in WinDump, 45
-X option in WinDump, 45, 47
x-token MIME encoding method, 497
XML (Extensible Markup Language), 529, 532

Z

Zone group, 596
zones
in DNS, 129
in security, 596, 600–601

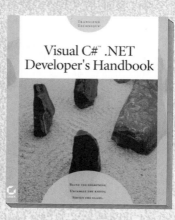